Gale Library of Daily Life

American Civil War

Gale Library of Daily Life

American Civil War

VOLUME 1

Steven E. Woodworth

EDITOR

GALE
CENGAGE Learning

Detroit • New York • San Francisco • New Haven, Conn • Waterville, Maine • London

GALE
CENGAGE Learning™

Gale Library of Daily Life
American Civil War

Steven E. Woodworth, Editor

Project Editor: Angela Doolin

Editorial: Mark Drouillard, Andrea Fritsch, Carly S. Kaloustian, Brad Morgan, Darcy L. Thompson, Ken Wachsberger

Rights Acquisition and Management: Beth Beaufore, Barb McNeil, Jackie Jones, Kelly Quin

Imaging: Lezlie Light

Product Design: Pamela A. Galbreath

Composition: Evi Seoud

Manufacturing: Drew Kalasky

For product information and technology assistance, contact us at
Gale Customer Support, 1-800-877-4253.
For permission to use material from this text or product, submit all requests online at **www.cengage.com/permissions.**
Further permissions questions can be emailed to
permissionrequest@cengage.com

Cover image credits:
"Color Lithography Showing the Battle of Gettysburg," © Bettman/Corbis
"Soldier from the 22nd New York State Militia near Harpers Ferry, Virginia, 1861," © Corbis
"Battle Damaged House in Atlanta," © Corbis

Text credits:
The excerpt on p. 226 by Bertram Wallace Korn is from *American Jewry and the Civil War*, Philadelphia, PA: The Jewish Publication Society of America, 1951. Copyright© 1951 The Jewish Publication Society, renewed 1979. Reproduced by permission.

Since this page cannot legibly accommodate all copyright notices, the credits constitute an extension of the copyright notice.

While every effort has been made to ensure the reliability of the information presented in this publication, Gale does not guarantee the accuracy of the data contained herein. Gale accepts no payment for listing; and inclusion in the publication of any organization, agency, institution, publication, service, or individual does not imply endorsement of the editors or publisher. Errors brought to the attention of the publisher and verified to the satisfaction of the publisher will be corrected in future editions.

Library of Congress Cataloging-in-Publication Data

American Civil War / Steven E. Woodworth, editor.
   p. cm. -- (Gale library of daily life)
   Includes bibliographical references and index.
   ISBN-13: 978-1-4144-3009-6 (set)
   ISBN-13: 978-1-4144-3010-2 (vol. 1)
   ISBN-13: 978-1-4144-3011-9 (vol. 2)
   1. United States--History--Civil War, 1861-1865--Social aspects. 2. United States--Social life and customs--1775-1865. 3. United States--Social conditions--To 1865. 4. Confederate States of America--Social life and customs. 5. Confederate States of America--Social conditions. 6. United States--History--Civil War, 1861-1865--Sources. I. Woodworth, Steven E.

E468.9.A46 2008
973.7'1--dc22   2007047017

Gale
27500 Drake Rd.
Farmington Hills, MI 48331-3535

ISBN-13: 978-1-4144-3009-6 (set)   ISBN-10: 1-4144-3009-4 (set)
ISBN-13: 978-1-4144-3010-2 (vol. 1)   ISBN-10: 1-4144-3010-8 (vol. 1)
ISBN-13: 978-1-4144-3011-9 (vol. 2)   ISBN-10: 1-4144-3011-6 (vol. 2)

This title is also available as an e-book.
ISBN-13: 978-1-4144-3012-6   ISBN-10: 1-4144-3012-4
Contact your Gale representative for ordering information.

Contents

Religion

Popular Culture

VOLUME 2

Preface

With its vast consequences and appalling cost the Civil War, the subject of a voluminous literature, can seem overwhelming. Lincoln, Lee, and all the rest bestride an almost mythical landscape, and even across the chasm of the intervening century and a half, the war seems larger than life. The war's grand scale is probably part of the reason that so many Americans find its study to be fascinating and exciting. Nonetheless, textbook histories of the Civil War can sometimes be a little unsatisfying, even unreal. As human beings, we naturally desire to know the past on a human scale. Somehow history seems more authentic when we can feel the humanity of the participants by learning the homely details of their daily lives—the kinds of things people usually did not write down, or alluded to only tangentially, mainly because such things simply seemed too obvious to mention. What would it have been like to have lived during those times—to have been a soldier, a civilian, or a slave? What did people wear, eat, read, or do in their spare time? What jobs did they pursue to earn their livings? What was important to them? The purpose of this text is to provide a reference source that will give ready answers to questions such as these and provide insights into how Americans lived and thought during the Civil War years.

This set aims at covering many facets of everyday life in the Civil War. The daily life of soldiers is considered, from recruitment—or conscription—to training, to what soldiers ate, what they wore, the weapons they carried, even the music their bands played. As for civilians, this set looks at family and community life, and considers the roles and experiences of men, women, and children, black and white. It describes what civilians ate and wore, and how they earned their living. Popular culture and leisure activities come in for attention, with articles or sections on literature, music, theater, minstrel shows, and the lyceum movement, among other topics. There is also a section on work and the economy, which gives attention to people in various walks of life—from farmers to factory workers to businessmen, planters, and slaves. For obvious reasons, political conflict loomed even larger than normal in the everyday lives of Americans during the Civil War era. Thus, this set devotes another section to that subject, dealing with election battles small and large, as well as with the political causes that inspired people's loyalty. Yet another topic the project explores is that of health and medicine during the Civil War. Both the practice of civilian physicians on the home front and the grim work of army surgeons in field hospitals are examined. Religion was extremely important to many Americans during the Civil War era, and so it too rightly claims attention within the pages that follow. Because the memory of the Civil War remained fresh and intense in the minds of Americans for generations after the guns fell silent, the war gave rise to such things as the institution of Memorial Day, the erection of monuments, and the founding of parks on some of the conflict's most famous battlefields. Thus, the last section of this set looks at such expressions of collective memory, as well as at the movement toward reconciliation between North and South.

Although this two-volume project was conceived as a reference book, readers will also find enjoyment in reading it from cover to cover. Rather than a stultifying list of alphabetical entries, as one finds in most reference works, this set offers a logically arranged progression of topics. Readers who wish to consult the set as a reference source may easily do so by using the table of contents and index, but those who simply want to learn more about everyday life in the Civil War era can read sequentially through the sections on various aspects of American life in the 1860s.

Finally, let me add that I am deeply grateful to a number of people for the indispensible help they have rendered to this project. Brad Morgan, an editor for Gale Cengage Learning, first suggested to me the idea of producing this work and oversaw the early stages of development. Later, Angela Doolin took over as the in-house editor at Gale and has done a splendid job with the really difficult and sometimes no doubt onerous work of shepherding the project through its various stages—the selection of authors, collection of articles, and assembly of the final manuscript—leaving me the much more pleasant tasks of writing about the Civil War and deciding which topics to cover and which authors to consult. David Slay took time out from the writing of a very promising doctoral dissertation (since completed) to serve as my assistant editor for this project, and the work has profited greatly from his keen editorial eye and voluminous knowledge of the Civil War era. I could not have done it without him. And, of course, the various authors who have shared their particular expertise by writing individual articles for the project have all made important contributions to its ultimate value.

Contributors

Christina Adkins

*Doctoral Candidate, Program
in the History of American
Civilization
Harvard University*
Civilian Photography
The Lost Cause
Newspapers and Magazines
War Photography

William Backus

Veterans' Organizations

Steven Barleen

*Doctoral Candidate,
Department of History
Northern Illinois University*
Factories
Manufacturing
Northern Manufacturing
Southern Manufacturing

Michael Kelly Beauchamp

*Doctoral Candidate,
Department of History
Texas A & M University*
Pacifism and Conscientious
Objectors
Prosecessionists/Southern
Nationalists
Proslavery Advocates

Megan Birk

*Doctoral Candidate,
Department of History
Purdue University*
Children and Childrearing

Anurag Biswas

Freelance Writer
Advances in Medicine
Alcohol
Triage and Surgery

Carol Brennan

Freelance Writer
Arms Manufacturing
Army Nurses
Education in the Confederacy
Fraternizing with the Enemy
Political Humor and Cartoons
Public Health and Sanitation
Rallies, Lectures, and Speeches
Refugees
Role of West Point
Sanitary Fairs
Surgeons
United States Sanitary
Commission
Volunteer Nurses

Jamie Bronstein

*Professor, Department of
History
New Mexico State University*
Child Labor
Labor
Paid Labor
Women Laborers

Deliah K. Brown

*Professor, Department of
History
Texas Southern University*
Judaism

William H. Brown

*Editor
North Carolina Office of
Archives and History*
Chickamauga
Draft Riots and Draft
Resisters
Slaves
Southern Union Loyalists
Unit and Regimental
Histories

Judith P. Bruce

Freelance Writer
Lectures and Speeches

Amy Crowson

*Instructor, Department of
History
Miles College*
Civilian Health Care

Jocelyn M. Cuffee

*Assistant Professor, Department
of Legal Research and
Writing
Western New England College
School of Law*
Abolitionists

Kwasi Densu

*Instructor, Department of
Political Science
Clark Atlanta University*
The Morrill Act
Plantation Life
Religion Practiced by Slaves

Ondra Krouse Dismukes
Doctoral Candidate,
Department of English
The University of Georgia
Dance among Slaves

Thomas J. Fehn
Undergraduate Student,
Department of History
Hinds Community College
Holidays

Rebecca J. Frey
Freelance Writer and Editor
Civil Liberties and Censorship
Family Separation and
 Reunion
Protestant Christianity

Carol J. Gibson
Independent Scholar
Army Bands

Lisa Guinn
Visiting Assistant Professor,
Department of Humanities
Ferris State University
Feminism

Scott Hancock
Associate Professor,
Departments of History and
Africana Studies
Gettysburg College
Free Blacks and Education

Keith S. Hébert
Historian
Georgia Historic Preservation
Division
Disease
Election of 1860
Nursing

David F. Herr
Associate Professor, Department
of History
St. Andrews Presbyterian
College
Agriculture
Propaganda
Support for the War

Allison E. Herrmann
Graduate Student, Department
of History
American University
Veterans

Kevin Hillstrom
Freelance Writer
Northern Lights Writers Group
African American Prisoners of
 War
African American Soldiers
Child Soldiers
Conscription
Desertion
Diaries and Letters from Soldiers
Drill Training
Equipment
Food and Rations
Foraging and Looting
Furloughs
Immigrant Soldiers
Interaction between Soldiers
 and Civilians
Living as a Prisoner of War
Mascots
Music
Native American Soldiers
Prisons and Prisoners of War
Recruiting
Resistance
Sanitation
Shelter
A Soldier's Pastimes
Spies
Sports
Uniforms
Vices
Volunteerism

Diane Hulett
Assistant Professor, Department
of English
Morris College
Volunteer Work to Support
 Troops

Jeffrey William Hunt
Director
Texas Military Forces Museum
Battlefield Wounds
Comrades and the Ambulance
 Corps
Field Hospitals
Gettysburg

Raymond Pierre Hylton
Dean, School of Humanities
and Social Sciences
Virginia Union University
Opposition to the War

Eric R. Jackson
Director, Institute for Freedom
Studies
Northern Kentucky University
Abolitionism
Minstrel Shows

Sandra Johnston
Lecturer, Department of
English and Modern
Languages
University of Maryland Eastern
Shore
Housing
Religious Tracts
The Young Men's Christian
 Association

Brian Matthew Jordan
Research Assistant,
Department of Civil War Era
Studies
Gettysburg College
Davis's and Lincoln's
 Inaugural Addresses

Mark S. Joy
Chair, Department of History
and Political Science
Jamestown College
Currency

Richard C. Keenan
Professor Emeritus, Department
of English and Modern
Languages
University of Maryland,
Eastern Shore
Blockade and Blockade
 Running
Photography

Pamela L. Kester
Freelance Writer
Common Schools
The Sunday School Movement
Textiles

Jenny Lagergren
Freelance Writer
Evacuation Hospitals
Games
Motherhood

Anthony A. Lee
Lecturer, Department of
History

University of California, Los Angeles
Culture and Leisure

Talitha L. LeFlouria
Doctoral Candidate, Department of History
Howard University
Women and Education

Jeanne M. Lesinski
Freelance Writer
Children's Literature
Diaries and Letters from Home
Immigration
Slave, Abolitionist, and Civil Rights Songs
Spirituals
Sports

Connie L. Lester
Assistant Professor, Department of History
University of Central Florida
Agricultural Fairs

Samuel Livingston
Assistant Professor, Department of History
Morehouse College
Plantation Life

Robert P. McParland
Assistant Professor, Department of English
Felician College
Reading and Reading Groups

Aileen McTiernan
Juris Doctor Candidate, School of Law
Rutgers University, Camden
Crime
Gambling

George A. Milite
Freelance Writer and Editor
Education
Party Politics
The Slavery Apologists
Technological Advances in Industry and Agriculture

Benjamin L. Miller
Doctoral Candidate, Department of History
University of Florida
Army Missionaries
U.S. Christian Commission

Matthew M. Mitchell
Graduate Student, Department of History
Tulane University
Jefferson Davis's Speech of Resignation from the U.S. Senate

Caryn E. Neumann
Visiting Assistant Professor, Department of History
Miami University of Ohio at Middletown
Clothing
Dancing
Diet
Food
Food Shortages
Obituaries and Local Memorials to the Dead
Prostitutes and Other Camp Followers
Religion and Slavery
Visiting Wives and Relatives
Women on the Battlefield
Women Soldiers

Jennifer Ann Newman
Doctoral Candidate, Department of History
Auburn University
Southern Domestic Life

Debra Newman Ham
Professor, Department of History
Morgantown University
Extended Family
Parenting and Childrearing
War Widows and Orphans

James Onderdonk
Associate Director, Institute for Computing in Humanities, Arts and Social Science
University of Illinois at Urbana–Champaign
Gettysburg Address
Revivals

Adrienne M. Petty
Assistant Professor, Department of History
The City College of New York
Smoking and Tobacco
Vices on the Home Front

Kerry L. Pimblott
Graduate Student, Department of History
University of Illinois, Urbana–Champaign
Lyceum Lectures
Music
Performing Arts

Adam J. Pratt
Graduate Student, Department of History
Louisiana State University
Fatherhood

John L. Reilly
Instructor, Department of Communications and Modern Languages
Cheyney University of Pennsylvania
Literature
Theater

Stephen Rockenbach
Assistant Professor, Department of History and Philosophy
Virginia State University
Biased Newspaper Reporting
Class Tensions
The Emancipation Proclamation
Men on the Home Front
Northern Copperheads
The Reconciliation Movement
War Music

Christopher D. Rodkey
Doctoral Candidate, Graduate Division of Religion
Drew University
Fraternal Organizations
War Profiteers

Donald Roe
Department of History
Howard University
Northern Support for the War

David W. Rolfs
Upper School Teacher, Department of History
Maclay College Preparatory School
Chaplains

Daniel Sauerwein
*Graduate Student, Department
of History*
University of North Dakota
Letters to the President
Souvenirs and Relics

Jodi M. Savage
*Equal Employment
Opportunity Officer, Coney
Island Hospital*
*New York City Health and
Hospitals Corporation*
Religion and Reform

Jeffery Seymour
Interim Curator
*The National Civil War Naval
Museum*
Shipbuilding

Robert S. Shelton
*Associate Professor, Department
of History*
Cleveland State University
Black Market

David H. Slay
*Doctoral Candidate,
Department of History*
Texas Christian Univeresity
African American
  Commemorations
Emancipation
Family

Free Blacks
Freedpeople
Hymns
Race and Racial Tensions
Slave Markets

Robbie C. Smith
Park Ranger
*Vicksburg National Military
Park*
Prisoner Exchange and Parole
Vicksburg

Timothy B. Smith
*Department of History and
Philosophy*
*University of Tennessee at
Martin*
Antietam
Battlefield Sites
Blue-Gray Reunions
Memorial and Decoration
  Days
National Cemeteries
Shiloh
Wartime Commemoration and
  Monuments

J. Douglas Tyson
*Teacher, Department of Social
Studies*
Ridley School District
Evacuation Hospitals
Recovery

Minoa Uffelman
*Assistant Professor, Department
of History*
Austin Peay State University
Unitarianism

Micki Waldrop
Freelance Writer
Courtship and Marriage
The Domestic Ideal
Northern Domestic Life
Shortages

Steven E. Woodworth
*Professor, Department of
History*
Texas Christian University
Effects of the War on Slaves
  and Freedpeople
Family and Community
Health and Medicine
Politics
Popular Culture
Reconciliation and
  Remembrance
Religion
A Soldier's Life
Work and Economy

Angela M. Zombek
*Doctoral Candidate,
Department of History*
University of Florida
Catholic Christianity

A Chronology of the Civil War

1858

August–October

Incumbent U.S. senator Stephen A. Douglas of Illinois and challenger Abraham Lincoln hold a series of debates. Douglas maintains that he does not care about slavery and is content to let the people in each western territory "vote it up, or vote it down." Lincoln counters that slavery is a moral wrong and should not be allowed to spread.

1859

October 16

Abolitionist John Brown leads nineteen men in a raid on the U.S. armory at Harper's Ferry, Virginia (now West Virginia). Ten of the raiders are killed. Brown and seven others are captured.

December 2

John Brown is hanged at Charlestown, Virginia, for murder, conspiring with slaves to rebel, and for treason against Virginia, though he had never been a citizen of that state.

1860

February 27

Abraham Lincoln delivers a speech at the Cooper Union in New York City, arguing that the goal of the Republican Party—preventing the further spread of slavery—is consistent with the thinking of the Founding Fathers.

May 3

The Democratic National Convention, meeting in Charleston, South Carolina, breaks up when Southern delegates use convention rules to block the nomination of the majority's choice, Stephen A. Douglas.

May 9

Southerners who had formerly belonged to the defunct Whig and Know-Nothing parties meet in Baltimore, Maryland, to form the Constitutional Union Party and nominate John Bell of Tennessee for president.

May 16

Abraham Lincoln wins the presidential nomination of the Republican National Convention, meeting in Chicago.

June 18

The Democrats meet again in Baltimore, Maryland, but Southern delegates walk out when the majority rejects their demand for a federal slave code for the territories. The remaining delegates nominate Douglas.

June 28

Southern delegates who had bolted the Democratic convention meet in Richmond, Virginia, and nominate Vice President John C. Breckinridge of Kentucky.

November 6

In the presidential election, Lincoln wins a majority of the electoral vote and a plurality of the popular vote.

November 10

The South Carolina legislature authorizes a special convention to consider the question of the state's secession. Both of South Carolina's U.S. senators resign their seats and leave Washington.

December 20

The South Carolina convention, meeting in Charleston, adopts an ordinance of secession.

1861

January 9

The unarmed steamer *Star of the West* attempts to enter Charleston Harbor carrying supplies and reinforcements for Fort Sumter, but Rebel cannon opens fire and forces it to turn back. Union gunners within Fort Sumter do not return fire.
Mississippi secedes.

January 10

Florida secedes.

January 11

Alabama secedes.

January 19

Georgia secedes.

January 26

Louisiana secedes.

February 1

Texas secedes.

February 8

A convention of the seceded states, meeting in Montgomery, Alabama, adopts a constitution for the new Confederate States of America.

February 9

The convention in Montgomery elects Jefferson Davis as president of the Confederate States.

February 11

Davis leaves his plantation in Mississippi to travel to Montgomery for his inauguration. Abraham Lincoln leaves Springfield, Illinois, to travel to Washington for his inauguration.

February 18

Jefferson Davis is inaugurated president of the Confederacy.

March 4

Lincoln is inaugurated.

April 6

Lincoln informs South Carolina governor Francis Pickens that U.S. ships will attempt to resupply Fort Sumter with food only and will not insert reinforcements unless resistance is made.

April 11

Brig. Gen. P. G. T. Beauregard, commander of the Confederate forces around Charleston, demands the surrender of Fort Sumter.

April 12

When Fort Sumter's commander, Maj. Robert Anderson, refuses Beauregard's order to surrender, Confederate guns open fire on the fort.

April 13

Fort Sumter is surrendered.

April 15

Lincoln calls on the states to muster 75,000 volunteers to put down the rebellion—the first of many calls for troops.

April 17

Virginia secedes.

April 19

A proslavery mob attacks Massachusetts militia passing through Baltimore on their way to Washington.

May 6

Arkansas and Tennessee secede.

May 20

North Carolina secedes.

June 10

A small force of Federal troops advancing from Fort Monroe meet defeat at Big Bethel, Virginia.

June 18

Lincoln signs legislation creating the United States Sanitary Commission, an organization tasked with coordinating the efforts of civilians who desire to aid Union soldiers by serving as volunteers in hospitals or by providing food, clothing, or other items.

July 21

A Federal army advancing from Washington toward the new Rebel capital at Richmond, Virginia, meets a humiliating defeat near a stream known as Bull Run.

July 27

Lincoln gives command of the Union troops in Virginia to Maj. Gen. George B. McClellan.

August 10

Union and Confederate troops clash at Wilson's Creek, Missouri, resulting in another Confederate victory.

August 28

Union naval forces capture Fort Hatteras on the North Carolina coast.

October 21

A Union reconnaissance probe suffers a disastrous defeat at Balls Bluff, Virginia, leading to the creation of the Congressional Join Committee on the Conduct of the War.

November 7

Union naval forces capture Port Royal Sound on the South Carolina coast.

November 8

Capt. Charles Wilkes of the U.S.S. *San Jacinto* stops the British mail steamer *Trent* and removes Confederate envoys James M. Mason and John Slidell, who had been bound for Europe. The incident creates a severe diplomatic crisis between the United States and Great Britain.

November 15

The national committee of the Young Men's Christian Association organizes the United States Christian Commission for the purpose of bringing comfort and Christian witness to the men of the Union armies.

1862

February 6

Union forces led by Brig. Gen. Ulysses S. Grant and Flag Officer Andrew H. Foote capture Fort Henry, in Tennessee, opening the Tennessee River to Union incursion as far south as northern Alabama.

February 8

Union amphibious forces capture Roanoke Island on the coast of North Carolina.

February 16

Grant strikes again, this time capturing Fort Donelson, Tennessee, and 15,000 prisoners and opening the Cumberland River all the way to Nashville. Along with the surrender of Fort Henry, this marks the most important turning point of the war.

March 7–8

A Union army under the command of Samuel R. Curtis defeats Confederates at the Battle of Pea Ridge in Arkansas.

April 6–7

A Confederate army commanded by Albert Sidney Johnston attacks Grant's Union army in what becomes known as the Battle of Shiloh, near the Tennessee River in the southern part of that state. Johnston is killed and Grant is victorious.

April 25

A Union fleet commanded by David G. Farragut captures New Orleans.

May 5

McClellan's Union army, advancing on Richmond from the east, fights and wins the Battle of Williamsburg, Virginia.

May–June

The small Confederate army of Thomas J. "Stonewall" Jackson wages a successful campaign in the Shenandoah Valley of Virginia, distracting Union attention from McClellan's campaign near Richmond.

May 31

The Confederate army defending Richmond, commanded by Gen. Joseph E. Johnston, attacks McClellan's army at what comes to be called the Battle of Fair Oaks (or the Battle of Seven Pines). The attack is a failure. Johnston is wounded and replaced by Robert E. Lee.

June 6

Union naval forces capture Memphis, Tennessee.

June 25–July 1

In a series of fierce attacks known as the Seven Days' Battles, Lee forces McClellan to withdraw from the outskirts of Richmond to Harrison's Landing on the James River, twenty-five miles away.

July 22

Lincoln reads the Emancipation Proclamation to his cabinet. Secretary of State William H. Seward suggests he delay public announcement of the proclamation until after the next Union victory, so that it will not be interpreted as an act of desperation.

August 28–30

Lee defeats the Union army of Maj. Gen. John Pope at the Second Battle of Bull Run.

September 17

Having crossed the Potomac River into Maryland, Lee's army faces its Union antagonist, this time once again under the command of McClellan, along Antietam Creek. The badly outnumbered Confederates narrowly escape destruction, and Lee finds that he has no choice but to retreat back into Virginia.

September 22

Lincoln publicly issues the preliminary Emancipation Proclamation: "That on the first day of January in the year of our Lord, one thousand eight hundred and sixty-three, all persons held as slaves, within any state, or designated part of a state, the people whereof shall then be in rebellion against the United States shall be then, thenceforward, and forever free."

October 3–4

Union forces under the overall command of Ulysses S. Grant defeat Earl Van Dorn's Confederate army at the Battle of Corinth, Mississippi.

October 8

The Union army commanded by Don Carlos Buell defeats Braxton Bragg's Confederate army at the Battle of Perryville, Kentucky.

November 4

The Democrats make significant gains in the mid-term Congressional elections.

November 7

For the last time, Lincoln removes the dawdling McClellan from command of the Union army in the East.

December 13

McClellan's successor, Ambrose Burnside, leads the Army of the Potomac to defeat at the Battle of Fredericksburg. Lee is once again victorious.

December 21

Confederate cavalry destroys Grant's supply depot at Holly Springs, Mississippi, forcing him to give up his attempt to reach the Confederate fortress of Vicksburg from the rear.

December 29

William T. Sherman leads a direct Union frontal assault on Vicksburg and suffers a severe defeat at the Battle of Chickasaw Bayou.

December 31

Union General William S. Rosecrans, the successor of Buell, clashes with Bragg's army at the Battle of Stone's River. Rosecrans wins a victory by the narrowest of margins.

1863

January 1

Lincoln issues the final Emancipation Proclamation: "I do order and declare that all persons held as slaves within said designated States, and parts of States, are, and henceforward shall be free."

March 3

Lincoln signs legislation setting up federal conscription.

April 2

In the so-called Richmond "Bread Riot," citizens of the Confederate capital, including many women, riot, complaining of lack of food but engaging in much looting of non-food items.

April 30

Grant's army lands on the east bank of the Mississippi River below Vicksburg and begins a rapid campaign to get at the Confederate fortress from the rear.

May 1–4

The Army of the Potomac, now under the command of Joseph Hooker, meets another humiliating defeat at the Battle of Chancellorsville, Virginia, though the battle results in the wounding of Stonewall Jackson.

May 10

Jackson dies.

May 14

Grant captures Jackson, Mississippi, and turns toward Vicksburg.

May 16

Grant defeats Confederate general John C. Pemberton in the Battle of Champion's Hill, fought between Jackson and Vicksburg.

May 18

Grant bottles up Pemberton and his 30,000 Confederate troops inside the Vicksburg defenses and lays siege to the fortress.

June 16

Lee's army once again crosses the Potomac into Maryland.

June 27

Lincoln removes Hooker as commander of the Army of the Potomac and appoints Maj. Gen. George G. Meade in his place.

July 1–3

Once again the eastern armies meet in a bloody but inconclusive clash. This time they fight in Pennsylvania, at Gettysburg. After the battle, Lee, who has gotten the worse of the encounter, has to retreat back into Virginia. Within a few weeks the armies are back in their pre-campaign positions, as has been the case with all of the other major campaigns east of the Appalachians.

July 4

In a stunning blow to the Confederacy, Pemberton surrenders Vicksburg and 30,000 troops to Grant. Within days the entire Mississippi River is under Union control, and the Confederacy is severed from its three westernmost states, Louisiana, Arkansas, and Texas.

July 13

Large mobs in New York City, including many Irish immigrants, riot against the draft, committing numerous atrocities against African Americans.

September 9

Union troops occupy Chattanooga, Tennessee.

September 10

Union troops take Little Rock, Arkansas.

September 18–20

In northwestern Georgia, Bragg's Confederate army, heavily reinforced by other Southern forces, attacks Rosecrans's advancing Union army and defeats it at the Battle of Chickamauga. Rosecrans retreats into Chattanooga, and Bragg virtually besieges him there.

October 13

In a widely watched election, Ohio voters resoundingly reject antiwar Democratic gubernatorial candidate Clement L. Vallandigham in favor of prowar Republican John Brough.

October 16

Lincoln gives Grant command of all Union armies west of the Appalachians, including Rosecrans's besieged force at Chattanooga.

October 27

Grant, having gone to Chattanooga in person, successfully reopens a supply line to the besieged army there.

November 23–25

Grant trounces Bragg in the Battle of Chattanooga, capturing dozens of cannon and thousands of prisoners. Bragg's battered army retreats to Dalton, Georgia, where Davis will soon replace Bragg with Joseph E. Johnston.

December 8

Lincoln issues his Proclamation of Amnesty and Reconstruction, offering pardons to low-ranking Rebels willing to take an oath of future loyalty to the United States.

1864

March 9

Lincoln makes Grant a lieutenant general, the highest rank in the Union army, and gives him command over all of the nation's armies.

April 12

Confederate troops under the command of Nathan Bedford Forrest massacre surrendering Union troops, many of them African American, at Fort Pillow, on the Mississippi River in Tennessee.

May 5–6

Grant's grand offensive begins. Grant accompanies the Army of the Potomac, still under the direct command of Meade, as it advances and tangles inconclusively with Lee's Confederates in the Battle of the Wilderness.

May 7

Sherman, now commanding the western Union armies, begins to advance from Chattanooga toward Atlanta.

May 8–21

Grant and Lee clash again at Spotsylvania Court House, ten miles closer to Richmond. As with the Battle of the Wilderness, casualties are appalling.

June 1–3

Grant and Lee meet yet again at Cold Harbor, Virginia, just outside Richmond. Once again fighting results in high casualties and no decisive outcome, but Grant is now scarcely ten miles from the center of Richmond.

June 8

The Republican Party, now styling itself the National Union Party, convenes in Baltimore and nominates Lincoln for a second term.

June 15

Sliding his army around behind Richmond, Grant strikes at Petersburg, nexus of the rail lines entering the Confederate capital from the south. Lee counters and a deadlock ensues, with both sides gradually extending their trench lines.

June 27

Sherman suffers a setback in his advance toward Atlanta, losing several thousand men in an unsuccessful attack on Kennesaw Mountain. Not long after, he finds a way to get around the mountain and its defenders, and his advance continues.

July 4

Congress adjourns, leaving the Wade-Davis Bill for Lincoln to sign. Instead, he pocket-vetoes it, believing its conditions for the reconstruction of the rebellious states are too harsh.

July 20

John Bell Hood, who had replaced Johnston as commander of the Confederate army in Georgia, attacks Sherman on the outskirts of Atlanta, in what comes to be known as the Battle of Peachtree Creek. Sherman's Federals prevail.

July 22

Hood attacks again, triggering the Battle of Atlanta. Again Sherman's men are victorious.

July 28

For the third time in eight days Hood launches a major attack on Sherman. Again Sherman wins, but he cannot get quite enough leverage to pry Hood out of Atlanta. Here, as at Richmond and Petersburg, deadlock ensues.

August 5

U.S. naval forces under the command of Rear Admiral David G. Farragut successfully take control of Mobile Bay, on the Gulf coast of Alabama, closing it as a port for blockade-runners.

August 23

Lincoln privately writes that he does not believe he will be reelected. The Democratic assertion that the war is a failure seems to be resonating with the voters.

August 31

The Democratic National Convention, meeting in Chicago, nominates George B. McClellan.

September 2

Sherman's troops march into Atlanta after forcing Hood's Confederates to evacuate. The Democrats' antiwar platform suddenly looks very foolish.

October 19

Union troops operating in the Shenandoah Valley under the command of Philip H. Sheridan administer a crushing defeat to the Confederate army of Jubal A. Early at the Battle of Cedar Creek.

November 8

Voters in the North give Lincoln a resounding victory at the polls in reelecting him for a second term.

November 16

Sherman sets out from Atlanta on the March to the Sea.

December 13

Sherman's army makes contact with Union naval forces near Savannah, having completed the March to the Sea.

December 15–16

Hood's Confederate army, which had slipped around into Tennessee, is routed by a Union army commanded by George H. Thomas.

December 21

Sherman's troops occupy Savannah following the retreat of the Confederate garrison.

1865

January 15

Union amphibious forces capture Fort Fisher, effectively closing Wilmington, North Carolina, as the last Confederate port open for blockade-runners.

January 31

The U.S. House of Representatives approves the Thirteenth Amendment, banning slavery throughout the United States. Already approved by the Senate, the amendment heads to the states for ratification.

Jefferson Davis, with the prompt approval of the Confederate senate, appoints Robert E. Lee commander of all Confederate armies.

February 1

Sherman's army marches north from Savannah, crossing into South Carolina, aiming to march across that state and North Carolina to join Grant in Virginia and finish off Lee.

February 3

Lincoln and Seward meet with three Confederate emissaries on board the steamer *River Queen* in Hampton Roads, just off Fort Monroe, Virginia, to discuss possible peace terms. Lincoln is prepared to make concessions but will not accede to the Confederates' non-negotiable demand that their states be treated as an independent nation.

February 17

Sherman's troops march into Columbia, South Carolina. That night the city burns, though it remains unclear whether the fires were set by Sherman's men, retreating Confederates, newly freed slaves, escaped prisoners of war, or all or some combination of the above.

March 19–21

Joseph E. Johnston, now commanding Confederate troops in the Carolinas, makes a desperate attempt to stop Sherman at the Battle of Bentonville, North Carolina, but is forced to withdraw. Sherman's army moves on inexorably.

April 1

At the Battle of Five Forks, a detachment of Grant's forces led by Philip H. Sheridan crushes Lee's western flank, gravely endangering the continued flow of supplies to Lee's army and Richmond.

April 2

Grant launches a predawn assault along the entire length of his lines, and the Confederate defenses crumble. Lee's troops resist just long enough to allow the Confederate government to flee Richmond, then make their own escape.

April 3

Union troops occupy Richmond while most of Grant's forces continue to pursue Lee's fleeing army west of the city.

April 6

Grant's leading units catch up with the rear of Lee's column and defeat it at the Battle of Sayler's Creek, capturing 8,000 Confederates —about a third of the men Lee has left.

April 9

Lee meets with Grant at Appomattox Court House, Virginia, and surrenders what is left of the Army of Northern Virginia.

April 14

In a formal ceremony, Robert Anderson, now a retired brigadier general, raises over Fort Sumter the flag he had lowered there four years and one day earlier.

That evening Lincoln is assassinated by pro-Confederate actor John Wilkes Booth while attending a performance of the play *Our American Cousin* at Ford's Theater in Washington.

April 18

Sherman and Johnston sign a preliminary agreement for the surrender of Johnston's army. A truce is maintained until the surrender is finalized eight days later.

April 26

Union cavalry catches up with John Wilkes Booth and an accomplice in rural Virginia. Booth refuses to surrender and is fatally shot.

May 4

Confederate Gen. Richard Taylor surrenders the forces of his Department of Alabama, Mississippi, and East Louisiana.

May 10

Union cavalry captures the fleeing Jefferson Davis near Irwinville, Georgia.

May 12

The last skirmish of the war is fought at Palmito Ranch, Texas.

May 26

Confederate Gen. Simon B. Buckner formally surrenders the remaining Confederate troops still at large west of the Mississippi.

Introduction

The Civil War was the most cataclysmic event in American history up to its time, and in some ways its impact remains unsurpassed. It changed America more than any other war—with the possible exception of the Revolutionary War. Yet even the Revolution did not create as much social change as did the conflict of the 1860s, and no other American war cost as much or left such deep scars on segments of American society. Understanding American history, and what the nation has become today, requires an understanding of the Civil War.

The Civil War was almost unique in the nation's experience in the degree to which it touched the lives of ordinary people. Never before had any war brought its destruction to the doorsteps of so many Americans. The Revolutionary War had been fought on American soil, but the Civil War was fought over a much broader expanse of territory and among a much larger population—and in the latter war the combatants on both sides were American. Since the Civil War, no organized enemy military force has fought on American soil (with the exception of a couple of small and sparsely populated islands in the Aleutians during World War II). The Civil War was the last time that Americans living in the interior of the country had the experience of hiding in their cellars to escape shelling or of seeing contending armies sweep past their houses in the midst of battle. It was the last time that Americans—whether citizens of Georgia or of Pennsylvania—experienced the entry of hostile, marauding soldiers into their homes or became war refugees in their own country. In a way and to an extent that remains unprecedented, the conflict of the 1860s brought warfare home to the average American. In doing so, it left deep scars and created animosities that have continued, in some ways, down to the present day. Southerners still complain of the devastation wrought by Sherman—even in places far from anywhere the general or his troops ever visited during the war.

The Civil War was also unparalleled in its impact on society. Some 3.5 million African Americans—40 percent of the population of the prewar Southern states—went from slavery to freedom as an immediate result of the war. Once they were free, the question facing the nation was what their status would be in postwar society. Northern abolitionists assumed that the freedpeople's status would and should be that of full participants in American society. White Southerners, with the support of many white Northerners as well, were determined that such should not be the case. The resulting political struggle, waged after the guns had fallen silent and the vast armies had disbanded, was at the heart of Reconstruction, which lasted for almost twelve years after the end of the war. In another sense, however, Reconstruction was simply a low-intensity continuation of the war, and one that white Southerners ultimately won. The task of transforming 3.5 million persons from slaves to full participants in American society proved to be more than one generation of Americans could accomplish, and completion of the process was left for a later generation. Still, the war had, in the space of four years, seen more progress toward the ultimate goal of racial equality than had occurred in the century before or would occur over a subsequent period nearly a century in length.

The Civil War also had massive economic effects. The economy of the South was devastated both by the physical destruction wrought by the war and by the end of slavery. Contrary to popular mythology, both Union and Confederate armies behaved in about the same way toward the territory of their enemies. The difference was that Union armies spent much more time and covered a great deal more ground inside enemy territory. The result was massive destruction of the Southern railroad network and of the South's relatively few factories. Warehouses and cotton gins were also targets for the torches of Union soldiers. This left the South's infrastructure badly damaged at war's end. Far more damaging, however, was the loss of almost all of the South's capital, which had been overwhelmingly invested in slaves. Along with this there was the unseen damage caused by the fact that European cotton mills had for four years been mostly cut off from their accustomed supply of Southern-grown cotton. During that time Europeans had discovered that Egypt and India were also good places from which to acquire the valuable fiber, and the market for American cotton was never as strong again. Thus, as the South struggled to rebuild its infrastructure and to reshape its entire economy on the basis of free labor, it also had to contend with perennially disappointing prices for its major cash crop. The process of economic recovery took a long time, and some of the economic effects of the war could still be felt in the South well into the twentieth century.

Finally, the Civil War stands out for its cost in lives. During the four years between 1861 and 1865, some 620,000 Americans died while fighting in the Union or Confederate armies—out of a total prewar population of about 32 million. Even in terms of raw numbers, that grim casualty figure has never been matched by any of America's subsequent wars, and as a percentage of the total population, the number of Civil War dead surpasses by many times American losses in any other conflict. As for anything that had gone before, the comparison is even more striking. The entire American loss of life in the Revolutionary War, the War of 1812, and the Mexican War—combined—was exceeded by the single 1862 Battle of Shiloh, and subsequent Civil War battles proved even more deadly. The conflict of the 1860s was on a scale unlike anything Americans had ever imagined. Never before or since has such a large percentage of the nation's population suffered bereavement.

As one might expect of an epoch that looms so large in the nation's history, the Civil War has been the subject of an enormous literature. It is doubtful if anyone really knows the total number of books that have been written on the war. Some estimates have placed that total as high as 70,000—more than one book per day since the war ended. Nor has the pace of publication slackened. Civil War books continue to appear at a rate that averages more than one per day. Battles, armies, generals, and political leaders have come in for much of this attention, but, especially in more recent years, almost every aspect of the war has been studied—including the participation of ethnic groups ranging from Germans to American Indians to Hispanics, the economy, labor, riots of various sorts, women on the home front, female nurses, and the impact of the war on various local communities, whether in the war's path or far from the scenes of conflict. Even the presence of women in both armies, neither of which allowed any female enlistment, has become a recent topic of more than one book. About four hundred women passed themselves off as men and enlisted under false pretenses, a subterfuge made possible by the cursoriness of the medical examinations Civil War soldiers received at the time of their enlistment. There are books on the lives of children during the Civil War, literature during the Civil War, and children's literature during the war. Quite naturally, the wartime experience of African Americans has also become an important subject of study. Clearly, each generation of Americans since the final surrenders at Appomattox and Durham Station has considered the Civil War eminently worthy of historical investigation.

How then did Americans experience the Civil War on a day-to-day basis? About 3.3 million men, or roughly one in ten Americans living at that time, spent at least part of the Civil War years as a soldier. The wartime lot of a soldier consisted of long periods of intense boredom punctuated by brief episodes of stark terror, along with a great deal of discomfort—cold, heat, drenching rain, little or very unpalatable food, parching thirst. Most Civil War soldiers, not surprisingly, were American-born whites, but the armies also included many soldiers with different backgrounds. Ten of thousands of recent German immigrants fought for the Union. Similar numbers of Irish immigrants also served, some on one side, some the other. Most significantly, 160,000 African Americans, most of them newly freed slaves, served in the Union armies.

The other 90 percent of Americans lived lives on the home front that were also profoundly affected, albeit more subtly, by the ongoing conflict. The strains that the war placed on family and community ties changed some things and left others the same. Family life during and after the Civil War continued to be shaped by the culture's domestic ideal, which cherished the concept of the home as a haven from the rigors and stresses of life. Women were seen as the pure guardians and cultivators of this sort of home. The stresses of war sometimes compelled women to depart from this ideal by taking on tasks around the farm that had previously been relegated to men or by working outside the home. Women saw this not as liberation, but as a burden and were happy to return to their accustomed domestic roles when their husbands came home.

Not surprisingly, medical care was much in demand in the midst of a war that killed or maimed hundreds of thousands of soldiers. Yet bullets and shells were not the chief killers, and soldiers were not the only ones who were in need of medical care. In the Civil War, as in all pre-twentieth-century wars on which we have solid information, disease killed more soldiers than did enemy action. Disease was somewhat less rampant outside the camps of the army, but even in settled civilian areas it could threaten the lives of citizens of any age or class to a degree that modern Americans would find shocking. While the state of medical science seems woefully primitive by today's standards, physicians of the Civil War era strove to provide the best possible care and made a number of significant improvements during the war years.

The Prussian philosopher of war Carl von Clausewitz famously noted, "War is politics carried on by other means." During the mid-nineteenth century it sometimes seemed that politics was war carried on by other means. Political difference as a motivator of conflict is central in any war, but in the American Civil War its importance was particularly significant. Absent barriers of language and nationality, differing political opinion was all that separated the opposing sides. Americans as a group paid far more attention to their politics than now, and political battles were hotly contested, even when the contestants were not bearing arms against one another in open warfare.

Throughout the war, the North continued to have a functioning two-party system. The presence of two parties helped channel political disagreement in relatively constructive ways, though Lincoln certainly had to contend with much opposition from Northern Democrats. The South, on the other hand, lacked a two-party system, and thus political differences within the Confederacy tended to become more radically polarized. Tensions between factions supporting and opposing Confederate president Jefferson Davis produced a political situation within the Confederate government that was, in at least some ways, more difficult than that faced by Lincoln in the North.

Despite the looming presence of the war, Americans still enjoyed many of the diversions and pleasures they had known during peacetime. Novels were written and eagerly read by many elements of the population. Theatergoing was popular as well, though some, especially the devout, tended to frown on both the theater and the novel as possibly degrading and of interest only to the idle. Lyceums, with their educational function, were seen as more edifying and were also highly popular.

Although perhaps one-fifth of the nation's male population would put on the uniform of the Union or Confederacy at some point during the conflict, the civilian economies of both sections had to continue to function if their societies were to continue to wage war. Fields had to be tilled, crops had to be harvested, and factory machinery had to be kept running. Farming, still the most common occupation in America, faced and met new challenges. Without the help of sons who were serving in the army, farmers produced bigger harvests than ever by using agricultural machinery, such as Cyrus McCormack's mechanical reaper. An increasing number of Americans worked in factories.

Especially in the textile industry, these workers included women as well as men. Either way, factory work was much more common in the North than in the South. Slaves, of course, continued in their accustomed prewar tasks until the war either freed them or prompted their masters to try to move them to places where they would be less likely to be in the path of the liberating Union army.

The United States in the mid-nineteenth century was strongly influenced by Christianity. The diaries and letters of Americans of that era clearly reveal how important a part religion played in daily life. The war disrupted worship in many civilian settings, as pastors went off to serve as army chaplains, or passing armies, primarily in the South, appropriated church buildings or engaged in conflict that made church attendance impractical. Religious practice was most severely disrupted in areas of the South not under the direct control of either army, as in these regions lawless bands of draft-dodgers and deserters from both sides made it risky to venture abroad for any purpose, religious or otherwise. Some churches saw substantial drops in civilian attendance and membership. On the other hand, within the armies themselves, both Northern and Southern, massive religious revivals took place. While some of these stirrings were more flamboyant than others and while postwar attention has tended to focus on the Confederate side, a substantial segment of virtually every field army of the war frequently engaged in religious meetings—preaching services, prayer meetings, or the like—whenever the opportunity was available. Even within the South, where wartime civilian religious observance had suffered the greatest setback, the influx of new converts from the armies assured that Christianity would be at least as strong after the war as it had been before.

The lives of Americans during the Civil War were a fascinating mix of the ordinary and the unusual. People of all types, civilians and soldiers alike, strove in many different ways simply to survive and to adjust their previous activities to the special demands of what proved to be the worst conflict in the nation's history.

Gale Library of Daily Life

American Civil War

A Soldier's Life

▪ A Soldier's Life Overview

During the course of the Civil War more than three million men served as soldiers in the armies of the North and South. For them, daily life during the conflict consisted of a multitude of new experiences, many of them unpleasant and most of them much different from anything the men would have encountered had they remained at their peaceful homes. For nearly one in ten Americans during the four years of the war, their status as a soldier was the prime factor that determined the contours of day-to-day existence.

The largest demographic cohort of the Civil War soldiers was composed of young white men born in the United States who had grown up on farms before the war. The typical soldier—if the concept of "typical" can even be applied to a group as diverse as the Civil War combatants—was in his early twenties. Yet those who wore the blue or the gray (or sometimes butternut and a variety of other colors, particularly in Confederate uniforms) varied broadly among themselves, and significant groups of soldiers differed in some notable way from the demographic profile of the majority of soldiers.

The most notable of these varied groups, by all odds, were the African Americans. They had a special motivation to fight because the war had come about as a result of the enslavement of their ethnic group and had become, by the time it was two years old, an open and direct struggle for the freedom of their people. More than 160,000 of them served exclusively in the Union Army and Navy. A handful were inducted into the Confederate Army in the closing weeks of the war, but the Confederate authorities never issued them rifles, and it remains highly debatable whether they would actually have fought for the Confederacy. The African Americans who did see combat with the Union Army showed just as much aptitude for soldiering as their white comrades—much to the surprise of some whites, whose racist assumptions had led them to believe that blacks would not fight. Nevertheless, black soldiers' experience of daily life during the war differed in a number of ways from that of their white counterparts.

Another notable group of Civil War soldiers were the immigrants. Of course, all Americans spring from immigrant stock, whether their ancestors crossed the Atlantic or Pacific by ship or walked across the Bering Strait during the Ice Age. These soldiers, however, were much more recent arrivals, having been born overseas or being the first generation born on American soil to immigrant parents. Especially numerous among them were the Germans, many of whom had come for economic opportunity in the New World, while some, especially the more prominent, had fled the repercussions of the unsuccessful German revolutions of 1848. A number of Union regiments were almost completely ethnically German; they marched and fought to orders given in the German language. The Union Army's Eleventh Corps, numbering in the neighborhood of 10,000 men, contained enough Germans to be known collectively as the "Dutch Corps." Its hard-luck reputation reinforced the prejudice in some nativists' minds that Germans made poor soldiers; however, the performance of many individual German regiments both in and out of the Eleventh Corps proved that idea to be mistaken.

The Irish also fought for the Union in large numbers; unlike the Germans, however, a smaller but still noticeable contingent of the sons of Erin also soldiered in the Confederate ranks. No one ever doubted that the Irishmen would fight, but their wartime service helped win them a little higher measure of respect than a nativist-influenced prewar society had shown them. The special circumstances of these German and Irish soldiers, and those of a smaller number of immigrants from such other countries as Italy or Poland, made their daily life during the war significantly different from that of the typical Civil War soldier.

While the Germans, Irish, and other nationalities in the Civil War armies represented the most recent immigrants to North American, another unusual group among the Civil War soldiers consisted of the descendents of the

1

earliest arrivals. American Indians served on both sides during the war. In some cases, they were able to put to use their special skills in woodcraft and scouting. At other times, especially in the region known as the Indian Territory (what later became the state of Oklahoma), Union Indian fought Confederate Indian, and the struggle took on all of the vicious characteristics that usually accompany internecine warfare among people of any ethnicity. Like the recent immigrants, American Indians had to ask themselves whether the conflict then dividing the continent was their own fight or someone else's.

Yet another group of Civil War soldiers who experienced daily life in ways that differed from the majority were the child soldiers. These could include boy musicians, especially drummers, or the large number of teenaged youth who successfully lied about their age in order to get themselves inducted into the army and experience the great adventure of war. Alonzo Woodworth was a strapping lad of fourteen in the fall of 1861 when he succeeded in convincing the mustering officer in his northeast Indiana community that he was four years older than he was. Duly inducted, he went to war as a member of the Forty-fourth Indiana Volunteer Regiment. His youth, however, made him particularly susceptible to the many diseases that afflicted Civil War soldiers, and he spent most of the war in and out of army hospitals and felt the effects of those years on his health for the rest of his life. The daily life of a soldier could be a different matter when a lad of tender years found himself in uniform.

As had been said of the soldier's lot in other wars, so the men who served in the Civil War armies experienced long periods of intense boredom punctuated by brief interludes of stark terror. A few of them wrote vivid accounts of their experiences in battle, but the daily life of the Civil War soldiers had much more to do with the mundane realities of camp, march, and drill. It was with details of such matters that the soldiers filled their diaries and their many letters home. Writing the letters themselves was one of the chief ways the soldiers beguiled the time and assuaged their often intense feelings of homesickness.

In the letters one reads of food and how it was prepared—such curious culinary creations as hardtack and salt pork fried together in grease or an item in the Union ration known as desiccated vegetables, sometimes referred to by the soldiers as "desecrated vegetables." Oddly enough, perhaps, desiccated vegetables became quite a favorite of many of the Union soldiers, rating just behind the highly esteemed ration of navy beans—or army beans, as that service preferred to call them. The most vital component of the ration as far as the soldiers were concerned, however, was coffee. Issued in the bean, coffee was ground with rifle butts and boiled in whatever container was handy. If constraints of time completely forbade the few minutes necessary to build a fire and make the liquid beverage, the soldiers would, on occasion, chew their coffee beans. Overall, the monotonous

and unpalatable nature of army rations predisposed some of the troops to engage in foraging—the taking of food from enemy civilians—and that in turn provided another pungent aspect to the daily life of those both in and out of the army.

The everyday lives of the soldiers also included such elements as drill—the seemingly endless hours of military exercises necessary for their units to maneuver effectively on the battlefield. Keeping reasonably warm and dry in inclement weather was another frequent concern of the men in blue and gray. Their ability to do so depended much on the equipment their armies issued them. Both sides usually had tents, and Union soldiers might also receive a poncho or a rubber or oilcloth sheet. Confederates usually had to obtain their supplies of such waterproofing equipment by capture.

For the long hours of idle time in camp, after they had written every word they could think of to the folks back home and had attended to the many chores involved in keeping fed and sheltered and maintaining military discipline, the soldiers resorted to a wide array of pastimes. Music, either informal from individual soldier-musicians or the more regular if not more skillful efforts of the regimental bands, helped keep spirits up, as did an assortment of mascots. Many regiments had dogs, but one Union regiment had an eagle, and one Confederate regiment, a camel. The new game of baseball, which the soldiers sometimes called "driveball," gained popularity from its frequent play in the camps, though it was not, as legend would have it, invented by General Abner Doubleday.

The daily life of the Civil War soldiers represented a mixture of the homely and the exotic, the boring and the terrifying, which made it strikingly different from that experienced by civilians before, during, or after the war. The essays that follow delve into some of the most interesting and important aspects of the circumstances the soldiers faced every day.

Steven E. Woodworth

■ Recruitment

RECRUITMENT: AN OVERVIEW

Of the approximately three million men who fought in the American Civil War, more than 620,000 did not survive. The majority of these fatalities—360,000 from the Union side, 260,000 from the Confederate rolls—

Volunteering down Dixie.   Confederate and Union armies were comprised of volunteers at the outset of the Civil War. However, as men began to see the brutality of a long fight, many became reluctant to enlist, compelling both armies to pass conscription laws to replenish their depleted ranks.   *The Library of Congress*

stemmed from disease and other causes rather than from battlefield wounds. But the carnage on the field of battle was nonetheless appalling. In one early clash, for example—the Battle of Shiloh of April 1862—more Americans fell than in all previous American wars combined.

While the soldiers who fought under the banners of the Union and Confederacy were not a monolithic group, most were young. About one-half of all Northern men who were between the ages of sixteen and twenty-four in 1860, for example, fought in the war at some point (Rorabaugh 1986, p. 696), and an even greater percentage of young Southerners took up arms for the Confederacy. But beyond this unsurprising preponderance of young recruits, there was no one type of Civil War soldier. Recruits were of many different nationalities and had widely different occupations; furthermore, while most troops were young, some were quite old—indeed, ages varied across a roughly fifty-year span (Sutherland 1989, p. 2).

The men who took up arms for the Blue and Gray also held a multitude of reasons for participating. Many on both sides were motivated by patriotism and other high-minded principles. Others were swept into the army by peer pressure and community expectations, the promise of adventure, or the prospect of proving their

manhood through the crucible of war. All of the aforementioned factors were pivotal in accounting for the initial rush of volunteers that filled the ranks of the Northern and Southern armies in the opening months of the war.

As the Civil War ground on, however, both armies suffered astonishing rates of attrition. With each passing month, the list of soldiers who had succumbed to enemy bullets or illness grew longer, and generals on both sides beseeched their political leaders for reinforcements. This posed a dilemma for both U.S. President Abraham Lincoln and Confederate President Jefferson Davis, for volunteers were by then few and far between.

Both administrations responded by imposing military drafts on their people. This decision to resort to the draft—widely known as *conscription*—was enormously unpopular and triggered outright rebellion in some areas, particularly in the North. Conscription measures were deeply flawed because they contained numerous service exemptions that were, by and large, only available to middle-class or affluent men. As the inequities of the conscription systems became evident in both the North and South, farming and working-class families without the financial resources to secure exemptions began to complain bitterly. Charges that the war had become "a rich man's war and a poor man's fight" were heard again and again during the last two years of the war, both around the campfires of marching armies and in homes where fathers, sons, and brothers had long been absent.

But while conscription measures in both the North and South became notorious for their divisiveness and corrupt implementation, they ultimately served their purpose of replenishing the ranks of the Blue and Gray. In the latter case, however, the replenishment was only temporary, and it never reached the level necessary for the Confederacy to continue the fight against a foe with superior military and industrial resources. Conscription actions in the South saw steadily diminishing returns, and by the end of 1864 it was clear to even the most optimistic Confederate partisan that defeating the Yankees was impossible if the South ran out of soldiers.

BIBLIOGRAPHY

Barton, Michael, and Larry M. Logue, eds. *The Civil War Soldier: A Historical Reader*. New York: New York University Press, 2002.

Catton, Bruce. *Reflections on the Civil War*, ed. John Leekley. Garden City, NY: Doubleday, 1981.

Donald, David Herbert, Jean Harvey Baker, and Michael F. Holt. *The Civil War and Reconstruction*. New York: W. W. Norton, 2001.

Mitchell, Reid. *Civil War Soldiers: Their Expectations and Their Experiences*. New York: Viking, 1988.

Rorabaugh, William J. "Who Fought for the North in the Civil War? Concord, Massachusetts, Enlistments." *Journal of American History* 73, no. 3 (1986): 695–701.

Sutherland, Daniel E. *The Expansion of Everyday Life, 1860–1876*. New York: Harper & Row, 1989.

Kevin Hillstrom

VOLUNTEERISM

In the first year of the Civil War, both the Union and Confederacy relied on volunteers to form the backbone of their armies. On March 6, 1861, the newly minted Confederate States of America (CSA) issued a call for 100,000 volunteers willing to defend the allied secessionist states against Northern "tyranny." Five weeks later, U.S. President Abraham Lincoln issued a similar call for 75,000 men to rally to the side of the existing federal army, which had shriveled to a mere 16,000 professional soldiers after thousands of Southerners resigned their commissions. Three weeks after this, the president issued an appeal for an additional 60,000 soldiers and sailors. Lincoln's first call to arms had required only ninety-day enlistments, but most of the men who answered his second call signed up for three-year enlistments.

A Rush to Join

The requests for volunteers issued by Lincoln and his Confederate counterpart, President Jefferson Davis, were met with a thunderous response. In fact, the mood was almost celebratory in the war's first few weeks. Thousands of men in both the North and South, their emotions at a fever pitch after years of steadily escalating tension and bombastic political rhetoric, were enormously relieved that the hour of reckoning seemed to finally be at hand. These men did not have to be convinced to volunteer; they went gladly, their steps lightened by patriotic pride and certainty of victory. Indeed, one key factor in the initial flood of applicants to join both armies was a pronounced fear that the war might end so quickly that the volunteer in question would not get an opportunity to snare his own share of combat glory. "The war was greeted in its first few weeks almost as a festival," confirmed one scholar. "People went out and celebrated, both in the North and the South. There were parades, bands playing, flags flying; people seemed almost happy" (Catton 1981, p. 40).

Volunteers for the Blue and Gray rushed to those colors for many of the same reasons. Countless idealistic and naive young men—including thousands of teen boys who lied about their age—enlisted not only to defend grand principles, but also out of a desire for adventure.

Another important factor in the initial flood of volunteer enlistments in both the North and South was peer and community pressure. The divided nation of the mid-nineteenth century was, despite the rapid growth of some cities, still predominantly an empire of villages, towns, and ethnically distinct neighborhoods. In most of these enclaves, neighbors were on a first-name basis with one another and anonymity was not an option. Healthy young men who did not join their peers in the enlistment line, then, were often subject to ridicule or outright condemnation. As one historian observed, "not a few fellows found their way to recruiting depots only after being pushed by the questioning glances of neighbors, disdainful jeers of uniformed swains, and resounding haughtiness of fair maids" (Sutherland 1989, p. 3).

In both the North and South, the importance of personal and family honor, and allegiance to town and county, were crucial incentives to enlistment. This was greatly intensified by the fact that platoons, companies, and regiments were usually composed of men from the same county—and often from the same town or village. The knowledge that one could enlist, train, and fight with other young men who had attended the same school or church, or even serve side by side with relatives and friends, was a powerful incentive to join the cause.

Preserving White Supremacy

While Northerners and Southerners volunteered for many of the same reasons, there was an additional

Appealing to help. Initial appeals by presidents Abraham Lincoln and Jefferson Davis garnered thousands of soldiers on both sides of the Mason-Dixon line. However, the Northern army did not accept free blacks in its ranks until the second year of the conflict. *Schomburg Center/Art Resource, NY*

rationale at work in the Confederacy. In the secessionist South, where a majority of military-age white males fought in the war at some point (and where an estimated 20 percent of that demographic group perished), much of the volunteer push was explicitly linked to the preservation of a "way of life" built on the twin foundations of white supremacy and black slavery.

As historian Gary Gallagher observed in *The Confederate War* (1997), the Confederate government was able to mobilize 75 to 80 percent of its white male population of military age over the course of the war. This success was due in no small measure to the "peculiar institution" of slavery—and the South's determination to defend the practice to its last breath. As a practical matter, the South's ability to gather such a high percentage of white males into its armies was directly attributable to the fact that the continued enslavement of an agricultural work force that included nearly 800,000 male slaves freed up white males to join the military in far greater numbers than otherwise could have been managed. The cultural mandate to preserve slavery, however, may have been just as great an impetus to enlistment in many areas of the South. Enlistees were motivated not just by the desire to preserve slavery as a system of labor, but by a fear of what might happen if the racial hierarchy were overturned. One young Confederate volunteer—a planter's son who joined the army with a slave servant in tow—offered a typical assessment

of the stakes involved in a letter home: "The time for action on the part of our entire race is *swiftly passing,* and unless [fellow white Southerners] all awake and get up on their feet like men, they may be compelled to forever crawl upon the ground like worms" (Logue 2002, p. 46).

Cogs in the Military Machine

Whether donning the colors of the Confederacy or the Union, soldiers in the first great wave of volunteers found themselves enmeshed in military machines that were quite similar in their structure and operating philosophy. For instance, both federal governments relied on individual states to raise their respective armies from the war's outset. These state-based regiments remained the cornerstone of both assembled forces for the war's duration, and though they had been raised for national service, their primary identification and allegiance was often to their home state.

This state of affairs put heavy pressure on state governors. They knew that they would get the credit if their state met its enlistment quota goal—and the blame if it failed to do so. With this in mind, governors in both the North and South tackled the task with zeal. They strong-armed state legislatures (who were generally compliant in this area anyway) to acquire additional funding with which to accelerate the enlistment process. Massachusetts Governor John Andrew (1818–1867), for

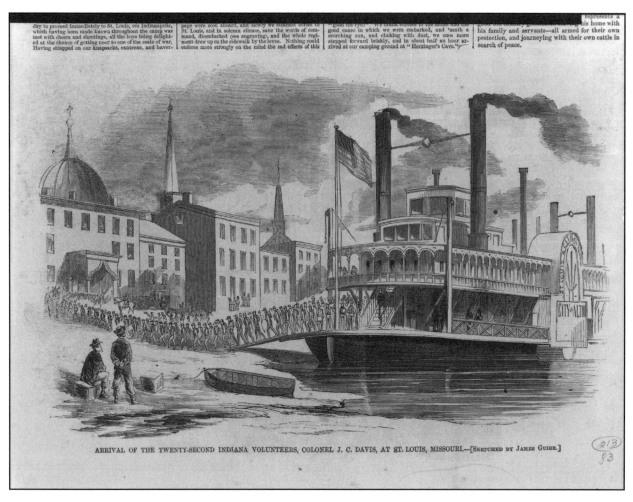

day to proceed immediately to St. Louis, via Indianapolis, which having been made known throughout the camp was met with cheers and shoutings, all the boys being delighted at the chance of getting near to one of the seats of war. Having strapped on our knapsacks, canteens, and haver-page were soon aboard, and slowly we steamed across to St. Louis, and in solemn silence, save the words of command, disembarked (see engraving), and the whole regiment drew up on the sidewalk by the levee. Nothing could enforce more strongly on the mind the sad effects of this "good old rye!" We drank success to the Union and the good cause in which we were embarked, and 'neath a scorching sun, and choking with dust, we once more stepped forward briskly, and in about half an hour arrived at our camping ground at "Herzinger's Cave." represents a his home with his family and servants—all armed for their own protection, and journeying with their own cattle in search of peace.

ARRIVAL OF THE TWENTY-SECOND INDIANA VOLUNTEERS, COLONEL J. C. DAVIS, AT ST. LOUIS, MISSOURI.—[Sketched by James Guire.]

Volunteer soldiers getting off a steamboat in Indiana. States throughout the Union and Confederacy sent soldiers to face the enemy. Troops in many volunteer army units often consisted of men from the same town or region, allowing soldiers to train, live, and fight with individuals with whom they were familiar. *The Library of Congress*

instance, used state funds to charter steamboats and railroad facilities for the transportation of enlistees, as well as to provide food, clothing, and shelter for volunteers until they received supplies from the federal government. His energetic leadership in these and other areas made Massachusetts one of the first Northern states to meet (and then exceed) its quota of volunteers.

Governors in both the North and South were also empowered to select various community leaders and military veterans to lead the recruitment process at the village, city, county, and district levels. Oftentimes, these community leaders received military commissions in return for their help. These commissions became official as soon as the regiment they were responsible for overseeing was raised and sworn in.

Of Companies and Regiments

In both armies, enlistees were assigned to fifty-man platoons, many of which were composed entirely of men from the same township or county. Two platoons com-prised a company, and ten companies formed a regiment. It was the regiment—consisting of roughly one thousand men of various ranks, many from the same region of the country—that was the basic military unit for both the Blue and the Gray. Regiments frequently had their own insignia and nicknames, and most carried unique battle flags, generally handmade by women from the soldiers' towns and villages.

Colorful sobriquets were not the exclusive domain of regiments, though. Within many Yankee and Rebel regiments, individual companies also christened themselves with cocky nicknames that often made explicit reference to the town or region from which the regiment's membership hailed. In his classic *The Life of Johnny Reb* (1943), historian Bell Irvin Wiley rattled off a representative sampling of company names that could be found sprinkled among the Confederate forces, including the Tallapoosa Thrashers, Bartow Yankee Killers, Chickasaw Desperadoes, Southern Rejecters of Old

Abe, Cherokee Lincoln Killers, and South Florida Bull Dogs.

Once a company was formally organized and recognized by the authorities, its soldiers went about the process of electing their own company officers. This odd procedure was commonplace in both the North and South, and underscores the improvisational quality that typified the frantic efforts of both sides to create a working military force. The positions that were most often filled in this manner were those of captains and lieutenants, but some regiments elected all of their non-commissioned and commissioned officers, from corporals to colonels. This led in some cases to the elevation of inept individuals, who were selected purely on the basis of their personal popularity.

After officers were elected, military training could begin in earnest. But the volunteers who filled the ranks of the Blue and Gray during the first two years or so of the Civil War were not professional soldiers, and frequently balked at efforts to rein in their proudly individualistic ways. This tension remained palpable in both armies from the opening days of the war to its conclusion.

An Overwhelming Response

The response to the call for volunteers to march under the Union and Confederate flags quickly swamped federal authorities. The war departments in both Washington, DC, and Montgomery, Alabama (Richmond, Virginia, did not become the Confederate capital until May 6, 1861) were completely unequipped to handle the flood of new soldiers, and the first few weeks of army-building became an administrative nightmare for both sides. The situation became so bad in the North that the War Department urged star recruiters such as Illinois Governor Richard Yates (1818–1873) to ease up on enlistment efforts until it was better prepared to accommodate new troops.

By early 1862 more than 700,000 troops had been enrolled in the Union army—all of them volunteers. But the initial ninety-day enrollment period for the first wave of volunteers had proven to be laughably optimistic, so by the time the War Department sent out the call for another 300,000 volunteers in early July 1862, the service commitment was for a much more realistic three-year term. Less than one year later, in March 1863, the continued demand for still more troops forced the U.S. government to take the momentous step of instituting the first of its military drafts. This controversial turn to conscription reflected a stark reality in the North: The first two years of the war had exhausted its supply of genuine "volunteers" and it would now have to turn to less enthusiastic men to fill the Union ranks. This is not to say that voluntary enlistment ended when the draft began; to the contrary, volunteerism continued to

account for the majority of new troops. Historians agree, however, that many of the men who technically volunteered for military duty during the draft era did so in reaction to the conscription threat, not out of patriotic pride or other high-minded motivations.

Down in the South, meanwhile, the initial call for 100,000 volunteers had also been easily met. But these enlistees had only been asked to serve for six months or a year. As it became evident that the war was going to drag on longer than many people on either side had believed, Confederate officials authorized in April 1862 the conscription of another 300,000 men who would serve for three years—or until the war ended. As in the North, the draft was hugely controversial in the South, but it was somewhat successful in replenishing the Confederacy's increasingly soldier-starved army. It encouraged thousands of draft-age men to volunteer rather than face the uncertainties of the draft, and conscription itself scooped up thousands of others.

BIBLIOGRAPHY

Catton, Bruce. *Reflections on the Civil War*, ed. John Leekley. Garden City, NY: Doubleday, 1981.

Catton, Bruce. *The American Heritage New History of the Civil War*, rev. ed. Ed. James M. McPherson. New York: Viking, 1996.

Donald, David Herbert, Jean Harvey Baker, and Michael F. Holt. *The Civil War and Reconstruction*. New York: W. W. Norton, 2001.

Gallagher, Gary W. *The Confederate War*. Cambridge, MA: Harvard University Press, 1997.

Logue, Larry M. "Who Joined the Confederate Army? Soldiers, Civilians, and Communities in Mississippi." In *The Civil War Soldier: A Historical Reader*, ed. Michael Barton and Larry M. Logue. New York: New York University Press, 2002.

Sutherland, Daniel E. *The Expansion of Everyday Life, 1860–1876*. New York: Harper & Row, 1989.

Wiley, Bell Irvin. *The Life of Johnny Reb: The Common Soldier of the Confederacy*. Indianapolis, IN: Bobbs-Merrill Company, 1943. Reprint, Baton Rouge: Louisiana State University Press, 1992.

Kevin Hillstrom

CONSCRIPTION

For much of the Civil War, both the Union and Confederate armies relied on conscription—mandatory military service—to replenish their battered companies and regiments. During 1861 and 1862 the Confederacy won the Battles of First and Second Bull Run, McDowell, First Winchester, Port Republic, Gaines Mill, and Fredericksburg, split honors at Antietam and Perryville, and lost at another eighteen engagements. The Confederacy's

Balloting for conscripts for the Union draft. During the Civil War, both the North and South relied on mandatory military service to rebuild their armies. The practice of drawing draftees was so unpopular it caused disillusionment and even violence. *The Art Archive/ Culver Pictures/The Picture Desk, Inc.*

casualties in 1861–1862 totaled a much greater percentage of its population than the percentage lost by the Northern states. Given this reality, the Confederacy was the first side to reluctantly turn to conscription, also known as "the draft" due to its many casualties in the first years of the war.

The Confederate Congress passed its first conscription act on April 16, 1862. This measure, designed to add another 300,000 soldiers to the Rebel ranks, required non-exempt white males between the ages of eighteen and thirty-five to sign up for possible military service. The United States followed suit eleven months later, on March 3, 1863, when the U.S. Congress passed the first of four wartime conscription acts. These conscription measures by the South and North ultimately accounted for about 20 percent of the soldiers who fought in the Civil War. More importantly, the mere threat of conscription convinced many other young men to claim some measure of direction over their own lives by "volunteering" for military service.

In both the North and South, however, the imposition of military drafts—and the exemptions that went primarily to the affluent or politically connected—proved to be enormously unpopular. Antidraft riots beleaguered many Northern cities, and in the South many citizens viewed the imposition of conscription as an affront to self-proclaimed values of personal freedom

and states' rights. "What will we have gained," Georgia Governor Joseph Brown (1821–1894) angrily declared, "when we have achieved our independence of the Northern States if in our efforts to do so, we have ... lost *Constitutional Liberty* at home?" (Robbins 1971, p. 93)

Conscription in the North

The 1863 conscription act passed by the U.S. Congress in March 1863 required all able-bodied male citizens between twenty and forty-five, as well as immigrants who had sworn their intention to be naturalized, to register for military service. Draftees, also known as *conscripts*, were required to serve three-year terms. They received the same pay and federal bounties as three-year volunteers. Federal conscription laws also provided mechanisms for enforcement of the draft, including funding for a new government agency that included enrollment officers (who were organized by congressional district), boards of enrollment, provost marshals, and a provost marshal general in Washington, DC.

The institution of a draft troubled many Northerners. By the time it took effect many had become alarmed by the war's slide into stalemate and by the shocking amount of blood already shed. Questions about the Lincoln administration's respect for personal liberty and constitutional freedoms also abounded. But as the historian David Williams (2005) notes, there was an economic dimension as well: Many feared that families would slide into destitution should breadwinners be drafted—and the soldier's measly pay of thirteen dollars per month did nothing to allay these fears or to serve as an inducement.

Lincoln and other Republicans were keenly aware of public opposition to conscription. Indeed, antiwar Democrats focused much of their political energy on denunciations of the draft, and this stance increasingly looked like a winning theme in their quest to make Lincoln a one-term president. Nonetheless, Lincoln issued four separate draft orders during the last two years of the war—in October 1863, March 1864, July 1864, and December 1864. The infusions of manpower they brought about proved pivotal in securing an eventual Union victory in the war. During this span of time, however, major flaws in the draft became starkly apparent. Most of these flaws were in the realm of exemptions.

Draft Exemptions

When the Lincoln administration, the U.S. Congress, and the War Department decided to impose a military draft, they recognized that certain service exemptions had to be included, both in the interests of military efficiency and public acceptance. As a result, exemptions were granted to men who were mentally or physically unfit, selected officials within state and federal governments, and only sons who provided primary support for widower mothers or infirm parents. The act also exempted aliens who had neither voted nor declared their intention to become American citizens. There was initially no exemption for conscientious objection based on religious beliefs, but exemptions were eventually added that permitted Quakers and other conscientious objectors to work in non-combat positions (such as hospital work).

None of these exemptions aroused widespread public indignation or protest. But two other exemptions folded into the 1863 conscription law were breathtakingly brazen in providing loopholes for middle-class and wealthy white men of draft age. The first of these loopholes was a stipulation that permitted a man who was drafted to pay a $300 commutation fee and thus be excused from service (until his number was drawn in a subsequent draft, at any rate). Because $300 amounted to a decent annual income for many American men, the price tag prevented all but wealthy men from exploring this loophole. This provision remained in effect until July 1864, when it was finally abolished in response to the public outcry. The second controversial loophole was one that allowed drafted men to hire substitutes to serve in their stead; if they could quickly find someone willing to serve, and could pay them the going market rate, they were off the hook. (Northerners who were conscripted had ten days in which to pay commutation, find a substitute, or report for duty.)

These two exemptions made it clear to many Northern soldiers—and their families waiting anxiously back home—that the Civil War was turning into "a rich man's war and a poor man's fight." Other citizens reached the same conclusion, and within weeks of passage of the 1863 conscription law, a new level of skepticism and cynicism about the war was detectable on many Northern city streets. During this time, for example, a parody of the patriotic recruiting song "We Are Coming Father Abraham" became popular in many urban areas. One representative verse of the parody, dubbed "Song of the Conscripts," went as follows:

We're coming Father Abraham, three hundred
thousand more,
We leave our homes and firesides with bleeding
hearts and sore,
Since poverty has been our crime, we bow to thy
decree,
We are the poor who have no wealth to purchase
liberty.
(Williams 2005, p. 274).

How the Draft Worked

Far from ending recruitment drives, in the North the military draft actually served to galvanize recruiting by states, cities, and other government organizations, because the draft was not imposed on any locality that had met its quota of recruits through volunteerism. The country was divided up into congressional districts, each of which was supposed to provide an apportionment of soldiers based on its population. If counties (or entire states) could meet their quota through volunteer enlistments, they did not have to use conscription to make up the "deficiency."

This state of affairs gave rise to a bounty system, in which towns and cities offered a lump-sum cash payment to any man who enlisted voluntarily. This "bounty" was often further supplemented by contributions from county boards of commissions, state legislatures, the federal government, and even private citizens or organizations. These bounties became as high as $1,000 in the latter stages of the war. Not surprisingly, these astounding sums led some ethically challenged but enterprising young men to become "bounty jumpers"—men who would enlist at one locale in order to collect the bounty, then disappear and do the same thing in another location. One bounty jumper reportedly executed this maneuver more than thirty times before he was finally apprehended and thrown into prison.

Another shady profession that blossomed in the wake of the United States' conscription laws was that of the substitute broker. For a fee, these men took on the task of finding substitutes for wealthy clients who had been served with draft notices. In many cases, however, brokers preyed on the most vulnerable members of society—alcoholics, the impoverished or homeless, the mentally ill—when rounding up substitutes. They then bribed doctors and other officials to get these down-and-out substitutes approved for military duty.

These and other men brought in by the substitute and bounty systems generally made for poor-quality soldiers. This reality did not go unnoticed by military leaders such as Union General Ulysses S. Grant (1822–1885), who lamented at war's end that not one soldier in eight who was brought in by the high-bounty system ever became a decent front-line soldier. Nor did it escape the notice of fellow soldiers, who loathed high-bounty troops, and often set out to make their lives miserable.

All told, more than three-quarters of a million names were enrolled during the two-year life of the Union conscription act. But only a little over 46,300 entered the army as actual draftees. In addition, almost 87,000 draftees evaded service by paying a commutation fee, and another 73,600 soldiers enrolled in the ranks as substitutes for wealthier countrymen (Donald 2001, p. 229). Thousands of others—possibly tens of thousands—avoided the draft by volunteering. And finally, there were those who responded to the threat of conscription with subterfuge or by fleeing.

Other Methods of Evading the Draft

Many Northern men evaded military service by ignoring conscription notices. This decision—whether it stemmed from cowardice, ideological opposition to the war, or concern for the welfare of family members—usually involved relocation to an area of the country that was inhospitable to conscription officers. The relatively unpopulated and thinly policed western territories were a particularly attractive destination for draft evaders, as was Canada. In these parts of North America, the vast spaces could easily swallow up a man or family that wished to disappear from the government's sight. For example, an officer stationed in California would find that tracking down deserters and draft dodgers was a nearly impossible task due to the sheer size of the state and the indifference of the population to the war (Williams 2005, p. 266).

Other draftees tried to avoid conscription by giving false identities or feigning blindness, deafness, or some other serious physical malady. Others hurriedly proposed to sweethearts or family friends in the mistaken belief that the Conscription Act excused married men from military service (in actuality, it merely put married men over the age of thirty-five on secondary draft status). Still others bribed draft administrators in order to avoid reporting for duty.

Another novel—and effective—response to the threat of conscription was the emergence of "draft insurance" societies or clubs. In these clubs, which popped up in Philadelphia, Boston, New York, Milwaukee, Indianapolis, and other larger cities of the North, each member contributed a sum of money that would be used to hire a substitute or pay a commutation fee should any fellow member receive a conscription notice. Members thus

diluted the financial pain while simultaneously receiving ironclad protection from the battlefield.

Violent Opposition to Conscription

In some parts of the North, public unhappiness with federal conscription laws boiled over into violence. Intimidation of draft officers was commonplace in many cities and counties—and in some cases the threats were so serious that it was difficult for authorities to find people willing to hire on as draft officers. Some of this hostility had an organizational basis, and conscription administrators sometimes voiced genuine alarm about the number of antidraft societies springing up in their midst. One provost marshal in New Jersey, for instance, reported that "organizations are formed or forming in nearly all the districts in New Jersey to resist the draft" (Murdock 1971, p. 85).

Tensions over the draft in some areas frequently became so great that bloodshed was virtually inevitable. One highly publicized explosion of draft-related violence occurred in the coal towns of Pennsylvania. According to historian Bruce Catton in *Reflections on the Civil War* (1981), mine workers in the region had long been trying to form unions in an effort to be more justly compensated for their dangerous and exhausting toil. When several leaders in the unionization effort were plucked from the ranks by the local provost marshal and carted off to the military, the frustrated miners lashed out in rage. Over the next several days they rioted across the countryside, reserving special violence for area draft offices.

The most deadly and infamous of the draft riots to afflict the Union, however, occurred in July 1863 in New York City. Many white city residents—and especially the city's large Irish population—opposed Lincoln and the emancipation cause in the first place, as they viewed free blacks as major competitors for scarce jobs, and after the passage of the Conscription Act their anger was further stoked by the bombastic rhetoric of anti-Lincoln city newspapers and political leaders such as Democratic Governor Horatio Seymour (1810–1886).

On July 11, 1863, the city's drawing of the first draftees' names commenced, and this proved to be the match that set off the powder keg. White mobs formed and marauded through the streets, cutting telegraph wires, burning the provost marshal's headquarters, and attacking police. Eventually, African Americans became the special focus of the mob's wrath, and throughout the city blacks were beaten and lynched, and had their homes burned to the ground. All in all, 119 New Yorkers were killed in the 1863 draft riots and more than 300 African Americans were wounded. In addition, thousands of African American families fled the city in fear for their lives.

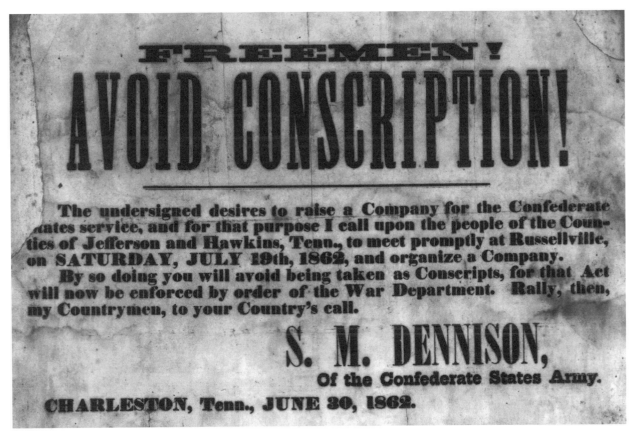

A conscription poster. Early Confederate success on the battlefield nonetheless resulted in heavy casualties. Starting with a smaller population from which to draw soldiers, the South began conscripting troops in early 1862 to augment their numbers. *MPI/Hulton Archive/ Getty Images*

The Cornerstone of the Union Army

Conscription thus was a mixed blessing for the Union cause. It did provide the army with much-needed infusions of new soldiers, either through outright conscription or volunteerism stemming from the threat of the draft. But the quality of the soldiers caught by the conscription net was uneven at best, and some commanders saw conscripts as little more than cannon fodder.

It was the volunteers who had first signed up for the Union cause in the heady days after Fort Sumter who remained the backbone of the army to the very end. Virtually all of them had lost close friends to the war and had been away from their families for nearly three years—but they reenlisted in early 1864 to finish the job when they could have gone home.

Conscription in the South

Saddled with significant disadvantages in terms of manpower, military equipment, and other resources, the Confederacy was forced to play the conscription card a full year before the Union did. First, however, the South needed to ensure that the soldiers it already had on hand stayed put. In the early spring of 1862, Confederate

president Jefferson Davis and the Confederate Congress were confronted with the looming possibility that much of the Southern army—comprised of volunteers who had accepted twelve-month enlistments the previous spring—might return to their homes. Determined to stave off this threat, lawmakers passed an act that offered lucrative signing bonuses and generous furloughs for veterans who reenlisted.

Then, on April 16, 1862, the Confederate Congress passed the first conscription law in American history. This act to legalize compulsory military service—service that Davis described as "absolutely indispensable" to the future of the Confederacy—applied to white men between the ages of eighteen and thirty-five (later amended to age forty-five). Eager to blunt the impact of the draft, the South sweetened the pot for potential enlistees before conscription even came into effect, by promising cash bonuses and choice of unit assignments to those who volunteered. These inducements had the desired effect, as thousands of Southerners who had not been moved to join in the war's beginning months now stepped forward. According to historian Albert Burton Moore, author of *Conscription and Conflict in the*

Confederacy (1924), the Confederate War Department later estimated that fully three-fourths of those who volunteered to march under the Rebel flag did so to avoid the stigma of conscription.

Within the army ranks, meanwhile, news of the conscription measures elicited a range of emotions. On the one hand, soldiers felt a measure of relief that new men would be arriving to help them shoulder the burden of warmaking. But many Rebel soldiers saw conscription as blatantly unconstitutional and as a sign of the South's desperate situation.

Exemptions to the Conscription Act

As was the case with the Union draft laws that followed a year later, Confederate conscription measures included a number of service exemptions. Eager to minimize disruptions on the domestic front and keep its army supplied with necessary staples, the Confederate conscription law permitted men engaged in a wide range of professions to be excused from enlistment. Schoolteachers (of at least twenty pupils), college professors, ministers, mail carriers and postmasters, druggists, assorted state and federal officials, telegraph operators, railroad and ferry workers, blacksmiths, tanners, millers, printers, newspaper editors, and workers in cotton mills, mines, and foundries all had the option of claiming an exemption. The announcement of these exemptions prompted a flurry of career changes in some parts of the South. For example, a number of men—including some with virtually no formal education—abruptly opened schoolhouses and promised to teach students for free if they could entice twenty students from the surrounding area to enroll.

In addition, wealthy Southerners—like their counterparts to the north—had the option of paying a commutation fee or hiring a substitute to serve in their stead. Finding a substitute was the preferred method of sidestepping military service, but this option soon became the sole province of the very rich. By the end of 1863, substitutes were demanding thousands of dollars for their services, and in some parts of the South the fee reached as high as $10,000. An advertisement for a substitute in one newspaper offered to pay "in cash, land, or negro property." Another offered a 230-acre farm. All told, at least 50,000 wealthy Southerners evaded military service by hiring substitutes (Williams 2005, p. 76).

The most unpopular and controversial exemption, however, was the "twenty-slave" exemption. This provision released one slave owner or overseer from military duty for every twenty slaves under their direction. Plantation owners with hundreds of slaves were thus able to excuse not only themselves but also their most valuable foremen from the army. Most wealthy Southern landowners were quick to take advantage of this loophole (though it should be noted that a number of them were exempt from the draft anyway because of their age). According to scholar William Kauffman Scarborough in

Masters of the Big House (2003), only thirty-one (11.4%) of the Confederacy's 272 largest slaveholders (those owning 250 slaves or more) saw military service during the Civil War, and only four of them died on duty. By contrast, nearly half of the South's military-aged white males served at one time or another, and one-third of those did not survive the war.

Anger and Disillusionment

Wealthy Southern landowners defended their absence from the Rebel ranks, noting that they played an important role as producers of food, clothing, and other essential goods for both the army and the wider public. But their emphasis on lucrative cotton production over badly needed staple crops such as corn diluted their claims that they were practicing their own brand of patriotism, and fellow Southerners recognized that every time a wealthy man evaded military service, the army turned more avidly to financially defenseless prospects such as poor farmers. As one Virginian angrily wrote to the Confederate War Department,

> It is impossible to make *poor* people comprehend the policy of putting able-bodied, healthy, Mr. A in such light service as collecting tithes and money *at home,* when the well known feeble & delicate Mr. B.—who is a poor man with a large family of children depending on him for bread—is sent to the front. ... I beseech you to be warned of the coming storm—the people will not *always* submit to this *unequal, unjust* and partial distribution of favor and wholesale conscription of the *poor* while the able-bodied & healthy men of property are all occupying *soft places.* (Escott 1978, p. 119)

Frustration with the inequities of the draft combined with other factors—fear, concern for vulnerable family members, disenchantment with the Davis administration—to create a significant draft evasion problem. Some men avoided the front lines by joining home guard or militia companies (which were supposed to be manned by seniors and teenage boys). Others fled to Mexico. But some, especially those living in communities that had become disillusioned about the war and the Confederate leadership, simply ignored the law. In these areas, convictions for draft dodging were few.

During the campaigns of 1864 the Confederate army became dangerously depleted, in part because desertion was emerging as a serious problem. Richmond responded by eliminating some exemption loopholes and expanding the age restrictions for enlistment to the minimum of seventeen and the maximum of fifty. But these measures took a toll on the South's factories and railroads, which increasingly struggled to operate with skeleton crews.

Mixed Feelings toward Conscripts

Meanwhile, Southerners who submitted to the draft or served as substitutes for more well-heeled countrymen were treated with suspicion or contempt by the dedicated veterans who had been wearing the Gray since the war's opening weeks. These attitudes were understandable, but they did not advance the Confederate cause, as they hardly made it likely that already unwilling conscripts would develop into first-class troops—and indeed, few did.

Despite these hard feelings, Rebel veterans often voiced a deep desire to force "stay-at-homes" into service. These battle-scarred soldiers recognized the truth of a basic equation: The larger the Confederate force was, the better its chances of victory over its foe. But even here, the Rebel veteran made exceptions for brothers, sons, and fathers who remained back home supporting their family. In the view of many soldiers, a family that sent one representative into the meat grinder of the Civil War had amply fulfilled its duty and defended its honor.

BIBLIOGRAPHY

Barton, Michael, and Larry M. Logue, eds. *The Civil War Soldier: A Historical Reader*. New York: New York University Press, 2002.

Catton, Bruce. *Reflections on the Civil War*, ed. John Leekley. Garden City, NY: Doubleday, 1981.

Catton, Bruce. *The American Heritage New History of the Civil War*, revised edition. Ed. James M. McPherson. New York: Viking, 1996.

Donald, David Herbert, Jean Harvey Baker, and Michael F. Holt. *The Civil War and Reconstruction*. New York: W. W. Norton, 2001.

Escott, Paul D. *After Secession: Jefferson Davis and the Failure of Confederate Nationalism*. Baton Rouge: Louisiana State University Press, 1978.

McPherson, James M. *For Cause and Comrades: Why Men Fought in the Civil War*. New York: Oxford University Press, 1997.

Mitchell, Reid. *Civil War Soldiers: Their Expectations and Their Experiences*. New York: Viking, 1988.

Moore, Albert Burton. *Conscription and Conflict in the Confederacy*. New York: Macmillan, 1924. Reprint, New York: Hillary House, 1963.

Murdock, Eugene C. *One Million Men: The Civil War Draft in the North*. Madison: State Historical Society of Wisconsin, 1971.

Robbins, John. "The Confederacy and the Writ of Habeas Corpus." *Georgia Historical Quarterly* 55 (Spring 1971): 83–101.

Scarborough, William Kauffman. *Masters of the Big House: Elite Slaveholders of the Mid-Nineteenth-Century South*. Baton Rouge: Louisiana State University Press, 2003.

Wiley, Bell Irvin. *The Life of Johnny Reb: The Common Soldier of the Confederacy*. Indianapolis, IN, and New York: Bobbs-Merrill Company, 1943. Reprint, Baton Rouge: Louisiana State University Press, 1992.

Williams, David. *A People's History of the Civil War: Struggles for the Meaning of Freedom*. New York: New Press, 2005.

Kevin Hillstrom

■ Drill Training

Drills and training were an integral part of Civil War military life, especially in the opening year of the conflict when both North and South were seeking to mobilize armies out of their respective civilian populations. Neither side distinguished itself in this regard, in part because each army was saddled with a large number of inexperienced officers who knew little or nothing about drill or military tactics. This was a vexing problem for both the Union and the Confederacy. Another complication in drill and training was the strong individualistic streak of many Yankee and Rebel soldiers. Accustomed to a hefty measure of independence and self-direction in their everyday lives, many enlistees chafed at the tedious hours spent at drill.

The Drill Routine

In both the Union and Confederate armies, drill exercises and other training were interspersed throughout the day at camp. By day's end, several hours had typically been devoted to drill (the amount of time spent on drill diminished significantly as the war intensified, however). Fighting formations were generally linear and had to be practiced to ensure that the soldiers could function in the necessary combat structures.

Company sergeants usually conducted the drills with supervision from company commanders and field officers. Veterans of the Mexican-American War and regular officers who had already been in the federal army prior to the war tended to be the biggest sticklers for training. These men had a greater appreciation for the importance of efficient movements on the battlefield, and they also saw drill as a way of building discipline and obedience. But even in units led by these men, training was often halting and haphazardly executed.

Whether directed by knowledgeable military veterans or novices appointed as a result of political connections or recruiting skills, drilling routines elicited reactions from the rank and file that ranged from patient understanding to fuming indignation. The latter reaction was particularly evident in the South, where many equated being forced to submit to military discipline with being reduced to the status of a slave.

Similar sentiments were also evident within the Union ranks. "We are almost drilled to Death now," complained one Pennsylvanian volunteer in a letter to a friend. "My Dear Boy, Playing Soldier and Soldiering in reality is two very different things I can assure you" (Sutherland 1989, p. 8). Writing to his sister, a private from Indiana cited drill as a perfect example of how

A company of infantry near Harpers Ferry. Turning civilians into soldiers often meant long hours of drill training in the field, a tedious task disliked by Union and Confederate troops alike. Recruits found the training dull and obeying orders challenging. *Hulton Archive/Getty Images*

[a] soldier is not his own man[;] . . . you fall in and start. You here feel your inferiority, even the Sargeants is hollering at you to close up, Ketch step, dress to the right, and sutch like, the man in youre reer is complaining of youre gun not being held up. Perhaps you will let this [cause you to] make some remark when you will be immediately tolde by a Lietenant to be silent in ranks or you will be put in the guard house. (McPherson 1997, p. 47)

The Importance of Drill

Most companies, whether marching under the Stars and Stripes or the Confederate flag, did not spent much of their time on target practice or other firearms-related drills. This decision was based on a widely held assumption that most soldiers were frontier types who were already proficient with the muzzle-loading rifles that predominated in the war. In reality, however, many enlistees came from urban areas in which hunting was not a widespread pastime, and some green soldiers did not even know how to load their muskets upon reporting for duty. The South, which had a more rural character than the North and a higher percentage of hunters and trappers in its ranks, was not hurt as badly as the North by this misconception, but even it fielded companies that were woefully undertrained in shooting and weapon maintenance.

Most drill activity was instead focused on marching and fighting formations. Specifically, a great deal of attention was paid to teaching soldiers how to efficiently switch from a marching formation (which was generally serpentine in character) to a fighting formation (which often required assumption of box-like or shield-like forms). Because these maneuvers involved the complex coordination of large numbers of men, and often had to be achieved under fire, few commanders ever considered their men to be adequately drilled and emphasized extensive practice.

BIBLIOGRAPHY

Catton, Bruce. *The American Heritage New History of the Civil War*, rev. ed. Ed. Bruce McPherson. New York: Viking, 1996.

Hummel, Jeffrey Rogers. *Emancipating Slaves, Enslaving Free Men: A History of the American Civil War*. Chicago: Open Court, 1996.

McPherson, James M. *For Cause and Comrades: Why Men Fought in the Civil War*. New York: Oxford University Press, 1997.

Mitchell, Reid. *Civil War Soldiers: Their Expectations and Their Experiences*. New York: Viking, 1988.

Sutherland, Daniel E. *The Expansion of Everyday Life, 1860–1876*. New York: Harper & Row, 1989.

Wiley, Bell Irvin. *The Life of Johnny Reb: The Common Soldier of the Confederacy*. Indianapolis, IN, and New York: Bobbs-Merrill Company, 1943. Reprint, Baton Rouge: Louisiana State University Press, 1992.

Kevin Hillstrom

■ Food and Rations

In the realm of food rations, the experiences of both Union and Confederate troops during the Civil War were similar in many respects. Each army set up commissary departments that in many operational aspects were mirror images of the other, and the typical soldier—whether a Yankee or a Rebel—endured periods in which food was scarce, particularly as the war progressed. Soldiers on both sides sought to supplement their army rations in similar ways as well, usually through foraging or visits to area sutlers (authorized civilian merchants). As the war progressed, it was the quantity of food (rather than quality) that most concerned the typical soldier (Sutherland 1989, p. 10).

The main difference in food rations between the armies of the South and North lay in the degree of deprivation. Whereas Union soldiers complained mightily—and with merit—about the rations they received, they nonetheless consumed sufficient food supplies to keep bellies full and malnutrition at bay, at least for the most part. Confederate soldiers were not as fortunate; as the war dragged on and the South's military fortunes turned for the worse, food scarcity became a significant problem for many Confederate troops.

Feeding the Troops

One of the first priorities of both sides in the weeks and months leading up to the Civil War was to set up commissary departments. In the North, the War Department was able to use the existing structure that was already in place for the federal army (though it had to overhaul it to accommodate the much greater demands of an expanded military). The Confederacy adopted a similar food distribution structure, in large measure because it was the system with which Southern officers who had resigned from the U.S. Army were familiar.

Boiled down to its essentials, the primary responsibility of these departments was to buy food for the soldiers and store and distribute the rations as needed. Because refrigeration (using blocks of ice) was not practical in camp or on the march, both armies relied heavily on salted or smoked meats and canned or dried vegetables. When the war began, the South adopted the official U.S. Army food ration structure for individual soldiers. The official daily ration for soldiers in camp included pork or bacon; fresh or salt beef; and cornmeal, bread, or flour. These staples were supplemented by rations that were doled out at the company level, such as beans, potatoes, peas, rice, coffee, tea, molasses, sugar, salt, pepper, and irregular dispensations of various types of vegetables or fruits. Fresh fruit, vegetables, and dairy products virtually disappeared from the soldiers' diet during the war, although some soldiers were able to "liberate" these goods from the civilian population during the course of military operations.

ON FEAST AND FAMINE

James H. Clark, a Union soldier of the 115th New York Regiment, details his quotidian wartime experience in his 1865 book *The Iron Hearted Regiment*. One of his daily concerns included food and rations. While the army did supply a ration to each soldier, he endured times of scarcity:

> September 16—I paid a silver quarter of a dollar for a poor breakfast, the same for dinner, and one quarter of a dollar for a little cider.

> September 18—Could not get anything to eat at any price. Money was of no value to purchase food, than grains of sand. The soldiers were ordered out of nearly every house which they stopped at (p. 31).

In contrast, soldiers' journeys also occasionally brought them to places where any palate could be satisfied. In Zenas T. Haines's 1863 book *Letters from the Forty-Fourth Regiment M.V.M.: A Record of the Experience of a Nine Months' Regiment in the Department of North Carolina in 1862-3*, Haines describes their trip through Newburn as a veritable trove of delicacies:

> Newburn has become quite a jolly place to live in. It is filled with Yankee jimcracks, ranging all the way from top-boots to preserved strawberries. The market supplies splendid Northern apples, Southern ditto, honey, cider, ginger cakes, crackers, fish, preserved meats and fruits, oysters, pickles, condensed milk, chocolate, sugar, tea, coffee. It is wonderfully convenient to be so near to all these little comforts ... gingerbread, pies, and even apple-dumplings, are brought to us by the negroes in profusion, while the sutlers furnish us with butter, cheese, sardines, and all the main essentials of luxurious living. Our regular rations are not to be sneezed at, although at present a scarcity of hops has thrown us back on hardtack. We are treated to beef steaks, excellent rice soups, fish, etc. (pp. 48–49).

In times of both famine and feast, food was always on the soldier's mind.

CARLY S. KALOUSTIAN

BIBLIOGRAPHY

Clark, James H. The Iron Hearted Regiment: Being an Account of the Battles, Marches and Gallant Deeds Performed by the 115th Regiment N.Y. *Albany, NY: J. Munsell, 1865. Sources in U.S. History Online: Civil War. Gale. Available from http://galenet.galegroup.com/.*

Haines, Zenas T. Letters from the Forty-Fourth Regiment M.V.M.: A Record of the Experience of a Nine Months' Regiment in the Department of North Carolina in 1862–3. *Boston: Herald Job Office, 1863. Sources in U.S. History Online: Civil War. Gale. Available from http://galenet.gale group.com/.*

Neither the U.S. army nor the Confederate one was able to meet its official ration-dispensation goals on a regular basis once the war started. Getting food to soldiers in semipermanent encampments, however, was much easier than keeping up with companies on the move. Many soldiers on the move became accustomed to operating on half-rations (or on even less). This was especially true in the South, which fell so far short of its ration-distribution goals by the spring of 1862 that it quietly reduced its official food-ration targets.

Food rations that did make it to the armies, whether they were encamped or on the march, were rarely prepared with much concern for making the food palatable. Commissary cooks and their supervisors were primarily concerned with stretching existing food resources as far as possible and delivering food to soldiers' plates with dispatch. Aesthetic considerations of taste and presentation were not primary in their food-preparation chores. "Our boys threaten a riot every day for the bad beef and spoiled bread issued to us," warned one unhappy Wisconsin soldier (Sutherland 1989, p. 10). Another Union soldier, a corporal from Illinois, no doubt spoke for many in his company when he bitterly wrote, "the boys say that our '*grub*' is enough to make a *mule* desert, and a *hog* wish he had never been born" (Donald 2001, p. 247). Ignorance and indifference about careful food handling and sanitation also took its toll; diarrhea and other intestinal ailments were commonplace in the ranks of both the North and South.

Salt Pork, Hardtack, and Coffee

The core staples in the diet of both Rebel and Yankee were salt pork (usually fried), the hard, square biscuits known as "hardtack," and black coffee. Salt pork was easily the most widely consumed meat during the war, although perennial salt shortages in the South (which during the prewar years had acquired most of its salt from the North) made the food difficult to come by in Southern camps as the war ground on.

Hardtack was widely reviled for its rock-like character and the frequency with which it became infested with weevils and other insects. Fresh hardtack could be chewed, but most hardtack was consumed weeks or months after it had been made. These batches were virtually impossible to choke down without first soaking them in bacon grease, condensed milk, coffee, soup, or water.

Black coffee, meanwhile, outranked even tobacco as a necessity for most soldiers. One of the most valuable items in the kit of just about every Civil War soldier, from the infantry private to the artillery captain, was a metal can (usually tin) that he could use to boil coffee. Coffee rations were usually doled out in bean rather than ground form because of concerns that contractors would dilute ground coffee—a legitimate precaution given the venality of some Civil War–era contractors. Soldiers were thus responsible for grinding their own coffee. Most accomplished this task by using rifle butts as a sort of pestle to mash the beans into powder. "In the morning, in camp, you could tell when the boys were getting up

by the rhythmic clinking, grinding noise that came up from in front of every tent" (Catton 1981, p. 42).

Supplemental Sources of Food

Occasionally, Civil War soldiers received packages of cookies, cakes, and other delights from loved ones back at home. These packages elicited a complex range of emotions in many recipients. On the one hand, soldiers savored the contents of these gift packages, which almost always were heavily weighted toward items that were known to be personal favorites. But such mail inevitably conjured up memories of the last meal the soldier had eaten back home before heading off to war—typically an extravagant feast from the family larder prepared by parents, wives, or siblings in the full knowledge that they might never see their departing relative again.

As the war progressed, Confederate and Union forces on the move also supplemented their army rations through fishing and hunting expeditions. Participation in these officially sanctioned expeditions was highly desirable, for it offered an escape from tedious camp chores and spiritually uplifted soldiers, who were reminded of past hours spent in the family fields and woods of Minnesota, Michigan, New York, Alabama, or Tennessee.

Many soldiers also turned to army sutlers, though this resource was beyond the financial means of some troops, especially in the last couple of years of the conflict. These civilian merchants sold a wide range of food and other items to soldiers with the official sanction of regimental commanders. Canny sutlers quickly realized that they could reap their greatest profits from the sale of food, and so they devoted a good percentage of their stockpile of goods to fresh fruit, onions, cheese, butter, condensed milk, cookies and cakes, and other products.

Union Foraging

For Rebel and Yankee companies moving through the country's eastern and western theaters, the civilian farms and general stores that lay in the vicinity of their camps and marching paths made up another resource. Both armies resorted to what was termed "foraging"—though this designation was little more than a self-serving euphemism for plundering the livestock and foodstuffs of civilians who could themselves be facing malnutrition or worse.

Some Union commanders forbade foraging, and many soldiers in the ranks looked at the practice as immoral and disgraceful. As the war progressed, however, and Union troops became increasingly weary of their meager, unappetizing, and unvarying commissary rations, the practice spread. As one soldier from Maine recounted, "despite most stringent orders against foraging, every morning the ground between the different encampments of the regiments was covered with sheep skins and feathers from turkeys, geese and hens that had given their lives,

Dinner in the camp. While troops in both blue and gray received only basic food provisions from their respective armies, many soldiers supplemented their meager rations with foods foraged from the forest or local farms. Union blockages and lack of diversification in agriculture led to greater problems in the South, where soldiers were chronically underfed and civilian larders were emptied by invading Union fighters. *Photograph by Mathew Brady. The Library of Congress.*

during the preceding night, for the relief of the hungry soldiers" (Robertson 1988, pp. 73–74).

Union plundering of Southern farms reached its greatest heights (or its nadir, depending on one's viewpoint) during General William Tecumseh Sherman's famous March through Georgia and the Carolinas in late 1864 and early 1865. As Sherman cut a methodical path through the heart of the Confederacy, he embraced foraging as official army policy. Seizing whatever they wished from the farms and stores that Sherman's army passed by, his men did destroy a great deal, including much livestock, but Sherman's orders directed that they should endeavor to leave each family enough food to get through until the next harvest. These orders were actually carried out at least some of the time. Armed with this official sanction, Sherman's troops routinely carried off food and other supplies by the wagonload from surrounding hamlets and farms. "We cannot change the hearts of those people of the South," the general declared. "But we can make war so terrible and make them so sick of war that generations would pass away before they would again appeal to it" (Grimsley 1997, p. 118).

Impressment and Hunger in the South

In the South, soldiers and civilians alike suffered from food shortages for much of the war. Factors responsible for the steadily diminishing availability of food included the effectiveness of Union naval blockades, the South's comparatively undeveloped railroad systems, and Federal occupation of vital agricultural areas, including Tennessee, Georgia, and large swaths of the Shenandoah Valley. Levels of hunger in the civilian population were further intensified by government impressments of crops and livestock for consumption by the army. "By the end of the war many staples had permanently disappeared from the southern diet. . . . Rats became a familiar item in many diets. President Davis was quoted as saying that he saw no reason for not eating them, for he thought they would be 'as good as squirrels.' But rats never became as popular as mule meat" (Donald 2001, p. 457). The food situation became so desperate that some Southern cities were rocked by food riots in the last two years of the war.

The diminishing availability of food inevitably had a negative impact on Confederate troops in the field. After the first year of war, Rebel soldiers were almost perpetually underfed. Their plight was further exacerbated by the incompetence and corruption of the commissary general of the Confederate Army, Lucius B. Northrop, who became widely hated.

In the latter stages of the Civil War, shortages of food rations became so severe that growing numbers of Rebel troops took to robbing fellow Southerners. "Impressment" of food was particularly commonplace among cavalry units, which had both greater mobility than their infantry counterparts and greater freedom from supervision. This grim development was difficult to witness for those Rebel soldiers who resisted the urge to plunder. "[Southerners] talk about the ravages of the enemy in their marches through the country," wrote one disillusioned Confederate soldier. "But I do not think that the Yankees are any worse than our own army" (Mitchell 1988, p. 163).

In the final analysis, however, most scholars agree that few Confederate military units ever succumbed to outright starvation or died as a direct result of acute malnutrition. But malnutrition undoubtedly was a contributing factor in the deaths of sick or wounded soldiers on both sides, and food shortages contributed to the cloud of dread that shadowed Southern troops in the latter stages of the war.

BIBLIOGRAPHY

Catton, Bruce. *Reflections on the Civil War*, ed. John Leekley. Garden City, NY: Doubleday, 1981.

Donald, David Herbert, Jean Harvey Baker, and Michael F. Holt. *The Civil War and Reconstruction*. New York: W. W. Norton, 2001.

Grimsley, Mark. *The Hard Hand of War: Union Military Policy toward Southern Civilians, 1860–1865*. Cambridge, NY: Cambridge University Press, 1997.

Linderman, Gerald F. *Embattled Courage: The Experience of Combat in the American Civil War*. New York: Free Press, 1987.

Mitchell, Reid. *Civil War Soldiers: Their Expectations and Their Experiences*. New York: Viking, 1988.

Robertson, James I., Jr. *Soldiers Blue and Gray*. Columbia, SC: University of South Carolina Press, 1988.

Shannon, Fred A. "The Life of the Common Soldier in the Union Army, 1861–1865." In *The Civil War Soldier: A Historical Reader*, ed. Michael Barton and Larry M. Logue. New York: New York University Press, 2002.

Sutherland, Daniel E. *The Expansion of Everyday Life, 1860–1876*. New York: Harper & Row, 1989.

Wiley, Bell Irvin. *The Life of Johnny Reb: The Common Soldier of the Confederacy*. Indianapolis, IN, and New York: Bobbs-Merrill Company, 1943. Reprint, Baton Rouge: Louisiana State University Press, 1992.

Williams, David. *Johnny Reb's War: Battlefield and Homefront*. Abilene, TX: McWhiney Foundation Press, 2000.

Kevin Hillstrom

■ Shelter

The ordinary Civil War soldier protected himself from the elements primarily through the use of tents that ranged in size from small "pup tents" to large Sibley tents capable of accommodating a dozen troops. Both training camps (especially early in the war) and field camps of armies that believed they would not be relocating any time soon were veritable "tent cities," composed of neat lines of tents stretching off into the distance. Within these tent quarters, soldiers either slept on cots or slept on the ground (sometimes on beds of straw). In either case, they usually warmed themselves with blankets and rubber ponchos to ward off the night chill.

While on the march or during battles that stretched on for more than one day, Civil War soldiers generally slept under the stars or under trees with nothing but a blanket—and sometimes a fire—to keep them warm. Rainy evenings spent in a cold trench were miserable experiences, especially because soldiers who found themselves in such circumstances usually knew that they would be facing enemy gunfire when dawn broke. Armies on the move also occasionally made use of barns or abandoned farmhouses for shelter.

Winter Camps

Accommodations for both Union and Confederate soldiers generally improved during the winter, a season of respite from the bloody battles that marked the rest of the year. Staying in one place for the winter afforded soldiers the opportunity to build one-room log cabins—some of which were outfitted with primitive but functional fireplaces and wooden floors. The interior of these structures often featured a smattering of mismatched chairs and battered furniture (usually empty kegs and ammunition chests and the like). Other soldiers created dugouts out of logs and canvas. These were typically just large enough to house two men. Other odd designs—many featuring some novel combination of straw, logs, fly tents, and rubber ponchos—also dotted many winter camps.

Tents remained a fixture of winter camps as well, especially in regions where building materials were scarce. But the Confederate Army never had enough tents, and many of its soldiers were forced to improvise their own makeshift protection (Wiley 1992 [1943], p. 62).

Finally, larger barracks were erected in some winter camps. These were typically of a twin-gabled "shotgun" design that slotted sleeping areas in long double rows. Such structures were favored by some commanders because they could house a large number of troops at one time, but soldiers were less enamored of these quarters because of their cramped conditions and the complete absence of privacy.

BIBLIOGRAPHY

Mitchell, Reid. *Civil War Soldiers: Their Expectations and Their Experiences*. New York: Viking, 1988.

Robertson, James I., Jr. *Soldiers Blue and Gray*. Columbia, SC: University of South Carolina Press, 1988.

Shannon, Fred A. "The Life of the Common Soldier in the Union Army, 1861–1865." In *The Civil War Soldier: A Historical Reader*, ed. Michael Barton and Larry M. Logue. New York: New York University Press, 2002.

HEADQUARTERS

Union and Confederate military commanders were responsible for the coordination of a host of wartime activities, including troop movements, resupply efforts, and the development of attack and defense strategies. General headquarters thus served as the "nerve centers" of the various armies roaming across the different sections, or "theaters," of the countryside during the war. The generals and other officers who manned these headquarters were responsible for overseeing the activities and affairs of all of the component parts of the army under their command, from the infantry, artillery, and cavalry corps that constituted the heart of their army to signalmen, engineers, and quartermaster and commissary departments.

When armies were on the move, large tents were often reserved to serve as headquarters at the end of the day, when camp was made. These tents had to be large because they not only provided shelter and administrative space for the commanding general and his staff officers, but also for a wide assortment of other support staff. These staffers included a variety of clerks, personal assistants and aides, couriers, and a cook assigned exclusively to feed the commander and his staff. Army headquarters in both armies were typically outfitted with a dedicated guard unit as well, which generally included an infantry battalion and a cavalry escort.

When wintering over—or when a suitable structure was discovered on the march—army commanders often utilized large stone farmhouses, barns, or plantation homes as their headquarters. These luxurious accommodations were savored by staff officers and other personnel attached to headquarters, and they departed these home-like surroundings with great reluctance. But whether headquarters was a stately mansion or a weathered canvas tent, the activities executed therein-preparation of battlefield reports, casualty lists, notes on sanitation, strategy sessions-were the same.

KEVIN HILLSTROM

Abraham Lincoln with George McClellan. When extended stays were expected, Union troops constructed tent cities to provide shelter. During times of travel and on the battle front, however, soldiers slept on the ground, exposed to the elements. © *Bettmann/Corbis*

BIBLIOGRAPHY

Catton, Bruce. The American Heritage New History of the Civil War, *revised edition. Ed. James M. McPherson. New York: Viking, 1996.*

Hagerman, Edward. *The American Civil War and the Origins of Modern Warfare. Bloomington, IN: University of Indiana Press, 1988.*

Wiley, Bell Irvin. *The Life of Johnny Reb: The Common Soldier of the Confederacy.* Indianapolis, IN, and New York: Bobbs-Merrill Company, 1943. Reprint, Baton Rouge: Louisiana State University Press, 1992.

Kevin Hillstrom

■ Uniforms

One striking element of the American Civil War was the way in which the characteristics, quality, and quantity of clothing and shoes made available to the soldiers that filled the ranks of the Union and Confederate armies reflected the overall progress and direction of the larger war. In the heady early days of the conflict, soldiers on both sides dressed in trousers, shirts, and coats that were so vibrantly colored they almost appeared celebratory. As

the conflict wore on, however, this finery disappeared, to be replaced by the dusty, tattered blue and gray uniforms long associated with the War Between the States. Clothing shortages deepened with each passing month, paralleling the growing death toll on both sides, and by the closing months of the war many members of the Confederate Army shuffling across the countryside were literally shoeless and clad in rags.

A Parade of Colors in the North

When the Union Army first gathered in the spring of 1861, the volunteer companies that poured into Washington, DC, and other training centers wore a wide range of uniforms. Some regiments arrived in the brilliant red pants, blue belts, and turbans and fezzes of the Algerian Zouaves, the famed French infantry units that had been created in Africa in the 1830s. Others cobbled together unique

Union army uniforms. Union army uniforms during the United States Civil War: (L–R) Private, Reg. Cavalry; General U.S. Grant's uniform; Line Officer, Artillery; Duryeas Zouave; Hawkin's Zouave; Private, Reg. Infantry; Line Officer, Duryea's Zouave; Campaign Uniform, Infantry; Private, Reg. Artillery. *The Art Archive/Culver Pictures/The Picture Desk, Inc.*

wardrobes based on local tastes, ethnic allegiances, and availability of materials. In numerous instances, regiments from the same state reported for duty in wildly varying colors.

In some cases, commanders devoted a fair amount of time and energy to questions of appearance. When John Gibbon (1827–1896) took command of a brigade of combined Wisconsin and Indiana troops in May 1862, for example, he determined that proper uniforms would lead to a boost in morale, pride, and greater cohesiveness. With these goals in mind, Gibbon authorized the issuance of new uniforms that included long, dark-blue frock coats, standard army hats, and white leggings. His troops accepted the dark blue coats and regulation headwear, but balked at the leggings—Gibbon's main effort to differentiate his soldiers from the larger Union force. As historian Jeffrey Wert noted in *A Brotherhood of Valor* (1999), Gibbon brushed aside his soldiers' complaints about the leggings until he awoke one morning to discover that sometime during the night, his horse had been outfitted with four of the leggings.

Many other Union soldiers, however, took peacock-like pride in their colorful and unique finery, and some of these outfits endured well into the second year of the war. As the months passed, though, Union soldiers— like their Confederate counterparts, who showed up for war in similarly variegated uniforms—came to recognize that the wide assortment of uniform types made it difficult to distinguish comrades from foes. As reports of deaths from friendly fire proliferated, especially after the Battle of Shiloh in April 1862, Northern troops became more favorably disposed to federal attempts to establish a more uniform dress code. All uniform colors except the regulation light and dark blue were banned by the War Department in 1862, and by the early winter months of 1863 most of the army had been supplied with uniforms of that color scheme.

Problems of Quality

Union soldiers maintained their allegiance to homespun clothing and broken-in work shoes in large part because the quality of government-issued uniforms and shoes in the war's opening months often was atrocious. *Harper's Weekly* reported that when it rained, Union troops "found their clothes, overcoats, and blankets scattering to the winds in rags, or dissolving into their primitive elements of dust" (Donald 2001, p. 238). Complaints of this sort were legion, and the War Department began shifting away from the most corrupt and venal of the clothing contractors.

Adding insult to injury, the common soldier frequently had to pay out of his own pocket for these poor-quality items. Each Yankee private had a clothing allowance of $3.50 per month; if he did not use the full allotment, he was free to pocket the remainder. But long hours of marching and explosive bouts of fighting took a heavy toll on clothing, which was usually substandard to begin with. Many soldiers were forced to spend more than their small clothing allowance to keep themselves outfitted, and any amount of additional spending was deducted from their regular monthly $13 paycheck.

Such stories became less commonplace after the first year of the war as the durability of government-issued uniforms dramatically improved. Still, the wool fabric was suffocating in the summertime—especially in the South—and many of the uniforms were somewhat ill-fitting. Soldiers could do nothing about the former issue, but they addressed the latter problem by embracing a haphazard but ultimately effective bartering system. When shipments of new coats, pants, and shoes reached regiments in camp or in the field, soldiers typically waded in a mad scramble and grabbed whatever they could, reasoning—usually accurately—that they could later trade for garments and footwear of a more suitable size and fit (Shannon 2002, p. 96).

Of all the items in a soldier's personal wardrobe, the one that often received the most attention was footwear. The quality and fit of a soldier's footwear determined whether a ten- or twenty-mile march would leave the soldier with tired but intact feet or a horror of bloody blisters. Most shoes resulted in the latter condition, for most of the footwear issued by the War Department was singularly unimpressive. In numerous instances, in fact, contractors did not differentiate between left and right shoes in their factories. They simply squared off the toe of every shoe they made, reasoning that the shoes could be used for either foot. Such shoes created an ideal environment for the cultivation of painful blisters.

Nonetheless, even shoes that fit poorly were prized by their owners, for the alternative—marching barefoot— was even more daunting scenario. This basic reality led many Union soldiers to steal shoes and boots off the feet of the battlefield dead, and when "foraging" of Southern farms and plantations became common in the last years of the war, functional shoes were among the most highly sought after items in any household.

Shortages in the South

In the South, the Confederate government had great difficulty obtaining uniforms for its soldiers from the war's outset. The newly formed Confederate army had no uniforms in stock, and it would take time to manufacture new ones or arrange for their shipment from Europe. Some troops received uniforms from state authorities, but this did not do much to offset the problem, as uniforms were in short supply at the state level as well. Civilian women pitched in to help fill the void, but many were not skilled seamstresses.

The Confederate army that took shape in 1861 thus featured a cornucopia of uniform styles and colors. Some arriving volunteers were garbed as though they were embarking on a hunting excursion into the woods behind their homes. Others arrived dressed in the colorful uniforms they had worn for parade purposes as members of militia organizations. And still others reported for duty in clothing created by local women's societies. When Virginians from the Shenandoah Valley arrived at their regional training center in Harpers Ferry, then, it was little surprise that each company had its own distinctive garb: red shirts and gray trousers for the Mountain guards; gray jackets and trousers for the West Augusta Guards and Augusta Rifles; and blue shirts, gray trousers, and U.S. Navy caps for the Southern Guards (Wert 1999, p. 14).

As was the case in the North, difficulties in differentiating friend from foe on the battlefield led the Confederate War Department to select gray as the official color of the army. The wide assortment of styles and splashes of colors that had previously marked Rebel encampments disappeared, to be replaced by a somber blend of gray and "butternut." The latter color was a direct result of Union blockades that forced the South to conjure up its own garment dyes. The butternut tint was a yellowish-brown color created by a dye made of copperas, walnut hulls, and other ingredients. This dye became so widely used that both Yankee and Rebel troops began to use the term *butternuts* for Confederate forces.

Competition for Clothing and Shoes

Throughout the South, shortages of coats, pants, shirts, and shoes continued for the duration of the war. The Confederate War Department's difficulties in this regard stemmed from several factors. Increased production by Southern factories offset losses caused by Union blockades to some degree, but the productivity of the Confederate manufacturing sector declined as the war dragged on, due to the conscription of workers and territorial gains by Northern troops. In addition, individual states shielded their uniform and footwear output

Confederate army uniforms. Civil War uniforms of the Confederate army: (L–R) North Carolina militia; Private, Reg. Infantry; Washington Artillery; Montgomery True Blue; Field Officer, Infantry; General Lee's uniform, Private, Reg. Cavalry; Louisiana Tiger; Louisiana Zouave; and Private, Reg. Artillery. *The Art Archive/Culver Pictures/The Picture Desk, Inc.*

from Richmond and from other states, to ensure that their own soldiers were adequately outfitted. This practice worked well for a state like North Carolina, which had many more textile factories than surrounding states, but it exacerbated shortages in states with less productive capacity.

These shortages became acute and constant in some parts of the army within the space of two years. When General Lee's Army of Northern Virginia set out for Maryland in August 1862, for example, one Virginian commented bleakly, "there is not a scarecrow in our cornfields that would not scorn to exchange clothes with [the passing soldiers]" (Williams 2000, p. 15). During the winters, the dearth of warm coats and other clothing sometimes became a matter of life and death. One Southerner recounted his shock when his regiment came across a group of Confederate sentries that had literally frozen to death:

> When we arrived there we found the guard sure enough. If I remember correctly, there were just eleven of them. Some were sitting down and some were lying down; but each and every one was as cold and as hard frozen as the icicles that hung from their hands and faces and clothing—dead! They had died at their post of duty. Two of them, a little in advance of the others, were standing with their guns in their hands, as cold and as hard frozen as a monument of marble. (Williams 2005, pp. 206–207)

Barefoot Soldiers

The direst shortages experienced in the Confederate army lay in the realm of footwear. As the Civil War progressed, many Rebel soldiers were reduced to marching barefoot or wrapping rags around their feet. "Most ... marches were on graveled turnpike roads, which were very severe on the barefooted men and cut up their feet horribly," recalled one Southern surgeon in a letter home. "When the poor fellows could get rags they would tie them around their feet for protection" (Dean 2002, p. 397). Shortages of shoes were so severe that some Confederate regiments became utterly dependent on scavenging shoes from the battlefield. As one historian observed, "the practice of reshoeing at the expense of dead and live Yankees was so common that the remark became trite among troops, 'All a Yankee is worth is his shoes'" (Wiley 1992, p. 115).

Perhaps the most infamous instance in which large numbers of Confederate soldiers were forced to go to war barefoot occurred in the winter of 1864–1865. Over the course of a long and arduous campaign through Tennessee, thousands of men in the bedraggled ranks of General John Bell Hood's army were forced to march barefoot through heavy sleet and snow. As they marched, their unprotected feet smeared tracks of blood through the white snow (Wiley 1992, p. 121).

BIBLIOGRAPHY

Dean, Eric T., Jr. " 'Dangled over Hell': The Trauma of the Civil War." In *The Civil War Soldier: A Historical Reader*, ed. Michael Barton and Larry M. Logue. New York: New York University Press, 2002.

Donald, David Herbert, Jean Harvey Baker, and Michael F. Holt. *The Civil War and Reconstruction.* New York: W. W. Norton, 2001.

Robertson, James I., Jr. *Soldiers Blue and Gray.* Columbia, SC: University of South Carolina Press, 1988.

Shannon, Fred A. "The Life of the Common Soldier in the Union Army, 1861–1865." In *The Civil War Soldier: A Historical Reader*, ed. Michael Barton and Larry M. Logue. New York: New York University Press, 2002.

Wert, Jeffry D. *A Brotherhood of Valor: The Common Soldiers of the Stonewall Brigade, C.S.A., and the Iron Brigade, U.S.A.* New York: Simon & Schuster, 1999.

Wiley, Bell Irvin. *The Life of Johnny Reb: The Common Soldier of the Confederacy.* Indianapolis, IN: Bobbs-Merrill Company, 1943. Reprint, Baton Rouge: Louisiana State University Press, 1992.

Williams, David. *Johnny Reb's War: Battlefield and Homefront.* Abilene, TX: McWhiney Foundation Press, 2000.

Williams, David. *A People's History of the Civil War: Struggles for the Meaning of Freedom.* New York: New Press, 2005.

Kevin Hillstrom

■ Equipment

Civil War soldiers on both sides of the conflict carried much of the same gear in their packs. Standard accouterments included such essential items as mess kits (plate, knife, fork, and spoon), cups and tin cans for drinking and grinding coffee, sewing kits (called *housewives* by Union troops), pocketknives, wool blankets, oilcloth groundsheets (which were much more common in Northern regiments than Southern ones), canteens, firearms, cartridge boxes, and bayonets. Rations were carried in the soldier's haverpack. Other commonplace but nonessential items toted by infantry soldiers in both the Union and Confederate armies included pipes and tobacco pouches, straight razors, Bibles, writing kits, family portraits, harmonicas and other small musical instruments, matchsafes, handkerchiefs, change purses, combs, towels, and soap. These personal items were supplemented by wagon-drawn supplies used by entire companies or regiments, like cooking materials, spades, tents, and the like.

Troops received staple items from federal or state authorities, but other supplies were either brought from home upon enlistment, delivered to grateful soldiers from home via mail service, lifted from the battlefield or civilian residences, or procured—usually at exorbitant rates—from civilian merchants known as *sutlers*. Soldiers also occasionally raided sutlers' tents late at night and helped themselves to what they needed.

As was the case with shoes and uniforms, both the North and South grappled with shoddy workmanship and perennial supply shortages in many equipment categories. Some Union blankets, for example, were so poorly made that they provided little warmth and quickly fell apart (Shannon 2002, p. 97). Confederate supply shortages were further exacerbated by a tendency on the part of many state authorities to hoard uniforms, blankets, and other supplies manufactured within their borders for the exclusive use of their own troops.

The North was able to use its vastly superior industrial capacity to address many of its supply shortages over time, but Southern problems with equipment quality and shortfalls became more acute as the war progressed. These problems—due to losses of territory (and hence manufacturing productivity), an inadequate transportation network, and severe shortfalls in raw materials for factory production—finally became so great that the Confederate Army became starved for many necessary types of equipment.

The Rifle: The Soldier's Most Important Piece of Equipment

The most valuable piece of equipment possessed by Rebel and Yankee soldiers was the rifle. At the war's outset, soldiers on both sides were almost exclusively armed with various types of smoothbore muskets that

AERIAL RECONNAISSANCE IN THE CIVIL WAR: THE UNION ARMY BALLOON CORPS

The Civil War saw the formation of the first organization for aerial reconnaissance, the Union Army Balloon Corps. Although the corps was considered a branch of the Union Army, it was organized and staffed by civilians, headed by the Chief Aeronaut, Thaddeus S. C. Lowe (1831–1913), appointed to that position by Abraham Lincoln in the summer of 1861. Lincoln became interested in employing balloons for military reconnaissance after hearing about their use by the French Army.

Lowe was an experienced balloonist who had financed his education in chemistry and meteorology by giving people rides in a balloon he had built himself as a teenager. He had become a noted weather expert by the time of the Civil War and was making plans for a transatlantic balloon crossing when the war broke out. Lowe brought his own balloon, the Enterprise, to Washington in June 1861 to demonstrate its potential to the president. Lowe's balloon contained a telegraph key and was connected by a telegraph wire to the White House. From a height of 500 feet above a nearby armory, Lowe sent a telegraph message to Lincoln:

> Balloon Enterprise
>
> Washington, DC
>
> June 18, 1861
>
> To the President of the United States:
>
> Sir: This point of observation commands an area nearly fifty miles in diameter. The City with its girdle of encampments presents a superb scene. I have pleasure in sending you this first dispatch from an aerial station, and in acknowledging indebtedness for your encouragement for the opportunity of demonstrating the availability of the science of aeronautics in the service of the country.
>
> Yours respectfully,
>
> T. S. C. Lowe. (Abbott 1864, p. 108)

Lowe selected a team of aeronauts who assisted him in observing battlefields around the Potomac River and the peninsula from 1861 through 1863, when the corps disbanded due to problems with military oversight of the civilian aeronauts. In those two years, however, the balloon corps demonstrated its ability to assist Union gunners in improving the accuracy of their artillery fire.

In addition to carrying out the first successful aerial reconnaissance during a major war, Lowe was also responsible for the invention of the aircraft carrier. Lowe had an old coal barge, the

Army inflates aerial balloon. Northern and Southern armies each used aerial balloons in a limited way to learn information about their opponent's troop strength and movements. *Mathew Brady Collection/US Army/National Archives/Time Life Pictures/Getty Images*

General Washington Parke Custis, converted for river transport of his balloons and a generator he had invented to produce the hydrogen gas used to inflate the balloons. The deck of the *Parke Custis* was cleared of everything that might entangle the ropes used to tether the balloons. From November 1861 through the spring of 1862 Lowe's barge was towed by a Navy gunboat, the U.S.S. *Coeur de Lion*, up and down the Potomac River so that Lowe and the other aeronauts could observe the movements of Confederate troops during the Peninsula Campaign.

Although the Union Army Balloon Corps was in operation for only two years, it was successful enough that the Confederate Army attempted to copy it, but failed because of the lack of skilled pilots and suitable materials for constructing balloons. Lowe's use of balloons for military purposes was revived by the U.S. Army Signal Corps during the Spanish-American War (1898) and by a balloon school operated by the Army at Fort Omaha in Nebraska during World War I.

REBECCA J. FREY

BIBLIOGRAPHY

Abbott, John Stevens Cabot. The History of the Civil War in America. *New York: Henry Bill, 1864.*

Hoehling, Mary Duprey. Thaddeus Lowe, America's One-Man Air Corps. *New York: Messner, 1958.*

were accurate to no more than 100 yards or so (many weapons had an effective range that was considerably less than this). This assortment of armaments included squirrel rifles, shotguns, muskets dating back to the War of 1812, so-called *Mississippi Rifles* (also known as the U.S. Army Model 1841 Rifle or the Whitney Rifle), and other privately owned firearms toted to the front by enlistees.

Around the same time that the Civil War broke out, however, a revolution in rifle technology was taking place. A new kind of bullet called the *Minié ball* was introduced; this new type of ammunition enabled the rapid and efficient loading of a muzzle-loading rifle, dramatically increasing range and accuracy. The Minié ball could also be loaded fairly quickly, which was another important consideration. Within a matter of months, this new firearms technology—which at the war's outset was limited primarily to sniper squads and other specialized regiments—was spreading like wildfire through the ranks of both the Federal and Confederate armies. It was not until 1863, however, that gun manufacturers in the North and South were finally able to catch up with the feverish demand for the new rifled weapons.

The two most popular rifle types to use the new Minie ball were the American-made Springfield rifle and the British-made Enfield rifle. The Springfield became the "workhorse weapon" of the Union army in particular, but even at war's end Springfields and Enfields accounted for only about 40 percent of all the shoulder arms used by the two governments (Davis 1991, pp. 54, 58). In 1863, in fact, the Union War Department officially recognized 121 different models of rifles, muskets, carbines, pistols, and revolvers and the Confederacy was even less discriminating. For both governments, however, this created logistical headaches, as a huge variety of types of ammunition had to be made available to troops (Davis 1991, p. 58).

Besides the Enfield and Springfield rifles, other specific models that were extensively used included breech-loading rifles such as the Sharps, Maynard, Burnside, Morse, and Star guns, the sixteen-shot Henry repeaters, and various short-barreled carbines (the latter were often used by cavalry). In addition, the Union Army purchased approximately 106,000 Spencer carbines and rifles. The Spencer repeating rifle fired a magazine of seven cartridges and could be reloaded in thirty seconds, even by a soldier on horseback. These weapons were so potent that Federal forces thus armed came to view themselves as virtually invincible on the field of battle—a belief that was substantiated by battlefield results at places like Gettysburg, Chickamauga, Atlanta, and Petersburg.

Changing the Face of War

The advent of new rifle technology during the Civil War might not have been so devastating had field commanders been quicker to adjust to the evolving tactical landscape. Soldiers armed with Springfield, Enfield, Spencer, and Henry rifles were transformed into deadly foes that could pick enemy soldiers off with far greater accuracy—and at far greater distances—than ever before. Close combat became a thing of the past; out of 245,000 wounds treated by surgeons in Federal hospitals during the course of the war, for example, fewer than 1,000 were saber or bayonet wounds (Hummel 1996, p. 188). Many generals preferred flank attacks, but these were not always possible. Instead, they were bound to keep using frontal attacks until a better way could be found of achieving results. And these attacks did sometimes prove effective, albeit at a high casualty rate.

As the months passed, however, army commanders and their lieutenants gradually adapted to the new reality and adjusted their infantry tactics. They abandoned fron-

tal assaults over open terrain, made greater use of forest and other natural cover, and made much more extensive use of man-made entrenchments.

BIBLIOGRAPHY

Davis, William C. *Rebels and Yankees: The Fighting Men of the Civil War.* New York: Smithmark Publishers, 1991.

Hagerman, Edward. *The American Civil War and the Origins of Modern Warfare.* Bloomington: University of Indiana Press, 1988.

Hummel, Jeffrey Rogers. *Emancipating Slaves, Enslaving Free Men: A History of the American Civil War.* Chicago: Open Court, 1996.

Robertson, James I., Jr. *Soldiers Blue and Gray.* Columbia, SC: University of South Carolina Press, 1988.

Shannon, Fred A. "The Life of the Common Soldier in the Union Army, 1861–1865." In *The Civil War Soldier: A Historical Reader*, ed. Michael Barton and Larry M. Logue. New York: New York University Press, 2002.

Wiley, Bell Irvin. *The Common Soldier of the Civil War.* New York: Charles Scribner's Sons, 1973.

Kevin Hillstrom

■ Mascots

Animal mascots were a fixture in many Union and Confederate camps during the Civil War. Dogs and horses were the most common mascots, but during the course of the war a virtual Noah's Ark of animals played this role, ranging from cats, domesticated raccoons, and sheep to such exotic good luck charms as a camel (belonging to the 43rd Mississippi Infantry) and a bear (mascot of the 12th Wisconsin Volunteers).

The morale-boosting benefits of keeping an animal mascot around were obvious to even the most dimwitted officer. These animals served as a reminder of pets back home, and playing with and caring for them gave troops a diversion from the tedium of camp and marching. Many mascots became strongly identified with their regiments, and some became legendary.

Famous Mascots

A number of the most famous and beloved of Civil War mascots were dogs. One such creature was Sallie, a brindle Staffordshire bull terrier that served as regimental mascot for the 11th Pennsylvania Volunteer infantry from the time she was a young pup. She accompanied the regiment at the Battle of Gettysburg but fell to Confederate fire in the war's final weeks, dying at the Battle of Hatcher's Run in Virginia in February 1865. Sallie is memorialized on the 11th Pennsylvania monument at the Gettysburg National Military Park.

Another legendary Union mascot was Jack, a bull terrier mascot of the 102nd Pennsylvania infantry. Jack reportedly accompanied his masters into several major battles, including the Wilderness campaigns and the siege of Petersburg. Some accounts even report that he was captured at one point by enemy soldiers, and that the regiment was so desperate to get him back that they exchanged a Confederate soldier for the dog.

The most famous of Civil War mascots, however, was probably "Old Abe," a bald eagle that served as official mascot for Company C of the 8th Regiment Wisconsin Volunteers. Raised by Chippewa Indians in northern Wisconsin, then sold to a Wisconsin family that gave the bird to the regiment, Old Abe was a regular fixture at recruitment events and parades. The eagle also accompanied the soldiers into battle, tethered to a perch alongside the regimental colors.

Confederate soldiers repeatedly tried to kill this "Yankee buzzard," believing its death would sap the enemy's morale. These attempts failed, but the regiment reluctantly decided that the eagle's days were numbered if it kept bringing the bird onto the battlefield. With this in mind, the members of the 8th Wisconsin retired Old Abe from active duty in September 1864 and presented the eagle to the state of Wisconsin as a gift. Authorities then used lithographic images of the bird to raise money for soldier relief and the Chicago Sanitary Commission. Old Abe lived for another sixteen years after the war ended. Kept in a cage in the state capital, he was a popular attraction for visitors. The eagle finally died in 1881.

BIBLIOGRAPHY

"Animal Mascots of the Civil War." Fort Ward Museum Online. http://oha.alexandriava.gov/.

Seguin, Marilyn W. *Dogs of War and Stories of Other Beasts of Battle in the Civil War.* Brookline Village, MA: Branden Publishing, 1998.

Kevin Hillstrom

■ Sanitation

Civil War army camps were notorious as filthy, fetid places and breeding grounds for disease. As one soldier lamented, a military camp in wartime was more often than not essentially "a city without sewerage" (quoted in Hummel 1996, p. 192). These conditions were created by a combination of indifference to basic hygiene, careless disposal of human and animal waste, limited access to clean water, close quarters, and complete ignorance of the ways in which disease-carrying bacteria could move from soldier to soldier.

OLD ABE

When soldiers left their homes, they deeply missed their families, wives, and neighbors. Such separation from the home and hearth was mitigated in many sectors of the military by the adoption of mascots, or regimental pets. Mascots have included such unusual pets as geese, hens, pigeons, owls, foxes, hedgehogs, bears, scorpions, raccoons, goats, llamas, and lion cubs as well as the usual dogs and cats (Cooper 2002, pp. 174–181). They have accompanied armies—and navies—into battle since at least the seventeenth century to bolster the troops' morale. Mascots were comforting objects for every soldier's affection far away from home. In addition, mascots were also thought to be symbols of good luck that would bring the soldiers or sailors who cared for them safely home from war (Cooper 2002, pp. 171–173). The Union Navy allowed mascots on board ship; the USS *Monitor* had a black cat as its mascot (Hoehling 1993, pp. 190–191), while a naval surgeon aboard the USS *Fernandina* was given a live owl that he kept as a mascot in the vessel's sick bay (Boyer 1963, p. 65).

Perhaps the most famous of these military mascots during the American Civil War, however, was a bald eagle, lovingly nicknamed "Old Abe" by the Eighth Wisconsin Infantry. As Adelaide Smith, an army nurse, recounts in her memoir, "Old Abe" was the soldiers' best friend and not only became a symbol of pride and victory for the men in his regiment, but also a legendary figure throughout the Union.

> The Eighth Wisconsin Infantry had some time before sent home their mascot "Old Abe," the hero of twenty battles and many skirmishes. The eagle was taken from its nest by an Indian and presented to Company C., where it became the pet of the regiment. During attacks he was carried at the front on a standard, near the flag—sometimes held by a long cord or chain—he would rise up flapping his great wings, and screeching defiance at the enemy loudly enough to be heard along the line. His reputation made thousands of dollars at fairs and elsewhere. His portrait was painted, and hangs in the Old South Church, Boston. The State pensioned Old Abe and supported an attendant to care for him. He died at last of old age, and his skin is stuffed and safely preserved in the state archives at Madison, Wisconsin. (Smith 1911, pp. 205–206)

CARLY S. KALOUSTIAN

BIBLIOGRAPHY

Boyer, Samuel P. Naval Surgeon: Blockading the South, 1862–1866, ed. Elinor and James A. Barnes. Bloomington: Indiana University Press, 1963.

Cooper, Jilly. Animals in War. Guilford, CT: Globe Pequot Press, 2002.

Hoehling, A. A. Thunder at Hampton Roads. New York: Da Capo Press, 1993.

Smith, Adelaide W. Reminiscences of an Army Nurse during the Civil War. New York: Greaves Pub. Co., 1911.

Louisa May Alcott (1832–1888), author and army nurse. While serving as an army nurse, *Little Women* author Louisa May Alcott recorded her experiences amid the filth, stench, and disease of a Union hospital. Without knowledge of how wounds become infected, hospital staff placed little priority on cleanliness and sanitation. *National Portrait Gallery, Smithsonian Institution/Art Resource, NY*

Squalid Conditions

Most military camps, whether flying the flag of the Union or the Confederacy, acquired a decidedly grimy appearance—and foul odor—over time. Nearby water supplies were often treated carelessly, resulting in contamination from the waste of soldiers or their horses. As long as the water looked relatively clean, soldiers (and cooks) believed that it was perfectly acceptable to use.

In addition, many camps failed to adequately separate privies from cooking tents, or to implement basic "housekeeping" measures that would have spared some troops from typhoid, dysentery, and other maladies that struck down thousands of soldiers during the course of the conflict. As a result, germ-spreading flies routinely transferred germs from human waste to food stores. One inspector touring Union camps outside Washington, DC, described a grim but typical scene:

In most cases the only sink is merely a straight trench some thirty feet long, unprovided with pole or rail; the edges are filthy, and the stench exceedingly offensive; the easy expedient of daily turning fresh earth into the trench being often neglected. ... From the ammoniacal odor frequently perceptible in some camps it is obvious that men are allowed to void their urine, during the night, at least, wherever convenient. (Williams 2005, pp. 208–209)

These failures, coupled with the crowded and poorly ventilated shelters in which soldiers were housed, enabled a wide range of dreaded diseases to stalk the Civil War camps of Rebel and Yankee soldiers. It also became fairly commonplace for new companies, upon reporting for duty, to endure outbreaks of childhood illnesses such as measles and mumps.

Virtually the only exceptions to these squalid conditions were the camps of the regular federal army or those led by West Pointers. In these camps, it was far more likely that at least a few sensible sanitation guidelines would be posted—and obeyed.

Perils for the Wounded

When Confederate and Union troops were on the move during the spring, summer, and fall, they gained respite from the more permanent camps that were such fertile breeding grounds for disease. But although the escape from crowded and poorly ventilated tents and barracks reduced exposure to airborne communicable diseases, it also increased exposure to the natural elements and often made clean drinking water harder to come by. More importantly, if an army was on the march, that generally meant that combat was approaching, and poor sanitation standards posed an enormous threat to wounded soldiers who managed to survive the battlefield.

During the Civil War, scientific and medical knowledge and training was far inferior to what it would be a mere generation later. This essential reality, combined with the sheer volume of casualties in the war, made medical treatment an extremely dicey proposition for wounded troops. Neither field surgeons nor doctors at hospital facilities hundreds of miles from the front lines had any knowledge of the root causes of infections or even basic germ theory. Indeed, army hospitals were notorious breeding grounds for disease. One glimpse at a typically overwhelmed facility explained why: "A more perfect pestilence box than this I never saw," exclaimed the author Louisa May Alcott, who served as an army nurse at Union Hotel Hospital in Washington, DC. "Cold, damp, dirty, full of vile odors from wounds, kitchens, and stables" (Robertson 1984, p. 94). Blood poisoning, erysipelas, pneumonia, and even the measles ravaged army hospitals, and with the medical knowledge and technology of that era, these diseases proved difficult, if not impossible, to treat (Ward 1994, p. 219).

"RULES FOR PRESERVING THE HEALTH OF THE SOLDIER"

On July 12, 1861, the U.S. Sanitary Commission published a report containing its "Rules for Preserving the Health of the Soldier." Written by William H. Van Buren, M.D., and signed by twelve other members of the commission, these rules were shortly afterward reprinted in Harper's Weekly.

Diet and food preparation were among the issues the report addressed. Food rations for the Union Army were generous by the standards of other nineteenth-century armies; as the commissioners noted, "the amount allowed for each man is greater in quantity than the similar allowance for any European soldier" (*Harper's Weekly,* August 24, 1861, p. 542). Some of the recommendations for food preparation, however, would no longer be accepted, given present-day knowledge that vitamins are destroyed by overcooking: "The bread must be thoroughly baked, and not eaten until it is cold. The soup must be boiled at least five hours, and the vegetables always cooked sufficiently to be perfectly soft and digestible" (p. 542). Similarly, the commission's recommendations about water intake are no longer followed:

> Water should be always drank [*sic*] in moderation, especially when the body is heated. The excessive thirst which follows violent exertion, or loss of blood, is unnatural, and is not quenched by large and repeated draughts; on the contrary, these are liable to do harm by causing bowel complaints. Experience teaches the old soldier that the less he drinks when on a march the better, and that he suffers less in the end by controlling the desire to drink, however urgent. (p. 542)

On the other hand, many of the commission's recommendations were sensible, such as their remarks concerning vaccination against smallpox: "Every officer and soldier should be carefully vaccinated with fresh vaccine matter, unless already marked by small-pox; and in all cases where there is any doubt as to the success of the operation it should be repeated at once" (p. 542). The vaccine in question was supplied by the Surgeon General.

Considerable detail was devoted to personal hygiene and camp sanitation:

> There is no more frequent source of disease, in camp life, than inattention to the calls of nature. Habitual neglect of nature's wants will certainly lead to disease and suffering. A trench should always be dug, and provided with a pole, supported by uprights, at a properly selected spot at a moderate distance from camp. ... The strictest discipline in regard to the performance of these duties is absolutely essential to health, as well as to decency. Men should never be allowed to void their excrement elsewhere than in the regularly established sinks. In a well regulated camp the sinks are visited daily by a police party, and a layer of earth thrown in, and lime and other disinfecting agents employed to prevent them from becoming offensive and unhealthy. ...

> The tents for the men should be placed as far from each other as the [Army] Regulations and the dimensions of the camp permit (never less than two paces); crowding is always injurious to health. No refuse, slops, or excrement should be allowed to be deposited in the trenches for drainage around the tents. Each tent should be thoroughly swept out daily, and the materials used for bedding aired and sunned, if possible; the canvas should be raised freely at its base, and it should be kept open as much as possible during the daytime, in dry weather, in order to secure ventilation, for tents are liable to become very unhealthy if not constantly and thoroughly aired. ...

> On a march, take especial care of the feet. Bathe them every night before sleeping, not in the morning. Select a shoe of stout, soft leather, with a broad sole, and low heel. (p. 542)

And the commissioners did not neglect morale: "The men should not be over-drilled. It is likely to beget disgust for drill, and to defeat its object. ... When practicable, amusements, sports, and gymnastic exercises should be favored among the men, such as running, leaping, wrestling, fencing, bayonet exercise, cricket, baseball, foot-ball, quoits, etc" (p. 542).

REBECCA J. FREY

SOURCE: *"Rules for Preserving the Health of the Soldier." In* Report of the U.S. Sanitary Commission. *Washington, DC: 1861. Reprinted in* Harper's Weekly, *August 24, 1861, p. 542.*

Conditions were particularly appalling around surgical tables. Equipment was never sterilized, and often water shortages prevented surgeons from even washing their hands. Instead, surgeons would wipe their hands and instruments on towels (Robertson 1984, p. 94). Thus, surgeons passed on diseases and caused infections in the patients they treated. Given these fundamental flaws in medical treatment, it is little wonder that for every Civil War soldier who lost his life on the battlefield, two others were felled by disease.

BIBLIOGRAPHY

Catton, Bruce. *The Civil War.* Boston: Houghton Mifflin, 1960.

Robertson, James I., Jr., and the editors of Time-Life Books. *Tenting Tonight: The Soldier's Life.* Alexandria, VA: Time-Life Books, 1984.

Shannon, Fred A. "The Life of the Common Soldier in the Union Army, 1861–1865." In *The Civil War Soldier: A Historical Reader*, ed. Michael Barton and Larry M. Logue. New York: New York University Press, 2002.

Ward, Geoffrey, with Ric Burns and Ken Burns. *The Civil War*. New York: Vintage, 1994.

Wiley, Bell Irvin. *The Common Soldier of the Civil War*. New York: Scribner, 1973.

Kevin Hillstrom

■ Desertion

Desertion and related lesser offenses, such as going AWOL (absent without leave), bedeviled both the Confederate and Union armies during the American Civil War. Estimates of the total number of desertions vary depending on historic sources and individual definitions of *desertion*, but historians generally put the number of Union desertions from military duty somewhere between 200,000 and 260,000 troops and the number of Confederate deserters at somewhere in excess of 100,000 troops. The North, however, had a far larger military in the first place, and a greater pool of potential replacements to replenish it with. As a result, desertions never threatened to cripple the overall Union war effort. By contrast, in the South the military margin for error was much less, and the pool of replacements much shallower. So while the number of deserters as a percentage of the total Confederate army was not that much greater than the percentage of deserters within the Union ranks, Southern desertion had a much more severe impact on military operations and morale. As the war turned decisively against the South in the last two years of the conflict, rates of desertion soared in many Confederate units, and historians cite desertion as a leading factor in the South's military collapse.

Answering Desperate Calls from Home

The great majority of Civil War soldiers—even those who endured horrendous battles and deadly skirmishes on multiple occasions—never abandoned their military obligations, even in their darkest hours of doubt and fear. Soldiers who rallied to the cause in the opening months of the conflict had a particularly low rate of desertion—and a correspondingly high intensity of loathing for those soldiers, whether volunteer or conscript, who slipped out of the line before the war was over. For these veteran soldiers, notions of honor and duty sustained their motivation throughout the years (McPherson 1997, p. 168).

Tens of thousands of other soldiers, however, left the ranks of the North and South before they had fulfilled their military obligations. The factors behind these premature departures were legion. Some slipped away out of cowardice—a failure to control and manage the fear that afflicted all Civil War soldiers. Many other soldiers deserted for more complicated reasons, however. For example, numerous soldiers reluctantly slipped away for home under cover of darkness or in the chaos of battle out of concern for loved ones. This was especially true of some Confederate soldiers, who knew in the war's latter stages that much of the South was being overrun by enemy troops and sought to protect their families back home.

This agony of divided loyalties was further deepened by beseeching letters from home. "It is useless to conceal the truth any longer," wrote one North Carolina soldier in early 1865. "Most of our people at home have become so demoralized that they write to their husbands, sons and brothers that desertion now is not dishonorable" (Robertson 1988, p. 136).

Some letters from loved ones even warned soldiers that failure to immediately set off for home meant certain doom for family members. One Alabama soldier, for example, received a letter from home in 1864 informing him that "if you put off a-coming, 'twont be no use to come, for we'll all hands of us be out there in the grave yard with your ma and mine" (Martin 2003 [1932], p. 172).

One of the better-known desertion trials of the Civil War concerned Confederate Private Edward Cooper, whose defense was based in part on one of these "please come home" letters—from his wife. This letter was reportedly a major factor in convincing authorities to spare Cooper's life. "I have been always proud of you, and since your connection with the Confederate army, I have been prouder of you than ever before," his wife's letter stated. "I would not have you do anything wrong for the world, but before God, Edward, unless you come home, we must die. Last night, I was aroused by little Eddie's crying. I called and said, 'what is the matter, Eddie?' And he said, 'O Mamma, I am so hungry.' And Lucy, Edward, your darling Lucy; she never complains, but she is growing thinner and thinner every day. And before God, Edward, unless you come home, we must die" (Moore 1880, p. 237).

This peril to loved ones—whether real or imagined—has been cited by historians as a contributing factor in the higher desertion rates among married soldiers than unmarried ones, as well as the higher desertion rates among privates than officers. Many of the latter came from comparatively affluent backgrounds and thus had families that were better able to sustain and protect themselves during the war.

Erosion of Morale

Myriad other factors contributed to soldiers' decisions to desert, either for home or for destinations that promised anonymity or opportunities to construct new lives. The Confederate Army's intensifying difficulties in procuring basic food and supplies for its soldiers undoubtedly played a role in rising desertion rates. In addition, the South had growing difficulty meeting its payroll obligations as the war went on. Both armies, meanwhile,

Execution of five deserters. Both the North and South realized early that desertion would plague their armies. The punishment for deserting varied by severity, ranging from paycuts and increased manual labor to branding and death. *Illustration by Alfred R. Waud. The Library of Congress.*

experienced greater problems with desertion when they tried to transfer soldiers far from home. In the case of Confederate troops, the desire to be close to home increased as the war progressed and Northern troops pushed further and further into Southern territory, possibly endangering family members. In some cases, opposition to transfers to distant locales was so strong that large-scale desertions occurred.

Another contributor to diminished morale—and thus higher rates of desertion—in both Union and Confederate units was the decision by each side to build up its military units in response to mounting casualties. As gaps in regiments and divisions were filled with conscripts and other replacements, the esprit de corps that had predominated in the all-volunteer force was supplanted by tensions between the new arrivals and veteran volunteers who viewed the former as useless and untrustworthy. In some instances, the hostility of fellow regimental members was enough to make already unenthusiastic conscripts want to desert.

Other desertions stemmed from a growing sense among the infantry rank and file that the Civil War was "a rich man's war and a poor man's fight." This conviction, which could be amply supported by even a cursory

glance at the socioeconomic inequities contained within the conscription acts of the Federal and Confederate governments, was further underscored by the furlough programs that both militaries instituted, which made it easier for wealthy soldiers to periodically return home. The failure of military authorities to grant deserved furloughs was especially commonplace in the increasingly soldier-strapped South. Confederate authorities tried to assuage the anger of troops with promises of future compensation, appeals to duty, and assorted excuses, but to little avail: Thousands of frustrated troops simply went home without permission (Wiley 1992, p. 139).

Punishments for Desertion

From the opening months of the Civil War, both the North and South recognized that desertion posed a potentially serious threat to their respective causes. With this in mind, the administrations of Jefferson Davis and Abraham Lincoln, as well as leading military officers from both armies, kept up a steady a drumbeat of entreaties and threats to keep their men from slipping away. Washington, DC, and Richmond, VA, even resorted to proclamations that promised pardons and general am-

"THE EXECUTION OF DESERTERS"

In September of 1863 *Harper's Weekly* published an illustration depicting the execution of five deserters, drawn by staff artist Alfred Rudolph Waud (1828–1891). Waud appended some brief remarks on the necessity of capital punishment for deserters:

> The crime of desertion has been one of the greatest drawbacks to our army. If the men who have deserted their flag had but been present on more than one occasion defeat would have been victory, and victory the destruction of the enemy. It may be therefore fairly asserted that desertion is the greatest crime of the soldier, and no punishment too severe for the offense. But the dislike to kill in cold blood-a Northern characteristic-the undue exercise of executive clemency, and in fact the very magnitude and vast spread of the offense, has prevented the proper punishment being applied. That is past; now the very necessity of saving life will cause the severest penalties to be rigorously exacted. The picture represents the [five] men who were sentenced to death in the Fifth Corps for desertion at the moment of their execution. Some of these had enlisted, pocketed the bounty, and deserted again and again. The sentence of death being so seldom enforced they considered it a safe game. They all suffered terribly mentally, and as they marched to their own funeral they staggered with mortal agony like a drunken man. Through the corps, ranged in hushed masses on the hill-side, the procession moved to a funeral march, the culprits walking each behind his own coffin. On reaching the grave they were, as usual, seated on their coffins; the priests made short prayers; their eyes were bandaged; and with a precision worthy of praise for its humanity, the orders were given and the volley fired which launched them into eternity. They died instantly, although one sat up nearly a minute after the firing; and there is no doubt that their death has had a very salutary influence on discipline.

REBECCA J. FREY

SOURCE: *"The Execution of Deserters."* Harper's Weekly, *September 26, 1863, p. 622.*

the sentence. For example, soldiers found guilty of being absent without leave usually were punished with some combination of pay forfeiture and increased manual labor. Those who were found guilty of the far more serious crime of desertion, however, might be sentenced to branding (often with a *C* to denote a Coward or a *D* to denote a Deserter), public flogging, extended imprisonment, or even death by execution.

According to historian Jeffrey Rogers Hummel in *Emancipating Slaves, Enslaving Free Men* (1996), the Union and the Confederacy executed a total of five hundred of their own troops during the course of the Civil War. This total exceeds the total number of executions in all other American wars combined. Two-thirds of the executions that took place during the Civil War were for the crime of desertion. Almost invariably, they were staged publicly, so as to send a harsh warning to anyone contemplating leaving ranks.

These executions undoubtedly had their intended effect in some cases. But in others, the brutal spectacles seemed to engender a deeper demoralization among some witnesses. A Rebel soldier from Florida, for example, was profoundly shaken after he witnessed the execution of a young deserter who spent the last moments of his life desperately begging for mercy. The soldier called the execution "one of the most sickening scenes I ever witnessed[;] ... [it] looked more like some tragedy of the dark ages, than the civilization of the nineteenth century" (Dean 2002, p. 414). A Union soldier from Indiana expressed similar sentiments after witnessing an execution of a deserter from his army. "I don't think I will ever witness another such a horror if I can get away from it," he wrote. "I have seen men shot in battle but never in cold blood before" (Dean 2002, p. 414).

Escalating Levels of Desertion

After the Civil War turned decisively against the South in mid-1863, rates of desertion from the Confederate forces rose dramatically. "In the wake of Gettysburg the highways of Virginia were crowded daily with homeward-bound troops, still in possession of full accouterments; and, according to one observer, these men 'when halted and asked for their furloughs or their authority to be absent from their commands, ... just pat their guns defiantly and say, 'this is my furlough,' and even enrolling officers turn away as peaceably as possible" (Wiley 1992, p. 143–44).

As the months passed, entire garrisons and companies quietly left the Confederate ranks. Many of these deserters separated and returned to their far-flung homes. Others banded together into outlaw groups that sustained themselves by robbing local communities or military stores. In some areas of the South, these guerrilla bands became so powerful that they became a threat to the Confederate detachments that were sent to neutralize them. The need to send such detachments put a

nesties to deserters willing to return to military duty and thus remove the "stain" upon their honor.

These official efforts met with some limited success, but punishment (and the threat thereof) quickly emerged as the primary officially sanctioned means of addressing the desertion issue. Punishments for desertion ranged greatly, depending on the perceived severity of the offense and the personal characteristics of the authorities imposing further drain on an army that was already groaning under the methodical, unrelenting pressure of a foe with superior resources.

By the time the final hours of 1864 were ticking away, desertion had reached epidemic levels in many Confederate units. Sentries walked away from their posts, infantrymen crept from their trenches under cover of darkness, and cavalrymen turned the heads of their mounts away from the front and toward home. Even Confederate General Robert E. Lee (1807–1870), the most respected and beloved military leader of the entire South, was powerless to stop some defections from the battered ranks of his Army of Northern Virginia. According to historian Bell Irvin Wiley's *The Life of Johnny Reb* (1992), the Confederate War Department reported that there were a total of 198,494 officers and men absent and only 160,198 present in the armies of the Confederacy on the eve of surrender (pp. 144–145). These figures confirm that although desertion constituted a problem for the North, its impact was far more crippling for the South.

BIBLIOGRAPHY

Alotta, Robert I. *Stop the Evil: A Civil War History of Desertion and Murder*. San Rafael, CA: Presidio Press, 1978.

Dean, Eric T., Jr. " 'Dangled over Hell': The Trauma of the Civil War." In *The Civil War Soldier: A Historical Reader*, ed. Michael Barton and Larry M. Logue. New York: New York University Press, 2002.

Donald, David Herbert, Jean Harvey Baker, and Michael F. Holt. *The Civil War and Reconstruction*. New York: W. W. Norton, 2001.

Hummel, Jeffrey Rogers. *Emancipating Slaves, Enslaving Free Men: A History of the American Civil War*. Chicago: Open Court, 1996.

Martin, Bessie. *A Rich Man's War, a Poor Man's Fight: Desertion of Alabama Troops from the Confederate Army*. Library of Alabama Classics Series. Tuscaloosa: University of Alabama Press, 2003. Originally published as *Desertion of Alabama Troops from the Confederate Army*, New York: Columbia University Press, 1932.

McPherson, James M. *For Cause and Comrades: Why Men Fought in the Civil War*. New York: Oxford University Press, 1997.

Mitchell, Reid. *Civil War Soldiers: Their Expectations and Their Experiences*. New York: Viking, 1988.

Moore, John W. *History of North Carolina: From the Earliest Discoveries to the Present Time*, Vol. 2. Raleigh, NC: Alfred Williams, 1880.

Power, J. Tracy. *Lee's Miserables: Life in the Army of Northern Virginia from the Wilderness to Appomattox*. Chapel Hill, NC: University of North Carolina Press, 1998.

Robertson, James I., Jr. *Soldiers Blue and Gray*. Columbia, SC: University of South Carolina Press, 1988.

Robertson, James I., Jr., and the editors of Time-Life Books. *Tenting Tonight: The Soldier's Life*. Alexandria, VA: Time-Life Books, 1984.

Ward, Geoffrey C., with Ric Burns and Ken Burns. *The Civil War*. New York: Vintage, 1994.

Wiley, Bell Irvin. *The Life of Johnny Reb: The Common Soldier of the Confederacy*. Indianapolis, IN, and New York: Bobbs-Merrill Company, 1943. Reprint, Baton Rouge: Louisiana State University Press, 1992.

Williams, David. *A People's History of the Civil War: Struggles for the Meaning of Freedom*. New York: New Press, 2005.

Kevin Hillstrom

■ A Soldier's Pastimes

A SOLDIER'S PASTIMES: AN OVERVIEW
  Kevin Hillstrom

SPORTS
  Kevin Hillstrom

MUSIC
  Kevin Hillstrom

VICES
  Kevin Hillstrom

A SOLDIER'S PASTIMES: AN OVERVIEW

Civil War soldiers spent relatively little time in actual combat. Most of their days were spent either on the march or in camp, where tedious chores and mundane interactions were the norm. Encampments, however, were not bereft of color or excitement. To the contrary, the fiercely individualistic and restless souls who filled the ranks of both the Union and Confederate armies devised a variety of means by which to relieve the boredom of camp. These pastimes took dramatically different forms, depending on the background, orientation, and character of the individuals involved. For example, both religious study and gambling thrived in this environment.

For both Rebel and Yankee soldiers, the campfire served as the military equivalent of the family hearth or local tavern when it came to social interaction. With the rising of the moon, wrote one Union soldier from New York State, "[e]very tent becomes a little illuminated pyramid. Cooking-fires burn bright along the alleys. The boys lark, sing, shout, do all these merry things that make the entertainment of volunteer service" (Sutherland 1989, p. 13). In these circles, men sang ribald lyrics, shared tales of hunting exploits from their pre–Civil War existences, speculated about enemy troop movements, and spoke with pride and longing about wives, sweethearts, and children back home. Frequently, they engaged in these conversations while simultaneously playing a game of checkers or mending frayed socks, shirts, or pants.

Bible Studiers and Amateur Thespians

Civil War soldiers frequently whiled away the hours by joining with their fellows to pursue some interest or diversion. For example, primitive but entertaining theatrical productions and minstrel shows were organized in many regiments, and some of these shows were so ambitious and spirited that they attracted local civilians as well as fellow soldiers. Occasionally, thespians in the ranks even organized benefit performances, with the profits earmarked for poor civilians or seriously wounded soldiers.

A great many soldiers found both spiritual replenishment and fraternal nourishment through formal religious services. Regimental chaplains were the most visible and essential members of these organized gatherings, for they not only led worship services on Sundays but spent the rest of the week tending to the private spiritual needs of soldiers and comforting maimed or wounded troops. Some religiously inclined men, however, held prayer meetings or Bible study sessions even without the guidance of a chaplain. Their efforts to maintain their spiritual ties to God were actively encouraged by a host of nondenominational religious organizations such as the American Tract Society and the Bible Society of the Confederate States. The principal mandate of these organizations was to place Bibles, hymnals, moral tracts, and other spiritually uplifting or comforting reading materials into the hands of war-weary soldiers. These societies found a ready audience for their efforts, in both the Union and Confederacy, when outbreaks of evangelical revivalism rippled through the ranks of increasingly disillusioned and desperate soldiers.

Finally, energetic and ambitious soldiers in both the Union and Confederate ranks organized army chapters of fraternal societies and benevolent associations. Of these various societies and associations, the freemasons were probably most adept at expanding their membership in wartime. In fact, extensive freemason networks existed in both the Northern and Southern armies by the time the war drew to a close in the spring of 1865.

Literature and Letters

Another major recreational pastime among literate Civil War soldiers was reading, and a smattering of regiments, such as the 13th Massachusetts, even maintained their own modest libraries of classic literature. Aside from the Bible, which was by far the most popular book in both armies, the majority of reading material in Union and Confederate tents consisted of popular contemporary periodicals such as *Harper's Weekly, Frank Leslie's Illus-*

trated Newspaper, and *Southern Illustrated News* or cheap and lurid novels of questionable literary merit. "Those reading materials that generally flooded an army were twenty-five cent thrillers, Beadle's famous 'Dime Novels,' and picture books offering 'spirited and spicy scenes,'" observed one Civil War historian. "While some field missionaries reported disgustingly that 'licentious books' and 'obscene pictures' were to be found in encampments, more men North and South simply read what was available. A Baptist missionary observed early in the war that 'the soldiers here are *starving* for reading matter. They will read anything'" (Robertson 1988, p. 84).

Civil War soldiers also spent a great deal of time poring over correspondence from loved ones back home. Notes from wives, children, parents, and friends were absolutely essential to the morale of countless soldiers on both sides of the conflict. "We can only pity the man who goes empty away from the little group assembled about the mail bag, and rejoice with him who strolls away with a letter near his heart," related one soldier (Catton 1996, p. 371). Indeed, soldiers read letters from home over and over again, and they jealously protected these fragile reminders of their prewar existence from the grime of camp and the elements as best they could. Rebel and Yankee soldiers also devoted a great deal of time to their own letter-writing, and many troops—from officers to newly arrived recruits—kept journals that documented their experiences in great detail.

Seeking Relief in Strange Places

Perhaps inevitably, given the loose, shambling quality of military discipline and the emotional need for a release from the grim business of war, practical jokes reached epidemic proportions in both the Union and Confederate armies. Some of these pranks were mild and unimaginative, such as hiding a fellow soldier's mess kit or rifle. But others were both clever and harrowing. For example, during wintertime pranksters occasionally covered the openings of chimneys with boards or other materials—creating clouds of black smoke guaranteed to chase a hut's coughing and angrily cursing inhabitants outside into the cold.

Soldiers sometimes even sought respite from the tedium of camp life or sentry duty through fraternization with enemy soldiers, with whom they felt a bond of shared experience. Evidence of this feeling of kinship is widely scattered throughout the letters and diaries of Civil War soldiers. "Although intercourse with the enemy was strictly forbidden," wrote one Pennsylvanian soldier, "the men were on the most friendly terms, amicably conversing and exchanging such commodities as coffee, sugar, tobacco, corn meal and newspapers" (Hays 1908, p. 271). Another Union soldier recounted similar tableaux—and emphasized that such fraternization was treated almost as standard operating procedure in some areas:

> It was a singular sight to see the soldiers of two great hostile armies walking about unconcernedly within a few yards of each other with their bayonets sticking in the ground, bantering and joking together, exchanging the compliments of the day and even saluting officers of the opposing forces with as much ceremony, decorum, and respect as they did their own. The keenest sense of honor existed among the enlisted men of each side. It was no uncommon sight, when visiting the picket posts, to see an equal number of "graybacks" and "bluebellies" as they facetiously termed each other, enjoying a social game of euchre or seven-up and sometimes the great national game of draw poker, with army rations and sutler's delicacies as the stakes. (Hays 1908, p. 271)

BIBLIOGRAPHY

Billings, John D. *Hardtack and Coffee; or, The Unwritten Story of Army Life.* Boston: G. M. Smith, 1887. Reprint, Alexandria, VA: Time-Life Books, 1982.

Catton, Bruce. *The American Heritage New History of the Civil War*, rev. ed. Ed. James M. McPherson. New York: Viking, 1996.

Davis, William C. *Rebels and Yankees: The Fighting Men of the Civil War.* New York: Smithmark Publishers, 1991.

Hays, Gilbert A. *Under the Red Patch: Story of the Sixty-Third Regiment, Pennsylvania Volunteers, 1861–1864.* Pittsburgh, PA: Sixty-Third Pennsylvania Volunteers Regimental Association, 1908.

Mitchell, Reid. *Civil War Soldiers: Their Expectations and Their Experiences.* New York: Viking, 1988.

Robertson, James I., Jr. *Soldiers Blue and Gray.* Columbia, SC: University of South Carolina Press, 1988.

Robertson, James I., Jr., and the editors of Time-Life Books. *Tenting Tonight: The Soldier's Life.* Alexandria, VA: Time-Life Books, 1984.

Shannon, Fred A. "The Life of the Common Soldier in the Union Army, 1861–1865." In *The Civil War Soldier: A Historical Reader*, ed. Michael Barton and Larry M. Logue. New York: New York University Press, 2002.

Sutherland, Daniel E. *The Expansion of Everyday Life, 1860–1876.* New York: Harper & Row, 1989.

Wiley, Bell Irvin. *The Life of Johnny Reb: The Common Soldier of the Confederacy.* Indianapolis, IN, and New York: Bobbs-Merrill Company, 1943. Reprint, Baton Rouge: Louisiana State University Press, 1992.

Woodworth, Steven E. *While God Is Marching on: The Religious World of Civil War Soldiers.* Lawrence, KS: University Press of Kansas, 2003.

Kevin Hillstrom

SPORTS

Throughout the Civil War, Yankee and Rebel troops alike turned to sports as one of the principal means of passing the interminable hours in camp. This was especially true during the warmer months. Many of the sporting contests held in army camps were individual in nature: shooting matches, footraces, wrestling matches, and boxing contests. But team sports, when they were organized, never lacked for willing participants. Moreover, team sports such as baseball, which was particularly popular in Union regiments, consistently attracted large audiences of soldiers who were more than happy to yell out encouragement—and pointed criticism.

Baseball, in fact, began as a gentlemen's team sport rather than a game for farmers, blue-collar workers, or urban immigrants. According to the Smithsonian Institution, baseball can be traced back to a group of well-to-do New Yorkers who met in a vacant lot in 1842 to play what quickly became a popular game. Other sources trace the game back to some upper-class young men from Philadelphia who crossed the Delaware in 1831 for regular games of what was called "two old cat" with teams from New Jersey (Kirsch 2003, p. 3). Within a few years there were other teams and organized leagues up and down the East Coast; Massachusetts players had their own distinctive set of rules. By 1861 there were at least 200 baseball clubs in the New York area (including northern New Jersey) alone. Baseball spread westward to Ohio and Kentucky by the late 1850s, but it remained a Northern team sport until after the Civil War; it did not interest the Southern aristocracy.

Baseball became a team sport for men of all classes when the Civil War began, when some of the well-off New York players came to Washington as Union soldiers. They discovered that some office clerks in the Treasury Department had already organized the Washington Base Ball Club, which had a team called the Washington Nationals. Soldiers and civilians quickly organized games, which the New Yorkers usually won. The games helped to break down class divisions, as players were valued for their skills rather than their social backgrounds. Officers played alongside enlisted men as equals rather than military superiors.

Supply shortages often necessitated a certain level of ingenuity when sporting contests were devised. Enterprising bowlers, for example, turned to cannonballs, while baseball equipment often consisted of little more than a farmer's fence rail (the bat) and a walnut or rock wrapped in fabric (the ball). In some cases rags were bundled together and tied with string to form a ball.

Soldiers posing before boxing match.   Observing and taking part in sporting events occupied soldiers during periods of quiet and provided a dose of levity to balance the horrors of the battlefield.   *George Eastman House/Hulton Archive/Getty Images.*

The playing field was located wherever there was a patch of reasonably flat ground; in Washington the teams played on the grounds of the Capitol, on the Ellipse, or inside the forts surrounding Washington.

When armies wintered over, participation in outdoor sports dwindled except for the odd day when unseasonably warm or sunny weather prevailed. During these winter months, poker tables and chess and checkers boards became the primary fields of competition. One exception to this rule, however, was the popularity of snowball fights. Most of these battles were brief skirmishes featuring a few soldiers on either side. On occasion, however, snowball fights blossomed into full-blown conflicts between entire companies. In these instances, soldiers followed the orders of officers just as they did on real fields of battle, and prisoners were sometimes taken. When serious snowball fights developed, participants often "loaded" their snowballs with rocks, bullets, or chunks of ice. These projectiles caused painful injuries on numerous occasions, but their use was generally regarded as completely in keeping with the brawling spirit of the contest. As one participant in a snowball clash between two New Hampshire regiments recounted, "tents were wrecked, bones broken, eyes blacked, and teeth knocked out—all in *fun*" (Robertson 1984, p. 71).

In spite of the occasional sports-related injury, sports were considered psychologically beneficial to the troops. It is noteworthy that the U.S. Sanitary Commission wholeheartedly recommended sports and "gymnastic exercises" as ways to maintain morale in camp in their 1861 report (*Harper's Weekly,* August 24, 1861) on preserving soldiers' health.

BIBLIOGRAPHY

Kirsch, George B. *Baseball in Blue and Gray: The National Pastime during the Civil War.* Princeton, NJ: Princeton University Press, 2003.

Mitchell, Reid. *Civil War Soldiers: Their Expectations and Their Experiences.* New York: Viking, 1988.

Robertson, James I., Jr., and the editors of Time-Life Books. *Tenting Tonight: The Soldier's Life.* Alexandria, VA: Time-Life Books, 1984.

Smithsonian Associates Civil War E-Mail Newsletter, 5 (10). "The 1860s—When Men Were Men and They Played Baseball in Washington." Available online at http://civilwarstudies.org/.

Sutherland, Daniel E. *The Expansion of Everyday Life, 1860–1876.* New York: Harper & Row, 1989.

U. S. Sanitary Commission. "Report of the U.S. Sanitary Commission: Rules for Preserving the Health of the Soldier." *Harper's Weekly,* August 24, 1861, p. 542.

Wiley, Bell Irvin. *The Life of Johnny Reb: The Common Soldier of the Confederacy*. Indianapolis, IN: Bobbs-Merrill Company, 1943. Reprint, Baton Rouge: Louisiana State University Press, 1992.

Kevin Hillstrom

MUSIC

As the Civil War progressed, music emerged as one of the primary means by which soldiers on both sides of the conflict passed the time and lifted their spirits. "Men left for war with a song on their lips," observed one scholar. "They sang while marching or waiting behind earthworks; they hummed melodies on the battlefield and in the guardhouse; music swelled from every nighttime bivouac" (Robertson 1988, p. 85). The music associated with the war, created in an era when singing in public was much more commonplace than it is today, provides a rich and evocative picture of the hopes, fears, and motivations of the common soldier. Many of the lyrics and melodies produced during—and inspired by—the war, in fact, continue to rank as among the most famous songs in American history.

Sentimental and Patriotic

Most Civil War songs that were popular among the infantry and artillery units—the companies that bore the brunt of the war's terror and destruction—were unabashedly maudlin in nature. To be sure, several songs with patriotic themes, such as "John Brown's Body," "Yankee Doodle," "Dixie," and "Battle Cry of Freedom," were quite popular. Other songs that struck a chord with soldiers and anxious loved ones alike directly addressed the brutal realities of war. For example, composer George F. Root's song "Just Before the Battle, Mother," includes the following lyrics: "Comrades brave are round me lying, / Filled with thoughts of home and God; / For well they know that on the morrow, / Some will sleep beneath the sod" (1863).

But if patriotic or otherwise war-themed songs were popular, so too were sentimental ones that celebrated the simple comforts of home or the lovely attributes of sweethearts, and, indeed, songs that dwelled on prewar life or imagined life after the war greatly outnumbered those devoted to military themes. Of the sentimental songs, "Home Sweet Home" was by far the most popular in both Union and Confederate camps. But the emotions it conjured up sometimes made commanders uneasy. In the winter of 1862–1863, for example, Union commanders forbade regimental bands with the Army of the Potomac from playing the song, for fear it would undermine the morale of homesick troops (Robertson 1984, p. 68).

Not surprisingly, separation from wives and sweethearts was a theme that repeated itself again and again in Civil War songs favored by soldiers. Popular Civil War songs with a wistfully romantic bent included "Lorena,"

"Annie Laurie," "All Quiet along the Potomac Tonight," "Annie of the Vale," "The Girl I Left Behind Me," "Her Bright Eyes Haunt Me Still," "Sweet Evelina," and "Juanita." Religion was another subject that drew soldiers in, and hymns emerged as popular expressions of Christian belief in both armies.

Soldiers who could play harmonica, fiddle, or banjo were highly prized at evening sing-alongs, and in some cases entire companies became emotionally invested in protecting the musical instruments possessed by these accompanists. Talented musicians in the ranks also became the cornerstones of organized dancing events and glee club performances. These bursts of merrymaking never failed to lift the spirits of tired and battle-worn men, and discerning military commanders actively encouraged song, dance, and music on the march or in camp. Confederate General Robert E. Lee (1807–1870) went so far as to bluntly assert that an army without music would be impossible.

Civil War Bands

Military bands sanctioned and supported by the War Departments in Washington and Richmond also served an important morale-boosting function. Military brass bands accompanied many companies into service during the opening months of the conflict, and as the war progressed company and regimental bands provided musical accompaniment for marching drills, evening concerts for soldiers (and sometimes civilians) at wintertime encampments, and even nights of musical escape for troops weary from a long day's march or battle.

The quality of many of these bands ranged from mediocre to poor, due to the difficulty of procuring instruments and a shortage of trained musicians. On occasion, even soldiers who were starved for entertainment voiced discontent with the quality of the music that band members coaxed from their instruments. One Mississippi soldier, for example, lamented that his regiment's band "has been practicing for more than a week but are not learning very fast. I think I am getting very tired of hearing the noise they make" (Moore 1959, p. 66).

Yet what the band members lacked in training and skill, they compensated for with enthusiasm and a keen understanding of the types of songs that could best rally and encourage the troops at the end of a tedious day of marching or during a cold snap in wintertime. Moreover, interspersed among the undistinguished company and regimental bands one could occasionally find groups of genuine skill and talent. Historian Bruce Catton (1996) noted that the 26th North Carolina Regimental Band was populated to a considerable extent by the sons of Moravian immigrants who had settled around Salem and nurtured a social culture that placed great emphasis on musical literacy and expression. These talented musicians were also dedicated soldiers, and at the Battle of Gettysburg they served as stretcher-bearers and assistants to field surgeons who were swathed from head to foot in blood and gore at the end of each day's fighting. Yet their greatest contribution to the regiment was as musicians. After the first bloody day of fighting at Gettysburg, the band performed a concert that reinvigorated flagging spirits throughout the regiment. "We ... found the men much more cheerful than we were ourselves," remembered one band member. "We played for some time ... and the men cheered us lustily" (Catton 1996, p. 356).

The songs and music of the Civil War also underscored the kinship that existed between the soldiers on both sides of the conflict. Songs like "Home Sweet Home" and "Annie Laurie" were equally popular with Rebel and Yankee soldiers, and on more than one occasion, band performances by soldiers from one army soothed the spirits not only of comrades, but also of the brave but homesick soldiers on the opposing front lines. In *Soldiers Blue and Gray* (1988), historian James I. Robertson Jr. recounts one of the most famous of these incidents. In December 1862 Union and Confederate forces gathered to face each other outside of Fredericksburg, Virginia. As evening fell over the land, bands from the two sides engaged in a sort of "battle of the bands," taking turns playing partisan favorites. The night air then became quiet for a time until a lone Union bugler played a mournful version of "Home Sweet Home" for the assembled armies. "As the sweet sounds rose and fell on the evening air," recalled one soldier from New Hampshire, "all listened intently, and I don't believe there was a dry eye in all those assembled thousands" (Robertson 1988, p. 85).

BIBLIOGRAPHY

Catton, Bruce. *The American Heritage New History of the Civil War*, rev. ed. Ed. James M. McPherson. New York: Viking, 1996.

Mitchell, Reid. *Civil War Soldiers: Their Expectations and Their Experiences.* New York: Viking, 1988.

Moore, Robert. *A Life for the Confederacy*, ed. James W. Silver. Jackson, TN: McCowat-Mercer Press, 1959.

Robertson, James I., Jr. *Soldiers Blue and Gray.* Columbia, SC: University of South Carolina Press, 1988.

Robertson, James I., Jr., and the editors of Time-Life Books. *Tenting Tonight: The Soldier's Life.* Alexandria, VA: Time-Life Books, 1984.

Root, George F. "Just Before the Battle, Mother." In *The Bugle-Call.* Chicago: Root & Cady, 1863.

Sutherland, Daniel E. *The Expansion of Everyday Life, 1860–1876.* New York: Harper & Row, 1989.

Wiley, Bell Irvin. *The Life of Johnny Reb: The Common Soldier of the Confederacy.* Indianapolis, IN: Bobbs-Merrill Company, 1943. Reprint, Baton Rouge: Louisiana State University Press, 1992.

Kevin Hillstrom

VICES

Civil War soldiers generally had access to only a limited number of diversions to help them pass the time when they were not marching, fighting, or attending to camp chores. Reading, letter-writing, and conversation filled some of the long idle hours, but many in the ranks of both the Confederate and Union armies were illiterate. For these men—and also for many of the more educated soldiers—filling the long hours required more exciting diversions.

Of all the so-called "vices" that infiltrated the fabric of both Union and Confederate armies, gambling was the most flagrant and ubiquitous. Various card and dice games were particularly popular, but as countless letters and journal entries attest, Yankees and Rebels alike rushed to wager their meager salaries on just about anything they could think of, from footraces and boxing matches to cockfights and raffles. Companies that were located near small rivers and streams even organized high-stakes sailing races by fashioning small boats out of scraps of wood and paper. And when playing cards could not be acquired due to paper shortages or lack of funds, enterprising soldiers simply fashioned their own, sometimes decorating them with the likenesses of political leaders (Wiley 1943, p. 53).

Many soldiers who were unlucky or unskilled in games of chance found themselves bereft of funds within a few days—or even hours—of receiving their pay. As one Union soldier lamented in a letter to a friend, "[I was] only paid a week ago and have not a cent now, having bluffed away all that I did not send home. I don't think I will play poker any more" (quoted in Robertson 1984, p. 62). This state of affairs further exacerbated the problem of theft in some companies, as cash-strapped soldiers turned to thievery to compensate for their losses at the gaming tables.

Throwing Away Evidence of Sin

Much of this fixation on poker and other forms of gambling would have scandalized family members or churchgoing neighbors back home—a fact of which soldiers were well aware. Indeed, the prevailing view among good Christian folk of the Civil War era was that cards were "tools of the devil." This led many soldiers to engage in behavior that might have seemed comical, had it not been driven by the fear of death in battle. Poker-playing Yankees and Rebels became notorious for tossing decks of playing cards into the woods as they made their way to the field of battle. They did this to ensure that cards would not be among the personal effects returned to loved ones should they not survive the fighting.

The scene at the end of a pitched battle, however, was markedly different. As dusk fell over the land, survivors of the day's carnage could often be found back in the woods, searching out the cards they had discarded

General Wilcox at a cockfight. Soldiers filled their free time with a number of diversions, including reading and writing letters for family members back home. Other soldiers looked to pass the time by gambling on nearly anything, from card games to cockfights. *Hulton Archive/Getty Images.*

earlier that day so that they could celebrate their survival with a long night of poker.

Brawling and Drinking

Fistfights between soldiers—and occasional clashes between entire units of soldiers—also bedeviled army commanders in both the North and South. Boredom, testosterone, and ethnic pride all contributed to the frequency with which brawling erupted in Civil War camps. Some outfits (such as certain Irish contingents) became notorious for their pugnacious ways, and a few regiments became so riddled with brawling that their capacity for fighting the enemy came into question. The 7th Missouri, for example, once had 900 fights break out in a single day. This is a remarkable tally on its face, but it is even more stunning given the fact that the entire regiment only had 800 soldiers in its ranks by that time.

Another incitement to brawling—and insubordination in general—was alcohol. Army regulations placed significant restrictions on the consumption of liquor or other forms of alcohol by enlisted men, and even officers were supposed to practice restraint in this area. Troop movements and limited discretionary income further discouraged purchases of whiskey from sutlers or other

merchants, and most camps experienced "dry spells" during which alcohol was virtually absent.

Most soldiers with a taste for whiskey, however, were not discriminating about the quality of the liquor they consumed. Some made their own liquor, fermenting pine boughs and other dubious materials in their goal to get drunk. Higher-grade alcohol, meanwhile, was obtained through foraging or clandestine purchase. And when troops did succeed in getting their hands on whiskey, they often overindulged.

Generals on both sides attempted to minimize the negative impact of alcohol abuse in their armies, but with limited success. Fines and various forms of corporal punishment simply did not provide sufficient deterrent to keep some soldiers from the bottle. At one point, Union General George B. McClellan (1826–1885) became so aggravated by the deleterious impact of whiskey on his troops that he opined that if he could somehow keep all liquor out of their hands "it would be worth 50,000 men to the armies of the United States" (Davis 1991, p. 154).

Rough Men and Rough Language

Army encampments were also typified by extensive and creative use of language of the foulest kind. Many of the men who wore the blue and gray were rough characters,

ALCOHOL ON THE FRONT

While soldiers engaged in periods of battle, most of their time was spent drilling, marching, and waiting for encounters with the enemy. During these lulls, some soldiers sought to fill their time with alcohol. As described in Confederate soldier William Stevenson's 1862 personal account *Thirteen Months in the Rebel Army: Being a Narrative of Personal Adventures in the Infantry, Ordnance, Cavalry, Courier, and Hospital Services,* the clandestine procurement and consumption of alcohol was a commonplace practice—as was turning a blind eye to it:

> Our rations at this time were neither very lavishly given nor very choice in quality, yet there was no actual suffering. For the first month whisky was served, and the men were satisfied to work for the promise of forty cents a day extra pay and three drams. In the fifth week the drams were stopped, and the extra pay never began... while the whisky ration was continued, there was little drunkenness. The men were satisfied with the limited amount given, and the general health of all was good. When the spirit ration was stopped, illicit trade in the "cra-thur" was carried by Jews and peddlers, who hung around the camp a short distance out in the woods. The search after these traders by the authorities was so vigilant, that at last there was no whisky vended nearer than the little town of Covington, eight miles distant. This, however, did not deter the men from making frequent trips to this place after it. Various expedients were resorted to, in order to bring it inside of the guard-lines. Some stopped the tubes on their guns, and filled the barrel with liquor. The colonel, while passing a tent one day, saw one of the men elevate his gun and take a long pull at the muzzle. He called out, "Pat, what have you got in your gun? Whisky?" He answered—"Colonel, I was looking into the barrel of my gun to see whether she was clean" (pp. 45–46).

CARLY S. KALOUSTIAN

SOURCE: Stevenson, William G. *Thirteen Months in the Rebel Army: Being a Narrative of Personal Adventures in the Infantry, Ordnance, Cavalry, Courier, and Hospital Services. New York : A. S. Barnes and Burr, 1862. Sources in U.S. History Online: Civil War. Gale. Available from http://galenet.galegroup.com/.*

hurled at one another or at God were the same ones that they had uttered in the taverns they frequented back home.

But for soldiers who were dedicated Christians, educated professionals, or recruits fresh from isolated farms, the incessant foul language could be quite demoralizing. "Around me is the gibber of reckless men & I am compelled to listen day and night to their profanity, filthy talk, and vulgar songs," grumbled one Union recruit. "I have some conception how Lot felt in Sodom when he had to listen to and be cursed by the filthy conversation of the wicked" (Glatthaar 1985, p. 96). A Confederate soldier from Mississippi painted a similarly bleak picture, asserting that "oaths, blasphemies, imprecations, obscenity, are hourly heard ringing in your ears until your mind is almost filled with them" (Wiley and Milhollen 1959, p. 190).

Some officers became so upset by the steady streams of profanity that issued from all corners of camp that they threatened soldiers with fines for excessive swearing. These threats proved impossible to enforce, however, and within a matter of days—or sometimes hours—they were inevitably abandoned.

In the end, too, profanity was the least of a soldier's troubles, and many of the most pious Yankees and Rebels were willing to overlook a foul mouth if other, more noble, characteristics were also present in their fellow soldiers. "Every one of [my comrades] is as a brother to me," wrote one Massachusetts soldier after a year of deadly battles, exhausting marches, and lousy food. "It is true many of them are very profane and the demon whiskey is not refused by many of them but with all their faults I love them because they are brave, generous, intelligent, and noble-hearted" (McPherson 1997, p. 88).

"Horizontal Refreshments"

Many Civil War soldiers also engaged in sexual activity—sometimes known by the euphemism "horizontal refreshments"—with prostitutes. Some men were naturally inclined to pursue this option anyway to satisfy their sexual urges. Others had wives and sweethearts back home to whom they had promised fidelity, only to find that their self-discipline fell apart after weeks, months, or years of enforced abstinence.

Early in the Civil War, camp followers were the main focus for soldiers looking to satisfy their urges for sex. Some of these camp followers were unabashed prostitutes, others served as cooks or laundresses on at least a part-time basis. Virtually all of them were sought for sexual satisfaction at one time or another, irrespective of their appearance or age. "Almost all the women are given to whoredom & are the ugliest, sallowfaced, shaggy headed, bare footed dirty wretches you ever saw," complained one Alabama soldier (Sutherland 1989, p. 16). As the war progressed, however, and troop movements accelerated, many of the camp followers fell away. At that point, both Union and Confederate soldiers became

and most enlisted men had little in the way of formal education. These factors, combined with the everyday frustrations and terrors of army life in a time of war, provided fertile soil for oaths of the most profane variety.

For many soldiers, the rough language swirling around them was no different than what they experienced back in the shipyards, factories, and stables that had employed them prior to the war. And the oaths they more dependent on furloughs or clandestine encounters with women from nearby communities. According to one historian, "men encamped near large towns and cities naturally had the best opportunities to enjoy female companionship, whatever their choice in women. They could meet utterly respectable ladies at church socials, Sanitary Commission fairs, and other civilized occasions. If a man sought more than polite conversation, he headed for the fleshpots. Every town had them" (Sutherland 1989, p. 16).

By the final months of the war, prostitution in numerous cities in both the North and South had greatly increased to accommodate the demand from soldiers on leave. Union soldiers, in general, enjoyed more generous furloughs, and they provided a steady flow of income into the red-light districts of places such as Boston, Chicago, Cincinnati, and New York. The nation's capital, meanwhile, supported hundreds of bordellos. Down in the South, the capital city of Richmond also became a center of prostitution.

Many soldiers who engaged in sexual relations with prostitutes and other women during the Civil War rationalized their behavior away as a necessary and harmless release from the pressures of war. But syphilis, gonorrhea, and other sexually transmitted diseases ravaged many units. In one study of sexual activity during the Civil War, historian Thomas Lowry (1994) determined that fully one out of three of the men who died in Union and Confederate veterans' homes were killed by the latter stages of venereal disease. Some of these men were bachelors—but some were not. Thus, an unknown number of women and children must likewise have been ravaged by gonorrhea, syphilis, and a host of other sexually transmitted diseases long after the war was over.

BIBLIOGRAPHY

Catton, Bruce. *Reflections on the Civil War*, ed. John Leekley. Garden City, NY: Doubleday, 1981.

Davis, William C. *Rebels and Yankees: The Fighting Men of the Civil War*. New York: Smithmark Publishers, 1991.

Glatthaar, Joseph T. *The March to the Sea and Beyond: Sherman's Troops in the Savannah and Carolinas Campaigns*. New York: New York University Press, 1985.

Hays, Gilbert Adams. *Under the Red Patch: Story of the Sixty-Third Regiment, Pennsylvania Volunteers, 1861–1864*. Pittsburgh, PA: Sixty-Third Pennsylvania Volunteers Regimental Association, 1908.

Lowry, Thomas P. *The Story the Soldiers Wouldn't Tell: Sex in the Civil War*. Mechanicsburg, PA: Stackpole Books, 1994.

McPherson, James M. *For Cause and Comrades: Why Men Fought in the Civil War*. New York: Oxford University Press, 1997.

Mitchell, Reid. *Civil War Soldiers: Their Expectations and Their Experiences*. New York: Viking, 1988.

Robertson, James I., Jr. *Soldiers Blue and Gray*. Columbia, SC: University of South Carolina Press, 1988.

Robertson, James I., Jr., and the editors of Time-Life Books. *Tenting Tonight: The Soldier's Life*. Alexandria, VA: Time-Life Books, 1984.

Shannon, Fred A. "The Life of the Common Soldier in the Union Army, 1861–1865." In *The Civil War Soldier: A Historical Reader*, ed. Michael Barton and Larry M. Logue. New York: New York University Press, 2002.

Sutherland, Daniel E. *The Expansion of Everyday Life, 1860–1876*. New York: Harper & Row, 1989.

Wiley, Bell Irvin. *The Life of Johnny Reb: The Common Soldier of the Confederacy*. Indianapolis, IN, and New York: Bobbs-Merrill Company, 1943. Reprint, Baton Rouge: Louisiana State University Press, 1992.

Wiley, Bell Irvin, and Hirst D. Milhollen. *They Who Fought Here*. New York: Macmillan, 1959.

Kevin Hillstrom

■ Diaries and Letters from Soldiers

Writing letters to loved ones and keeping personal journals was one of the primary ways in which Civil War soldiers passed the time in camp or at the end of a long day's march. These activities relieved the tedium of a soldier's life and served as the main vehicle through which Rebels and Yankees maintained their emotional ties to family and friends back home. Penning correspondence to loved ones and the exercise of diary keeping also had significant therapeutic benefits for many battle-scarred soldiers.

The themes that the soldiers explored in these notes, letters, and journal entries were repeated again and again. Recollections of battlefield experiences and emotions were a major and often cathartic focus, but far more sentences were devoted to wistful expressions of love for wives, girlfriends, parents, siblings, and children back home. Accounts of daily life in camp also took up a lot of space in letters and dairies. One historian observed that "[t]hey used ink and pencil, even crayons. They wrote on foolscap and parchment, in the margins of newspapers and on the back of wallpaper. When a precious sheet of paper was filled, if there was more to say they gave the sheet a quarter turn and cross-wrote over what they had already written" (Davis 1991, p. 39).

Pining for Loved Ones

Of all the topics that soldiers wrote about during the Civil War, perhaps none were written about with the same fervor as those of homesickness and love for absent family. Some soldiers maintained some measure of restraint and formality on these topics in their letters and journal entries, but many other war-weary Rebels and Yankees wrote with emotional abandon. "I am sick and tird [*sic*] of the war and I want to see you and the children the worst in the world," wrote one private in the Ohio 1st in 1862. "I wood [*sic*] give my monthly wages and my hundred dollars bounty to be at home" (McPherson 1997, p. 256).

Like many other men caught up in the conflict, Confederate surgeon Harvey Black showed a fondness for reliving past days of domestic bliss in his letters home. In a November 1863 letter to his wife Mollie, for example, he recalled the joys of their courtship:

> The happy day of our marriage arrived and since then, hours, days, and years of time, confidence & happiness passed rapidly away, and only to make us feel that happy as were the hours of youthful days, they compare not with those of later years and perhaps even these may not be equal to that which is in reserve for us. I don't know how much pleasure it affords you to go over these days of the past, but to me they will ever be remembered as days of felicity. And how happy the thought that years increase the affection & esteem we have for each other to love & be loved. May it ever be so, and may I ever be a husband worthy of your warmest affections. (November 1, 1863)

Honor and Sacrifice

Patriotism was another favorite topic in the correspondence and journal entries of soldiers fighting under the Union and Confederate banners. One of the most famous letters of the entire war was written by Union soldier Sullivan Ballou to his wife Sarah on July 14, 1861. In this letter, which is suffused with powerful expressions of love for his wife, Ballou nonetheless signals his willingness to sacrifice himself to the Union cause.

> If it is necessary that I should fall on the battlefield for my country, I am ready. ... My courage does not halt or falter. I know how strongly American Civilization now leans upon the triumph of the Government, and how great a debt we owe to those who went before us through the blood and suffering of the Revolution. And I am willing—perfectly willing—to lay down all my joys in this life, to help maintain this Government, and to pay that debt. (Ballou 1888, p. 1058)

Ballou did remain true to his word, and sacrificed himself to the Union cause a week after this letter was written to his dear wife Sarah.

Many Confederate soldiers expressed equally heartfelt feelings about the importance of duty and honor. In one letter home, a Georgia native gently rebuked his wife for a previous letter in which she had told him that his daughters were pleading for their father's return.

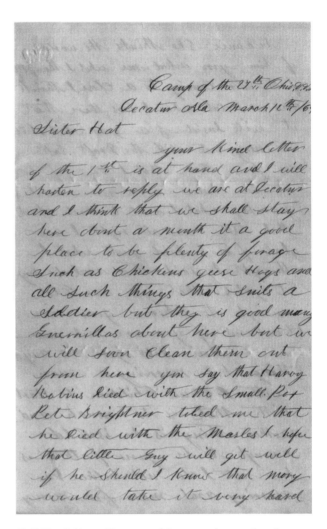

Civil War letter. First page of three-page letter written by a Michigan soldier, Ed Webb, to his sister, Hattie Webb Wyman, on March 12, 1864. *Monroe County, Michigan, Historical Commission Archives*

> I came to the war because I felt it to be my duty. ... I am not going to run away[;] if I never come home I had rather di[e] without seeing them than for pe[o]ple to tell them after I am dead that their father was a deserter. ... It [is] every Southern man[']s duty to fight against abolition misrule and preserve his Liberty untarnished which was won by our fore Fathers [*sic*]. (McPherson 1997, p. 138)

Soldiers in both armies also expressed profound anger at men back home who avoided military service. They equated such evasion with cowardice and absence of moral scruples, and reserved special scorn for wealthy countrymen who used various draft exemptions to avoid shouldering their fair share of the burden.

> I have come here and left everything that is dear to me on earth to fight and suffer all manner of hardships to protect property, not my own, whilst many of them who have property are still at home

with their families—in fact they are the ones as a general rule that stay at home," wrote one bitter Rebel from South Carolina. "Will we poor soldiers ever be recompensed for what we are doing? I fear not (Reid 1892, p. 13).

An Alabama soldier voiced similar sentiments, denouncing "the miserable gilded coward who remains in the rear to fatten like a hyena over the grave of his country" (Williams 1981, p. 146).

Soldiers' ink also turned venomous on the subject of civilian critics of the war (known as "Copperheads" in the North). "It is outrageous and abominable that the Army must be slandered and abused by the cowards that stay at home," wrote a Massachusetts officer in 1864 (Brewster 1992, p. 298).

Tales of Hardship and Horror

Another recurring topic in the letters, journals, and diaries that survived the war was everyday discomfort, hunger, and hardship. In one representative passage from a Confederate soldier's diary, a long march to Chattanooga that was interrupted by a wonderful and unexpected bounty is described: "I remember I found some apples about the size of a quail's egg, under an apple tree and I ate about as many as I could hold, and that night we were notified that we could draw some rations but I was too tired and sleepy to get up. I was about petered out and had done without rations so long I was not hungry" (Robertson 1988, p. 110). Sentiments such as these were legion, in letters and journals written by Yankee and Rebel alike.

Such excerpts provide important insights into the everyday experiences of hungry, poorly equipped, weary, and—in many cases—disillusioned soldiers. But they pale next to the vivid descriptions of battle found in many letters and journal entries. Some soldiers, clinging to conventions of masculinity, were loathe to admit the fear they undoubtedly felt, but other were frank about their terror and anguish.

Nonetheless, the historical record is generously sprinkled with letters and diary entries that make it clear that "seeing the elephant"—experiencing combat firsthand—was a terrifying experience. After the epic Battle of Antietam, for example, a Union officer with a New York regiment acknowledged that "I don't pretend to say I wasn't afraid, and I must say that I did not see a face but that turned pale or hear a voice that did not tremble" (McPherson 1997, p. 37) in the moments leading up to the battle. A captain in a North Carolina regiment was similarly candid, noting that even after acquitting himself well in several battles, he still approached every battle "*badly scared* ... I am not as brave as I thought I was. I never wanted out of a place as bad in my life" (McPherson 1997, p. 37).

Some soldiers writing about actual battle scenes, meanwhile, were not inclined to spare their readers from the brutal realities of war. Writing in his journal, a Ten-

nessee infantryman recalled one harrowing Union assault on his company's position:

> A solid line of blazing fire right from the muzzles of the Yankee guns [was] poured right onto our very faces, singeing our hair and clothes, the hot blood of our dead and wounded spurting on us, the blinding smoke and stifling atmosphere filling our eyes and mouths, and the awful concussion causing the blood to gush our of our noses and ears, and above all, the roar of battle, made it a perfect pandemonium. Afterward I heard a soldier express himself by saying that he thought 'Hell had broke loose in Georgia, sure enough' (Watkins 1882 [1987], p. 157).

On the whole, however, soldiers were hesitant to recount the gritty details of war and hardship with their relatives and friends back home.

Survivors of these orgies of bloodletting often could not help but comment on the hellish tableaus that prevailed after the rifles and cannons finally fell silent. One soldier at the Battle of Chancellorsville wrote that

> [O]ur line of battle extended over some eight miles and for that distance you see the dead bodies of the enemy lying in every direction, some with their heads shot off, some with their brains oozing out, some pierced through the head with musket balls, some with their noses shot away, some with their mouths smashed, some wounded in the neck, some with broken arms or legs, some shot through the breast and some cut in two with shells (Linderman 1987, p. 125).

Army surgeons offered similarly bleak perspectives in their journals and letters. "Oh! It is awful," wrote one field surgeon. "It does not seem as though I could take a knife in my hand to-day, yet there are a hundred cases of amputation waiting for me. Poor fellows come and beg almost on their knees for the first chance to have an arm taken off. It is a scene of horror such as I never saw" (Bowen 1884, p. 304).

Brothers in Arms

Soldiers also wrote at length about the officers who commanded them. Some passages sang the praises of captains who were brave, knowledgeable, and attentive to the needs of the men under their commands. At times, however, the lines written about officers dripped with anger and disillusionment. Special bitterness was reserved for those officers who did not share in the hardships experienced by common soldiers. One Confederate soldier, for example, griped that his regimental commanders

> had their black cooks, who were out foraging all the time, and they filled their masters' bellies if there was fish or fowl to be had. The regimental wagons carried the officers' clothes, and they were never half-naked, lousy, or dirty. They never had to sleep upon the bare ground nor carry forty

Northern soldiers at Potomac during respite. In letters to family and personal journals, soldiers often used their limited free time to record their thoughts about the war, their memories of home, and their hopes about the future. *Hulton Archive/Getty Images.*

rounds of cartridges strapped around their galled hips; the officers were never unshod or felt the torture of stone-bruise" (Hunter 1905, p. 517).

A far different tone prevailed when Union and Confederate soldiers wrote about their fellow enlisted men, however. These descriptions of comrades-in-arms were usually littered with references to brotherhood, shared sacrifice, and mutual respect. After the epic Seven Days battles, for example, a private from the 83rd Pennsylvania—which suffered 75 percent casualties—wrote that "it seems strange how much the rest of our company has become united since the battles. They are almost like brothers in one family now. We used to have the 'aristocratic tent' and 'tent of the upper ten,' and so on, but there is nothing of that kind now. We have all lost dear friends and common sorrow makes us all equal" (McPherson 1997, p. 87).

Letters and journals also provide ample evidence that fraternization between armies was not uncommon, at least in some theatres, especially in the latter stages of the Civil War. After a friendly meeting between the troops near Kenesaw Mountain in 1864, a member of Sherman's army in a letter to his parents remarked:

We made a bargain with them that we would not fire on them if they would not fire on us, and they were as good as their word. It seems too bad that we have to fight men that we like. Now these Southern soldiers seem just like our own boys ... They talk about ... their mothers and fathers and their sweethearts just as we do. ...Both sides did a lot of talking but there was no shooting until I came off duty in the morning. (Wiley 1943 [1992], p. 356)

A final subject that was frequently discussed was the character of the people and land that came under occupation. Yankee troops were convinced of the superior industry and culture of the North, and when they traveled through the South they searched for evidence to support that notion. Their letters described, at length, the Southern climate, agriculture, housing, cities, and civic populations, both white and black (Mitchell 1988, p. 90). One of the recurring topics in their narratives of Southern life was evidence of the depravity of slavery. Not surprisingly, soldiers from rural areas of the North who had little experience with blacks also wrote at length about their impressions of the blacks they encountered.

Many of these letters and diaries exhibited little sympathy for Southerners and the difficult conditions in which they existed during the last years of the war. Union soldiers saw the straits in which Southerners found themselves as a fitting punishment for their rebellion. But empathy for hungry Southern civilians could still be found in some letters and journals. "All I pity are the little children," wrote one New York soldier stationed in Virginia in December 1864. "They look up so sad with so much astonishment wondering, I presume, why we are all armed, filling their little hearts with terror, & why they are all so destitute & why Papa is not at home attending to their wants in this bleak, cold winter weather. Poor children! They know not they are suffering the curse of treason" (Mitchell 1988, p. 117).

Mail Call

Civil War soldiers also treasured letters they received from wives, children, parents, and friends. "For soldiers in the field," observed one historian, "an unreliable postal service was the only link to home. When mail did get through, each letter was treated almost as a sacred relic. ... If soldiers felt great joy on receiving a cherished letter, they also experienced deep depression when no word came" (Williams 2005, p. 239–40). Indeed, one Confederate soldier reported that "those who received letters went off with radiant countenances. If it was night, each built a fire for light and, sitting down on the ground, read his letter over and over. Those unfortunates who got none went off looking as if they had not a friend on earth" (Worsham 1912, p. 98).

Mail call became more psychologically important as the war progressed as well. As memories of home and loved ones became hazier with time, tangible evidence that people back home still had the weary soldiers in their thoughts was crucial to shoring up morale. As one Union soldier bluntly stated in a letter to his sister, "I had rather have letters now than clothes" (Gordon 2002, p. 328). But just as messages of love sent spirits soaring, tales of woe—usually in the form of financial hardship—eroded the spirits of soldiers whose psyches were already frayed by war and its many discomforts and brutalities.

BIBLIOGRAPHY

Ballou, Adin. *An Elaborate History and Genealogy of the Ballous in America.* Providence, RI: Ariel Ballou and Latimer Ballou, 1888.

Bowen, James Lorenzo. *History of the Thirty-Seventh Regiment, Mass., Volunteers in the Civil War of 1861–1865.* Holyoke, MA: Clark W. Bryan & Company Publishers, 1884.

Brewster, Charles Harvey. *When This Cruel War Is Over: The Civil War Letters of Charles Harvey Brewster,* ed. David W. Blight. Amherst, MA: University of Massachusetts Press, 1992.

Davis, William C. *Rebels and Yankees: The Fighting Men of the Civil War.* New York: Smithmark Publishers, 1991.

Gordon, Lesley J. " 'Surely They Remember Me': The 16th Connecticut in War, Captivity, and Public Memory." In *Union Soldiers and the Northern Home Front: Wartime Experiences, Postwar Adjustments,* ed. Paul A. Cimbala and Randall M. Miller. New York: Fordham University Press, 2002.

Harvey Black to Mary (Mollie) Black, November 1 1863. "My Precious Loulie...": Love Letters of the Civil War. Virginia Tech University Digital Library and Archives. Available from http://spec.lib.vt.edu/.

Hunter, Alexander. *Johnny Reb and Billy Yank.* New York: The Neale Publishing Company, 1905.

Linderman, Gerald F. *Embattled Courage: The Experience of Combat in the American Civil War.* New York: Free Press, 1987.

McPherson, James M. *For Cause and Comrades: Why Men Fought in the Civil War.* New York: Oxford University Press, 1997.

Mitchell, Reid. *Civil War Soldiers: Their Expectations and Their Experiences.* New York: Viking, 1988.

Reid, Jesse Walton. *History of the Fourth Regiment of S.C. Volunteers from the Commencement of the War until Lee's Surrender.* Washington, DC: Jesse Walton Reid, 1892.

Robertson, James I., Jr. *Soldiers Blue and Gray.* Columbia, SC: University of South Carolina Press, 1988.

Robertson, James I., Jr., and the editors of Time-Life Books. *Tenting Tonight: The Soldier's Life.* Alexandria, VA: Time-Life Books, 1984.

Watkins, Sam R. *"Co. Aytch": Maury Grays, First Tennessee Regiment.* Nashville, TN: Cumberland Presbyterian Publishing House, 1882. Reprint, Wilmington, NC: Broadfoot, 1987.

Wiley, Bell Irvin. *The Life of Johnny Reb: The Common Soldier of the Confederacy.* Indianapolis, IN, and New York: Bobbs-Merrill Company, 1943. Reprint, Baton Rouge: Louisiana State University Press, 1992.

Williams, David. *A People's History of the Civil War: Struggles for the Meaning of Freedom.* New York: New Press, 2005.

Williams, James M. *From That Terrible Field: Civil War Letters of James M. Williams, Twenty-First Alabama Infantry Volunteers,* ed. John Kent Folmar. University, AL: University of Alabama Press, 1981.

Worsham, John H. *One of Jackson's Foot Cavalry: His Experience and What He Saw during the War, 1861–1865.* New York: Neale Publishing, 1912.

Kevin Hillstrom

■ Furloughs

Furloughs were formal leaves from military service granted to enlisted men from the Union or Confederate armies. These furloughs, whether bestowed on Yankee or Rebel soldiers, could only be granted by commanding officers attached to the soldier's company or regiment. Military officers also could apply for furloughs, but the rules that applied were often at least nominally different, and officer furloughs were more commonly called "leaves."

How the Furlough Programs Worked

Furlough requests in both the Northern and Southern armies were torturous affairs. Requests were subject to approval from a long list of offices, and it could take months to receive a definitive answer. Moreover, this long wait often ended in disappointment, with the request refused. Perhaps inevitably, the seeming capriciousness of commanders in determining who would and would not receive furloughs led to conspiracy theories among the rank and file. "There always seemed to be grounds for finding partiality in cases where furloughs were granted, and these were seized upon and magnified by those who were disappointed," wrote one scholar in describing the prevailing sentiments in Confederate units. "Married men complained that single comrades were preferred, and vice versa; poor men were convinced that wealthy men were favored, privates grumbled that officers received a disproportionate share of leaves" (Wiley 1992, p. 139).

Soldiers who did receive furloughs typically received leave of several weeks, in part to accommodate the extensive travel time that was often required simply to get to and from home. Men on furlough were required to leave government-issued firearms and other equipment behind. They were also required to carry army documents that provided beginning and ending dates for the furlough, detailed description of the furloughed soldier's physical appearance and unit affiliation, and a record of pay and subsistence allowances furnished. Furlough papers clearly warned soldiers that failure to return to military service by the date specified would result in their classification as a deserter.

Anger and Dismay

As the Civil War progressed, both armies used promises of generous furloughs to encourage reenlistment. Entire Union regiments, for example, were offered "veteran's furloughs" if they reenlisted. This inducement had its desired effect, for it gave veterans a means by which they could simultaneously remain committed to military duties and check on family and property back home. Some soldiers who took these veteran's furloughs, however, found it difficult to depart again from home once they were back in the loving arms of family.

Another problem was that the armies broke their furlough promises to some soldiers. As the war progressed and Union forces moved deeper into Southern territory, Federal commanders increasingly turned down furlough requests on the grounds that the soldiers were too far from home to make furloughs practical. In the Confederate Army, meanwhile, troop shortages and military setbacks in various theatres of operation made it increasingly difficult for soldiers to coax furlough approvals from commanders. This in turn created significant morale problems in many Rebel units. As Confederate General Daniel H. Hill (1821–1889) opined, "If our brave soldiers are not permitted to visit their homes, the next generation in the South will be composed of the descendants of skulkers and cowards" (quoted in Robertson 1984, p. 55).

Military authorities in both the North and South had a ready assortment of responses to these complaints. When they denied furloughs that had been previously promised in return for reenlistment (or for procuring recruits or returning deserters to their units), they patiently explained that rising desertion rates and the evolving military situation made it impossible for them to make good on their promises. In the face of this disappointment, thousands of soldiers simply went home anyhow.

BIBLIOGRAPHY

Robertson, James I., Jr. *Soldiers Blue and Gray.* Columbia: University of South Carolina Press, 1988.

Robertson, James I., Jr., and the editors of Time-Life Books. *Tenting Tonight: The Soldier's Life.* Alexandria, VA: Time-Life Books, 1984.

Wiley, Bell Irvin. *The Life of Johnny Reb: The Common Soldier of the Confederacy.* Indianapolis, IN, and New York: Bobbs-Merrill Company, 1943. Reprint, Baton Rouge: Louisiana State University Press, 1992.

Williams, David. *A People's History of the Civil War: Struggles for the Meaning of Freedom.* New York: New Press, 2005.

Kevin Hillstrom

■ Prisons and Prisoners of War

PRISONS AND PRISONERS OF WAR:
AN OVERVIEW
Kevin Hillstrom

LIVING AS A PRISONER OF WAR
Kevin Hillstrom

AFRICAN AMERICAN PRISONERS OF WAR
Kevin Hillstrom

PRISONER EXCHANGE AND PAROLE
Robbie C. Smith

PRISONS AND PRISONERS OF WAR: AN OVERVIEW

The history of the American Civil War is rife with examples of hardship and pain, but perhaps nowhere were conditions harsher than in the prisoner-of-war camps that dotted the interiors of both the North and South during the final two years of the conflict. Some of these prisons managed to provide enough food and shelter to sustain the physical health of their populations for the war's duration. Many others, however, became notorious for their squalid living conditions and meager rations. In the worst cases—such as at the Andersonville facility in Georgia and the Elmira camp in New York—Civil War prison camps became incubators of disease, centers of malnutrition or outright starvation, and warrens of treachery, thievery, and brutality.

Paroles and Exchanges

In the early stages of the Civil War, feeding and sheltering captured enemy soldiers did not constitute a heavy burden for either the Federal or Confederate government. Large battles occurred infrequently compared to later years, which served to limit the number of prisoners. In addition, despite President Abraham Lincoln's initial refusal to authorize prisoner exchanges—a stance that stemmed from his belief that such negotiations might give the Confederacy a veneer of legitimacy as a distinct nation and erode Washington's efforts to frame the secessionists as a collection of treasonous agitators within an already established sovereign state—field commanders frequently arranged informal prisoner exchanges. Canny administrators on both sides of the conflict welcomed this approach, for they recognized that both the North and South were ill-equipped to handle large numbers of prisoners.

In the summer of 1862 the North and South agreed to a formal parole arrangement for prisoners of war. Under this agreement, prisoners were traded on a one-for-one basis, while officers were traded in accordance with equations that took varying ranks into consideration. "Leftover" soldiers were paroled—that is, they were released with the understanding that they would not take up arms again until they were figured into the mathematics of some future prisoner exchange. Once paroled, soldiers went home or reported to parole camps operated and maintained by their own governments until they were formally "exchanged." This system was mutually beneficial, though to function it required that each side had confidence the other would act in good faith.

The parole system was not without its problems, however. The main complaint leveled by military commanders was that many soldiers on parole—which in many ways was a sort of administrative limbo—came to feel as if they were not really in the army anymore. Not surprisingly, then, the prevailing environment in parole camps was often undisciplined and characterized by inattention to military decorum. In addition, some paroled men simply wandered off to nearby towns that promised more recreational opportunities than the spartan accommodations of camp could provide. Paroled prisoners who returned home were even more difficult to round up, even though they were still technically members of the military and subject to its orders. It was extremely difficult for many of these men to uproot themselves from the comforts and routines of home and return to a military life that, in most cases, no longer seemed nearly as romantic or glorious as it had back in the heady weeks after Fort Sumter.

Expanding Prison Systems

Despite its various imperfections, this state of affairs kept the prisoner-of-war populations low in both the North and South, and it ensured that most soldiers who were captured only had to spend a matter of days or weeks in enemy hands before they were exchanged or paroled.

Events in 1863 and early 1864, though, shattered this arrangement beyond repair and ushered in grim new methodologies for dealing with prisoner populations that exploded in size in a matter of months. The first major blow to the parole system came in 1863, when the administration of Confederate President Jefferson Davis threatened to take all captured black soldiers from the Union Army and place them into slavery in the factories and fields of the South. The administration further declared that it was considering executing captured white officers from black regiments for fomenting "servile insurrection." Finally, the government in Richmond announced that it would not include black Union troops in future prisoner exchanges. This stand was unacceptable to Lincoln, and it constituted the first major rupture in the parole system.

A second blow to the system came when the South unilaterally—and falsely—claimed that some of its parolees had been exchanged and were thus eligible to return to military service. This brazen move, which stemmed from the Confederacy's increasingly desperate need for men to replenish its dwindling military ranks, led the

Andersonville Prison, Georgia.   Perhaps the most notorious prisoner of war camp in the Confederacy, Andersonville became the final resting spot for thousands of Union soldiers who died there. Lack of food, clean water, and medical care created conditions that killed more than one hundred men per day.   *The Library of Congress.*

Union to further curtail its participation in the exchange and parole programs. It was at this time that both the North and South began hurriedly converting military barracks, forts, and tobacco warehouses into prisoner-of-war camps to house the growing number of captured troops.

Finally, Ulysses S. Grant's promotion to commander of all Union forces in March 1864 marked a complete end to the prisoner-exchange programs that had worked so well during the first two years of the war. Grant knew that by the spring of 1864 the South was suffering from increasingly acute shortages of manpower, and that his army enjoyed clear and growing numerical superiority over the enemy. Grant held firm to the Union decision not to exchange only white soldiers, abandoning their black comrades to slavery.

Filling Up the Prisons

When the parole system fell apart, the number of prisoners of war in both armies accelerated rapidly. Captured soldiers typically spent their first hours of captivity knotted together in crowded holding pens or in places that could easily be converted into temporary corrals, such as gullies. After officers recorded their names, ranks, and unit affiliation, provost marshals sent captured prisoners off to various prison facilities. Some fortunate prisoners were delivered to the gates of their prisons by train or boat, but most captured soldiers had to endure long marches on foot to reach their destination. By the end of the war, virtually all prisoners—especially Union prisoners of the Confederate military, which was squeezing every last bit of logistical support out of its unraveling transportation network—had to travel by foot to prison.

Captured officers generally received far better treatment than enlisted men. Union and Confederate prison authorities sometimes found space in their own quarters for captured officers, and the rations captured officers received was often a cut above the fare given rank-and-file prisoners. Other officers, however, found themselves in the general prisoner-of-war population, and shared facilities that were crowded, filthy, and disease-ridden.

All told, approximately 195,000 Federal soldiers were subjected to imprisonment in wartime, while about 215,000 Confederate troops were captured and imprisoned over the course of the war. According to official reports, of these more than 400,000 prisoners, approximately 56,000 died in captivity. The mortality rate in Union prisons was about 12 percent, while the rate in Confederate prisons reached almost 16 percent. These shockingly high mortality rates stemmed from prison conditions that were, more often than not, perilous and dehumanizing.

"Hell on Earth"

Malnutrition and hunger were typical of many of the Civil War prison camps. Food allocations were meager to begin with, and withholding rations emerged as a common means of reining in or otherwise modifying the behavior of prisoners. Tales of malnutrition or starvation in enemy prison camps also prompted some reductions in food rations.

Shelters, blankets, stoves, and other resources offering protection from the elements were also in short supply at many prison installations. This was particularly problematic in the North, where many Rebel prisoners endured long, cold winters in threadbare tents and tattered clothing. Sanitary conditions were notoriously poor in many prison camps in both the North and South as well, with many captives forced to drink, bathe, and dispose of human waste in the same areas—sometimes using the same water source. Medical care at these facilities ranged from poor to barbaric.

One of the worst of the Civil War camps was Andersonville in southern Georgia. Historian William C. Davis described a typical scene at the hospital there thusly: "Stewards cleaned wounds with dirty water poured on them, forming pools on the ground where insects bred in the moist filth. Inevitably, millions of flies swarmed over the helpless patients, relentlessly laying eggs in their open wounds and sores. Scores of men went mad from the pain of maggots eating their way through their inflamed flesh" (Davis 1991, p. 176).

All of these forces—hunger, crowded and unsanitary conditions, exposure to the elements, vulnerability to disease and depression—combined to make the prison camps horrible places. Little wonder, then, that numerous accounts of prisoner of war experiences, whether penned by Confederate or Union soldiers, describe Civil War prison camp environments as literal "hells on earth."

The Worst of the Prison Camps

Andersonville Prison, mentioned above, was the most notorious of all the Civil War prison camps. This sixteen-acre tract in southwestern Georgia, composed of open fields and swamps, housed approximately 41,000 Union prisoners during the war. Of that number, 12,000 to 15,000 perished inside Andersonville's fences. In August 1864, 100 prisoners per day were dying in that nightmarish stockade. At the end of the war, Andersonville's superintendent, Henry Wirz, became the only

ANDERSONVILLE PRISON

The Confederate prison of Andersonville, Georgia, became one of the most notorious during the Civil War. Prisoners faced untold hardships: lack of rations, disease (dysentery was widespread due contaminated water), brutal guards, and hostile fellow inmates. In his 1865 book *Life-struggles in Rebel Prisons: A Record of the Sufferings, Escapes, Adventures and Starvation of the Union prisoners*, Joseph Ferguson describes the architecture of the prison and life within its walls for the prisoners:

> The Andersonville prison was created for enlisted men, and only a few officers were taken to this pen, who were recaptured after escape, or who desired to pass for privates, believing they would have a better opportunity among so many to get away from the rebels. The pen was about two hundred yards long, and one hundred wide. Some thirty-five thousand human beings were huddled together in this small space. It was a mean-looking stockade, about seventeen feet high, the posts being sunk into the ground some four or five feet. The ground selected was on the side of a hill, part of it being a marsh... the position selected was such an [*sic*] one as fiends would pick out to accomplish dark crime of which the cruel keeper of Andersonville stands charged. In the enclosure there were no tents, huts, barracks or houses, to protect the inmates from the scorching rays of tropic sun of a Southern summer, or the cold and biting frost of a dreary winter. As prisoners came to the pen they were robbed of their clothing, blankets, shelter-tents, shoes, and even shirts. They were deprived of everything... and then put into the slaughter house to run around like lost sheep (pp. 75–76).

CARLY S. KALOUSTIAN

SOURCE: *Ferguson, Joseph*. Life-struggles in Rebel Prisons: A Record of the Sufferings, Escapes, Adventures and Starvation of the Union Prisoners. *Philadelphia, PA: J. M. Ferguson, 1865. Sources in U.S. History Online: Civil War. Gale. Available from http://galenet.galegroup.com/.*

Confederate to be tried and executed by the Federal government for war crimes.

Andersonville was by no means the only death trap maintained by Southern authorities, however. The mortality rate among prisoners at a Confederate stockade in Salisbury, North Carolina, in fact, was higher than that at Andersonville, according to historian Robert Eberly (Eberly 1999).

Several of the Union camps, meanwhile, were nearly as deadly as the infamous Andersonville. Places such as Camp Randall (in Wisconsin) and Camp Douglas (in Illinois) claimed thousands of soldiers' lives. But even these awful places paled next to Camp Elmira in upstate

Confederate prisoners of war. During the early stages of the Civil War, enemy soldiers captured on the battlefield were frequently paroled and allowed to return home on the condition that they would not take up arms for the remainder of the conflict. *The Library of Congress*

New York. At Elmira, nearly 800 of the 8,400 prisoners housed there died of disease within three months of their arrival, in large part because the river that flowed through the grounds quickly became fouled. All told, the death rate at Elmira, where the prison population was subjected to freezing winters, reached 24 percent (Williams 2005, p. 239).

Attempts to escape these horrible camps were launched by both Union and Confederate soldiers, but most of these desperate bids for freedom failed. Many would-be escapees were unable to get beyond the fences, and most of those who did make it out by using underground tunnels or other means were tracked down by bloodhounds and rifle-wielding guards. Over the course of the war, though, a few hundred clever and intrepid prisoners did succeed in their escape attempts. Most of these successful escapes from prison camp horrors were carried out by individuals or small groups of two to three, not by large groups of prisoners. When these fortunate individuals passed through enemy lines to safety, their accounts of inhuman conditions and brutal guards were seized on as propaganda tools by both sides. On the whole, though, few Civil War prisoners ever mounted escape attempts, as most were too worn down physically and mentally to conceive of or carry out viable plans.

The Final Months

In early 1865 Grant and the Federal authorities finally relented and resurrected the prisoner-exchange policies that had kept prisoner-of-war numbers down during the first half of the war. By this time, however, advancing Union troops were already seizing control of large swaths of the Southern countryside—including the stockades contained therein.

By March, many Confederate units had abandoned any pretense of holding on to enemy prisoners. Instead, Rebel commanders simply paroled them and sent them on their way. Around that same time, desperate lawmakers in Richmond authorized the recruitment of 300,000 slaves and promised full emancipation of slaves after the war if the British and French governments would give the tottering Confederacy diplomatic recognition. But these measures did nothing to stem the tide of Union military victories washing over the South. By the time Confederate General Robert E. Lee finally surrendered to Grant at Appomattox in Virginia on April 9, 1865, military prisons across both the North and South were preparing to release their long-suffering inmates.

Historians frequently cite the prison camps of the Civil War as one of the conflict's darkest elements. But most scholars agree that the devastating death toll in these facilities was not rooted in human malevolence or even indifference to the plight of those unfortunate enough to wait out the war's final months or years in captivity. In most cases, it was simply that each side felt compelled to channel the bulk of its scarce resources to its own fighting men, leaving very little for prisoners of war. "With very few exceptions, like perhaps Wirz at Andersonville, the men in charge of the camps did the best they could," wrote historian Bruce Catton. "The big trouble was that in North and South alike, as far as the authorities were concerned, the prison camps came last. They got what was left over when all of the other needs had been met. They were last on the line for food supplies, for medical supplies, for doctors, for housing, for clothing, for guards, for all of the things that are needed to run a prison camp. ... The prisoner of war got the dirty end of the stick not because anybody wanted to mistreat him, but simply because it worked out that way" (Catton 1981, p. 69).

BIBLIOGRAPHY

Barton, Michael, and Larry M. Logue, eds. *The Civil War Soldier: A Historical Reader*. New York: New York University Press, 2002.

Catton, Bruce. "Prison Camps of the Civil War." *American Heritage* 10, no. 5 (1959): 4–13.

Catton, Bruce. *Reflections on the Civil War*. Garden City, NY: Doubleday, 1981.

Catton, Bruce. *The American Heritage New History of the Civil War*, rev. ed. Ed. James M. McPherson. New York: Viking, 1996.

Davis, William C. *Rebels and Yankees: The Fighting Men of the Civil War*. New York: Smithmark Publishers, 1991.

Donald, David Herbert, Jean Harvey Baker, and Michael F. Holt. *The Civil War and Reconstruction*. New York: W. W. Norton, 2001.

Eberly, Robert E., Jr. "Prison Town." *Civil War Times Illustrated* 38 (March 1999): 30–33.

Hesseltine, William Best. *Civil War Prisons: A Study in War Psychology*. New York: F. Ungar, 1964.

Horigan, Michael. *Elmira: Death Camp of the North*. Mechanicsburg, PA: Stackpole Books, 2002.

Marvel, William. *Andersonville: The Last Depot*. Chapel Hill: University of North Carolina Press, 1994.

Mitchell, Reid. *Civil War Soldiers: Their Expectations and Their Experiences*. New York: Viking, 1988.

Mitchell, Reid. "Our Prison System: Supposing We Had Any: The Confederate and Union Prison Systems." In *On the Road to Total War: The American Civil War and the German Wars of Unification*, ed. Stig Förster and Jörg Nagler. New York: Cambridge University Press, 1997.

Speer, Lonnie R. *Portals to Hell: Military Prisons of the Civil War*. Mechanicsburg, PA: Stackpole Books, 1997.

Williams, David. *A People's History of the Civil War: Struggles for the Meaning of Freedom*. New York: New Press, 2005.

Kevin Hillstrom

LIVING AS A PRISONER OF WAR

More than 400,000 Civil War soldiers spent at least part of the conflict as prisoners of war. Tens of thousands more were paroled after capture and thus evaded prison; these soldiers—most of them captured during the opening months of the war—were the fortunate ones, for the men who were captured in the last two and a half years of the conflict endured many challenges to both body and soul. In fact, parole was fairly common up through the surrender of Vicksburg in 1863, in which 30,000 Confederates prisoners were paroled. The average soldier, from either the North or South, headed off to war with a host of new hopes and fears for his new military duties, but left home without the faintest conception of the nightmarish trials that would await him if captured and held captive by his enemies.

Days of Crushing Boredom

One of the most difficult if mundane aspects of being a prisoner of war during the Civil War was the utter lack of military or recreational activities to help pass the time. The crowded prisons in both the North and South offered no diversions of any kind for prisoners, and countless men spent their days shuffling or sitting and thinking about the bitter and miserable turn that their lives had taken. As one Union soldier wrote of his stint in a Confederate prison in South Carolina, many of his fellow prisoners sat "moping for hours with a look of utter dejection, their elbow upon their knee, and their chin resting upon their hand, their eyes having a vacant, faraway look" (Cooper 1888, p. 267). Thoughts of delicious food and loved ones back home seeped into every waking moment, and with nothing to take their minds off such torturous subjects, many soldiers struggled with profound depression.

Soldiers who could read and write sought some relief from the tedium through letter writing, but shortages of paper limited this option, and censorship by authorities was so heavy-handed that many letters were rendered senseless by blacked-out marks or scissor cuts. The uncertainties of wartime mail delivery further contributed to the anxiety of prisoners desperate for even a moment of relief from the dark environment that enveloped them. "Will no one send a little word to cheer us in our gloomy hours of activity?" wailed one Southern prisoner. "Oh, God! How dreadful are these bitter feelings of hope deferred. Thus we linger, thus we drag the slow, tedious hours of prison life" (Clark 1901, p. 677).

Religious services also helped pass the time for some soldiers and gave many religiously inclined soldiers a

Florence Military Prison.   With supplies limited by fighting, troops on the battlefront received priority over prisoners of war. Consequently, men held in enemy stockades suffered from scarce amounts of food, clothing, and medicine, with many of them dying from disease and starvation rather than battle-related injuries.   *Photograph by James E. Taylor. The Library of Congress.*

badly needed spiritual boost. An even greater number of imprisoned soldiers passed the time in conversation. These conversations—sometimes desultory, other times passionate—ranged over every conceivable subject, from the prewar lives that they had left behind to the character of fellow prisoners. But perhaps no topic preoccupied the soldiers as much as the question of when and under what circumstances their deliverance might come. Not surprisingly, then, newly arrived prisoners were barraged with requests for information about the progress of the war, and the prospects for a prisoner exchange.

Battling Hunger and Disease

Civil War prisoners from both the Union and Confederate ranks often found their worst suspicions about the other side confirmed once they were in the clutches of the enemy. In reality, however, the mistreatment and hardships that prisoners of war endured stemmed less from sanctioned policies of brutality than from individual acts of cruelty and, most pertinently, coldly logical decisions on the parts of the Federal and Confederate

governments to divert the bulk of their limited resources to the armies still operating out in the field.

Food rations in virtually all stockades were insufficient to stave off at least mild malnutrition, and scurvy and other diet-related maladies became epidemic. In some prisons, however, food rations were so meager that outright starvation was a genuine possibility for some soldiers. Ghastly levels of emaciation prevailed in these places, and the intellectual, emotional, and physical health of countless men became eroded or shattered by what they endured in these hopeless locales. Starvation was a particular risk for prisoners who had neither the physical strength nor allies to keep their rations from predatory men with whom they were incarcerated, but in some prisons starvation threatened virtually the entire population. Hunger led captives to take desperate measures:

> Many captives supplemented their diet with anything in the form of nutrition they could get their hands on, cats and dogs included. Some were strays, but others were pets of the guards or officers. … To be caught eating someone's pet could

result in severe punishment, so rats were more often the targets of hungry soldiers. Besides, they were much more abundant. (Williams 2005, p. 238)

The plight of Confederate prisoners of war was worsened by the fact that the Union commissary general of prisoners was Colonel William Hoffman (1807–1884). A bureaucrat with little regard for the welfare of the prisoners in his charge, Hoffman ordered a succession of cold-hearted measures during the course of the war. These ranged from dramatic reductions in rations in retaliation for reports of similar reductions in Southern prisons (which had far fewer resources to begin with) to burning packages of blankets and clothing sent to inmates at Elmira by loved ones (Hoffman reportedly only allowed clothing and blankets that were gray to be used by the inmates at Elmira, one of the coldest locations in the entire Union prison system). Even Hoffman's reduced rations were more generous than what Union soldiers received in most Confederate prisons, especially Andersonville. At war's end, Hoffman proudly returned to the Federal Treasury nearly $2 million he had saved through reductions in the rations given to Confederate prisoners.

In both Northern and Southern prisons, clean water was in short supply. Water used for drinking and washing was taken from streams and wells fouled by human waste. Given the circumstances, all stockades inevitably deteriorated into squalid pits. Maintaining a reasonable level of personal hygiene was impossible, and the stench of sweat and human waste hung over every prison. Clouds of fleas, mosquitoes, biting flies, and other insects tortured countless men during the summertime, and during the winter Southerners in particular struggled with the crushing cold. One Confederate prisoner, for example, recalled that the camp where he was imprisoned allotted only one stove per barracks, even though the barracks was crammed with 200 or more prisoners. Every morning, remembered the soldier, "the men crawled out of their bunks shivering and half frozen, when a scuffle, and frequently a fight, for a place by the fire occurred. God help the sick or the weak, as they were literally left out in the cold."(Robertson 1984, pp. 128–129)

Preyed on by Comrades

Thievery, assaults, and intimidation among prisoners were unfortunate realities in the inmate populations of many Civil War prisons. These dark events played out on a routine basis in many stockades in both the North and South, but the most grimly spectacular example of this sort of in-fighting took place at the Confederate prison at Andersonville, Georgia. Conditions there were so awful that normal rules of civilized behavior and military brotherhood fell by the wayside. Survivors recalled that the daily food allotment at Andersonville generally con-

---

HARD LIVING

William Harris, a Yankee soldier who was imprisoned during the Civil War details his captivity in his 1862 book *Prison-life in the Tobacco Warehouse at Richmond*. His sufferings focus on the day-to-day injustices and hardships. Here he describes the exorbitantly inflated prices for food, which soldiers had to pay to supplement their meager rations:

> The Confederate government furnishes the rations of bread and beef, with salt and brown soap. All other articles of food are provided by the prisoners, at the following prices:—Tea, $4 per pound; coffee $1 per pound; brown sugar, 20 cents; butter, 60 cents; potatoes, $2 per bushel; molasses, $1.25 per gallon. The cost of extra rations, which are confined to the foregoing articles, averages $2.50 per week for each officer. (p. 23)

At other times, however, Harris's account turns toward the emotionally crushing realities of captivity. Aside from the physical pangs of empty stomachs and exposure, boredom and depression wore on the prisoners, who dreamed of being reunited with their loved ones:

> The avidity with which each man gnawed his crust was ample evidence of his hunger. But a few moments elapsed before we received our allowance of boiled beef without salt; yet the bread by this time, in many cases, was all devoured. Breakfast being over ... [the prisoners] seated themselves on our only chair (the floor) and engaged in an exciting game of "penny poker"; others pitched pennies, played euchre, draughts, etc. But the main portion would for a while gaze at the capital of Rebeldom, and then, taking the floor for a stool, sit like "Patience on a monument, smiling at grief." In retired spots could be seen the more thoughtful, perusing with manifest delight a Bible or Testament, rendered doubly sacred by being the last token of the affection of a doting parent or loving sister ... it is here that we feel the loss of home comforts, our jovial associates, and all we once held dear. (pp. 58–59)

CARLY S. KALOUSTIAN

SOURCE: *Harris, William C. Prison-life in the Tobacco Warehouse at Richmond. Philadelphia, PA: G. W. Childs, 1862. Sources in U.S. History Online: Civil War. Gale. Available from http://galenet.galegroup.com/.*

---

sisted of three tablespoons of beans, a teaspoon of salt, and half a pint of unsifted cornmeal. A Confederate doctor who worked at Andersonville, meanwhile, reported that "from the crowded conditions, filthy habits, bad diet, and dejected, depressed condition of the prisoners, their systems had become so disordered that the smallest abrasion of the skin, from the rubbing of a shoe, or from the effects of the sun, the prick of a splinter or the scratching of a mosquito bite, in some cases took on a rapid and frightful ulceration and gangrene" (Davis 1991, p. 176).

The deterioration of conditions at Andersonville became so great that even the most partisan Southerners began to feel as if they were party to a great moral wrong. As one woman from the Andersonville area admitted, "My heart aches for these poor wretches, Yankees though they are, and I am afraid God will suffer some terrible retribution to fall upon us for letting such things happen" (Williams 2005, p. 238).

Meeting the Enemy

One of the less remarked-upon aspects of the Civil War prison camps was that the capture and incarceration of prisoners afforded soldiers with opportunities to meet and size up the enemy face-to-face. Reactions to captives and their circumstances ran the gamut of human emotions. Some Yankee and Rebel soldiers gloried in seeing the enemy humiliated and helpless. Many others recognized the similarities between themselves and the captured men before them, and their interactions were suffused with empathy for their plight. Surviving journals and letters from the war, for example, indicate that the tattered and shoeless appearance of Confederate captives in the last years of the war made a particularly deep impression on Union soldiers.

Prisoners who became acquainted with guards, meanwhile, sometimes fell prey to the temptation to befriend the enemy, thus risking retribution from fellow prisoners. This temptation was particularly great for conscripts and other prisoners who had not entered the war with enthusiasm. But it also bedeviled veteran Confederate prisoners, especially during the last months of the war when Southern defeat looked inevitable.

BIBLIOGRAPHY

Barton, Michael, and Larry M. Logue, eds. *The Civil War Soldier: A Historical Reader*. New York: New York University Press, 2002.

Catton, Bruce. *Reflections on the Civil War*, ed. John Leekley. Garden City, NY: Doubleday, 1981.

Clark, Walter, ed. *Histories of the Several Regiments and Battalions from North Carolina, in the Great War 1861–'65*. Goldsboro, NC: Nash Brothers, 1901.

Cooper, Alonzo. *In and Out of Rebel Prisons*. Oswego, NY, 1888.

Davis, William C. *Rebels and Yankees: The Fighting Men of the Civil War*. New York: Smithmark Publishers, 1991.

Donald, David Herbert, Jean Harvey Baker, and Michael F. Holt. *The Civil War and Reconstruction*. New York: W. W. Norton, 2001.

Eberly, Robert E., Jr. "Prison Town." *Civil War Times Illustrated* 38 (March 1999): 30–33.

Hesseltine, William Best. *Civil War Prisons: A Study in War Psychology*. New York: F. Ungar, 1964.

Horigan, Michael. *Elmira: Death Camp of the North*. Mechanicsburg, PA: Stackpole Books, 2002.

Marvel, William. *Andersonville: The Last Depot*. Chapel Hill: University of North Carolina Press, 1994.

Mitchell, Reid. *Civil War Soldiers: Their Expectations and Their Experiences*. New York: Viking, 1988.

Mitchell, Reid. "Our Prison System: Supposing We Had Any: The Confederate and Union Prison Systems." In *On the Road to Total War: The American Civil War and the German Wars of Unification, 1861–1871*, ed. Stig Förster and Jorg Nagler. New York: Cambridge University Press, 1997.

Robertson, James I., Jr., and the editors of Time-Life Books. *Tenting Tonight: The Soldier's Life*. Alexandria, VA: Time-Life Books, 1984.

Speer, Lonnie R. *Portals to Hell: Military Prisons of the Civil War*. Mechanicsburg, PA: Stackpole Books, 1997.

Williams, David. *A People's History of the Civil War: Struggles for the Meaning of Freedom*. New York: New Press, 2005.

Kevin Hillstrom

AFRICAN AMERICAN PRISONERS OF WAR

When the Civil War erupted in the spring of 1861, thousands of African American men in the North asked to take up arms as part of the Union Army. They did so in part because of their hatred of the Confederacy and its allegiance to the "peculiar institution" of slavery, and in part because they believed that proving their mettle on the battlefield would advance their quest to gain American citizenship. It was not until July 1862, however, that the U.S. Congress passed legislation that permitted black men to serve as soldiers in the Union Army. This legislation specified that all-black units were to be led by white officers.

The entrance of black soldiers into the conflict was a great boon to the Union war effort, but Southern reaction to this development triggered a series of events that greatly increased the number of prisoners of war held by both sides. Prior to the summer of 1862, North and South had cobbled together a prisoner exchange and parole system that, despite some flaws, kept prisoner numbers relatively low. But the Confederacy flatly refused to even consider exchanging captured black soldiers. Instead, the administration of Jefferson Davis threatened to enslave captured blacks and execute their white officers. President Abraham Lincoln responded by vowing to reciprocate in kind: For every white officer the South executed, the North would execute a Confederate prisoner; for every black soldier reenslaved, the North

Ku Klux Klan Grand Wizard Nathan Bedford Forrest (1821–1877). Confederate cavalrymen, led by Nathan Bedford Forrest, later the first Grand Wizard of the Ku Klux Klan, killing unarmed black Union soldiers after the surrender of Fort Pillow in Tennessee, August 12, 1864. *MPI/Hulton Archives/Getty Images.*

would assign one of its prisoners hard labor. Federal authorities also suspended Union participation in the exchange system until the Confederacy agreed to exchange black soldiers. This deadlock produced a tremendous upsurge in the number of prisoners held by both sides.

New Heights of Fury

Official Confederate policy called for captured black Union soldiers to be incarcerated and prepared for eventual enslavement in Southern fields or factories. Many Confederate officers in the field, though, encouraged the men under their command to kill all black soldiers who came in their sight, even if they were wounded or attempting to surrender. Some Rebel soldiers objected to these instructions on moral grounds, but others reveled in brutalizing their black foes. In a few cases, outright massacres of captured black soldiers took place. The most infamous of these events occurred at Fort Pillow, Tennessee, on April 12, 1864. On this day, Rebel soldiers under the command of Nathan Bedford Forrest (1821–1877) killed nearly 300 black Union troops—including dozens who had reportedly surrendered.

For black Union soldiers who were thrown into Southern stockades, conditions were so bleak that some lamented not dying on the battlefield. Life for all prisoners of war was marked by pain, hunger, and feelings of

hopelessness, but for black prisoners conditions were particularly harsh. "We were kept at hard labor and inhumanely treated," recalled one black Unionist. "If we lagged or faltered or misunderstood an order we were whipped and abused. ... For the slightest causes we were subjected to the lash [and] we were very poorly provided for with food" (Speer 1997, p. 113). Medical treatment for black prisoners was virtually nonexistent as well, and the shelter they received was frequently even more negligible than that provided to white prisoners. All told, blacks held in Confederate prison camps died at a rate of 35 percent, more than twice the average for white captives (Speer 1997, p. 113).

Black prisoners also sometimes endured the indignity of mistreatment at the hands of white inmates. Hostility to black soldiers stemmed partly from bigotry, but it also was rooted in the knowledge that the prisoner exchange system had fallen apart as a direct result of the introduction of black soldiers into the conflict. Other white Yankee prisoners, however, firmly supported the Lincoln administration's decision to refuse exchanges until Richmond agreed to include black prisoners in such trades. "Anyone, whatever may be his color, who wears the blue of Uncle Sam is entitled to protection," wrote one captain imprisoned in a Georgia stockade (Mitchell 1988, p. 49).

BIBLIOGRAPHY

Cimprich, John, and Robert C. Mainfort Jr., eds. "Fort Pillow Revisited: New Evidence about an Old Controversy." *Civil War History* 28, no. 4 (1982): 293–306.

Davis, William C. *Rebels and Yankees: The Fighting Men of the Civil War.* New York: Smithmark Publishers, 1991.

Glatthaar, Joseph T. *Forged in Battle: The Civil War Alliance of Black Soldiers and White Officers.* New York: Free Press, 1990.

Mitchell, Reid. *Civil War Soldiers: Their Expectations and Their Experiences.* New York: Viking, 1988.

Speer, Lonnie R. *Portals to Hell: Military Prisons of the Civil War.* Mechanicsburg, PA: Stackpole Books, 1997.

Kevin Hillstrom

PRISONER EXCHANGE AND PAROLE

Conflict on the scale experienced during the Civil War found North and South alike ill-prepared. The magnitude of the war's repercussions were exposed dramatically in the administration of captured combatants. Hurriedly improvised measures to accommodate an unforeseen number of prisoners resulted in appalling living conditions. Civil War prisons have become synonymous with deprivation, hardship, and a lack of the basic necessities to sustain life: food, clothing, hygiene, and shelter.

Stephen Minot Weld, a Union officer captured during the Seven Days campaign, described the rations served in Richmond's Libby Prison: "The only food furnished us was sour bread, meat, and salt, and at times a little vinegar. The meat was made into greasy soup, entirely unfit for a human being's stomach. If we had not had some money, we should have starved" (Weld 1979 [1912], p. 126). The menu available to Confederate prisoners was little, if any, better. Confederate Captain John Dooley, held captive in the Federal prison at Johnson's island in Ohio relates, "many go to the slop barrels and garbage piles to gather from the refuse a handful of revolting food" (Dooley 1945, p. 165).

In some instances, in both Union and Confederate prisons, the captives were treated to slightly better fare. Ambrose Spencer lived near Andersonville, the Confederate prison in Georgia. He penned an account of conditions faced there by Union prisoners. Making mention of the victuals, Spencer observed, "the rations for one day generally consisted of two ounces of bacon, a sweet potato when is season, a piece of bread two and a half inches square, composed of corn and cowpeas ground together into meal and unsifted" (Spencer 1866, p. 75). Sergeant Bartlett Malone of the 6th North Carolina infantry noted, "our rations at Point Lookout was 5 crackers and a cup of coffee for Breakfast. And for dinner a small ration of meat 2 crackers three Potatoes and a cup of Soup" (Malone 1987 [1960], p. 93). South Carolinian Berry Benson confirms the frequency of meals at the Federal Point Lookout, Maryland site. He mentioned, "we were given only two meals a day, breakfast at eight, dinner at two" (Benson 1992, p. 93). Commenting on the late meal, Benson went on to say, "... we had dinner, but it seemed to me very scanty. As a whole, I don't think Confederate prisoners suffered greatly for food, tho' we had none too much truly" (p. 94).

Food, while at a minimum was at the same time at a premium. In some instances prisoners were able to supplement their meager fare of rations by purchasing surplus food items or scavenging nearby resources. Dooley related, "Rats are found to be very good for food, and every night many are captured and slain. So pressing is the want of food that nearly all who can have gone into the rat business, wither selling these horrid animals or killing them and eating them" (1945, p. 163). Dooley recounted a favorite Johnson's Island story that called into question even the supply and survival of rodents: "... one night it was so cold in ... block 2 that a little mouse starting from its hole to run across the floor, was unable to complete its journey and expired frozen to death in the middle of the room" (p. 166). Although Dooley recounts this tale somewhat facetiously, it demonstrates prisoners' efforts to alleviate extreme conditions through humor and exaggeration.

During the early months of hostilities, both sides struggled to provide housing for captured combatants. Union prisoners captured in early engagements in Virginia were transported to the fledgling Confederacy's capital at Richmond. Corporal William H. Merrell of the 27th New York remembered conditions in Richmond's Tobacco Warehouse:

> There were no artificial conveniences for either eating or sleeping. At night the prisoners stretched themselves upon the bare floor, uncovered; and at meal time — if the irregular and melancholy farce of eating may be thus interpreted — they sat upon the floor, ranging against the wall, and (in primitive style) devoured whatever they could obtain. A more gloomy and revolting spectacle can hardly present itself to the imagination, than was afforded by these filthy quarter (1862, p. 25).

As the war progressed, facilities for holding captives were chosen for convenience with an appreciation for size and security, as in the case of Point Lookout, Fort Delaware, Belle Isle, and Tobacco Warehouse. Little if any thought was given however to providing prisoners with the basic necessities much less anything to ease an otherwise severe existence. In addition, existing prisons became overcrowded adding to the occupants' discomfort. Merell commented, "... I was transferred from the general hospital to Prison No. 1 — a tobacco warehouse

... its interior dimensions being seventy feet in length by twenty-six in width. It was in a most crowded state, as may be inferred from the fact that at no time were there less than one hundred and thirty, and often as many as one hundred and fifty occupants" (1862, p. 25). Private William Oake, of the 26th Iowa Infantry had a similar experience: "In the room in which we were there were about three hundred prisoners, and although the room was 40 x 100 feet I can assure my readers there was not much room for rent" (Oake 2006, p. 122).

In some instances prisoners were barely, if at all, afforded shelter. Vermont private Charles Fairbanks remembered such conditions at one of the more infamous Confederate prisons near Richmond: "... We were taken to Belle Island, about one-half mile from the city. Here we were surrounded by earth works, within an enclosure of four acres, where were confined over four thousand prisoners without shelter, except a few 'Cibley tents', the majority of the prisoners being exposed to the weather day and night" (Fairbanks 2004, p. 71). According to Benson, a similar situation existed at Point Lookout: "The prison was a rectangular enclosure of about ten acres ... Inside the fence were rows of tents with streets between ... In the tent where I was placed, were 15 others, and it may be well believed that 16 men, even in a Sibley tent, were badly crowded" (Benson 1992, pp. 90–91).

Even though additional housing was acquired and prisoners were separated according to rank, conditions improved little. Captives faced not only extreme overcrowding, but complications incident to that condition. Weld recounted, "My chief annoyance was from the lice. Every morning for over six weeks I looked over my clothes carefully, and as regularly found two or three of the disgusting old fellows besides any amount of nits and young ones. The building was full of them and whenever any one hammered on the floor above, down came lice. I have always had a great horror of them, and found them rather hard to bear" (1979 [1912], p. 128). Dooley noted, "Mice and roaches gamboled round our heads, performing feats of wondrous skill to astonish us who were now in this dismal world of theirs. No pillows and no blankets to cover up, and then the vermin!" (1945, p. 125).

Under such conditions it is not surprising that hygiene was non-existent, although prisoners made a valiant effort in the attempt. Oake related, "We of course had an abundance of water but having no soap we did not as a general thing do a very good job in our laundry work, but still it would freshen up our old rags, and for a short time would feel quite comfortable until the heat of our bodies began to revive the greybacks that had for a short time been put out of commission by being immersed cold water" (Oake 2006, p. 122). Dooley noted,

We have great trouble to get water for washing and cooking purposes. Two holes in the enclosure have been furnishing us with drinking, washing and cooking water. This water being clearer in the morning we try to furnish each room with a supply of drinking water for the day; but after some few thousands of buckets have been plunged in may be used only for washing and cooking purposes. At present one of the holes is out of order, and all come down to our small well, which refused to accommodate all as abundantly as it did a few. (1945, p. 145).

Merrell commented, "Let the reader picture a hundred haggard faces and emaciated forms — some with hair and beard of three months growth — so miserably clothed, in general, as scarcely to subserve the purposes of decency; and many limping about with pain from healed wounds ..." (1862, p. 25). "It was utterly impossible to keep clean. The only clothing I had was what I had on when captured, which consisted of a woolen shirt, blouse and pants. Each day as long as I was able to sit up, I took off my shirt and pants and killed the lice between my thumb nails," wrote Fairbanks (2004, p. 77).

By the end of June 1862, there was a growing accumulation of captives that were becoming increasingly unmanageable. Consequently, the Union and Confederate governments agreed to a plan for prisoner exchange known as the Dix-Hill cartel. "Immediately following the fights around Richmond in 1862, General D. H. Hill, of the Confederate Army and General Jno. A. Dix, of the Federal Army, were chosen by their respective governments to arrange a cartel for the exchange of prisoners" (Ratchford 1971 [1908], p. 27). The effect of potential exchange is found in numerous memoirs, letters, and diaries. The thought of exchange gave captives hope not only of relief from suffering but also for their very survival. Private Fairbanks, who was not expected to survive his ordeal to see parole, remembered his experience:

Ten days later ... word was passed around that another squad was to be paroled, and only those who were sick, one hundred eighty six men, were to be selected from the four thousand. My heart almost stopped its action when the thought came, 'what if I am left behind this time' but I did not give up ... as the number increased and my name was not called, I began to grow weak. When one hundred eighty had been called, one hundred eighty-one, one hundred eighty-two, and I knew there were only three more, I heard my name ..." (Fairbanks 2004, p. 81).

Disagreements between the contending governments over United States Colored Troops, the alleged abuse of the cartel by Confederate bureau chief Robert Ould, and the recognition by Union General Ulysses S. Grant that returning prisoners strengthened the enemy, forced a halt to the exchange program. Regular exchanges dwindled in late 1863 and were discontinued in 1864, not to be resumed until the final months of the war. The impact is reflected in the writings of John Dooley: "New Year's Day 1865. Gloom—blood—and repining everywhere ... All things appear so very dark and sad I feel like writing no more." Over the course of the next seven days his outlook changed considerably because of the hope of exchange: "News somewhat more cheering for us ... Trans-Mississippi prisoners ordered to be prepared to leave at a moment's notice ... One hundred and seventy prisoners of the trans-Mississippi department ... left today for exchange. This is cheering indeed ... it gives us some hope that they will not be the only ones who may be exchanged and once having set the ball in motion we may all be rolled to our homes..." (1945, p. 165).

Conditions in terms of food, clothing, shelter, and hygiene barely sustained existence. Treatment at the hands of the enemy, however, varied widely. Treatment encompassed the kindest compassion and the most wanton cruelty. Benson remembered with appreciation the compassion of some Union soldiers: "The Sergt. Of the guard, a tall, fine-looking fellow ... had been very kind to us, giving us his own rations when we could draw none... We might have suffered severely for food, if our guards had not been good fellows and divided with us" (Benson 1992, p. 90). Weld noted both extremes in treatment:

> In regard to my treatment in Richmond, I met with very kind treatment from the officer in charge, Lieutenant Trabue. The first officer who had charge of us, Captain William Read, was as conceited a puppy as ever lived. He was impudent to the officers, and was consequently removed. Trabue then had charge of us and was very kind and obliging... Most of the officers who had anything to do with us, treated us personally in a very kind manner... (Weld 1979 [1912], pp. 125–126).

Malone recalled more than one account of seemingly unjustified cruelty: "A Yankey shot one of our men the other day wounded him in the head shot him for peepen threw the cracks of the planken ... aYankey Captain shot his Pistel among our men and wounded 5 of them; since one has died — he shot them for crowding arond the gate" (Malone 1987 [1960], p. 94).

Civil War military prisons were synonymous with deprivation, suffering, and death. Some of the more notorious were Libby Prison, Point Lookout, Belle Island, Elmira, and Andersonville. Andersonville prison in Georgia is remembered, arguably, as the most egregious example of utter destitution among them. Ambrose Spencer was a staunch Unionist who lived near Andersonville. In his account of conditions at the prison, Spencer noted:

> meanwhile the crowds within the stockade had attained the highest limits as to numbers which was reached during its continuance, there being ... thirty-six thousand four hundred and eighty ...

With this increase there was a corresponding augmentation of their sufferings. The rains ...together with the constant tread of so many men, converted the interior at times into one vast bed of muddy slush nearly a foot deep — an aggregation of semi-liquid filth, through which the miserable prisoners unceasingly tramped in the unvarying round of pointless existence. Then for some days the hot sun would pour down upon this quagmire, feculent with putrefaction, and draw from its depths vapors saturated with fetid stench that it exhaled, and which corrupted the air they had to inhale. With their faces begrimed with smoke and dirt, their clothes in tatters and impregnated with vermin, shoeless and hatless, now up to their knees in mud, then breathing the pestilential atmosphere which a September sun had evoked, the wonder is that human nature did not succumb more rapidly and in greater numbers than the irresponsible death registers indicated" (1866, p. 109).

Spencer, like most of Northern America at that time, held the Confederate authorities of the prison, and especially its commandant Henry Wirz responsible. Wirz was convicted and hanged by the United States government as a result.

In contrast to the perspective of Spencer as an outsider looking into the horror that was Andersonville, is the actual experience of Edward Boate who, as a prisoner, suffered its reality. Boate was a captive at Andersonville and a parolee who served his sick comrades by working in the Surgeon General's Headquarters. Boate, therefore, offers a unique perspective on his enemy's efforts on behalf of Andersonville's imprisoned: "I know the efforts that were being daily made to sustain the prisoners. The country for twenty and fifty miles around was being laid under contribution for meat and meal for our men. The surgeon in charge daily employed messengers to scour the country for vegetables for our sick men; for straw for their tents; and for every necessary that could contribute to their comfort, but too often without success." (Boate 2004, p. 22). On behalf of Wirz, Boate said,

> When I became a paroled prisoner, I had to alter my opinions of Captain Wirz. What I thought harsh in him was more assumed than real; while what was kind in the man was real, not assumed. He had the least amount of sectional feeling I met in the South. He would often say: 'If the d—d fanatics on both sides were put into a barrel and thrown into the sea and if they could escape through the bung-hole, let them do so; but it if they sank to the bottom the country at large would be the better of it (Boate 2004, p. 35).

Boate went on to comment on the accusations of atrocities committed by Wirz: "Among Wirz's 'atrocities,' was a principle he adopted and acted upon throughout, that whenever there was a chance of giving fresh air, an additional or better ration or an opportunity of purchasing a little vegetables, it was reserved for men who came from Belle Island, as they were the men who[se] incarceration had been the most protracted" (Boate 2004, p. 37).

The harshness of prison life was a reality attested to almost without exception in surviving accounts of prison life. Prison existence was however, recalled with an admirable lack of animosity and in a detached, objective manner by those who suffered within its grasp. Edward Boate, as an example, processed his experience and considered his captors in a most compassionate and non-judgmental fashion. Similarly, what grace the pages of a surprising number of letters, diaries and memoirs in spite of the baseless inhumanity of living conditions, is the endurance of the human will and the resilience of the human spirit.

BIBLIOGRAPHY

Benson, Berry. *Berry Benson's Civil War Book: Memoirs of a Confederate Scout and Sharpshooter.* Edited by Susan Williams Benson. Athens: University of Georgia Press, 1992.

Boate, Edward Wellington. *An Andersonville Prisoner's Defense of Captain Henry Wirz: The New York Daily News Letters and Washington Testimony of Edward Wellington Boate.* Compiled by James West Thompson. Jackson: Jackson Civil War Roundtable, 2004.

Butler, Benjamin F. *Butler's Book.* Boston: A. M. Thayer & Co., 1892.

Dooley, John. *John Dooley Confederate Soldier.* Georgetown: The Georgetown University Press, 1945.

Fairbanks, Charles. *Notes of Army and Prison Life 1862–1865.* Edited by Janet Hayward Burnham. Bethel: My Little Jessie Press, 2004.

Grant, Ulysses Simpson. *The Papers of Ulysses S. Grant. Vol. 10. January 1–May 31, 1864.* Edited by John Y. Simon. Carbondale: Southern Illinois University Press, 1982.

Malone, Bartlett Yancey. *Whipt' em Everytime, the Diary of Bartlett Yancey Malone: Co. H, 6th N. C. Regiment.* 1960. Reprint, Edited by William Whatley Pierson, Jr. Wilmington: Broadfoot Publishing Company, 1987.

Merrell, W. H. *Five Months in Rebeldom, or, Notes from the Diary of a Bull Run Prisoner, at Richmond.* Rochester, NY: Adams and Dabney, 1862.

Oake, William Royal. *On the Skirmish Line Behind a Friendly Tree.* Edited by Stacy Dale Allen. Helena: Farcountry Press, 2006.

Ratchford, J. W. *Some Reminiscences of Persons and Incidents of the Civil War.* 1908. Reprint, Austin: Shoal Creek Publishers, 1971.

Spencer, Ambrose. *A Narrative of Andersonville: Drawn from the Evidence Elicited on the Trial of Henry Wirz the Jailer: With the Argument of Colonel N. P. Chipman, Judge Advocate.* New York: Harper and Brothers, 1866.

Weld, Stephen Minot. *War Diary and Letters of Stephen Minot Weld 1861–1865.* 1912. Reprint, Boston: Massachusetts Historical Society, 1979.

Robbie C. Smith

■ Women on the Battlefield

WOMEN ON THE BATTLEFIELD: AN OVERVIEW

While their numbers were relatively small, the Civil War battlefield included women in addition to men. Thousands of Union and Confederate women aided their country's war effort as nurses, laundresses, and cooks. Some of the more daring served as local scouts, spies attached to the military, and, in rare cases, as soldiers.

Spies and Scouts

Advances in military technology meant that the Civil War battlefield could extend over a wide span of territory, particularly in such situations as the siege of Vicksburg. Spies crossed battlefields to provide critical information on troop movements; their job was just as dangerous as soldiering (Blanton 2002, p. 120). Women spies could more easily evade detection than men partly because they did not raise the same degree of suspicion. A Confederate spy, Mary Ann Pitman (alias Molly Hays, Charles Thompson, and Second Lieutenant Rawley) of Tennessee, often slipped through Union lines by pretending to be a loyal citizen who had information that she would impart only to the commanding officer. Once inside the lines, Pitman had little trouble persuading younger staff officers to show her the defenses and positions of troops and fortifications (pp. 89–90).

Prostitutes also visited battlefields to ply their trade, but at the risk of being mistaken for spies. Shortly after the conclusion of the Battle of Nashville in 1864, two prostitutes took a carriage out to the battlefield. The women ventured so far out that they were captured by Confederate cavalrymen who suspected them to be spies. The women were briefly jailed in Franklin, Tennessee, before being escorted back to Nashville (Blanton 2002, pp. 124–125).

Combatants and Support Personnel

Some women worked in male guise on the battlefield as combatants, teamsters (drivers of teams of horses used to pull cannon and other heavy equipment), or mule drivers, but many more appear to have served as musicians in regimental bands. Drummers did not need the upper body strength required in other battlefield occupations. Edmonia Gates spent six months as a Union teamster as well as a stint as a drummer boy in Wilson's Zouaves, the One Hundred and Twenty-first New York Infantry Regiment. Rebecca Peterman served as a drummer in the Seventh Wisconsin Infantry before abandoning music to become a scout. An anonymous Union woman wounded at Gettysburg served as a drummer, as did Fanny Harris of Indiana, who reportedly "passed through a dozen battles." Because many women looked like teenaged boys too young for regular enlistment, their only possible entry into the army was through the ranks of the musicians. At least a half-dozen women are known to have served through the war as drummers (Blanton 2002, pp. 50, 57, 71).

In addition to serving in the ranks, women also served in various headquarters commands. A Union soldier, Ida Remington, spent part of her two-year enlistment detailed as an officer's servant. Two girls from Pennsylvania, including one using the alias of Charles Norton of the One Hundred and Forty-First Pennsylvania Infantry, also served in regimental headquarters as personal aides to officers. Norton cooked, nursed, kept guard over the property of the officers, and did whatever other jobs were assigned to her. During the Battle of Fredericksburg, Sarah Edmonds served as an orderly to General Poe. Ella Hobart Gibson was elected chaplain of the First Wisconsin Regiment of Heavy Artillery in 1864 and served for nine months in that capacity (Blanton 2002, pp. 41, 157).

Soldiers who were discovered to be women often persuaded officers to permit them to stay with their regiment as nurses or laundresses. If they could not be soldiers, they would be useful in other ways while still remaining with their loved ones. Thomas L. Livermore reported that a laundress attached to the Irish brigade advanced with the unit at the Battle of Antietam in 1862 and "swung her bonnet around and cheered on the men" (Wiley 1952, p. 339) At the Battle of Port Hudson in 1862, Mrs. Bradley, the "wife of a 2d sergeant in a company of Miles' Legion was struck in the leg by a piece of shell . . . She suffered amputation, but died soon after" (Hewitt 1983, p. 80).

Elizabeth Finnern stayed with her regiment after she was discovered to be a woman. She worked both as a battlefield nurse and a surgeon's assistant in the regimental hospital. One veteran recalled some years later that Finnern "went through all Marches and battles with us" (Blanton 2002, p. 116–117). Another declared that she

Mary Ann Ball "Mother" Bickerdyke. A volunteer nurse from Illinois, Mary Ann Ball "Mother" Bickerdyke organized the nursing of wounded Union soldiers on the battlefield, earning respect from soldiers and generals alike for her practical determination to help the injured. She continued to help soldiers after the war, becoming an attorney and assisting veterans with legal matters. *© Bettmann/Corbis.*

"was on every march and every battle field with the 81st Ohio" (p. 117). For practical reasons, Finnern stayed in male attire even after her sex was known to everyone in the regiment. She was also a pragmatist who "in times of danger . . . carried a musket just as did the soldiers" (p. 117). Finnern drew no army pay for her work as a nurse and surgeon's assistant. Sarah Satronia enlisted in an Iowa regiment with her husband and remained undiscovered for about two months. Her commanding officer then allowed her to stay with the unit as a battlefield nurse. Mary Brown, the wife of Private Ivory Brown of the Thirty-First Maine Infantry, also stayed with the regiment when she was discovered to be a woman. She worked as a nurse and surgeon's assistant (p. 117).

Battlefield Nursing

In the mid-nineteenth century, professional nursing was largely a male occupation. Fewer than four thousand women served as paid nurses for the Union Army. Neither the number of paid Confederate nurses nor the women on both sides who nursed without compensation is recorded with any accuracy. Frances Jamieson, also known as Frank Abel, left her Union cavalry regiment after the death of her husband at First Bull Run and joined the Hospital Corps as a nurse. Jamieson assisted with amputations as well as other surgical theater nursing duties. The assistant surgeon of the Twelfth Indiana Cavalry was a woman.

Clara Barton (1821–1912) is undoubtedly the most famous woman who ever walked on a battlefield. Determined to serve the soldiers in the field, Barton hoped to become as close to being a soldier as conditions permitted. Barton had filled a warehouse with a variety of goods that the army could use, including food and medicine. Moving throughout Virginia and Maryland, Barton and her supplies aided the wounded and dying at Cedar Mountain, Second Bull Run, Chantilly, South Mountain, Antietam, Charleston, and in the Wilderness campaign. When Barton appeared at Cedar Mountain in August 1862, convention dictated that she should wait until the came to the rear to be treated. Refusing to wait for authorization, something that she was unlikely to receive, Barton moved onto the battlefield after the fighting had subsided. Accompanied by two civilian helpers, she saw men in the throes of death. The soldiers, lying helpless on the field, were suffering from sunstroke, dehydration, and shock. Over the next two days, Barton cooked meals, washed wounds, applied dressings, assisted the surgeons in their gruesome tasks, distributed medicine, and offered kind words to the frightened soldiers. Her ministrations led to the nickname, "Angel of the Battlefield."

At Antietam, Barton used a pocket knife to extract a bullet from the jaw of a young soldier, the procedure carried out without chloroform for the boy and with some trepidation on Barton's part. Shortly thereafter, as she was giving a wounded man a drink of water, a bullet passed through the sleeve of her dress and struck the soldier dead. Ranging along the battlefield, Barton continued to provide aid to the other wounded. At the 1863 Battle of Fort Wagner during the siege of Charleston, South Carolina, Barton waded ashore despite the danger of flying bullets and ministered to the men as they lay bleeding. To many soldiers, it seemed as if Barton's courage had no limits (Oates 1994, pp. 112–115, 136).

Mary Ann Ball ("Mother") Bickerdyke (1817–1901) of Illinois nursed soldiers during the Civil War as part of a private effort to relieve the suffering of the troops. Next to Barton, she is the most famous battlefield nurse of the war. Bickerdyke gained some national renown at Fort Donelson in February 1862 by using a lantern to search the battlefield for wounded men at midnight before they froze to death. After helping evac-uate the wounded, Bickerdyke decided that the most pressing need for nursing assistance was at the front. She joined General Ulysses S. Grant's army as it moved to take control of the Mississippi River. For seven months, Bickerdyke worked at Union field hospitals in Savannah, Tennessee; Iuka, Mississippi; and Corinth, Mississippi. When challenged by an army surgeon who asked under whose authority she fed the wounded men, Bickerdyke famously replied that she received her authority from the Lord God Almighty and did he have anyone ranking higher than that? (Baker 1952, p. 119). After the war, Bickerdyke became an attorney and helped Union veterans with legal issues.

Battlefield and Home Front

With so much of Civil War fighting conducted close to homes, some women found themselves on the battlefield even though they had no intention of getting so close to the fighting. Lucy Rebecca Buck of Virginia wrote in her diary in 1864 that "While I write the hostile armies confront each other at the river in a menacing attitude but everything seems unnaturally still—the quiet so dull and dead broken only at intervals by the distant beating of the tattoo or the wail of a bugle. ... We shall not undress tonight for there's no knowing when we may be aroused to a renewal of strife" (Baer 1997, p. 292). Buck witnessed the killing of seven of Mosby's Rangers, members of a Virginia infantry battalion that carried out small raids and what would now be called psychological warfare, by Union troops on September 23, 1864. Buck's neighbor Sue Richardson reported that "Poor Henry Rhodes—hadn't been long in service—was shot in our field, nearly in front of our door. We could see the crowd assembled around him ... Mr. Carter and Mr. Overby of Fauquier were hung in the Mountain field on a large walnut tree.... It almost kills us to witness it" (Baer, 1997, p. 309). By the end of the Civil War, Southerners could no longer sharply differentiate between the battlefield and the home front.

BIBLIOGRAPHY

Baer, Elizabeth R., ed. *Shadows on My Heart: The Civil War Diary of Lucy Rebecca Buck of Virginia.* Athens: University of Georgia Press, 1997.

Baker, Nina Brown. *Cyclone in Calico: The Story of Mary Ann Bickerdyke.* Boston: Little, Brown, 1952.

Blanton, DeAnne, and Lauren M. Cook. *They Fought Like Demons: Women Soldiers in the American Civil War.* Baton Rouge: Louisiana State University Press, 2002.

Denney, Robert E. *Civil War Medicine: Care and Comfort of the Wounded.* New York: Sterling, 1994.

Hewitt, Lawrence L. *Miles' Legion: A History and Roster.* Baton Rouge: Elliott's Bookshop Press, 1983.

Livermore, Mary. *My Story of the War: A Woman's Narrative of Four Years Personal Experience as a Nurse in the Union Army.* Williamstown, MA: Corner House, 1978.

Oates, Stephen B. *A Woman of Valor: Clara Barton and the Civil War.* New York: Free Press, 1994.

Wiley, Bell Irvin. *The Life of Billy Yank: The Common Soldier of the Union.* Indianapolis, IN: Bobbs-Merrill, 1952.

Caryn E. Neumann

WOMEN SOLDIERS

When Johnny went marching off to war, quite a few Janes joined him. Women warriors had taken the field in previous conflicts, and the Civil War proved no exception. There was no public recruitment of women into the army, yet significant numbers of women decided to enlist anyway.

Letters written home by only three women soldiers have surfaced; only two women soldiers published memoirs of their experiences; and no diaries of women soldiers have been found. Like the men with whom they served, the majority of women soldiers hailed from agrarian, working-class, or immigrant backgrounds, where no premium was placed on education for girls. Women probably had a lower literacy rate than men. Additionally, when they assumed male identities and joined the army, women soldiers usually severed contact with family and friends at home. Scholars have identified 250 women soldiers in the ranks of the Union and Confederate armies. There were, undoubtedly, many more distaff soldiers.

The start of the Civil War aroused martial passions in women as well as men. Many women who wanted to join the army did not because war was a man's business. Lucy Breckinridge of Virginia lamented that "I wish that women could fight. I would gladly shoulder my pistol and shoot some Yankees if it were allowable" (Robertson 1994, p. 26). According to DeAnne Blanton and Lauren M. Cook in *They Fought Like Demons: Women Soldiers in the American Civil War* (2002), Sarah Morgan of Louisiana declared, "O! If I was only a man! Then I could … slay them with a will." Also, a Mrs. Black of Boston, mistakenly drafted by the Union, showed up as ordered and declared that she "wished no substitute" and was ready to "take position in line." When the men of Richland, Ohio, failed to volunteer in sufficient numbers, seven young women tried to volunteer, and stated that, "as soon as they could be furnished with uniforms, they would leave their clothing to the young men, who lacked the manliness to defend the flag of their country when it was assailed." Lastly, in September 1864, an Ohio woman wrote to President Abraham Lincoln that "I could get up a Regiment in one day of young Ladies of high rank" (p. 22). Most women aided the war effort by contributing supplies, nursing the wounded, or encouraging men to enlist.

Women who sought more excitement became soldiers. It proved easy to enlist: All a woman needed to do was cut her hair short, don male clothing, pick an alias,

Female soldier Sarah Emma Edmonds. Sarah Emma Edmonds (1841–1898) applied to Congress for a soldier's pension, supported by many fellow soldiers and their strong recommendations. Edmonds refused medical treatment during wartime in order to keep her sex a secret and continue in the army. *© Bettmann/Corbis.*

and find the nearest recruiter. In the mid-nineteenth century individuals did not carry personal identification, and most lacked a birth certificate. In theory, all recruits were subjected to a physical examination; in reality, the pressure to quickly fill regimental ranks militated against finding reasons to reject a volunteer. Physicians generally looked only for reasonable height, at least a partial set of teeth with which to tear open powder cartridges, and the presence of a trigger finger. In the case of Franklin Thompson of the Second Michigan Infantry, the examiner simply took Thompson's hand and asked, "Well, what sort of a living has this hand earned" (Blanton and Cook 2002, p. 36). Thompson said that he had focused on getting an education, and was duly enlisted on May 25, 1861. Thompson had been born Sarah Emma Edmonds. Jennie Hodges of the Ninety-fifty Illinois Infantry, also known as Albert Cashier, showed only her hands and feet to the examiner. She served a full three-year enlistment, mustering out with her regiment on August 3, 1862.

A large number of women soldiers joined the army with a husband, brother, sweetheart, or father, much as male soldiers joined up with a male relative. Mary Siezgle originally went to the front and served as a nurse, but decided to stay with her husband in a New York regiment. The only way for her to do so was to put on male clothing and do "her share of actual fighting" (Blanton and Cook 2002, p. 43) . During the Atlanta campaign, Major William Ludlow encountered a wounded Confederate who explained to her doctor that "she belonged to the Missouri Brigade ... had a husband and one or two brothers in one of the regiments, and followed them to war" (p. 54). All of her relations were killed, and "having no home but the regiment," she took a musket and served in the ranks. When John Finnern returned home and then decided to reenlist in the Eighty-first Ohio Infantry, his wife Elizabeth decided that he was not leaving her again. Both Finnerns signed up on September 23, 1861.

Once in the army, it was not terribly difficult to attend to the necessities of life in private. Women soldiers undoubtedly answered the call of nature by heading to the woods or some other private place. This behavior did not arouse suspicion because so many men did the same thing. It is probable that many women stopped menstruating because of the intense athletic training, substantial weight loss, poor nutrition, and severe psychological stress associated with being a Civil War soldier. Soldiers on the march often went for months at a time without a change of clothing or a bath. Herman Weiss of the Sixth New York Heavy Artillery explained to his wife how a woman in his regiment had maintained her male persona for nearly three years: "It is no wonder at all that her tent mates did not know that she was a woman for you must know that we never undress to go to bed. On the contrary we dress up, we go to bed with boots, overcoat and all on and she could find chances enough when she would be in the tent alone to change her clothes" (Blanton and Cook 2002, p. 57).

Female soldiers did not differ in any fundamental way from male soldiers, including their strength under fire. When Sarah Edmonds applied to Congress for a soldier's pension, a number of her comrades testified on her behalf. First Lieutenant William Turner stated in an affidavit that Edmonds "bore a good reputation, behaved as a person of good moral character, and was always ready for duty" (Blanton and Cook 2002, p. 155). Edmonds blamed her wartime injuries on her failing health. She wrote, "Had I been what I represented myself to be, I should have gone to the hospital .... But being a woman I felt compelled to suffer in silence ... in order to escape detection of my sex. I would rather have been shot dead, than to have been known to be a woman and sent away from the army" (p. 155). Frank Martin was shot in the shoulder at the Battle of Stones River, discovered to be a woman, and discharged. When she left the hospital, she enlisted in another regiment. Women accepted the risks of soldiering for the same mix of reasons that motivated men, including the desire to serve their country.

BIBLIOGRAPHY

Blanton, DeAnne, and Lauren M. Cook. *They Fought Like Demons: Women Soldiers in the American Civil War*. Baton Rouge: Louisiana State University Press, 2002.

Robertson, James I., ed. *A Confederate Girl's Diary*. Bloomington: Indiana University Press, 1960.

Robertson, Mary D., ed. *Lucy Breckinridge of Grove Hill: Journal of a Virginia Girl, 1862–1864*. Columbia: University of South Carolina Press, 1994.

Caryn E. Neumann

VISITING WIVES AND RELATIVES

The Civil War separated wives and husbands, sisters and brothers, and parents and children for years as the fighting continued far longer than anyone had initially expected. The separation damaged intimacy between spouses and left wives feeling anxious and lonely. Parents and other relatives wondered if disease or a bullet would claim the soldier in the family before they could see him again. With camps set up within travel distance for many Americans, wives and relatives took the opportunity to visit soldiers.

Women often expressed their loneliness in letters to soldiers and in their diaries, such as the following women included in Nina Silber's *Daughter of the Union: Northern Women Fight the Civil War* (2005). Anne Cotton told her husband Josiah, a surgeon in an Ohio regiment, "You do not miss me half so much as I do you. You are all the time surrounded by so many and do not get time to feel lonesome while I am alone most of the time and have nothing to do but think of you and wish you back." Elizabeth Caleff wrote to her fiancé James Bowler in the First Minnesota that "You have something exciting all the time, but you never can imagine how lonely I feel when I think of you being away." Mary Baker wrote in her diary in July 1861, "Am so lonely, miss Elliot every minute. Don't know what I shall do so long without him" (pp. 37–38).

Letter writing helped to maintain contact, but it could not substitute for personal contact. Jane Thompson wrote to her husband in September 1862, "Oh, how I wish I could sleep with you tonight. Would you like to sleep with me?" (Silber 2005, p. 44). Clara Wood wrote to her husband Amos in 1862 that "I have got your pictures in front of me. I write a few lines and then look at them and think and even say how I wish how much I wish he was here" (p. 42). Some women managed to ease their loneliness by visiting male relatives, but not every woman could pay a visit.

Civil War armies usually suspended operations between November and April. In the long periods when troops were holed up in winter quarters, wives and relatives took the opportunity to visit. These visits eased the homesickness and boredom of the soldiers. The troops also found entertainment by visiting locals during these long winter camps. A young New Yorker in Virginia recorded in his diary that "At night after taps, run the Picets and went out in the country to see the girls" (Wiley 1952, p. 215). A Minnesota private wrote, "When not on post we sit in the house [of a Southern planter] by the fire conversing with the old gentleman's daughters and enjoying ourselves hugely. It is a long time since I was in a private house ..." (p. 216). Alvin Buck, a Confederate soldier, cheered his sister with a visit in September 1864. "Darling Brother! This visit of yours will give me strength to endure much of sorrow and disappointment the coming winter," she wrote in her diary (Baer 1997, p. 138). Soldiers also called on relatives and friends in other regiments, with eating, drinking, and talk of home as the principal activity.

Men could not always obtain furloughs to return home. George Shepherd, a Wisconsin farmer, explained to his wife Mary that "You know when I was your man I would come when I could and see you. But now I am Uncle Sam's man and can't come only just when he pleases" (Silber 2005, p. 30). When Fighting Joe Hooker took command of the Army of the Potomac he restored morale by instituting a policy of liberally granting furloughs (Hunt 1992, p. 63). Frank Dickerson of Maine reported to his father in January 1863 that he had applied for a furlough, but his commanding officer refused to approve it until one of the furloughed officers returned to duty; he expected to return home for a short visit at that time (Hunt 1992, p. 63). The liberal furlough policy did not last long. It proved easier for wives to travel to visit husbands.

The visits of wives often enlivened camp routine. Frank Dickerson of Maine reported that when General Stoneman and his wife visited his camp at Buford, Maryland, in September 1863, the men fixed up the camp with evergreens and cedars so that it looked like a garden. Dickerson wrote that, "We had an excellent cold dinner, gotten up by a celebrated caterer in Washington, which we sat down to about 5 o'clock. Several of the officers had their wives present. Mrs. Capt. Mason, Mrs. Dr. Porter, Mrs. Sweetman, and Mrs. Paden" (Hunt 1992, p. 76). The wives of Mason and Porter boarded at a house about a mile from camp. Dickerson told his father that, "On the whole the entertainment was one of the most pleasant I have ever witnessed and everything passed off with great éclat. The band enlivened the scene with their fine music and the General appeared to be very much pleased and his wife also" (Hunt 1992, p. 76).

Generally, visits to Union troops took place while troops remained encamped in their Northern quarters, before they departed for battlefields in the South. The poor communications of the day and the difficulties of traveling across battle zones could complicate travel to the South. The father of the Indiana officer Ovid Butler attempted to visit his son in Tennessee, without success. The senior Butler wrote,

> We left here on the train ... but owing to obstructions on the track did not get to Louisville till 11 OClock the next day. There we were refused a pass from Gen Granger. We got that pass but too late to leave Louisville till the morning of Saturday the 21st. We arrived at Nashville the night of that day and found upon inquiry that the Signal Corps party had left for the front on the day we left home. This was a great disappointment to us as we had hoped and much desired to see you there. (Davis 2004, p. 54)

Travel also proved costly. When Emily Elliott of Ohio joined her major husband in Nashville, Tennessee, in January 1864, she had not seen him for sixteen months. She wrote in her diary, "I want to get Dentons clothes all in good order for maybe I will not stay long. Living here is very expensive" (Woodworth 2000, p. 169).

Once Union regiments moved South, camp visits were less likely for enlisted men, unless medical circumstances compelled a woman to come and attend to a soldier's needs. E. Anne Butler left her home in Indiana to visit a wounded relative recuperating at Franklin, Tennessee, in 1864. She expected to see the lieutenant's wife as well and catch up on family news. In January 1865, she again traveled to Nashville to aid another wounded relative. "When through a letter from Mrs. Scovel we learned the condition of Capt. It was thought best that I should come to him as Nettie was too feeble either to take the trip or to render him any service in the way of nursing," she wrote to her son (Davis 2004, p. 89). Officers' wives often stayed with their spouses for extended periods, even in Southern camps, so long as the military situation allowed and the women could cope with the inconveniences.

Southern women did not necessarily find it any easier than Northern women to visit relatives. Although the travel distance to Confederate camps certainly was shorter, the collapse of the Southern economy and the severe transportation problems of the South made visiting difficult. The fiancée of Confederate general John Morgan ran a Union blockade of Nashville to marry him in November 1862 (*Chicago Tribune*, August 6, 1863). Other women visited camps close to home. Laura Beecher Comer brought cakes to friends stationed at a nearby camp in Georgia (Clinton 2000, p. 144). Leila Willis, heavily pregnant with her third child, could not even manage to see her husband in a nearby camp because of her condition (p. 125).

Southern women, generally the better-off wives of officers, did travel some distances to visit. Mrs. Morgan joined her husband in Murfreesboro, Tennessee. The August 9, 1863, *Chicago Tribune* reported that Mrs. Morgan joined her husband at a great ball, dressed in a green silk dress and bonnet that Morgan had brought back from one of his raids. On July 17, 1864, the *New*

Brigadier General John A. Rawlins and his family. When soldiers expected to remain at camp for an extended period of time, many women set out to visit their absent husbands, brothers, and sons, particularly during the quiet winter months. *The Library of Congress*

York Times reported that the summer season in St. Louis, Missouri, was marked by the arrival of numerous women from the South: "They are wives of officers in the rebel service and come hither, as they say, to settle business affairs and visit relatives." The women were arrested for failing to comply with the military order requiring persons crossing into Union territory to report to the nearest provost-marshal.

It is possible that some visiting wives brought back vital military information when they returned home.

Many Southerners certainly suspected Northern visitors. The *Richmond Dispatch*, reprinted in the *New York Times*, reported in February 1863 that many Northern women had crossed Confederate lines to visit husbands. The women were suspected of being spies by the editor of the *South Carolinian*, who wrote,

> We had supposed that the object of the flag of truce permits was to persons returning to their domicile, and had no idea that Northern women whose husbands had been caught in our workshops

when the war commenced were to be allowed to visit them. It may be all well, but they certainly should not be allowed to communicate again with the North until the war is over. (reprinted in *New York Times*, February 8, 1863)

The *Charleston Courier* editorialized that

We have good reason for suspecting, if not believing, that many spies and doubtful characters ... are among the subjects of the late flag of truce. We beg that a strict watch be kept over all who have recently arrived within our lines, and are not well known. We have been too often betrayed by the credulous courtesy accorded to flags of truce, and to female apparel. (reprinted in the *New York Times*, February 8, 1863)

Northerners also discovered suspected spies. Mrs. Cheatham of Nashville, the sister-in-law of Confederate General John Morgan, tried traveling under a flag of truce to visit her sister. While returning to her home in Alton, Illinois, she was captured with suspected smugglers and jailed (*Chicago Tribune*, August 6, 1863).

Some Northern women, especially those in border states, were sent South because they were viewed as enemies of the Union. Such women aided Confederate officers and soldiers revisiting border states, boasted that they were enemies of the Union, and publicly wished ill to the Union.

The *New York Times* reported on August 8, 1863, that:

Only the open, avowed, incorrigible and dangerous enemies of the United States, and those detected in secret acts of correspondence with them, were ordered beyond the Union lines, and forbidden to return. No "children" have been ordered away—no women have been sent except those convicted of disloyal acts and refusing to cease their guilt, and those asking to be sent away because their husbands or protectors are already in the South, bearing arms against the Government.

As the Missouri women who asked to be sent South show, many women, especially Southerners, were accustomed to being cared for by others. Forced to fend for themselves without the assistance of men or slaves, some Southern women were lost and, if able, went to visit relatives for extended periods of time. The *New York Times* reported on November 2, 1862 that a former resident of Key West, Florida, returned to the island in November 1862 because while her husband served in the Confederacy, she could not support herself, and she returned to live with her father.

Some women in war zones refused to leave their homes to visit relatives because of fears of what might happen in their absence. Mrs. John S. Phelps of Springfield, Missouri, the wife of a commander of Missouri troops loyal to the Union, declined to travel to see friends in New York City. In a letter reprinted in the January 24, 1862, *New York Times*, Phelps wrote,

You very kindly invite me to visit New-York. Nothing would afford me more pleasure, were these not "war times;" but now I cannot leave Missouri. There may be a battle at Springfield, and my husband may be wounded; if he should escape, unhurt, others will not; and if I cannot engage in battle, because of my sex, I will have the honor of dressing the wounds of those who have left their homes and friends to fight for our glorious Union.

Other women remained at home to care for ailing relatives, maintain the farm, and take care of other business that could not be suspended, even briefly.

Women occasionally became ensnared in a tug-of-war between the desires of their soldier husbands and their parents' anxieties about their safety. Leila Turpin Willis was the wife of Larkin Willis, a Richmond tobacco agent and an engineer for the Confederate army. Between July 1861 and January 1864 Leila Willis made at least eight trips—many of several months' duration—between the home of her parents and the house that she shared with her husband and two small children. Leila's mother, Rebecca Turpin, pressured her daughter to visit by citing her own poor health and the threat of nearby Union troops. In one letter she warned, "I am glad you are all well and safe ... but you may be deprived of your husband and everything else soon .... Your father says if you can get home you had better come" (Clinton 2000, p. 125).

Some visitors came to military camps for sightseeing. Early in the war, a Richmond girl took a tour of the Carolina encampment in her city. She wrote on May 22, 1861, "We had a delightful walk and when we got there the place was so pretty that we did not want to come home until very late. The tents were fixed in rows under trees, and the soldiers were gathering in groups preparatory to dress parade, we saw that before we came away" (Clinton 2000, p. 123). Later in the war, Demia Butler traveled from Indiana to Nashville, Tennessee, to see the place that her soldier brother had long been encamped. Butler wrote that she had taken several rides in different directions to see the place that she termed "a city of Soldiers" (Davis 2004, pp. 96–97).

Once in a great while, the life of a Union or Confederate soldier would be brightened by the visit of wife, relative, or friend from home. Such visits, however, were rare. Soldiers mainly had to be content with letters and newspapers from home as well as whatever recreation they could provide for themselves.

BIBLIOGRAPHY

Baer, Elizabeth R., ed. *Shadows on My Heart: The Civil War Diary of Lucy Rebecca Buck of Virginia*. Athens: University of Georgia Press, 1997.

Clinton, Catherine, ed. *Southern Families at War: Loyalty and Conflict in the Civil War South*. New York: Oxford University Press, 2000.

Davis, Barbara Butler, ed. *Affectionately Yours: The Civil War Home-Front Letters of the Ovid Butler Family.* Indianapolis: Indiana Historical Society Press, 2004.

"Flags of Truce." *New York Times.* February 8, 1863, p. 2.

"FROM MISSOURI.; Rebel Invasion of the State Condition of Affairs in Different Localities The Machinations of Rebel Women A Skull Gatherer The 'Conservatives' of Missouri Missouri's Governor." *New York Times,* July 17, 1864. Available from http://proquest.umi.com/.

Hunt, H. Draper, ed. *Dearest Father: The Civil War Letters of Lt. Frank Dickerson, a Son of Belfast, Maine.* Unity, ME: North Country Press, 1992.

"Key West Correspondence." *New York Times.* November 2, 1862, p. 1.

"Mrs. John Hunt Morgan." *Dayton* (OH) *Journal,* reprinted in *Chicago Tribune.* August 6, 1863, p. 3.

"News From Washington." *New York Times.* August 8, 1863, p. 1.

Silber, Nina. *Daughter of the Union: Northern Women Fight the Civil War.* Cambridge, MA: Harvard University Press, 2005.

"The Wife of Hon. John Phelps Loyal." *New York Times.* January 24, 1862, p. 3.

Wiley, Bell Irvin. *The Life of Billy Yank: The Common Soldier of the Union.* Indianapolis, IN: Bobbs-Merrill, 1952.

Woodworth, Steven E. *Cultures in Conflict: The American Civil War.* Westport, CT: Greenwood Press, 2000.

Caryn E. Neumann

PROSTITUTES AND OTHER CAMP FOLLOWERS

Men were not the only ones moving from camp to camp during the Civil War. Camp followers, including the families of soldiers, cooks, launderers, and sutlers, were present throughout the war. Although some individuals recognized business opportunities in camp following, others simply had no other place to go. Women with husbands in the military sometimes lacked the resources or the emotional strength to live apart from their spouses. African Americans, newly escaped from plantations, had no place to go and no means of earning a living except by serving Union soldiers. Camp followers dressed wounds, cooked food, mended clothing, provided sexual services, and shared the fears of the soldiers.

Although men at war were granted a certain amount of moral leeway, the same could not be said for the women they left behind at home. A woman's behavior was often read by her neighbors and relatives as a barometer of her commitment and support for her husband's wartime sacrifice. Eliza Otis aroused her family's

Mary Tepe, vivandiere. Often lacking income at home due to the death of a husband, women frequently accompanied traveling armies, providing domestic services such as washing laundry, preparing meals, and mending clothes. Because neither the Union or Confederate armies provided much support services while at camp, these women fulfilled a need while earning a living. *Charles J. and Isaac G. Tyson/National Park Service/National Archives/Time Life Pictures/Getty Images*

suspicions by traveling frequently without a male escort (Silber 2005, p. 35). Rose Stone, the wife of a Minnesota soldier, was categorized as "loose" for allowing another man to take her to a party and for flirting at the party (Silber 2005, p. 37).

Over the course of history, only a handful of women have recorded their experiences as prostitutes because of the shame associated with the activity. If a prostitute was literate, it is unlikely that she would have recorded her sexual activity for posterity to condemn her. Likewise, a soldier who visited a prostitute would not include such a detail in a letter back home that would likely be read by his parents, wife or sweetheart, sisters, and other loved ones. Much of the history of prostitution during the war is lost.

It is certain, however, that prostitution was widespread. Many individuals believed that there was a connection between masculinity and sexual activity. A rite of passage from boy to man in nineteenth-century America was sometimes marked by a first visit to a prostitute, who initiated him into the sexual world. Men were thought to require frequent sexual activity, and in the Civil War era, masturbation was heavily condemned by religious and medical authorities. When wives were absent, many individuals expected that soldiers would visit prostitutes.

In contrast, when husbands were absent, wives were expected to remain chaste, but many people suspected lone wives of making themselves sexually available to other men. Julia Underhill relocated to Massachusetts in part because the number of men approaching her in public with unwanted sexual advances made it increasingly difficult for her to maintain a respectable reputation (Silber 2005, p. 35). Northern society found it difficult to determine the extent to which unchaperoned women could be considered instigators, as opposed to victims, of inappropriate sexual behavior.

The number of prostitutes during the war is likely relatively high. In times of economic downturn or personal economic emergency, poor women often have turned to prostitution to survive. Prostitution stemmed from desperate circumstances rather than some innate predisposition. In 1858, the physician William Wallace Sanger released a survey of 2,000 women who had been incarcerated at the venereal disease hospital at the Houses of Correction on Blackwell's Island, New York. Nearly 47 percent were very young (median age of fifteen), foreign-born (mostly recent Irish or German immigrants), and unskilled, though 38 percent were native-born (Gilfoyle 1992, p. 117). Although most were themselves unskilled, more than half were the daughters of skilled workers. Male desertion, widowhood, single motherhood, and, especially, the death of a male wage-earner, made prostitution the only viable economic choice. Casual prostitution was a way to supplement low-wage employment. It is unlikely that the pattern of prostitution changed much with the coming of the war.

The collapse of the Southern economy during the Civil War may have forced many women into prostitution as a means of survival for themselves and their families. The enlistment or death of a Union soldier also resulted in economic loss for Union women, and possibly forced widows or abandoned wives into prostitution. After 1800, prostitution branched out from houses of prostitution to hotels, cafes, dance halls, music halls, and the streets. Clandestine commercial activity could be a one-time affair or a long-term pattern. The absence of brothels made it difficult to monitor and regulate illicit sexual activity.

Military authorities tacitly accepted prostitution during the Civil War, in part because they could do little to prevent it. Some officers themselves patronized prostitutes and were tolerant of the illicit sexual activity of the troops. Major General Joseph "Fighting Joe" Hooker (1814–1879) remained enormously popular with his men throughout the war, even though his personal habits frequently brought condemnation from his peers—Hooker's fellow officers did not hold him in high regard. A hard-drinking bachelor, Hooker notoriously visited brothels. Charles Francis Adams Jr. famously commented that under Hooker, "the headquarters of the Army of the Potomac was a place to which no self-respecting man asked to go, and no decent woman could go. It was a combination of bar-room and brothel" (Silber 2005, p. 80).

Many men regarded visits to prostitutes as one of the benefits accorded to those risking life and limb. The Minnesota soldier, James Bowler, chastised his new bride, Elizabeth, for seeking to deny him "what few privileges" he was "able to secure" (Silber 2005, p. 84). Those privileges included keeping company with black women, who, in the eyes of many Union men, seemed to be the most readily available sexual partners in the South. When Lizzie Bowler replied that such activity was "not to be tolerated among respectable people," James quickly retreated and stated that he had written "a jesting, frolicking letter" only to see how she would respond (p. 84). Racial boundaries in prostitution typically crossed only one way. Although white men had access to black women, black men generally did not have access to white women—the most reviled prostitutes were white women who sold sex to men of color.

Prostitutes in other eras have observed that business increases during times of war and the threat of war. The Union soldier James Beatty seemed resigned to the idea that he might give in to "some kinds of temptations to evil" that "will be much stronger in me now than ever before," and implied that visits to prostitutes were the inevitable result of war and would be little affected by women's home-front counseling (Silber 2005, p. 83).

Temptation seemed to plague soldiers at every turn. Not surprisingly, in cities throughout the North and West, and especially in areas where Union soldiers clustered, prostitution increased dramatically. Most of the prostitutes were probably young and single, if the demographics of prostitutes in the West hold true for camp-following prostitutes in the South and North. For most women, fading beauty was a liability, and by the age of thirty, many had turned to other ways of making a living. Some prostitutes did escape this line of work by marrying former clients.

Women also served the army in respectable occupations such as laundress, cook, and seamstress. Civil War authorities did not provide much support staff for soldiers, particularly in the first months of the war. Soldiers often were given uncooked food and were expected to prepare it themselves, but typically, they had not received any instruction in cooking because such work was women's labor. Confronted with raw beans and raw meat, they were baffled. Some of the sickness that befell men in the early months of the war came from consuming undercooked or poorly prepared food. Similarly, men did not have any training in sewing or laundering. Camp followers were tolerated by the military because they provided critical services to the troops.

Camp-following laundresses, seamstresses, and cooks also sometimes supplemented their earnings by selling sexual services to decamped soldiers. The number of women seeking "respectable" work exceeded the demand, forcing women to compete for jobs and driving down wages, and as a result, some laundresses and seamstresses turned to prostitution. The link is seen in the use of the words *laundress* and *seamstress* as euphemisms for *prostitute* in U.S. military records, where several "laundresses" or "seamstresses" listed as sharing living quarters generally may be assumed to represent prostitutes in a brothel.

Camp followers also included people who had no link to prostitution. For example, when slaves escaped from plantations, the Union army faced the problem of housing and caring for them, and they numbered in the thousands. The army put men to work as drivers, cooks, blacksmiths, and construction workers. Black women, many of whom had fled with children, often were denounced as prostitutes and lazy vagrants. The denunciations likely had roots in the age-old stereotype of black women as sexually promiscuous Jezebels, an image that permitted the sexual abuse of slave women. It is not clear if any "contrabands," as escaped slaves were called by the Union, worked as prostitutes; some newly freed black women found jobs as cooks and laundresses in and around Union camps. However, employment proved difficult to find. Many black families spent the remainder of the war living in wretched conditions. At Camp Nelson, Kentucky, in late 1864, white soldiers leveled the shantytown erected by black women and left 400 freedpeople homeless while the black men of the camp fought a battle against Confederates (White 1999, p. 167).

Camp followers were a part of wars well before the modern era. They provided services that the military either could not or would not offer to the soldiers. Generally valued by the soldiers, they were sometimes viewed as a necessary evil by civilians and military authorities.

BIBLIOGRAPHY

Butler, Anne M. *Daughters of Joy, Sisters of Misery: Prostitutes in the American West, 1865–90.* Champaign: University of Illinois Press, 1985.

Gilfoyle, Timothy. *City of Eros: New York City, Prostitution, and the Commercialization of Sex, 1790–1920.* New York: W.W. Norton, 1992.

Silber, Nina. *Daughters of the Union: Northern Women Fight the Civil War.* Cambridge, MA: Harvard University Press, 2005.

White, Deborah Gray. *Ar'n't I a Woman?: Female Slaves in the Plantation South.* New York: W.W. Norton, 1999.

Caryn E. Neumann

■ Child Soldiers

The majority of Civil War soldiers who participated in the conflict were eighteen or older. But a sizable number of Yankee and Rebel troops were minors. This was especially true in the opening months of the war, when motivations such as family honor, duty to country, the prospect of adventure, and proving one's manhood prompted thousands of boys to join older siblings and neighbors and descend on recruiting stations. The percentage of minors in the armed services of the Union and Confederates armies, however, dwindled in the latter stages of the war, when military drafts became the primary means of replenishing depleted regiments and underage soldiers already in the ranks reached their eighteenth birthdays.

Johnny Clem (1851–1937), child soldier. While the majority of soldiers enlisted in both the Union and Confederate armies were over the age of eighteen, many youngsters lied about their age to gain entry into the conflict. Young soldiers often served as field musicians, relaying orders to the troops by fife and drum. *MPI/ Hulton Archive/Getty Images*

A UNION DRUMMER BOY WRITES HOME

Felix Voltz was a boy from Buffalo, New York, who had been apprenticed to a trade he did not like. In February 1865, he decided to enlist as a drummer boy with the 187th New York Volunteer Regiment. Felix's father was upset by his son's impulsive decision, which he described in a letter written to the boy's uncle:

> [Felix] went and looked for some Recruiting [sic] Offices[;] … the last one of all he found at the Arcade Buildings and there the Bounty Brockers [broker] by the name of Weaver took him to the Provost Marshalls [sic] Office where he was sworn in U.S. Service for one Years [sic] in the 187th Reg[imen]t N.Y. Vol[unteer]s. … Felix left the house Monday morning and we did not know what had become of him untill [sic] the letter carrier brought us a letter Wednesday Evening from Felix.

Felix was at first happy to serve as a drummer boy, because doing so relieved him of picket duty and other more dangerous assignments. On March 3, 1865, he wrote to his family:

> Dear Parents Br[o]th[er]s & Sisters: I take the Pen in Hand this Evening to write you a few lines. … The first thing I will let you know about Me being in the Drum Chor [Corps]. … I had to go on Picket Duty the other day and when I came back I got sick for two or three days but I got over that and then I went to Tony the Orderly and ask him if they had A Drummer for our Company Says he No sir then he told me to wait A day or two. … Please tell Mother not to wearry [sic] herself about Me for I am all right yet and I hope will be so for the next year and tell

here [her] I am in no danger what so ever all I have to do is to take care of Me and my Drum and learn how to Drum as soon as possible I must not do no more guard or Picket Duty nor I must not take care of no Musket at all. … So no more this time give my best Respects to all inquiring Friends.

By May 1865, Felix was openly expressing homesickness. After telling his brothers about falling sick the day the army marched through Richmond after the fall of the Confederacy, Felix wrote the following:

> D[ea]r Br[o]th[ers] I wish you would Answer soon and send me some Post[age]. St[amps]. and some paper and Envelops I know no more news at Present. I will close my writing with sending my best Regards and love to you all in the Family tell Mother not weary herself about me because I am as healthy as ever I was and tell Father that I beg him to forgive me for being so Ugly and Headstrong tell him that I have found out what A home is and that there is nobody on this world thank Father & Mother and A Home and tell him if God safe my Health and lets me get Home Safe again that I will try and behafe [sic] and mind my Parents better than I have.

REBECCA J. FREY

SOURCE: *"The Letters of Felix Voltz, MS 93-021." Special Collections Department of the University Libraries of Virginia Tech, Digital Library and Archives. Available from http://spec.lib.vt.edu/voltz/.*

Lying to Get into the Fray

In both the North and South, the minimum age for enlistment was eighteen. Over the life of the war, about 80 percent of the soldiers who fought in the Civil War were between eighteen and twenty-nine. Older men dotted the ranks of both armies, but both sides also featured a fair number of boy soldiers who boldly misrepresented their age in order to join the war effort. It became a common practice, for example, for earnest teens to write the number "18" on a scrap of paper, which they then placed in one of their shoes. This little ceremony enabled them to "truthfully" respond that they were "over eighteen" when the recruiting officer asked them their age.

Civil War historians believe that, all told, tens of thousands of boys under the age of eighteen served in both militaries during the conflict, while thousands of others were active participants in the guerrilla warfare that erupted in the border states and some sections of the South during the course of the war. Writing in *A People's History of the Civil War* (2005), historian David Williams asserted that as many as 76,000 children under the age of eighteen served in Civil War regiments—and

that this figure probably underestimates the number of soldiers who lied about their age in order to enlist. Historian Bell Irvin Wiley reported similar findings in his classic *The Life of Johnny Reb* (1943), which shows that fully 5 percent of Confederate infantry privates in a sampling of ninety-four regiments were under age eighteen at their time of enlistment, compared to the only 1.6 percent of Union soldiers who were under eighteen.

Musicians and Drummer Boys

When it came to military band membership, neither the Confederate nor the Union army instituted any age limitations. Boys barely into their teens could routinely be found in music groups or serving as buglers or drummer boys. Some children were even younger; Private Edward Black, for example, joined the 21st Indiana as a musician at the tender age of nine. Another group of underage soldiers that nonetheless had a consequential impact on the war were cadet drillmasters who helped train raw recruits. The Confederate army made particularly extensive use of this resource, borrowing youthful instructors from the Virginia Military Institute (VMI) and other Southern military schools. These cadets were usually held in reserve, but there were several occasions on which they were assigned to frontline positions on the field of battle.

Aging Quickly

Minors who managed to insinuate themselves into the military ranks of the Union and Confederate armies lost their innocence quickly. Daily exposure to the myriad vices practiced by older soldiers stripped them of whatever naiveté they may have had upon enlistment, and the grueling regimen of Civil War soldiering hardened them. Though this hardening made them better soldiers, their plight filled many observers with deep sympathy and sorrow. The writer Walt Whitman (1819–1892), who served as a hospital nurse in Washington, recalled an encounter with a fifteen-year-old child soldier from Tennessee whose father was dead, and whose mother had been chased from her home by the ravages of war. Whitman watched the boy march out of the city with the rest of his regiment the next day. "My boy was stepping along with the rest," Whitman said. "There were many boys no older. There did not appear to be a man over thirty years of age, and a large proportion were from 15 to 22 or 23. They all had the look of veterans, stain'd, impassive, and a certain unbent, lounging gait" (Whitman, p. 778).

BIBLIOGRAPHY

Smith, Page. *Trial by Fire: A People's History of the Civil War and Reconstruction*. New York: McGraw-Hill, 1982.

Wiley, Bell Irvin. *The Life of Johnny Reb: The Common Soldier of the Confederacy*. Indianapolis, IN, and New York: Bobbs-Merrill Company, 1943. Reprint, Baton Rouge: Louisiana State University Press, 1992.

Whitman, Walt. *Whitman: Poetry and Prose*. Ed. Justin Kaplan. New York: Literary Classics of the United States, Inc., 1996.

Williams, David. *A People's History of the Civil War: Struggles for the Meaning of Freedom*. New York: New Press, 2005.

Kevin Hillstrom

■ African American Soldiers

During the course of the Civil War, approximately 200,000 African American men served under the Union banner. These troops included large numbers of free men from Northern cities, but also featured a significant contingent of slaves who were absorbed into the military directly off plantations along the Mississippi River and the Southern coast. African American soldiers, segregated by race and commanded by white officers, were initially confined to garrison duty or manual labor details, and for much of the war they received lesser pay than their white counterparts. As the months passed, however, a number of black units distinguished themselves in combat. Many military scholars believe, in fact, that it was the addition of African Americans to the Union side that allowed the North to increasingly dominate the war. In addition, the valiant performance of black Civil War soldiers marked one of the first significant steps that African Americans took in their long and arduous journey from enslavement to equality in American society.

Fighting for the Right to Fight

When the Civil War erupted in the spring of 1861, thousands of free black men in the North volunteered for military service. They did so not only because they wanted to see their Southern brethren freed from the shackles of slavery, but also because they recognized that the war presented them with the opportunity to advance their efforts to gain greater legal rights. As abolitionist Frederick Douglass (1818–1895) declared, "Once let the black man get upon his person the brass letters, *U.S.*, let him get an eagle on his button, and a musket on his shoulder and bullets in his pocket, and there is no power on earth which can deny that he has earned the right to citizenship in the United States" (Douglass 1999, p. 536).

Opposition to enlisting African Americans was strong, however. President Abraham Lincoln had framed the federal government's response to the secessionist threat as one of opposition to rebellion, not slavery. He and others were also greatly concerned that the Union would lose Kentucky and other border states if the government armed blacks. Racism also saturated the white ranks of the Union Army, although pockets of support for the idea of recruiting blacks did exist.

Blocked from enlisting in the army, some blacks tried to support the war effort by signing up as cooks, carpenters, and nurses. In addition, thousands of black men enlisted in the Union Navy, which had no racial restrictions in its enlistment policies. By the end of the war, about 29,000 black men served in Union shipyards, on warships, and on other vessels.

Meanwhile, black leaders and their allies in the abolitionist movement continued to lobby Washington for a change in policy that would permit African Americans—both free men and freed slaves—to join the war effort as soldiers. Some progressive-minded white officers expressed puzzlement and outrage that the Lincoln administration continued to relegate such a potentially powerful military resource to the sidelines. "Isn't it extraordinary that the Government won't make use of the instrument that would finish the war sooner than anything else, —viz the slaves?" wrote Robert Gould Shaw (1837–1863), who would later command the all-black 54th Massachusetts Volunteers to glory in its famous assault on Fort Wagner outside Charleston. "What a lick it would be at them [the Confederates], to call on all the blacks in the country to come and enlist in our army! They would probably make a fine army after a little drill, and could certainly be kept under better discipline than our independent Yankees" (Duncan 1992, p. 123).

By the summer of 1862, federal authorities had become more receptive to these arguments. A string of military setbacks, growing difficulties in filling holes in battle-scarred regiments, and growing confidence in the allegiance of the slaveholding border states convinced Lincoln that black enlistment was a politically achievable goal. In July Congress passed laws paving the way for the entrance of African Americans into the Union Army, albeit in segregated units under the command of white officers. Six months later, Lincoln's formal issuance of the Emancipation Proclamation, which freed all slaves in Confederate territory, further underscored the government's evolving thinking on blacks and their importance in the conflict.

Doubt and Conviction

Reaction to black enlistment among white Union companies and regiments was mixed. Some white troops harbored profound doubts about the military capabilities and bravery of blacks; others declared angrily that they were fighting to suppress a rebellion, not to free the slaves—much less to serve alongside them. One Indiana private offered a fairly representative perspective when he explained his decision to forego reenlistment: "[T]his war has turned out very Different from what I thought it would," he wrote. "It is a War ... to free the Nigars ... and I do not propose to fight any more in such a cause" (Smith 2002, p. 6).

African American men, on the other hand, rushed forward to prove doubters wrong. Many enlisted for practical reasons as well. The promise of a regular paycheck, combined with bounties and other monetary incentives, contributed to the decision of many poor blacks to enlist. Others, however, were primarily motivated by abolitionist sentiments. In addition, many fugitives from slavery regarded military service with the

Attack on Fort Sumter. The Confederate army took advantage of African American labor throughout the Civil War, as seen in this illustration, based on a photograph, of the 1861 attack of the Union-held Fort Sumter, marking the outbreak of the War between the States. *Photograph by William Waud. The Library of Congress.*

Union Army as a means to secure the freedom of their family members. Finally, countless soldiers were motivated by racial pride and a consuming desire to prove that blacks were worthy of American citizenship. As J. G. E. Hystuns, a black noncommissioned officer with the 54th Massachusetts, asserted, "if there is one spark of manhood running in the blood of the Race that has resisted the … waves of oppression, the school of the soldier will fan it to a glowing flame" (Salvatore 1996, p. 115).

Training and Deployment

When black enlistees entered the army, they were subjected to an intensive regimen of drill and firearms training (the latter was emphasized in part because so few African American recruits had any experience handling firearms). Some naive enlistees entered the army with the assurances of recruiters of free and equal treatment still ringing in their ears, but they were quickly stripped of such comforting illusions. In reality, most United States Colored Troops (USCT) camps were marked by harsh and demeaning modes of training and discipline. Anger and resentment quickly blossomed. In some cases, these reactions were unwarranted, as they were based on unrealistic expectations about aspects of military life that pertained to *all* soldiers, whether they were white or black. In many other instances, however, black soldiers were subjected to more exhausting and punitive treatment than were their white counterparts. In the worst cases, abusive treatment at the hands of white officers evoked memories of servitude on Southern plantations.

In some camps, the demeaning treatment of black soldiers aroused the ire of white officers and enlisted men who believed that such rough handling was both unfair and counterproductive, as it undermined fighting spirit and cohesiveness. A number of camp chaplains were also strong defenders of the rights of black troops.

The white officers who commanded black regiments during the Civil War varied enormously, both in quality and in motivation. Some volunteered out of ambition, their interest sparked by War Department policies that offered early promotions to officers who were willing to take command of black troops. The best of the white officers to command black units harbored abolitionist sentiments—or at the very least were capable of revising racist preconceptions about the limited military aptitude of black troops when confronted with evidence to the contrary. A few white officers actually embraced the opportunity to help blacks in advancing their cause. As Nathan W. Daniels, commander of 2nd Louisiana Native Guard, declared, "Thank God it hath been my fortune to be a participator in the grand idea of proclaiming freedom to this much abused & tortured race. Thank God my Regiment an African one" (Weaver 1998, p. 68).

Daily Trials and Tribulations

Military life during the Civil War was frightening, dangerous, and exhausting for virtually every soldier in the Union and Confederate armies. But for African American troops wearing the blue uniform of the Union, conditions were even more difficult to endure. Race enveloped virtually every aspect of black military life. During their service, many blacks received inferior assignments, poor training, and deficient care, not to mention insults from white soldiers. Discriminatory treatment seeped into virtually every realm of daily existence. Many African American enlistees were not surprised to find that the arms, equipment, and uniforms they received were often inferior to those distributed to white regiments. But they were openly dismayed when they came to recognize that prevailing beliefs that they were ill-suited to combat meant they were in danger of spending the entire war toiling at thankless chores and duties far from the front lines, often replacing white units for these jobs.

At times, this demeaning exploitation of black soldiers who desperately wanted to contribute to the war effort in more meaningful ways prompted protests from sympathetic white officers and enlisted men. "They are put at the hardest as well as the meanest kinds of work," wrote one disgusted white soldier from New York. "I have seen them policing (cleaning up filth and rubbish) white regiment camps. If a spirited white soldier were to do this except as punishment for some offense I think he would die first" (Palladino 1997, p. 44).

The discriminatory treatment that most angered African American soldiers, however, was the inequality of pay. Whereas white enlisted men received $13 per month, black soldiers in the Union Army only received $10 per month. This situation infuriated black soldiers, especially after black units took on greater combat roles in the conflict. "It seems strange to me that we do not receive the same pay and rations as the white soldiers," wrote one battle-hardened black soldier. "Do we not fill the same ranks? Do we not cover the same space of ground? Do we not take up the same length of ground in a grave-yard that others do? The [musket] ball does not miss the black man and strike the white, nor the white and strike the black. … [T]he black men have to go through the same hurling of musketry, and the same belching of cannonading as white soldiers do" (Redkey 2002 [1992], p. 48). Another African American soldier, Corporal James Henry Gooding of the 54th Massachusetts, wrote in a letter published in the *New Bedford Mercury* on November 21, 1863, that

as men who have families to feed, and clothe, and keep warm, we must say, that the *ten* dollars by the greatest government in the world is an unjust distinction to men who have only a black skin to merit it. To put the matter on the ground that we are not soldiers would be simply absurd, in the

Flag of the 84th Regiment, U.S. Colored Infantry. Many historians believe the Union's enlistment of African American troops gave the North a decisive advantage during the Civil War. Though initially denied admittance to the army, more than 200,000 African American soldiers eventually served under the Union flag, offering evidence they deserved to be accorded equal rights as full citizens of the United States. © *Smithsonian Institution/Corbis*

face of the existing facts. A soldier's pay is $13 per month, and Congress has nothing to do but to acknowledge that we *are* such—it needs no further legislation. To say even, we were *not* soldiers and pay us $20 would be injustice, for it would rob a whole race of their title to manhood.

This situation endured until June 1864, when the War Department grudgingly eliminated the disparity after years of protests from black soldiers, white officers, and sympathetic lawmakers and newspaper editors.

Brothers in Arms

Within many black military units, shared experiences and hardships created strong feelings of kinship and community. This sense of brotherhood and heightened racial solidarity was honed not only in moments of harrowing combat or hours of marching, but also during days in camp. Black Union soldiers passed their free time in

many of the same ways that white soldiers did. African American troops indulged in the same vices—gambling, drinking, and escapades with prostitutes—and engaged in the same long, meandering conversations about politics, prewar life, and various aspects of the soldier's existence. The social environment in most black encampments, however, was unique in a number of notable respects. For example, virtually every black regiment included a handful of "storytellers" who regaled audiences with campfire tales, just as they had in slave communities. These tales served not only to entertain, but also to shape communal identity and give symbolic form to a range of events and experiences.

Music also played an important recreational role in many black camps. But whereas white musicians and listeners used music primarily as a way to just pass the time, the activities of black singing groups and glee clubs, which were commonplace, were often freighted with deeper meaning and significance. African American musicians and singers took great pride in both their abilities and the cultural traditions upon which they drew. Significantly, music often increased camp unity and boosted camp morale, and helped blacks strengthen relations with white officers and soldiers.

The literacy rate in black regiments was far lower than it was in white units, a direct result of Southern laws against educating slaves and limited opportunities for education even among black people in the North. As a result, reading, letter-writing, and journal-keeping were not as prevalent among USCT soldiers as they were with white troops. Nevertheless, some black regiments established debating and literary societies. These were promoted by noncommissioned officers, many of whom had received sound educations and been politically active prior to the war. In addition, educated black noncommissioned officers and enlisted men frequently volunteered their reading and writing services to illiterate comrades.

In some black camps, formal instruction in reading and writing was established. These "schools" did not lack for students, as many soldiers badly wanted to be able to independently communicate with wives, sweethearts, parents, children, and other loved ones back home. Many white officers supported these "schools," because they thought it would improve military performance, others supported the "schools" because they thought that such work would help prepare attendees for the rights, responsibilities, and privileges of citizenship. Teachers included chaplains, noncommissioned officers, wives of white officers, and volunteers from missionary societies and freedmen aid societies. Elementary textbooks used in Northern common schools were extensively used in camp schools, as were donated publications from charitable religious presses.

For those soldiers who could read, preferred reading material ranged from the Bible to works of literature to newspapers. Of the latter, black newspapers such as the *Weekly Anglo-African* and the *Christian Recorder* were particularly popular, as they reported extensively on the hardships and triumphs of African American troops. A few regiments even launched their own newspapers, which served multiple functions: They provided entertainment to their black audience, reassured black troops that their sacrifice of toil and blood was in service to a great cause, and gave instruction on how to endure a military experience that often seemed bleak and emasculating.

On the Field of Battle

More than 68,000 of the 200,000 black soldiers who served in the Union Army—one out of every three men—died during the Civil War. More than 2,750 of these deaths occurred on the battlefield, but a far greater number of African American troops were felled by a toxic combination of disease and terrible medical care. According to historian Joseph T. Glatthaar in *Forged in Battle* (1990), inadequate or incompetent medical care contributed to the deaths of more than 29,000 black soldiers from pneumonia, dysentery, typhoid fever, and malaria. All told, approximately one out of five black soldiers died from disease. By contrast, only one out of twelve white Union soldiers were felled by disease (Smith 2002, p. 41).

Until mid-1863, black units rarely found themselves on the front lines. Instead, they usually toiled in rear areas that became incubators of disease. Other black units, such as the seven regiments of U.S. Colored Cavalry (USCC) that served during the Civil War, carried out assignments that involved manning remote outposts, scouting, and reconnaissance.

From mid-1863 forward, however, black Union troops were increasingly thrown into battle—in large measure because they performed so well in early engagements. At Milliken's Bend, Louisiana, in June 1863, for example, three regiments of black troops—most of them with hardly any military training at all—served as the backbone of a successful Union effort to beat back an assault from a larger Confederate force. In the aftermath of the battle, journalist and government official Charles Dana (1819–1897) wrote that the "sentiment ... [in] regard to the employment of Negro troops has been revolutionized by the bravery of the blacks in the recent Battle of Milliken's Bend. Prominent officers, who used in private to sneer at the idea, are now heartily in favor of it" (Trudeau 1998, p. 59). Conversely, word of the performance of the black troops in the battle sent a shudder of apprehension through many Confederate camps and communities. "It is hard to believe that Southern soldiers—and Texans at that—have been whipped by a mongrel crew of white and black Yankees," wrote one bewildered and shaken Confederate woman in her journal. "There must be some mistake" (Trudeau 1998, p. 59).

The most famous battle involving significant numbers of black troops occurred in the summer of 1863, when the all-black 54th Massachusetts volunteers commanded by Colonel Robert Gould Shaw (1837–1863) led an assault against Battery Wagner, a Confederate fortress guarding the entrance to Charleston Harbor. The assault ultimately failed, but the bravery and Herculean effort shown by the 54th Massachusetts—which lost nearly half its men in the battle—became one of the most famous episodes of the entire war.

As Dana suggested, the bravery shown by black troops in battle led many white Yankees to abandon their doubts about the suitability of African Americans for military service. Colonel Thomas W. Higginson (1823–1911), who led the all-black First South Carolina Volunteers, reported after one battle along the Florida-Georgia border that "nobody knows anything about these men who has not seen them in battle. I find that I myself knew nothing. There is a fiery energy about them beyond anything of which I have ever read" (Smith 2002, pp. 313–314). And after the Battle of Nashville in December 1864, Union General James B. Steedman (1817–1883) declared that he "was unable to discover that color made any difference in the fighting of my troops. All, white and black, nobly did their duty as soldiers, and evinced cheerfulness and resolution such as I have never seen excelled in any campaign of the war in which I have borne a part" (Smith 2002, p. 63).

The Impact of Black Military Service

The solid performance of black soldiers during the Civil War improved the lives of black Americans in the North in a host of areas. As word of their sacrifices on the front lines filtered back to Northern communities, antipathy toward black civilians lessened in some aspects (though bigotry remained commonplace, as the 1863 draft riots showed in stark detail). The nation's first antidiscriminatory laws were passed before the war even ended, such as one that permitted blacks to testify as witnesses in federal court.

The sacrifices borne by the Union's black regiments also marked an important early step in the African American quest for acceptance and equality in American society. As President Lincoln observed, African Americans had "heroically vindicated their manhood on the battlefield, where, in assisting to save the life of the Republic, they have demonstrated in blood their right to the ballot" (Arnold 1866, p. 656).

Black Soldiers in the Confederacy

In the Confederate South, meanwhile, the use of blacks as beasts of burden intensified. In support of the war effort, slaves were used to construct trenches and other fortifications, repair railroads, haul artillery and other military equipment, and harvest crops. This freed up white men to fight, but it further exacerbated manpower shortages later in the war, when the number of black runaways soared.

By mid-1863, some pragmatic individuals in the South were cautiously raising the prospect of adding slaves to the Confederate Army—even if such a drastic step meant an end to slavery. "[Slavery should not be] a barrier to our independence," declared an August 1863 editorial in the *Jackson Mississippian*. "If it is found in the way—if it proves an insurmountable object of the achievement of our liberty and separate nationality, away with it! Let it perish! ... We must make up our minds to one solemn duty, the first duty of the patriot, and that is to save ourselves from the rapacious North, whatever the cost" (Hummel 1996, pp. 280–281). Even General Robert E. Lee (1807–1870) expressed support for this idea near the end of the war.

In March 1865, the demoralized Confederate Congress narrowly authorized the recruitment of 300,000 slaves to add to the depleted ranks of the Rebel army. At around this same time, President Jefferson Davis and other top officials sent the British and French governments frantic promises to fully emancipate Southern slaves in exchange for formal diplomatic recognition of the Confederacy. The Confederates even agreed to treat black prisoners of war like white prisoners in the context of prisoner exchanges (the South's prior refusal to exchange black prisoners had slowed all prisoner exchanges to a trickle, which in turn created horrendously overcrowded prisoner of war camps in both the North and South during the last two years of the conflict). All of these measures were borne of palpable desperation, however, and they all came to naught.

BIBLIOGRAPHY

Arnold, Isaac Newton. *The History of Abraham Lincoln, and the Overthrow of Slavery*. Chicago: Clarke & Co. Publishers, 1866.

Berlin, Ira, Joseph P. Reidy, and Leslie S. Rowland, eds. *Freedom's Soldiers: The Black Military Experience in the Civil War*. New York: Cambridge University Press, 1998.

Blight, David W. *Race and Reunion: The Civil War in American Memory*. Cambridge, MA: Belknap Press of Harvard University Press, 2001.

Cornish, Dudley Taylor. *The Sable Arm: Negro Troops in the Union Army, 1861–1865*. New York: Longmans, Green, 1956. Reprint, New York: W. W. Norton, 1966.

Douglass, Frederick. *Frederick Douglass: Selected Speeches and Writings,* ed. Philip S. Foner and Taylor Yuval. Chicago: Lawrence Hill Press, 1999.

Duncan, Russell, ed. *Blue-Eyed Child of Fortune: The Civil War Letters of Colonel Robert Gould Shaw*. Athens: University of Georgia Press, 1992.

Glatthaar, Joseph T. *Forged in Battle: The Civil War Alliance of Black Soldiers and White Officers*. New York: Free Press, 1990.

Glatthaar, Joseph T. "Black Glory: The African-American Role in Union Victory." In *Why the Confederacy Lost*, ed. Gabor S. Boritt. New York: Oxford University Press, 1992.

Gooding, James Henry. Letter. *New Bedford Mercury*, November 21, 1863.

Hansen, Joyce. *Between Two Fires: Black Soldiers in the Civil War*. New York: Franklin Watts, 1993.

Hargrove, Hondon B. *Black Union Soldiers in the Civil War*. Jefferson, NC: McFarland, 1988.

Hummel, Jeffrey Rogers. *Emancipating Slaves, Enslaving Free Men: A History of the American Civil War*. Chicago: Open Court, 1996.

Palladino, Anita, ed. *Diary of a Yankee Engineer: The Civil War Story of John H. Westervelt.* New York: Fordham University Press, 1997.

Redkey, Edwin S., ed. *A Grand Army of Black Men: Letters from African-American Soldiers in the Union Army, 1861–1865.* New York: Cambridge University Press, 1992, 2002.

Salvatore, Nick. *We All Got History: The Memory Books of Amos Webber.* New York: Times Books/Random House, 1996.

Smith, John David, ed. *Black Soldiers in Blue: African American Troops in the Civil War Era.* Chapel Hill: University of North Carolina Press, 2002.

Trudeau, Noah Andre. *Like Men of War: Black Troops in the Civil War, 1862–1865.* Boston: Little, Brown, 1998.

Weaver, C. P., ed. *Thank God My Regiment an African One: The Civil War Diary of Colonel Nathan W. Daniels.* Baton Rouge: Louisiana State University Press, 1998.

Wilson, Keith P. *Campfires of Freedom: The Camp Life of Black Soldiers during the Civil War.* Kent, OH: Kent State University Press, 2002.

Kevin Hillstrom

■ Immigrant Soldiers

Most soldiers who fought in the Civil War, whether wearing the blue garb of the Union Army or the gray colors of the Confederates, were native-born Americans. These men, however, were joined by tens of thousands of foreign-born soldiers from virtually every part of the globe. In the case of the Federal military in particular, immigrant soldiers came to comprise a sizable portion of the overall force. By the end of the war in 1865, one out of four men who fought for the Union were foreign-born.

Foreign-Born Yankees

The American Civil War erupted at a time when families were emigrating from Europe to U.S. shores in never before seen numbers. This exodus from Europe, spurred by political upheaval, the Irish potato famines, and America's blossoming reputation as a meritocracy, funneled huge numbers of immigrants into the North. Most immigrants chose Northern cities and states because industrialization—and the associated promise of jobs—was proceeding at a far more rapid pace in those places than in the South, and because farm land was both more abundant and more affordable in the North than in the plantation-oriented South. By 1860 nearly one out of three men living in the North was foreign-born.

This resource could not be ignored when it came time for the Federal government to muster an army to put down the insurrection in the South. President

Federal recruiting poster designed for Irish immigrants. The North took advantage of their larger foreign-born population, enlisting thousands of immigrants to fight the Confederates. Immigrants' reasons for joining the fight ranged from a sense of obligation to their new country to a Federal decree that men must register for military service if they wished to acquire citizenship. *Private Collection/Peter Newark American Pictures/The Bridgeman Art Library.*

Abraham Lincoln handed out military commissions to immigrant generals, which proved an effective tool in increasing enlistments in immigrant neighborhoods. Of course, many foreign-born Americans did not need such inducements to volunteer; swayed by financial and patriotic considerations, immigrants flooded many Union recruiting offices in the opening months of the conflict. Another burst of immigrants joining the military occurred in 1863, when Congress passed conscription laws that required immigrants who had sworn their intention to become naturalized citizens to register for military service.

Armies of Multiple Nationalities

As the war progressed, some Union camps became highly polyglot. As historian Bell Irvin Wiley reported in his

General Robert Nugent (d. 1901) and staff of the Irish Brigade.   Though sometimes subject to prejudice by native-born Union soldiers, immigrant soldiers, such as those from General Robert Nugent's Irish Brigade, readily volunteered to defend their newly-adopted country. By Civil War's end, foreign-born troops comprised nearly twenty-five percent of Federal troops, providing an important manpower advantage over the Confederacy.   *The Library of Congress.*

seminal *The Life of Billy Yank*, Company H of the 8th Michigan included seven Canadians, five Englishmen, four Germans, two Irishmen, one Dutchman, one Scotsman, and one enigmatic individual who listed his nationality as "the ocean." This assortment of nationalities was by no means unusual. One Union regiment had so many men of different nationalities in its ranks that the commanding officer had to give orders in seven languages. On more than one occasion, these language barriers hindered the performance of Union units in battle.

Other Yankee regiments consisted almost entirely of foreign-born soldiers. The 79th New York infantry, for example, was made up primarily of Scottish immigrants—a fact that led them to become known simply as "the Highlanders." Similarly, every soldier in the 9th Wisconsin infantry was from Germany, and both New York State and Ohio produced several regiments that were almost entirely composed of German immigrants. All told, it is believed that over 200,000 Germans marched under the Union banner.

Another 150,000 Irish immigrants fought for the Union, and at least twenty regiments were composed almost entirely of men from Ireland. Throughout the war, numerous Union generals remarked on the unique aspects of handling Irish soldiers. They griped about their bluster and resistance to authority, but also spoke admiringly of their cheerful and resilient demeanor in the face of war's myriad horrors and discomforts.

In addition to the German and Irish contingents, other nationalities well represented in the Union military included Englishmen and Canadians (an estimated 60,000 soldiers combined). Immigrants from France, Hungary, Sweden, Norway, and even various Asian nations further fleshed out the Yankee ranks.

The number of foreign-born soldiers in the Confederate ranks was much smaller. The Rebel army included one brigade of Irishmen, several German regiments, and even boasted a Louisiana brigade with a strong French presence that was commanded by a French count with the colorful name of Camille Armand Jules Marie, Prince de Polignac.

Motivations

Foreign-born soldiers were sometimes treated with disdain by their native-born counterparts. The latter's hostility was in many cases nothing more than bigotry, though in other instances animosity stemmed from impatience with language barriers and other perceived impediments to efficient military performance.

Despite the sometimes cold reception they received from American-born comrades, however, few foreign-born soldiers seemed to question their decision to take up arms in defense of the Union and the republican principles it represented. A German soldier attached to the 8th Missouri, for example, declared that he "grasped the weapon of death for the purpose of doing my part in defending and upholding the integrity, laws and the preservation of my adopted country from a band of contemptible traitors who would if they can accomplish their hellish designs, destroy the best and noblest government on earth" (Wiley 1975, p. 79). An Irish immigrant attached to the 28th Massachusetts expressed similar sentiments about the stakes involved in the War between the States. "This is my country as much as the man who was born on the soil," he declared. "This is the first test of a modern free government in the act of sustaining itself against internal enemys. ... If it fail all tyrants will succeed[;] the old cry will be sent forth from the aristocrats of Europe that such is the common lot of all republics. ... Irishmen and their descendents have ... a stake in [this] nation" (Welsh 1986, pp. 65–66). These strongly held convictions were essential to the morale and brave performance of the great majority of the Civil War's foreign-born troops.

BIBLIOGRAPHY

Davis, William C. *Rebels and Yankees: The Fighting Men of the Civil War.* New York: Smithmark Publishers, 1991.

McPherson, James M. *For Cause and Comrades: Why Men Fought in the Civil War.* New York: Oxford University Press, 1997.

Welsh, Peter. *Irish Green and Union Blue: The Civil War Letters of Peter Welsh*, ed. Lawrence Frederick Kohl and Margaret Cossé Richard. New York: Fordham University Press, 1986.

Wiley, Bell Irvin. *The Life of Billy Yank, the Common Soldier of the Union.* Indianapolis: Bobbs-Merrill, 1951.

Wiley, Bell Irvin. *The Common Soldier of the Civil War.* New York: Scribner, 1975.

Kevin Hillstrom

■ Native American Soldiers

An estimated 16,000 to 20,000 Native American men took part in the American Civil War in an official capacity, with the vast majority—probably three-quarters of the total—fighting on the side of the Confederacy. Native American soldiers were most prominent and important in the lightly populated Trans-Mississippi

West, but Native Americans also participated in battles in the Eastern theaters of the war.

Indian Troops in the East

East of the Mississippi River, Native American membership in the Confederate military consisted primarily of a few hundred soldiers scattered among white regiments hailing from Kentucky, North Carolina, and Tennessee. As Laurence Hauptman detailed in *Between Two Fires* (1995), the most prominent tribes to formally cast their lot with the Confederacy were the Catawba of South Carolina, who became particularly proficient at scouting and tracking down runaway slaves, and the Eastern Band of Cherokee, who guarded mountain passes and conducted raids against Union positions in the Smoky Mountain region. Many of these Native American soldiers eschewed the uniform worn by white Confederate soldiers. "Their faces were painted, and their long straight hair, tied in a queue, hung down behind," wrote one Confederate soldier from Missouri. "Their dress was chiefly in the Indian costume—buckskin hunting-shirts, dyed of almost every color, leggings, and moccasins of the same material, with little bells, rattles, ear-rings, and similar paraphernalia. Many of them were bareheaded and about half carried only bows and arrows, tomahawks, and war-clubs" (Davis 1991, p. 22).

Within the Union ranks, the most notable tribes to make their presence felt included members of Virginia's Pamunkey tribe, who served as river pilots for George B. McClellan's Army of the Potomac in 1862 during the Peninsula campaign, and Lumbee warriors from North Carolina, who waged guerrilla campaigns in the swamp country of their native lands in the last months of the war. The pro-Union tribes most deserving of mention, however, are Michigan's Ottawa and Ojibwa tribes. Warriors from these tribes became Company K of the 1st Michigan Sharpshooters, a group that distinguished itself at the bloody Battle of the Crater and several other engagements.

What motivated these Native Americans to become involved in the Civil War, which was fought for purposes that had nothing to do with them? The answer, in essence, was that their tribal leaders hoped that participation in the war would help them negotiate more favorable treaties to protect their traditional homelands from white incursion (similar motivations prompted other far-flung tribes, such as the Pequots of Connecticut and the Seneca of western New York, to assist the Federals).

Fighting in Indian Territory

In the Trans-Mississippi West, many Indian tribes avoided any involvement in the white man's war. Union forces, though, did receive the support of Delaware Indian leaders who hoped to parlay that support into a reasonable

A group Native American soldiers nursing injuries. Hoping their sacrifices would prove an advantage when negotiating treaties, Native American soldiers fought on both sides of the Mason-Dixon line, with the majority of the troops joining the Confederate side. Native American soldiers endured poor treatment, however, and were often regarded as expendable. *The Library of Congress*

land treaty with officials in Washington. More importantly, the Cherokee became deeply involved in the Civil War. The war opened a deep schism among the Cherokee. The majority of the Cherokee nation, under the leadership of chief John Ross, tried to steer a neutral course. "I am—the Cherokees are—your friends and the

friends of your people," he wrote to Confederate officials. "But we do not wish to be brought into the feuds between yourselves and your Northern Brethren. Our wish is for peace. Peace at home and Peace among you" (Moore 1862, p. 394). Over time, however, some Cherokees from Ross's group drifted into the Union camp. A sizable

A NATIVE AMERICAN AT APPOMATTOX: ELY SAMUEL PARKER (1828–1895)

Ely (pronounced *E-lee*) Samuel Parker was a Seneca-Iroquois Indian who not only served in the Union Army during the Civil War but rose to the rank of brigadier general. Parker was born in 1828 in Indian Falls, New York, on what was then the Tonawanda reservation. His mother had been told by a tribal elder before Ely's birth that her son would become a great warrior and peacemaker. Parker's original tribal name was Hasanoanda, which means "The Reader." A gifted child, he learned English rapidly and was sent to an academy in western New York; there he won prizes for his speaking skill. His tribal leaders thought so highly of him that they sent him to Washington at the age of eighteen to represent the Iroquois and Seneca in treaty negotiations with the United States. In 1852, Parker was made the sachem (chief) of the Seneca tribe and given the name Donehogawa, which means "Keeper of the Western Door."

After graduation from the academy, Parker wished to study law but was rejected by Harvard because he was an Indian. He prepared for the New York bar examination by working for three years in a law firm, but was not allowed to take the test on the grounds that he was not an American citizen (Native Americans were not given citizenship rights until 1924). Parker then became a civil engineer; after working on the Erie Canal, he was sent west to Galena, Illinois, where he met Ulysses S. Grant. When the Civil War broke out, Parker contacted the governor of New York and offered to raise a regiment of Iroquois volunteers to fight on the Union side. His proposal was rejected.

Grant did not forget Parker, however. When Grant was promoted to major general in 1863, he gave Parker an appointment in the Union Army as a captain of engineers. Parker served under Grant at the siege of Vicksburg in 1863 and returned east with him when Grant was made commander of all Union forces in March 1864. As Grant's adjutant, Parker used his legal training to help draft the surrender document that Robert E. Lee signed at Appomattox in April 1865. The document, now in the National Archives, is in Parker's handwriting. After the war, Parker was promoted to the rank of brigadier general, his promotion being backdated to the date of Lee's surrender.

While Lee was signing the surrender papers, he apparently mistook Parker for a black man, and tried to apologize by saying, "I am glad to see one real American here." Parker is said to have replied, "We are all Americans, sir" (Armstrong 1978, p.178).

REBECCA J. FREY

BIBLIOGRAPHY

Armstrong, William H. *Warrior in Two Camps: Ely S. Parker, Union General and Seneca Chief. Syracuse, NY: Syracuse University Press, 1978.*

Gilmore, Gerry J. "Seneca Chief Fought Greed, Injustice." U.S. Department of Defense, Armed Forces Press Service, 2002. Available from http://www.pentagon.gov/specials/nativeam02/injustice.html.

faction led by Stand Watie, however, joined the Confederate cause. Watie's followers became the foundation of a sizable Native American force for the Confederacy; the South ultimately raised eleven regiments and seven battalions of Indian cavalry in the region.

The clashes between these forces occurred primarily in Indian Territory (modern-day Oklahoma), which both Confederate and Union officials recognized as key to the Rebels' western defenses. White military leaders pushed the Indians into bloody confrontations with one another again and again, with little regard for the spiraling death toll. As the war progressed, Indian Territory became a notoriously bloody and savage killing ground. Stories of scalpings and other savagery were seized on by white officials and settlers who were eager to push Indians elsewhere in the West off their traditional lands.

Almost without exception, white military strategists with the Union and Confederacy treated the Native American warriors under their charge with a combination of contempt and disregard. Wages, food, clothing, and weapons that had been earmarked for the Indians were routinely diverted to white troops. Many Indians had to scavenge clothing from the field, by foraging, or make do with the rags provided from depleted commissaries. In addition, corruption and fraud remained hallmarks of government contracts for various services earmarked for the tribes as a whole. The violence in Indian Territory also roiled the internal politics and society of myriad tribes, making them even more vulnerable to the mighty tide of westward settlement rolling over their lands. The spilling over of the Civil War into Indian Territory, then, was a negative development for the Native Americans living in the region, and the conduct of both Union and Confederate leaders toward Native American soldiers marching under their banners remains one of the most shameful chapters in the entire conflict.

BIBLIOGRAPHY

Berg, Gordon. "Inured to Hardships, Fleet as Deer." *Civil War Times* (June 2007).

Civil War Society. "Native Americans in the Civil War." *Encyclopedia of the Civil War.* New York: Wings Books, 1997.

Davis, William C. *Rebels and Yankees: The Fighting Men of the Civil War.* New York: Smithmark Publishers, 1991.

Franks, Kenny A. *Stand Watie and the Agony of the Cherokee Nation.* Memphis, TN: Memphis State University Press, 1979.

Hatch, Thom. *The Blue, the Gray, and the Red: Indian Campaigns of the Civil War.* Mechanicsburg, PA: Stackpole, 2003.

Hauptman, Laurence M. *Between Two Fires: American Indians in the Civil War.* New York: Free Press, 1995.

Josephy, Alvin M., Jr. *The Civil War in the American West.* New York: Random House, 1991.

Moore, Frank, ed. *Rebellion Record: A Diary of American Events.* New York: G. P. Putnam, 1862.

Kevin Hillstrom

■ Spies

Spies and saboteurs occupy an ambiguous place in the pantheons of Civil War history and legend. Those to whom their services were provided often perceived them as heroic figures who supplied vital information at considerable personal peril—and with little prospect that their sacrifices and efforts would ever be publicly acknowledged. For some military strategists, political leaders, and citizens in both the North and South, these spies working behind enemy lines were the ultimate patriots.

The population in both the North and South viewed any spy in their midst as the worst sort of treasonous scoundrel. A few spies and saboteurs—usually women—were regarded a little more mildly, as misguided fools rather than immoral traitors. But most agents caught gathering intelligence, serving as couriers of classified information, or otherwise hindering the domestic war effort were dealt with harshly. Executions of convicted spies were commonplace.

Cobbling Together Spy Networks

When the fireworks at Fort Sumter erupted in the spring of 1861 and ushered in the Civil War, both the Union and the Confederacy scrambled to cobble together intelligence-gathering networks that could track enemy movements, report on enemy resources and strategies, and monitor the strengths and weaknesses of supply lines and assorted military operations maintained by the other side.

In this realm, Union military strategists did not enjoy a significant advantage over their counterparts in the South. In 1861 the federal authorities in Washington did not have any sort of well-established intelligence apparatus in place to which they could turn; prior to the war there simply had never been a pressing need for such an entity (though a smattering of U.S. diplomats and other officials in Europe and elsewhere did provide some basic information-gathering functions). Moreover, as Donald Markle (1994) points out, the Union had an established government with various departments that could be infiltrated, whereas in the initial stages of the war there was essentially no centralized Confederate government to infiltrate (1994, p. xvii).

Despite this edge, however—and despite their ability to line up a network of safe houses and courier lines in the North within months of the onset of war—the Confederates never really managed to gain a decisive advantage in the realm of espionage.

Confederate Spies

The man charged with developing a Confederate spy network capable of infiltrating the North was Major William Norris (1820–1896), who also served the government in Richmond in a far more public role as head of the Confederate Signal Bureau. During the course of the war, Norris and his cohorts in Richmond benefited enormously from the efforts of Confederate agents such as E. Porter Alexander (1835–1910) and Thomas Nelson Conrad (1837–1905). Some of the most effective spies for the Confederacy, however, were women. Rose O'Neal Greenbow (1817–1864), who was a Washington

Confederate spy Mrs. Rose Greenbow (1817–1864). Female spies, including Rose Greenbow, often took advantage of nineteenth-century stereotypes that regarded women as less able to participate in the intricacies of war. Using their social connections to learn important information about enemy movements, fortifications, and strategies, successful women spies proved to be excellent sources of detailed information during the Civil War. *The Library of Congress*

"BELLE" BOYD AND PAULINE CUSHMAN

Some of the most notorious—and successful—spies on both sides of the Civil War were women. Perhaps the most colorful was Maria Isabella "Belle" Boyd (1844–1900), known as "the Cleopatra of the Secession." Born in Martinsburg in what is now West Virginia, Boyd began her espionage work at the age of seventeen. When some drunken Union soldiers entered the family home on July 4, 1861, and insulted Belle's mother, the teenager drew a pistol and shot one of them. As a result, a detachment of Union soldiers was posted around the house and the family's activities were monitored. Belle took advantage of this close contact to charm one of the officers into revealing military secrets. It was a pattern she followed on other occasions, along with eavesdropping on Union officers through a knothole in the upper floor of the local hotel.

Boyd was not universally admired in the Confederacy in spite of her repeated success in obtaining Union military secrets. She was a flamboyant dresser, preferring richly colored clothes and wearing a feather in her hair. She also traveled alone, often on horseback, and visited Southern officers in their camp tents—behavior that shocked other women. Arrested twice and imprisoned for espionage, Boyd was released both times. In 1864 she went to England, where she met and married an officer in the Union Navy, Samuel Wylde Hardinge. After his death, she remained in England and began a career as an actress.

In 1869 she returned to the United States and remarried. She divorced her second husband in 1884 and married a third husband in 1885. A year later, Boyd began to give lecture tours across the United States about her adventures as a Confederate spy. She died in Wisconsin of typhoid fever in 1900.

Boyd's most celebrated counterpart on the Union side was Pauline Cushman (1833–1893), who had become an actress before the Civil War. Cushman's husband, a musician who had joined the Union Army, was killed in 1862. While on tour with a theatrical troupe in Louisville, Kentucky, Cushman began to fraternize with Confederate officers. She obtained battle plans and, concealing them in her shoes, attempted to carry them back to the Union lines. Cushman was caught by Braxton Bragg's troops and sentenced to death by hanging, but was saved three days before her scheduled execution by a Union advance and Confederate retreat.

According to some sources, Cushman then disguised herself as a Union cavalry major and became known as Miss Major Cushman. By the spring of 1865 she was already giving lectures around the country on her work as a Union spy. Cushman's later years were unhappy, however. Her children both died in 1868. She moved to San Francisco and married a second husband in 1872, but was widowed again in less than a year. She married a third husband in 1879 and moved with him to Texas but separated from him in 1890. By 1892 she had moved back to San Francisco and was living in poverty.

Cushman's last days were spent working as a seamstress and cleaning lady. She became addicted to opium to relieve the pain of severe arthritis, and died of an overdose in December 1893. Cushman is buried in the national cemetery at the Presidio in San Francisco, where her gravestone identifies her as a Union spy.

REBECCA J. FREY

BIBLIOGRAPHY

Christen, William J. *Pauline Cushman, Spy of the Cumberland: An Accounting and Memorandum of Her Life. Roseville, MN: Edinborough Press, 2005.*

Scarborough, Ruth. *Belle Boyd, Siren of the South. Macon, GA: Mercer University Press, 1983.*

socialite with access to some of the capital's most important political operators, was perhaps the most famous of these agents, but others such as Antonia Ford (1838–1871) and Maria "Belle" Boyd (1843–1900) also delivered valuable information on Union troop movements, defensive priorities, and military strategies to grateful recipients down South.

Women were particularly effective agents—for the Union as well as the Confederacy—precisely because nineteenth-century notions of female inferiority were so deeply ingrained in the thoughts and attitudes of Northern and Southern men. It was hard for many to imagine that women could possibly be engaged in espionage, and for those female spies that were caught, treatment was far more lenient: Not one of the women caught spying for either side was threatened with execution (Williams 2005, p. 139).

As the war progressed, Southern spymasters also became adept at gleaning important military intelligence from Northern newspapers, some of which were stunningly careless about revealing Federal troop movements and other information about Yankee military operations (the South did not hemorrhage important military information in the same way, mostly because it had far fewer papers). In addition, Rebel military commanders and scouts in the field received a steady diet of intelligence on enemy movements, strength, and morale from members of the civilian population. This information, provided by farmers, field hands, housewives, hunters, storeowners, and other Southerners from every walk of life, became a veritable flood during the last two years of the war, when Union troops were making ever deeper incursions into the Confederate heartland. This intelligence ultimately was insufficient to stem the Yankee tide, but it did make Union military objectives considerably harder to achieve.

Union Spies

Leading architects of Union intelligence-gathering efforts during the Civil War included Allan Pinkerton (1819–

1884), founder of the legendary Pinkerton Detective Agency, and Provost Marshal Marsena R. Patrick (1811–1888). These and other administrators not only coordinated the activities of Union spies in the South, such as Philip Henson and Timothy Webster (1821–1862) (the latter was perhaps the most famous of the male spies utilized by the North), they also worked to ferret out spies and saboteurs in their own midst. In the latter regard, Northern spymasters were much more effective than their Confederate counterparts. Their greater level of success was attributable in part to the fact that even before the war began, the Federal government had identified many Southern sympathizers in Washington, DC, and other population centers. In addition, the South's ability to detect spies became progressively weaker as the war went on as Confederate difficulties with virtually every aspect of military operations intensified.

Like the South, the North had its share of notable women spies, including Mary Gordon, Carrie King, and Pauline Cushman (1833–1893). Perhaps the most famous woman to gather meaningful military intelligence for the North was Elizabeth Van Lew (1818–1900). A wealthy socialite, Van Lew cultivated a reputation for bizarre behavior that helped disguise her involvement in the Underground Railroad and increased her ability to pass on important information involving Confederate strategies and troop movements. Van Lew's chief "lieutenant" in these efforts was Mary Elizabeth Bowser (c. 1840–??), a former slave educated by Van Lew who managed to obtain employment as a dining room attendant to Confederate President Jefferson Davis (1808–1889).

Another important source of military intelligence was a spy network nurtured into an effective weapon by Union General Ulysses S. Grant (1822–1885). Under the guiding hand of Grant and General Grenville M. Dodge (1831–1916), this networkevolved into an effective provider of military and political intelligence. By the latter stages of the war, "a large secret service force operated all over the Confederacy," recalled Union Colonel George E. Spencer (1836–1893). "It was probably the most effective secret service in the federal army and General Grant came to rely on the information received from it" (Perkins 1929, p. 105).

As Federal armies made deeper incursions into the South, the information provided by undercover spies was also supplemented by information from antisecessionist Southerners, as well as those looking to curry favor with the new authorities in the region. In the early years, these ordinary Southerners were furtive in providing assistance, but they became increasingly bold in the war's final months, when the Confederacy's death rattle had become audible to all. Finally, Yankee armies in the field received a great deal of valuable intelligence from fugitive slaves, many of whom carried valuable information about enemy positions and dispositions. Some of these "informers" were so eager to help defeat

Major Pauline Cushman (1833–1893), spy and actress. An unsuccessful actress, Pauline Cushman was caught as she attempted to smuggle information about Confederate plans. Sentenced to death, she escaped from enemy hands during the confusion of a Union military attack and later toured the United States telling her story. *Hulton Archive/Getty Images.*

the slaveholding South that they delayed their journey northward in order to guide Union forces to vulnerable supply depots and other potential military targets.

BIBLIOGRAPHY

Bakeless, John. *Spies of the Confederacy.* Philadelphia: Lippincott, 1970.

Davis, William C., and the editors of Time-Life Books. *Spies, Scouts, and Raiders: Irregular Operations.* New York: Time-Life Books, 1985.

Feis, William B. *Grant's Secret Service: The Intelligence War from Belmont to Appomattox.* Lincoln, NE: Bison Books, 2004.

Fishel, Edwin C. "The Mythology of Civil War Intelligence." *Civil War History* 10, no. 4 (1964): 344–367.

Freehling, William W. *The South vs. the South: How Anti-Confederate Southerners Shaped the Course of the Civil War*. New York: Oxford University Press, 2001.

Gaddy, David W. "Gray Cloaks and Daggers." *Civil War Times Illustrated* July 14, no. 4 (1975): 20–27.

Leonard, Elizabeth D. *All the Daring of the Soldier: Women of the Civil War Armies*. New York: Penguin Books, 1999.

Markle, Donald E. *Spies and Spymasters of the Civil War*. New York: Hippocrene Books, 1994.

Massey, Mary Elizabeth. *Women in the Civil War*. Lincoln: University of Nebraska Press, 1994.

Perkins, Jacob Randolph. *Trails, Rails and War: The Life of General G. M. Dodge*. Indianapolis: Bobbs-Merrill, 1929.

Varon, Elizabeth R. *Southern Lady, Yankee Spy: The True Story of Elizabeth Van Lew, a Union Agent in the Heart of the Confederacy*. Oxford University Press, USA, 2005.

Williams, David. *A People's History of the Civil War: Struggles for the Meaning of Freedom*. New York: New Press, 2005.

Kevin Hillstrom

■ Foraging and Looting

The practice of foraging by military personnel increased exponentially during the course of the American Civil War. At the outset of the conflict, Rebel and Yankee soldiers alike mostly viewed the civilian populations in North and South—and the property they owned—as firmly outside the sphere of military action. As the war progressed, however, these restrictions on contact with civilians—some self-imposed on moral grounds, others in adherence to explicit military rules prohibiting foraging and looting—became frayed and in many cases were discarded altogether.

There are very important differences between foraging and looting. Foraging was sanctioned by the laws and customs of war, although it was approached with some squeamishness at the beginning of the war. Looting involved taking non-food items for non-military uses, and was sanctioned neither by the laws and customs of war nor by officers on either side. This gradual turn to foraging and looting was especially true of Union soldiers operating in the Confederate states, where most of the war was fought. This is not to say that Union soldiers were the only culpable party; Confederates were no less likely to forage and loot, given the opportunity. In the

South, however, the Union army faced shifting attitudes about war strategy and increased frustration about perceived civilian culpability in guerrilla activity that prompted an outright embrace of looting and foraging.

Foraging in the Countryside

Food was the first area in which soldiers engaged in large-scale theft from civilians. In its earliest stages, the practice of "living off the land" as a way of supplementing meager and unvaried commissary rations was done lightly and with an almost quaint concern for propriety and ethics. For example, soldiers in both armies freely picked apples, pears, cherries, and other fruit from trees they passed while on the march, but they were less sanguine about consuming field crops because they knew that production of the latter was directly due to the exertions of farmers and farmhands. The same ethical issues confronted soldiers who came across cellars and smokehouses containing private food stores. Because many soldiers came from rural circumstances themselves, they knew the long, hot hours that went into raising field crops and filling storage cellars and smokehouses, and the thought of absconding with the fruits of those labors troubled many a conscience.

Over time, however, the attitudes of many soldiers toward supplementing their diet with food found on the march changed markedly. Food rations from the military commissaries of both armies were notoriously meager, of limited variety, and wretched in taste, and soldiers who had been choking down hardtack and salt pork for weeks at a time understandably were tempted by the livestock, fruit, and vegetables that they came across in enemy territory. Once individual members of a company or regiment crossed an ethical line by taking food from civilians for their own consumption, the behavior almost inevitably spread to other members of the company or regiment, like a fast-spreading virus.

Another one of the key elements in the institutionalization of foraging within military units was gaining approval—or at least tacit acceptance—of the practice from officers. Many enlisted men accomplished this by implicating officers as beneficiaries of their predation. Officers who received and kept a portion of the bounty from foraging expeditions were in no position to rein in the practice. As accomplices, their main concern was to maintain appearances. As a result, some officers who were "on the take" engaged in elaborate charades in which they publicly exhorted troops in their charge to kept their hands off private property, then waited in their tents for soldiers to bring them their share of the spoils.

Lee in the North

The two major occasions on which Confederate forces had the opportunity to forage at length came in 1862 and 1863, when General Robert E. Lee (1807–1870) led invasions into Maryland and Pennsylvania. During both these campaigns, some Southern voices urged Lee's Army of Northern Virginia to be an apocalyptic force laying bare Northern hearths and fields. The *Richmond Dispatch*, for instance, expressed a fervent wish that Rebel "troops will turn the whole country into a desert" (Royster 1991, p. 37).

Some Confederate forces refrained from foraging, and Lee himself took pains to use Confederate currency to procure salt and other important supplies. But proud Rebel declarations that all private property in the North was treated with the utmost respect were demonstrably false. Many prosperous farmers across Pennsylvania—as well as some who were not so prosperous—were raided by Rebel parties in 1862 and 1863, and Lee was forced to issue a formal injunction against foraging after it became clear to him and his lieutenants that plundering of civilian property was threatening to get out of hand. Despite his order, seizure and destruction of Northern food and property continued. As scholar Edwin B. Coddington wrote in *The Gettysburg Campaign: A Study in Command*, "writing confidentially in their letters or diaries and later in memoirs, Southerners mentioned not only thefts of horses but of other kinds of property as well. . . . One soldier noted in his diary that nearly half the men in his regiment were out foraging" (Coddington 1997, p. 177).

Yankees in the South

Early Union campaigns into Confederate territory likewise were marked by unauthorized foraging, but these transgressions were initially carried out by only a minority of soldiers. Many Federal regiments and companies actively enforced rules against foraging with systems of fines and other punishments, and a number of them actually assigned soldiers to guard Rebel property from foragers. Some Union officers actively worked to stamp out foraging as late as the summer of 1864. And of course many Yankee soldiers refused to engage in foraging at any time during the war despite their comrades' actions, usually because they found the practice to be both morally indefensible and personally degrading.

Formal rules and moral qualms about foraging began to erode in some parts of the Union Army as early as mid-1862, however. The lifting of restrictions on foraging gladdened the hearts of many Yankee soldiers. In July 1862, for example, a Union soldier in the Army of Virginia expressed delight when the army's new commander, General John Pope (1822–1892), issued orders permitting foraging and ending guarding of Rebel property.

> Guarding of the property of the rebels has been the greatest Curse to us in this army that could have been thought of for the men had got so mad about it that a good many of them did not care whether they did anything or not. . . . The soldiers begin to think that we are going to have war in earnest and that we are to be supported by the

Government and that no false notions of mercy are to save the scoundrels that have caused this war. (Mitchell 1988, p. 139)

Indeed, rank-and-file Yankees realized early on that destruction of food and other provisions far behind enemy lines had the potential to be deeply injurious to supply-starved Rebel armies in the field.

Union foraging, though, quickly took on a darker hue, deteriorating into outright looting, vandalism, and destruction of Confederate property. In some cases, military considerations merely served as a pretext for engaging in vicious or heartless behavior. Factors driving this turn by Union troops toward wanton theft of jewelry and other valuables and indiscriminate arson against homes and fields included mounting frustration and disillusionment with the war, heightened anger and concern about guerrilla activity by Southern civilians, and rationalizations that soldiers deserved some spoils of war, given the hardships and dangers that they were enduring. In numerous cases, Union troops attacked Confederate property with implacable fury. One Union soldier with the Army of the Potomac recalled the pillaging of a stately plantation in December 1862: "What the troops could not use they demolished; the men smashed mirrors, fine china and alabaster vases; mutilated books, paintings and embroidered draperies; and chopped up antique furniture for firewood" (Thomas 1990, p. 194).

Such ceremonies of demolition—sometimes conducted in a strangely festive, carnival-like atmosphere—were not carried out exclusively or even primarily by hardened criminals in uniform. Some of the vandals were God-fearing men from good homes who took pains to explain their behavior in letters to loved ones and personal diaries. "If any of your readers should think that there was too much Vandalism in any of these acts," wrote one Union soldier in an August 1863 letter home,

> [L]et them think of the necessity which requires our army to be down here, of the danger to Life and Limb, each one is subject to, besides doing as our brave fellows did, march and fight under a hot sun upon seven or eight hard crackers for two weeks, and do as some of our men actually did, rifle the haversacks of the *Dead* for food, and give from half a dollar to a dollar for a single cracker! (Mitchell 1988, p. 140)

Defending Home and Hearth

Even the Yankee regiments that most flagrantly marauded the countryside generally followed a set of guidelines governing their behavior. Reported incidents of rape, for instance, were relatively rare. Myriad accounts from both Yankee soldiers and Southern civilians indicate that because abandonment was taken as evidence of treasonous sympathies, abandoned homes and property were treated much more harshly than the homes and property of homeowners who stood fast. Indeed, many Southern

After the foraging. By war's end, Union taboos toward foraging and looting loosened, as many soldiers justified their destruction of the countryside as punishment for the South's determination to preserve slavery and their decision to secede from the United States of America. *The Library of Congress.*

homeowners—and especially women whose fathers and husbands were off at war—convinced would-be looters to spare their homes, usually by appealing to their sense of fair play and chivalry.

Southern civilians were usually cognizant of the impending arrival of enemy troops. Some had days to weigh whether to flee or stay and hope for the best. No matter what the decision proved to be, many affluent planters and other homeowners tried to hide their valuables—money, livestock, jewelry, valued heirlooms—from the approaching Yankees. On sizable plantations, elaborate preparations were taken. As one scholar explains:

> What supplies were movable were carried off and hidden. When the master did not feel he could trust his slaves, or felt they might be frightened into revealing hiding places, he had to do this work himself, and probably at night. The women decided what to do with jewelry and household valuables and sometimes put on an extra dress and clothed their children with a superfluity of garments—in case the house was burned or garments carried off they would have a change of clothing. The master or the overseer had the stock driven off and horses and mules hidden, and then stood ready to depart himself on short notice. ... When

there was no white man on the plantation, the woman would try to carry out these measures herself. (Kennett 1995, p. 298)

Sometimes these desperate measures worked. On other occasions, suspicious soldiers relied on intimidation or violence to find out where valuables had been placed or livestock had been taken. Few Southerners subjected to outright terrorism at the hands of enemy soldiers were capable of holding out for long. Moreover, many slaves happily informed Union troops about where their masters' valuables and livestock could be found. In addition, their accounts of deprivation and heartbreak at the hands of slave owners elicited greater levels of destruction from some Yankee units, who cast their acts of arson and other demolition as righteous blows against an ungodly and disloyal people.

Sherman's Hard War

One of the most notorious Union military commanders to officially sanction foraging and destruction of enemy private property was General Philip Sheridan (1831–1888). As chief of cavalry of the Army of the Potomac in the summer and fall of 1864, Sheridan oversaw the annihilation of large swaths of crops in Virginia's

Shenandoah Valley, the so-called "breadbasket of the Confederacy." Sheridan's men destroyed crops, burned houses and barns, and drove off or captured livestock with ruthless efficiency. "The people [of the Shenandoah Valley] must be left nothing but their eyes to weep with over the war," Sheridan famously declared (Hutton 1999, p. 204).

General William Tecumseh Sherman (1820–1891) is another infamously aggressive general who battled through Georgia and the Carolinas in late 1864 and early 1865. During the course of this "March to the Sea," which began in earnest with the burning of Atlanta, Sherman made a reputation for himself as the embodiment of the most ruthless and brutal side of war.

Earlier in the war, Sherman had indicated a profound distaste for visiting war's horrors on civilians. "War at best is barbarism, but to involve all—children, women, old and helpless—is more than can be justified," he stated. "Our men will become absolutely lawless unless they can be checked" (Nevin 1986, p. 117). By the time he arrived on the doorstep of Atlanta in September 1864 with 60,000 troops behind him, his views had changed. "War is cruelty, and you cannot refine it" he wrote in a letter to Atlanta's city leaders:

> Those who brought war into our country deserve all the curses and maledictions a people can pour out. I know I had no hand in making this war, and I know I will make more sacrifices to-day than any of you to secure peace. But you cannot have peace and a division of our country. ... You might as well appeal against the thunder-storm as against these terrible hardships of war. They are inevitable, and the only way the people of Atlanta can hope once more to live in peace and quiet at home, is to stop the war, which can only be done by admitting that it began in error and is perpetuated by pride. We don't want your negroes, or your horses, or your houses, or your lands, or any thing you have, but we do want and will have a just obedience to the laws of the United States. That we will have, and, if it involved the destruction of your improvements, we cannot help it. (Simpson 1999, p. 708)

In the same letter, Sherman also made pointed reference to Confederate incidents of foraging and looting in the border states that remained loyal to the Union:

> I myself have seen in Missouri, Kentucky, Tennessee, and Mississippi, hundreds and thousands of women and children fleeing from your armies and desperadoes, hungry and with bleeding feet. In Memphis, Vicksburg, and Mississippi, we fed thousands upon thousands of the families of rebel soldiers left on our hands, and whom we could not see starve. Now that war comes home to you, you feel very different. You deprecate its horrors, but did not feel them when you sent car-loads of

soldiers and ammunition, and moulded shells and shot, to carry war into Kentucky and Tennessee, to desolate the homes of hundreds and thousands of good people who only asked to live in peace at their old homes, and under the Government of their inheritance. (Simpson 1999, p. 708)

Looting and Destruction during the March to the Sea

After leaving Atlanta's factories and public buildings in smoking ruins, Sherman fed and supplied his army by taking whatever he needed from Georgia's farms and towns on his way to the coastal city of Savannah. He also directed his troops to destroy whatever they could not use themselves. "Evidently it is a material element in this campaign to produce among the people of Georgia a thorough conviction of the personal misery which attends war, and of the utter helplessness and inability of their 'rulers,' State or Confederate, to protect them," wrote Major Henry Hitchcock, a member of Sherman's staff. "And I am bound to say that I believe more and more that only by this means can the war be ended" (Nevin 1986, p. 163).

Sherman's own instructions regarding foraging made it clear that Union soldiers had a lot of latitude in terms of what they could take for themselves. The army did establish a basic framework for foraging: Parties were to be organized by brigade commanders and they were to keep on hand a ten-days' supply of meat, vegetables, and other food for soldiers and a three-day ration of forage for horses and mules. But whereas some units followed these guidelines fairly faithfully, others departed from it in sometimes dramatic fashion. For example, Sherman instructed foraging parties to leave some basic foodstuffs and other necessities for civilian families, but these instructions were skirted or ignored in some cases.

When Sherman's army took control of Savannah in December 1864, the city was largely spared from violence and destruction. But when the Union army passed over the Savannah River and into South Carolina—the first state that had seceded from the Union—looting, vandalism, and arson reached new heights. This level of violence and destruction was due in no small measure to soldiers' desire to punish South Carolinians for their rebellious ways. Each night, the skies surrounding the army were alight with homes and fields burning into cinders. Chimneys were often the only thing left standing in the morning, and these charred remains came to be known as "Sherman's sentinels." The residents of the state capital of Columbia suffered particularly harsh treatment at the hands of the Yankees. "That is the way we carry on the war now," wrote one Wisconsin soldier in Sherman's army. "Raze, burn, and destroy everything we come to" (Bropst 1960, p. 103).

Sherman's troops loot a Georgia plantation. James E. Taylor's 1888 print depicts the widespread looting enjoyed by victorious soldiers during General William Tecumseh Sherman's "March to the Sea." While soldiers tended to be more respectful of private property during the early stages of the conflict, by war's end military strategy changed to include consuming or destroying all of the opposition's resources. © *The New York Public Library/Art Resource, NY*

Bandits, Bummers and other Camp Followers

Much of the worst violence and predation visited upon Georgians and South Carolinians during Sherman's March to the Sea was actually not carried out by Union troops. Many of the most deplorable and vicious excesses were committed by *bandits*—civilian criminals and army deserters who trailed behind the marching army and fed on the remains of plantations and communities they passed. These lawless pillagers seldom displayed any restraint based on moral considerations, and some of these bands committed brazen atrocities. In many cases the bandits operated with impunity, as Union officers could do very little to counter them. *Bummers*, on the other hand, had not left the army but engaged individually in freelance foraging before returning to the ranks. Later, the term came to encompass all of Sherman's soldiers. Any bummer who committed an atrocity and was found out was liable to the severest of punishment by his officers.

To the great shame of Southerners, some Confederate cavalry units shadowing Sherman's movements also became notorious for preying on helpless civilians. "Impressment" of civilian food, clothing, and other provisions became standard operating procedure with units such as the First Alabama Cavalry, one of the many regiments commanded by General Joseph Wheeler (1836–1906). Earlier in the war this unit had distinguished itself, but by the time Sherman exited Georgia, many Georgians considered Wheeler's cavalry to be even worse than the Yankees.

Scarred Land and Defeated People

Increased incidence of foraging, looting, and destruction in the war's latter stages left many landowners and communities utterly bereft and emotionally devastated. Fields that had once teemed with cotton and other lucrative crops and stately plantations that had once been festooned with lace and finery now lay in ruins. These sights were utterly demoralizing to battered and disillusioned Confederate troops. As one Rebel soldier wrote after traveling through a war-ravaged section of Tennessee, "it almost steels a man's heart against mercy to see the fair habitations of this once proud and prosperous State smouldering in desolation" (Mitchell 1988, p. 175).

The stunned and heartsick citizens victimized by foraging soldiers also struggled to come to terms with the new reality of their lives. One Southerner wrote that after her household had been terrorized by a mob of foragers and bummers, "we could hardly believe it was our home. One week before it was one of the most beautiful places in the state. Now it was a vast wreck. Gin-houses, packing screws, granary—all lay in ashes. Not a fence was to be seen for miles … the army had turned their stock into the fields and destroyed what they had not carried off. Burning cotton and grain filled the air with smoke, and even the sun seemed to hide its face" (Davis 1988 [1980], p. 86). Another Southern women offered a similarly mournful account of a grim visit from Union cavalry. "They fed their horses at M's barn, ripping off the planks that the corn might roll out," she recalled.

> The door was opened by the overseer, but that was too slow a way for thieves and robbers. While they were filling the wagons, four officers went over every part of the house, even the drawers and trunks. These men wore the trappings of officers! While I write, I have six wagons in view at my brother's barn, taking off his corn, and the choice spirits accompanying them are catching the sheep and carrying them off. This robbery now goes on every day. (Davis 2007, p. 204)

Whatever the moral implications of this predation on civilian resources, however, the practice of foraging and looting undoubtedly accelerated the South's reluctant course toward surrender. This fact alone convinced many Union commanders and privates alike that "hard war" played an important and ultimately beneficial role in bringing the destructive war to a close.

BIBLIOGRAPHY

Brobst, John F. *Well, Mary: Civil War Letters of a Wisconsin Volunteer*, ed. Margaret Brobst Roth. Madison: University of Wisconsin Press, 1960.

Casler, John O. *Four Years in the Stonewall Brigade*, 2nd rev. ed. Girard, KS: Appeal Publishing Company, 1906.

Coddington, Edwin B. *The Gettysburg Campaign: A Study in Command*. New York: Simon and Schuster, 1997.

Davis, Burke. *Sherman's March*. New York: Random House, 1980. Reprint, New York: Vintage Books, 1988.

Davis, William C. and James I. Robertson. *Virginia at War, 1862*. Lexington: University Press of Kentucky, 2007.

Glatthaar, Joseph T. *The March to the Sea and Beyond: Sherman's Troops in the Savannah and Carolinas Campaigns*. New York: New York University Press, 1985.

Hutton, Paul Andrew. *Phil Sheridan and his Army*. Norman: University of Oklahoma Press, 1999.

Kennett, Lee B. *Marching through Georgia: The Story of Soldiers and Civilians during Sherman's Campaign*. New York: HarperCollins, 1995.

Linderman, Gerald F. *Embattled Courage: The Experience of Combat in the American Civil War*. New York: Free Press, 1987.

Meyers, Augustus. *Ten Years in the Ranks, U.S. Army*. New York: Stirling Press, 1914. Reprint, New York: Arno Press, 1979.

Mitchell, Reid. *Civil War Soldiers: Their Expectations and Their Experiences*. New York: Viking, 1988.

Nevin, David, and the editors of Time-Life Books. *Sherman's March: Atlanta to the Sea*. New York: Time-Life, 1986.

Robertson, James I., Jr. *Soldiers Blue and Gray*. Columbia, SC: University of South Carolina Press, 1988.

Royster, Charles. *The Destructive War: William Tecumseh Sherman, Stonewall Jackson, and the Americans*. New York: Knopf, 1991.

Simpson, Brooks D. *Sherman's Civil War*. Chapel Hill: University of North Carolina Press, 1999.

Starr, Stephen Z. *Union Cavalry in the Civil War: The War in the West, 1861–1865*. Baton Rouge: Louisiana State University Press, 1985.

Thomas, Dianne Stine, and the editors of Time-Life Books. *Brother against Brother: Time-Life Books History of the Civil War*. New York: Time-Life, 1990.

Walters, John Bennett. *Merchant of Terror: General Sherman and Total War*. Indianapolis: Bobbs-Merrill, 1973.

Kevin Hillstrom

■ Interaction between Soldiers and Civilians

Relations between Civil War soldiers and civilians—both on the home front and during incursions into enemy territory—became progressively more strained as the long and bloody war dragged on. In the former case, many soldiers in both the Northern and Southern armies became angry with people back home who second-guessed strategic decisions or, in the view of some troops, did not fully appreciate the sacrifices they were making. These feelings intensified as the celebratory aspect of the war's early months faded and the comforting ties to hearth and home came to feel more tenuous.

Soldiers and Civilians Back Home

The psychological well-being of most Civil War soldiers was grounded in two beliefs that sustained them even during the grimmest moments of the conflict. The first of these beliefs was in the fundamental justness of the cause for which they were fighting. The second was the conviction that their sacrifices were respected and valued by the family, friends, and communities that they had left behind.

Visible gestures of appreciation and respect for Yankee and Rebel soldiers were in abundance in the early stages of the Civil War. Many regiments of patriotic volunteers were sent off to war with the cheers of fellow citizens ringing in their ears. Indeed, spirited public celebrations of their bravery and impending victory were commonplace in both the South and the North. Countless memoirs, letters, and newspaper accounts from the period attest to the carnival-like atmosphere that marked the departure of excited troops. And as the troops moved through the countryside, spontaneous celebrations of their progress erupted in myriad appreciative communities.

As the months passed, though, and the conflict became a grim deadlock, the novelty of the Federal and Confederate uniforms faded away in both regions. Instead, civilians quite naturally became preoccupied with daily routines and—in the South especially—the mounting challenges of providing food and other basic necessities for children and the elderly. More significantly, soldiers became increasingly cognizant of grumbling on the home front from disillusioned civilians who recognized that the optimistic assurances of imminent victory that they had heard at the war's outset had been in error.

By the war's midpoint, some Yankee and Rebel troops experienced a growing sense, reflected palpably in their memoirs and correspondence, of alienation from civilians. These men, many of whom had endured horrific battles, unsatisfying rations, and exhausting months of exposure to the elements, became convinced that people back home had no conception of what they were enduring. Further, some of them came to feel that the civilians for whom they were putting their lives on the line were a singularly ungrateful and cowardly lot. "I hate and despise [the] puny cravens at home, whose fears make them tremble at shadows," fumed one Union officer with the 5th New Jersey in mid-1862. "These poltroons deserve the scorn of all true patriots" (Acton 1965, pp. 37–38).

Special contempt also was reserved for critics of the war itself (such as the "Copperheads" in the North and "Tories" in the South) and for civilians who criticized the way in which the war was being prosecuted. As one disillusioned Confederate soldier wrote in a letter home,

> I saw a gentleman who left DeSoto Parish about two weeks since. He says the old men at home are all generals now—gather in groups in the little towns over there and talk about the war and discuss the abilities of our Generals—Know more than any of them—Except General Lee only—They admit him to be a great man, but all the others do wrong all the time. Our soldiers have all come to the conclusion that they have no friends out of the army except the ladies. (Mitchell 1988, p. 67)

During the last two years of the war, the alienation that some Rebel and Yankee soldiers felt from their countrymen and countrywomen back home was so profound that they felt, ironically enough, greater kinship with enemy soldiers—who, after all, had endured many of the same hardships and tribulations that they had.

Soldiers and Civilians in Enemy Territory

Interactions between Civil War soldiers and civilians of the opposition changed dramatically during the course of the conflict. During the first two years of the war, military commanders and enlisted men alike saw the civilian population as "off-limits," and foraging among the civilian population was officially prohibited in both armies.

These prohibitions proved increasingly difficult to enforce as the war progressed, however. In 1862 and 1863, when General Robert E. Lee led invasions into Maryland and Pennsylvania, Lee's troops were astounded by the wealth they encountered as they moved through the countryside—wealth in the form of vast fields of thriving wheat, long expanses of rich pastureland, and impressive buildings of stone and brick. A fair amount of foraging and "living off the land" occurred during these incursions, in part because Lee had no supply lines connecting his army to Southern supply centers. Moreover, all blacks captured by the invading Rebels were shipped south for enslavement.

Yankee troops, for their part, were unimpressed by Northerners' largely passive response to invasion. They chafed at reports that some civilians were assuring Rebel troops that they were Copperheads, as well as at accounts that most Northerners displayed greater measures of curiosity or fear than defiance when confronted by enemy soldiers. Indeed, Lee's progress through Pennsylvania was met with very little civilian resistance. By contrast, Yankee troops moving through the South during this same time had learned to be wary of guerrillas lurking among the civilian populace. The regional contrast in civilian response to invasion was both stark and dismaying to Union soldiers. "They [Confederate forces] ride through Penna. Without molestation—while we cannot go a hundred yards outside of the picket line without being fired at," complained one Union soldier (Mitchell 1988, p. 152).

Northern Soldiers in the South

The vast majority of the conflict took place in the South. Northern communities, for the most part, did not have to worry about enemy soldiers showing up on their doorstep—although occasional eruptions of violence such as the July 1864 burning of Chambersburg, Pennsylvania, at the hands of Confederate troops under the command of General John McCausland ranked as dramatic exceptions to this rule.

Franklin County Court House.   In the early years of the Civil War, both Northern and Southern soldiers generally refrained from abusing the private property of opposing citizens. By 1864, however, soldiers had become hardened by vicious fighting and set out to consume anything of value that could be used to help the enemy side.   *The Library of Congress*

In many parts of the South, meanwhile, enemy troops—or the threat thereof—became a pervasive presence. This state of affairs would not have been so frightening and unnerving for Southern civilians if the rules of military-civilian interaction were as they had been in 1861. By 1864, however, these rules had changed. The horrors of war had hardened Union soldiers and stripped away some of the inhibitions that had previously constrained their willingness to engage in looting and foraging. More importantly, Union commanders such as General Philip Sheridan (1831–1888) and General William T. Sherman

(1820–1891) embraced military policies explicitly designed to punish Southern civilians for the transgressions of the Confederacy as a whole. Rather than tolerating Looting, Union armies actively encouraged it as a way to bring the secessionists to their knees and bring the war to an end.

The response of Northern soldiers to this so-called "hard war" against Confederate women, children, and elderly varied considerably. "This thing of foraging is hard for a bashful young man," admitted one Union soldier. "The old women storm, the young women cry, beg, entreat that you will not take their subsistence, but it must

Saying goodbye. Though a serious event, during the early stages of the Civil War, townspeople often celebrated as they sent their soldiers to fight. As the war progressed, however, citizens became more concerned with providing for themselves in the absence of so many fathers and husbands, and less excited about seeing their departure. *© North Wind Picture Archives*

be done and you have to turn a deaf ear to every plea" (Mitchell 1988, p. 175). A Northern officer was even more succinct, writing that "we take everything from the people without remorse" (Kennett 1995, p. 236).

This formal sanctioning of foraging was ruthless, but it was also effective, especially as Union military victories over valiant but overmatched Confederate forces became more frequent and decisive. By early 1865 large swaths of the South had been burned or looted by Union armies, and civilian support for continuing the war had plummeted. As one resident of Columbia, South Carolina, stated to a Union officer after Northern troops captured the city in February 1865, "Sir, every life that is now lost in this war is murder; murder, sir. We have fought you bravely, but

our strength is exhausted; we have no resources; we have no more men. The contest was unequal. You have conquered us, and it is best to submit and make wise use of the future" (Nichols 1865, p. 172).

BIBLIOGRAPHY

Acton, Edward. " 'Dear Molly': Letters of Captain Edward A. Acton to His Wife, 1862." *Pennsylvania Magazine of History and Biography* 89 (1965).

Ash, Stephen. *When the Yankees Came: Conflict and Chaos in the Occupied South.* Chapel Hill, NC: The University of North Carolina Press, 1999.

Coddington, Edwin B. *The Gettysburg Campaign: A Study in Command.* New York: Simon and Schuster, 1997.

Glatthaar, Joseph T. *The March to the Sea and Beyond: Sherman's Troops in the Savannah and Carolinas Campaigns.* New York: New York University Press, 1985.

Grimsley, Mark. *The Hard Hand of War: Union Military Policy toward Southern Civilians, 1860–1865.* New York: Cambridge University Press, 1997.

Kennett, Lee B. *Marching through Georgia: The Story of Soldiers and Civilians during Sherman's Campaign.* New York: HarperCollins, 1995.

Linderman, Gerald F. *Embattled Courage: The Experience of Combat in the American Civil War.* New York: Free Press, 1987.

McPherson, James M. *For Cause and Comrades: Why Men Fought in the Civil War.* New York: Oxford University Press, 1997.

Mitchell, Reid. *Civil War Soldiers: Their Expectations and Their Experiences.* New York: Viking, 1988.

Nichols, George Ward. *The Story of the Great March: From the Diary of a Staff Officer.* New York: Harper & Brothers Publishers, 1865.

Kevin Hillstrom

◾ Resistance

Civilian resistance to enemy soldiers operating in their midst was an important factor in the South during the second half of the Civil War. In contrast to the North, which experienced only brief invasions by Southern forces in 1863 and 1864—many regions in the South grappled with the presence of enemy soldiers in the vicinity on a regular basis for the duration of the war. Clashes between Union troops and Southern civilians intensified during this period, and in many instances, civilian resistance took violent form. Those who took up arms to smite the Yankee invaders believed in the rightness of their cause, but in the end their activities brought more suffering to the South. Historians believe that their guerrilla actions further hardened the harsh Union attitude toward Southern civilians and private property during the latter stages of the war.

Ruins in Richmond, Virginia. With much of the fighting occurring in the South, the civilian population often came in direct contact with Union troops. Some of them, eager to see the soldiers leave quickly, cooperated with the men in blue, though others engaged in guerrilla warfare, earning the ire of Northern soldiers. © *Corbis*

Defending the Heartland

The majority of Southern civilians adopted passive or cooperative attitudes when forced to interact with Northern units. Many Southern families and communities, their ranks greatly thinned by the Confederate Army's desperate appetite for healthy young white men, simply wanted to do whatever was necessary to get the enemy soldiers moving on. Acts of defiance were not likely to accomplish this goal. Furthermore, most understood that resistance or shows of hostility would likely serve only to provoke greater destruction. "Most women understood that when the enemy appeared, any hostile or provocative gesture on their part could cost them heavily—thus a woman who rushed out and cut her own well rope as thirsty Northern soldiers came through her gate could well have her house burned by the furious bluecoats" (Kennett 1995, p. 298).

In some areas of the South, in fact, acts of sabotage or violence against Federal troops in the region was strongly opposed by the majority of community members. They reasoned that partisan acts of resistance would keep the invaders in the area longer as they sought to apprehend the culprits. And the longer that an enemy army stayed in an area, the more resources it would consume. Writing in *Marching through Georgia* (1995), historian Lee B. Kennett recounts at least one instance in which Southerners were so angered by a local man's decision to burn a bridge in the path of Union troops—thus delaying their departure from the region—that community members set fire to his home and fields.

Nonetheless, many Southerners embraced guerrilla activity when Federal troops entered their lands. Guerillas operated either as members of spontaneously formed groups, or as part of already-existing home guard or militia units (Linderman 1987, p. 196). The first notable instances in which guerilla activity occurred came during the 1862 Peninsula campaign in Virginia, and ambushes, sniper attacks, acts of sabotage, and other forms of "irregular warfare" became more frequent from that point forward. Most of these rifle-toting defenders of the Southland lacked formal military training, and the squirrel rifles and other modest firearms at their disposal limited their ability to inflict significant casualties on the enemy. But their familiarity with the local terrain, their implacable hatred for the invading Yankees, and their ability to melt into the general population combined to make them a force to be reckoned with in some districts.

Union concerns about Southern irregulars further intensified when it became clear that Confederate authorities were sanctioning—and in some cases providing material support to—some guerrilla activity. The most notable instance of official government assistance to irregulars came in the region of Virginia that came to be known as "Mosby's Confederacy," in homage to the charismatic John Singleton Mosby and his guerrilla followers.

Rooting Out the Guerrillas

Confederate partisans viewed their actions as noble and valorous acts of defiance against an oppressive foe. Ordinary soldiers in the Northern ranks, however, harbored a much different view of these resisters. Seizing on the dominant methodologies of the partisans—bushwhackings, sniper attacks, nighttime arson attacks, and the like—Yankee troops overwhelmingly described the guerrillas as cowardly and amoral. They also saw these partisan activities as a violation of basic tenets of war.

It did not take long for Union commanders and soldiers alike to see all local civilians as potential enemies. This evolving view of civilians made it much easier for Union soldiers to rationalize their looting and destruction of Southern households and personal property. The increasingly ruthless behavior of the federal army in turn prompted new acts of bushwhacking and sabotage from outraged partisans. A spiraling cycle of violence thus came into being, and it became more powerful with each act of partisan sabotage or Union attack on Southern property. Inevitably, Southerners who were innocent of any acts of hostility against Union soldiers sometimes suffered at the hands of angry and suspicious Yankees.

An Unstoppable Tide

Confederate guerrilla activity against Union troops was most sustained during Union General William T. Sherman's notorious "March to the Sea" in 1864 and early 1865. During this march, as Sherman's army cut a wide and destructive path through the heart of the Confederacy, bands of Confederate partisans bedeviled the enemy force in their midst through sniper attacks, attacks on bridges and trestles, sabotage of railroad tracks and telegraph wires, and raids on supply depots and other outposts. These actions never threatened to derail Sherman's march, but they did constitute an annoying nuisance. "Our armies traverse the land," Sherman fumed, "and the waves of disaffection, sedition and crime close in behind as our track disappears" (Kennett 1995, p. 98).

Determined to reverse this state of affairs and punish the South for its stubborn resistance, Sherman embraced the idea of neutralizing guerrilla activity in captured territory through the deportation of agitators and irreconcilables. This policy of displacement of sympathizers of Confederate guerrillas actually originated while Sherman commanded Memphis in the fall of 1862, in retaliation for sniping at Union steamboats. From mid-1864 forward, Union forces moving through Confederate lands expelled thousands of people from their homes. Most were deported to locales in the North, where it was thought that their poisonous attitudes would be so diluted as to render them harmless. By some accounts an estimated 20,000 Southerners were unloaded at the harbor in Cairo, Illinois, without any provision for their shelter or other needs. Other Union commanders adopted similarly harsh measures to address the guerrilla issue. Union General Ulysses S. Grant, for example, became so fed up with Mosby's predations that he ordered the arrest of all men under fifty living in Loudon County—the heart of Mosby's Confederacy.

Rank-and-file Union soldiers were largely supportive of these measures. Rebel troops, though, expressed profound disgust at the Union Army's increased use of "hard war" tactics to smash partisan activity and destroy the will of Southern civilians. "I try to restrain my bitterness," wrote one member of Stonewall Jackson's famed Stonewall Brigade. "[But] it is an insult to civilization and to God to pretend that the Laws of War justify such warfare" (Douglas 1940, pp. 315–316).

BIBLIOGRAPHY

Douglas, Henry Kyd. *I Rode with Stonewall.* Chapel Hill: University of North Carolina Press, 1940.

Glatthaar, Joseph T. *The March to the Sea and Beyond: Sherman's Troops in the Savannah and Carolinas Campaigns.* New York: New York University Press, 1985.

Grimsley, Mark. *Hard Hand of War.* Cambridge, UK: Cambridge University Press, 1997.

Kennett, Lee B. *Marching through Georgia: The Story of Soldiers and Civilians during Sherman's Campaign.* New York: HarperCollins, 1995.

Linderman, Gerald F. *Embattled Courage: The Experience of Combat in the American Civil War.* New York: Free Press, 1987.

Mitchell, Reid. *Civil War Soldiers: Their Expectations and Their Experiences.* New York: Viking, 1988.

Robertson, James I., Jr. *Soldiers Blue and Gray.* Columbia, SC: University of South Carolina Press, 1988.

Royster, Charles. *The Destructive War: William Tecumseh Sherman, Stonewall Jackson, and the Americans.* New York: Knopf, 1991.

Woodworth, Steven E. *Nothing but Victory: The Army of the Tennessee, 1861–1865.* New York: Vintage, 2006.

Kevin Hillstrom

Family and Community

Family and Community Overview

The Civil War put unique strains and pressures on American families and communities, and yet what the war changed was hardly more noticeable than what it left the same. Sometimes the war brought subtle changes in the way Americans thought about family and community relationships. At other times the stresses of war served only to show how resilient and durable were the ties that bound American society together in a densely woven network of families and communities.

It was in part the presence of strong family ties that has enabled scholars to know as much as they do about the Civil War. When the soldiers—by war's end some three million of them—went off to fight, most of them suffered severe homesickness. They sought to assuage that malady by writing long and frequent letters, and they exhorted family members back home to write equally frequent letters in return. Many of these letters have been preserved, especially those from the soldiers to those who had remained at home. Taken together, all of these letters have told historians much about life in the nineteenth century.

Family life during the Civil War era was influenced by the prevailing cultural domestic ideal, celebrating the home as a refuge from the cares of the world. Women's literature of the time encouraged wives to make their homes pleasant and comfortable places for their husbands and children. Talk of the war raging in the country hardly surfaced at all in such publications as its concerns played no part in the shaping of the ideal home. The nineteenth-century domestic ideal made women the chief agents of civilizing mankind, lifting aspirations and encouraging attentiveness to spiritual concerns.

The war, however, also placed new stresses on domestic life. Even in the North, women found themselves in some cases pressed into tasks they had not previously performed, including farm labor. An anonymous 1862 songwriter celebrated the willingness of Northern women to undertake such work in order to free their men for military service: "Then take your gun and go," says the patriotic wife in the song, "Yes, take your gun and go, For Ruth can drive the oxen, John, And I can use the hoe." Wives and daughters took on the extra labor as a form of service to their country and as a necessity of life with their normal breadwinners gone. It was a temporary expedient, gladly relinquished when the war ended.

Yet home life was not all misery during the war, especially in the North. Workingmen on the home front fared tolerably well. Although wartime inflation totaled as much as 100 percent, incomes for many workers (although notably not soldiers) kept pace or even gained ground in the midst of a wartime economic boom. Some women, at least, read parts of the extensive literature on how to make their home ideal, and many no doubt strove to implement some of the suggestions. Children could enjoy a small but growing selection of books and periodicals in the relatively new genre of children's literature, some of which strove to explain the war to young minds in simple terms. Many children, like their parents, enjoyed the comfort and encouragement of religion, as the Sunday school movement was in full swing during the mid-nineteenth century and did not slow down during the war. Many adults attended the services of local churches or synagogues.

The pressures on Southern domestic life were far greater than those in the North, because the South was the scene of most of the war's fighting. Like their Northern counterparts, Southern women had to undertake unfamiliar tasks in the absence of husbands. For some Southern women—a minority—the war brought enemy soldiers directly into their neighborhoods with attendant loss of livestock and food supplies. Even beyond the reach of the armies, the families of Confederate soldiers suffered severely in the absence of breadwinners, and because the Confederate government was woefully in arrears with its soldiers' pay, the families simply had to get by as best they could. Because the Confederacy chose to finance its war largely by printing more money, massive inflation swept the South, creating economic hardship and prompting even the government to resort to demanding payment in kind rather than in cash when it levied taxes. Hunger in several of the South's cities, including Richmond, led to bread riots. By the end of the war, letters from wives throughout the South to their soldier husbands in the field often urged the men to come home even if returning meant desertion.

Of course the war meant something entirely different for slave men, women, and children throughout the South. Though the conflict ultimately brought their freedom, it could also bring hardship for former slaves who fled their plantations to follow the Union armies to freedom. The army lacked the means and in some cases the desire to care for the freedpeople, and the former slaves often suffered much from hunger and exposure. Arriving in the so-called contraband camps set up by the federal Freedmen's Bureau might have brought some relief, but conditions for black families could still be difficult there. Nevertheless, they were free. For many former slaves the first priority upon obtaining their freedom was to search for family members previously separated by sale. For slave families that remained on the plantation throughout the war and were located outside the zone of the armies' operations—as many were—the conflict brought little change to the unrelenting routine of labor for men, women, and children.

In short, as the essays that follow illustrate in many ways, the Civil War brought novel circumstances and new stresses for some families but left many others in the enjoyment of more or less the same style of life they had known before the guns opened fire at Fort Sumter in April 1861.

Steven E. Woodworth

■ The Domestic Ideal

THE DOMESTIC IDEAL: AN OVERVIEW

The mid-nineteenth-century domestic ideal as espoused in the popular women's press saw the home as a sacred refuge from military and political upheavals. A well-kept home was also the source of the nation's strength. For, as an editorial in the *New York Evangelist* noted, "the

Family dinner in camp. Wealthier women in the North and South often used additional help in running their households. Affluent Northern families could generally afford to hire servants to assist with domestic labors, while Southern slaveholding families typically relied on house slaves to perform tasks such as cooking, cleaning, and serving meals. *© Corbis*

more they [housewives] can build up at the domestic hearth a reverence for family and social amenities, the more solid will be the foundation upon which the Republic is built" ("The Home," June 27, 1861, p. 7). A "cheerless home" is "no home at all in the true sense of the word," the Evangelist admonished, "whilst a Home that is imbued with the sentiment of domesticity will be quitted with regret, and returned to with rejoicing" (p. 7). "[I]n the midst of the troubles that environ us," the article concludes, "cultivate the Home, adorn it neatly within, adorn it tastefully without . . . then draw the family around the substantial board, treat every member kindly, accept your lot in life with a reverential spirit, and thank God for a happy Home" (p. 7).

The American domestic ideal was patterned after the British one—in both countries, the culture of domesticity arose from Utilitarian and Evangelical philosophies that idealized the home. Historians cite the industrial revolution as a root cause of this new focus: The more work and home became separate spheres, the more home life was idealized. Also significant was the growth of a well-off middle class that could afford to make the home a comfortable retreat.

The nineteenth century also saw a new focus on the separateness of male and female realms. Women were seen as dominating the private sphere of home and the parts of society that touched on the domestic sphere, whereas men were thought to properly dominate the public sphere of work and politics. The public sphere could be bruising, and in the nineteenth century women were fashioned into domestic angels, whose duty it was to soothe, regenerate, and morally improve their husbands—and by extension the nation. Women dominated the private sphere by maintaining discipline, enforcing frugality, and upholding cleanliness.

Throughout the war, publications such as *Godey's Lady's Book* and various newspapers and magazines—*Flag of Our Union, Ohio Cultivator, Southern Cultivator*, and *Ballou's Dollar Magazine*, to name but a few—ran articles about the proper management of the domestic sphere. *Godey's*, in particular, had an enormous circulation and was enjoyed by women all over America.

Many articles in the women's press concentrated on newlyweds. For example, a two-part article that ran in the December 1860 and January 1861 issues of *Godey's* offered advice first to new husbands, then to new wives. It declared that a well-bred and well-trained woman was a prudent creature who would use "cleverness...[to] economize, and endeavor to abridge her expenses; sitting down with such cheerfulness to her scanty meal... concealing their poverty from the world and endeavoring to gild it over with genteel and respectable appearance" ("A Whisper to a Newly-Married Pair. A Whisper to the Husband on Expenditure," p. 503).

It was imperative for a new wife to be a good housekeeper; otherwise, problems in the home might develop. "A Young Wife's Sorrow," a humorous article by T. S. Arthur published in July 1861 in the *American Phrenological Journal*, focused on one newlywed with poor housekeeping skills. This woman, named Martha, had been experiencing difficulties in her marriage of several months. When Martha's mother came to visit, hoping to grasp the source of her daughter's marital troubles, she realized immediately that "the basis of the difficulty lay in the total unfitness of Martha for the position she had assumed—that of housekeeper....[I]n consequence [of her failings] her young husband, in whose ideal of home perfect order had been included, found everything so different from his anticipation, that his grateful acquiescence was impossible" (p. 6). With her mother's help, Martha came to realize "that in holding herself above domestic duties and manipulations, she was governed more by pride and indolence, than a just regard for wifely or womanly dignity." She now understood that "to hold fast to her husband's love, she must do something more for him than offer loving words;

for, life being real and earnest, demands earnest work from all" (p. 6). In the end, Martha becomes the picture of the domestic ideal, and made her house into a Home.

The lack of preparation for domestic duty exhibited by some newly married women was not solely their own fault. It was also the fault, Arthur declared, of mothers who "bring up their daughters to listless, lounging, ladyhood, attending themselves to all the cares and drudgery of domestic affairs, and when their daughters marry, though they may be versed in music, light literature, ornamental artistic idle-work, they know literally nothing of those *realities of the home*" (p. 6). Daughters should instead be given the opportunity to play house and occasionally take charge in their childhood homes, Arthur asserted, so that they may learn the necessary skills before they become wives.

Many other cautionary tales of wives who disappointed and embarrassed themselves in front of family and friends were recounted in newspapers and magazines that targeted a female readership. Whether it was a wife's inability to organize and govern her home, her negligence in managing her servants, or her squandering of money and resources, such failings were always painted in a harsh light: No woman should act as such women did.

Economy was the cornerstone of the nineteenth century domestic ideal. As the May 7, 1864, edition of the *Friends' Intelligencer* averred, "as a rule, the financial success of any family depends more upon the economy of the wife than upon the earnings or business income of the husband" (p. 141). Columns advised readers on such matters as how to make cheap coffee, stew prunes, cure scurvy, and even make a "Cheap and Excellent Ink" by mixing bi-chromate of potash with logwood extract (*Southern Cultivator*, May 1861, p. 167). An article entitled "Yankee Economics—Pork and Beans," published in the August 1, 1861, edition of the *Ohio Cultivator*, made it clear how much thought was required for true economy. A Mr. Blood of Waltham, Massachusetts, the article informed readers, "will call at the houses of all those who will send word to him, on Saturday afternoons, and take their beans, bake them nicely, and return them early on Sunday morning, for the small sum of six cents" (p. 251). Why was it that the wives of Waltham did not cook their own beans, the *Cultivator* asked rhetorically? Economy was the answer:

> [T]o cook beans well, as well as they are always cooked for Sunday dinners in New England, requires many hours of steady heat; and in families where only a small cooking stove is used, this would be expensive; too much wood and too much time in attending to them would be consumed....[I]t would be poor economy for them to be troubled about the beans, when sixpence will bring them nicely baked up on the table, smoking hot, browned to a *t*. (p. 251)

The June 1864 edition of *Dollar Monthly Magazine* tried to convince the reader that soup can provide a healthful and pleasantly filling meal, as well as an economical one: "[A] Frenchman can make a soup out of materials which some of our housewives would scorn, and commit to the offal barrel, and in fact is sufficient to show us that we have much to learn if we would live well and economically at the same time" ("Soup as an Article of Food," p. 500).

Some female authors attempted to counter popular conceptions of domesticity. In the March 2, 1861, edition of the *Flag of Our Union*, for example, Sarah Soewell commented that men who wrote housekeeping guides "seem to think that one word covers the whole ground and that is—work" (p. 4). Soewell, however, was not rebelling against the life of the housewife; she merely sought to rationalize it: Anyone could "do the hard, rough work, but not every one [sic] can plan it rightly; and this planning, management, or whatever you please to call it, is the grand secret of perfect housekeeping" (p. 4).

Besides making a home, a wife was also supposed to cultivate her mental faculties. As J. Atwood wrote in "Advice to Young Women," published in the February 26, 1863, edition of the *Christian Advocate and Journal*, a young wife should not merely look after her household's economy, manage the servants, and work industriously in the home—she should also further her education. After all, women "hold the destinies of the world in a measure in their hands; for the training and fireside education we all receive is principally from mothers....[If a woman's] mind and heart are not properly trained, how can she train her child!" (p. 67). In order to accomplish their betterment, women were to exercise "the mind and heart...by reading, meditation, and prayer," so that their minds become "stored with valuable ideas and useful information" (p. 67). Furthermore, this improvement of the mental faculties would also make a wife a better helpmeet for her husband, for "a sensible young man desires for a wife a lady of some intelligence; one whom he can converse on various subjects" (p. 67).

In order not to jeopardize the work she performed throughout the day to make the home a tranquil and orderly retreat, the housewife was charged with keeping her temper, even if her husband did not show her the same kindness. The good wife and homemaker was always to be amiable and pleasing to her husband, despite any flaws she might perceive in him. J. Atwood, in the *Christian Advocate and Journal* article mentioned above, counseled women to "attend, also, to your spirit and manner in your daily intercourse with those around you, and with whom you mingle in life[;]...be pleasant and cheerful, kind and sweet-tempered...never suffer yourself to be angry" (February 26, 1863, p. 67). An article in the April 1861 edition of *Godey's* called on young wives to "strain every nerve, use constant prayer

for strength and power to become really a helpmeet, really a companion, really a helper-on, really a guardian angel in human guise to husband and children" ("Domestic Management," April 1861, p. 313). Especially in the beginning of a marriage, after the blinders of courtship have been removed, counseled the author of "Ladies on the Point of Marriage" in the May 1862 edition of *Godey's*, a wife should recall that

> your tact, your best good humor, must be exerted....[T]he admiring man on whom you have bestowed your hand will be too much gratified in observing this conduct not to meet it more than halfway, own perhaps his hasty remark, kiss off a soft, indignant tear, and mutual forgiveness of each early petty offence may prevent the growth of many a future grievance. (p. 456)

Women were encouraged to look at their own behavior if they were unhappily married. According to the March 1864 edition of *Godey's*, the fault could be the woman's own:

> When I see a woman, with that beautiful countenance which has won the heart of her husband, darkened by a frown, constantly fretting and making all about her uncomfortable...I am tempted to exclaim 'Hush, dear woman, these useless, sinful repinings! Examine yourself, perchance the blame lies at your own door after all....[T]here is a talisman possessing a magic charm that will scatter all these evils...it is cheerfulness. ("Don't Fret," p. 252).

This, then, was the burden the domestic ideal placed on women. Not only were they charged with creating a sacred and orderly refuge from the outside world, they were also held responsible should any disharmony intrude. In the real world, of course, women did the best they could to run their households, feeling alternately inspired and oppressed by the images of ideal womanhood their society held up for them to emulate.

BIBLIOGRAPHY

Arthur, T. S. "A Young Wife's Sorrow." *American Phrenological Journal* 34, no. 1 (1861): 6–8.

Atwood, J. "Advice to Young Women." *Christian Advocate and Journal* 38, no. 9 (1863): 43.

Blunt, Alison. "Imperial Geographies of Home: British Domesticity in India, 1886–1925." *Transactions of the Institute of British Geographers*, n.s., 24, no. 4 (1999): 421–440.

"Cheap and Excellent Ink." *Southern Cultivator* 19, no. 5 (1861): 69.

"Domestic Management." *Godey's Lady's Book* 62 (April 1861): 313.

"Don't Fret." *Godey's Lady's Book* 68 (March 1864): 252.

Gage, Frances D. "Home Department: Ways of a Good Housekeeper." *Ohio Cultivator* 17, no. 2 (1861): 60.

Gage, Frances D. "Yankee Economics—Pork and Beans." *Ohio Cultivator* 17, no. 8 (1861): 251.

"The Home." *New York Evangelist* 32, no. 26 (1861): 7.

"Ladies on the Point of Marriage." *Godey's Lady's Book* 64 (May 1862): 456.

Nobel, Thomas, et al. *Western Civilization: The Continuing Experiment.* Boston: Houghton Mifflin, 2005.

"Small Leaks in the Household Ship." *Friends' Intelligencer* 21, no. 9 (1864): 141.

"Soup as an Article of Food." *Dollar Monthly Magazine* 9, no. 6 (1864): 500.

Sowell, Mrs. Sarah S. "Good Housekeeping." *Flag of Our Union* 16, no. 9 (1861): 4.

"A Whisper to a Newly-Married Pair. A Whisper to the Husband on Expenditure." *Godey's Lady's Book* 61 (December 1860): 503.

"A Whisper to a Newly-Married Pair. A Whisper to the Wife." *Godey's Lady's Book* 62 (January 1861): 27.

Zlotnick, Susan. "Domesticating Imperialism: Curry and Cookbooks in Victorian England." *Frontiers: A Journal of Women Studies* 16, nos. 2–3 (1996): 51–68.

Micki Waldrop

NORTHERN DOMESTIC LIFE

The upheaval of the Civil War was not confined to politics, the military sphere, and the economy; the home front—domestic life—was just as affected as the other aspects of national life. In the North, this meant that some women stepped into the shoes of male relatives who were away fighting, while others found alternative methods to support the war effort.

Women in Agriculture

Women on Northern farms were forced by circumstances to go beyond their traditional domestic duties—providing their families with a comfortable home, provisioning and preserving food for the winter, caring for animals and attending small kitchen gardens—and became full-scale farmers. With many able-bodied men away at war, farmers' wives and daughters plowed fields and planted and harvested crops. Luckily, they were not alone in their efforts, as they were able to turn to other women in the area for support. For example, the *Lowell (MA) Daily Citizen* for October 16, 1862, relates that "Mrs. H. Beard and Mrs. C. Beard of Waterville, Lamoille county, Vt., whose husbands have both gone to the war, having harvested the corn raised on their farms, made a 'husking bee,' and invited some eight or ten of the women of the neighborhood, and husked out some thirty of forty bushels of ears" (n.p.).

Many did not like the idea of female farmers, however, even during the Civil War; they saw these women as an affront to defined gender roles. One Mr. J. Talcott, for example, lamented the entrance of women into farm work as detrimental to their mental, physical, and social health. His opinion prompted various rebuttals from female farmers, such as a letter from Della Roberts published in the July 1863 issue of the *New England Farmer*, claiming that in three years of farming she had "never known it to have the slightest effect upon the minds of any whose friendship was worth having" (Roberts 1863, p. 229). According to Roberts's references to Talcott's letter, he was not completely adverse to women working outdoors; in fact, he advised country women to garden and ride on horseback in their free time. Taking a team of horses out to plow the fields, however, was too degrading and out of character for a woman—the crux of Talcott's argument.

In response to Talcott, Roberts remarks that according to detractors "women may do anything they please in the world that *amounts to nothing*" (p. 229). Men had monopolized almost all of the work that would enable women to earn a good living—but farming was one occupation that was not completely closed to them. However, when women started farming, people like Talcott "raised the frightful bear-in-the-corner of masculine women, vulgarity, ignorance, and all of the other bug-a-boos that are commonly used to frighten children" (p. 229). Roberts implies that she and her kind are not likely to be farmers for life, and insists that the lessons learned from farming will allow them to be "just as loveable, just as good, and watchful, and kind" as any other woman. Indeed, as the farmwoman "grows stronger and more healthy (as she cannot avoid doing), she will be more patient and far more competent to fulfill the office of wife and mother with credit to herself, and bring honor to her husband and children" (p. 229). While the Civil War does not enter into Roberts's argument, the war's effect on gender roles and expectations is implicit. Despite the Talcotts of the world, society at large during the war tacitly acknowledged the need for some women to step into traditionally masculine roles in order to survive. However, the gender status quo had to be maintained if only in thought; hence Roberts's assertion that farming would make women *better* wives and mothers.

Not all men were opposed to women working on farms. In the July 19, 1862, *Saturday Evening Post* article "Women Farmers," for example, an anonymous author marveled at the industry of the Roberts family women: Four daughters, one niece, and the mother, Paulina Roberts, all labored on the farm. It is not definitely known whether this family is the same as Della Roberts's family. In any case, the Roberts women "ploughed 75 acres, dragged 100 acres 3 times, sowed, broadcast 100, and rolled 100" (p. 8). The article notes that "housework is considered by them the hardest and most difficult to perform [;]...they all prefer out-door farm-work" (p. 8). The example set by the Roberts women, the author asserts, will cause some women to become "practical farmers; and ploughing, dragging, sowing, rolling, planting, hoeing and harvesting will become the pleasant, healthful and remunerative occupation of women as well as men" (p. 8).

Mechanization of agriculture helped many of the women farmers to perform their tasks, as Della Roberts points out in her letter to the *New England Farmer*: "Machinery has very much facilitated farming of late—so we are able to do a great deal of work without injury to ourselves" (Roberts 1863, p. 229). Machines like the reaper and the thresher not only made harvesting less labor-intensive, they allowed women to do twice as much in a day as their fathers had been able to do.

Urban Women: New Jobs and the War Effort

Upheaval of the status quo was not confined to the countryside; the cities too saw women stepping into the public workplace during the Civil War—left on their own to feed a family on soldiers' wages, many women had to find new ways to make ends meet. For women, work outside the home was mostly limited to teaching, sewing, office work, or work as a domestic. Women who worked out of necessity were not well paid for their toil. For example, one sewing woman described in an "appeal" from an anonymous female clerk published in the April 22, 1864, issue of the Boston *Liberator* "toiled from 7 a.m. to 9 p.m. [but] earned but nine and a half cents" (n.p.). The wages of the other seamstresses were also grievously inadequate: "[T]welve and a half cents was found to be more than the average, and eighteen cents a princely sum" (n.p.). Women who worked in offices were similarly underpaid. Nonetheless, the little bit of money such women managed to amass helped them survive. In addition, many women felt that their work was an expression of patriotism and contributed to the war effort.

At the beginning of the war, middle- and upper-class women—those who did not need to work—were expected to remain in the home. Northern women sewed, wrapped bandages, and helped raise money for the war effort. "Young creatures whose fingers have been too dainty all their lives long to do a useful thing," asserted an anonymous letter writer in the January 1863 issue of *Godey's Lady's Book*, "heartily...[entered] into the making of coarse shirts and drawers, and knitting coarse yarn for stockings...patiently and industriously working away, week after week, at common clothes and the making of comfortable garments for the sick and the wounded" ("Letter from a Lady of New England," p. 93). As the war raged on, however, middle- and upper-class women began to leave their homes to work directly or indirectly for the war effort.

Another letter published in *Godey's* in December 1862, argues that while society is "much averse to masculine women and to those who unsex themselves by assuming the privileges of men and pushing forward into man's work," there are nonetheless "occupations and professions in which women would be fully competent and which they can fulfil [*sic*] with propriety and efficiency" ("Letter from a Lady of Pennsylvania," p. 605). Women could be employed by the postal service, for example. This type of work alone would allow "thousands of mourning widows, bereaved mothers, daughters, and sister's left destitute of their natural protectors, by this wasting war...to sustain themselves and those dependant on them, [and] be useful to the community in which they reside" (p. 605).

Many women who were adamant about working directly for the war effort chose to become nurses. Some did so in response to Abraham Lincoln's 1861 communiqué "To the Loyal Women of America," which asked women to help the war effort by signing up to do volunteer work for the United States Sanitary Commission (USSC)—a department within the War Department. Although female nurses initially served on a volunteer basis with the USSC, the commission did begin to pay them salaries later in the war. Female nurses were largely welcomed into field hospitals, as before their arrival convalescing soldiers often had to help nurse those whose wounds were worse than their own. In his memoir *Leaves from the Diary of an Army Surgeon* (1863), Thomas Ellis commented that the arrival of women nurses "did much to alleviate the sufferings of the brave fellows....[When] their parched lips received the cup of tea, gruel or lemonade, or as in many cases, a stimulating drink, they were truly grateful and expressed their thanks to the lady nurses in a very flattering manner" (p. 71). All manner of women volunteered in wartime hospitals and after the war had ended they led the movement to open nursing schools for women.

BIBLIOGRAPHY

"An Appeal." *The Liberator* (Boston), April 22, 1864.

Ellis, Thomas T. *Leaves from the Diary of an Army Surgeon; or, Incidents of Field, Camp, and Hospital Life*. New York: J. Bradburn, 1863.

"Letter from a Lady of New England." *Godey's Lady's Book*, January 1863, p. 93.

"Letter from a Lady of Pennsylvania." *Godey's Lady's Book*, December 1862, p. 605.

Lowell (Mass.) *Daily Citizen and News*, October 16, 1862.

Roberts, Della A. "Woman Farming." *New England Farmer*, July 1863, p. 229.

United States Sanitary Commission. *To the Loyal Women of America*. Washington, DC: Author, 1861.

"Women Farmers." *Saturday Evening Post*, July 19, 1862, p. 8.

Micki Waldrop

SOUTHERN DOMESTIC LIFE

The magnitude of the destruction and devastation wrought by the Civil War infiltrated every aspect of American society and left few untouched by its horrors. The outbreak of war dramatically altered domestic relations in such a way that home life itself played a role in the outcome of the conflict. It was probably one of the many factors that contributed to Confederate desertion, which was in turn one of the many reasons for the Confederate defeat.

In the Confederacy, the home front was often touched directly by the realities of the battlefield; Southerners experienced the war in a way that most Northerners could not. As white Southern men left their families to fight, the structure of the family itself, which was central to the social order of the antebellum South, was altered for the duration of the war. Women and children were left to perform tasks previously done by men. The absence of the male coercive power that enforced the institution of slavery meant that the institution was under strain. Southern families also faced external pressures as a result of the war. Survival became a daily challenge for some families in the later stages of the war. The Northern blockade, which President Abraham Lincoln called for on April 19, 1861, forced families to come up with innovative substitutes for luxury goods, military supplies, and some of the familiar necessities of life. For example, elite white women who were used to purchasing fabric for their dresses, were now forced to rely on innovative substitutes, such as homespun cloth, which became a popular fashion statement of one's patriotism and devotion to the Confederacy. As the Confederate government implemented harsh policies deemed necessary to winning the war, many people worn down by hardship became bitter. They complained that their government favored the wealthy. While women helped sustain the war effort, the horrors and deprivations of the war disillusioned many of them. All of these internal problems ultimately contributed to the defeat of the Confederacy.

Historians' Views on Domestic Life in the South

While historians traditionally focused on major battles and leaders of the Civil War, in recent decades some have turned their attention to events on the home front as part of an attempt to explain at least part of the reason for the Confederacy's defeat. This emphasis on domestic life began in the 1970s with the work of such social historians as Drew Gilpin Faust, George Rable, Laura Edwards, and David Williams. Some scholars eventually argued that for the Confederacy, the war was lost on the home front long before the South's military defeat on the battlefield. Although this view is certainly not shared by all historians of the Civil War, an examination of

Southern woman whipping a field slave. With much of the white male population fighting the North, slave-owning women were forced to take charge of daily plantation operations, a task some cruelly fulfilled. *Snark/Art Resource, NY*

Southern domestic life is essential to understanding the American Civil War.

Gender Norms

The patriarchal society of the antebellum South depended on a carefully defined system of gender norms in which everyone had their place. The Southern social construct of manhood was based on the enslavement of blacks as well as on the simultaneous protection and subordination of women. White men controlled not only their families but also society as a whole. White women in turn defined themselves in relation to men—as wives, mothers, daughters, and, most importantly, as dependents. Although barred from leadership positions, most elite Southern white women were content with their social position and valued the security that the paternalistic hierarchy of the antebellum world provided; they were not closet feminists who opposed slavery or the paternalistic social structure. Feminism by and large was a Northern concept that had not taken hold in the South. Initially, white men and women alike ardently supported the Confederacy because they believed that the North threatened the security of their respective social positions. Men enlisted to protect their position as freemen, whereas women encouraged men to fight to protect their own privileged positions in society. The irony of this situation is that the decision to go to war ended up causing Southern gender ideals to be weakened during the duration of the war as women were temporarily forced to take on new leadership roles in the absence of men.

The Outbreak of War

The Civil War officially began with the shelling of Fort Sumter on April 12, 1861, and Lincoln's call for 75,000 troops the following day. Excitement and enthusiasm for the Confederacy spread like wildfire throughout the South. White men throughout the South flocked to join the Confederate army, eager to defend their homes, their families, and their honor against the North, abolitionists, and the threat of Lincoln's presidency. While many white women were no less enthusiastic than the men, some also predicted bloodshed and heartache. Months before the outbreak of war, Elizabeth Rhodes of Eufaula, Alabama, for example, expressed deep anxieties in her diary entry for December 31, 1860:

> There are dark clouds overspreading our National Horizon and we cannot yet know whether the fringes of prosperity will dispel them and the bright rays of peace and happiness once more beam upon us...[or] grow darker and denser until proved out in wars and bloodshed on our once prosperous and happy nation. Time alone can unfold these things. We can only wait and pray God to overrule all things for His glory and the good of mankind. (Unpublished diary)

Nevertheless, white women actively rallied to support the volunteers. They immediately formed sewing circles to provide their soldiers with uniforms and flags. Local communities turned out en masse to watch the ladies present their soldiers with a banner or flag. Parties were thrown for the soldiers in the days before they left their towns, and when it finally came time for them to depart, they were sent off amid cheering crowds and prayerful, teary goodbyes. Once the initial exhilaration of the war passed and reports of battles began reaching home, however, the realities of daily life during the war set in.

Women and War

Traditional Southern gender norms dictated female subordination to men within the family. Women traditionally worked in the home and were not involved in managing farms or plantations. Because the majority of men were absent during the war and thus no longer able to provide daily management of farms or plantations, women were forced to take up the task—a significant change to gender norms. As one Southern woman aptly observed, "everything is entirely reversed" (Whites 1995, p. 131). Women indeed were forced to take on many of the roles and responsibilities previously relegated to men. Many letters from husbands to wives contained detailed advice on when to plant certain crops and how to manage slaves. Yet these letters did not substitute for men's former active daily management of the farm or plantation.

Many women also were thrust into the labor market and worked for pay for the first time in their lives. Those white women who worked outside their homes did so to support their families and their work did not lead to a radical social change in their postwar social positions. Women assumed public roles as they organized volunteer relief associations to provide for the poor. They turned to other female friends and kinship networks for support while becoming more self-reliant and autonomous individuals. Yet as everything else in their lives changed, white women clung desperately to the social order they knew from the prewar world. Indeed, the Civil War both profoundly changed women's lives and, ironically, further entrenched the ideals of the preexisting Southern social order. Thus for white Southern women, the war altered society in a variety of ways as the conflict progressed, but did not result in a radical overthrow of the traditional values that produced Southern society and women's roles within it. Southern women clung to their traditional beliefs long after the end of the war.

Religion

One of the traditional sets of belief that many Southern women steadfastly held to was their religion, which provided support and constancy in the troubled and uncertain world around them. Many Southerners went to war firmly believing that God was on their side. Southern religious leaders drew upon Biblical principles and metaphors, claiming that the South was God's chosen nation. Women sent their loved ones off with God's blessings and prayed daily for their protection. Religion and daily life cannot be separated. Indeed, religion and the belief in a life after death provided a sense of comfort and reassurance in a society surrounded by death. Women in particular turned to the hope of again meeting departed loved ones in Heaven in order to cope with the increasing number of deaths surrounding them as the war progressed.

Children

While women had traditionally been expected to care for children, the absence of husbands meant that they now carried the entire burden of managing their families. Women longed for the support of their husbands as they faced the daily challenges of raising children. Such difficulties as illnesses common to childhood became topics of constant discussion in letters from wives to their husbands.

Children themselves experienced the tribulations of life during wartime no less than adults. They faced daily hardships and the absence of their fathers, brothers, and other male relatives. The Civil War politicized children by making them more aware of the events that were taking place around them. Young boys sometimes formed home guard units and carried wooden guns while practicing drilling maneuvers copied from older male relatives. The Civil War also displaced hundreds of children and left thousands more orphaned.

Southern children who came of age during the political and social upheaval that marked wartime and postwar reconstruction were profoundly shaped by their experiences. After the war they felt a need to legitimize the South's role in the conflict, an urge that influenced their political and racial attitudes. Indeed, as James Marten aptly pointed out in his book *The Children's Civil War* (1998), many of the worst Southern racial policies of the 1890s were enacted by white men who had been children during the Civil War.

Slavery

Slavery was another aspect of Southern domestic life that the Civil War forever altered. Slavery as an institution had begun to weaken long before its abolition. The master-slave relationship, which depended heavily on force and the threat of punishment, changed as masters left to fight and were no longer physically present. Many slaves did not respect their mistresses in the same way that they respected their masters. They also knew that a Northern victory meant their freedom, and therefore did all they could to undermine the chances of a Confederate victory. Furthermore, the fear of slave insurrections forced desperately needed men to stay home to help protect against revolts. In their diaries as well as in letters to their husbands, white women daily recorded their fears of slave insurrections. Women were left with the day-to-day management of slaves, which cast them in a role that defied traditional concepts of the weak, subordinate woman. Many women petitioned the Confederate government to provide assistance to them. The government responded with the Twenty Negro Law, which stated that any slave owner with more than twenty slaves was exempted from military service. While this measure alleviated some of the problems elite planter women faced, it also led many poorer women to feel discriminated against.

Disillusionment and Desertion

As families struggled to survive and attempted to maintain established gender norms, external pressures caused by the war itself and the policies of the Confederate government added to their hardships. The Union blockade, which Lincoln called for in 1861, made it difficult for Southerners to get imported goods. For many, problems caused by rampant inflation and the lack of food, medicine, clothes, and shoes were only compounded by the policies of the government, which the poor perceived as favoring the elites. These policies led to a belief that Jefferson Davis, president of the Confederacy, cared little for the common person. Indeed, many Confederate policies, such as creating a stronger central government, conscription, government intervention in the economy, and direct taxation, led to general disillusionment with the government.

By the end of 1864, the helplessness that many Southerners felt in the face of poverty, speculation, and governmental mistreatment led to general despondency throughout the Confederacy, which in turn led to widespread desertion from the army. Over two-thirds of the army had deserted by the end of 1864. Many women who had initially encouraged men to fight now became disheartened with the war and begged their husbands to return home. Yet desertion cannot be viewed simply as the result of disillusionment or as a cowardly act of treason, because many men believed that their first duty was to protect their families. Many soldiers away from home worried about being unable to provide this protection. This concern was especially strong in Union-occupied areas of the South. Once Union armies occupied an area, many of the Confederate soldiers who had been conscripted into the Confederate army from that area felt the need to return to protect their homes and families, which led to desertion from the Confederate army.

In various ways, then, the pull of domestic bonds and the strains caused by temporary reversals in gender norms can be said to have played a role in the South's defeat.

BIBLIOGRAPHY

Ash, Stephen V. *When the Yankees Came: Conflict and Chaos in the Occupied South, 1861–1865.* Chapel Hill: University of North Carolina Press, 1995.

Attie, Jeanie. *Patriotic Toil: Northern Women and the Civil War.* Ithaca, NY: Cornell University Press, 1998.

Clinton, Catherine, ed. *Southern Families at War: Loyalty and Conflict in the Civil War South.* New York: Oxford University Press, 2000.

Edwards, Laura F. *Scarlet Doesn't Live Here Anymore: Southern Women in the Civil War Era.* Urbana: University of Illinois Press, 2000.

Escott, Paul D. *After Secession: Jefferson Davis and the Failure of Confederate Nationalism.* Baton Rouge: Louisiana State University Press, 1978.

Faust, Drew Gilpin. *The Creation of Confederate Nationalism: Ideology and Identity in the Civil War*

South. Baton Rouge: Louisiana State University Press, 1988.

Faust, Drew Gilpin. *Mothers of Invention: Women of the Slaveholding South in the American Civil War.* Chapel Hill: University of North Carolina Press, 1996.

Genovese, Eugene D. *Consuming Fire: The Fall of the Confederacy in the Mind of the White Christian South.* Athens: University of Georgia Press, 1998.

Inscoe, John C., and Gordon B. McKinney. *The Heart of Confederate Appalachia: Western North Carolina in the Civil War.* Chapel Hill: University of North Carolina Press, 2000.

Leonard, Elizabeth D. *Yankee Women: Gender Battles in the Civil War.* New York: W. W. Norton, 1994.

Marten, James. *The Children's Civil War.* Chapel Hill: University of North Carolina Press, 1998.

McCaslin, Richard B. *Tainted Breeze: The Great Hanging at Gainesville, Texas, 1862.* Baton Rouge: Louisiana State University Press, 1994.

Noe, Kenneth W., and Shannon H. Wilson, eds. *The Civil War in Appalachia: Collected Essays.* Knoxville: University of Tennessee Press, 1997.

Rable, George C. *Civil Wars: Women and the Crisis of Southern Nationalism.* Urbana: University of Illinois Press, 1989.

Rhodes, Elizabeth. Diary. 5 vols. Vols. 1–3 at the Auburn University Library. Vols. 1–5 at the Carnegie Library in Eufaula, Alabama. Original handwritten diaries in the possession of the Shorter Mansion and Museum, Eufaula, Alabama.

Thomas, Emory M. *The Confederate Nation, 1861–1865.* New York: Harper & Row, 1979.

Whites, LeeAnn. *The Civil War as a Crisis in Gender: Augusta Georgia, 1860–1890.* Athens: University of Georgia Press, 1995.

Williams, David. *Rich Man's War: Class, Cast, and Confederate Defeat in the Lower Chattahoochee Valley.* Athens: University of Georgia Press, 1998.

Jennifer Ann Newman

■ Clothing

Clothing fashion essentially came to a standstill during the Civil War. Many civilians, especially those in the South or the wives of Union soldiers, could no longer afford the latest styles. Material for clothing, such as cotton, could no longer be as easily obtained as before the war. In an era filled with enormous death and misery, it became socially unacceptable in many circles to dress elaborately as if the war did not exist. Clothing had importance as a necessity, but not as a fashion statement.

The styles of the 1850s continued to some degree during the 1860s. The prosperity that the Industrial Revolution brought to the United States enabled Americans in the 1850s to travel relatively easily to Europe and it became fashionable to take such a trip. Americans who went on the "Grand Tour" returned with stylish new wardrobes from France (in the case of women) or England (in the case of men). At the same time, the 1846 invention of the sewing machine permitted the emergence of a fashion industry in New York City, as dressmakers could now work more easily and quickly. Many New York dressmaking firms imported French and English originals to copy and sell. Magazines such as *Godey's Lady's Book* and *Harper's Bazaar* explained the latest European styles to American women.

American men wore tailcoats or frock coats only for formal or evening wear. Waistcoats were made of colorful embroidered or brocade fabric. Creased trousers appeared in the 1860s. During the day, men wore trousers that were only a shade paler than their coats; these were often made of checked or plaid fabric. For evening wear, they tended to choose lighter-colored trousers, but dark, matching trousers and jackets were beginning to become popular. The most common colors for daytime clothing were soft browns, olive, amber, and vanilla.

Like their European counterparts, American women in the 1850s relied on tightly laced bone corsets to shape their figures. The most fashionable strove to have a fifteen-inch waist. In contrast, their full, bell-shaped skirts were quite wide, measuring as much as ten yards around. Underneath a skirt, women wore long, lace-trimmed white muslin drawers, a crinoline or petticoat of calico (quilted and reinforced with whalebone), and several starched muslin petticoats with flounces. In winter, there might be an additional petticoat. These multiple petticoats began to be replaced by the cage crinoline in the mid-1850s. By 1860, the crinoline and bell-shaped skirt were already in decline, although still common enough. By the beginning of the Civil War, the customary bonnet had been generally replaced by a small hat worn forward, a style introduced by Empress Eugenie of France.

The petticoats that many women wore provided secret places for gold coins, jewelry, and paper. Hoop petticoats also provided hiding places, as a Confederate sympathizer in Missouri noted: "Mrs. Houston took dozens of pairs of good warm socks to our loved ones, and we could slip in a little money and medicine wrapped up. She wore hoop skirts, and I tell you they were fine ladders to hang things on" (Brackman 2000, p. 72). Sara Pryor, the wife of a Confederate officer, reported that she met a woman in a wagon who lifted the edge of her hooped petticoat to reveal "a roll of army cloth, several pairs of cavalry boots, a roll of crimson flannel, packages of gilt braid and sewing silk, cans of preserved meats, a bag of coffee!" (p. 77). Men of the Victorian era were far too chivalrous to carefully search women, as smugglers well knew.

GODEY'S FASHIONS FOR DECEMBER 1861.

Civil war fashion. For many reasons related to money and materials, clothing became less trendy and ornate as the war continued. *The Library of Congress*

Smugglers found a market in the South because needles, pins, thread, and cloth became very scarce as a result of the effective Union naval blockade. The collapse of the Southern economy had the additional result of reducing interest in the latest fashions.

Confederate diarist Mary Chesnut noticed that new clothes were no longer a priority for Southern women. "We were all in a sadly moulting condition," she wrote in mid-1863. "We had come to the end of our good clothes in three years and now our only resource was to turn them upside down or inside out—mending, darning, patching" (DeCredico 1996, p. 88). Many Southern women disassembled their own wardrobes to make shirts, trousers, and underwear for their soldiers.

Confederate troops were worse off than white civilian women. Chesnut watched 10,000 Confederate soldiers march through Richmond in 1863. "We had seen nothing like this before," she reported. "Hitherto, it was only regiments marching spic and span in their fresh clothes, just from home, on their way to the army. Such rags and tags—nothing alike—most garments and arms taken from the enemy—such shoes!" (DeCredico 1996, p. 88). A new machine for sewing leather had made possible the mass production of boots, a great advantage for an army, but only the Union had the resources to carry out such production. Most of the fabric mills were also in the North. There were disadvantages to mass production, however: Uniforms were often ill fitting. Many Union soldiers spent their free time tailoring their jackets, shirts, and trousers.

African Americans in the South who had escaped from slavery or been newly freed often had little but rags on their backs. In response, various African American charitable networks collected and sent clothing. The Relief Association of Elmira, New York, a black women's organization, sent a barrel with 114 pieces of clothing to the Union Relief Association of the Union Bethel

African Methodist Episcopal Church in Washington, DC. The women of Baltimore sent 575 pieces of clothing to the church. The First Female Contraband Aid Society of Alexandria, Virginia, was a sewing circle established to "furnish aid and comfort" to the freed people. On February 6, 1862, African American women in New York City held a Grand Calico Dress Ball and asked for donations of clothing "for the relief of those who in the joy of their new born Freedom, are now appealing to the world for assistance and recognition" (Forbes 1988, p. 191). Clothing not only protected freedpeople from the elements, it also served as a symbol of their worth as human beings.

BIBLIOGRAPHY

Brackman, Barbara. *Civil War Women: Their Quilts, Their Roles, Activities for Re-Enactors.* Lafayette, CA: C & T Publishing, 2000.

DeCredico, Mary A. *Mary Boykin Chesnut: A Confederate Woman's Life.* Madison, WI: Madison House, 1996.

Forbes, Ella. *African American Women during the Civil War.* New York: Garland, 1998.

Tierney, Tom. *Historic Costume: From the Renaissance through the Nineteenth Century.* Mineola, NY: Dover, 2003.

                                        Caryn E. Neumann

■ Food

FOOD: AN OVERVIEW

Food during the Civil War tended to be plain and simple. Cooking styles in both the North and South did not vary dramatically from the colonial era. Differences in climate, terrain, and produce from state to state led to differences in cuisine, however. The New Englander, the Louisiana Cajun, and the Virginia tidewater aristocrat all dined on distinct cuisines. The foods of this era are difficult to replicate, partly because some of the varieties of fruits and vegetables are no longer sold and partly because many dishes were considered too common to record. Only foods prepared for special occasions typically appeared in cookbooks prior to the twentieth century.

There are some broad similarities in Civil War foods. American cuisine is based on English, African, and Native American cuisines. English cookbooks appeared in America with the first colonists. The recipes, rich with herbs, included dishes that would become American staples, such as fruitcake, pound cake, and butter sauces. Africans, who as slaves cooked for the wealthier Southern households, cooked okra in pots along with tomatoes. Sesame seeds and bean pilaus are other traditional African foods. The popularity of peanuts and sweet potatoes in the Southern diet may also reflect African influence, although these foods are native to the New World. Most Native American contributions to American cuisine came in the form of produce, such as squash, tomatoes, and, most famously, corn.

The kitchens and preservation styles of Americans in the Civil War era differed little from those of Europeans in centuries past. Cooking continued to be centered around open hearths and brick ovens. An adjustable spit was used for roasting, while a series of cranes and pulleys made it possible to move pots closer or farther from the flame. Pots were typically made of iron or tin. Only the wealthiest households could afford copper pots and pans. Most homes had at least four saucepans of various sizes, several skillets, a waffle iron, bread pans, a toasting iron, and a teakettle. Cooks used iron skillets called *spiders*, which were fitted with long legs that could be set among the coals. Dutch ovens were also common. These pots had legs and deep-rimmed lids so that coals could be piled both above and beneath for even heating. A chafing dish—a table-high tripod with a receptacle for coals—would be used for delicate dishes, such as boiled custard, or for the finishing of fricassees and sauces. American kitchens also generally held tin cake pans, pie pans, an oilcan, a candle box, a funnel, an egg boiler, scoops, dippers, a colander, breadboxes, and cake boxes. Woodenware in the home would typically include a breadboard, spice boxes, and a saltbox. Earthenware jars with lids kept pickles, butter, and salt. Baskets of various sizes held fruit, vegetables, and eggs.

The use of kitchen equipment required considerable skill as heat could not be regulated with the flick of a knob or push of a button as it can be today. Advice on frying food appeared in the March 1864 issue of *Godey's Lady's Book*, the most popular magazine for women in the nineteenth century, with a circulation of 150,000 during the 1860s. Cooks were told to use a pan that was about four inches deep, with a perfectly flat and thin bottom, twelve inches long and nine inches wide. The editors warned women to be very particular about what they used for frying. Clean, fresh, salt-free oil, butter, lard, or drippings were most advisable. Additionally, cooks in large kitchens could use clarified mutton or beef suet, preferably from the kidney area. (Southern cooks used sunflower seed oil when animal fats became scarce.) The fire under the pan needed to be clear and sharp, while the light in the kitchen had to be good enough to judge the color of cooked food. To determine when the frying pan had reached the proper heat, a

Hunger in New Orleans. "The Starving People of New Orleans Fed by the United States Military Authorities," illustration from *Harper's Weekly*, 1862. *The Library of Congress.*

cook was advised to throw a little bit of bread into the pan. If it fried crisp, the fat was ready. If it burned the bread, the fat was too hot. Knowing when fat was at proper heat was the key to frying. The magazine warned that although frying was one of the most common culinary operations, it was one that was rarely performed perfectly well.

Large brick ovens were easier to use than fry pans. These ovens were either freestanding or housed in a separate outbuilding, especially in hot Southern regions where additional heat in the home was not appreciated. Brick ovens were heated by coals; the coals were then swept out, and bread was placed directly on the oven floor. A dome of clay bricks above held the heat and the bread cooled gradually, forming a crisp, chewy crust. Pastries and other baked goods, as well as baked meats—often encased in pastry—also benefited from the radiant heat of the brick floor.

Iceboxes were sold commercially during the Civil War, but they were a luxury. For most Americans, the 1860s remained an era before refrigeration. Preservation methods included drying and smoking. Extra fruits and vegetables were bottled in Mason jars, a device perfected in 1859. Home canning did not become widespread until the development of the pressure cooker in 1874. As a result, *Godey's Lady's Book* offered numerous food storage tips. In August 1864, the magazine advised readers that vegetables kept best on a stone floor and apples could be preserved for a long period by packing them in large barrels with dry sand.

Coarse nets suspended in a storeroom worked well to preserve finer fruits, such as lemons. Women were advised to purchase and prepare large quantities of lemons and oranges when they were cheap. The peels were saved for sweetmeats (organ meat) and grating, as they were commonly used in various dishes. Onions, shallots, and garlic were also hung up for winter use, in ropes from the ceiling, as were dried parsley, basil, savory, and, knotted together, marjoram, thyme, and tarragon.

Most of the recipes in *Godey's Lady's Book* were contributed by middle-class readers and were meant for family meals. Unlike cookbooks, these recipes were not intended for banquets or fine dining. The recipes indicate that the average American ate mostly meat and baked goods. The largest number of meat recipes in the magazine during the war were for beef, followed by those for pork, veal, wildfowl, chicken, turkey, lamb, and wild game. Chicken was only served in the summer, perhaps because that was the most appropriate time for thinning a flock. Because the United States was primarily rural, most of the consumed meat came from animals killed on the farm or brought in from the hunt. Accordingly, a cook would not want to waste any part of the animal. Tongue, brains, feet, and sweetmeats were regularly eaten. Seafood was also popular. Overall, Americans ate a wider range of meats than is common in the twenty-first century. These meats may have been well seasoned. Cayenne pepper was popular, and archeological examinations of sunken ships from the

Civil War era have revealed that sailors used Worcestershire sauce in considerable quantities. The word "gravy" in Civil War recipes usually meant stock, not a sauce.

Civil War Americans ate comparatively few vegetables and fruits. In rural areas, people grew their own vegetables but the variety was not particularly great. Potatoes were most popular, followed by cabbages, onions, and turnips. Potatoes appear to have been served with every meal. The ease with which root vegetables could be preserved over the winter undoubtedly contributed to their popularity. Fresh vegetables were usually not available in the winter. Salads were not eaten, except for chicken salad and lobster salad. Southerners ate a number of different corn products, including hominy, a crude ash bread called pone, and ears of corn roasted in ashes. Everyone ate *succotash*—a mixture of corn and lima beans—as well as corn fritters, corn mush, boiled and baked corn puddings, and corn chowder.

The typical American ate little fruit, except for apples and pears. Oranges and lemons were usually special treats, as they were expensive imports. Coconuts and pineapple, brought in from Cuba, could be found in markets. Watermelon, berries, and grapes were sometimes grown locally. Both apples and pears were pressed into cider and perry, healthier beverages than water. (Cholera, a major nineteenth-century killer, was spread through water consumption, as were a number of other nasty parasitic diseases.) Although the North had dairies and bottled milk had been sold in New York City since the 1850s, milk consumption nationally was less than half a pint a day. Canned condensed milk, perfected by Gail Borden, was only available to the troops, as the U.S. government commandeered Borden's entire factory output. The alcoholic beverage most favored by Americans at mid-century was beer, followed by whiskey and wine. Coffee was just becoming popular at the start of the war. When it became rare, drinkers drank mock coffees, brewed from a wide range of substances: parched and ground acorns, beans, chicory, corn, cottonseed, dandelion roots, groundnuts, okra seed, peanuts, parched rice, rye, sweet potato, and wheat. Eating chocolate was largely unknown and baking chocolate did not become available until later in the century. Hot chocolate, however, was consumed. In the South, when chocolate became unavailable, cooks invented a substitute made from roasted peanuts blended with boiled milk and sugar. Common teas included black alder, blackberry, currant, holly, huckleberry, raspberry, and sassafras. Confederate soldiers made mock tea from corn bran, ginger, or various herbs.

Breads were a staple of the American diet. When Europeans arrived in the New World, they discovered maize, also called Indian corn. (The Old English word for grain is *corn.*) This popular Indian food was so closely linked with the Native Americans that it became known as *injun*. By the nineteenth century, the bread known as *rye 'n injun* filled the stomachs of many Northerners. By the time of the Civil War, most Northern households used fine white flour. Corn and rice, not wheat, were the major grain crops of the Confederate states. Cornbread, not wheat or rye bread, was found in the majority of Southern homes.

Leaven made for a lighter bread product. Hardtack, the infamously unpalatable staple food of the Civil War soldier, stayed in the "eat-it-or-starve" category because it lacked leavening. Accordingly, leaven was actively pursued. Commercial yeast did not reach the market until 1868. Civil War cooks used potash, a potassium carbonate leeched out of burned wood ash. Partially refined, it was known as *pearlash* and had been exported by the ton since the late eighteenth century. Saleratus, a leavening agent, became available to cooks in the first half of the nineteenth century. Combined with cream of tartar (an acid) to make it work, it evolved into baking powder in 1856. Yeast became commercially available around 1868, although other versions were commonly made at home before that time. *Godey's* often included recipes for yeast. In 1863 the magazine included directions for making peach-leaf yeast, potato yeast, and hop-beer yeast.

Civil War desserts were typically puddings. Common Northern fare included corn, plum, and pumpkin puddings, whereas Southerners enjoyed sweet potato and rice puddings. Custards, creams, and fruit desserts also enjoyed popularity. Molasses custard and huckleberry pie were common in the South. Tarts, made of apples, lemons, or cranberries, were often baked in a crock with only a pastry lid. The term *cake* was used interchangeably for breads and cookies. Northerners baked Boston cream cakes and Vermont currant cake. Both regions enjoyed rhubarb fool and strawberry soufflé.

The Civil War did not have a large effect on the food habits of Northerners. It did, however, drastically affect the nature of the foods available to Southerners. Following the war, food habits returned to normal in the South by the start of the 1870s.

BIBLIOGRAPHY

Evans, Meryle, et al. *The Southern Heritage Breads Cookbook*. Birmingham, AL: Oxmoor House, 1983.

Fowler, Damon Lee. *Classical Southern Cooking: A Celebration of the Cuisine of the Old South*. New York: Crown, 1995.

Grover, Kathryn, ed. *Dining in America, 1850–1900*. Amherst: University of Massachusetts Press, 1987.

Johnson, Sharon Peregrine, and Byron A. Johnson. *The Authentic Guide to Drinks of the Civil War Era, 1853–1873*. Gettysburg, PA: Thomas, 1992.

McIntosh, Elaine N. *American Food Habits in Historical Perspective.* Westport, CT: Praeger, 1995.

Spaulding, Lily May, and John Spaulding, eds. *Civil War Recipes: Receipts from the Pages of Godey's Lady's Book.* Lexington: University Press of Kentucky, 1999.

Caryn E. Neumann

DIET

During the Civil War, the average American had a diet centered on meat and bread in both the North and South. There was, however, an increasing interest in changing general eating patterns. Vegetarianism was promoted, and many foods were used for medicinal purposes. The safety of food preparation was re-evaluated, and women were encouraged to become more educated in cooking and to approach cooking scientifically. The feeding of children was studied, as well, and new ideas on scheduling and rationing a child's food were implemented.

The nineteenth century witnessed a health reform movement that placed food at the heart of its philosophy. Vegetarians, encouraged by the theories of Sylvester Graham, argued that the killing and eating of animals contaminated and brutalized the human soul, making meat-eaters murderous and bloodthirsty. In 1860, as the United States stood on the brink of war, the prominent health reformer Russell Trall criticized the presidential contenders for failing to address a vitally important topic: vegetarianism—or, as he put it, the issue of "beef versus bread, hog v. hominy, or mutton v. squash" (Whorton 1982, p. 62). Like other vegetarians of the time, Trall held that true emancipation meant the liberation of all Americans from an appetite for flesh.

Other reformers saw different dangers in the nations kitchens. A certain Dr. Hill, for example, quoted in *Godey's Lady's Book* in August 1865, warned of the cost of inadequate food preparation practices: "Bad cookery kills multitudes, and makes miserable dyspeptics and suicides innumerable. It would be an inestimable boon to humanity to make cookery an indispensable branch of public school learning." A proper diet of properly prepared food was essential for good physical and mental health.

Food preparation had long been regarded as women's work and as not requiring education or analysis, while cookbooks were simply collections of recipes. The publication in 1846 of Catherine Beecher's *Treatise on Domestic Economy,* however, did much to change American attitudes toward diet. Beecher encouraged women to learn all they could about contemporary science and to use that knowledge to decide how to best feed their families. Other publications, such as advice

Catherine Beecher (1800–1878), renovator of food preparation. Catherine Beecher wrote the book *Treatise on Domestic Economy,* which encouraged women of the Civil War era to use science in order to mitigate the dangers of poor food preparation. *The Granger Collection, New York.*

books, home medical manuals, and women's magazines, emphasized that women needed scientific education to be good wives and mothers. All of these ideas remained in vogue during the Civil War.

As mentioned above, meat and baked goods predominated in the average American diet of the 1860s. A New England breakfast often consisted of cornmeal mush with cream, perhaps with some maple syrup as a sweetener. The same table might include corn dodgers (cornmeal griddle cakes), tea, and doughnuts made from locally ground wheat. Dinner, the largest meal of the day and served at noon, typically consisted of boiled potatoes and ham, fresh pork, or corned beef. Pie would always be served with apple in the winter, rhubarb in the spring, and berry in the summer and fall. Mincemeat pie, perhaps made with venison and boiled cider, appears to have been more common in the fall and winter. A Saturday dinner would consist of boiled salted codfish. A Sunday dinner might be baked beans, brown bread, and Indian pudding. In the evening, supper was served. This was typically a light meal of johnnycake and milk, bread and milk with maple syrup, or flapjacks sprinkled with brown sugar, followed by custard.

Meals were equally as plain in the South. Although meat was scarce in the South during the war, beef and pork were heavily favored. In 1861, for example, one South Carolina inn served hog and hominy (pork and boiled corn) for breakfast, dinner, and supper. The Southern upper classes did usually consume a greater variety of foods, however. A woman in Georgia lamented during the summer of 1865 that on her plantation

> We have no kind of meat in our house but ham and bacon, and have to eat hominy instead of rice at dinner. . . . Cornfield peas have been our staple diet for the last ten days. Mother has cooked them in every variety of style she ever heard, but they are cornfield peas still. All this would have been horribly mortifying a year or two ago, but everyone knows how it is now, and I am glad to have even cornfield peas to share with the soldiers. (Spaulding 1999, p. 6)

Medicinal foods also formed part of the diet. Until the advent of antibiotics in the mid-twentieth century, there was little that physicians could do for people sick with wasting diseases, chronic illnesses, or any other type of serious illness. Family members, chiefly women, were expected to care for the ill as well as possible, usually by treating them with patent medicines or home remedies. Vanilla, for example, was used as an aid for stomach distress, as a stimulant, and as a calmative for hysteria. For invalids, jelly was recommended, according to the May 1862 *Godey's Lady's Book.* Isinglass jelly contained one ounce of isinglass (gelatin) shavings, forty Jamaica peppers, and a bit of brown crust of bread that was boiled and then strained. Bread jelly required that the crum of a penny roll be cut into thin slices, toasted to pale brown, boiled gently in a quart of water, strained on a bit of lemon peel, sweetened with sugar and, perhaps, strengthened with wine. Strengthening jelly contained an ounce of pearl barley, an ounce of sago, an ounce of rice, and an ounce of eringo root reduced in two quarts of soft water to one quart. It was to be taken by teacupful in milk, morning, noon, and night.

The feeding of children was of particular interest. The "Health Department" of *Godey's Lady's Book* warned that half of all children died before reaching the age of eighteen because of inattention to their diet. The magazine advised that children past age six be limited to three meals a day, augmented by snacks of apple or cold, dry, coarse bread. Children were to be taught to eat slowly, though they could eat as much as they wanted, and hard food was to be cut up into pieces no larger than a pea. To provide the lime needed for the development of good teeth, the magazine suggested that children should eat whole-grain brown bread instead of white bread.

BIBLIOGRAPHY

"Editor's Table." *Godey's Lady's Book and Magazine,* 71, August 1865.

Kamminga, Harmke, and Andrew Cunningham, eds. *The Science and Culture of Nutrition, 1840–1940.* Atlanta, GA: Rodopi, 1995.

Spaulding, Lily May, and John Spaulding, eds. *Civil War Recipes: Receipts from the Pages of Godey's Lady's Book.* Lexington: University Press of Kentucky, 1999.

Whorton, James C. *Crusaders for Fitness: The History of American Health Reformers.* Princeton, NJ: Princeton University Press, 1982.

Caryn E. Neumann

FOOD SHORTAGES

Food shortages became a fact of life in the Confederacy during the Civil War. The Confederacy suffered from a constant and critical lack of provisions, a situation stemming from a number of factors ranging from its economy to enemy actions. The Union blockade of the seas, successful Union invasions, the occupation of key agricultural areas, and the fighting of battles on prime farmland resulted in a sharp reduction in Southern food production. Army rations, already sparse at the beginning of the war, were cut back as the conflict progressed. As historians have noted, the South's ultimate defeat came in part because of the ever-present hunger suffered by soldiers and civilians. The North, in contrast, did not experience a food shortage to any degree.

The South suffered from a severe shortage of food crops. Prior to the Civil War, the main crops of the South were tobacco and cotton. Neither crop filled stomachs. In 1863, Joseph Brown, the governor of Georgia, issued a proclamation calling on Georgians to plant food crops instead of tobacco and cotton. He also urged that farmers "prevent the destruction of food" by turning stored foodstuffs into alcoholic beverages (*New York Times,* October 25, 1863). Before the war, many Southern farmers produced corn and other grains for home consumption. When these men went off to war, their households lost an irreplaceable source of family support. Without slave ownership or the funds to replace the labor of absent husbands, ordinary Southern white women experienced great deprivation. Many were forced to rely on the charity of town councils and similar groups.

As the war continued and more Southerners required food aid, the pool of food resources continued to shrink and prices rose. Additionally, Confederate currency rapidly lost its purchasing power. In 1864, a bushel of potatoes that cost $2.25 in the North cost $25 in Richmond (Moore 1996, p. 242). Confederate diarist Mary Chesnut reported spending $800 for two pounds of tea, forty pounds of coffee, and sixty pounds of sugar in June 1864 (DeCredico 1996, p. 163).

Rising levels of desertion from the Confederate army were frequently blamed on the fact that many

DISTRIBUTING RATIONS.

Distributing rations in the South. Both soldiers and civilians suffered from a persistent lack of necessities caused by both the economy and the enemy. The Union blockade, their occupation of Confederate farmland, and the battles on fertile soil all contributed to the crisis. *Schomburg Center/Art Resource, NY*

men could no longer bear the thought of the destitution their wives and children were facing. In response, the Confederacy and state governments took steps to support the dependents of soldiers. Charleston, for example, established a free market to supply provisions to the needy families of soldiers and sailors. These governmental bodies were not always successful, however. By January 1864, the Charleston market had exhausted its funds and could no longer provide help to several thousand dependent women and children. Even when food was available, it often failed to reach its destination because of problems with the Confederate railroads. By the mid-point of the war, most Southern rails were deteriorating rapidly and routine maintenance had become almost impossible because of a shortage of iron.

In the spring of 1863, the Confederacy was rocked by food riots. The Richmond Bread Riot involved a group of women, estimated at anywhere from a few hundred to several thousand, who marched to Capitol Square in search of food and answers as to why their families were starving. The mob looted the business district until President Jefferson Davis calmed the situation by threatening to have a militia infantry unit fire on them. The next day, the Richmond city council established a free city market for the meritorious poor. For those in reduced circumstances as a result of inflation and shortages, the council created a city depot where low-cost provisions could be sold. Bread riots also broke out in Atlanta and in High Point, North Carolina.

While much of the damage to fields resulted inadvertently from fighting, punishing civilians became the goal of Union troops marching with General William T. Sherman. As part of Sherman's policy of hard war, his men were ordered to destroy civilians' food supply, leaving just enough food for the people to eat. Even those Southerners with money found it difficult to obtain food. Eliza Mason Smith, a member of a prominent planter family from the low country outside of Charleston, South Carolina, fled to Augusta, Georgia, in 1864. She reported that prices in the market were high beyond belief, that many foods could not be bought at any price, and that no goods were secure because of widespread theft, including daily street robberies (Whites 1995, p. 99). Catherine Rowland of Augusta reported a similar situation in the winter of 1865. In her diary she observed, "I was startled and amazed to find out how greatly the price of everything had advanced, it is awful, and how the poor can *live* I cannot imagine" (p. 99). The *Charleston Mercury* reported on February 10, 1865, that Captain Julian Mitchell, under the authority of the South Carolina governor, aimed to save food from the hands of the enemy for the use of South Carolinians. "The garden of the State is now the battle ground of two armies," the newspaper explained, "and not a plough will, in all probability, be struck in this whole region of country again until the end of the war" (*New York Times*, February 11, 1865). According to the May 6, 1865, issue of the *New York Herald*, despite the

FOOD SHORTAGES IN THE LAST DAYS OF THE CONFEDERACY

Mary Boykin Miller Chesnut (1823–1886), the daughter of a governor of South Carolina and wife of a senator, James Chesnut Jr., kept a diary from February 1861 until August 1865 in which she recorded her impressions of the Civil War and of life on the Southern home front. The Chesnuts were living in Charleston, South Carolina, when the Civil War began in 1861. James Chesnut became a brigadier general in the Confederate Army after he resigned his seat in the U.S. Senate. In her diary, Mary chronicled the growing hardships experienced on the Southern home front, especially after 1863. The following excerpts from early 1865 describe the effects of food shortages on even well-to-do Southerners in the last year of the war.

> February 16th, 1865. . . . The day I left home I had packed a box of flour, sugar rice, and coffee, but my husband would not let me bring it. He said I was coming to a land of plenty-unexplored North Carolina, where the foot of the Yankee marauder was unknown, and in Columbia they would need food. Now I have written for that box and many other things to be sent me . . . or I shall starve.

> February 18th. . . . As we came up on the train from Charlotte a soldier took out of his pocket a filthy rag. If it had lain in the gutter for months it could not have looked worse. He unwrapped the thing carefully and took out two biscuits of the species known as "hard tack." Then he gallantly handed me one and with an ingratiating smile asked me "to take some." Then he explained, saying, "Please take these two; swap with me; give me something softer that I can eat; I am very weak still." Immediately, for his benefit, my basket of luncheon was emptied, but as for his biscuit, I would not choose any.

> February 26th. —Mrs. Munroe offered me religious books, which I declined, being already provided with the Lamentations of Jeremiah, the Psalms of David, the denunciations of Hosea, and, above all, the patient wail of Job. Job is my comforter now. I should be so thankful to know life never would be any worse with me. My husband is well. . . . I am bodily comfortable, if somewhat dingily lodged, and I daily part with my raiment for food. We find no one who will exchange eatables for Confederate money; so we are devouring our clothes.

> February 29th. Ellen [Mary's maid] and I are shut up here. It is rain, rain, everlasting rain. As our money is worthless, are we not to starve? Heavens! how grateful I was to-day when Mrs. McLean sent me a piece of chicken. I think the emptiness of my larder has leaked out. To-day Mrs. Munroe sent me hot cakes and eggs for my breakfast.

> March 5th. . . . The rain, it raineth every day. The weather typifies our tearful despair, on a large scale. It is also Lent now—a quite convenient custom, for we, in truth, have nothing to eat. So we fast and pray, and go dragging to church like drowned rats to be preached at. . . . Ellen said I had a little piece of bread and a little molasses in store for my dinner to-day.

> March 6th. To-day came a godsend. Even a small piece of bread and the molasses had become things of the past. My larder was empty, when a tall mulatto woman brought a tray covered by a huge white serviette. Ellen ushered her in with a flourish, saying, "Mrs. McDaniel's maid." The maid set down the tray upon my bare table, and uncovered it with conscious pride. There were fowls ready for roasting, sausages, butter, bread, eggs, and preserves. I was dumb with delight. After silent thanks to heaven my powers of speech returned, and I exhausted myself in messages of gratitude to Mrs. McDaniel.

REBECCA J. FREY

SOURCE: Chesnut, Mary Boykin Miller. *A Diary from Dixie*. New York: D. Appleton, 1905, pp. 348–357.

---

efforts of Mitchell and others, starvation did come to the South.

Food shortages forced Southerners to make substitutions for products that had been easily accessible before the war. Typical substitutions included artichoke leaves for hops in the manufacture of yeast, peach tree leaves for vanilla, and sorghum for sugar. Salt pork and bacon grease were common seasonings in Southern cookery prior to the Civil War. With meat scarce and poverty rampant during the war, it became usual to supplement the meager diet of field peas, greens, sweet potatoes, and grits with cheap salt pork fat. The North, in sharp contrast, had enough food to be able to export the surplus to Europe.

With the end of the war came food for the Confederacy. When Robert E. Lee surrendered at Appomattox, he reported that his men had been without food for two days and asked Ulysses S. Grant to feed them. Lee's soldiers reportedly sent up a rousing cheer when wagons of food appeared. The May 6, 1865, *New York Herald* reported that only the fact that U.S. commissaries were furnishing them with food was preserving the people of Virginia from starvation. "At present," the newspaper warned, "the farmers generally are without the implements or seeds necessary to do their planting, and unless these can be speedily procured there will be no crops forthcoming in the State in the summer and fall." The war's outcome depended as much on stomachs as it did on bullets.

BIBLIOGRAPHY

"Amnesty Offered to the Southern People." *New York Herald,* May 6, 1865, p. 1, col. 1.

"Black Flag Raised South, by Starving Women." *New York Times*. February 11, 1865, p. 4, col. 3, quoting the *Charleston Mercury*, February 10, 1865.

Davis, William C. *A Taste for War: The Culinary History of the Blue and Gray*. Mechanicsburg, PA: Stackpole Books, 2003.

DeCredico, Mary A. *Mary Boykin Chesnut: A Confederate Woman's Life*. Madison, WI: Madison House, 1996.

Dickson, Paul. *Chow: A Cook's Tour of Military Food*. New York: New American Library, 1978.

Moore, Jerrold Northrop. *Confederate Commissary General: Lucius Bellinger Northrop and the Subsistence Bureau of the Southern Army*. Shippensburg, PA: White Mane, 1996.

"Report on Defeat of Shelby in Missouri (War)." *New York Times*. October 25, 1863, p. 6, col. 5.

Whites, LeeAnn. *The Civil War as a Crisis in Gender: Augusta, Georgia, 1860–1890*. Athens: University of Georgia Press, 1995.

Caryn E. Neumann

■ Education

EDUCATION: AN OVERVIEW

The Civil War had a serious impact on the progress of education, particularly in the Confederate states. Before the war, most children were educated either privately, in private schools or at home, or in public schools. The more rural areas had no public schools, or just rudimentary ones; in larger cities, public schools were generally available. Colleges and universities were generally reserved for people going into specific professions, such as the law and the ministry, but interest in what would be called in the early twenty-first century a liberal arts curriculum gradually grew throughout the nineteenth century.

When war came, both state and federal government priorities toward education were put on hold. Schools received little attention. A number of colleges and universities, especially in the South, were virtually emptied out during the war years because so many students had volunteered for or been conscripted into the armed forces. Many of them closed, only to reopen after the war.

Not a Uniform System

Elementary and secondary education, in both the Union and the Confederacy, was not universal and had never been. This was an era during which many people received their training as apprentices, even in such professions as law or medicine. With the advent of the Industrial Revolution in the nineteenth century, factories shot up, particularly in the North, and many people learned the skills that could afford them factory jobs.

In rural areas throughout the nation, education was not a priority except among the wealthy. Schools only stayed open a few months out of every year, in most places, to allow children to be home to help on the farm. The South's economy was primarily agrarian, and most people worked on farms and plantations (Catton 1971, p. 179). Contrary to the *Gone With The Wind* portrait of an aristocratic and elite Southern society, in truth few were wealthy enough to own plantations. Of those who owned slaves, the vast majority owned fewer than 20 and worked with them on the land (Salzberger and Turck 2004, p. 10). Education, even at its most rudimentary levels, was a luxury for most people.

Slaves, meanwhile, received no formal education, outside of, perhaps, being taught passages from the Bible at their masters' pleasure. In fact, it was illegal in every Southern state to teach a slave to read, although some people broke the law and did so anyway. In his classic work *Up From Slavery* (1901), Booker T. Washington (1856–1915) paints a typical picture of how a slave child, even a very young one, might pass his time on the plantation: "During the period that I spent in slavery I was not large enough to be of much service, still I was occupied most of the time in cleaning the yards, carrying water to the men in the fields, or going to the mill, to which I used to take the corn, about once a week, to be ground." Like other slaves, he had no formal schooling. "I remember," he writes, "on several occasions I went as far as the schoolhouse door with one of my mistresses to carry her books." He imagined that being able to attend school was "about the same as getting into paradise" (Washington 1901, pp. 4–5).

Washington makes a telling point about the formal education of even well-to-do white Southerners—one which in part explains why the Confederacy was at such a disadvantage from almost the beginning. "The slave

Misses Cooke's school room, Freedman's Bureau, Richmond, Virginia, 1866. Deprived of the right to pursue an education while in bondage, many former slaves, young and old, took advantage of their new freedoms by attending school. Northern aid societies, in conjunction with the Freedmen's Bureau, sent teachers throughout the South to staff schools serving the African American population, much to the disapproval of local whites. *Sketch by Jas. E. Taylor. The Library of Congress.*

system," he writes, "in a large measure, took the spirit of self-reliance and self-help out of the white people. My old master had many boys and girls, but not one, so far as I know, ever mastered a single trade or special line of productive industry." Thus, while they did receive "book learning," they lacked practical experience. Except for formal book education, he notes, "when freedom came, the slaves were almost as well fitted to begin life anew as the master" (Washington 1901, p. 9).

Formal Education for Children

In both the North and the South, schoolchildren were given instruction in reading and writing, as well as general mathematics and science. Books such as the seventeenth-century *New England Primer* and later texts such as the *New York Reader* and Noah Webster's *Blue-Back Speller* were typical of the period throughout the Union and the Confederacy (Knight 1922, p. 269). One of the most popular series of textbooks was the *McGuffey's Eclectic Reader* books, written by educator William Holmes McGuffey (1800–1873), who was born in Pennsylvania, educated in Ohio, and taught at the University of Virginia from 1845 to 1873. These books, which combine lessons in grammar, spelling, and pronunciation with moral education, were reprinted and used well into the twentieth century. The books are apolitical and make no reference to the Confederacy or

slavery. Typical of the lessons in McGuffey's fifth *Eclectic Reader* (1857) are stories such as "The Poor Widow," a story about how a family receives a benefactor who turns out to be George Washington and fables such as the well-known poem "The Spider and the Fly" (pp. 40–46, 60–61). McGuffey offers instructions to students to assist them in their reading: "Pronounce correctly. Do not say *put-tt-est* (pro. prit-ti-est) for prit-ti-est; *creature* nor *critter* (pro. creat-yure) for crea-ture; *ful-lish* for fool-ish . . ." (p. 60).

A number of Southern educators, aware that their emerging nation would do well to have a moral heritage of its own, created textbooks in the McGuffey style. While continuing to emphasize traditional lessons, these books also provided positive references, which some might call propaganda, to the Confederacy and the Southern way of life.

In Raleigh, North Carolina, Levi Branson (1832–1903) of the publishing firm Branson, Farrar & Co. produced textbooks that strove to do precisely that. One textbook, titled *First Book in Composition, Applying the Principles of Grammar to the Art of Composing, Especially Designed for the Use of Southern Schools* (1863), uses a number of generic examples to provide examples of grammar and usage. A number of his sentences, however, are clearly geared toward the ongoing war and the

Confederacy's strength as a nation. For example, he finishes his preface to the book with, "In the hope that it may be useful to the young of our great rising Confederacy, the work is respectfully offered to the public" (Branson 1863, p. 3).

In an exercise asking students to choose the correct pronoun, sentences such as these appear: "Jefferson Davis defended [his] country bravely, and deserves great applause for [his] patriotism" (Branson 1863, p. 14). Other exercises mention the Confederacy and its products, in particular its cotton crop. To show that the Confederacy did not abandon its ties to the colonial forces who fought the American Revolution and, in fact, strongly identified with the noble bravery of the colonists, sentences such as this also appear: "Washington, in [his] youth, and throughout [his]whole life, adhered strictly to the truth, and thus set an example, which [we] ought to follow" (Branson 1863, p. 14).

In another Branson, Farrar book for young readers, titled *The Dixie Reader*, designed to follow an introductory book called *The Dixie Primer*, author Marinda B. Moore provides reading samples not unlike the generic offerings of McGuffey. But she also includes examples that play up the moral strength, and perhaps superiority, of the South, as the following passage about an elderly slave illustrates:

> 1. Here comes old aunt Ann. She is quite old. See how she leans on her stick. 2. When she was young she did good work, but now she can not work much. But she is not like a poor white woman. 3. Aunt Ann knows that her young Miss, as she calls her, will take care of her as long as she lives. 4. Ma-ny poor white folks would be glad to live in her house and eat what Miss Kate sends out for her din-ner. (Moore 1863, p. 22)

Even with the drawbacks and setbacks the South faced before and during the war, formal education was not neglected; in fact, in many ways education in the South was quite progressive. In North Carolina, for example, the public school system improved dramatically during the twelve-year tenure, from 1853 to 1865, of Calvin H. Wiley (1819–1887), the state's first Superintendant of Public Instruction. In his first seven years in office the number of public schools rose from 2,500 to more than 3,000, the number of students from 95,000 to nearly 119,000, and the number of teachers from 800 to nearly 2,800 (Johnson 1937, p. 280). At the beginning of the Civil War, North Carolina was considered to have the third best state public school system in the United States, after Massachusetts and Connecticut (Jarrett 1964, p. 276).

Education for Freedmen

It should be remembered that often, even among the staunchest opponents of slavery, racial inequality was nonetheless a reality. Free black men and women in the North were often denied the educational opportunities available to white Northerners. In particular, higher education was essentially closed to them; between the founding of the United States and the signing of the Emancipation Proclamation in 1863, only twenty-nine black students graduated from white colleges (Lucas 1994, p. 158). Although many white Northerners and Southerners believed in segregated schools, many did believe that black students should have access to higher education. In the 1850s and 1860s, white religious groups founded colleges for black students, including Cheney State College (founded by the Quakers) and Lincoln University (founded by the Presbyterians), both in Pennsylvania; and Wilberforce (founded by the Methodists) in Ohio (Lucas 1994, pp. 158–159).

Younger free black children were able to attend segregated schools as they existed. It was rare for a black student to wind up in a grammar school whose primary population was white.

Higher Education

Higher education, both before and during the Civil War, was, in general, the purview of the wealthy. Neither the factory worker in the North nor the farmer in the South or Midwest saw higher education as a necessity. The role of colleges and universities in American life would undergo significant changes throughout the remainder of the nineteenth century and into the twentieth. For the average person living through the Civil War, college education held little practical value.

Among those who did attend college, higher education in the North benefited from the economic boom that accompanied the Civil War. A number of colleges and universities that would achieve national renown were founded in the North during the Civil War years: Cornell, Lehigh, Swarthmore, the Massachusetts Institute of Technology, the University of Massachusetts, and Vassar, which was chartered in 1861 but opened in 1865. In the territories, several colleges opened, including the University of Colorado and the University of Washington (Trager 1994, pp. 486, 483, 496, 500).

The South saw virtually no such activity during the Civil War years. Most of the Southern colleges were faced with limited enrollments, especially after the Confederacy issued conscription notices to those of college age and many of their professors, and closed for the duration of the war (Lucas 1994, p. 141). A typical scenario: When the 1863 session began at the University of Georgia, there were forty students in attendance. A few weeks after the term began, the state of Georgia called those students into service, so the school was left with no alternative but to close (Reed 1949, p. 692). Some, such as the University of Virginia, managed to remain open, albeit with a significantly abridged program of study.

Interestingly, some of the earliest efforts at creating advanced schools for women took place in the South.

Beginning in the early nineteenth century and continuing during the war years, such schools provided women with a liberal arts education focusing on such topics as English, French, and Latin (Farnham 1994, pp. 72–73). Higher education for women was looked upon by many as a frivolity, and during the war, most women had to remain at home because so many men had gone off to battle. But the spark clearly did not die, in part perhaps because women were put in the position of having to run their homesteads singlehandedly. Over the next few decades after the war, women's colleges opened in several states.

In 1862, President Abraham Lincoln signed the Morrill Land Grant Act into law. Under this law, each state was allotted the equivalent of 30,000 acres of land per Congressional representative for the purpose of creating a land-grant college that would focus on providing higher education for farmers and those engaged in mechanical trades. In part, the Morrill Act was enacted to provide farmers with an opportunity to learn the latest techniques for their profession so that they could increase crop yield and become more efficient farmers (Catton 1971, pp. 173–174). Kansas State University, chartered in February 1863 in Manhattan, Kansas, was the first land-grant school to open under the Morrill Act. The Confederate States had no such program, although after the war they were included in the Morrill program.

When the war ended, Southern colleges re-opened and resumed their courses of study. Colleges and universities in both the South and the North, however, suffered from the tragic losses of life on both sides, with combined losses of more than 600,000 young men (Trager 1994 p. 498).

BIBLIOGRAPHY

Branson, Levi. *First Book in Composition, Applying the Principles of Grammar to the Art of Composing, Especially Designed for the Use of Southern Schools.* Raleigh, NC: Branson, Farrar & Co., 1863.

Catton, Bruce. *The Civil War.* New York: American Heritage Press, 1971.

Farnham, Christie Anne. *The Education of the Southern Belle: Higher Education and Student Socialization in the Antebellum South.* New York: New York University Press, 1994.

Jarrett, Calvin D. "Calvin H. Wiley: Southern Education Leader." *Peabody Journal of Education,* Vol. 41, No. 5 (Mar., 1964), pp. 276–288.

Johnson, Guion Griffis. *Ante-Bellum North Carolina: A Social History.* Chapel Hill, NC: University of North Carolina Press, 1937.

Knight, Edgar W. *Public Education in the South.* Boston: Ginn and Company, 1922.

Lucas, Christopher J. *American Higher Education: A History.* New York: Palgrave Macmillan, 1994.

McGuffey, William H. *McGuffey's New Fifth Eclectic Reader: Selected and Original Exercises for Schools.* Cincinnati: Winthrop B. Smith & Co., 1857.

Moore, Marinda B. *The First Dixie Reader; Designed to Follow the Dixie Primer.* Raleigh, NC: Branson, Farrar & Co., 1863.

Reed, Thomas Walter. *History of the University of Georgia.* Athens: University of Georgia Press, 1949.

Salzberger, Ronald P. and Mary Turck. *Reparations for Slavery: A Reader.* Lanham, MD: Rowman & Littlefield, 2004.

Stewart, Kensey Johns. *A Geography for Beginners.* Richmond, VA: J. W. Randolph, 1864.

Stout, Harry S. *Upon the Altar of the Nation: A Moral History of the Civil War.* New York: Viking, 2006.

Texas Public Schools: One Hundred Fifty Years 1854–2004. Austin, TX: Texas Education Agency, 2004.

Trager, James. *The People's Chronology.* New York: Henry Holt, 1994.

Washington, Booker T. *Up From Slavery.* New York: Doubleday, Page, 1901.

George A. Milite

WOMEN AND EDUCATION

Prior to the Civil War, most white American women, Northern and Southern, labored in the domestic sphere. The enlistment of male soldiers into the Union army, in particular, however, left a large cavity in the male-dominated teaching profession in the North. Hence, the rise of northern female educators during the Civil War era was in direct response to the increased need for teachers in American schools. The feminization of the education field was also significantly impacted by the massive number of freedmen seeking to learn to read and write.

During the antebellum period (1830–1860), movements to expand the American educational system through the creation of common (public) schools and to advance the status of women's education took shape. Nineteenth-century women were traditionally excluded from secondary and post-secondary education, largely substantiated by the belief in female intellectual inferiority. The basis of female progress was largely measured by a woman's capabilities as a wife and mother, not by the extent of her classical knowledge. In 1862, one columnist for the *Boston Investigator* remarked in the article "Female Education" that "…a well furnished mind, a well governed temper, love of domestic pleasures, and an inclination and capacity to pursue domestic employments, are the first requisite in a woman and the foundation of her respectability and enjoyment."

During the Civil War, secondary education was largely private. The development of a mainstream public education system did not evolve until the decade

Teachers educate newly-freed blacks in the South. With the departure of men to fight in the Civil War, many women filled their positions in schools, taking on the responsibility of educating students. After the war ended, many women journeyed to the South in hopes of offering literacy to the former slaves. *© Corbis.*

"The great toil of brain and body in educating our children comes almost entirely upon women, who cannot obtain, as their reward, enough to live upon; while 'modest,' 'wise,' 'considerate,' man delegates a little more than a baker's dozen of his sex to *superintend* us in our labor, and pays himself by the lion's share" (Smith 1864, p. 3).

Female educational and professional advancement sometimes stood outside of racial boundaries. The commitment to educating former slaves was often biracial, drawing black and white women together for a common cause. The Sea Island "experiment" was demonstrative of this universal struggle, but also exposed underlying racial tensions and mixed motives. In September 1862, Laura Towne and Ellen Murray, two white, educated northerners, opened Penn School in the Port Royal District of the Sea Islands off the South Carolina coast. Penn School was South Carolina's first school for African Americans, and was largely funded with Quaker support. Both Towne and Murray committed their lives to edifying former slaves, but were arguably participating in an educational trend that was largely paternalistic.

When Charlotte Forten, an educated black Philadelphian belonging to a prestigious free black family, arrived on the Sea Islands, she was met with mixed reception. Her refinement and musical capabilities caused great astonishment and admiration among her peers and students. Yet Forten, a product of her time, privately expressed her mistrust of whites, stating in her diary *The Journal of Charlotte Forten: A Free Negro in the Slave Era* that "...it is hard to go through life meeting contempt with contempt, hatred with hatred, fearing, with too good reason to love and trust hardly anyone whose skin is white,—however lovable, attractive, and congenial in seeming" (p. 10).

BIBLIOGRAPHY

"Female Education." *Boston Investigator* (Boston, MA), May 14, 1862, issue 2, col. B.

Forten, Charlotte. *The Journal of Charlotte Forten: A Free Negro in the Slave Era*, 3rd ed. Ed. Ray A. Billington. London: Collier Books, 1969.

Katz, William Loren, ed. *Two Black Teachers during the Civil War: Mary S. Peake; the Colored Teacher at Fortress Monroe [by] Lewis C. Lockwood. Life on the Sea Islands [by] Charlotte Forten.* New York: Arno Press, 1969.

Selleck, Linda. *Gentle Invaders: Quaker Women Educators and Racial Issues During the Civil War and Reconstruction.* Richmond, IN: Friends United Press, 1995.

Smith, John, Mrs. "Mrs. John Smith Gives an Opinion upon the Salaries of School Teachers, Male and Female." *Daily Evening Bulletin.* Issue 68. San Francisco: CA, June 24, 1864.

following the war. One of the principal arguments that stemmed from the common school movement emphasized the training of female teachers. Scant numbers of middle class and elite girls from the North and South attended female seminaries as a substitute for secondary and higher education. Female seminaries prepared female teachers, while at the same time allowing young women to study male-dominated subjects such as mathematics, science, and Latin.

Although the extent of women's education was sometimes limited, the Civil War era was marked by a large influx of women into the teaching profession. Few southern women possessed the educational training to fill teaching positions vacated by southern men, while northern women found greater success in the profession. In many cases, female educators were the preferred transmitters of knowledge and American values, but earned wages that were usually less than half of a male teacher's pay. Unequal compensation was a pressing concern for women throughout the United States. Even in the West, female teachers drew public attention to the wage discrimination. In 1864, Mrs. John Smith wrote,

Williams, Heather Andrea. *Self-taught: African American Education in Slavery and Freedom.* Chapel Hill: University of North Carolina Press, 2005.

Talitha L. LeFlouria

FREE BLACKS AND EDUCATION

The story of freed people's efforts to gain an education begins in slavery. *Education* is a loaded term—there are many kinds of education, and in one sense, Africans did not come to the Americas uneducated. But most were not literate, and few possessed the kinds of formal European education that many of their masters and other whites had received. For this essay, the term *education* signifies the somewhat narrow meaning of literacy and the formal instruction received in a typically organized American school system.

From Slavery to Freedom

Knowledge is power. Slaves recognized that their lack of knowledge limited their power over their own lives and protected their master's control over them. Slave owners and white elites recognized this, too, and therefore often made it illegal to teach slaves to read and write. In *Bullwhip Days*, the former slave Sarah Wilson recalled that "our white folks didn't believe in niggers larnin' anything. Dey thought hit would make de niggers harder to keep slaves, an to make dem wuk" (Mellon 1988, p. 197). Nonetheless, at times slaves found the means to become literate. Marshall Mack, born a slave in 1854 in Oklahoma, remembered how his uncle acquired literacy while taking his owner's children to school every day: "On sech trips, the chillun learned my uncle to read and write. Dey slipped and done this, for it was a law among slave-holders that a slave not be caught wid a book" ("Marshall Mack" 1941). Mack's uncle recognized an opportunity and took full advantage. For him and other slaves, educating themselves was a form of resistance. In his autobiography, Frederick Douglass made this clear. When his owner declared that "Learning would spoil the best nigger in the world," Douglass became all the more determined to learn: "What he most dreaded, that I most desired. What he most loved, that I most hated. . . . [The] argument he so warmly urged, against my learning to read, only served to inspire me with a desire and determination to learn" (Douglass 1845, p. 37). Literacy and education opened up a new world for Douglass, and sharpened his desire to be free. After escaping slavery, Douglass's desire to learn continued to burn, and helped propel him into the leadership of the abolitionist movement before the Civil War. Douglass was a staunch advocate for the education of freed people both during and after the war.

Many free black Southerners also pursued an education when they were able, though they had to do so carefully and usually clandestinely: In the eyes of white

A freedman's school riot. Not all Southerners readily accepted freed slaves as citizens possessing equal civil rights. Many attempts made by African Americans after the war to vote, find employment, and earn an education were prevented by white Southerners, fearful of losing their privileged status. © *North Wind Picture Archives.*

Southerners, educated free blacks threatened to destabilize slavery and increase the chances of insurrection. Denmark Vesey (1767–1822), a literate free black man in Charleston, had done exactly that in 1822—his planned slave revolt came close to fruition before the plot was discovered and quashed. But some blacks did manage to obtain a formal education. Mary Peake, a young free black woman from Virginia, was sent by her parents to Washington, DC, for schooling during the 1830s. Congress eventually decided that Virginia's law prohibiting formal education for African Americans should apply to free blacks, but Mary Peake put to good use the ten years of education she had acquired. Lewis Lockwood, a Northern missionary who wrote Peake's biography, recounted that for years before the Civil War "she was engaged in instructing children and adults, through her shrewdness and the divine protection eluding the vigilance of conservators of the slave law, or, if temporarily interfered with, again commencing and prosecuting her labors of love with cautious fearlessness" (Lockwood 1969, p. 14).

Black Education in the North

Because slavery died in the Northern states long before it did in the South, free black Northerners had a greater ability to educate themselves through literary societies and schools. Their efforts at times received support from a few white Northerners, but generally they struggled with insufficient resources. As a result, many free black Northerners pushed for racially integrated schooling. William C. Nell, one of the leaders of Boston's black community, argued for years that African Americans' long history of contributing to the military, economic, and political security of their country meant that "the descendants of such citizens [are] entitled to the same educational facilities that are so freely guaranteed to all other children" throughout the North (Wesley and Uzelac 2002, p. 465).

Some African Americans, however, believed that integration was a chimera, and pushed for black control of black schools. In cities such as Boston and Cleveland, the majority of black parents and leadership pushed hard for integration, whereas in other cities black communities believed self-determination was best achieved by maintaining control over a separate school system. The historian Nikki Taylor notes that in Cincinnati, for instance, the black school board managed to be "a powerful advocate for educational access and equality" from the 1850s into the 1870s. For them, "integration was, at times, at odds with the larger objectives of equality and self-determination" so long as they could control the schools (Taylor 2006, p. 297). That was often the key—in many locations, African Americans were too few in number, or opposition was too strong for them to secure anything close to equal resources for their students and teachers. In such cases, the tendency was to seek integration.

This debate within black communities persisted long after the Civil War. Nevertheless, like their enslaved brothers and sisters, free black Northerners established a pattern of formal schooling that helped provide a foundation for future efforts at black education. They placed a high value on education, which they believed could help them achieve equality and full citizenship rights. The *National Era*, a Washington, DC–based black newspaper, noted in 1854 that "Slavery denies self-ownership, education, wages, all political rights to its subjects" (November 9, 1854). Fighting against this injustice was a call to arms. The North Carolina–born David Walker, a fiery black shop owner in Boston, had made this explicit years before when he published the incendiary tract "Appeal to the Coloured Citizens of the World" in 1829. He believed simple literacy was not enough: African Americans had to "seek after the substance of learning." They had to be desperate and determined to learn. "I would," he declared, "crawl on my hands and knees through mud and mire, to the feet of a learned man, where I would sit and humbly supplicate him to instill into me, that which neither devils nor tyrants could remove, only with my life—for coloured people to acquire learning in this country, makes tyrants quake and tremble on their sandy foundation" (Walker 1830, p. 34).

Education during the Civil War

Within months of the outbreak of war in 1861, word spread among slaves that if they could get behind Union lines, the Union Army would not return them to slavery. Enslaved women, men, and children by the thousands walked, ran, rode, and even swam toward Union lines and freedom. They poured into military encampments, small towns, rural outposts, and cities such as Washington, DC. The *Christian Recorder*, a Philadelphia-based black newspaper of the African Methodist Episcopal (A.M.E.) Church, reported that by summer 1865, almost 10,000 African Americans had escaped slavery from Virginia. They built two schoolhouses and employed twenty teachers for their children, and according to one white observer, were "giving more earnest and general attention to education than the white people of this city" (*Christian Recorder*, July 22, 1865). These African Americans made it clear right away that they wanted to improve their education. A reporter for the *Atlantic Monthly* who spent summer 1861 among the contrabands at Fort Monroe in Virginia wrote that

> there was a very general desire among the contrabands to know how to read. A few had learned; and these, in every instance where we inquired as to their teacher, had been taught on the sly in their childhood by their white playmates.... I remember of a summer's afternoon seeing a young married woman, perhaps twenty-five years old, seated on a door-step with her primer before her, trying to make progress. ("The Contrabands at Fortress Monroe," p. 639)

Mary Peake was one of their teachers. Her class at first had only about a half dozen students, but once word got out, within days there were more than fifty. Other schools were set up in response to the demand, and Mary Peake also began teaching adults at night (Lockwood 1969, pp. 14–16). Harriet Jacobs, who, before escaping slavery in 1842, had spent seven years in a crawlspace hiding from a sexually abusive master (she chronicled her story in the gripping narrative *Incidents in the Life of a Slave Girl: Written by Herself*), told similar stories of working with freed people during and after the Civil War (Yacavone 2004, p. 199). Donald Yacovone's superb reader of Civil War documents contains a letter Jacobs wrote in March 1864, when she was in Alexandria, Virginia, working with her daughter and two white teachers from Massachusetts. In fall 1863, they had needed room for a school, so "one of the freedmen, whose cabin consisted of two rooms, gave it up to us for our school. We soon found that the clamor of little voices begging for admittance far exceeded the narrow limits of this establishment" (Yacavone 2004, p. 199). The freedpeople in this community raised $150 and built a schoolhouse to answer the growing demand. In January 1864, seventy-five students were attending; by March there were 225 and an evening school for adults. Jacobs told her Northern supporters that "you would be astonished at the progress many of them have made in this short time. Many who less than three months ago scarcely knew the A. B. C. are now reading and spelling in words of two or three syllables. When I look at these bright little boys, I often wonder whether there is not some Frederick Douglass among them, destined to do honor to his race in the future" (Yacavone 2004, pp. 199–200).

African Americans' resolute determination to be educated inspired many white Northerners and religious organizations to send teachers south. One of the teachers assisting Harriet Jacobs was from the Education Commission of Boston, which eventually merged with similar organizations to form the American Freedmen's Aid Union, the largest volunteer organization from the North. In *Christian Reconstruction*, the historian Joe M. Richardson noted that as soon as word of contrabands reached leaders in the American Missionary Association, they began organizing efforts to send teachers south. They found that "few teachers have had more responsive students than those who went away among the contrabands." The teacher H. S. Beale was impressed that "plowmen hurry from the field at night to get their hour of study." That responsiveness knew no age limits; one man who was said to be 108 years old and had only been free for a few weeks, came to learn to read (Richardson 1986, pp. 13–14).

After 1863, once African Americans were permitted to enlist in the Union Army, black soldiers, many of whom had been contrabands, also were emphatic in pursuing opportunities to learn. One of the American Missionary Association's chaplains noted in 1864 that "a majority of the men seemed to regard their books an indispensable portion of their equipment, and the cartridge-box and spelling book are attached to the same belt" (Richardson 1986, p. 25). Education, like being able to fight against the Confederacy, emboldened black men. James Alexander, a free black man helping to set up an Arkansas A.M.E. Church in 1864, described education as weapon received from the schools that the black troops of the Fifty-sixth and Sixtieth U.S. Infantry regiments had established for themselves. The "quiet, well-behaved set of men," had made rapid progress, "daily acquiring a better and more efficient use of that most deadly weapon, with which they have chastised the rebels, while here, on more than one occasion" (*The Christian Recorder*, December 31, 1864). Members of these regiments often took up formal and informal leadership roles in their communities in the North and South when they returned home from service, building on and contributing to the foundation of education that hundreds of free African Americans had established.

There were many white-led organizations that made immeasurable contributions to the efforts to provide sound education to African Americans, especially during and after the Civil War. The Freedmen's Bureau, a federal agency established in March 1865, was given the monumental task of assisting freedpeople in virtually every area of transitioning from slavery to freedom—including acquiring land, obtaining medical care, resolving legal disputes, providing basic necessities, protecting civil rights, and accessing education. The Bureau was grossly underfunded and understaffed. Churches and missionary agencies helped, sending thousands of men and women into the South. Their efforts have been well documented.

Free and enslaved black women and men had always been at the center of the black educational mission. Sometimes with their own money and their own hands, sometimes with the help of white missionary organizations, and sometimes with the help of the Freedmen's Bureau, they built and populated schools all over the South, just as free blacks had done in the North before the war. The Civil War and emancipation provided unprecedented and dramatic new access to education, and hundreds of thousands of free African Americans took advantage of the opportunity.

BIBLIOGRAPHY

"Arkansas Letter." *Christian Recorder*, December 31, 1864.

Belt-Beyan, Phyllis M. *The Emergence of African American Literary Traditions: Family and Community Efforts in the Nineteenth Century.* Westport, CT: Praeger, 2004.

Butchart, Ronald E. *Northern Schools, Southern Blacks, and Reconstruction: Freedmen's Education, 1862–1875.* Westport, CT: Greenwood Press, 1980.

Christian Recorder. Philadelphia, 1861–1898.

"The Contrabands at Fortress Monroe." *Atlantic Monthly* 8 (November 1861): 626–641.

Douglass, Frederick. *Narrative of the Life of Frederick Douglass, an American Slave.* Boston: Anti-Slavery Office, 1845.

Lockwood, Lewis. "Mary S. Peake, the Colored Teacher at Fortress Monroe 1863." *Two Black Teachers during the Civil War.* New York: Arno Press and the *New York Times,* 1969.

"Marshall Mack." *Born in Slavery: Slave Narratives from the Federal Writers' Project, 1936-1938.* Oklahoma Narratives, Vol. 13, pp. 212-214. Washington, DC: 1941. Available from http://memory.loc.gov/.

Mellon, James, ed. *Bullwhip Days: The Slaves Remember: An Oral History.* New York: Avon Books, 1988.

National Era. Washington, DC, 1847–1860.

Richardson, Joe M. *Christian Reconstruction: The American Missionary Association and Southern Blacks, 1861–1890.* Athens: University of Georgia Press, 1986.

Taylor, Nikki. "African Americans' Strive for Educational Self-Determination in Cincinnati Before 1873." *The Black Urban Community: From Dusk till Dawn,* ed. Gayle T. Tate and Lewis A. Randolph. New York: Palgrave Macmillan, 2006.

Walker, David. *Appeal to the Coloured Citizens of the World.* Boston: Author, 1830.

Wesley, Dorothy Porter and Constance Porter Uzelac, eds. *William Cooper Nell: Selected Writings 1832-1874.* Baltimore: Black Classic Press, 2002.

Williams, Heather Andrea. *Self-Taught: African American Education in Slavery and Freedom.* Chapel Hill: University of North Carolina Press, 2005.

Yacovone, Donald, ed. *Freedom's Journey: African American Voices of the Civil War.* Chicago: Lawrence Hill Books, 2004.

Scott Hancock

THE MORRILL ACT

The Morrill Act of 1862, introduced by Vermont Congressman Justin Morrill, was a federal mandate to provide funding for the development of "public" institutions of higher education in states loyal to the Union. The Morrill Act was originally titled "An Act Donating Public Lands to the Several States and Territories Which May Provide Colleges for the Benefit of Agriculture and the Mechanic Arts."

Vermont congressman Justin Smith Morrill (1810–1898). As Western territories filled with farmers taking advantage of the Homestead Act of 1862, Vermont congressman Justin Morrill proposed the opening in those areas of public universities devoted to agriculture and mechanics. After the Civil War, the Second Morrill Act allowed Southern states to take advantage of the program, with separate universities established for both white and African American students. © *Corbis*

Following the secession of the South and the onset of the Civil War in 1861, the Union's economic and political focus began to turn heavily toward western expansion. New territory in the West, many felt, would compensate for the temporary loss of Southern agricultural lands and raw materials. The federal Homestead Act of 1862 granted persons at least twenty years of age title to farm 160 acres for five years before purchasing the land for a nominal price from the federal government. The intent of the act was to encourage the development of a large "yeoman farmer" class that would replace the practice of slave labor on Southern plantations with small, independently owned, family farms (Foner 1989, p. 9). The passage of the Homestead Act paralleled the passage of the Pacific Railway Act of 1862, which provided federal support for the development of the transcontinental railroad system. This railway system connected the industrial centers of the Northeast to the pacific coast. Both the Homestead Act and the Pacific Railway Act guaranteed the free flow of manufactured goods and raw materials across Western states and territories, strengthening America's emerging industrial economy (Foner 1989, pp. 200–203). "Every acre of the fertile soil is a mine which only waits for the contact of labor to yield its treasures," Congressman Samuel Hooper of Massachusetts remarked, "and every acre is opened to that fruitful contact by the Homestead Act" (Hooper 1862, p. 36).

The Morrill Act of 1862 was passed to give "intellectual" support to westward expansion. The agricultural, technological, and commercial challenges associated with linking Western territories to Northern industries needed to be studied thoroughly. This study was of particular importance to ensuring the stability of emerging, yeoman farming communities. The Morrill Act granted 30,000 acres of federally controlled land to each congressman representing states in support of the Union. The acreage was to be sold to generate revenue that would be used to build public institutions of higher education dedicated to instruction in agricultural and mechanical fields. Iowa State University, the University of Illinois, Cornell University, Purdue University, the Massachusetts Institute of Technology, Rutgers, and the University of Missouri are a few examples of educational institutions that had their origins in the Morrill Act. An important aspect of the act was its intent to provide formal education to those traditionally excluded form America's liberal arts–based institutions. Subsequently, "land grant institutions," as they are commonly called, have served as intellectual centers for the states that they serve, particularly in the area of agriculture.

At the end of the Civil War, the former rebel states of the South came under the purview of the Morrill Act. As a result, the University of Georgia, the University of Florida, Clemson University, North Carolina State University, and the University of Tennessee, among others, were all designated as land grant institutions. Many of the Southern land grant institutions had actually been founded much earlier, in the seventeenth and eighteenth centuries, but their new status meant they would henceforth be supported economically by the federal government. The University of Georgia, for example, had been in existence since 1785, while the University of Tennessee was founded in 1794, but did not receive land-grant status until 1879.

Along with the need to expand access to education, another challenge associated with the end of the Civil War was the problem of dealing with the history of slave labor and white racism in the Southern states. Following the infamous Hayes-Tilden Compromise of 1877, the former Confederacy gained de facto control over the South. The gains made by African Americans in the areas of politics, economics, and education were challenged when Hayes-Tilden effectively ended the period in American history known as Reconstruction. Segregation laws, popularly known as Jim Crow laws, were passed at the state level to prevent African Americans from voting and becoming economically independent. In addition, the post-Reconstruction era witnessed the emergence of organizations like the Ku Klux Klan. The Klan, by force and under the cover of night, terrorized African Americans who sought to participate in state politics, build schools, own land, or escape from the labor conditions associated with sharecropping. These developments led to the passage of a second Morrill Act in 1890.

BIBLIOGRAPHY

Foner Eric. *Reconstruction: America's Unfinished Revolution, 1863–1877*. New York: Harper & Row, 1989.

Hooper, Samuel. *Banking Association and Uniform Currency Bill: With Extracts from Reports of Secretary of the Treasury*. Washington, DC, 1862.

Schwartz, John A. "Land-Grant Act: History and Institutions." Available from http://www.higher-ed.org/.

Kwasi Densu

EDUCATION IN THE CONFEDERACY

During the American Civil War, several textbooks were produced for schoolchildren in the Confederate states with content designed to build a sense of national identity. Some of them used strong, anti-Northern language, with one oft-cited example appearing in the title *Elementary Arithmetic*, for North Carolinian children: "If one Confederate soldier can whip 7 Yankees, how many soldiers can whip 49 Yankees?" (Wiley 1978, p. 123). Aside from such propaganda, more common to these schoolbooks were lessons in sacrifice and duty to one's country, along with the contention that slavery was both a moral and economically justified system.

Fewer School Districts

By contrast to the Northern states in the Union, the Confederate states were predominantly rural, with an economy based on agriculture, not manufacturing or commerce. Hence there were fewer urban centers and correspondingly fewer organized school districts. Most Southern whites—for it was illegal in the Southern states to teach a slave to read or write—were educated at home, if they were wealthy, or in local one-room schoolhouses for households. The school year was usually arranged around the planting and harvest seasons, which was also a commonplace schedule in rural communities of the Northern states. The term usually began in December after the last harvest, and ended in March, just before the spring planting required the help of all available household members.

With the outbreak of the Civil War, maintaining the secessionist cause took on paramount importance, and all resources were marshaled for the war effort. In the first half of the nineteenth century, most schoolteachers were male, following a belief that male teachers were better able to provide the necessary discipline. It was only after the war that more women took up the profession, as a result of the conviction that females were better suited to providing moral guidance for young minds. When the war began, conscription went into effect in the Confederate states, and many male teachers were called to serve, though there were some exemptions allowed. Furthermore, the number of pupils able to attend school on a regular basis also dwindled, as economic hardships became a fact of life. Children were needed to help on their families' farms, and in some cases households were forced to relocate to cities like Richmond, where youngsters helped support their families by working in munitions factories.

Moral Lessons

For the students who did remain in class in the South during the war years, their textbooks attempted to create a sense of national identity and culture, along with providing moral lessons in citizenship, family honor, and Christian duty. The illustrations reflected a nation at war, with cannons, soldiers, and Confederate flags used freely in illustrations. A Richmond publishing house, George L. Bidgood, issued a large number of these books, including *The Confederate First Reader: Containing Selections in Prose and Poetry, as Reading Exercises for the Younger Children in the Schools and Families of the Confederate States*, by Richard McAllister Smith. Designed for slightly advanced readers, its reading selections borrowed heavily from the Bible and such similar classics as the ancient Greek tale of the tortoise and the hare. As Smith writes in his preface, "The pieces have been selected with a view to interest and instruct the pupils, and at the same time to elevate their ideas, form correct tastes, and instil proper sentiments" (Smith 1864, p. 3).

Stronger language could be found in the *Confederate Speller and Reader*, written by a minister named John Neely and registered as copyrighted material in Augusta, Georgia, in 1864. Its tone was clear: "Troops who enter a State with hos-tile purpose, are in-va-ders. Let all who are able, take up arms to drive them back" (Rubin 2005, p. 31). These primers also addressed issues relating to the loss of family members. In a passage titled "The Dead Baby" from Marinda Branson Moore's *The First Dixie Reader*, the cause of death is explained:

. . . croup. It was well two days a-go, and could play as you do; but now see its pale white face. 3. Take its lit-tle white hand in yours and feel how cold it is. You ask what made the ba-by die. I will tell you. 4. God saw it would be best to take it to heav-en now. Per-haps he looked away in the fu-ture, and saw that the child would not be good if it grew to be a man (Moore 1863, p. 56).

Proslavery Propaganda

Moore also addressed slavery and its moral implications in her "Dixie" series of books, issued by her Raleigh, North Carolina, publisher, Branson & Farrar. In her *First Dixie Reader*, one passage reads:

1. Here comes old aunt Ann. She is quite old. See how she leans on her stick. 2. When she was young she did good work, but now she can not work much. But she is not like a poor white wo-man. 3. Aunt Ann knows that her young Miss, as she calls her, will take care of her as long as she lives. 4. Ma-ny poor white folks would be glad to live in her house and eat what Miss Kate sends out for her din-ner (Moore 1863, p. 22).

These pro-Dixie books were quickly abandoned after the war, replaced by texts either issued in the North or vetted by Reconstruction officials as fostering a more healing mood for the nation.

BIBLIOGRAPHY

Moore, Marinda Branson. *The First Dixie Reader: Designed to Follow the Dixie Primer*. Raleigh, NC: Branson & Farrar, 1863.

Rubin, Anne Sarah. *A Shattered Nation: The Rise and Fall of the Confederacy, 1861-1868*. Chapel Hill: University of North Carolina Press, 2005.

Smith, R. M. *The Confederate First Reader: Containing Selections in Prose and Poetry, as Reading Exercises for the Younger Children in the Schools and Families of the Confederate States*. Richmond, VA: G. L. Bidgood, 1864.

Sutherland, Daniel E. *The Expansion of Everyday Life, 1860-1876*. New York: Harper & Row, 1989.

Wiley, Bell Irvin. *The Life of Johnny Reb: The Common Soldier of the Confederacy*. Baton Rouge: Louisiana State University Press, 1978.

Carol Brennan

COMMON SCHOOLS

In 1671 Virginia's colonial governor, Sir William Berkeley (1606–1677), famously wrote to his British overseers with regard to his North American dominion: "I thank God there are no free schools or printing . . . for learning has brought disobedience, and heresy, and sects into the world, and printing has divulged them" (*Percy Anecdotes* 1847, p. 181). Unfortunately for Berkeley and his

British superiors, the Puritan belief in education as a means of preserving both religious faith and moral culture inspired much of the revolutionary activities that ultimately led to the formation of the United States of America.

It was another Virginian, Thomas Jefferson (1743–1826), who systematized the education of young Americans through his *Bill for the More General Diffusion of Knowledge* (1779). Jefferson envisioned a district system in which all children would benefit from primary education in a local school. In addition to reading and mathematics, schools should teach history to provide pupils with the moral and civic understanding required of an informed electorate. As Jefferson wrote to James Madison (1751–1836) in 1787, "Educate and inform the whole mass of the people. Enable them to see that it is their interest to preserve peace and order, and they will preserve them. And it requires no very high degree of education to convince them of this. They are the only sure reliance for the preservation of our liberty" (Bergh 1903, p. 392).

The common school movement that took root in the first decades of the 1800s revolutionized American education. Prior to this change, most children learned what few academic skills they possessed at home; farming or an apprenticeship in a trade were of greater importance. Common schools, in contrast, were open to all children. Their focus was the "three R's"—reading, writing, and arithmetic—skills that addressed the more sophisticated needs of an increasingly industrialized economy with a rising urban merchant class and a manufacture-based economy. In an article titled "What Schools Should Do," a writer for the *Milwaukee Sentinel* emphasized the link between vocation and education, noting of farmers that "the fruitfulness of the soil does not depend so much upon its richness, as it does upon the intelligence of those who cultivate it." "The mechanic should cultivate his mind, that his head may help his hands," the writer added, while for the merchant, a sufficient education would ensure that "his employment . . . would never descend to a system of higgling" ("What Schools Should Do," October 9, 1838).

While responding to changing workforce demands, common schools were also promoted as a way to fight the moral decay associated with urbanization. American workers and their families were now migrating from farms to cities and were coming into contact with immigrants from many other countries. Echoing Jefferson, common schools were viewed as a means of instilling the Protestant work ethic and civic values in future citizens, thereby strengthening the economy and political framework of the still-young nation. Such exemplary Americans as Eli Whitney (1765–1825), the inventor of the cotton gin and the concept of interchangeable parts in machinery, were often cited by advocates of public education. As Horace Greeley (1811–1872)

Connecticut schoolmaster and state legislator Noah Webster (1758–1843). Noah Webster, Connecticut schoolmaster and state legislator, was an advocator of Jefferson's common schools program. He believed education to be the most imperative institution in a democracy. He wrote three books, *American Spelling Book* (1786), *Elementary Spelling Book* (1829), and *American Dictionary of the English Language* that became staples in American classrooms. *Portrait by James Sharples, Sr., photograph. National Archives and Records Administration.*

noted in his *The American Conflict*, the enterprising young Whitney devoted "his summers to the labors of the farm, attending the common school of his district through its winter session," where he was "noted for devotion to, and eminent skill in, arithmetic. At fourteen, he was looked upon by his neighbors as a very remarkable, energetic, and intelligent youth" (Greeley 1866, p. 59).

Jefferson's system of common schools was taken up by several noted reformers. The Connecticut schoolmaster and state legislator Noah Webster (1758–1843), whose "blue-back" *American Spelling Book* (1786), *Elementary Spelling Book* (1829), and *American Dictionary of the English Language* (1828) became fixtures in most American classrooms during the nineteenth century, viewed education as the most crucial undertaking of a democratic government. A major advocate for common schools, the Boston attorney and legislator Horace Mann (1796–1859) became secretary of the Massachusetts Board of Education in 1837 and also founded the influential *Common School Journal.* Viewing the common-school system as a way to attain economic equality and instill respect for work and its fruits (or the private property of others), Mann argued that an education is the God-given right of every human being, regardless of wealth, race, or gender. Other reformers included James G. Carter (1795–1849), who helped establish normal schools to train competent teachers, and the attorney Calvin H. Wiley (1819–1887), who became North Carolina's superintendent of common schools in 1852.

By the 1830s the common-school movement had deep roots in New England, and Massachusetts was a leader in advancing general education. As a Vermont-based journalist noted with some chagrin in assessing the advances of his Southern neighbor, "it must be some consolation to know that the neighboring states are making such improvements in their common-school systems . . . that Vermont cannot very long remain blind to the light that is shining around her" (*Vermont Chronicle,* March 23, 1827, p. 198). Further to the south and west, in Ohio and Pennsylvania, the establishment of common schools was also actively pursued. "Whatever excuse the first settlers may have had amidst the multiplied difficulties with which they had to contend, we have no such excuses now," observed the editor of the *Ohio Observer* in advocating a common-school program modeled after that of Massachusetts (*Ohio Observer,* November 2, 1833, p. 7).

Although common schools were welcomed by most Americans, some families chose to opt out. As Charles Wheeler Denison noted in *The Tanner-Boy and How He Became Lieutenant-General,* a contemporary biography of Union General Ulysses S. Grant (1822–1885), the mother of the future U.S. president "was not content to leave him, as many mothers leave their children, to the routine instruction of the common-school of the neighborhood. . . . Her lessons of duty as a mother were learned from the Holy Book" and the "book of nature" (Denison 1864, p. 12). While strongly held religious beliefs or fear of inadequate moral guidance inspired resistance to public education for some parents, others took issue with the regional authority of school boards and the system of broad public taxation that funded such boards. Still others recoiled from sending their children to common schools due to fears of the consequences of coming into contact with members of other races or the poorer classes. Despite such objections, most state legislatures in the North and West had a system of publicly funded common schools in place by 1860.

Common Schools in the South

In contrast with the North and West, by 1860 few Southern states had taken such large strides toward establishing public education. Their efforts were hampered in some areas by the plantation system, which divided some parts of the South into large estates rather than the regional clusters of easily taxable homesteads present in the North. While common schools existed in a few Southern cities, the sons and daughters of many affluent Southern families attended private academies, were educated by tutors and governesses, or were educated in the Northern states or in Europe. Although the institution of slavery was perhaps the largest barrier to the establishment of a common-school system, the relative unimportance of education among the Southern populace must also be noted. Although the South Carolina legislature established a public school district system in 1821, ten years later the state could boast only 8,390 students from a population of 594,400 residents. In contrast, Massachusetts could then claim 149,222 students in a state population of 737,699 ("Common School Education," July 28, 1842, p. 51). By the time war broke out in 1862, 11,881 district school libraries had been established in Northern states, but only 186 existed in the South (Sumner 1870–1883, p. 42).

During the Civil War, Southern schools fared far worse than their Northern counterparts, as the Confederacy requisitioned all available monies for the war effort. "A large number of male teachers were among the first to volunteer in the army of the Confederacy," school superintendent Wiley noted in an 1862 report to Raleigh, North Carolina's *Weekly Raleigh Register.* Supplying textbooks was also difficult, and some children were given outdated editions of Webster's classic "blueback" speller, all positive references to Northern states dutifully redacted. Some pro-Confederate textbooks were published locally with homemade paper and pasteboard. Wiley did not consider paper shortages and the like to be setbacks. "The continued and absorbing contemplation of a long war tends to depress the mind of the country," the superintendent maintained, adding that "the diversion of thought to . . . our industrial interests . . . " because of such shortages "gives new spring and elasticity to our hearts, enabling us the better to . . . appreciate the immense forces at work for our final independence, and thus to engage with more intelligent, determined and persevering efforts in the struggle before us" (Wiley 1862, p. 2).

Unlike some Confederate states, the indefatigable efforts of North Carolina's school superintendent helped it keep its schools open throughout the war. As Wiley noted in a report to the state's governor in January of 1866, "the common schools lived and discharged their useful mission through all the gloom and trials of the conflict, and when the last gun was fired, the doors were still open and they numbered their pupils by the scores of thousands" (Abercrombie 1910, vol. 13, p. 5809). The desegregation efforts following the war fueled the common-school programs of the South, and by the end of the nineteenth century almost all children in the United States could obtain a primary education.

BIBLIOGRAPHY

Abercrombie, John W., ed. *Library of Southern Literature*, vol. 13. Atlanta, GA: Martin & Hoyt, 1910.

Bergh, Albert Ellery, ed. *The Writings of Thomas Jefferson*, Vol. 6. Washington, DC: Thomas Jefferson Memorial Association, 1903.

Carlton, Frank Tracy. *Economic Influences upon Educational Progress in the United States, 1820-1850*. Madison: University of Wisconsin, 1965.

"Common School Education: Two Slave States," *Emancipator and Free American* (New York, NY), July 28, 1842, p. 51.

Cremin, Lawrence A. *The Republic and the School: Horace Mann on the Education of Free Men*. New York: Teachers College Press, 1957.

Denison, Charles Wheeler. *The Tanner-Boy and How He Became Lieutenant-General*. Boston: Roberts Brothers, 1864.

Gould, Benjamin Apthorp. *Sanitary Memoirs of the War of the Rebellion*, vol. 2: *Investigations in the Military and Anthropological Statistics of American Soldiers*. New York: Arno Press, 1979 [c. 1869].

Greeley, Horace. *The American Conflict: A History of the Great Rebellion in the United States of America, 1860-1864: Its Causes, Incidents, and Results*, vol. 1. Hartford, CT: O. D. Chase & Co., 1866.

Kaestle, Carl F. *Pillars of the Republic: Common Schools and American Society, 1780–1860*. New York: Hill & Wang, 1983.

Mondale, Sarah, and Sarah Patton, eds. *School: The Story of American Public Education*. Boston: Beacon Press, 2001.

Nasaw, David. *Schooled to Order: A Social History of Public Schooling in the United States*. New York: Oxford University Press, 1979.

Ohio Observer (Hudson, OH), November 2, 1833, p. 7.

The Percy Anecdotes: American Anecdotes, rev. ed., vol. 1. New York: Harper & Brothers, 1847.

Sumner, Charles. *The Works of Charles Sumner*, vol. 5. Boston: Lee & Shepard, 1870–1883.

Vermont Chronicle (Bellows Falls, VT), March 23, 1827, p. 198.

"What Schools Should Do," *Milwaukee Sentinel* (Milwaukee, WI), October 9, 1838.

Wiley, C. H. "Editorial." *Weekly Raleigh Register* (Raleigh, NC), November 26, 1862, p. 2.

Pamela L. Kester

ROLE OF WEST POINT

Graduates of the federal military academy at West Point, New York, played a crucial role in the American Civil War as commanding officers of both Union and Con-federate forces. Even Jefferson Davis, the president of the Confederate States of America (CSA), was a graduate of the United States Military Academy at West Point. When the war began in April 1861, the U.S. Army's list of active-duty officers showed 1,080 men, of whom 824 were West Point graduates (Office of the Chief of Military History 1989, p. 189). The academy had been established by the third U.S. president, Thomas Jefferson, in part to build a sense of national identity among its military officers that would, it was hoped, prevent the sort of regional factionalism that led to the outbreak of civil war. Among those 824 West Point alumni recorded in 1861, 184 left the U.S. Army to serve in the Confederate Army (Office of the Chief of Military History 1989, p. 189).

As an elite training ground for military personnel, West Point developed strong bonds among cadets over the course of an arduous four-year stint, and that camaraderie in many cases resulted in lifelong friendships. The war compelled officers to command regiments whose weapons were aimed against forces commanded by fellow West Pointers. Taking up arms against men with whom they had trained and served was a gross violation of the military code of honor, and for these officers it proved one of the more heartbreaking aspects of the American Civil War.

Trained Army Engineers

Founded in 1802 on a scenic perch overlooking the Hudson River some fifty miles distant from New York City, West Point was modeled after France's famous military academies. Its counterpart was the U.S. Naval Academy at Annapolis, Maryland, which had been founded in 1845. Relatively early in its history, however, West Point became the target of critics, who claimed the school was an elitist institution open only to the sons of the wealthy or prominent. To gain admission, a potential cadet had to be appointed by a member of Congress, making entrance entirely dependent on family connections.

In the era before the Civil War, West Point offered such military training as drilling and artillery practice, but its curriculum was mainly a practical, engineering-focused course of studies that graduated men who went on to staff the Army Corps of Engineers. Because in this era institutions of higher learning focused on the arts or sciences, and the field of engineering had not yet fully developed as a profession, West Point was a rare training ground in this new field. Cadets were educated at taxpayer expense, and often resigned their military commissions after a few years to take lucrative jobs with the railroads or in other new sectors of the Industrial Revolution. This development led some to declare that West Point was a waste of taxpayer money and should be eliminated altogether. In response, Congress mandated that after 1838 graduates would be required to serve four years of active duty in the Army. Most entered as a second lieutenant, the entry level for commissioned officers.

Despite its critics' claims of elitism, West Point was a difficult, isolated place where cadets spent fifteen hours per day either on military drills or in classes. Freshmen cadets, or *plebes* (after *plebeian*, Latin for "commoner"), began their first year living in tents in a summer encampment on the Plain, the academy's immense forty-acre parade ground. They learned the rudiments of marching, drills, and army rules of deportment and conduct, and took part in incessant artillery training. When September arrived, they entered the classroom and moved into one of two stone barracks buildings that were icy and drafty for a good part of the year. Each of the buildings housed 250 cadets and were lit only by whale-oil lamps, which gave off a rank fishy odor. Cadets were furnished with their own iron bed, mattress, chair, table, mirror, and mattress.

A Regimented Routine

Life at West Point was regulated by drum signals that woke cadets every morning, and announced the onset of the next scheduled activity. At a drumbeat, cadets marched into a mess hall for their three daily meals, and stood at attention until the command to take their assigned seats was issued. Twenty minutes was allotted for each meal, and talking was forbidden. Fare consisted chiefly of boiled meat and vegetables, though some professors and their wives took pity on cadets, who were often homesick during their first year, and invited them to their homes on weekends for such treats as Virginia ham and fresh-baked pie. Cadets were granted a single two-month-long furlough midway through their four-year course, but could receive permission to leave in the event of a death in the family. Leaving campus on the weekend required formal permission.

Classes at West Point were rigorous, and focused on math and science. Cadets were also expected to develop a fluency in French, required for reading Napoleon Bonaparte's famous tracts on warfare and strategy. Cadets were tremendously isolated, and because of the school's location on a bluff above the Hudson River, they were cut off almost entirely from the rest of the world during colder months. Illicit skating or rowboat parties, however, sometimes made the trek up the Hudson to a tavern they had been expressly forbidden to visit. This tavern was operated by the Havens family, and served buckwheat pancakes and a specialty drink, the hot rum flip. Occasional raids of the tavern by West Point teachers resulted in students receiving demerits; these were also handed out for the most insignificant infractions, such as a minor flaw in a uniform. The accumulation of two hundred demerits in a single year resulted in automatic dismissal.

First Battle Led by Two Alumni

The Civil War began on April 12, 1861, when Confederate forces opened fire on Fort Sumter, South Carolina.

WEST POINT'S FIGHTING BISHOP

Leonidas Polk (1806–1864) graduated from West Point in the Class of 1827, one year ahead of his roommate, Jefferson Davis, and two years ahead of Robert E. Lee. A third cousin of President James K. Polk, Leonidas Polk was baptized during his senior year by the Episcopal chaplain of West Point and decided to enter the ministry. After graduating from the military academy, he resigned his commission as a second lieutenant of cavalry and entered the Virginia Theological Seminary. In 1831, he was ordained in the Episcopal Church. He was appointed as missionary bishop of the Southeast in 1838, and became the first Episcopal bishop of Louisiana in 1841. Over the next nineteen years, he established new churches throughout Louisiana.

In 1860, Polk laid the cornerstone of the University of the South in Sewanee, Tennessee. He intended the school to be an American version of Oxford and Cambridge—in his words, "a home for all the arts and sciences and of literary culture in the Southern states" (Parks 1962, p. 135). Polk had already been thinking of secession when he was planning the foundation of his university, as is reflected in his correspondence with other bishops as early as 1856. When the Civil War began in 1861, Polk withdrew his diocese from the Episcopal Church of the United States and accepted a commission from his old friend Jefferson Davis as a major general in the Confederate Army. He saw no conflict between his calling to the Christian ministry and his role as a battlefield commander.

Polk was not, however, a talented military leader. He helped to drive the border state of Kentucky toward the Union side by sending troops into the state in September 1861. He was transferred to a command in Mississippi after a series of disagreements with Braxton Bragg, but later returned to assist Joseph E. Johnston during the Atlanta campaign of 1864. Polk was killed by a Union artillery shell at the battle of Pine Mountain in Georgia in June 1864. In spite of Polk's poor record as a tactician, he was popular with his troops; it is said that hundreds of Confederate soldiers wept openly when they heard of his death.

REBECCA J. FREY

BIBLIOGRAPHY

Parks, Joseph Howard. *General Leonidas Polk, C.S.A., the Fighting Bishop*. Baton Rouge: Louisiana State University Press, 1962.

Robins, Glenn. *The Bishop of the Old South: The Ministry and Civil War Legacy of Leonidas Polk*. Macon, GA: Mercer University Press, 2006.

The secessionist troops were led by a New Orleans native, General Pierre Gustave Toutant Beauregard, who was an 1838 graduate of West Point. Beauregard had even been appointed as West Point's superintendent, but served just a week in that office before resigning when his home state of Louisiana joined South Carolina in seceding from the union. When Beauregard issued the order to fire on the

West Point. Graduates of the United States Military Academy at West Point commanded troops for both the Confederate and Union armies. Many officers found taking the battlefield against a fellow West Point graduate a difficult task. *The Library of Congress.*

fort, he was attacking a garrison commanded by U.S. Army Major Robert Anderson, Class of 1825, who had returned to the school as an artillery instructor in the 1830s; Beauregard had been one of his students.

Like Beauregard and Anderson, many of the leading officers on the Union and Confederate sides were already veterans of combat thanks to their service in the Mexican-American War of 1846–1848. In that conflict, their supervising officer was General Winfield Scott, famously known as "Old Fuss and Feathers" for his insistence that his men rigorously adhere to the Army's rules of dress and deportment. Scott was general-in-chief of the U.S. Army from 1841 to 1861, and was a rarity among high-ranking Army officers of the era for not having attended West Point. He was a strong supporter of the school, however, and regularly turned up at the semiannual oral examinations informally referred to by cadets as "the Agony." During the Mexican War, several West Point–trained officers served as key members of his staff and aided in what was considered Scott's greatest military achievement, the 1847–1848 conquest of Mexico. Those men included Robert E. Lee, Ulysses Grant, and Thomas "Stonewall" Jackson.

When the Civil War began, Scott was seventy-four years old, and thus too aged to serve in battle. Scott recommended Lee (Class of 1829 and superintendent of West Point from 1852 to 1855) to command the Union Army. Lee, however, was a native of Virginia and declined President Abraham Lincoln's official appointment to the post, instead heading south to become military advisor to Jefferson Davis, who made him commander of the Confederate Army in 1862. Davis was one class ahead of Lee but had a less illustrious career at the academy, becoming the first cadet ever subjected to court-martial for being caught drinking at the Havens tavern. In his defense, the future Confederate president claimed that malt liquor, hard cider, and porter were not "spirituous liquors."

The bitter divisions of the Civil War were most starkly evident in the graduating class of 1861, several of whose members left early to join the Army of the Confederacy. Their departure was viewed as an egregious violation of the oath of loyalty to the United States and its Constitution that they had sworn as plebes. Congress quickly added a second oath in August 1861, requiring incoming cadets to pledge to "maintain and defend the sovereignty of the United States," and to swear that this responsibility would be "paramount to any and all allegiance, sovereignty, or fealty" they might owe "to any state, county, or country whatsoever" (Callan 1863, p. 483).

Ties That Bind

The number of West Point graduates whose names entered into military history for their service during the war is a long one, beginning with the First Battle of Bull Run on July 21, 1861, where "Stonewall" Jackson (Class of 1846) led a Confederate brigade and earned his enduring nickname. Union Army Major General Ambrose Burnside (Class of 1847) commanded the Army of the Potomac after 1862, and the fortunes of the war hinged on decisions made by him and his Confederate nemesis, General Lee. Confederate Brigadier General Thomas Lafayette Rosser, one of the Southerners who left before graduation in 1861, captured several troops from a cavalry division led by his former classmate, Union Army Brigadier General George Armstrong Custer (Class of 1861), during the Battle of Trevilian Station in 1864, but the two renewed their friendship while working for the Army Corps of Engineers in the early 1870s.

Custer—infamous for graduating last among the thirty-four members of his class—was also involved in one of the more unusual episodes of the war: In 1862 he served as best man at the wedding of his classmate, Confederate Army Captain John Lea. Lea, furthermore, had been wounded in the May 1862 battle for Williamsburg, in which Custer had served under Union General George McClellan (Class of 1846). The Union victory was immensely aided when General William T. Sherman (Class of 1840) captured Atlanta in September 1864. Seven months later, General Lee surrendered to Union Army Lieutenant General Ulysses S. Grant (Class of 1843, and the first West Point graduate to be elected President of the United States) at the Appomattox Courthouse in Virginia.

In his *Civil War Memoirs*, Grant recounts an anecdote that also appeared in *The Spirit of Old West Point*, a 1907 book by Morris Schaff, an historian and 1862 West Point graduate. The story involves Schaff's journey from Alabama to Atlanta across a war-ravaged South not long after the war's end. "Late one night...the ramshackle train stopped at a lonely station. Charles Ball [Class of June, 1861], still in Confederate gray, entered. As soon as he recognized me, he quickened his step and met me with such unaffected cordiality that the car seemed to glow with new lamps. In view of what had gone before I would not have been hurt had he merely bowed and passed on, for I realized how much there had been to embitter. Yet he sat, and we talked over old times half the night. I could not help wondering, as he parted from me, whether I could have shown so much magnanimity had the South conquered the North, and had I come home in rags, to find the old farm desolate" (Grant 2004, p. 524).

BIBLIOGRAPHY

Ambrose, Stephen E. *Duty, Honor, Country: A History of West Point*. Baltimore, MD: Johns Hopkins University Press, 1966. Reprint, 1999.

Callan, John F. *The Military Laws of the United States*. Philadelphia: George W. Childs, 1863.

Carhart, Tom. *West Point Warriors: Profiles of Duty, Honor, and Country in Battle*. New York: Warner Books, 2002.

Crackel, Theodore J. *West Point: A Bicentennial History* Lawrence: University Press of Kansas, 2002.

Grant, Ulysses S. *The Civil War Memoirs of Ulysses S. Grant*, ed. Brian M. Thomsen. New York: Tor/Forge, 2004.

Office of the Chief of Military History, United States Army. Chapter 9: "1861." In *American Military History* (Army Historical Series). Washington, DC: Center of Military History, United States Army, 1989.

Patterson, Gerard A. *Rebels from West Point: The 306 U.S. Military Academy Graduates Who Fought for the Confederacy*. Mechanicsburg, PA: Stackpole Books, 2002.

Carol Brennan

■ Family Separation and Reunion

The effects of the Civil War on American family life were not as disruptive as those of some later conflicts, in spite of the strains caused by geographical separation and postwar reunion. The American family at all social levels was already different from its European counterparts by the early 1830s, a fact often remarked on by visitors from abroad. Alexis de Tocqueville (1805–1859) was a French political theorist and historian who visited the United States in 1832, publishing his impressions in 1835 under the title *De la démocratie en Amérique*, translated into English as *Democracy in America*. De Tocqueville saw the American family, along with religion and a democratic form of political participation, as one of three social forces that helped to hold the young nation together. He laid particular emphasis on the role of American women within the family:

> For my part, I have no hesitation in saying that although the American woman never leaves her domestic sphere and is in some respects very dependent within it, nowhere [in the world] does she enjoy a higher station...if anyone asks me what I think the chief cause of the extraordinary prosperity and growing power of this nation, I should answer that it is due to the superiority of their women. (de Tocqueville 1969 [1835], p. 603)

Moreover, de Tocqueville regarded women as the primary sources of the influence of religion on the American family. He noted that American men were often driven primarily by economic considerations:

> ...religion is often powerless to restrain men in the midst of innumerable temptations which fortune offers. It cannot moderate their eagerness to

enrich themselves ... but it reigns supreme in the souls of the women, and it is women who shape mores. Certainly of all countries in the world, America is the one in which the marriage tie is most respected and where the highest and truest conception of conjugal happiness has been conceived. (de Tocqueville 1969 [1835], p. 291)

In addition to the strength of their family life, however, pre–Civil War Americans were also noted for making a virtue of individualism and self-sufficiency. J. Hector St. John de Crèvecoeur (1735–1813) was a French army lieutenant from an aristocratic family who settled in upstate New York after the French defeat in 1759 and took out citizenship in what was then the colony of New York. He married an American woman in 1770, purchased a sizable farm, and took up writing about the new type of citizen that was emerging in North America. In *Letters from an American Farmer* (1782), Crèvecoeur observed that Americans were more active and self-reliant than Europeans, and less impressed by social rank or ancient customs. He described the change that occurred when a European immigrant became an American: "From nothing to start into being; from a servant to the rank of a master; from being the slave to some despotic prince, to become a free man, invested with lands, to which every municipal blessing is annexed! What a change indeed! It is in consequence of that change that he becomes an American" (Crèvecoeur 1981 [1782], p. 83).

These two features of nineteenth-century American society, a high valuation of the family (often strengthened by religious convictions) on the one hand and an emphasis on personal independence on the other, not only predated the Civil War but have persisted into the present century (Bellah et al. 1985, pp. 87–89). One important difference between the nineteenth century and the twenty-first, however, is the changes in technology that have made it easier for separated family members to keep in touch.

Coping with Separation

People who were separated from their families at the time of the Civil War did not have the benefit of rapid, reliable, and affordable transportation to visit their loved ones; they also lacked the modern telecommunication devices that are taken for granted in the twenty-first century.

To begin with transportation, although the railroads played an important part in military strategy and troop transport during the Civil War (Gable 1997, pp. 1–4), they were not as readily available to the civilian population. In January 1862, Congress authorized President Lincoln to take over civilian railroad lines for military use. People who wanted to visit or care for relatives in either army frequently had to travel in horse-drawn carriages or wagons. The scarcity of efficient transportation

also often complicated family reunions after the war was over. Maria Jackson, a former slave, told of her family's move to Georgia after her father returned from the war:

My daddy was named Jim Neely, and he comed all the way to Alabamy to marry my mammy.... Mammy and daddy got back togedder atter the war and it was a long time 'fore us come to Georgy. My granddaddy sent fer us then, yes that he did. He sent a one horse waggin plum to Alabamy to brung us back.... I don't 'member how long it tuk 'em to git back in that waggin but I does member dat ... it sho' a long hard trip 'cause it warn 't lak times is now, and folks lived a long ways apart, and somepin' t'eat was hard to git, and dey was hungry plenty times. (Jackson 1938, pp. 268–269)

In the absence of face-to-face visits, people kept in touch through the mail. Recent advances in photography allowed Civil War soldiers and their families to enclose small photographs known as *cartes de visite* in their letters; but the earliest telephone would not be invented until 1871, and the telegraph system was, like the railroads, taken over for military use in May 1861. Telegrams were sent to inform Civil War families of a soldier's injury or death, but these were only brief official communications, not personal messages.

The letters exchanged between separated family members during the Civil War were handwritten. The first commercially successful typewriter was invented in 1867 but not produced in quantity until 1873. Thus the letters so eagerly awaited by soldiers and their relatives during the war took much longer to write than a modern letter composed on a word processor or sent as an e-mail message. In addition, the slowness of the postal system and interruptions in mail delivery resulting from the war meant that people worried about their loved ones often had to wait months for news. Kate Douglas Wiggin (1856–1923), a children's author and educator born a few years before the Civil War, wrote a novel that included an account of the way in which one woman first heard of her fiancé's mortal injury:

[Jane] was engaged to marry young Tom Carter... Then the war broke out. Tom enlisted at the first call. Up to that time Jane had loved him with a quiet, friendly sort of affection, and had given her country a mild emotion of the same sort. But ... the anxiety of the time set new currents of feeling in motion ... Men and women grew fast in those days of the nation's trouble and danger ... Then after a year's anxiety, a year when one never looked in the newspaper without dread and sickness of suspense, came the telegram saying that Tom was wounded; and ... she packed her trunk and started for the South. She was in time to hold Tom's hand through

MARY TODD LINCOLN AND SPIRITUALISM

Mary Todd Lincoln (1818–1882) was one of the most controversial First Ladies in American history. Born into a slaveholding family in Kentucky, she left for Illinois at the age of twenty to escape a domineering stepmother. Although she was courted by Stephen A. Douglas, Mary Todd was more attracted to Abraham Lincoln, Douglas's fellow lawyer, and married him in November 1842. They had four sons, only one of whom outlived both parents. By the time Lincoln was elected to the presidency, their second son, Eddie, had already died at the age of four. Their third son, Willie, died of typhoid fever in the White House in April 1862.

Mary Todd Lincoln had already been under considerable stress as First Lady because of her Southern background. Two of her stepbrothers and her brother-in-law were killed fighting for the Confederacy, and she was accused of being a Confederate spy. After Willie's death, she began to look for comfort in the teachings of spiritualism, a movement that had begun in upstate New York in the 1840s. Spiritualists believed that a person could make direct contact with God, angels, or the spirits of the dead through clairvoyants or mediums.

The movement's first leaders were the Fox sisters of Hydesville, New York, who reported in 1848 that they had made contact with the spirit of a murdered peddler who communicated with them by rapping on tables. Spiritualism was appealing to many women because it offered them opportunities for leadership as mediums or as lecturers. Following the Fox sisters, such women as Cora L. V. Scott and Achsa W. Sprague lectured widely throughout the United States and held séances. Séances are meetings in which the participants sit around a table in a darkened or semi-darkened room while the medium goes into a trance and receives communications from the dead. Some twenty-first century spiritualists refer to these trance messages as channeling. Spiritualism surged in popularity during and after the Civil War because there were so many bereaved families longing for some kind of contact with or message from soldiers who had died in the war.

Mary Todd Lincoln apparently began to visit the Lauries, spiritualists living in the Georgetown section of Washington, in the spring of 1862 after Willie's death. She hoped to be able to communicate with her two dead sons. She later wrote to her half-sister that she had been visited by Alexander, her half-brother killed at Baton Rouge in 1862, as well as her boys. "Willie lives. He comes to me every night and stands at the foot of the bed with the same sweet adorable smile he always has had. He does not always come alone. Little Eddie is sometimes with him, and twice he has come with our brother, Alex." It is thought that there were at least eight spiritualist séances held in the White House itself between 1863 and Lincoln's assassination in April 1865. Lincoln is said to have attended one of these meetings in April 1863.

After Mary Todd Lincoln left the White House, she frequently visited spiritualists under an assumed name in order to test their abilities. On one trip to Boston, she attended a séance in which Lincoln appeared before her. She then visited the studio of William Mumler, a "spirit photographer," who produced a photograph in which the figure of Lincoln can be seen behind that of his widow, his hands on her shoulders. The picture is said to have given Mrs. Lincoln great comfort in her later years. Unfortunately for Mumler, he was sued for fraud in 1869, the prosecution charging that the "spirit photographs" were made by using double exposures and other tricks of the photographic trade.

REBECCA J. FREY

BIBLIOGRAPHY

Ahlstrom, Sydney E. *A Religious History of the American People. New Haven, CT: Yale University Press, 1972, pp. 488–490.*

"Do You Believe? The Mumler Mystery." *American Museum of Photography.* Available at http://www.photographymuseum.com/mumler.html.

Carter, Paul A. *The Spiritual Crisis of the Gilded Age. DeKalb: Northern Illinois University Press, 1971, pp. 99–106.*

hours of pain . . . to put her arms about him so that he could have a home to die in, and that was all;— all, but it served. (Wiggin 1903, p. 67)

Military Families

There was one group of American families that had become accustomed to postponed weddings and periodic family separations before the Civil War, and that was the families of career military officers. Ulysses S. Grant and his wife Julia had to wait four years to marry after they met in 1844. Julia and "Ulys" became secretly engaged in 1845; her father, a wealthy Missouri slave owner, had his reservations about the match because Grant's family was relatively poor. After graduating from West Point, Grant served in the Mexican War until 1848, when he could finally marry Julia. She accompanied him to various garrisons in the West until 1852, when she returned to Illinois to live with Grant's parents

in order to care for the first two of their four children. Grant resigned his military commission in 1854 in order to rejoin his growing family.

During the Civil War, Julia visited her husband as often as possible, often moving their children to new schools in order to keep the family together. In October 1861, Grant wrote to his sister from Cairo, Illinois, that he expected Julia to arrive within the week. In 1862, he wrote to his sister from Tennessee that he was looking forward to a week-long visit from his wife. During the last year of the war, Grant wrote to his father that he and Julia had been offered a house in Philadelphia and that they planned to move there permanently (Grant 1912, letters of October 25, 1861; October 16, 1862; and September 5, 1864).

There was the same kind of family loyalty on the Confederate side. Robert E. Lee visited his wife Mary

African American Union soldiers return home to Little Rock at war's end. African American troops in the Union came from both the free North and the enslaved South. These men had to fight for the right to fight, then fight for equal treatment in the segregated army. © *North Wind Picture Archives*

Anna, who suffered from rheumatoid arthritis and was confined to a wheelchair by 1861, as often as he could during the conflict. On Christmas Day of the same year, he sent his daughter a letter expressing how much he missed his family in Virginia:

> My Dear Daughter: Having distributed such poor Christmas gifts as I had to those around me, I have been looking for something for you. Trifles even are hard to get these war-times, and you must not therefore expect more. I have sent you what I thought most useful in your separation from me, and hope it will be of some service ... To compensate for such 'trash'[money], I send you some sweet violets, that I gathered for you this morning while covered with dense white frost, whose crystals glittered in the bright sun like diamonds, and formed a brooch of rare beauty and sweetness, which could not be fabricated by the expenditure of a world of money ... Among the calamities of war, the hardest to bear perhaps, is the separation of families and friends. (Lee 1861)

Slave Families

The ambiguous legal status of slave marriages prior to the Civil War meant that some former slaves who had joined the Union Army or fled to the North during the war either took new wives or returned to their homes to find that their wives had remarried. Those who had been married in a formal religious ceremony—which some

slave owners encouraged—generally had less complicated reunions. One former slave recalled her wedding:

> When I growed up I married Exter Durham. He belonged to Marse Snipes Durham who had de plantation 'cross de county line in Orange County. We had a big weddin'. We was married on de front po'ch of de big house.... Dat was some weddin'. I had on a white dress, white shoes an' long while gloves dat come to my elbow, an' Mis' Betsy done made me a weddin' veil out of a white net window curtain. When she played de weddin' ma'ch on de piano, me an' Exter ma'ched down de walk an' up on de po'ch to de altar Mis' Betsy done fixed. Dat de pretties' altar I ever seed.... Uncle Edmond Kirby married us. He was de nigger preacher dat preached at de plantation church.... [Before emancipation Exter saw his wife only on weekends.] I was glad when de war stopped kaze den me an' Exter could be together all de time 'stead of Saturday an' Sunday. (Durham 1941, pp. 287–289)

Another former slave was less fortunate. Years later, his daughter recalled that when her father "... came back from the war—in the old time way of jumping the broom handle—my mother had married again, so he didn't disturb her, and the little children she had then" (Holmes 1945, p. 175).

Popular Music

Popular music was one way of coping with the pain and frustration of family separation. Many of the camp songs of the Civil War, both Northern and Southern, expressed a longing for an end to the conflict and anticipation of reunion with families. "Goober Peas," a Southern song attributed to A. Pindar, reflects not only the dietary hardships of the Confederate soldier ("goober peas" is an old term for boiled peanuts, considered an emergency ration), but also his homesickness:

> Sitting by the roadside on a summer's day,
> Chatting with my mess-mates, passing time away,
> Lying in the shadows underneath the trees—
> Goodness, how delicious, eating goober peas.
>
> *Chorus*: Peas, peas, peas, peas,
> Eating goober peas.
> Goodness, how delicious,
> Eating goober peas....
>
> Just before the battle, the General hears a row
> He says, 'The Yanks are coming, I hear their rifles now.'
> He looks down the roadway, and what d'ya think he sees?
> The Georgia Militia cracking goober peas. *Chorus.*
>
> I think my song has lasted just about enough.
> The subject is interesting, but the rhymes are mighty rough.
> I wish the war was over, so free from rags and fleas—
> We'd kiss our wives and sweethearts, say good-bye to goober peas. *Chorus.* (Pindar 1866)

On the Union side, soldiers sang "Just before the Battle, Mother," written by George F. Root:

> Just before the battle, Mother, I am thinking most of you.
> While upon the field we're watching, with the enemy in view.
> Comrades brave are 'round me lying, filled with thoughts of home and God;
> For well they know that on the morrow, some will sleep beneath the sod.
>
> *Chorus*: Farewell, Mother, you may never press me to your breast again;
> But, oh, you'll not forget me, Mother, if I'm numbered with the slain.
>
> Oh, I long to see you, Mother, and the loving ones at home,
> But I'll never leave our banner till in honor I can come.
> Tell the traitors all around you that their cruel words we know,
> In every battle kill our soldiers by the help they give the foe. *Chorus.*
>
> Hark! I hear the bugles sounding, 'tis the signal for the fight,
> Now, may God protect us, Mother, as He ever does the right.
> Hear "The Battle Cry of Freedom," how it swells upon the air,
> Oh, yes, we'll rally 'round the standard, or we'll nobly perish there.
>
> *Chorus.*

Closure

For thousands of American families in 1865, the only reunion they could expect with their loved ones was on the other side of the grave. Some mourners turned to spiritualism, hoping to receive ghostly messages from their dead (Carter 1971, pp. 85–108). Others read popular novels about the afterlife, mostly forgotten by contemporary readers, but best sellers in the years following the war. Elizabeth Stuart Phelps (1844–1911), a clergyman's daughter, wrote a novel about heaven called *The Gates Ajar*, which opens with the news of the narrator's brother's death in combat:

> They tell me that it should not have been such a shock. 'Your brother has been in the army so long that you should have been prepared for anything.'...I suppose it is all true; but that never makes it any easier. The house feels like a prison. I walk up and down and wonder that I ever called it home.... It seems to me as if the world were spinning around in the light and wind and laughter, and God just stretched out His hand one morning and put it out. (Phelps 1868, pp. 5–6)

The fact that *The Gates Ajar* went through fifty-five printings between 1868 and 1884 indicates that a good many bereaved Americans found comfort in Phelps's picture of the afterlife.

Confederate soldiers returning home from war often had difficult reunions with their families. A recent historian has described the mood of the defeated Southerners as "relief and dejection and smoldering rage" (Ahlstrom 1973, p. 682). In many cases the men had to cope with the destruction of their homesteads and other property as well as the disruption of their family life. Mary Boykin Miller Chesnut (1823–1886), the wife of a former senator from South Carolina, recorded in her diary a conversation she had with a fellow displaced Southerner in March 1865:

> ... as Captain Ogden is a refugee, has had no means of communicating with his home since New Orleans fell, and was sure to know how refugees contrive to live, I beguiled the time acquiring information from him. 'When people are without a cent, how do they live?' I asked. 'I am about to enter the noble band of homeless, houseless refugees, and Confederate pay does not buy one's shoe-strings. To which he replied, 'Sponge, sponge. Why did you not let Colonel Childs pay your bills?' 'I have no bills,' said I. 'We have never made bills anywhere, not even at home, where they would trust us, and nobody would trust me in Lincolnton.' 'Why did you not borrow his money? General Chesnut [Mary's husband] could pay him at his leisure?' 'I am by no means sure General Chesnut will ever again have any money,' said I. (Chesnut 1905, pp. 367–368)

A Civil War soldier returns home to his family. The American family was not as affected by the strain of the Civil War as it would be by later wars. French political theorist, Alexis de Tocqueville, claimed that the American family, religion, and democracy helped hold the young nation together. *The Library of Congress.*

Some former Confederates found a measure of comfort in the nostalgic ideology of the Lost Cause; others returned as best they could to their former occupations or moved to the West to seek new fortunes there.

For Union veterans, family reunions were sweetened by the additional satisfaction of military victory. Patrick Gilmore (1829–1892), an Irish American bandmaster serving in the Union Army, wrote one of the best-known Union songs in 1863, two years before the end of the war, in anticipation of a Northern victory. "When Johnny Comes Marching Home" is Gilmore's reversal of an Irish antiwar song, "Johnny I Hardly Knew Ye," in which a soldier's wife laments her returning husband's injuries: "Ye're an armless, boneless, chickenless egg, Ye'll have to be put with a bowl out to beg, Oh Johnny I hardly knew ye." Gilmore rewrote the message of the song to comfort his sister Annie, who was engaged to a captain in the Union light artillery named John O'Rourke:

When Johnny comes marching home again,
Hurrah! Hurrah!
We'll give him a hearty welcome then,

Hurrah! Hurrah!
The men will cheer and the boys will shout,
The ladies they will all turn out,
And we'll all feel gay when Johnny comes marching home....

Get ready for the Jubilee,
Hurrah! Hurrah!
We'll give the hero three times three,
Hurrah! Hurrah!
The laurel wreath is ready now
To place upon his loyal brow,
And we'll all feel gay when Johnny comes marching home.

Let love and friendship on that day,
Hurrah, hurrah!
Their choicest pleasures then display,
Hurrah, hurrah!
And let each one perform some part,
To fill with joy the warrior's heart,
And we'll all feel gay when Johnny comes marching home. (Gilmore 1863)

In addition to individual reunions with their loved ones, Union soldiers were also welcomed home by the nation as a whole in the first mass victory parade in the country's history. Known as the Grand Review of the Armies, it took place on two successive days, May 23 and 24, 1865, in Washington. On the first day, 80,000 infantrymen from General Meade's Army of the Potomac marched down Pennsylvania Avenue twelve abreast, along with pieces of artillery and a seven-mile-long line of cavalrymen. On the second day, 65,000 men from General Sherman's Army of Georgia passed in review, the infantrymen followed by the medical corps and civilians—black families who had escaped from slavery. Within a week both armies were officially disbanded. The Grand Review was so moving to the participants, however, that it was repeated by 40,000 surviving veterans 50 years later—in 1915, when Europe was in the midst of a new war that the United States would enter within two years (*New York Times*, August 16, 1915).

BIBLIOGRAPHY

Ahlstrom, Sydney E. *A Religious History of the American People*. New Haven and London: Yale University Press, 1973.

Bellah, Robert N., Richard Madsen, William M. Sullivan, Ann Swidler, and Steven M. Tipton. *Habits of the Heart: Individualism and Commitment in American Life*. Berkeley, CA: University of California Press, 1985.

Carter, Paul A. *The Spiritual Crisis of the Gilded Age*. DeKalb: Northern Illinois University Press, 1971.

Chesnut, Mary Boykin Miller. *A Diary from Dixie*, edited by Isabella D. Martin and Myrta Lockett Avery. New York: D. Appleton & Company, 1905.

de Crèvecoeur, J. Hector St. John. *Letters from an American Farmer*. New York: Penguin Books, 1981 [1782].

Durham, Tempe Herndon. Interview in *Slave Narratives: A Folk History of Slavery in the United States from Interviews with Former Slaves: Typewritten Records*, vol. 14, pp. 284–290. Washington, DC: Federal Writers' Project, 1941.

Gable, Christopher R. *Railroad Generalship: Foundations of Civil War Strategy*. Fort Leavenworth, KS: U.S. Army Command and General Staff College, 1997.

Gilmore, Patrick. "When Johnny Comes Marching Home." Boston: Henry Tolman, 1863 [sheet music]. A MIDI file is available at http://kids.niehs.nih.gov/lyrics/johnny.htm.

Grant, Ulysses S. *Letters of Ulysses S. Grant to His Father and His Youngest Sister, 1857–78*, edited by Jesse Grant Cramer. New York: Putnam, 1912.

Holmes [no first name given]. *The Unwritten History of Slavery: Autobiographical Accounts of Negro Ex-Slaves*. Interview in Fisk University Social Science Institute, vol. 18, pp. 175–180. Nashville, TN: Fisk University, 1945.

Jackson, Maria. Interview recorded December 13, 1938. In *The American Slave: A Composite Autobiography*, edited by George P. Rawick, Suppl. Series 2, vol. 1, pp. 267–274. Westport, CT: Greenwood Press, 1972–1979.

Lee, Robert E. Letter to his daughter, December 25, 1861. Available online at http://www.stratford hall.org/decdoc/letter.html.

Phelps, Elizabeth S. *The Gates Ajar*. Boston: Fields, Osgood, & Co., 1868.

Pindar, A. "Goober Peas." New Orleans: A. E. Blackmar, 1866 [sheet music]. A MIDI file is available at http://kids.niehs.nih.gov/lyrics/gooberp.htm.

Root, George F. "Just before the Battle, Mother." Text in the public domain. A MIDI file is available at http://civilwarpoetry.org/union/songs/justbefore.html.

"To Repeat Grand Review: 40,000 Veterans of Civil War Will March on Fiftieth Anniversary." *New York Times*, August 16, 1915, p. 10.

de Tocqueville, Alexis. *Democracy in America*, tr. George Lawrence, ed. J. P. Mayer. New York: Doubleday, 1969 [1835].

Wiggin, Kate Douglas. *Rebecca of Sunnybrook Farm*. Boston & New York: Houghton Mifflin & Co., 1903.

Rebecca J. Frey

■ Parenting and Childrearing

PARENTING AND CHILDREARING:
  AN OVERVIEW
    Debra Newman Ham

MOTHERHOOD
    Jenny Lagergren

FATHERHOOD
    Adam J. Pratt

CHILDREN AND CHILDREARING
    Megan Birk

EXTENDED FAMILY
    Debra Newman Ham

PARENTING AND CHILDREARING: AN OVERVIEW

In addition to their horror over the tragic cessation of young lives, Civil War parents had to face increased difficulty in every type of childrearing role. Many young people had to take on adult roles years before they were ready. Parents watched as hundreds of thousands of teenage sons went off to war with Union or Confederate troops. Far more deadly than guns and mortar were the diseases that fell eleven of every twelve who died in the military camps. In the southern war theaters, Confederate parents tried to protect their children from Union soldiers and armaments, as well as from the ravages of a devastated economy, while more than five thousand members of the enslaved population dubbed "contraband of war" sought means to escape with their children to the Union lines. The wives and children of men who joined the United States Colored Troops, especially from the border states, sometimes had to face the wrath of their owners against themselves and their offspring. In both the border and southern states, some whites attempted to kidnap, sell, or illegally apprentice African American children so that they could retain them as unpaid laborers. Families themselves fought for custody of orphans or struggled through separation and custody battles, and almost all parents wanted their children to be educated.

Diaries and Reminiscences

A ten-year-old girl, Carrie Berry, whose diary is at the Atlanta History Center, vividly captured the horrors and complexities of the war experience for childrearing. The child's diary clearly shows that her mother was attempting to train her in household tasks and send her to school and church, in spite of the violence near their home. It was impossible for her mother or father to return her home to normalcy amidst the warfare surrounding them. Young Carrie explained that on Monday, August 1, 1864, she had to care for her younger sister "but before night we had to run to the cellar" for cover during an assault. She later reported, "We did not feel safe in our cellar because the shells fell so thick and fast." She stated that they could "hear the canons and muskets very plane [*sic*], but the shells we dread. One has busted under the dining room which frightened us very much. One passed through the smoke-house and a piece hit the top of the house and fell through but we were at Auntie Markham's, so none of us were hurt. We stay very close in the cellar when they are shelling." Wednesday, August 3, was Carrie's birthday. She wrote, "I was ten years old, But I did not have a cake times were too hard so I celebrated with ironing. I hope by my next birthday we will have peace in our land so that I can have a nice dinner" (*Carrie Berry Diary, August 1, 1864–January 4, 1865*).

In her 2000 article "'Of Necessity and Public Benefit', Southern Families and their Appeals for Protection," Amy E. Murrell looks at letters from a South Carolina woman named Margaret A. Easterling. Trying to run the family plantation, care for her children, slaves, and her aged mother in "a neighborhood which [N]egroes number twenty to one," Easterling asked Confederate officials to keep her oldest and strongest son, Willie, who was seventeen in the military, but send home her "feeble" son,

Josiah. She wrote, "I know our cause is worthy of every and any sacrifice... but I am not mistress of my fears."

Another schoolgirl diary once more points to a loss of youth and growing bitterness because of the violence and changes around her. Kept by sixteen-year-old Alice Williamson in 1864 in Gallatin, Tennessee, and held by the Atlanta History Center, the thirty-six page diary describes the violent occupation of the area by Union forces led by General Eleazar A. Paine and details her disgust of Union sympathizers, African American soldiers, and ambitious contrabands who also wanted to be educated. It is obvious that Williamson's parents were trying to keep her in school, but by the time that her journal closes, the school has shut down and she speculates that her teacher is going to teach the contrabands. Williamson accuses General Paine of a number of atrocities. She stated that on March 11, Paine

> went up the country a few miles to a Mr. Dalton's whose son came home from the Southern Army the day before and had the same day taken the Amnesty Oath. Riding up to the door he enquired of Mr. Dalton if his son was at home but before he answered his son came to the door. Old Nick then told him to get his horse and go with him. After insulting the father he carried his son a half mile away and shot him six times. Bidden to rise and go home, the young man has never been heard of since. (*Alice Williamson Diary*)

This account is most likely untrue because the general would almost certainly have had an enlisted man shoot him, if he had wanted him shot.

On June 5, Williamson reported that "the Tennesseans set fire to the contraband school." By June 10, she is relating that

> The country is overrun with Yanks: they are camped in the woods in front of us and have already paid us several visits killed sheep, goats and chickens Our new yankees are very neighborly. They come over to see us every few minutes in the day. Some came today and demanded their dinner at two o'clock but did not get it. They went off cursing us for being d__n rebels.

On September 16, she lamented, "Todays paper brings sad news, Atlanta has certainly been taken: Sherman has ordered every man, woman and child from that place...." (*Alice Williamson Diary*).

An African American Perspective

Susie King Taylor was a teen, a wife, a mother, a laundress and a nurse during the Civil War. She published a memoir in 1902 entitled *Reminiscences of My Life in Camp with the 33rd U. S. Colored Troops. Late 1st South Carolina Volunteers*. In the book, she relates how her mother, a market woman, and her grandmother helped provide her with a clandestine education, since it was illegal for slaves to learn to read. Susie wrote that by 1861, she had heard a great deal about freedom, President Abraham Lincoln (1809–1865), and the Yankee soldiers. After the Civil War began, the slaves believed that Lincoln and the Yankees were soon coming to set them free. As Union soldiers moved into the South, slaves flocked to their camps and Susie was among them. President Lincoln, however, remained as reluctant to allow black men to enlist as soldiers as he was to declare the slaves free. Blacks were allowed only a limited role in the war effort for the first three years. Nevertheless, slaves from miles around left their owners and sought refuge behind Union lines wherever the troops moved, and free black men independently or under Union soldiers' direction began to train for combat and practice military drills. Because Fort Sumter, South Carolina, and the surrounding area were recaptured by the Union early in the war, blacks began to converge upon that area to join with and work for the Union troops.

At the arrival of the Yankees in the South, Susie, just fourteen years old, left with her uncle and his family for the South Carolina Sea Islands in order to find the Union army. Susie wrote that she was overjoyed to see the Yankees. She, like thousands of other slaves, believed that her liberation was at hand. She was willing to help in the struggle for freedom in any way that she could.

The Union officers were surprised to find that Susie could read and write and pressed her into service as a teacher of slave children and some adults. She also tutored some of the soldiers who were eager to learn how to read and write. In the camp, she met and married Sergeant Edward King of the first South Carolina Volunteers. They had one son.

Lincoln announced that the proclamation would take effect on January 1, 1863. The Emancipation Proclamation proclaimed that all slaves in the Confederate states would be "forever free." Although scholars argue the effectiveness of the proclamation, Susie, her family, and the other recruits and contrabands who were with them felt that they were free from that moment and were willing to fight and die to keep their liberty.

The government promised that U.S. Colored Troops would get equal pay, but it did not fulfill that promise. Susie's husband and the other troops and their officers were extremely disappointed, and many black men refused to take any pay that was less than that of white soldiers. Eventually, the government reversed its position and agreed, again, to give the soldiers full pay with all of the back pay due, but by that time many members of the Colored Troops, Susie sadly reported, had died without receiving one dime for their service.

Traveling with her husband and the Colored Troops, Susie worked alternately as a teacher and nurse, never receiving any pay for her services. She traveled with them as far south as Florida and camped with them in Georgia. She nursed sick and wounded men according to their needs and worked alongside Clara Barton

(1821–1912) in the Sea Islands for several months. Susie, still a teenager, marveled over how quickly she got over the sight of bloodied, maimed, and mangled bodies. She recounted that whenever she would see wounded soldiers her only thoughts were about how to alleviate their suffering.

After the war, Susie and her husband, Edward, returned to Savannah, where she opened a school. Edward died in 1866, leaving Susie as a widow at only eighteen years old.

BIBLIOGRAPHY

Alice Williamson Diary. Special Collections, Duke University. Available from http://scriptorium.lib.duke.edu/williamson/.

Berlin, Ira, and Leslie S. Rowland, eds. *Families and Freedom: A Documentary History of African-American Kinship in the Civil War Era.* New York: New Press, 1997.

Carrie Berry Diary, August 1, 1864–January 4, 1865. Special Collections, Duke University, Durham, NC. Available from http://www.americancivilwar.com/women/carrie_berry.html.

Higginson, Thomas Wentworth. *Army Life in a Black Regiment.* [1870.] New York: Collier Books, [1962.]

Murrell, Amy E., "Of Necessity and Public Benefit: Southern Families and their Appeals for Protection." In *Southern Families at War: Loyalty and Conflict in the Civil War South,* ed. Catherine Clinton. New York: Oxford University Press, 2000.

Quarles, Benjamin. *The Negro in the Civil War.* Boston: Little, Brown, [1969.]

Taylor, Susie King. *Reminiscences of my Life in Camp with the 33rd U.S. Colored Troops, Late 1st South Carolina Volunteers.* [Boston: S K. Taylor, 1902.], ed. Patricia W. Romero. New York: Markus Wiener Publishing, 1988.

Debra Newman Ham

MOTHERHOOD

At the start of the Civil War in 1861, the conventional roles of women shifted to include new practical responsibilities and social positions. Before the war, husbands often established household rules and provided families with security, while few women worked outside of the home. As the primary caretakers of children and spouses, women already had full-time work inside their households. With the onset of the war, however, it became necessary for many mothers to become leaders of the household and pursue jobs outside their homes. In addition to the changes in practical responsibilities, the war forced women to examine their identities as mothers.

ARMY NURSES AS MOTHERS

Many soldiers and women were initially recoiled from the new interactions between the sexes in Civil War hospitals, but duty necessitated that they make the best of it. In order to do so, women, who had never taken care of anyone other than family members, and soldiers, who had never been taken care of by anyone but their mothers, fused these roles together to form public families. Soldiers could therefore be taken care of by their "mothers" and nurses could take care of their "children."

Several nurses, most notably Mary Ann Bickerdyke (1817–1901), were known to all as "Mother." Mother Ransom of Indiana and Grandmother Newcomb of Illinois are other prominent examples. Mother Bickerdyke dispensed motherly care for the soldiers, leading the mother of a wounded soldier to remark, "It is no wonder you are called 'mother'" (Holland 1895, p. 525). Nurses not officially known as "mother" were often given that title, though, and they saw their patients as their children in many cases. According to the editor of the diary and letters of Hannah Ropes, Civil War nurses often saw themselves as responsible surrogate mothers for the soldiers in their care (Brumgardt 1980, p. 15). As for Ropes herself, she once said that "the poor privates are my children for the time being" (p. 77).

Emily Elizabeth Parsons also often referred to her soldiers as children, stating her role in the hospitals as that of "see[ing] after the many wants of my children, so my men seem to me" (Parsons 1880, p. 22). Parsons referred to her job of making forty-four beds every day as analogous to the endless work of a well-known nursery rhyme character, as she remarked that she had "more children than the old woman in the shoe" (p. 52). Ada W. Bacot, a Confederate nurse, often referred to her patients as "poor children" and comparing her devotion to the Southern cause to the love of a "fond mother" (Berlin 1994, p. 51). Bacot claimed to be a child of Southern ideals herself, demonstrating the blurring of family lines between public and private, real and idealistic. Fannie Beers, another Confederate nurse, also discussed her conceptions of family in the Civil War hospitals. She referred to all her patients as her "boys," regardless of their age. Beers even pointed out that some were upset that she took the liberty of referring to men who were husbands and fathers as "her boys," but to Beers, "these are *my boys*—still—always my boys" (Beers 1888, p. 311).

JOHN FRENCH

BIBLIOGRAPHY

Beers, Fannie A. *Memories: A Record of Personal Experience and Adventure during Four Years of War. Philadelphia: J.B. Lippincott Company, 1888.*

Berlin, Jean V, ed. A Confederate Nurse: The Diary of Ada W. Bacot, 1860–1863. *Columbia: University of South Carolina Press, 1994.*

Brumgardt, John R, ed. Civil War Nurse: The Diary and Letters of Hannah Ropes. *Knoxville: University of Tennessee Press, 1980.*

Holland, Mary A. Gardner, compiler. Our Army Nurses. *Boston: B. Wilkins & Co., Publishers, 1895.*

Parsons, Emily Elizabeth. Memoir of Emily Elizabeth Parsons, *ed. Theophilus Parsons. Boston: Little, Brown, 1880.*

Divided Families and Changes in Family Relationships

As the country was divided through war, families' relationships shifted as well. Some families grew closer; the emphasis on emotional attachments within families and moral development in children during the nineteenth century, including during the Civil War years, was stronger than the earlier, stricter perspectives on children's statuses, although one historian has noted that this shift in emphasis could be seen as early as the American Revolution (Marten 1998, p. 22). Children were relied on less for earning and contributing to household incomes, and were instead regarded as central family members to be nurtured. Mothers were increasingly interested in the growth and personal development of their children.

Pressures generated by the war influenced and expanded the responsibilities of mothers. As many households lost male family members temporarily or permanently to the war, mothers were faced with new challenges in raising their children alone. Without the support of husbands, or a mother's concurrent daily concerns as a wife, women had to reexamine their domestic duties. Therefore, they often took on work typically performed by males, such as physical tasks around the home. Mothers also became accountable for disciplining children, which had traditionally been the fathers' task (Sutherland 1989, p. 63). The uncertainties of the war, including its duration and practical consequences, forced mothers to make such rapid changes in daily living.

Explorations of self-identity and purpose added strains to the already difficult circumstances of experiencing a period of national upheaval. Family relationships were stressed and tested in a variety of ways during the years of the Civil War. One historian maintains that women not only often felt frustrated by or unequal to their new responsibilities but also began to question men's supposedly superior competence and wisdom (Faust 1996, p. 134). As the contours of personal identities shifted, wives could no longer count on their menfolk to buffer them from harm or to serve as the foundation of the family. Naturally, major life events could not be put on hold simply on account of a spouse's prolonged absence. Mothers often had to experience or endure such significant events as the birth or death of a child without the feelings of safekeeping conferred by a united family or any male support.

Additional Roles and Responsibilities

Mothers often acted as links or channels of communication between an absent father and the children. They tried to shorten the distances between soldiers and their homes by reporting the mundane events or changes in their children. Documenting such pieces of news as language development or new lessons learned at school helped mothers hold their families together, even across distances. In a letter written to her husband shortly after he enlisted with the Union Army in 1863, Martha Glover, a slave in Missouri, said that "The children talk about you all the time. I wish you could get a furlough & come to see us once more. We want to see you worse than we ever did before . . ." (Berlin et al. 1987, p. 12). Mothers like Ms. Glover who were legally slaves faced tremendous burdens—including the unpredictability of personal safety—in addition to worrying about their children's well-being and future. Glover's letter clearly expresses the uncertainties many mothers were forced to endure: ". . . I do not know what will become of me & my poor little children" (Berlin et al. 1987, p. 12). Concurrently, concerns about spouses held by other slave owners or recruited to fight for emancipation added to many daily difficulties and apprehensions about the future as slave families were separated by events beyond their control.

Mothers also frequently had the responsibility of explaining the life-changing events of the early 1860s to the children. Children in the South and the North were exposed to many realities of war directly through family members leaving for battle and society's preoccupation with the war. While families living in the South confronted dangers that few Northern families faced because so much of the war was fought in Southern territory, both sides endured the difficulties of divided families, which often included the loss of fathers, spouses, or sons (Marten 1998, p. 21).

Regardless of where the families lived—in Northern or Southern states—mothers were forced to realize that the subject of war was often at the forefront of children's minds. Even young children experienced the rhetoric of war in multiple forms—games, books, toys, theater performances, and newspapers were among the many forms of entertainment and mass media influenced by the topic. Women had to help their young ones to understand a dangerous and changing world, while communicating a sense of safety and protection that the majority of mothers in any period of time work to convey. With the younger generation's futures as the motivation for many soldiers to fight for the Union or Confederate armies, or the encouragement for many slaves to fight for emancipation, mothers had the complex task of explaining why fathers had to be away from home while comforting their children and reassuring them of their importance and safety. Likewise, wives often reassured their husbands that they would help the young family members remember their fathers and the causes for which they fought (Marten 1998, pp. 11–13).

Another responsibility mothers confronted was working outside the home. With many males away at war during the early 1860s, the United States experienced an increase in the number of female workers. Mothers who had devoted their energies to raising a family and maintaining a home abruptly assumed financial challenges without the husband's income. While there was no massive or permanent displacement of men in most occupations, the tradition that woman's only legitimate place was in the home had been weakened by the end of the war (Sutherland 1989, p. 62). The rise in the number of female workers occurred together with the increased burdens mothers were taking on inside the home. Although some mothers could delegate certain household chores to older and responsible children, the war changed the composition of family life, both inside and outside the home—financially, practically, and personally. Many women, including mothers and daughters, particularly in the South, found jobs that supported the war effort by working in government jobs, such as positions in the Treasury Department or in factories (Marten 1998, p. 172). Such employment often helped them to establish a new sense of self-worth as well as connections to the military causes of their regions. However, finding employment overall was a difficult task. Most mothers were not accustomed to looking for work or spending a majority of the day outside the home. The availability of jobs varied, with greater potential for paid employment in larger cities. Also, the cost of living was increasing, which added economic stresses to the already intense realities of guiding a family through a period of war.

Motherhood in the North and South

Mothers in the North experienced a different range of lifestyle adjustments from those in the South. With the exception of southern Pennsylvania and some of the border states, most Northern households were located at a safe geographical distance from the battlefields. Therefore, families could feel a type of abandonment and confusion about the future without the ability to see conflicts firsthand. In addition, because Northern mothers were not able to help with the immediate impacts of war, they often felt uneasy and lonely remaining in the North, far from sons or husbands (Silber 2005, p. 91). Domestic life was turned inside out. Overall, a mother's world, whether trying to maintain a home in the North or the South, became much more difficult.

Living in the South generated distinct challenges and reputations for mothers as well. Being located closer to areas of fighting created constant worry of invasion by Northern troops. The sense of safety within the home became a daily concern. In addition to the practical challenges of living near war sites Southern women had distinguished reputations for being strong nationalists, willing to put aside their domestic traditions to support sons and husbands. They felt the fighting was for a greater purpose than their domestic world and were often admired for such devotion to their cause (Silber 2005, p. 91). On the other hand, the war also forced them to examine the racial divisions that had persisted, which they had accepted. Up until the war, privileged and wealthy white mothers in the South had relied on the work of slaves to maintain family estates and to help in raising their children.

Women also questioned their moral duties as mothers. A common concern was how to retain an influence on sons while they were away from the home environment with its strong maternal presence. One way for mothers to prolong their influence and maintain a sense of responsibility for grown sons was to write letters that communicated the values they had worked to instill during their sons' childhoods. In many cases these letters included reminders of religious beliefs and principles (Silber 2005, p. 96). It comforted mothers to some extent to continue such instruction of values through long-distance communication with their children. The connections through letters, however, were small substitutions for the strong presence mothers had had in their sons' lives before the separations.

Up until the war, many mothers had devoted their energies and identities to raising children and maintaining a household. When the composition of the households shifted, along with the social structure of the country, mothers reevaluated their multiple responsibilities to their families, homes, and personal identities.

BIBLIOGRAPHY

Berlin, I., F. C. Cary, S. F. Miller, and L. S. Rowland. "Families and Freedom: Black Families in the American Civil War." *History Today* 37, no. 1 (1987): 8–15.

Faust, D. G. *Mothers of Invention, Women of the Slaveholding South in the American Civil War.* Chapel Hill: University of North Carolina Press, 1996.

Marten, J. M. *The Children's Civil War.* Chapel Hill: University of North Carolina Press, 1998.

Silber, N. *Daughters of the Union: Northern Women Fight the Civil War.* Cambridge, MA: Harvard University Press, 2005.

Sutherland, Daniel D. *The Expansion of Everyday Life, 1860–1876.* New York: Harper & Row, Publishers, 1989.

Jenny Lagergren

FATHERHOOD

In 1861 Joseph Hopkins Twichell enlisted in the Army of the Potomac as a chaplain. Feeling a call from God to participate in the nation's great struggle, Twichell prom-

ised to serve his regiment faithfully and guide them on their quest to victory. Twichell had written every week to his father since his days as a seminary student; thus the two men had a strong emotional bond that transcended distance. The father had also served as a chaplain, and one of Joseph's primary reasons for his enlistment was the encouragement offered by his father. Two years later, Twichell received a disturbing telegram telling him to rush home because his father had died. Not only had the younger man's hero and source of inspiration been snatched away from him, but so too had his primary correspondent—someone with whom he could share his innermost feelings. When Twichell recovered from the unexpected loss, he sat down to write to his mother but found the task more hurtful than helpful. "I shall never write—'Dear Father' again—never . . . . How many times, when I was . . . disturbed, has the mere writing of them called me to peace and a better mind" (Messent and Courtney 2006, pp. 229).

The grief he felt cascaded over him; Twichell had to reassure himself that he had lived up to his father's expectations. "I only wish he had known how much I loved him. I hoped to show it someday, but now, Oh God! Blankness gathers about the future." Without his father's direction, the uncertainty of the future weighed upon Twichell and he longed for the reassurance and stability his father had once provided: "Oh! For another touch of his hand!—and hour of his company—the sound of his voice! Would that I could hear him call me 'Joe' again. Nobody ever did, or ever can speak it as he did" (Messent and Courtney 2006, pp. 230–231).

American Ideals of Fatherhood

The genuine grief articulated by Twichell upon learning of his father's death demonstrates the important position that fathers maintained in everyday life during the Civil War. Tradition dictated that fathers act as their families' leaders, decision makers, and primary breadwinners. Prior to the Civil War, small family-owned shops and farms dominated the rhythm and pace of life. Fathers often managed their family members as they would employees. In the decades leading up to the Civil War, however, growing sentimentality surrounding family life also demanded that fathers take on a more nurturing and loving role within the family.

The growing cultural influence of the middle class was primarily responsible for this challenge to the traditional role of fatherhood. The middle-class ideal perpetuated throughout antebellum America glorified the nuclear family consisting of father, mother, and children. The ideal family, according to the historian Amy Murrell Taylor in *The Divided Family in Civil War America*, "was meant to be an emotional sanctuary, a small and child-centered refuge from public life that replaced

The soldier's dream of home.   Fathers who sent their children to war as well as fathers who left their children behind suffered from the long separation. Antebellum attitudes encouraged fathers to take an actively affectionate role in the raising of children, resulting in feelings of loneliness when the loving family unit was shattered by war.   *The Library of Congress*

traditional patriarchal authority with affection and love"(Taylor 2005, pp. 1–12).

By the middle of the nineteenth century, American fathers presided over their families in a stern but loving manner. They played important roles in the development in their children and spent much of their lives instructing their offspring. For example, fathers taught their sons the importance of ambition and manly independence, yet both of those qualities were necessarily bound by the father's authority. This confrontation between an established authority figure and an upstart youth defined many father-son relationships and likewise prevented a family from realizing the ideal. Fathers similarly raised their daughters to continue the traditions of domesticity but also encouraged limited forays into greater independence (Rose 1992, pp. 162–177).

The antebellum notions of the father as authority figure were complicated by the war because fathers were often called away from home to serve in the military for men from all realms of society. Other domestic responsibilities also made the ideal difficult to realize. Poor farmers were forced to put sons and daughters to work in order to both plant and harvest crops. Northern factory workers watched as their youngest children went to work in textile and other factories. African American slaves in the South never had the opportunity to create ideal families. Forced into bondage, black slaves found family life tenuous at best. Without the ability to protect their families, black fathers remained at a loss until they earned their freedom.

Effects of Civil War

With the onset of the Civil War in 1861, Abraham Lincoln's declaration that "a house divided against itself cannot stand" rang true not only for the political existence of the American nation but also for households across the country. Hundreds of thousands of men enlisted to serve in both the Union and Confederate armies, which created a great crisis in the nature of family life. No longer able to realize their vision of the ideal family, fathers and sons across the nation still sought to retain emotional bonds with their family despite their inability to remain a cohesive unit. Many young men who went off to fight kept in close contact with their fathers and reassured them not only of their decisions to enlist but also that they had been raised well.

In April 1862, just before partaking in his first action of the war, a young soldier from Louisiana, Jared Sanders, wrote home to his father about the hardships he had encountered so far in the field. "Our march was very trying to our men, for the day before we had marched until midnight, & were tired down before we started. Our men stood the march better that I expected." Lest his father think that he had raised an unmanly son, the green recruit affirmed that he was "determined to *fight now & forever* & to *"rough it"* like a man. I stood the walk like a man of *25 miles in 24 hours*" (Sanders 2001, pp. 65–66).

Other sons focused on more mundane matters to prove their manhood and also to show their fathers that their prewar lessons had not been lost on them. Will McKee of Georgia sent his father seventy-five dollars to use as his father saw fit. Despite that sum of money, McKee could sense his father's displeasure for not sending larger sums during such difficult times: "I expect you think hard of me for not sending my money home where it would be taken cear of." Not wanting his father to worry that some of his money might be spent on vices rather than on food for his family, McKee guaranteed his father that "I try and be saven for the futer" (McKee 2000, p. 56.). Though having been thrown into a life-and-death struggle, McKee sought to show his father that he had learned lessons of thriftiness from his parent's example.

But McKee's letter also demonstrated how the war, rather than a father's tutelage, had shaped a generation of men. So far from home, many soldiers became the effective heads of their families and their fathers relied on them not just for monetary support but for advice as well. Oliver Wilcox Norton of Pennsylvania wrote home to his father when he learned that his brother sought to enlist. "I expect that when the call is made and recruiting commences in your vicinity, he will want to enlist, but don't let him. . . . One representative from the family will do." Norton remained convinced that his younger brother would not last long in the army. "Let him see a ditch half full of dead and wounded men piled on each other; let him see men fall all round him and hear them beg for water; let him see one-quarter of the awful sights of the battlefield, and he would be content to keep away" (Norton 1903, p. 99). The experiences that young men had witnessed during the Civil War legitimized their elevated stature in their family. By asking for his son's advice in family matters, a father also recognized his son's passage from boyhood into manhood. Though warfare was brutal and terrible, it served as a more effective rite of passage than a father's teachings.

Thus a generation of young men took on a greater measure of authority because of their experience during wartime. On the other hand, many families, usually wealthy ones, had the luxury of maintaining prewar family standards. The politically powerful Clay family of Kentucky remained loyal to the Union during the war, but none of Brutus J. Clay's sons enlisted. Instead, all three of his sons obeyed the authority of their father and stayed out of the fighting. One son, Cash, enrolled at Yale and was appalled at his treatment by what he considered abolitionist students and professors. "A man who has the least respect for his own feelings and honor cannot attend the societies. They declare all Southern men barbarians. They say ignorance and vice reign supreme in all the slave states and that we are not half as good as cannibals." For young Cash, his loyalty to his father's wishes and to the Union cost him abuse and social humiliation (Berry 1997, pp. 362–373).

For the slaves, however, the Civil War provided an opportunity for freedom and for separated families to reunite. One slave, Ms. Holmes, recalled that her father, Frank, had left her with his owner's family while he went to fight for the Confederate Army as a replacement for the youngest son of the planter's family. Only three months after joining the Confederate Army, Frank deserted and made his way to the Union lines. There he became a Union soldier and began fighting for his freedom. While he was gone, his wife married another man and effectively abandoned Ms. Holmes, who had now come under the care of her owners. While living with her white surrogate family, Ms. Holmes learned rudimentary reading and writing but she also came into a family situation for the first time and she commented that "they took care of me just like I was their own people." This improvement in her life lasted only briefly; when her father returned from war, he took his daughter and tried to make a new life (*American Slave Narratives: An Online Anthology*).

Fatherhood in the Civil War became intimately connected to the happenings on the battlefield. As fathers and sons gave their lives in the conflict, families were torn apart and had to recreate the ideal family as best they could. Though not all families were harmed by the war, most sent at least one son into combat. The loss of family cohesion created a rupture in family life that antebellum Americans had worked hard to avoid. Though the family remained the integral unit of social organization after the war, the ideal family seemed to have less credibility than before. With so many fathers and sons lost to death or injury, families were forced to organize themselves in new ways directly following the war's outcome. While fathers still held authority, the generation of soldiers who survived the conflict had experienced more hardship and was granted their own form of authority. African American fathers also had the opportunity to earn their freedom and to provide a more stable and secure home life for their families.

BIBLIOGRAPHY

American Slave Narratives: An Online Anthology. Available from http://xroads.virginia.edu/.

Berry, Mary Clay, ed. *Voices from a Century Before: The Odyssey of a Nineteenth-Century Kentucky Family.* New York: Arcade Publishing, 1997.

McKee, Hugh, ed., *The McKee Letters, 1859–1880: Correspondence of a Georgia Farm Family during the Civil War and Reconstruction.* Milledgeville, GA: Boyd Publishing Company, 2000.

Messent, Peter, and Steve Courtney, eds. *The Civil War Letters of Joseph Hopkins Twichell: A Chaplain's Story.* Athens: University of Georgia Press, 2006.

Norton, Oliver Wilcox. *Army Letters, 1861–1865.* Chicago: O.L Deming, 1903.

Rose, Anne C. *Victorian America and the Civil War.* Cambridge, U.K.: Cambridge University Press, 1992.

Sanders, Mary Elizabeth ed., *Letters of a Southern Family, 1816–1941.* Lafayette, LA: Center for Louisiana Studies, 2001.

Taylor, Amy Murrell. *The Divided Family in Civil War America.* Chapel Hill: University of North Carolina Press, 2005.

Adam J. Pratt

CHILDREN AND CHILDREARING

The Civil War disrupted the lives of children regardless of their proximity to the fighting. Household routines, schooling, and family dynamics changed for children in the United States while parents coped with the realities of a country divided. News about the war came from adults, newspapers, and local discussion. Children wrote about their feelings and experiences, corresponded with family members in military service, and received information tailored to them in newspapers and schoolbooks.

Northern Children

Children living in the North did not suffer many of the war-related problems endured by children in the South. Food continued to flow to family tables, schools stayed open, and routines were maintained. But even with few disruptions, children could not ignore the war. With many men gone to war, children did more to help on farms and in their homes. Some, such as those in areas of Pennsylvania and in border states, witnessed short periods of violence. Newspapers featuring children's columns attempted to explain the conflict in language children understood.

Children participated in the war effort, supplementing their daily routines with aid to soldiers. Public acknowledgments of their efforts came with graphic descriptions of how their gifts were used. In the *Lowell Daily Citizen and News* James E. Yateman, president of

the Western Sanitary Committee, thanked a young St. Louis girl for saving her money to send snacks to soldiers. He explained that the men who received her snacks had lost limbs in the battle of Pittsbugh Landing, and that they cried tears of joy to know that little children remembered them and sacrificed on their behalf. Jane Bradbury, who sent envelopes to Union soldiers stationed in Tennessee, received a thank-you letter from a Wisconsin man who told her the donation would allow other men to write to loved ones (Bohrnstedt 2003, p. 227). Adults did not refrain from providing children with descriptions of battle injuries, making the realities of war stand out as a stark reality to the undisturbed calm of most Northern homes.

Although the war was a central feature of their lives, children still faced the same hazards typical to children in peacetime. Often they were separated from their parents by sickness, accidents, and death unrelated to the war. Both President Abraham Lincoln (1809–1865) and General William T. Sherman (1820–1891) lost children during the war. Parents who suffered this plight were encouraged to celebrate the innocence of children at such a dark time in the nation's history.

Despite the troubled times, children in the North did not suffer the same level of educational disruption that took place in the South. William Morse of Woodbury, Vermont, managed to attend school the entire winter of 1864 despite the death of his mother and the absence of his soldier father (Silber 1996, p. 165). Northern children made sacrifices through donations and hard work; their counterparts in the South struggled with daily necessities.

Southern Children

Notwithstanding their enthusiasm for the Confederate cause, many white children living in the South were subject to drastic changes in their daily routines in addition to the stresses of missing male family members. Bombardments of Vicksburg and Atlanta brought the kind of deprivation experienced by soldiers directly into the lives of children for extended periods of time. As cities such as Richmond ran low on supplies and food, children were sent out to collect scraps of useable materials. Some took on added responsibilities because their families had fled encroaching battles. Some families, such as the Bosses of Virginia, moved into the homes of relatives when the head of their household died in the war. Such extended kin networks helped parents and children struggling without a breadwinner (Cashin 2002, p. 115). Many Southern colleges and country schools shut down; those that stayed open changed their curricula to reflect the spirit of the Confederacy (Werner 1998, p. 53).

The Confederate cause required all able-bodied people to help, and children were no exception. A reminder

African American women and children reading the Bible at the Freedman's Village school, Arlington Heights, Virginia, 1864. The village was established by the Federal Government across the Potomac River from Washington, DC, to address the needs of the growing number of slaves who escaped from the South during the Civil War. *The Art Archive/National Archives, Washington, DC/The Picture Desk, Inc.*

in the Savannah, Georgia, *Daily News and Herald* encouraged children to use every open space to plant corn. Northern observers remarked on the adamant loyalty expressed by Southern women and children who would rather suffer than surrender. But for many, by the end of the war their suffering had gradually eclipsed the enthusiasm of earlier years. Many children had to work in the fields because of the lack of laborers, tools, food, and animals.

Some children professing Confederate loyalty lived in Union states. In Maryland, their typical war games pointed to split affections, as children on both sides of the fight emulated their favorite generals and soldiers. For some children, this play connected them to family and the larger cause.

Slave Children

Besides facing their usual amount of work and deprivation, slave children had to work harder to compensate the loss of labor and lack of supplies as the war lengthened. They received information about the progress of the war by listening to adults, both white and black, and many eagerly anticipated freedom. Slave families who fled to Union lines could expect little help. The "contrabands," as escaped slaves became known, received the fewest supplies and and the least medical care from the army, and those encamped with the troops suffered outbreaks of disease, starvation, and exposure.

Northern newspapers printed touching stories of slave children aiding the Union cause. The San Francisco *Daily Evening Bulletin* published a short song for children about a small slave girl riding to freedom on a federal cannon. Other stories of daring escapes from slavery reached Northern readers. Slave children who survived were used to teach important lessons about the themes of the war. Plymouth, Massachusetts, celebrated the baptism of a small girl born into slavery who had been rescued by a Northern nurse. Reverend Beecher reminded his congregation that the youngest victims of Southern power needed the continued efforts of all Northerners. The Union soldier William Bradbury, who visited a school for freed slaves during his service, told his children that black children varied in color and that "the whitest were not always the smartest" (Bohrnstedt 2003, p. 290).

Many slave children were separated from their families as a result of the war. Some masters liquidated their assets during the war, resulting in the sale and dispersal of their slaves, or otherwise sent their slaves away from the fighting. During Confederate forays into the North, freed people were captured, moved south, and sold into slavery. African American women and children were the most likely victims of this wartime profiteering because most of their men had left home to aid the army. As the Union army pushed farther south, an increasing number of slaves escaped to the freedom of the battle lines.

Former slaves who joined the Union army often brought their families along to ensure their freedom and care, but camp following often led to dangerous outbreaks of smallpox, and the lack of supplies for these civilians brought illness and death. Some children benefited from their time in military camps, though, because it afforded them the beginnings of an education. The *Liberator* printed the accounts of camp teachers impressed by the enthusiasm of freed slave children despite their frequent illnesses (Silber 1996, p. 94).

Other slave families needed to be rebuilt at the end of the war. Adults separated from their children tried to locate them, and to keep older children under their control. The Freedman's Bureau handled numerous cases of parents fighting to control the labor of their own children under constant pressure from white landowners seeking laborers (Berlin and Rowland 1997, ch. 7).

Corresponding with Children

Parents separated from their children because of the war offered advice and continued parenting via letters. Fathers serving the army in particular used letters to stay connected with the children they had left behind at home; without these expressions of affection and guidance between fathers and their children, some worried they would be forgotten. Fathers often requested information about the education and behavior of their children, who responded with news of momentous occasions such as the loss of a tooth, a sibling's first words, or the arrival of a new farm animal. Eight-year-old James Cabot of Boston asked his father to send a cannonball or a secession dollar. The fascination with memorabilia worried some fathers, who understood the true brutality of fighting (Cashin 2002, p. 237).

Many fathers used their correspondence to inform their children of the dangers of the war. Grant Taylor of Texas reminded his children that he might not return home, and looked to the afterlife for a reunion: "O dear children be good and meet me in Heaven where we will never part anymore" (Blomquist and Taylor 2000, p. 194). William Bradbury, a Union soldier, wrote poems for his children so they could recite the simple rhymes that included his fondest memories of home life.

The frustration of separation was evident in family correspondence. Major General Lafayette McLaws expressed annoyance that his two young sons failed to write him even though they were old enough to do so (Oeffinger 2002, p. 166). Isaac Brooks from Rhode Island gently chastised his children for not writing to him, and reminded them to obey their mother. In attempting to explain his absence, he wrote, "I think it is for the best and it is the duty of us all, to do what we can for our country and to preserve its integrity even to the sacrifice of our lives" (Silber 1996, p. 60). Fathers also worried about what happened in their absence. McLaws asked his wife and children to send news of his sons' fishing and hunting expeditions, and sent specific instructions to ensure safe handling of firearms: "keep it fired off in the house...he must be careful in loading so as to keep the muzzle away from his body" (Oeffinger 2002, p. 174).

Mothers shared news of daily activities in letters, too. Malinda Taylor wrote to her Confederate soldier husband frequently, telling him the difficult truth about the effect his absence had on their children. Their children missed him badly and often told people he was "outside"; the youngest child stopped asking for him a few months after his departure (Blomquist and Taylor 2000, p. 6). Some women told their husbands that their young children did not recognize their fathers from photographs. Jane Bradbury's worried mother described the girl's nightmares in letters to her father. Jane's father, William Bradbury, constantly reminded his wife Mary to keep close watch of the children's penmanship, education, and compositions. In some of his letters he chastised his children and wife for their lack of care with their writing (Bohrnstedt 2003, p. 34).

Pregnant women and those with newborns had a particularly difficult time because they were forced to depend on older children, neighbors, or extended family to care for their families during their confinements. The Bradbury family faced this situation, and William encouraged his daughter Jane to help her mother with two infants. Basic aspects of parenting such as the naming of a new baby might require frequent letters to resolve a disagreement. Many fathers never met their infant children, and others waited many months before meeting new additions to their families.

Children continued to play, learn, grow, and explore despite the stresses of war. Mothers accepted new tasks, and young people took on new responsibilities around the home. Newspapers, letters, and regular discussions kept children connected to the war effort even when the fighting happened hundreds of miles away. Fathers who feared they might never return home did not limit their parenting to reminding children to be good and respect their mothers; often they tried to explain the reasons for their absences and the potential dangers of their situation. Children away from the front lines played war games, and those closer to danger experienced the war in a much more realistic way. White Southern and slave children experienced deprivation and loss on a scale not known in the North, but no child lived through the war without changes to their daily routines.

BIBLIOGRAPHY

"A Child's Offering." *Lowell Daily Citizen and News*, May 13, 1862.

Berlin, Ira, and Leslie Rowland, eds. *Families and Freedom: A Documentary History of African-American Kinship in the Civil War Era*. New York: New Press, 1997.

Blomquist, Ann K., and Robert A. Taylor, eds. *This Cruel War: The Civil War Letters of Grant and Malinda Taylor, 1862–1865*. Macon, GA: Mercer University Press, 2000.

Bohrnstedt, Jennifer Cain, ed. *While Father is Away: The Civil War Letters of William H. Bradbury*. Lexington: University Press of Kentucky, 2003.

Cashin, Joan E., ed. *The War Was You and Me: Civilians in the American Civil War*. Princeton, NJ: Princeton University Press, 2002.

Clinton, Catherine, ed. *Southern Families at War: Loyalty and Conflict in the Civil War South*. Oxford, U.K.: Oxford University Press, 2000.

"Let Every Man, Woman, and Child." *Daily News and Herald*, February 26, 1863.

Marten, James. *The Children's Civil War*. Chapel Hill: University of North Carolina Press, 1998.

"Northern and Southern Lyrics." *Daily Evening Bulletin*, November 11, 1862.

Oeffinger, John C., ed. *A Soldier's General: The Civil War Letters of Major General Lafayette McLaws*. Chapel Hill: University of North Carolina Press, 2002.

Silber, Nina, and Mary Beth Sievens, eds. *Yankee Correspondence: Civil War Letters between New England Soldiers and the Home Front*. Charlottesville: University Press of Virginia, 1996.

Werner, Emmy E. *Reluctant Witnesses: Children's Voices from the Civil War*. Boulder, CO: Westview Press, 1998.

Megan Birk

EXTENDED FAMILIES

Thousands of homes were adversely affected by the Civil War as men left for extended periods or were wounded or killed. Mothers, grandmothers, grandfathers, aunts, and uncles had to pull together to meet the needs of their children and their communities. A letter to Abraham Lincoln from Kentucky Union sympathizer, William Davenport, dated January 11, 1864, tells of Brigadier General James Shackelford's family grief and turmoil. Soon after Shackelford had gone home for his wife's funeral and returned with a heavy heart to his post, he related discouraging news about the members of the family he had just left. Davenport sent Lincoln Shackelford's petition to return home permanently to his extended family. Davenport wrote: "On reaching home...he [Shackelford] found his mother—a widowed lady 74 years old—confined to bed and in a helpless condition—his Mother-in-law very old and Blind—his Sister a widow far gone with consumption—and his four infant children in a very dependent condition. These persons constitute[d] his family...." Davenport explained that these family members required Shackelford's "personal attention and care

and therefore he asks to be relieved of his Command and tenders his Resignation" (Davenport 1864). Davenport assured Lincoln that Shackelford remained loyal to the Union cause and to the president.

The American Civil War—the proverbial "house divided"—often led to great havoc and suffering within extended families. Sidney George Fisher warned in his diary in February 1861 that "one of the evils of civil dissentions is that they produce discord between families & friends & great care should be taken to avoid disputes which may cause ill feelings to arise" (Fisher 2007, p. 379). Nothing was simple during this war. There were some people who lived in the North who sympathized with or fought for the Confederacy and some who lived in the South who remained with the Union. African Americans fought on the Union side and went to war with the Confederates. Black workers were instrumental on both sides of the divide.

Impact of Military Service

Documents and diaries from the period provide example after example of family discord. The most obvious cause of division was that one or more members of the same family split their allegiance, some joining the Union and others the Confederacy. An article by Judith Lee Hunt, "'High with Courage and Hope': The Middleton Family's Civil War," chronicles the difficulties of a family that had relatives in the North and South with divided loyalties. One sister lived in the North and her husband sought to assure her loyalty to the Union, while a brother in Charleston, South Carolina, tried to keep her allegiance with the South. The sister was in South Carolina when Fort Sumter was bombarded but left immediately, saying that it would most probably be "her last visit to friends and family in the South" for a while. One brother was killed in the war, while another member of the family, a South Carolina naval officer named Edward Middleton, decided to remain with the Union although the majority of his extended family supported the Confederacy and felt that he was shaming them by his behavior. Middleton did request to be assigned to naval patrols in the Pacific Ocean so that he would not have to participate in Civil War combat. Yet when the Confederate government attempted to seize "land, tenements...goods and chattel" held by Union sympathizers, Middleton's Confederate brothers had to fight to keep their property (Hunt 2000, p. 107).

A diarist reports another case in which some members of the same family fought in blue and others in gray. As the Confederate soldiers made their way through Chambersburg, Pennsylvania, toward Gettysburg, a young man who was from Pennsylvania but had joined the Rebel cause came through town and visited a relative. The observer, Rachel Cormany, records what happened on June 24, 1863:

Home from the war. Civil War service placed great strains on family relations in several ways. In some families, women and children were forced to assume duties regularly taken up by men, while other families were splintered as brothers and cousins often joined the fight on opposing sides. *The Library of Congress*

I was sitting on Jared's poarch [*sic*] when a young man (rebel) came & shook hands with Mr. Jared—a relative, his brother is in this army too. He was raised here—His mother is burried here—Mr. Jared told him he ought to go & kneel on his Mothers grave & ask for pardo[n] for having fought in such a bad cause. against such a good Government. tears almost came, he said he could not well help getting in, but he would not fight in P[ennsylvani]a. he told his officers so, he was placed under arrest awhile but was released again. Now he said he is compelled to carry a gun & that is as far as they will get toward making him fight. He was in Jacksons Brig[ade] (*Diary of Rachel Cormany*, June 24, 1863).

African American Families

In 1861, the Union General Benjamin F. Butler refused to return several slaves who had sought refuge at Fort Monroe in Virginia, declaring them to be "contraband of war" (Butler 1861, p. 72). Subsequently, Union leaders vacillated between allowing so-called contrabands to travel and camp with Union troops as support workers and at other times returning them to their owners. No matter what the official policy, the Union troops could not keep thousands of African American extended families from running away to their camps.

After the Emancipation Proclamation officially declared the end of slavery in the Confederacy and called for the enlistment of United States Colored Troops, black extended families often followed the soldiers. Parents and their children, grandparents, aunts, and uncles lived in contraband camps near the Union troops and received some support. In the Border States, contraband families were not as well received by the Union troops and had to provide for their needs as best as they could. Some families were hired by the Union Army or paid by individual soldiers.

Frederick Law Olmsted (1822–1903), a member of the United States Sanitary Commission (USSC), recorded his impressions of contraband families in *Hospital Transports: A Memoir of the Embarkation of the Sick and Wounded from the Peninsula of Virginia in the Summer of 1862*:

We have on two of our boats nine contraband women, from the Lee estate...excellent workers... The Negro quarters are decent and comfortable little houses, and a wide road between them and the bank which slopes to the river. [Black children] are rushing about, and tipping into the washtubs. In one cabin two small babies were being taken care of by an old woman who said she was their grandmother.... Babies had the measles, which wouldn't 'come out' on one of them. So she had laid him tenderly in the open clay oven, and, with hot sage-tea and an unusually large brick put to his...feet, was proceeding to develop the disease. (Olmsted 1863, p. 124)

A document from the Library of Congress provides Asa Fiske's reminiscences about African American family life during the war. Fiske, who was assigned in 1863 to serve as assistant superintendent of contrabands for the Department of West Tennessee, directed the care of several thousand former slaves. This involved procuring food, clothing, bedding and medical supplies for them. He was also concerned about their moral and spiritual lives and on one occasion performed one marriage ceremony for 119 contraband families simultaneously. Fiske later wrote to his granddaughter, "This great Wedding day produced most remarkable results on the good order and morality of the entire camp" and he remarked that the "sacredness of the Marital compact was...rigidly observed" (Fiske 1914).

As more and more African Americans were freeing themselves by simply walking away from the plantations where they lived, whites in the South and Border States often tried to apprentice black children legally so that they would not lose their service. The families of freedmen and women, however, usually felt that apprenticeship was simply another word for slavery. A note from Lt. James DeGrey, an agent from the Freedmen's Bureau, dated January 29, 1867, appears in *Families and Freedom*. Commenting on a woman's attempt to have a child released from an apprenticeship, DeGrey wrote, "My belief is, the old lady wants the boy because he is now able to do Some work. The binding out of children Seems to the freedmen like putting them back into Slavery. In every case where I have bound out children thus far, some grandmother or fortieth cousin has come to have them released" (Berlin and Rowland 1997, p. 242)

In addition to trying to make African Americans remain on the plantations, Confederate armies often compelled African American families to travel with them. Rachel Cormany's diary relates information about blacks who had come with the Confederates as they traveled to Gettysburg. She reported that the rebels

> ...were hunting up the contrabands & driving them off by droves. O! How it grated on our hearts to have to sit quietly & look at such brutal deeds—I saw no men among the contrabands—all women & children. Some of the colored people who were raised here were taken along—I sat on the front step as they were driven by just like we would drive cattle. Some laughed & seemed not

to care—but nearly all hung their heads. One woman was pleading wonderfully with her driver for her children—but all the sympathy she received from him was a rough 'March along'— at which she would quicken her pace again. It is a query what they want with those little babies— whole families were taken. Of course when the mother was taken she would take her children. I suppose the men left thinking the women & children would not be disturbed. (*Diary of Rachel Cormany*, June 18, 1863)

On June 17, 1863, Cormany wrote that among the last to leave were some with soldiers with African Americans "on their horses behind them. How glad we are they are gone—None of our Soldiers came." The next day Cormany admitted that the townspeople "have to be afraid to go out of our houses. A large wagon train & 500 or 600 Cavalry have just passed & it is now about 3 1/2 o'clock. hope all are through now. Many of the saddles were empty, & any amount of negroes are along" (*Diary of Rachel Cormany*, June 28, 1863).

Letters from Home

Some extended families simply relied on extensive correspondence during the war. One Confederate soldier, Thomas Smiley of Augusta County, Virginia, heard from his mother, father, sister, aunts, uncles, and cousins during his enlistment. Ellen Martin, one of Smiley's aunts, warned her nephew to "prepare to meet thy God." She also mentions that she was doing community work on behalf of the soldiers. On April 28, 1861, she wrote her beloved nephew about the state of his soul:

> Permit me to enquire whether you have made this preparation or not. Meet God you must, whether prepared or unprepared And how soon you know not, Death may summons to his presence But God has often met you, Both by his providence and by his Spirit, I cannot believe you have lived to be almost nineteen without often feeling the gentle wooings of Gods Spirit. (Ellen Martin to Thomas Smiley, April 28, 1861)

Thomas received similar admonitions from his uncle, James J. Martin, on June 4, 1861, while his cousin, Letitia Berry, wrote about the family and community events shortly afterward:

> Your fathers folks were well this morning father saw Cousin Billie in Newport. Capt Curries Company started yesterday I was in Middlebrook when they passed they all looked very lively went to Staunton in wagons, there was about twenty wagons I think. They were very well fixed, the best of any of the companies from about here, had their tents, knapsacks canteens and almost every thing necessary for a soldier, the ladies have been sewing for them in Brownsburg for two week about sixty there every days and five sewing machines. We have been sewing for you all this week in middlebrook made 61 pants, your tents

started today (Letitia Berry to Thomas Smiley, June 6, 1861).

Another cousin, Maggie Berry, wrote in July 1861, to "Dear Cousin Thomas," and chided,

"You have no doubt come to the conclusion that I have forgotten you as I have not written to you sooner but not so my good Cousin. Your letter was written the 27th of June came to NewPort & has lain there until yesterday. I was glad to receive one more letter from my good but absent Cousin" (Maggie Berry to Thomas Smiley, July 12, 1861). This family exchanged many additional letters in which the family's love and concern for this young soldier is evident.

The great volume of Civil War extended family official records, personal letters, diaries and reports clearly indicate that preserving the family was of paramount importance to Americans, white and black, North and South.

BIBLIOGRAPHY

Berlin, Ira, and Leslie S. Rowland, eds. *Families and Freedom: A Documentary History of African American Kinship in the Civil War Era*. New York: The New Press, 1997.

Butler, Benjamin F. *The Rebellion Record: A Diary of American Events*, ed. Frank Moore. New York: G. P. Putnam, 1861.

Cormany, Rachel. *Franklin Diary: Diary of Rachel Cormany (1863)*. Virginia Center for Digital History, the Rectors and Visitors of the University of Virginia, 1998. Available from http://etext.lib. virginia.edu/.

Davenport, William, to Abraham Lincoln, January 11, 1864. *Abraham Lincoln Papers*, Manuscript Division, Library of Congress, Washington, DC.

Fisher, Sidney George. *A Philadelphia Perspective: The Civil War Diary of Sidney George Fisher*, ed. Jonathan W. White. New York: Fordham University Press, 2007.

Fiske, Asa, to "Little Villuines," May 1914. *Hand, Fiske, and Aldridge Family Papers*, Manuscript Division, Library of Congress, Washington, DC.

Ham, Debra Newman, ed. *African American Mosaic: A Library of Congress Resource Guide for the Study of Black History and Culture*. Washington DC: Library of Congress, 1993.

Hunt, Judith Lee, "'High with Courage and Hope': The Middleton Family's Civil War," in *Southern Families at War: Loyalty and Conflict in the Civil War South*, ed. Catherine Clinton. New York: Oxford University Press, 2000.

Letters of the Smiley Family, 1861–1865. *Valley of the Shadow*, http://valley.vcdh.virginia.edu/.

Olmsted, Frederick Law. *Hospital Transports: A Memoir of the Embarkation of the Sick and Wounded from the Peninsula of Virginia in the Summer of 1862*. Boston: Ticknor & Fields, 1863.

Debra Newman Ham

■ Courtship and Marriage

In general, courtship and marriage in the United States in the nineteenth century were conducted along well-developed lines. Among the monied classes especially there existed prescribed methods for men to meet eligible women, become engaged to them, and marry them. To have a socially sanctioned marriage meant following these norms, which were reinforced and disseminated by the popular press. The media instructed readers on proper behavior and the best method for catching a prospective spouse, and also on how to conduct oneself once married. Many publications written for male and female audiences weighed in on the question of courtship and marriage rituals.

The October 1864 edition of *Godey's Lady's Book* discussed some of the methods that young nineteenth-century girls used to divine the identity of their future spouse. In a dispatch titled "From a Correspondent," an anonymous author asserts that "All Hallow E'en...[is] supposed particularly efficacious for the practice of charms of all kinds relating to love and marriage" (p. 358). One of the more interesting methods of discovering the identity of one's future husband involved the sowing of hempseed in one's garden or a nearby field. "I have heard many of my mother's juvenile friends trying the experiment," the author claims, "and have performed my own part, years ago, in such a ceremony, as the clock tolled the midnight hour, pale with fear and trembling.... [N]o spectre [*sic*] came mowing after me, and the only result was an extraordinary crop of thistles in our garden" (p. 358). Such activities were largely pursued by young girls, as older ones ready for marriage were too busy refining their manners and trying to find a husband.

Courtship and Character

The *American Phrenological Journal*, a publication devoted to the notion that a person's character traits can be determined by an analysis of the shape of the head, seemed especially interested in courtship procedures. John Henry Hopkins (1792–1868), who was the Episcopal Bishop of Vermont for many years and became the eighth Presiding Bishop of the Episcopal Church in the United States in 1865, contributed an article titled "Choosing a Wife" to the September 1863 issue of the journal. The bishop instructed men on the methods of finding the right spouse. Courtship should begin when a young man finds a woman of his acquaintance interesting. The bishop suggests that the suitor "should commence at once the work of judgment, before his feelings are too far engaged" (Hopkins 1863, p. 73). He should prudently consider whether the woman has the qualities and attributes that would make him happy. Additionally, the prospective bridegroom should question whether "she be blessed with true religious principals," those being sweetness, good sense, discretion, and modesty, and being free from "envy, vanity, censoriousness, and affectation" (p. 73).

Bishop Hopkins also suggests that the best way to judge a woman is to observe her at home. Is she disobedient, unfeeling, and imperious to her siblings, and unwilling to help with the domestic work in her own home? Is she "lazy and indolent, fond of reading novels, and full of affected sentimentality, while she is without relish for useful information"? Does she "look down with proud

disdain upon honest labor"? If the answer to any of these questions is affirmative, then she is most likely not the right choice for marriage (p. 73). The bishop does admit, however, that people can change. If a man offers criticism to his intended and she "receive[s] it in good part, and display docility and energy enough to conquer her evil habits, and attain a higher and a better character, he may safely calculate on the happiest result" (p. 73).

Engagement and Marriage

Hopkins claimed that an early marriage, despite the misgivings of some doctors and economists, is "the true and normal condition of our race," and added that the shorter the engagement the better (p. 73). Hopkins's preference for brief engagements was shared by other commentators as well. In "Engagements," published in March 1863 by *The Knickerbocker Monthly*, an anonymous male author complains that it is as hard for a man to announce his marriage as it is for his friends to hear about it. Upon the inevitable proclamation, "the only

Marriage at camp, 7th New Jersey Volunteer Army, Potomac, Virginia. During the Civil War, women were encouraged to display self-sacrificing patriotism by prodding their suitors and husbands to enlist in the hostilities, thereby openly demonstrating their masculine qualities. *The Library of Congress.*

obvious and unexceptionable question is to ask whether it is to be soon, and to hear whether there is to be an engagement, or an immediate marriage" (p. 202). If no lengthy engagement is expected, then the man is looked on as a hero for "any thing like an engagement is a diminution of the glory of matrimony" (p. 202). Marital bliss depends "but merely on that power of adaptation which enables any two human beings who are forced to live together to get on pretty well, and fall in with each other's ways"; therefore, "there is no object in forming an engagement" (p. 202). Experts agree, the author asserts, that "however marriages are commenced, they all end in about the same average of happiness—great trials arise from worldly incontinences being avoided, as many married people will get on as well if they meet for the first time at the altar, as if they have spent a couple years in eager flirtation" (p. 202). A lengthy engagement would be appropriate only for those couples whose preference was for the man to establish himself financially and socially before getting married.

Some aspects of nineteenth-century courtship and engagement came under attack. In her June 1865 article "Courtship As It Should Be," printed in the *American Phrenological Journal*, Mrs. George Washington Wyllys objected to the practice of secret engagements. "If you have won the heart of a strong, steadfast man, you should rather glory in your prize.... [W]e have no patience with the sickly sentimentalism of modern days that consider courtship as something to be prosecuted in a stealthy, underhand sort of way, and an engagement of marriage as a secret that should be wrapped in impenetrable mystery" (Wyllys 1865, p. 178). In "A Bad Way to Get Married," written for the October 1862 issue of the *New York Monthly Magazine*, an anonymous author criticized "the method of seeking a husband or a wife by advertisement." He suggested that "no girl of well-regulated mind, and with a proper feeling of delicacy and self-respect, would think of responding to the public overtures of a man whom she had never met, and of whom she knew positively nothing; and, therefore, the women who usually answer such advertisements may be considered as likely to make undesirable wives" (p. 351).

Once married, a woman was expected to maintain order in her family and household. Gone was the need for flirting, dancing, and singing; instead, a young wife should become economical and industrious. She was to endeavor to be "pleasant and cheerful, kind and sweet-tempered; not morose and reserved on the one hand, or giggling and trifling on the other," suggested J. Atwood in "Advice to Young Women," written for the *Christian Advocate and Journal* (February 26, 1863, p. 67). Men, for their part, were expected to be the sole breadwinners for their families.

Effects of the Civil War

The Civil War caused some changes in the role of women and in the formation of relationships. Women showed their patriotism by acting like recruitment officers for the military. They encouraged their husbands, sons, and beaus to enlist, and shunned suitors who were unwilling to join the war effort. Later in the war, when the suffering was at its worst, especially in the South, women were expected to send loved ones who deserted back to the front. According to *Southern Field and Fireside*, it was women who made "the Confederate soldier a gentleman of honor, courage, virtue and truth, instead of a cut-throat and a vagabond" (April 11, 1863; quoted in Faust 1990, p. 1204). In the Confederacy, women who willingly encouraged men to join the military were seen as performing a self-sacrificial act, in support of a higher cause. Alice Fahs suggests that women in the North were also encouraged by popular media outlets to renounce and chastise any man who refused to enlist in the military (Fahs 1999, p. 1468). Women's attempts to persuade beaus or husbands to enlist allowed them to share in the patriotic fervor of the war and changed the dynamics of courtship, engagement, and marriage.

The nineteenth-century United States produced many prolific letter writers, and the war had little effect on their productivity. Susan Albertine suggests that many women used letter writing to test the strength of their romantic bonds with absent soldiers. Hence love letters became a larger part of the courtship, engagement, and marriage process than they would have been without a war (Albertine 1992, pp. 143–147). Besides writing love letters to brave soldiers, women—and men as well—collected keepsakes of their beloveds or betrotheds. One of the most popular keepsakes in the nineteenth century was hair, especially when made into jewelry. Throughout the war, *Godey's Lady's Book*, for example, offered to convert hair sent by readers into such items of jewelry as bracelets or fob chains. Hair jewelry was used not only as a token of affection but also to commemorate wartime triumphs (Navarro 2001, pp. 1–2).

BIBLIOGRAPHY

"A Bad Way to Get Married." *New York Monthly Magazine*, October 1862.

Albertine, Susan. "Heart's Expression: The Middle-Class Language of Love in Late Nineteenth-Century Correspondence." *American Literary History* 4, no. 1 (1992): 141–164.

Atwood, J. "Advice to Young Women." *Christian Advocate and Journal*, February 26, 1863.

"Engagements." *Knickerbocker Monthly*, March 1863.

Fahs, Alice. "The Feminized Civil War: Gender, Northern Popular Literature, and the Memory of the War, 1861–1900." *Journal of American History* 85, no. 4 (1999): 1461–1494.

Faust, Drew Gilpin. "Altars of Sacrifice: Confederate Women and the Narratives of War." *Journal of American History* 76, no. 4 (1990): 1200–1228.

"From a Correspondent." *Godey's Lady's Book*, October 1864, p. 358.

Hopkins, John Henry. "Choosing a Wife." *American Phrenology Journal* 38, no. 3 (1863): 73.

Navarro, Irene G. "Hairwork of the Nineteenth-Century—Hair Jewelry: Nineteenth-Century United States and Europe." *Magazine Antiques* 159, no. 3 (2001): 484–493.

Wyllys, Mrs. George Washington. "Our Social Relations." *American Phrenology Journal* 41, no. 6 (1865): 178.

Micki Waldrop

■ Men on the Home Front

During the American Civil War popular conceptions of manhood and honor dictated that men volunteer to serve their country. Not all men, however, could or would serve in the military during the conflict. Some men joined the army for short periods of time, but avoided long-term enlistment. Many civilian men in the Union and the Confederacy performed important tasks, such as running the government, providing home defense, and operating essential wartime industries. Other civilian men objected to the war and refused to fight or simply believed that protecting their homes and providing for their families were more important.

Businessmen who stayed home during the war risked having their neighbors brand them as profiteers, but some occupations were considered too important for men to leave vacant. Many businessmen and merchants supported the war effort through community leadership and financial donations. Prominent businessmen donated to relief funds that benefited soldiers' families and donated money to provide bounties to encourage men to enlist. The United States Sanitary Commission, a northern civilian organization formed to benefit the physical and moral well-being of soldiers, was organized and staffed by civilian men, although women did most of the fund raising. The officers of the Commission included Unitarian minister Henry W. Bellows, New York lawyer George Templeton Strong, and well-known architect Frederick Law Olmstead (1822–1903). Shortly after the war, northern writer Frank B. Goodrich, quoted by James Marten in his 2003 book *Civil War America: Voices from the Home Front*, defended those who profited from staying home by alluding to "the records of money given, not money earned; a labor of love, not of labor for hire and salary; of self-assessment, of tribute rendered always willingly, often unasked" (p. 135). It cannot be denied, however, that some northern men avoided military service because there was more money to be made on the home front through speculation or illicit trade with the South.

In the Confederacy industry and agriculture were doubly essential, considering the reality of fighting the war and establishing a new nation at the same time. Joseph Reid Anderson, proprietor of the important Tredegar Iron Works in Richmond, Virginia, resigned his commission as a brigadier general in the Confederate Army in 1862. In his letter of resignation, dated July 14, 1862, and reproduced on the Web site *Civil War Richmond* Anderson cited several pressing issues at his factory and stated that, "Since these changes have occurred I cannot doubt as to where I can render most service to the Country." Anderson spent the rest of the war working for the Confederate Ordnance Department in Richmond, where he could oversee his business. The government also considered plantations essential to the wartime economy and therefore exempted from the draft men who owned at least twenty slaves. This exemption was later expanded to also cover men who owned between fourteen and nineteen slaves, but working-class southerners, who still would not qualify, resented this distinction. Henry Steele Commager relays in his 2000 edited work *The Civil War Archive: The History of the Civil War in Documents* how John Beauchamp, a clerk for the war department in Richmond, remarked that "the avarice and cupidity of the men at home could only be excelled by the ravenous wolves, and most of our sufferings are fully deserved" (p. 501).

Men who stayed home often considered their responsibility to their families more important than joining the army, but these men were not necessarily opposed to the war effort. Men on the home front formed militias and drilled regularly in order to defend their homes from the enemy. There were several occasions in the North and South where civilians' preparedness was tested. In July 1863, Confederate cavalry led by General John Hunt Morgan raided through Indiana and Ohio and were met by militia who skirmished with the Confederates. In southern Indiana the rebels were opposed by the state military organization, the Indiana Legion, which was composed of men of military age who protected their rural border communities while continuing to labor on farms and in workshops. During the crisis, however, all available men were needed, and Indiana's governor, Oliver Hazard Perry Throck Morton (1823–1877), declared "that all able-bodied white male citizens will form themselves into companies, and arm themselves with such arms as they can procure," as Flora E. Simmons recorded in her 1863 book *A Complete Account of the John Morgan Raid through Kentucky, Indiana and Ohio, in July, 1863* (p. 16). White men in the Confederacy also answered the call to fight the enemy when needed. On June 9, 1864, about 2,500 hastily formed militia, composed of those too young or old for military service, held off approximately 4,500 Union cavalry outside Petersburg, Virginia. Residents later dubbed the engagement, which caused the Union army to begin a lengthy and costly siege of the city, the

"Battle of Old Men and Boys." Black male civilians were willing to volunteer to protect their homes, but in 1862, when Cincinnati, Ohio, was endangered by Confederate troops, city authorities only allowed black citizens to dig trenches and build earthworks.

Both the Union and Confederate drafts often forced military-age men to serve unless they could provide a substitute. The Confederacy began to conscript men in 1862, and the Union followed suit the following year. The draft did not necessarily mean that civilian men were forced to leave their communities. Wealthy men could afford to hire a substitute, and in the North, draftees could pay a $300 commutation fee to avoid conscription. This infuriated workers who could not pay the fee. As noted by editor Michael Perman in his 1998 book *Major Problems in the Civil War and Reconstruction: Documents and Essays*, a New Jersey official wrote to Secretary of State William Seward on July 18, 1863, reporting that "the minds of the poor, even of Republicans, are terribly inflamed by the $300 clause in the enrolling act" (p. 192). Some civilian men resisted the draft, refusing to serve. This was especially common in the Confederacy during the last two years of the war. Jones County, Mississippi, became a center for local resistance to conscription and a refuge for deserters to such an extent that it became known as "The Free State of Jones." A strong sense of duty to family and community caused men in both the North and the South to avoid military service or to leave before their term had ended.

BIBLIOGRAPHY

Anderson, Joseph R. to General S. Cooper. Richmond, VA. July 14, 1862. *Civil War Richmond*. Available from http://www.mdgorman.com/.

Bynum, Victoria E. *The Free State of Jones: Mississippi's Longest Civil War*. Chapel Hill: University of North Carolina Press, 2001.

Cashin, Joan E., ed. *The War Was You and Me: Civilians in the American Civil War*. Princeton, NJ: Princeton University Press, 2002.

Commager, Henry Steele, ed. *The Civil War Archive: The History of the Civil War in Documents*. New York: Black Dog and Leventhal, 2000.

Marten, James. *Civil War America: Voices from the Home Front*. Santa Barbara, CA: ABI-CLIO, 2003.

Perman, Michael, ed. *Major Problems in the Civil War and Reconstruction: Documents and Essays*. Boston: Houghton Mifflin, 1998.

Simmons, Flora E. *A Complete Account of the John Morgan Raid through Kentucky, Indiana and Ohio, in July, 1863*. [Louisville, Ky.]: F.E. Simmons, 1863. Sources in U.S. History Online: Civil War. Gale. Available from http://galenet.galegroup. com/.

Stephen Rockenbach

■ War Widows and Orphans

In President Abraham Lincoln's oft-quoted second inaugural address in1865, he stated:

> With malice toward none; with charity for all; with firmness in the right, as God gives us to see the right, let us strive on to finish the work we are in; to bind up the nation's wounds; to care for him who shall have borne the battle, and for his widow, and his orphan—to do all which may achieve and cherish a just, and a lasting peace, among ourselves, and with all nations.

The most obvious widows and orphans during the war were those who lost husbands and fathers in battle. Yet there were also women who were widowed before the war whose sons went off to fight and left them in hard straits with themselves and other siblings to support. Many widows, black and white, wrote letters seeking jobs, pensions, other types of financial aid, or the exemption of their sons from military duty so that they could come home to support their families. Soldiers themselves appealed to the government for aid for widowed parents or for release from service to care for them. African American women who had been enslaved and therefore could not legally marry during their period of enslavement had the additional problem of proving that the soldier from whom they expected support or because of whose military service they requested a pension was indeed their husband. Women often had to fight to be given a chance to work because the custom of the day expected that some male in the extended family would become the primary supporter of widows and their children.

Letters to Lincoln

The Abraham Lincoln papers in the Library of Congress provide a rich trove of information about Northern widows and orphans during the Civil War. Some letters like this one dated, requested honor for fallen heroes rather than material support. Isaac Newton Arnold (1815–1884), Illinois Congressman and Lincoln friend and biographer, wrote to Lincoln:

> … earnestly requesting that a commission of Brigr. General might be forwarded to the widow of my friend, & law student Col. James A. Mulligan.... [T]he Board of Trade voted his widow $1000. & citizens have subscribed much more. His last words 'Lay me down & save the flag,' expressed his unselfish devotion to the country. If you will cause such a commission to be sent, I shall deem it one of the most grateful acts of my life to present it to his widow. (August 4, 1864)

In another letter thanking Lincoln for benefits received, Anna E. Jones, widow of John Richter Jones, wrote

Draft riots in New York.   While many men went to war willingly, others in both the North and the South protested, sometimes violently, over being forced to join the military. Riots broke out in the North among lower income immigrants as they feared they might eventually lose their employment to African Americans for whose freedom they were being conscripted to fight.   *The Library of Congress.*

from Eaglesmeare, Pennsylvania, that it was "with heart-felt gratitude that I venture to address you in order to thank you for your kindness to the widow and orphan in nominating my son Horatio M. Jones as a Cadet at West Point. May you be rewarded for your kindness by his emulating his late father, Col J. Richter Jones, in his love and devotion to his country" (September 24, 1863).

Many letters to Lincoln requested passes for widows to travel between the Union and the Confederate states. Samuel P. Lee, an officer in the Union Navy, North Atlantic Blockading Squadron, wrote to Lincoln from the flagship, U.S.S. *Minnesota* "off Newport News," Virginia, requesting safe conduct for:

> . . . the widow of the late Secretary [of State Abel P.] Upshur, who, with her grand-child (a mere boy), and her sister, desires to return to her home in Washington City. Formerly I was on terms of friendship with this then influential, now helpless, family, and I ask your Excellency, as an act of humanity, to approve and return to me the enclosed, which authorizes Major General Butler to issue the necessary passports, on the usual con-

ditions, to these ladies and this child. (February 27, 1864)

Lincoln also issued a pass on one occasion to permit his wife's stepsister to travel across Union-held territory. "It is my wish that Mrs. Emily T. Helm, (widow of the late Gen. B. H. Helm, who fell in the Confederate service,) now returning to Kentucky, may have protection of person and property, except as to slaves, of which I say nothing" (December 14, 1863). Sadly, Mary Todd Lincoln's relationships to several Confederate soldiers through her extended family led to considerable criticism of the First Lady.

A very different kind of petition was addressed to Lincoln from Mary Mann, the widow of the educational reformer Horace Mann (1796–1859), then living in Concord, Massachusetts. She sent a "Petition of the children of the United States; (under 18 years) that the President will free all slave children." Mann wrote, "These children understand the social relations, father, mother, brother and sister; and the thought of separation is distressing, and when they are instructed to know that little slave children are constantly liable to be sold away—fathers and mothers also, their sensibilities are wrought up to the highest indignation" (April 1864). Interestingly, Lincoln drafted an answer to Mann, stating:

> Madam, The petition of persons under eighteen, praying that I would free all slave children, and the heading of which petition it appears you wrote, was handed me a few days since by Senator Sumner. Please tell these little people I am very glad their young hearts are so full of just and generous sympathy, and that, while I have not the power to grant all they ask, I trust they will remember that God has, and that, as it seems, He wills to do it. Yours truly, A. Lincoln. (April 5, 1864)

J. Andrews Harris of Philadelphia, Pennsylvania, wrote to Lincoln on behalf of women working to supply the Union Army as well as to support their families:

> I venture to appeal to you directly, without the intervention of red tape, on behalf of about thirty thousand suffering people in the city of Philadelphia, who can, by a word from you . . . be relieved of at least one half of their misery. They are women who sew, (on army work), and their children. These women are now forced, instead of getting their work and their pay direct from the arsenal, to be at the mercy of contractors who give them sometimes not one half of the government rates . . . If an order were given . . . that they be allowed to get their work & their pay directly from the arsenal, instead of its being given to contractors in the first place, the difficulty they labour under would be done away. These women are, very many of them, the wives or widows of American Soldiers; & all they need is the show of fair play at the hands of the government for which their husbands are fighting or have died . . . The hand which by a stroke of the pen gave freedom to an oppressed race can . . . secure, at the least, fair dealing with those who are dear to men who left them at home, unprotected, to be able to back up your Emancipation proclamation at the risk of their lives. The prayers of a poor wife, a helpless widow, & destitute children, will surely call down a blessing from Heaven upon you if you will but interpose in their behalf. (January 23, 1865)

Some of the Lincoln letters request exemptions from military service. A telegram from John Williams of Springfield, Illinois, to Lincoln requested that "Chas A Trumbo Co K one hundred fourteen (114) Ills only stay of his widowed mother wishes to put an acceptable substitute in his place Can you grant permission [?]" (January 4, 1865). Another letter not only requested that Lincoln relieve her son from service but also explained why the writer could not return his signing bonus. Ann Bowden from Washington, DC, wrote,

> Our Most worthey presedent please Excuase Me for takeing this Liberty But I Cannot Express my Grate gratitude for your kindness in granting Me

the order for My Son john H Bowden's of Chicago discharge what Goverment Bounty he has receved I have that Unbroken to refuned But the 1 hundred Dollers County Bounty I have Not Got It as I had to Use it Last winter to Maintain My Sick Boy and a dependant Sister I have Bin a widow Eleven years My Oldest Son a Loosing his health on Cheat Mountain Makes it Vary Bad for Us our kind president If you Can releave Me So that I Can take My Boy home with me I feel that God will reward you and I No he will Bless all your Undertakings please Answare[.]. (June 12, 1864)

Another widow asked Lincoln's help with another kind of arrangement. Mary Buckley of Washington, DC, wrote to explain that she was:

> . . . the widow of Dennis Buckley who was employed for several years as a laborer in the Arsenal in this city, and whose excellent character is vouched for by officers of the Army, in letters which I have in my possession I am poor and the mother of six children, the oldest of whom is not more than 12.years of age. I ask for employment for my brother Michael Donovan, who has been out of work for two months and who kindly helps to support me. He is well known, as an industrious, honest man, who has been employed at the Arsenal, and in various Departments of the Government and has who is very poor. (October 10, 1861)

Lincoln directed that some military officers find work for Donovan.

Lucretia S. Hickman of Washington, DC, asked Lincoln for employment for herself:

> Sir—Being the orphan daughter of an officer of The U. S—and reft of all means of support—by your Liberation proclamation—which I must say—I never, the-less, most cordially approve—as the World of enlightened men—must now—and in all coming time—Yet the inconvenience to me is—that every Nephew—and male relative I have is now in the front—battling for the Unity and very National existence of their country—And I—and their widowed mother utterly destitute of resources. Yet I am able and willing to write & maintain us honorably. Will you not—guided by your native instincts of high justice and benevolence give me an order on some of your able functionaries [to help find suitable employment] (May 23, 1864)?

A letter from Lincoln to Secretary of War Edwin M. Stanton requests the commutation of a soldier's punishment. Lincoln wrote,

> A poor widow, by the name of Baird, has a son in the Army, that for some offence has been sentenced to serve a long time without pay, or at most, with very little pay—I do not like this punishment of withholding pay—it falls so very hard

upon poor families—After he has been serving in this way for several months, at the tearful appeal of the poor mother, I made a direction that he be allowed to enlist for a new term, on the same conditions as others—She now comes, and says she can not get it acted upon. Please do it. (March 1, 1864)

African American War Widows

One of the obvious sources for information about Civil War widows is the Veterans Administration records in the National Archives. White women could usually prove their marital status by providing marriage certificates issued by the church or the state. Even family Bibles were sometimes accepted as proof of marital unions. Formerly enslaved women, on the other hand, did not usually possess such documents. African American war widows had to make their claims in a more roundabout fashion. At first the United States recognized only legal marriages and ignored slave marriages. Yet Congress was aware that slave couples had lived together and raised families; thus the members began to write guidelines to allow former slave wives to receive pensions for their husbands' service in the United States Colored Troops. In 1864 Congress amended the pension bill by allowing,

> ... that the widows and children of colored soldiers ... shall be entitled to receive the pensions now provided by law, without other proof of marriage than that the parties had habitually recognized each other as man and wife, and lived together as such for a definite period, not less than two years, to be shown by the affidavits of credible witnesses (U. S. War Department 1861, p. 66).

This act was amended on June 6, 1866; the new act required no "other evidence of marriage than proof, satisfactory to the Commissioner of Pensions, that the parties have habitually recognized each other as man and wife, and lived together as such" (Harmon 1867, p. 276). Legislation passed on June 15, 1873, however, stated that the widow was required to supply evidence that she and her husband "were joined in marriage by some ceremony deemed by them obligatory" (p. 267).

One example of a pension file is that of Lucy Brown. While enslaved to one of the wealthiest slave owners in Mississippi, Lucy Brown married a fellow slave, Thomas Brown, and bore him several children. According to Henry Young, who had resided on the same plantation as the Browns, "Thomas and Lucy lived together as husband and wife continually after they were married up to the time that he enlisted" (Frankel 1999, p. 100–101). During the war, while Lucy's husband served in the Union Army, Lucy lived in a federal camp established for former slaves. Reunited in Vicksburg, Lucy and Thomas were legally married with a Union Army chaplain officiating. According to Lucy Brown, "We were married again by the chaplain of the regiment and he gave me a certificate" (Frankel 1999, p. 101).

After her husband died during the war, Lucy, accompanied by her only surviving child, Clara, found work as a field hand and a domestic servant after the war.

During and after the Civil War thousands of formerly enslaved family members went in search of one another. Reunions, however, sometimes indicated that African Americans had taken more than one spouse. This unintentional bigamy occurred because enslaved people had often had no say in marriages arranged by their owners. A typical instance is reflected in a letter from Willie Ann Grey of Salvisa, Kentucky, on April 7, 1866, to her "Dear Husband":

> I received your letter the 5 of this month and was very glad to hear from you. You wish me to come to Virginia. I had much rather you would come after me but if you cannot make it conveniently you will have to make some arrangement for me and my family. I have 3 little fatherless girls. My husband went off under Burbridge's command and was killed at Richmond Virginia. If you can pay my passage I will come the first of May ... For if you love me you will love my children and you will have to promise me that you will provide for them as well as if they were your own ... (Sterling 1984, pp. 315–316).

It seems that the couple had had one child together, Maria; Grey knew that he wanted that child but wanted more assurance that her husband truly wanted her and the whole family.

Another example is a letter from a nineteen-year-old African American soldier, Richard Henry Tebout on September 26, 1865, in which he requests a thirty-day furlough to see his mother in New York. He said, "I want to go home to stay for my mothr is sick." He explains that he has not seen his fifty-three-year-old mother for two years. "My mother lost all her children this fall whill I was in the serveice U. S. ... My father is dead. My mother farther is deaed my mother is a widow and so here left alone for ever" (Berlin 1997, pp. 206–208). Tebout, who was in the hospital suffering from wounds he had received at Petersburg when he penned this letter, was subsequently mustered out.

War Orphans

The war left many children orphaned and left some who were already orphaned in worse condition that they had been in before the conflict affected the area where they lived. Extended family members often took in orphans, but there were still many children who ended up in group homes. The military, the Freedmen's Bureau, concerned groups of soldiers, and a variety of church and civic organizations banded together to try to help these destitute children. For example, Mrs. Wade H. Burden of Springfield, Missouri, wrote to Lincoln to ask for help:

> I appeal to you in behalf of the destitute Orphans of this town and vicinity many of them children of

Soldiers deprived of their Fathers by this 'Cruel War' others refugees who have fled to us for protection leaving all their worldly goods behind them many of them are living in tents and others are without shelter living as best they can The ladies of Springfield have organized a society for the purpose of providing for these homeless little ones they propose to purchase a farm with as good buildings as can be had but in order to do this we must have money and there is very little of that in the Treasury not more than $700. We wish to get a shelter for these children before winter and are compelled to solicit subscriptions from abroad Our Citizens will do all they can but they have been heavily taxed during the war and are unable to raise the whole amount—We need at least $4000. Our farm will cost us $5000. Will you not assist us? (August 15, 1864)

D. G. Klein, a minister of the German Reformed Church, also petitioned Lincoln to request an exemption from the draft because he had,

> . . . been engaged in the work of founding an Orphans' Home, for the sheltering, clothing, feeding and educating of poor orphan children, especially such as have become orphans through the present, wicked rebellion against our government and its constitutional administrators. Being subject to the draft, he finds himself greatly embarrassed, on account of the uncertainty of being able to go on with the work, and therefore, he would respectfully, but earnestly, pray his Excellency, the President, and the Honorable Secretary of War, to grant him the favor of a special exemption from the impending draft, and from any future draft, should it be come necessary to make any. (October 10, 1864)

In 1864, the *First Annual Report of the National Association for the Relief of Destitute Colored Women and Children* in Washington, DC, stated that the organization originally attempted to raise funds for sixty-two children and two aged women. "The want of house room has hitherto prevented our admitting many of the aged. Of the children received twelve were infants. But few of the entire number were in a healthful condition when admitted. Several . . . were in a nearly dying state from consumption, scurvy, and chronic diarrhea" (p. 8). The administrators explained that they were trying to leave unhealthy children in the hospital but the surgeons had induced them "to receive some whom we could hardly hope to save . . ." (p. 8). Those who did survive—thirty-seven—were regularly schooled.

The Rev. Horace James, superintendent of the North Carolina Department of Negro Affairs, prepared the *Annual Report of the Superintendent of Negro Affairs in North Carolina, 1864.* In it he mentions both widows and orphans. For example, in his description of the state of affairs for blacks in the town of New Berne, North Carolina, he reported that 10,872 blacks resided in the

vicinity of the town and of this number, 2,798 lived in a freedmen's village near the town. . . . "Thirteen hundred and fifty-one members of colored soldiers families are now fed in New Berne, 660 being adults, and 691 children. In addition to the wives and children of soldiers, I am now supplying food to 2,149 persons in New Berne who are very poor, or aged, infirm, widows or orphans, or for other reasons dependent on the charity of the government. This class of persons is therefore twenty-three per cent." (pp. 6–7).

African American Orphans and the New York Draft Riots

Probably the most discussed event concerning Civil War orphans did not relate to the war-torn South but to the Colored Orphan Asylum in New York City. White laborers who were angry about being drafted into the Union Army rioted for several days in mid-July 1863. They perceived the Union's role in the war as fighting for the abolition of slavery—the Emancipation Proclamation was in force as of January 1, 1863—and equal rights for African Americans. Thus they vented their anger against any person of color they could find.

Harper's Weekly, a popular magazine of the period, described the incident this way:

> The Orphan Asylum for Colored Children was visited by the mob about four o'clock [on July 13, 1863]. This Institution is situated on Fifth Avenue, and the building, with the grounds and gardens adjoining, extended from Forty-third to Forty-fourth Street. Hundreds, and perhaps thousands of the rioters . . . entered the premises, and in the most excited and violent manner they ransacked and plundered the building from cellar to garret. The building was located in the most pleasant and healthy portion of the city. It was purely a charitable institution . . . . The building was a large four-story one, with two wings of three stories each . . . . After the entire building had been ransacked, and every article deemed worth carrying away had been taken—and this included even the little garments for the orphans, which were contributed by the benevolent ladies of this city—the premises were fired on the first floor. (August 1, 1863)

David Barnes's report of the event provides more information:

> While Sergeant Petty was in charge of the station on the evening of Monday, July 13, Superintendent Davis, of the Colored Orphan Asylum, led into the station two hundred and sixteen of the children, none over twelve years of age, who had escaped from their home by the rear as the dastardly and infamous mob forced an entrance in front and fired the building. The little ones would undoubtedly been assailed had they not been hurriedly guided away. (Barnes 1863, p. 70)

The number of people involved in the attack on the asylum and the composition of the crowd is described in "An Eyewitness Account of the New York Draft Riots," written by a scholar, John Torrey, who was living with several of his daughters at Columbia College when the attack took place. He discussed the rioters saying that the "whole road way & sidewalks filled with rough fellows (&some equally rough women) who were tearing up rails, cutting down telegraph poles, & setting fire to buildings." Torrey described the attack on the Orphan Asylum this way:

> Towards evening the mob, furious as demons, went yelling over to the Colored-Orphan Asylum in 5th Avenue . . . & rolling a barrel of kerosene in it, the whole structure was soon in a blaze, & smoking ruin . . . Before this fire was extinguished, or rather burned out, for the wicked wretches who caused it would not permit the engines to be used, the northern sky was brilliantly illuminated, probably by the burning of the Aged Colored-woman's Home in 65th St. (Dupree & Fishel 1960, p. 476).

The crowds yelled their support of the Democrats and Jefferson Davis, President of the Confederacy, and threatened to destroy the homes of any known Republicans and abolitionists.

Some whites also plotted against African American orphans in the South. They did not want to destroy them; however, rather they wanted to apprentice them legally so that they could retain their labor for many years. In a statement dated November 11, 1867, written for Adam Woods and signed with his "X," Woods tells of his efforts to get custody of his brother's children, three boys. He says that they were in the possession of their former owner, Franklin Ditto, in Mead County, Kentucky. The children's father died while serving in the Union Army and their mother had predeceased him. Woods explains that after he received word of his brother's death, "he immediately made arrangements" to come from Kansas, where he had settled, to see about the children. "He called to see Mr. Ditto and asked Mr. Ditto for the children and was answered that he could not get them unless he had a legal right to them. He says Mr. Ditto knows him well and knows that he is the brother of Pleasant." Woods names his brothers and sisters living in the area who could vouch for his identity. Stating that he and his wife are both industrious but childless, "and that he is well able to raise and educate" his brother's children, he "wanted to get possession of them and take them home to Kansas" (Berlin 1997, pp. 206–208). There were many such cases that came before Freedmen's Bureau officials throughout the South.

Communities in both North and South banded together to try to meet the needs of widows and orphans by providing a variety of such support networks as homes for children, help for widows applying for pensions, or employment for those who needed paid work. African Americans in the South were diligent in their efforts to remove children of color from the clutches of former masters. Churches and religious groups were also tireless in their efforts to help those who were in need.

BIBLIOGRAPHY

Barnes, David. *The Draft Riots in New York, July 1863: The Metropolitan Police: Their Service During Riot Week*. New York: Baker & Godwin, Printers and Publishers, 1863.

Berlin, Ira, and Leslie S. Rowland, eds. *Families and Freedom: A Documentary History of African American Families in the Civil War Era*. New York: The New Press, 1997.

"Colored Orphan Asylum." *Harper's Weekly*, August 1, 1863.

Davis, Rodney O., Matthew Norman, Joel Ward, et al., eds. *Abraham Lincoln Papers at the Library of Congress*. Available from http://memory.loc.gov/.

Dupree, A. Hunter, and Leslie H. Fishel, Jr. "An Eyewitness Account of the New York Draft Riots." *Mississippi Valley Historical Review* 47, no. 3 (1960): 472–479.

Frankel, Noralee. *Freedom's Women: Black Women and Families in Civil War Era Mississippi*. Bloomington: Indiana University Press, 1999.

Frankel, Noralee. "From Slave Women to Free Women: The National Archives and Black Women's History in the Civil War Era." *Prologue* 29, no. 2 (1997). Available from http://www.archives.gov/.

Harmon, Henry C. *A Manual of the Pension Laws of the United States of America*. Washington, DC: W. H. and O. H. Morrison, 1867.

James, Horace. North Carolina Department of Negro Affairs, *Annual Report of the Superintendent of Negro Affairs in North Carolina, 1864*. Boston: W. F. Brown & Co. Printers, 1865.

Sterling, Dorothy. *We Are Your Sisters: Black Women in the Nineteenth Century*. New York: W.W. Norton, 1984.

U. S. War Department. *Annual Reports of the War Department*. Section 14. Washington: Government Printing Office, 1861.

Debra Newman Ham

■ Volunteer Work to Support Troops

When President Abraham Lincoln called up 75,000 Union volunteers after the surrender of Fort Sumter (April 13, 1861), civilians in Philadelphia were there to meet the trains and provide "coffee and sandwiches from their own homes to the men in the streets" (Library Company of Philadelphia 2006). As more and more troop trains arrived, local barrel makers William Cooper and Henry Pearce donated the use of a two-story brick building, designated thereafter as the Cooper Shop Volunteer Refreshment Saloon. Local merchant Barzilai S. Brown started a second facility, the Union Volunteer Refreshment Saloon. Operational by late May 1861, the Refreshment Saloons provided reading materials, bathing facilities, changes of clothing, letter writing materials, and other comforts, as well as meals. Indeed, by the time the saloons closed in December 1865, they had served more than one million meals (Library Company of Philadelphia 2006).

The immediate response of Philadelphians is one early example of the great outpouring of volunteer support for Civil War soldiers and their families. Civilian support was immediate, universal, and heartfelt. As men from the North and South mobilized to fight, their service was mirrored by the family members they left behind, primarily women.

In the North, Union soldiers were supported by more than 10,000 volunteer aid societies that provided blankets, food, supplies, and medical aid (Massachusetts Foundation for the Humanities). On April 20, 1861, the Soldier's Aid Society of Northern Ohio formed in Cleveland, supplying blankets and clothing to Union volunteers from the Ohio area. Rebecca Rouse served as its first president (Ohio Historical Society). On April 25, 1861, Dr. Elizabeth Blackwell, Dr. Dorothea Dix, and others established the New York Women's Central Association of Relief (WCAR) to train nurses for work in army hospitals and to raise funds for medical supplies (Giesberg 2006, p. 32).

Often the unpredictability of troop movements prevented effective delivery of supplies. As a result, two commissions—the United States Sanitary Commission (USSC) and the United States Christian Commission (USCC)—were formed to expedite efficient delivery of goods and services. Many of the individual soldiers' aid societies in the North immediately allied themselves with one of these commissions. In its first report, the USSC acknowledged that

> The present is essentially a people's war. The hearts and minds, the bodies and souls, of the whole people and of both sexes throughout the loyal States are in it. The rush of volunteers to arms is equaled by the enthusiasm and zeal of the women of the nation, and the clerical and medical professions view with each other in their ardor to contribute in some manner to the success of our noble and sacred cause. (Bellows, Harris, Harsen, et al. 1861)

The USSC is credited with cutting the disease rate of the Union army by half and raising almost $25 million in support for the Northern war effort (United States Sanitary Commission 2005). Katherine Wormeley, who

was active in the work of the USSC, called it "the great artery which bears the people's love to the people's army" (United States Sanitary Commission 2005). USSC volunteers "tirelessly canvassed neighborhoods for donations, worked as nurses, organized diet kitchens in the camps, ran hospital ships, knitted socks and gloves, sewed blankets and uniforms, baked food, and organized Sanitary Fairs that raised millions of dollars worth of goods and funds for the Federal Army" (United States Sanitary Commission 2005).

What motivated these outpourings of support? The novelist Louisa May Alcott (1832–1888) wrote in her Civil War journal, "As I can't fight, I will content myself by working for those who can" (Massachusetts Foundation for the Humanities). Alcott herself worked for a month during the winter of 1862 to 1863 at the Union Hotel Hospital in Georgetown, DC. Although she contracted typhoid pneumonia and was forced to give up her nursing work, she used her experiences at the hospital to write "Hospital Sketches," serialized in the *Boston Commonwealth* and published in book form in August 1863. In "Hospital Sketches" she wrote, "All that is best and bravest in the hearts of men and women, comes out in scenes like these; and, though a hospital is a rough school, its lessons are both stern and salutary; and the humblest of pupils there, in proportion of his faithfulness, learns a deeper faith in God and in himself" (Alcott 1863, p. 84).

In the South, the reality of war hit closer to home. Because most of the war was fought on Southern soil, civilians were more intimately involved in battlefield realities, particularly nursing and hospital care.

The Ladies Aid Society of Montgomery, Alabama, was the first group organized to meet the medical needs of Confederate soldiers. The Young Ladies Hospital Association of Columbia, South Carolina, formed after the first Battle of Bull Run, instituted the Columbia Wayside Hospital in one room of the state capitol building. An observer at the time noted that the young women were "unused to labor, but willing minds made up for their lack of skill, and it was wonderful how soon they learned to cut out and make up homespun shirts, knit socks, roll bandages, and etc., and before long many a box of substantial comforts was sent to the boys in the army from the girls at home" (Marten 2003, pp. 310–311).

Confederate nurse Kate Cumming wrote this moving account of her work:

> This morning, when passing the front door, a man asked me if I had anything to eat, which I could give to some men at the depot awaiting transportation on the cars. He said that they had eaten nothing for some days. Some of the ladies assisting me, we took them hot coffee, bread and meat. The poor fellows ate eagerly, and seemed so thankful. One of the men, who was taking care of them, asked me where I was from. When I

Students of Academy of Fine Arts. Many volunteers found patriotic uses for their skills, such as the young women who used their sewing talents to create a flag for the Academy of Fine Arts in Philadelphia. *Hulton Archives/Getty Images.*

replied Mobile, he said that Mobile was the best place in the Confederacy. (Cumming 1866)

Southern women also planned and attended bazaars, fairs, concerts, raffles, and dances to raise money for army supplies, and even sponsored specific Confederate gunboats through fund-raising drives (Frank 2004).

Occasionally, volunteers had to be cajoled into making personal sacrifices. In her Civil War journal for October 13, 1871, the Southerner Mary Boykin Chesnut

wrote of dear friends who refused to allow their seamstresses to work on garments for the soldiers until their own winter clothes had been finished. Boykin wrote,

I told them true patriotesses would be willing to wear the same clothes until our siege was raised. They did not seem to care. They have seen no ragged, dirty, sick and miserable soldiers lying in the hospital, no lack of woman's nursing, no lack of woman's tears, but an awful lack of a proper

A *Harper's Weekly* composite depicting volunteers filling cartridges. Men and women on the home front often supported the soldiers by making supplies that would be used in battle. *The Library of Congress*

change in clean clothes. They know nothing of the horrors of war. One has to see to believe. They take it easy, and are not yet willing to make personal sacrifices. The time is coming when they will not be given a choice in the matter. (Chesnut 1973, p. 1693)

At the conclusion of the war, Frank B. Goodrich compiled *The Tribute Book: A Record of the Munificence, Self-Sacrifice and Patriotism of the American People during the War for the Union* (1865). In it he noted "the records of money given, not money earned; of a labor of love, not of labor for hire and salary; of self-assessment, of tribute rendered always willingly, always unasked" (Marten 2003, p. 3). Volunteer support during the Civil War, in all its forms, is a testament to the willingness of Americans, from both the North and South, to support their soldiers.

BIBLIOGRAPHY

Alcott, Louisa May. *Hospital Sketches*. Boston: J. Redpath, 1863.

Bellows, Henry W., Elisha Harris, J. Harsen, and W. H. Van Buren. "U.S. Sanitary Commission Report No. 1: An Address to the Secretary of War." May 18, 1861. Disability History Museum Web site. Available from http://www.disabilitymuseum.org/.

Chesnut, Mary Boykin. "A Diary from Dixie." In *American Literature: The Makers and the Making*, Book C, ed. Cleanth Brooks, R. W. B. Lewis, and Robert Penn Warren. New York: St. Martin's Press, 1973.

Cumming, Kate. "A Nurse's Diary." In *A Journal of Hospital Life in the Confederate Army of Tennessee, From the Battle of Shiloh to the End of the War: With Sketches of Life and Character, and Brief Notices of Current Events during That Period*. Louisville, KY: John P. Morgan, 1866. Available from http://www.pbs.org/.

Donald, William J. "Alabama Confederate Hospitals." *Alabama Review* 15 (October 1962): 271–281; 16 (January 1963): 64–78.

Frank, Lisa Tendrich. "Women during the Civil War." *New Georgia Encyclopedia*. Athens: Georgia Humanities Council and University of Georgia Press, 2004. Available from http://www.georgiaencyclopedia.org/.

Giesberg, Judith Ann. *Civil War Sisterhood: The United States Sanitary Commission and Women's Politics in Transition*. Lebanon, NH: University Press of New England, 2006.

Library Company of Philadelphia. "Civil War Volunteer Saloon and Hospitals Ephemera Collection 1861–1868." McAllister Collection, Library Company of Philadelphia, 2006. Available from http://lcpdams.librarycompany.org:20018/.

Marten, James Alan. *Civil War America: Voices from the Home Front*. Santa Barbara, CA: ABC-CLIO, 2003.

Massachusetts Foundation for the Humanities. "Fitchburg Forms Ladies Soldier's Aid Society: September 16, 1861." Mass Moments Web site. Available from http://www.massmoments.org/.

Ohio Historical Society. "Soldiers' Aid Society." *Ohio History Central: An Online Encyclopedia of Ohio History*. Available from http://www.ohiohistorycentral.org/.

United States Sanitary Commission. "The U.S.S.C." 2005. Available from http://www.forttejon.org/.

Diane Hulett

■ Refugees

The American Civil War, during which large sections of the nation became literal battlegrounds for the armies of the North and South, resulted in a massive displacement of citizenry that remains a singular event in U.S. history. The states whose populations endured the greatest upheaval were those in the secessionist South, followed by border states whose citizens were divided in their sympathies, such as Missouri and Tennessee. The refugees largely fell into three groups: white Southerners who fled their homes as Union troops advanced; white Southern refugees driven from their homes by secessionists; and slaves. Of the third category, some were captured as contraband by victorious Union troops, while other blacks in bondage seized the opportunity presented by the chaos of war and their suddenly absentee owners, and escaped to the North and freedom—where many then joined the Union Army and the fight to vanquish the Confederacy. There were also a number of Native Americans uprooted by the war, some of whom chose to fight for the Union or Confederate cause.

White Southerners

Few reliable figures exist that provide a concrete total for the number of Americans displaced by war between 1861 and 1865. Some of the wealthiest Southern families were able to book passage on vessels bound for Europe, Honduras, and Brazil, but many other members of the Confederate elite remained at home, where the situation was perilous. The wife of Confederate Army general Robert E. Lee was part of the first wave of internal refugees in May 1861, when she fled her home in Arlington, Virginia, to which she was never able to return. Another woman, Virginia Clay-Clopton, despite being married to a prominent politician and being close to the family of Confederate States of America (CSA) president Jefferson Davis, was forced to spend most of the war years in transit. She stayed in hotels or with members of her extended family, and paid Confederate soldiers to serve as escorts for her and her sister on

Former slaves move north.   As Union troops marched across the deep South, newly-freed slaves were left to fend for themselves. Some headed for the North and enlisted in the Union army, while others remained in the South hiring themselves out to their previous owners.   *The Library of Congress*

routes that were dangerous for unaccompanied women, or indeed for any noncombatant.

Born in North Carolina, Clay-Clopton settled in Huntsville, Alabama, after her 1843 marriage to Clement Claiborne Clay, and lived part of the year in Washington after her husband was elected to the U.S. Senate in the 1850s. She was in her mid-thirties when war broke out, and spent four years staying with various friends and family members in the South, often accompanied only by her sister; the two passed the time sewing and knitting garments for their husbands, because warm clothing was at a premium due to wartime shortages. Clay-Clopton initially headed to Richmond, the Confederate capital, like many residents of Southern states who had been forced to flee their homes at the war's onset. In 1860 Richmond's population was 40,000, but it swelled to 100,000 during the war (Gallagher 2001, p. 95). Overcrowded conditions bred disease, and epidemics of smallpox and scarlet fever periodically swept though the city, forcing those who had the means, such as Clay-Clopton, to flee once again.

In her 1905 memoir, *A Belle of the Fifties*, Clay-Clopton recalled making her way to Georgia by train with her sister. The two "rode from Stevenson to Chattanooga on the freight train, the baggage-cars on the passenger-train being unable to receive a single trunk. Arriving at Chattanooga, we would have been forced to go to the small-pox hotel or remain in the streets but for the gallantry of an acquaintance of ours, an army officer of Washington memory, who gave up his room to us" (p. 192). Clay-Clopton later returned to Richmond, but conditions there were now abysmal:

> Patients in the hospitals suffered, even for necessary medicines. Sugar was sold at fifty Confederate dollars a pound. Vegetables and small fruits were exceedingly scarce. My visits to the hospital wards were by no means so constant as those of many of my friends, yet I remember one poor little Arkansas boy in whom I became interested, and went frequently to see, wending my way to his cot through endless wards, where an army of sick men lay, minus an arm, or leg, or with bandaged

heads that told of fearful encounters. The drip-drip of the water upon their wounds to prevent the development of a greater evil is one of the most horrible remembrances I carry of those days. (p. 201)

Pro-Union Refugees

Life during wartime presented even greater perils for Union sympathizers caught behind enemy lines. A young woman named Cora Mitchel was the daughter of a wealthy Connecticut cotton merchant who had, with other Northern entrepreneurs, helped to make the city of Apalachicola, Florida, the third busiest port on the Gulf of Mexico, after New Orleans and Mobile. The Apalachicola River had two tributaries, the Flint and Chattahoochee rivers, each of which went deep into Georgia almost to the border of South Carolina. In the years before the war, New England traders with ties to Europe made Apalachicola into an important way station for cotton shipments between the plantations and lucrative foreign markets.

At the outbreak of war, Mitchel and her brother first went to Columbus, Georgia, where her married sister was living, and attended school there. Her brother was soon conscripted by force into the Confederate Army—despite the fact that he was underage—and became ill from one of the fevers that regularly swept through Army camps on both sides due to poor sanitary conditions. When he returned home on leave, Mitchel's father fled north with him. The fact that her brother was a deserter became well known in Apalachicola, and Mitchel's mother, Sophia, began to fear for her safety as well as that of her younger children. Sophia Mitchel then decided to travel to Columbus to retrieve Cora, in preparation for the family's final flight north.

The 300-mile trip up the Chattahoochee River the Mitchels planned to make was a perilous one, as part of the waterway had been blockaded by Confederate forces. On the journey back to Apalachicola, Mitchel and her mother had to pick up CSA passports, recently required for travel to Gulf Coast ports in order to prevent further Confederate army desertions. "Immediately on our arrival at Fort Gaines mother went to the arsenal for the passport," Mitchel wrote. "She was met by a very agreeable young adjutant, who said he had not the power to give us one, but he was expecting the major back at any moment and he would give it." Over the next two days, Sophia Mitchel repeated the four-mile round-trip walk, with no success. On the fourth day, Cora asked her mother if she might try instead; when she returned, she had the travel documents in hand. "My youth probably appealed to the young man, and he could not help feeling that I ought not to be detained," she wrote in her memoir. "We did not know it then, but found out afterwards that he had orders to detain us till the major came, as we were not to be allowed to go on" (1916, pp. 18–19).

Because of the blockade, part of Mitchel's journey had to be made through the bayou, which

> had been widened and deepened by the force of the strong current, but as the stream carried off the banks the trees would fall in, making it much more dangerous, and the utmost care and skill were necessary to bring us through in safety. Mother and I lay in the bottom of the boat with strict orders not to move, while the little boat was tossed about by the swift current. If we had hit one of the projecting trees, we would have sunk immediately. (1916, pp. 20–21)

At night, after getting back on the river itself, they went ashore to rest. Mitchel remembered feeling "excited by the novelty and beauty of the scene":

> The moon was full, and though just before Christmas, the weather was mild. The air was heavy with the scents of the forest behind us, from which could be heard, from time to time, the calls of owls, panthers and wildcats. We saw none, but there was always the expectation that one would appear. We roasted peanuts in the coals and toasted bacon and corn pones. These were our only food during the entire journey. The river water, muddy though it was, satisfied our thirst. Supplies of all kinds had long been very scarce, and we had learned to be very thankful for little, and that of the simplest. (1916, p. 22)

At Apalachicola, Mitchel and her mother gathered the remaining children and managed to get aboard a ship bound for Key West, at the tip of Florida—no easy feat. There, "another problem presented itself," Mitchel wrote. "The town was full of refugees. The one hotel was crowded to its fullest capacity, and no boat from New Orleans [was] in sight" because of a yellow fever outbreak in Key West (1916, p. 36). Finally, one appeared, and Mitchel's mother was able to convince the captain to let her family of six have the only available stateroom, which had no natural light and flooded every morning when the decks were washed. "We were only one group among many forlorn refugees. We were shabby and neglected. Part of the time we were seasick, and always [we were] uncomfortable in our cramped quarters," she wrote, but they arrived safely in New York and then headed to Rhode Island, where they reunited with her father and brother (1916, p. 41).

A Lutheran Pastor in Tennessee

Border states such as Kentucky and Tennessee, where loyalties were divided, also produced a torrent of refugees. It was in the towns and villages of these states that the divisiveness of the war was felt most immediately, as once-cordial neighbors turned bitter toward one another. Hermann Bokum, a German immigrant who had settled in the Cumberland Mountains region as a pastor, provided one account of the war in his 1863 book, *The Testimony of a Refugee from East Tennessee*. He described how local men eager to aid Confederate forces joined regiments that were beginning to form at the war's onset. Union loyalists in the area, however, set fire to some of the bridges that these regiments would need to pass over to reach Virginia; in reprisal, state officials sympathetic to the Confederate cause meted out harsh punishments to ordinary civilians. "A man named Haun had been taken to prison, because he had taken part in the burning of the bridges," Bokum recounted. "The names of the persons who tried him have never been made public. . . . Others beside him were hung, still others were shot down or otherwise murdered" (p. 8).

Bokum had traveled to Washington to plead the case of Union sympathizers in Tennessee, but when he returned home he was troubled by rumors his friends reported back to him—that he, too, might be hanged without a trial. In June 1861 Tennessee became the last of the border states to secede from the Union, and a conscription law then went into effect. Bokum failed to report to the mustering site, after which he received word that a party of five were heading to his home to arrest him:

> I had made up my mind to go to prison. I could not bear the thought of leaving the atmosphere where my wife and my children were breathing, but my wife prevailed on me to go to our friends in the North. Her last words were: "Fear not for me, I trust in God"; I begged her to kiss our children, and I turned into the mountains. Never I trust, shall I cease to be thankful for the gracious manner in which I was shielded from harm in that perilous journey. Six months later my wife and my children arrived in Cincinnati, having crossed the Cumberland Mountains in the rear of the two contending armies, and having made more than 300 miles in an open buggy." (1863, p. 10)

They eventually relocated to Philadelphia, where Bokum became chaplain at Turner's Lane Hospital.

An Ozark Ballad's Tale

There were also significant numbers of men who joined the Union Army after fleeing home states that had seceded. One of them was Daniel Martin, an Arkansas man whose story survives in a well-known Ozark Mountains folk song, "The Battle of Elkhorn Tavern," which cultural historians believe Martin likely wrote himself and passed on to his descendants. A farmer who was probably in his early twenties when the war broke out, Martin left the Confederate state to join the pro-Union Missouri Infantry volunteers at Rolla, Missouri. The ballad, which recounts Martin's two years of service, begins with the stanza, "My name is Daniel Martin, I was born in Arkansas / I fled from those bad rebels who fear not God nor law / I left my aged parents. I left my loving wife / I was forced to go to Rolla to try and save my life." The song goes on to recount the events of the

Battle of Elkhorn Tavern, as well as those of the March 1862 Battle of Pea Ridge, which finally gave the Union side firm control of Missouri. The lyrics conclude with the observation, "And if ever I get through this war you may call me roasted done / I'll never go to fight again for money, love or fun."

The Plight of Slaves

Untold numbers of blacks were caught up in the Civil War, and while many were too fearful of reprisals to strike out on their own once chaos descended on the South, others fled north to freedom. Many sought shelter and protection at Union Army camps, and the federal government found itself struggling to care for thousands of displaced persons who had neither homes nor income to provide for their families. When Union forces captured the strategic North Carolina city of New Bern in March 1862, General Ambrose Burnside appointed a superintendent of the poor to oversee relief efforts. Fifteen months later, government officials sent to investigate conditions in the area filed a report stating that "7,500 colored persons and 1,800 white persons received relief" through the efforts of the superintendent, but that

> the average proportion dealt out in each of the staple articles of food—as flour, beef, bacon, bread, &c.—was about as one for each colored person relieved to sixteen for each white person to whom such relief was granted. At the time this occurred work was offered to both blacks and whites; to the whites at the rate of $12 a month, and to the blacks at the rate of $8 a month. (Owen, McKaye, and Howe 1863, n.p.)

A horrific incident at Camp Nelson, a Union Army camp in Kentucky, captured the plight of former slaves in newly mustered black regiments after the Emancipation Proclamation was issued in 1863 and separate army units for black soldiers were created. The wives and children of these former slaves, having no place else to go, came with them to Camp Nelson and other sites, despite vehement local opposition. Camp Nelson's commanding officer, Brigadier General Speed S. Fry, referred to the problem as "the [Expletive] Woman Question," and feared that food rations would run out, diseases would kill soldiers before they even got to battle, and the presence of families nearby would lead to a quick breakdown of military discipline (Wilson 2002, p. 187). After several attempts to get rid of them, on November 23, 1864, Fry succeeded in expelling 400 women and children. They had nowhere to go, almost no possessions, and were driven out into cold weather. The African American soldier Joseph Miller recounted the details of that day: "[M]orning was bitter cold. It was freezing hard. I was certain it would kill my sick child to take him out in the cold. I told the man in charge that it would be the death of my boy. I told him my wife and children had no place to go and I told him that I was a soldier of the United States. He told me that it did not make any difference" (quoted in Wilson 2002, p. 187). Miller's family was ejected, and when he finally found them they were "shivering with cold and famished with hunger. They had not received a morsel of food during the whole day" (p. 187), and his child was indeed among the scores of casualties that resulted from Fry's decision.

The Camp Nelson incident was widely reported in the Northern papers and stirred outrage. To make amends for the atrocity, federal officials established formal refugee housing at the camp, called the *Home for Colored Refugees*. Nearly a hundred duplex cottages housed families, and there was also a school, mess hall, and hospital. The site was taken over after the war ended in 1865 by the Bureau of Refugees, Freedmen, and Abandoned Lands, a federal agency usually referred to in shortened form as the Freedmen's Bureau. A sympathetic West Point graduate, civil rights supporter, and Union general named Oliver O. Howard (1830–1909) was installed as director of the Freedmen's Bureau. Howard's field agents, however, were notoriously corrupt in their duties, which included monitoring the newly defeated Southern areas for incidents of abuse that appeared to be continuations of bondage, and overseeing the creation of a free labor market.

Once freed from slavery, many of the South's blacks became refugees, and many were desperate for any kind of work, even if it entailed returning to plantations. The *Preliminary Report of the American Freedmen's Inquiry Commission* included the account of one young Confederate sympathizer, Frederick A. Eustis, who had returned home to take over the family's South Carolina plantation. He was met by former slaves eager to work for wages:

> I never knew during forty years of plantation life so little sickness. Formerly every man had a fever of some kind, and now the veriest old cripple, who did nothing under secesh [Confederate] rule, will row a boat three nights in succession to Edisto, or will pick up the corn about the corn-house. There are twenty people whom I know were considered worn out and too old to work under the slave system, who are now working cotton, as well as their two acres of provisions; and their crops look very well. (Owen, McKaye, and Howe 1863, n.p.)

BIBLIOGRAPHY

"The Battle of Elkhorn Tavern." Available from http://musicanet.org/.

Bokum, Hermann. *The Testimony of a Refugee from East Tennessee*. Philadelphia, 1863.

Clay-Clopton, Virginia. *A Belle of the Fifties: Memoirs of Mrs. Clay, of Alabama, Covering Social and Political Life in Washington and the South, 1853–66*. New York: Doubleday, Page & Company, 1905.

Gallagher, Gary W. *The American Civil War: The War in the East 1861–May 1863*. Oxford: Osprey Publishing, 2001.

Massey, Mary Elizabeth. *Refugee Life in the Confederacy*. Baton Rouge: Louisiana State University Press, 1964. Reprint, 2001.

Mitchel, Cora. *Reminiscences of the Civil War*. Providence, RI: Snow & Farnham, 1916.

Owen, Robert Dale, James McKaye, and Samuel. G. Howe. *Preliminary Report of the American Freedmen's Inquiry Commission to the Secretary of War*. New York: 1863.

Wilson, Keith P. *Campfires of Freedom: The Camp Life of Black Soldiers during the Civil War*. Kent, OH: Kent State University Press, 2002.

Carol Brennan

■ Fraternizing with the Enemy

Fraternization is a term defined as "to become like brothers" and undermines the goals and objectives of war. Providing covert aid or even extending cordiality to the enemy is usually prohibited in most military codes of conduct and is subject to harsh punitive measures. During the American Civil War, an unusually high degree of fraternization occurred but often went unpunished.

Shared Values

Incidents of fraternization were rarely reported during the war years, but many came to light afterward in the personal recollections of soldiers on both sides. Historians note that in addition to speaking the same language, Union and Confederate participants in the war shared even stronger bonds, including a Judeo-Christian religious upbringing and an essentially identical value system—with the exception of slavery—that made perception of the other as a deadly enemy more difficult to justify. Furthermore, soldiers on both sides had signed up to fight with the belief that the war would be over within a few short months—but as those months dragged into years, soldiers and officers alike came to realize they were, as most soldiers in history before them, pawns in a much larger political and ideological struggle. As one officer noted in 1864, "If the settlement of this thing were left to our armies there would be peace and good fellowship established in two hours" (Rolph 2002, p. 3).

Incidents of fraternization were reported at nearly every major engagement between Union and Confederate forces. During the First Battle of Manassas in July 1861, Confederate soldiers gave water to fallen Union soldiers. A year and a month later, during what became known as the Second Battle of Manassas or the Battle of Bull Run, a Union eyewitness to its aftermath watched as Confederate soldiers walked around the body-strewn battlefield and bayoneted the Union casualties. As these

"Rebs" approached a fallen member of the Second Wisconsin Infantry Regiment, one Union soldier saw that "his enemy hesitated . . . and finally raised him carefully up, and gave him water from his canteen. He was afterwards removed to the hospitals of Richmond, where he received careful treatment, and at last was exchanged and allowed to return home" (Rolph 2002, p. 29).

Such poignant acts occurred on both sides. In East Tennessee a Union soldier was stationed on picket duty, or holding ground already taken, during a particularly cold stretch of weather. A poorly dressed Confederate soldier approached him and told him there were neither overcoats nor blankets to be had on his side. The following night, the man returned, and the Union soldier had six blankets to give him. At this, the Confederate "fell down on his knees . . . and I never heard anybody pray such a prayer as the Southern soldier prayed for me, kneeling there in the snow in his ragged old uniform. I took off my hat and stood still till he was through, and then he faded away in the darkness" (Rolph 2002, p. 49).

The Freemasons, also known as the Masonic Order, played a role in the relatively high degree of fraternization during the war. Captured or wounded soldiers might identify themselves as members of the organization and provide one of the secret words, grips, handshakes, or other signs of membership, such as placing the thumb on the tip of the nose and waving the fingers of that hand. Although Union soldiers occasionally set fire to homes and crops as Confederate territory was taken, soldiers who entered one mansion in Maury County, Tennessee, saw the portrait of its owner wearing a Masonic ring. The Union commanding officer, himself a Mason, ordered his men to let the house stand.

Belle Boyd

Civilians also fraternized with the enemy, with locals providing medical care to soldiers from the other side, but accusations of espionage inevitably arose. One of the most notorious cases of fraternization was that of Belle Boyd, the teenage daughter of a hotel-keeper in Martinsburg, West Virginia. When her town was seized by Union troops who went on a Fourth of July drinking binge and then went from house to house to seize Confederate memorabilia and install Union flags above each, Boyd and her mother resisted, and after insults were exchanged, Boyd shot and killed one of the Union men. A board of inquiry cleared her of criminal charges, but sentries were posted at the family-run inn to keep watch over her. An attractive young woman, Boyd became friendly with her guards, and managed to glean useful information on troop movements and plans. She would then send her slave, Eliza, to Confederate camps to deliver the messages. Eventually, after several more arrests and escapes, Boyd convinced her Union guard to marry her and switch sides, but soon divorced him when she learned he was penniless. Enormously famous in her

Belle Boyd (1843–1900), Confederate spy. Belle Boyd was a teenager when the Union army took over her town of Martinsburg, West Virginia. After killing a Union officer, Belle became friendly with the guards placed outside her home and shared the Union battle plans they had relayed with the Confederate Army. *© Bettman/Corbis*

day, Boyd was even awarded the Southern Cross of Honor, the highest civilian honor of the Confederate States of America, and after the war worked as an actress on the London and New York stages.

There were also instances of fraternization between Northerners who supported the Confederate side. These were derisively called Copperheads, after the copper Liberty-head coins they sported as badges, and were usually Democratic Party members who advocated an end to the war via an immediate peace settlement. They issued venomous propaganda against the North's abolitionists, whom they blamed for starting the war, and even against Abraham Lincoln (1809–1865), who was sometimes caricatured in Copperhead pamphlets as an African. Their counterpart in the Confederacy was a more loosely knit group called the Red Strings, or Heroes of America, who also hoped for a cessation of hostilities and the return of the Southern states to the Union. Many of them were Quakers and identified their houses by means of a red string hung from a window.

The Southern Claims Commission, a congressional body established to validate and reimburse Southerners for property damage inflicted by Union troops during the war, operated between 1871 until 1880. In some cases, however, the Commission heard claims from those who stated they had willingly provided food, medical care, shelter, or other prohibited acts of fraternization during the war because they supported the Union side. Many of the claims reimbursed involved the taking of horses, but in the case of a black couple, Thomas and Nancy Jefferson of Waynesboro, Virginia, who filed claim No. 15385, they requested reimbursement for one hog, three barrels of flour, and seven weeks of nursing care provided by Nancy to one adjutant assistant general named Fry from Sherman's army. The documents relating to their claim quote the Jeffersons as asserting,

> Our Loyalty is indisputable, as we are colored persons, and only suffered our House to be used as a Hospital, and furnished sustanance and the attendance upon the sick soldier, because he was wouned at our door, and the Confederates would have striped and murdered him…had he not been cared for by us. It would only be an act of Justice to pay us. ("Two Communities in the American Civil War")

Newspapers on both sides of the conflict rarely reported incidents of fraternization, but in the postwar era reunions of former enemies were a staple of every major battle anniversary. Regiments that had once fought one another organized meetings to hand over captured flags, and newly created veterans' organizations tended to and decorated graves of fallen soldiers from the other side of the battle. In a famous photograph from 1913, taken at the fiftieth anniversary of the Battle of Gettysburg, two elderly men are shown with their hands clasped in friendship: They reconnected at the reunion as each was telling their story to comrades about the infamous Pickett's Charge. A. C. Smith, a member of the Fifty-sixth Virginia Infantry, was wounded in the charge, and a Union soldier gave him water, then took him to the field hospital. As Smith was recounting his tale, at the same wall was Albert Hamilton of the Seventy-second Pennsylvania Infantry, who was saying "it was right here that a Johnny [Reb, a nickname for Confederate soldiers] fell into my arms. I lifted him up and gave him a swig of water, then got him on my shoulders and carried him off" (Rolph 2002, pp. 115–116). At this point, the two men overheard each other's recollections and jubilantly embraced.

BIBLIOGRAPHY

Lowell Daily Citizen and News (Lowell, MA), September 8, 1864.

Power, J. Tracy. *Lee's Miserables: Life in the Army of Northern Virginia from the Wilderness to Appomattox.* Chapel Hill: University of North Carolina Press, 1998.

Rolph, Daniel N. *My Brother's Keeper: Union and Confederate Soldiers' Acts of Mercy during the Civil War.* Mechanicsburg, PA: Stackpole Books, 2002.

Sutherland, Daniel E. *The Expansion of Everyday Life, 1860-1876.* New York: Harper & Row, 1989.

"Two Communities in the American Civil War." *The Valley of the Shadow.* Available from http://valley.vcdh.virginia.edu/.

Carol Brennan

■ Diaries and Letters from Home

As evidenced by the number of surviving letters and diaries, the daily life of Civil War soldiers and civilians are well documented. The written word was still the primary means of communication, as the telephone had yet to be invented, and literacy rates had been rising steadily throughout the century. Although the North had the highest literacy rates in the world at that time, in the South literacy rates were much lower because only free white children and children of the wealthy families were permitted to attend school (Werner 1998, p. 3). While telegraph services were largely reserved for military use, the U.S. Postal Service was expanding and improving in reliability, albeit slowly. Memoirs and other accounts of wartime events on and off the battlefield began appearing in published form during the war itself. After completing military drills or during breaks from battle, soldiers wrote and read letters from loved ones. These letters were a source of emotional support, as were the objects that many received along with them: blankets, boots, books, foodstuffs, and so on. Enlisted men's wives, children, and parents asked for advice, prayed for loved ones' safety, and reported news of families and friends.

Diaries and letters trace the war from its very beginning stages. Upon hearing news of the Confederacy's secession from the Union, an anonymous young Southern woman wrote in her diary that New Orleans "was very lively and noisy this evening with rockets and lights in honor of secession. Mrs. F., in common with the neighbors, illuminated. We walked out to see the houses of others gleaming amid the dark shrubbery like a fairy scene" (Straubing 1985, p. 183). Fourteen-year-old Thomas Upson of Indiana recalled in his journal the shock the beginning of hostilities caused: "Grandma wanted to know what was the trouble. Father told her and she began to cry, 'Oh, my poor children in the South! God knows how they will suffer.'…She and Mother were crying. I lit out for the barn. I do hate to see women cry" (Werner 1998, p. 7). The onset of war was hardly less shocking for adults, especially women who depended on their husbands to be providers and helpers in the home. Only a month after giving birth to

Female family members write and embroider. With mail delivery operating slowly, but regularly, troops looked forward to news they received from home. Many of the letters expressed not only affection for the distant soldier, but also details of hardship family members endured in the absence of fathers, sons, and husbands. *Hulton Archives/Getty Images.*

their child, Rachel Bowman of Chambersburg, Pennsylvania, wrote in her September 21, 1862, journal entry about her husband Samuel joining Sulenbergers Cavalry company:

> It went hard to see him go . . . for he is more than life to me. When he told me that he had enlisted, I felt an indescribable heaviness in my heart. . . . We prayed earnestly over it. I became calm & felt more resigned, at times still I am overcome, tears relieve me very much, my heart always seems lighter after weeping freely[.] In daytime I get along very well but the nights seem very long. (Cormany 1982, p. 253)

For soldiers and their loved ones, night only exacerbated the loneliness they felt. While emotions ran high and were mixed, most people, both Northerners and

Southerners, believed in the righteousness of their cause and that the conflict would last for only a short time.

Commentary on political and military matters filled the pages of many letters. One example of this is the January 1, 1863, letter that Henry A. Ritner wrote to his son Jacob, a captain in the First Iowa Infantry. Referring to President Lincoln's initial assertion that the war was not being fought to free the slaves but to preserve the Union, the elder Ritner commented:

> My opinion of the war is that it is an abolition war got up for the purpose of abolishing slavery and that God is its author. . . . and the object is to abolish slavery and punish the nation for its sins, especially that of slavery and to install the black man in to his natural and inalienable rights, and the sooner the government [and] army recognize this aspect and act upon it the sooner we will have

peace.... But if we as a nation refuse to acknowledge the rights of the black man then it may cost us our national existence. (Larimer 2000, p. 87)

Women Take on New Roles

With many men called away to war, women and children had to take on additional responsibilities. These new duties included a wide variety of household chores, as well as work outside the home. An October 14, 1864, letter from a young girl named Lodema Anderson, written to her father, L. Merrit Anderson, refers to some of this strenuous household work, and to the pain of separation:

Ma has been diging [*sic*] potatoes to dry ... and she is pretty tired to night [*sic*] to pay for it.... [M]a is pounding salt to salt her butter squate [*sic*] down on the flore [*sic*] and aunt Dorit is siting [*sic*] by the stove knitting and pa I want to [have you] here[,] you had better believe that[,] but I have one of your photographs and I half [*sic*] to kiss it[;] it does me a good deal of good but still it is[,] and you nor near it[,] hey pa ... but it has to do. (Seidman 2001, p. 121)

Emeline Ritner of Iowa wrote to her husband Jacob about the heat and drought they were experiencing in July of 1863, and about how it was affecting her health:

We are still all well. I am not very stout but think I will get along if I don't "work" too hard. Every little thing I do or walk up town I feel tired nearly to death.... I am getting "grey." It is time. If you don't come back pretty soon, you won't know me. I will be an old woman. (Larimer 2000, pp. 193–195)

Many women who were in dire straits wrote letters to government officials, asking for aid. In January of 1864, Hattie L. Carr of North Evans, New York, pleaded in a letter to Abraham Lincoln:

Honored Sir ... I come with a request trusting that out of the goodness of your heart you will grant it. It is but a breath to you. While to me [it is] as life and death. I beg you for the discharge of my Husband.... He has faithfully served our common cause for eighteen long months, while I have struggled with sickness and poverty at times[.] I can do that no longer, for I am sick—dying, for the sight of that dear face[.] I can labor no more and I could starve [for] I am alone and friendless. (Seidman 2001, p. 125)

Though a son under the age of eighteen might be discharged if he had entered the service without his parents' consent, the laws did not allow the discharge of adult men.

In addition to taking on their husbands' responsibilities in homes and businesses, many women, Union and Confederate alike, joined *bonnet brigades*—organizations that supported the war effort with money and medical and other supplies. "During these sad days there was no time or place for private griefs," Sarah Hill, the wife of an Army Corps of Engineers officer, wrote in her journal. "Loyal women in St. Louis had their hearts and hands full ministering to the many needs which were constantly arising. Every loyal household became a soldiers' aid society" (Hill 1980, p. 48). Hill recalled the many bed ticks, comforters, socks, and sleeping caps the women had sewn and knit. She also recounted that at Christmas time,

there were no festive gatherings or merry making. We as a family devoted all our efforts and what means we could spare, toward the cheer of our

Union soldiers reading letters from loved ones. Letters and other packages from home were important for emotional support and morale among soldiers. They read and wrote letters after military drill and between battles. *The Art Archive/Culver Pictures/The Picture Desk, Inc.*

boys in E. M.'s Company D. The younger girls made "Betties," or housewives, for each man in the company. They were small cases that could be rolled up and carried in the pocket, containing thread, needles, pins and buttons. (p. 56)

Others generated funds by staging benefit theatrical and musical shows, as described by Hill in her diary: "Many entertainments were planned and given by the loyal women of St. Louis for the benefit of the Soldiers' Aid Society during the winter of '61 and '62" (p. 59).

Women in the free states took part in efforts to help newly emancipated slaves. In a letter to her husband Jacob, Emeline Ritner described one such effort at a Methodist church: "After the sermon, a collection was taken up [that] amounted to 117.00 for the "Freedmen's Relief Association." It is for the purpose of clothing the Negroes that are freed by the war. Those that are away down where they can't get work to do" (Larimer 2000, p. 255).

Women could also be found in local hospitals behind the lines, where they helped treat wounded and sick soldiers. Nurses often wrote letters for soldiers who were illiterate or too wounded to write. Louisa May Alcott, who would go on to write the classic novel *Little Women*, worked as a nurse and recalled in *Hospital Sketches* (1863) writing for a shy man named John (p. 59).

Women Witness to Wartime Suffering

Maria Isabella Johnson described the situation in Vicksburg, Mississippi, shortly before its capture by Union forces on July 4, 1863: "Most of the caves that the frightened citizens of Vicksburg were scooping in the surrounding hills were just large enough to admit a small mattress, on which the family, be it large or small, huddled up together, in a way that was injurious alike to comfort and health" (Head 2003, p. 26). A little more than a year later, Rachel Cormany described the destruction of Chambersberg, Pennsylvania, by Confederate soldiers who had demanded $100,000 in gold:

[W]hen they were informed of the impossibility, they deliberately went from house to house & fired it. The whole heart of the town is burned. They gave no time for people to get any thing out. . . . [E]ach had to escape for life & took only what they could first grab. . . . Some saved considerable. . . . others only the clothes on their backs— & even some of those were taken off as they escaped from their burning dwellings. (Cormany 1982, p. 446)

By the end of their long ordeal, many men and women had left written records—letters and diaries— which provide later generations with glimpses into this difficult period in United States history.

BIBLIOGRAPHY

Alcott, Louisa May. *Hospital Sketches*. Boston: James Redpath, 1863.

Chesnut, Mary Boykin Miller. *Mary Chesnut's Civil War*, ed. C. Vann Woodward. New Haven, CT: Yale University Press, 1981.

Clare, Josephine. *Narrative of the Adventures and Experiences of Mrs. Josephine Clare: A Resident of the South at the Breaking Out of the Rebellion, Her Final Escape from Natichitoches, La., and Safe Arrival at Home, in Mariette, Pa*. Lancaster, PA: Pearson & Geist, 1865.

Cormany, Rachel Bowman. *The Cormany Diaries: A Northern Family in the Civil War*, ed. James C. Mohr. Pittsburgh, PA: University of Pittsburgh Press, 1982.

Custer, Elizabeth Bacon. *The Civil War Memories of Elizabeth Bacon Custer, Reconstructed from Her Diaries and Notes*, ed. Arlene Reynolds. Austin: University of Texas, 1994.

Eastman, Mary H. *Jenny Wade of Gettysburg*. Philadelphia: Lippincott, 1864.

Head, Tom, ed. *Voices from the Civil War: Women and Families*. San Diego, CA: Blackbirch Press, 2003.

Hill, Sarah Jane Full. *Mrs. Hill's Journal: Civil War Reminiscences*, ed. Mark M. Krug. Chicago: R. R. Donnelley & Sons, 1980.

Jackson, Henry W. R. *The Southern Women of the Second American Revolution: Their Trials, and Yankee Barbarity Illustrated*. Atlanta, GA: Intelligencer Steam-power Press, 1863.

Larimer, Charles F., ed. *Love and Valor: The Intimate Civil War Letters between Captain Jacob and Emeline Ritner*. Western Spring, IL: Sigourney Press, 2000.

Leonard, Elizabeth D. *Yankee Women: Gender Battles in the Civil War*. New York: Norton, 1994.

Moore, Frank. *Women of the War: Their Heroism and Self-Sacrifice*. Chicago: R. C. Treat, 1866. Reprint, Alexander, NC: Blue Gray Books, 1997.

Peter, Frances Dallam. *A Union Woman in Civil War Kentucky*, ed. John David Smith and William Cooper Jr. Lexington: University Press of Kentucky, 2000.

Powers, Elvira J. *Hospital Pencillings: Being a Diary While in Jefferson General Hospital, Jeffersonville, Ind., and Others at Nashville, Tennessee, as Matron and Visitor*. Boston: Edward L. Mitchel, 1866.

Seidman, Rachel Filene. *The Civil War: A History in Documents*. New York: Oxford University Press, 2001.

Straubing, Harold Elk, ed. "Diary of a Pro-Union Woman of the Confederacy." In *Civil War Eyewitness Reports*, ed. Harold Elk Straubing. North Haven, CT: Archon Books, 1985.

Werner, Emmy E. *Reluctant Witnesses: Children's Voices from the Civil War*. Boulder, CO: Westview Press, 1998.

Jeanne M. Lesinski

■ Immigration

Through the years of colonization and then nationhood, the United States has benefited from periodic influxes of newcomers that coincided with fluctuations in the country's business cycles. In the countries of origin, such factors as increased population; the inability of farmers to feed this population; the inability of industry to provide jobs; religious intolerance, prejudice and other social factors; and political upheavals prompted people to leave their homelands. Poverty, however, was the strongest incentive for immigration. There were no laws regulating immigration to the United States until 1875; thus immigrants had unrestricted access to the country if they could pay the cost of passage.

Two periods of concentrated immigration took place around the time of the Civil War: From 1845 to 1854 more than three million foreigners arrived, and from 1865 to 1875 almost 3.5 million more came to America. While not all of them remained, an overwhelming majority became permanent citizens (Dinnerstein and Reimers 1977, pp. 12–13). Most immigrants—about 86.6 percent—settled in the free states. This figure indicates that there were eight immigrants in the free states for every one who settled in a slave-holding state. This imbalance was the case partly because the slave states did not need unskilled white laborers (Kennedy 1864, p. xxx).

Although it would be more precise to speak of the various immigrant peoples according to their ethnicity, nativists (people who favor established inhabitants over new immigrants) often identified newcomers by the language they spoke. Thus while German-speaking people might come from Prussia, Bavaria, Saxony, the Rhineland, Austria, or Switzerland, they were all called Germans. According to the census of 1860, the average age for both men and women was twenty years when they arrived on American shores (Kennedy 1864, p. xx).

Scottish, Irish, German, and Chinese immigrants made up the majority of those arriving prior to and immediately after the Civil War. During the war years, the number of arrivals from any ethnic group slowed to a fraction of those from previous years as few people wanted to immigrate to a country at war. Nevertheless, 121,282 foreign passengers arrived in 1859; 153,640 in 1860; 91,919 in 1861; and 91,987 in 1862 (Kennedy 1864, p. xxv).

British Immigrants

English and Scottish settlers had been coming to North America since its earliest days of colonization, dispersing themselves throughout the territory, yet the 1860 census indicated that the largest populations of Britons settled in New York, Pennsylvania, Illinois, Wisconsin, Ohio, Michigan, and Massachusetts. The Scots settled in New York, Pennsylvania and Illinois (Kennedy 1864, p. xxix). Many wanted to flee the rapidly industrializing society of Great Britain, to own land, to farm independ-ently, and to escape the onerous burden of British taxation. Immigrants from the British Isles were able to take up work in the skilled trades as well as in farming and laboring.

German Immigrants

After the English, the Germans made up the largest immigrant group to arrive on American shores. Over the period from 1820 to 1870, 6 million German foreigners came to the United States due to the high cost of living and political unrest in their native country. Germany was not a united country until 1870; meanwhile, the population had grown so swiftly that starvation threatened in some areas. Many of these immigrants were of the peasant, artisan, or the middle class (Coppa and Curran 1976, p. 44). In the decade immediately prior to the outbreak of the Civil War, nearly 1 million Germans arrived, and after the war's end another 1.5 million made the journey. They represented both Roman Catholic and Protestant denominations and settled primarily in Ohio, New York, Pennsylvania, and Illinois, where they took up farming in rural areas or skilled and unskilled labor in the cities. The immigrants tried to retain the use of their language; they set up German-language schools and published newspapers. Nevertheless, the German immigrants generally assimilated as readily as their British counterparts.

Irish Immigrants

Another immigrant group that significantly changed the complexion of the country was the Irish, who had long suffered under English rule after the formation of the United Kingdom. When they found themselves unable to make a living because of new land laws and a blight that destroyed their main food crop—potatoes—they left in droves during the years of famine (1845–1847). Between 1845 and 1855 more than one million Irish immigrants arrived at the seaports of the Northeast. By 1860 Massachusetts, New York, and Pennsylvania had Irish populations that numbered more than 100,000; the Irish eventually made up 20 percent of the population of New York City. They were largely unskilled workers; in addition, most were members of the Roman Catholic Church. These two factors aroused the prejudice of the nativists, who were overwhelmingly Protestant. During the war many Irishmen fought for the North as part of the Irish Brigade as well as many other units, and even a writer for the *Charleston Courier, Tri-Weekly* argued, albeit preferentially: "The Irish were the best troops in the Yankee armies" (May 23, 1863). Yet these efforts gained the Irish only limited acceptance. In 1865 the song "No Irish Need Apply" could still be heard, though by this time the ebullient Irish had themselves recast it as a humorous song. Although prejudice against the Irish population was reduced during the Civil War, it was by no means eradicated.

"Chinese railroad workers in Sacramento, California. In the 1860s thousands of workers left their villages in China and immigrated to the western United States. Many worked on railroad crews, while others took jobs as miners, merchants, field hands, or household help."

Chinese Immigrants

Asians too, particularly the Chinese, were coming to the United States, beginning in 1848 when gold was discovered in California. By 1851, 25,000 Chinese, mostly from the southern coastal province of Kwangtung, had come to California. Between 1851 and the outbreak of the Civil War, another 41,000 arrived, with still another 64,000 emigrating during the 1860s. Some California newspapers, such as the *Daily Evening Bulletin* (San Francisco), routinely noted new arrivals in the shipping news: "The *Jacob Bell*, which came into port on Saturday, brought from Hongkong 320 Chinese immigrants" (February 12, 1861).

Unlike other immigrants, the Chinese did not intend to settle permanently in the United States, so they came without their families. This group of men worked in the gold fields, labored on farms, opened stores, and served as mechanics. Taking jobs that others thought too menial, they also did laundry and worked as household servants, proving themselves good workers. In 1863,

when the federal government began the construction of the first transcontinental railroad, the Chinese proved to be hardworking and conscientious laborers. As a result they were hired by the thousands (Coppa and Curran 1976, p. 194).

The Civil War and the economic depression it caused had an overall dampening effect on immigration; yet as soon as the economy improved, America again became the destination for thousands of immigrants. Finally the U.S. government thought it necessary to regulate immigration. In 1875 Congress passed a law commonly known as the Asian Exclusion Act, which prohibited the importation of Chinese workers against their will and for illegal purposes. Yet even stricter controls did not daunt potential newcomers, who continued to view America as an opportunity to better themselves or as an escape from unfavorable conditions in their homelands.

BIBLIOGRAPHY

Charleston Courier (Charleston, SC), May 23, 1863, column E, n.p.

Coppa, Frank J., and Thomas J. Curran. *The Immigrant Experience in America*. Boston: Twayne Publishers, 1976.

Daily Evening Bulletin (San Francisco, CA), February 12, 1861, issue 107, col. B.

Dinnerstein, Leonard, and David M. Reimers. *Ethnic Americans: A History of Immigration and Assimilation*. New York: New York University Press, 1977.

Erickson, Charlotte. *Invisible Immigrants: The Adaptation of English and Scottish Immigrants in Nineteenth-Century America*. Coral Gables: University of Florida Press, 1972.

"Immigration." *Law Library of Congress*. Available from http://memory.loc.gov/.

Kennedy, Joseph C. G. *Population of the United States in 1860: Compiled from the Original Returns of the Eighth Census Under the Direction of the Secretary of the Interior*. Washington, DC: U.S. Government Printing Office, 1864.

Jeanne M. Lesinski

■ Crime

The Civil War wrought much atrocity, dishonesty, and depravity upon the civilian population. As an editorial in the November 21, 1865, *Little Rock Daily Gazette* pointed out, before the war news of the discovery of an assaulted dead body would have horrified the community. Yet, the editorial continued, by war's end scenes of blood and violence had become so commonplace that they hardly attracted any notice at all—and, in fact, following the war such instances had increased in prevalence. The six months following the end of the war saw an almost exponential increase in crime, and, according to the *Gazette*, the streets became filled with a great number of "disreputable women," gamblers, and thieves. By late November 1865, however, this postwar crime wave had abated. Reflecting on the horror of the six months following the end of the war, the *Semi-Weekly Telegraph* observed: "That the public have noticed so large an increase in this fatal species... may be sensibly attributed to the lapse of a great war, and the revelation and recoil of the passions which it absorbed" (November 30, 1865).

Throughout the war, criminals perpetrated crimes of all sorts. For example, the Nashville *Dispatch*'s crime log for a single day included the following items: "Robbery of an actress"; "Highway robbery"; "A whole family poisoned with arsenic"; "A bloody street fight"; "Horrible tragedy: a man kills his wife, and is shot by his neighbors"; "Another desperate and bloody street fight" (*New Haven Daily Palladium*, October, 18, 1865). The San Francisco *Daily Evening Bulletin* noted that between December 1, 1863, and February 17, 1864,

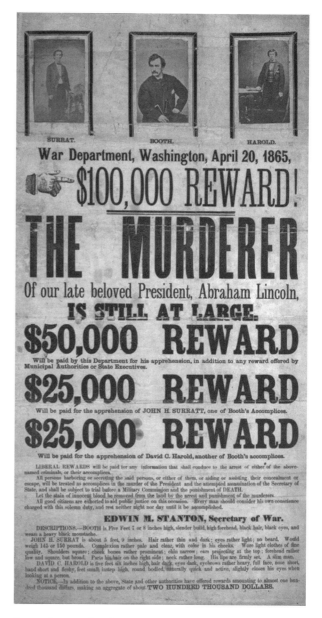

Reward poster for the assassins of President Lincoln. After the cessation of fighting between the North and South, the brutality of the battlefield found its way into civilian life, with recorded crime exploding during the first six months after the war. Public officials throughout the nation limited by law the consumption of alcohol, established a curfew for youths, and even installed street lights in order to curb crime. *The Library of Congress*

"at least, an average of one person daily has lost his life by assassination, or in brawls, or by the hands of the Vigilante Committees" (February 17, 1864). The *Bulletin* called for reform of criminal law—specifically, the jury system. Another factor contributing to rampant criminality, the *Bulletin* declared, was the laxness of justices who freed the accused once they had confessed their crimes and paid a $5 fine.

Many crimes were committed by children. "Children are every year born in vice, nursed in wretchedness, and cradled in infamy," declared the San Francisco *Daily Evening Bulletin*. "Change their conditions and we changed their destination in life" (January 8, 1864). Proactively seeking to prevent children's development into criminals, the chief of police of San Francisco issued an ordinance permitting arrest of all youths found loitering or violating curfews (*Daily Evening Bulletin*, January 8, 1864). In April 1864, the *Lowell Daily Citizen and News* noted in its analysis of arrest statistics that most crimes committed the previous year were related to alcohol consumption: " 'We should not have done it, if we had not been drinking,' is the almost universal plea of criminals" (April 15, 1864). The Lowell city marshal attributed nine-tenths of arrests in the city to rum drinking.

If alcohol contributed to crime, so too did poorly lit streets. In an attempt to decrease opportunities to commit crime in Washington, DC, the mayor and city council approved an act to increase lighting on the city's streets (*Daily National Intelligencer*, April 15, 1864).

The April 5, 1862, *Wisconsin State Register* reported one rather ingenious crime that posed a quandary for authorities. Nathan Levi, a Northerner, was found to have printed large quantities of counterfeit Confederate treasury notes. When officers arrived to arrest the man, he asserted he was only trying to cripple the rebel treasury by flooding the South with spurious currency. Considering Confederate tender was not legal money and not authorized by law, the secretary of war declared Levi's case to be "one of the toughest cases he met with during the war." In the end, Levi was freed without charge (*Newark Advocate*, September 19, 1862).

The "Great Crime of the Age," of course, was the assassination of President Abraham Lincoln on April 14, 1865. As the *Milwaukee Daily Sentinel* rightly remarked, "Mr. Lincoln was absolutely indispensable to the nation's future life and true greatness…[and] his victories… gave assurances of peace, of national honor, of national integrity, and national prosperity as their fruits" (April 17, 1865). "Sum up all the crimes in the calendar," the *Daily Cleveland Herald* declared, "and they fail to express that of the man who stabs his country" (April 20, 1865).

BIBLIOGRAPHY

"The Carnival of Crime." *Semi-Weekly Telegraph* (Salt Lake City, UT), November 30, 1865.

"Crime in California." *San Francisco Daily Evening Bulletin*, February 17, 1864.

Crime and Lawlessness. *Little Rock Daily Gazette*, November 21, 1865.

"The Great Crime." *Daily Cleveland Herald*, April 20, 1864.

"The Great Crime of the Age." *Milwaukee Daily Sentinel*, April 17, 1865.

"Intemperance and Crime." *Lowell* (MA) *Daily Citizen and News*, April 15, 1864.

"School of Crime." *San Francisco Daily Evening Bulletin*, January 8, 1864.

"A Shrewd Yankee Trick—Is It a Crime?" *Wisconsin State Register*, April 5, 1862.

Untitled. *New Haven Daily Palladium* (New Haven, CT), October 18, 1865.

Untitled. *Newark Advocate* (Newark, OH), September 19, 1862.

Aileen E. McTiernan

■ Class Tensions

During the mid-nineteenth century, distinctions of wealth and status divided American society. The Civil War exacerbated those divisions, as working-class citizens and yeoman farmers pondered the war's consequences. In both the Union and Confederacy, members of the upper classes urged their less privileged neighbors to support the war effort. However, workers, laborers, farmers, and craftsmen often believed that the war affected them more than it did the upper classes, which included merchants, businessmen, and plantation owners. Historians have questioned whether or not the conflict was a "rich man's war, and a poor man's fight." Even though citizens of all classes fought, volunteered, and supported the war, men and women at the lower end of the social spectrum often believed they had more to lose.

Northerners were quick to point out the inequality inherent in the slaveholding South; however, some Southerners also noticed that some citizens of the Confederacy fared better than others. One wartime Northern author summed up the class conflict in the slave states by concluding that the "political economy of the Slave States of the South…is attended with social consequences of the most important kind" (Cairnes 1862, p. 49). This was true at least for the plantation South, where the best land was owned by planters and the work was done primarily by slaves instead of wage earners. The plantation system, this writer observed, resulted in "a numerous horde of people, who, too poor to keep slaves and too proud to work, prefer a vagrant and precarious life…to engaging in occupations which would association them with the slaves whom they despise" (Cairnes 1862, p. 49). Even Confederate officials believed that some men were getting wealthy while others were fighting and dying. John Beauchamp Jones, a clerk in the Confederacy's War Department, complained that some clerks "procure exemptions, discharges, and contracts for the speculators for heavy bribes and invest the money in real estate…so that their own prosperity will be secure" (Jones 1866, p. 332).

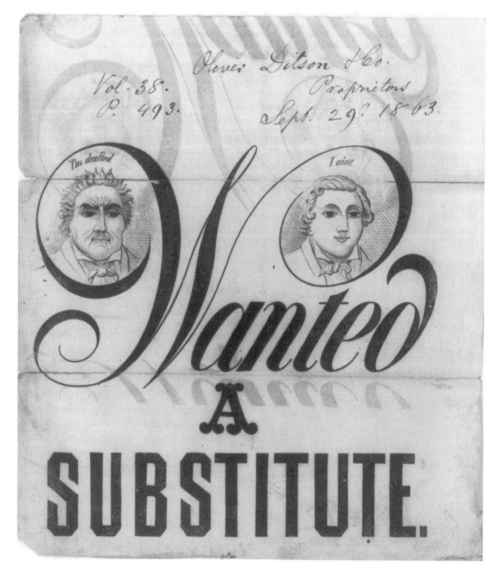

"Wanted: A Substitute."   An illustrated sheet music cover, which protests the inequities of the draft or proscription system enacted under the Enrollment Act of 1863. The act allowed drafted men to purchase an exemption or to furnish a surrogate or "substitute" in lieu of their own service. The unfairness of the measure to the economically disadvantaged is dramatized in the illustration to this piece, showing the bust portrait of one man, "I'm drafted," in contrast to that of an obviously more well-to-do young man, "I aint."   *The Library of Congress*

Confederate Military Draft

The Confederacy turned to conscription to meet its military needs in 1862, which intensified class tensions. The poor and working class were unable to avoid service whereas wealthy citizens could bribe officials or send substitutes. Planters who owned more than twenty slaves and men who held positions essential to the war effort, including government officials, were exempt from the draft. Some influential men paid as much as $500 to obtain appointments as postmasters, clerks, coroners, or other government positions that exempted them from military service (Williams 2005, p. 77). Confederate sol-

diers who served in spite of hardships at home resented fighting for the interests of others. The twenty-slave law, as it was known, made slaves even more valuable in the Confederacy, as some citizens attempted to increase their slaveholdings to gain exemption from military service.

Some young men who could not afford to purchase an exemption or a substitute refused to serve. The son of Mrs. E. C. Kent, for example, was arrested and imprisoned by the Confederate Army for avoiding the draft. Mrs. Kent tried desperately to convince the Confederate government to free her son, and wrote President Jefferson Davis on her son's behalf. Davis replied that he could only free her son if the young man agreed to serve in the army. The boy would not agree to go, so Mrs. Kent visited him in prison. She observed that her son was in a room with several Rebel officers and a well-known lawyer, but noted that "men of this class were generally not retained very long" (Kent 1865, p. 22).

During the war desertion and draft resistance in the Confederacy demonstrated that some common people believed that the wealthy and influential were not doing their part in the war, while the poor and less fortunate were expected to bear the brunt of the fighting. Others were simply tired of the war or considered the South's defeat inevitable.

Poverty and the War

The Confederacy's unsuccessful attempt to establish itself as a new nation came at a cost, and many citizens believed most of the burden fell on the common folk. Josepine Clare, a Unionist whose husband fled the Confederacy and joined the Union Army, described the condition of common soldiers in Mississippi. Upon seeing train cars loaded with soldiers, she remarked that "their clothing was all tattered and torn, and their general appearance was shabby in the extreme" (Clare 1865, p. 13). Clare lamented the war and suffering "brought on these poor illiterate people by a diabolical class of men who wanted to crush the poor man and sink him beneath the level of the negro" (Clare 1865, p. 13). The suffering of war was not limited to the lower classes of society, but those civilians who had little to begin with faced dire situations as the war continued.

The Union blockade of Confederate ports combined with Southern planters' continued focus on cotton production (instead of planting much-needed corn and wheat) caused a food shortage in the Confederacy. In 1863 women living in cities throughout the South were unable to afford food because merchants were charging outrageous prices for scarce commodities. Faced with watching their children starve, women took to the streets, often breaking into shops and taking what food they needed. The most famous bread riot occurred in the capital of the Confederacy, Richmond, Virginia, in April 1863. When city authorities were unable to disperse the women, Jefferson Davis appeared and offered his own money to the crowd, but also threatened to order the militia to fire on those women who did not return home.

The war intensified the class divisions in the Confederacy and ultimately led many common citizens to criticize the Confederate government and call for an end to the war. Even the presence of the dreaded Yankees seemed better than starvation.

Union Military Draft

As the war went on longer than most Northern citizens had hoped it would, a growing need for troops caused the Union Government to call for conscription. The only men who were exempt from the draft in the North were those who were too ill, too old, or who could claim that service would be an undue hardship. As in the Confederacy, wealthy men could avoid being drafted by hiring a substitute, but the Enrollment Act included an additional provision allowing conscripts to pay a commutation fee of $300 to avoid serving. This loophole angered some working-class men, not just because only the rich could afford the fee, but also because it put a limit on the amount paid to substitutes. Martin Ryerson of Newton, New Jersey, wrote to William H. Seward, then Secretary of State, complaining that "a rich man, who without this might have had to pay $1,000 or $2,000, or more, for a substitute, can now get off for $300, and the poor, and those of middling circumstances, say they ought to have been left to make their own bargains" (Perman 1998, p. 192). Ryerson believed that the exemption clause was well meant but had the unintended consequence of increasing class tensions and was therefore "an unfortunate mistake."

New York Draft Riots

Class tensions surrounding conscription resulted in violence during the New York draft riots of July 1863. Workers in the city, mostly Irish laborers, reacted angrily to the Emancipation Proclamation of January 1863 and the Enrollment Act of March 1863. These white workers resented the idea of being forced to fight to free slaves. Many feared former slaves would move to the North to compete with white workers for jobs. The rioters attacked draft officials, African Americans, and any men who looked wealthy enough to pay the commutation fee. Ellen Leonard was visiting relatives in the city and witnessed the first night of the riot. On the following morning, Leonard wrote, she saw "rough-looking men" and "hordes of ragged children" roaming the streets and concluded that "the 'dangerous classes' were evidently wide awake" (Leonard 1867?, p. 5). A member of a family wealthy enough to visit New York on a shopping trip, Leonard did not understand the class tensions that caused the destruction and violence. This lack of understanding is also evident in a report on the New York Police Department's role in suppressing the violence. This account suggested that although "the riot which commenced on the first day of the draft, was ostensibly in opposition to it . . . [it] early took the character of an outbreak for the purpose of pillage, and also of outrage upon the colored population" (Barnes 1863, p. 5).

Such perceptions of the riot were colored by common stereotypes of the poor and working class, especially immigrants, who were viewed as being less intelligent, less moral, and prone to violence. The rioters, however, were not merely committing random acts of violence and looting: They were lashing out at the people they perceived to be benefiting most from the war—African

Americans and the wealthy. Union troops eventually had to be called in, after which peace was restored. The draft lottery in New York City, however, was suspended.

Class Divisions in the Union

The North had distinct social divisions that fostered different opinions of the war's purpose and meaning. Even patriotic workingmen were concerned about volunteering for the army and leaving their families to fend for themselves. As a result, state and local governments offered bounties to men who were willing to enlist. Within some communities, citizens took up collections to help the family members of soldiers, particularly widows and orphans. There were, however, always individuals who took advantage of these arrangements, which caused some citizens to criticize volunteers who sought bounties rather than enlisting from pure patriotism.

In addition, there was a type of fraud known as bounty jumping, which consisted of enlisting, collecting the bounty, and then deserting the army—often to travel to another city and enlist again for another bounty payment. Frank Wilkeson, the son of a journalist, ran away from home before he was sixteen and enlisted in the Union Army by lying about his age. Wilkeson was scandalized by the number of bounty jumpers he encountered. From his privileged point of view the recruits who accepted bounties were "blackguards, thieves and ruffians." Wilkeson remarked that "if there was a man in all that shameless crew who had enlisted from patriotic motives, I did not see him" (quoted in Commager 2000, p. 96). Wilkeson eventually earned an officer's commission, which allowed him to rise above the ranks of the enlisted men, whom he believed mostly "belonged to the criminal classes" (Commager 2000, p. 96).

Class and Politics

The Democratic and Republican parties both exploited class tensions in an attempt to get the support of the working class. The Republicans appealed to the ideals of free labor, which valued the work of independent men who could rise up and progress by their own efforts. Free labor stood in opposition to slave labor, which privileged the wealthy slave owner. During the war Republicans and their spokesmen in the media continued to assert that a war to end slavery benefited common laborers. The *Milwaukee Daily Sentinel*, for example, ran an article that summarized the war as a conflict between Northern free labor and Southern slave labor, and asserted that "no classes are so vitally interested in the great conflict now waging . . . as the working classes" (April 29, 1863). Some farmers and laborers in the Union agreed with this sentiment, believing that ending slavery would provide opportunities for all workingmen.

By contrast, the Democratic Party used fear and racism to urge white workers to oppose emancipation and the Republican Party. Many white laborers, particularly in areas bordering slave states, were afraid of losing their jobs to emancipated slaves who could be expected to move northward after the war. In Indiana, the *New Albany Daily Ledger* fueled tensions by condemning the proposed Emancipation Proclamation and encouraging Unionists not "to spill their blood or squander their hard earnings for the purpose of giving freedom to four millions of Negroes, who would soon overrun them by hundreds of thousands" (October 27, 1862). Republican newspapers attempted to counter such assertions, although their efforts were not always very enlightened. The *Cincinnati Gazette*, for example, claimed that after the war former slaves would return to their former homes, because "with freedom in the South the natural drift of the blacks is towards the tropics" (September 25, 1862).

While emancipation's future impact was a contentious issue, many in the working class had more immediate reason to be concerned about the war's economic repercussions. Everyday items increased in price, including staples such as milk and butter, which by 1864 had increased in cost by almost 600 percent (Williams 2005, p. 115). Most lower-class families, regardless of their political leanings, were eager for the war to end so that they could resume daily lives less marked by deprivation and suffering.

BIBLIOGRAPHY

Barnes, David M. *The Draft Riots in New York, July, 1863: The Metropolitan Police: Their Services during Riot Week, Their Honorable Record.* New York: Baker & Godwin, 1863.

Cairnes, John Elliott. *The Slave Power: Its Character, Career, and Probable Designs: Being an Attempt to Explain the Real Issues Involved in the American Contest,* 2nd ed. New York: Carleton, 1862.

Clare, Josepine. *Narrative of the Adventures and Experiences of Mrs. Josepine Clare, a Resident of the South at the Breaking Out of the Rebellion.* Lancaster, PA: Pearson & Geist, 1865.

Commager, Henry Steele, ed. *The Civil War Archive: The History of the Civil War in Documents.* New York: Black Dog & Leventhal, 2000.

Jones, John Beauchamp. *A Rebel War Clerk's Diary at the Confederate States Capital,* vol. 1. Philadelphia: Lippincott, 1866.

Kent, E. C. *"Four Years in Secessia": A Narrative of a Residence at the South Previous to and during the Southern Rebellion, up to November 1863,* 2nd ed. Buffalo, NY: Franklin Printing House, 1865.

Leonard, Ellen. *Three Days Reign of Terror, or the July Riots in 1863, in New York.* New York, 1867.

Marten, James. *Civil War America: Voices from the Home Front.* Santa Barbara, CA: ABC-CLIO, 2003.

Perman, Michael, ed. *Major Problems in the Civil War and Reconstruction*, 2nd ed. Boston: Houghton Mifflin, 1998.

Shanks, John P. C. (John Peter Clever). *Vindication of Major General John C. Fremont, Against the Attacks of the Slave Power and Its Allies.* Washington, DC: Scammell, 1862.

Williams, David. *A People's History of the Civil War: Struggles for the Meaning of Freedom.* New York: New Press, 2005.

Stephen Rockenbach

Housing

Housing during the Civil War era varied depending on one's social and economic status, whether one was free or enslaved, and whether one lived in the North or the South, in the city or in the country.

Urban Housing

Beginning in the 1840s and 1850s the North became increasingly urbanized and modern as people sought jobs in factories. Those who could not afford their own houses lived in apartments, boardinghouses, or tenements. The better one's income, the better the housing one could afford. The lower class in the North was comprised mostly of very poor immigrants, the largest group of which was the Irish Catholics, who lived in crowded slums ridden with crime and disease.

Andrew Miller, a boardinghouse keeper in Charleston, South Carolina, lived in his boardinghouse along with "several other White lodgers occupying different rooms," (p. 90) relays Bernard L. Herman in his article "Slave and Servant Housing in Charleston, 1770–1820." The bottom front room was occupied by a nearby grocer, while Miller lived in the bottom back room. Behind the boardinghouse approximately fifty feet away was the kitchen (a separate building), and the upstairs room above the kitchen was occupied by a slave.

Townhouses were a step up from the boardinghouse. Typical townhouses, Herman notes, contained "a ground-floor commercial area and upper-story living spaces" (p. 90). The front entrance led directly from the street into the front shop area, while a back or side entrance led into the ground-floor back room and stairs

Susan Downey House, Harpers Ferry, Jefferson County, West Virginia. Susan Downey's house in Harpers Ferry, West Virginia, provides a useful example of the housing available to urban dwellers at the time of the Civil War. *The Library of Congress*

leading to the upper level. On the upper level, living quarters included a front parlor and a smaller back dining room. The kitchen was often a separate building behind the townhouse. The plots of urban townhouses usually also contained a washhouse, privy, stable, carriage house, and other buildings such as a garden shed or warehouse.

Urban homeowners lived in single-family dwellings rather than townhouses. Residences ranged from mansions to multistory houses to cottages or cabins, depending on one's income. Typical middle-class homes had public rooms for receiving guests. These included a hall, parlor, dining room, and possibly a library in wealthier homes. The parlor was used to receive visitors and also as a gathering place for the family to read, write, play games, talk with one another, or do needlework. Bedrooms were considered private rooms and were located upstairs in multistory dwellings, so as to be inaccessible to guests. Wealthier families had nurseries for the children, often on the third floor. Work rooms included the kitchen, pantry, laundry, scullery and cellar. Foodstuffs were stored in the pantry or cellar and prepared in the kitchen. Vegetables and dishes were washed in the scullery. In less well-to-do homes, the kitchen also served as the scullery and the laundry. Cooking was usually done on wood-burning stoves, which were standard in Northern middle-class homes, but in rural and lower-class homes, food was prepared on an open fireplace hearth. Heating was usually provided by one or more fireplaces. Wealthier families had wallpaper and carpeting.

Country Homes North and South

Rural homes in the North were frame or log farm houses, one or two stories, and were heated by fireplaces

Marye's House, Fredericksburg, Virginia. Housing and property throughout the South was damaged both by fighting and by Union troops as they sought to destroy anything that could be of aid to the Confederacy. *The Library of Congress*

or woodstoves. Like urban homes, the number of rooms and type of furnishings varied with the income of the owners, but farmhouses were surrounded by much more land than urban homes. Floride Clemson, a Southern aristocratic woman, kept a diary during the Civil War and also wrote letters to her mother, who had married and moved to the North. These letters were edited by Charles M. McGee Jr. and Ernest M. Lander Jr. in the 1989 collection *A Rebel Came Home: The Diary and Letters of Floride Clemson, 1863–1866*. Describing one of the houses she saw in Altoona, Pennsylvania, Floride wrote, "The scenery about here is magnificent. . . . They have a beautiful view of the mountains, and some intervening rolling ground. There are trees at the back of the house, a lovely garden at one side, nice grounds on the other, and terraces and the view in front" (p. 123).

Southern rural homes ranged from similar small farms to large plantations. Plantation homes were larger than typical farmhouses. A small plantation might have seventeen rooms and sit on a few hundred acres. One of the largest plantations was Nottoway Plantation, built in 1858 in southeastern Louisiana. Sitting on 6,200 acres, the sugar-cane plantation was once worked by 155 slaves. The 53,000-square-foot house had sixty-four rooms, seven staircases, and five galleries.

Housing for Slaves

Urban slave holders had few slaves, usually domestic workers, so often no special housing existed for the slaves. Because slave owners wanted their slaves to be close at hand whenever they required something of them, their sleeping quarters were close to where they worked, in rooms above the kitchen, storehouse, shops, and carriage houses, or in attic spaces. According to John Michael Vlach in his article "Evidence of Slave Housing in Washington," by 1850 Southern cities also had "large shanty towns occupied principally by blacks, both slave and free" (p. 67).

On large plantations in the South, Willis D. Weatherford relates in the 1910 book *Negro Life in the South, Present Conditions and Needs*, housing for slaves consisted of "long rows of log cabins—mostly one-roomed" that stretched away form the plantation house (p. 62). Albert Castel in 2000 compiled *Tom Taylor's Civil War*, drawing on Taylor's letters and diaries. In writing to his wife about his travels down the Mississippi River on the steamer *Silver Moon*, Taylor described the "fine large plantations with capacious one story residences surrounded by village of [slave] cabins all neatly white-washed and generally located in groves that dotted the shores" (pp. 59–60).

Little care was taken to ensure the comforts of slaves. Weatherford quotes Booker T. Washington (1856–1915) describing his cabin as having a door that contained large cracks and hung on "uncertain hinges" (p. 63). Washington also describes his cabin as having a dirt floor with a large, deep hole in the center of the dirt floor that was covered with boards and used to store sweet potatoes for the winter. W. D. Weatherford, in his travels in 1908, found that housing conditions for the "negro farmer have not changed since slavery" very much. He writes, "I have traveled throughout the country in almost every section of the South, and the negro farm houses consist usually of one, two, or three rooms, poorly furnished, poorly kept, with no pictures, and with the barest necessities for living" (pp. 63–64). Housing for civilians during the Civil War ranged from luxurious to austere; lower-class civilians and slaves occupied even more basic domiciles.

BIBLIOGRAPHY

Adams, Jessica. *Wounds of Returning: Race, Memory, and Property on the Postslavery Plantation*. Chapel Hill: University of North Carolina Press, 2007.

Castel, Albert, compiler. *Tom Taylor's Civil War*. Lawrence, Kansas: University Press of Kansas, 2000.

Fitts, Robert K. "The Landscapes of Northern Bondage." *Historical Archaeology* 30, no. 2 (1996): 54–73.

Herman, Bernard L. "Slave and Servant Housing in Charleston, 1770–1820." *Historical Archaeology* 33, no. 3 (1999): 88–101.

McGee, Charles M. Jr., and Ernest M. Lander, Jr., eds. *A Rebel Came Home: The Diary and Letters of Floride Clemson, 1863–1866*. Columbia, SC: University of South Carolina Press, 1989.

Nottoway Plantation House. Available from http://www.nps.gov/.

Vlach, John Michael. "Evidence of Slave Housing in Washington." *Washington History* (Fall/Winter 1993–94): 64–74.

Volo, Dorothy Denneen, and James M. Volo. *Daily Life in Civil War America*. Westport, CT.: Greenwood Press, 1998.

Weatherford, Willis D. *Negro Life in the South, Present Conditions and Needs*. New York: Young Men's Christian Association Press, 1910.

Sandra Johnston

Religion

■ Religion Overview

America's predominant religion in the Civil War era was Protestant Christianity, specifically Protestant Christianity of the Reformed (Calvinist) or Free Church (Anabaptist) traditions. The same is true of America in the early twenty-first century but to a lesser extent. The great waves of immigration that were to come during the late nineteenth and early twentieth centuries increased the proportions of Americans who were Jewish, Roman Catholic, Lutheran, or Eastern Orthodox. The late twentieth century brought the appearance in America of religions that stand outside the Judeo-Christian tradition, such as Islam, Hinduism, Buddhism, Wicca, and secular humanism. In the early twenty-first century the non-Judeo-Christian religions still claimed only minorities of adherents in America—and except for secular humanism, tiny minorities—but at the time of the Civil War, all the American adherents of these non-Judeo-Christian faiths could probably have been gathered comfortably in a single room, if not a broom closet.

Alongside America's large Protestant majority in the Civil War era was a small but thriving Jewish minority and a much larger and more rapidly growing minority of Roman Catholics. Adherents of the Catholic faith had come to America since colonial times, when seventeenth-century Maryland had harbored a significant minority of Catholic settlers. During the decades immediately preceding the Civil War, America's Catholic population had burgeoned thanks to massive Irish and German immigration. Aside from the factors that had drawn Europeans to America for more than two centuries by that time, the Irish were driven by famine and poverty in their native land and the Germans by political upheavals in theirs. The influx of so many foreign-born persons of a religious persuasion hitherto marginal in America prompted some Americans in the 1850s to question whether the country's free institutions would continue to thrive if a large segment of the populace came to hold a different religious and philosophical allegiance. Such con-

cerns were briefly reflected in the mid-decade popularity of the American Party (labeled the "Know-Nothing Party" by its critics). It soon faded from the national scene as a result of the growing intensity of the slavery debate.

America's large Protestant majority was in some ways unusually unified in the mid-nineteenth century, thanks in large part to a series of religious revivals spanning the previous half century known collectively as the Second Great Awakening. The original Great Awakening had occurred in the early to mid-eighteenth century. The second got under way shortly after the beginning of the nineteenth century. In what were then the western portions of settled America—the regions between the Appalachians and the Mississippi, the Second Great Awakening was marked by fervent camp meetings and indefatigable circuit riders. Cane Ridge was the largest example of the frontier camp meetings. Held in 1801 on a ridge in Kentucky that had been named by Daniel Boone a generation before, the Cane Ridge meeting drew perhaps as many as 10,000 worshippers, seekers, or just plain curious visitors. Its size and exuberant emotionalism assured its fame, but also made it atypical of the many camp meetings that followed throughout the country—smaller and less sensational gatherings but no less fervent.

The most famous of the itinerant preachers known as circuit riders was Peter Cartwright (1785–1872). First active in Kentucky, Cartwright subsequently moved to Illinois. Forthright, fearless, and sometimes flamboyant, Cartwright preached to Andrew Jackson and once ran for U.S. Congress against an ambitious young man named Abraham Lincoln. He and many others like him, less colorful if no less courageous, helped spread fervent Bible-based Christianity throughout regions in which the first generation of pioneer settlers had sometimes left at least the practical elements of their religion behind when they moved westward.

In the East the revivals took a somewhat more familiar form, though even there religious leaders were quick to innovate in their methods if not in their doctrine. Chief of the innovators was Charles Grandison Finney (1792–1875), the most prominent preacher of the Second Great Awakening. He encouraged those interested in conversion to Christianity to sit in a special pew known as the "Anxious Bench," situated near the front of his auditoria, and he urged all who had not done so to take action immediately in seeking the forgiveness of their sins through Jesus Christ. Finney's protracted meetings featured preaching in the same town every evening for as much as six weeks. By the time his Rochester, New York, meeting came to end, local saloonkeepers were complaining that Finney was putting them out of business by converting all their erstwhile patrons.

The vibrant Christianity of the revivals tended to blur denominational lines among most Protestants and create a sense of unity among earnest believers. The Methodists were the largest denomination in America, followed by the Baptists, with the Presbyterians a distant third. The Cane Ridge camp meeting saw the cooperation of all three denominations; in this respect it was not unusual. During the Civil War it was not at all unusual for soldiers to avail themselves of relatively rare opportunities for worship in established churches by attending a Methodist, a Baptist, and a Presbyterian service at different times during a single Sunday. Some of the clergy might occasionally quibble about the relative merits of infant baptism as opposed to the biblical version of that ordinance, but the men and women in the pews seemed to take little interest in such disputes.

Yet at the same time that the era of the Civil War saw an unusual degree of unity among Christians of the various Protestant denominations in America, it also witnessed a sharp and deep divide—a veritable chasm—between North and South. Many Southerners had long professed that there was no conflict between their Christianity and their ownership of slaves and support for the system of slavery, and they had had little use for Christians who claimed the contrary. Methodism had not grown in the South as it had in the North because of that denomination's strong stand against slavery. Not until the American Methodist leader Francis Asbury's decision to direct his preachers to keep quiet about slavery, at least in the South, did Methodism begin to grow rapidly in that region as it had already been doing in the North.

But Northern Christians did not remain silent. The abolitionist movement, born in the 1830s, became almost a religious crusade, with more than 85 percent of its membership within the ranks of evangelical Christians and one of its most vocal leaders none other than Charles Finney. Southerners expressed outrage that anyone could question their Christianity or condemn the institution of slavery. For a time, denominational leaders in the North, in contrast to the more independent Finney, tried to suppress the antislavery zeal of their

members. When Methodist bishops tried to squelch members' agitation for a stronger denominational position against slavery in 1843, the disgruntled antislavery zealots within the denomination consulted their Bibles, found justification there neither for slavery nor for bishops and broke away to form a small new denomination called the Wesleyan Methodists, uncompromisingly opposed to slavery—and without bishops.

Enough antislavery Methodists remained in the larger denomination to precipitate a showdown at the Methodist general conference the following year. Proslavery Methodists from the South were determined to make no concession to any sort of suggestion that the South's "peculiar institution" was sinful. The result was a complete split of the denomination into separate Northern and Southern wings. The following year the Baptists broke along the same lines, and the Presbyterians subsequently became similarly polarized. The Episcopalians followed suit in March 1861, after several states had already seceded to form the Confederacy. The complete sectional division of all the largest denominations in a country where religion was as important as it was in the United States was a major harbinger of the coming clash between North and South, freedom and slavery.

Though divided between North and South, Americans continued to show much interest in their religion and to take much solace from it. The late 1850s saw another wave of revival in the North, known as the Businessmen's Revival, because of a strong response in many cities. When the war broke out, Americans on both sides were quick to invoke God's aid and to hope, and sometimes assume, that He would be on their side. Both sides took active steps to promote the moral and spiritual welfare of the young men who went off to fight. In the Confederate armies this spiritual nurture took the form of a few chaplains and a number of preachers who traveled through the army's camps as "army missionaries." In the Union armies there was a larger number of chaplains (including some Roman Catholic priests and several Jewish rabbis) and the well-organized ministrations of the United States Christian Commission (USCC), whose delegates circulated through the armies, preaching and handing out Christian literature. Both sides experienced vigorous religious revivals within their armies during the war.

Thus even in the nation's deepest division, its religious faith continued to be a common bond between the warring factions, even if they were not always quite aware of the fact.

Steven E. Woodworth

■ Protestant Christianity

Religion in the United States from the colonial period through the Civil War was dominated by Protestant forms of Christianity. The Protestant churches as a group were not only religious institutions but also a major influence on the general culture of the United States. Such shared values as a belief in the importance of hard work, the notion that virtue should be rewarded, and the concept of religion as the cornerstone of civilized society, were taught in homes and public schools as well as in the churches. As the church historian George Marsden has noted, the most popular textbooks in American grade schools after 1826, *McGuffey's Eclectic Readers*, were thoroughly Protestant in content. They included lessons with such titles as "No Excellence without Labor," "Respect for the Sabbath Rewarded," "The Bible, the Best of Classics," and "The Righteous Never Forsaken" (Marsden 1991, pp. 10–11).

It is important to remember, however, that Great Britain, a colonial power with a Protestant state church, was not the only European nation that established settlements in North America. The thirteen British colonies along the Eastern seaboard had been preceded by the Roman Catholic missions of New Spain in the American Southwest and New France in what is now Canada. Given the rivalry between France and Great Britain for possession of the northern portion of the continent, as well as the bloody history of religious wars in Western Europe in the sixteenth and seventeenth centuries, the settlers of New England and the Middle Atlantic colonies were often defensive about their Protestantism. Fear of the "Popish menace" associated with the French and Spanish monarchies led to widespread anti-Catholic feeling that persisted among American Protestants well past the end of the Civil War in 1865 (Ahlstrom 1973, p. 53). Thus in the period between the Revolutionary War and the Civil War, Protestantism was closely linked with patriotism as well as with civic virtue in the minds of many Americans.

It is also important to recall that some of the original colonies as well as the mother country had established churches. Because the early settlers of New England and the colonies further south were accustomed to having a state church as part of the general pattern of European government, the question in their minds was not *whether* to have an established church but rather *which* church to establish. By degrees Congregationalism became the established church of Massachusetts, Connecticut, and New Hampshire, while the Anglican (Episcopal) Church was established in Virginia and received some degree of public support in the Carolinas, New Jersey, Georgia, and New York. Of the original thirteen colonies, only Rhode Island and Maryland were founded without a state church, and in Maryland the religious freedom originally guaranteed in the colony's 1649 Act of Toleration did not last.

By the middle of the eighteenth century, however, the colonial state churches were moving toward disestablishment. By 1775, Connecticut, Massachusetts, New Hampshire, Maryland, and Virginia were the only colonies that still had official state churches at all, and even

they generally practiced an informal toleration of other bodies. The Revolution brought an end to the establishment of the Anglican Church in Virginia. Congregationalism lasted a bit longer in New England, however; it was not until 1818 that Connecticut finally adopted a state constitution that disestablished the Congregational Church. Connecticut's example was followed by New Hampshire in 1819 and Massachusetts in 1833. The existence of state churches in the thirteen original colonies, however, is part of the background for understanding the Second Great Awakening of the nineteenth century. People who had found the older churches lacking in spiritual vitality after the Revolution were open to religious revivalism as well as the various moral crusades (particularly abolitionism and the temperance movement) of the 1820s and 1830s.

Changing Denominational Mix

The decades preceding the Civil War were marked by several other changes in the denominational landscape of American Protestantism. One was the explosive growth of the churches that were able to adapt most readily to the challenges of the frontier—the Baptists, Methodists, and Disciples of Christ (Marsden 1991, p. 12). By 1844, when the Methodist churches divided between North and South over the issue of slavery, they represented the largest religious body in the United States (Ahlstrom 1973 p. 437). The denominations that had dominated American Protestantism in the late eighteenth century—the Episcopalians, the Presbyterians, and the Congregationalists—also grew in numbers, but much more slowly (Ahlstrom 1973, p. 454).

An important reason for the slower growth of the more traditional churches was their insistence on an educated ministry. The oldest colleges in the United States, including Harvard (1636) and Yale (1701), had been founded specifically to train clergy. Thomas Clap (1703–1767), the fifth rector and first president of Yale, revised the college's constitution in line with his conviction that "the Principal Design of the Institution of this College was to educate Persons for the Work of the Ministry" (Bainton 1985, p. 12). Emphasis on education as a prerequisite for ordination, however, led to a growing division between churches that accepted this principle and those that regarded personal conversion and charismatic preaching as the primary qualifications for ministry. Even during the first Great Awakening, Clap and his like-minded colleagues opposed the open-air preaching of George Whitefield and other itinerant revivalists.

The educational requirements for ordination in the Congregational, Episcopal, and Presbyterian churches were raised further by the establishment of theological seminaries alongside medical and law schools as graduate institutions at the beginning of the nineteenth century. By 1812 Princeton had separated its seminary from its

Lutheran Theological Seminary, Gettysburg, Pennsylvania, 1863. The Lutheran Theological Seminary saw fierce fighting on its grounds during the Battle of Gettysburg. Both Union and Confederate soldiers used seminary buildings during the fight, transforming the multi-storied dormitory pictured here into a observation tower and hospital. *The Library of Congress*

undergraduate college, followed by Harvard in 1815 and Yale in 1822 (Bainton 1985, pp. 79–81). The General Convention of the Episcopal Church voted to establish the General Theological Seminary in New York City in 1817, although the first buildings were not constructed until 1827. The Lutherans, separated from the mainstream of American Protestantism by their liturgical forms of worship as well as language differences, founded a theological seminary at Gettysburg in 1826 (Nelson 1980, pp. 128–129). The school's campus later became

the site of fierce fighting on the first day of the Battle of Gettysburg, July 1, 1863.

The relative informality of Methodist and Baptist worship, as well as their deemphasizing of formal education as preparation for ministry, helped these churches to thrive on the western frontier. Peter Cartwright (1785–1872), a Methodist circuit rider and one of the outstanding preachers of the Second Great Awakening, even regarded higher education as a hindrance to the spread of the Gospel. Converted at a camp meeting in

1801, Cartwright said, "I have seen so many educated preachers who forcibly reminded me of lettuce growing under the shade of a peach-tree, or like a gosling that had got the straddles by wading in the dew, that I turn away sick and faint" (Ahlstrom 1973, p. 438).

Another change in the denominational composition of American Protestantism prior to the Civil War was the emergence of separate black churches. In 1816, Richard Allen (1760–1831), a former slave, became the first bishop of the African Methodist Episcopal (AME) Church, a denomination organized in Philadelphia that had about 25,000 members by 1860. In 1821 another black Methodist body, the African Methodist Episcopal Church Zion (AME Zion) was formed in New York City. As the Union armies moved deeper into the South toward the end of the Civil War, both AME churches opened missions among the freedpeople. They grew exponentially over the next few decades, the AME counting 452,725 members by 1896 and the AME Zion 349,788 (Ahlstrom 1973, pp. 708–709). The first black Baptist denomination, the Colored Primitive Baptists, was organized in 1866, a year after the end of the Civil War.

Sectarianism

The nineteenth century witnessed a growth in the number and variety of denominations and smaller groups (sects) within American Protestantism as well as an overall increase in the number of church members. European visitors to the United States from the 1830s onward remarked on the sheer number of different religious bodies in the country. Even in the 1930s, the German theologian Dietrich Bonhoeffer, then a graduate student in New York City, recorded in his diary, "It has been granted to the Americans less than any other nation on earth to realize the visible unity of the Church of God" (Bonhoeffer 1965, p. 94).

The distinction between a denomination and a sect is not always easy to draw, but in general a denomination can be defined as a socially and theologically stable body of Christians with a conventional church structure, whereas a sect is a group that develops on the periphery of a religion or denomination and eventually secedes from it, developing its own set of doctrines and religious practices as it separates from the parent body (Stark and Bainbridge 1979, pp. 121–122). Moreover, while denominations typically attract people from a range of social backgrounds, occupations, and educational levels, sects are more likely to appeal to those who feel disadvantaged or marginalized (Ahlstrom 1973, pp. 473–474).

In the period between the 1820s and the outbreak of the Civil War, the Second Great Awakening and other revival movements helped to prepare the ground for new sects that emerged from mainstream Protestantism but differed from it in a number of ways. The emphasis of nineteenth-century revivalists on "heart religion" rather than theological precision and on immediate spiritual experience rather than a sense of the historical continuity of the Church favored the growth of movements led by charismatic individuals who were not ordained by or identified with the traditional churches. Many of these persons developed their own idiosyncratic interpretations of the Bible or, as in the case of Joseph Smith (1805–1844), claimed to be recipients of a new set of inspired writings.

William Miller (1782–1849) was a Vermont farmer who had left the Baptist Church as a young adult but returned to it after a conversion experience in 1816. He began an intense study of the Bible and came to the conclusion that the Second Coming of Christ would occur in 1843. He did not begin to preach or lecture publicly about his calculations, however, until 1831. By 1840 Miller's ideas had gained national attention, and local meetings were organized all over the United States to summon people to repentance and preparation for the Lord's return. Although Miller initially predicted the Second Coming to occur at some point between March 21, 1843, and March 21, 1844, he was persuaded by some of his followers to revise his calculations and set the final date as October 22, 1844. When that day—known as the Great Disappointment—came and went, most of Miller's followers abandoned the movement.

Some, however, followed a new leader, Ellen H. White (1827–1915). White had earlier left the Methodist Church to join Miller's movement in 1842. After the Great Disappointment of 1844, White began to have visions and claimed to have a spirit of prophecy. In 1863, in the middle of the Civil War, White and her followers formally established the Seventh-day Adventist Church, known in the twenty-first century for its distinctive views on diet and health as well as for its general cultural conservatism.

The other major sect to emerge from American Protestantism in the 1840s was the Church of Jesus Christ of Latter-day Saints, better known as the Mormon Church. Joseph Smith, the founder of Mormonism, claimed to have been guided by the angel Moroni to a set of golden plates buried in a hillside near Palmyra, New York, in 1827. Smith spent the next three years translating the plates and published the result as the Book of Mormon in 1830. His new revelation, whose language echoes that of the King James Bible, began to attract followers within weeks of its publication. By the early 1840s the first Mormon colonies had begun their westward migration, chased from one Midwestern town after another by citizens offended by Smith's threats of violence against opponents, his claims to be a "Second Mohammed" (Ahlstrom 1973, p. 506), and by the Mormon practice of plural marriage. After Smith was lynched by a mob in Carthage, Illinois, in June 1844, Brigham Young (1801–1877) led the Mormons further west to what was then Utah territory, becoming its first governor as well as the second leader of the Latter-day Saints.

Missionary Activity

The period from 1815 to 1914 has sometimes been described as the "great century" of Christian missions (Latourette 1970, p. 225). In the United States, missions to the Indians began in the colonial period and continued as settlers moved westward in the years preceding the Civil War. Jonathan Edwards (1703–1758), an important figure in the first Great Awakening and an eminent theologian, served as a missionary to the Housatonic Indians in western Massachusetts (then a frontier area) from 1750 until 1757, when he left Stockbridge reluctantly to assume the presidency of the College of New Jersey (later Princeton). By 1798 Connecticut had its own Missionary Society, which described its purpose as "Christianiz[ing] the heathen in North America" (Bainton 1985, p. 132).

In addition to converting the Native Americans to Christianity, nineteenth-century Protestant clergy also saw missions in the West as a way of slowing the growth of Roman Catholicism in the newly opened territories. Lyman Beecher (1775–1863), another leader of the Second Great Awakening and the founder of Lane Theological Seminary in Ohio, preached a sermon in early 1834 on the importance of keeping the West safe for Protestantism (Beecher 1835, pp. 10–12). Tragically, Beecher's sermon led to the burning of a Roman Catholic convent in Boston in August 1834 (*Boston Evening Transcript*, August 12, 1834).

Protestant missionaries were also sent to Native Americans in the southeastern states by the American Board of Commissioners for Foreign Missions (ABCFM), a Congregationalist body chartered in 1812 as an outgrowth of the Second Great Awakening. Many of these missionaries, in particular Jeremiah Evarts (1781–1831), the secretary of the ABCFM, were opponents of President Andrew Jackson's policy of Indian removal and lobbied Congress to protect the Indians from forced deportation to the West.

Evarts was also instrumental in opening missionary work to unmarried women. Under his leadership, the ABCFM sent Ellen Stetson (1783–1848) as the first single woman missionary to the Indians in 1821 and Betsey Stockton (1798?–1865), an African American born in slavery, as a missionary to the Sandwich Islands (now Hawaii) in 1822 (Maxfield 1998, pp. 172–175). Evarts's acceptance of women as missionaries inspired Mary Lyon (1797–1849) to open Mount Holyoke Female Seminary in 1837 to give women their first opportunity for higher education equal to that offered by the men's colleges. Lyon hoped that many of the school's graduates would enter the mission field. Writing to her fellow New Englanders in 1843 to support missions at home and abroad, Lyon singled out the work of the ABCFM:

I took a survey of Modern Missions. What a sublime spectacle! I glanced over the history of the American Board of Commissioners for Foreign Missions—the glory of our country—the corner stone of all our voluntary benevolent associations. I love to go back in its history more than thirty years... Though I was but a child [in 1812], I love even now the very thought that I can remember even the beginnings of this great and glorious enterprise (Lyon 1843, p. 15).

Although Lyon's seminary was not chartered as a college until 1888, it paved the way for the women's colleges founded during or shortly after the Civil War, including Vassar (1861), Smith (1875), and Wellesley (1875).

Women's Ministries

In addition to the opening of the mission field, the nineteenth century witnessed other new developments in the ministries of women outside as well as inside the Protestant churches. It was ironic, given the opposition of many American Protestants to Roman Catholicism, that one of the pioneers of women's ministries in the early nineteenth century was Elizabeth Ann Seton (1774–1821), an Episcopalian who became a Roman Catholic in 1805. Seton founded the Sisters of Charity of St. Joseph in 1809, the first women's religious order that began in the United States. She was also the first native-born American to be declared a saint by the Roman Catholic Church, being canonized by Pope Paul VI in 1975.

Women in the Lutheran and Episcopal churches in the 1850s had a new opportunity for service as deaconesses. The office of deaconess had existed in the early Christian churches, as is evident in the New Testament, but had largely disappeared in the European churches by the end of the thirteenth century. In the nineteenth century, however, some clergy in the Church of England and the Lutheran churches of Germany decided to revive the ancient office. As the early deaconesses had cared for the sick and helped to prepare women converts for Christian baptism, the nineteenth-century founders of deaconess movements trained women for service as teachers (particularly in girls' schools and foreign missions), lay ministers, and nurses. The first Episcopal deaconesses in the United States were consecrated in the Diocese of Maryland in 1855 (Rich 1907, n.p.). William Passavant (1821–1894), a devout Lutheran layman, founded an Institution of Protestant Deaconesses in Philadelphia modeled on the pattern of the deaconess motherhouse established by Theodor Fliedner in Kaiserswerth, Germany, in 1836. The first American Lutheran deaconesses began their work in Passavant's institution in 1849 (Weiser 1962, pp. 54–55).

Although the ordination of women to the ministry was unthinkable in most American Protestant churches at the time of the Civil War, Antoinette Louise Brown

(1825–1891), an ardent abolitionist and a leader of the women's suffrage movement, was ordained by the Congregational Church of South Butler, New York, in 1853. She was thus the first clergywoman in a mainstream Protestant denomination in the United States.

Alternatives to Orthodox Protestantism

The Civil War affected the American churches by the sheer number of its casualties as well as by the splits that divided most mainstream Protestant bodies during the abolitionist controversies of the 1840s and 1850s. It is often forgotten that the Civil War cost more American lives (363,000 Union, 200,000 Confederate) than any other conflict in the nation's history, including World War II (408,000). Moreover, this loss occurred when the total population of the country was only 31.5 million, including slaves (Census of 1860). There were many families in both South and North that had to cope with profound grief as well as with the economic dislocations and hardships associated with war.

People who had been raised as Protestant Christians responded in various ways to the human devastation resulting from the war. Some, such as the writer and journalist Ambrose Bierce, were so traumatized by their combat experiences as to give up belief in any meaning to life at all, let alone a religious significance. Bierce wrote toward the end of his life that he had basically given up the traditional Christian belief in an afterlife:

> In this matter of immortality, people's beliefs appear to go along with their wishes. The man who is content with annihilation thinks he will get it; those that want immortality are pretty sure they are immortal; and that is a very comfortable allotment of faiths. The few of us that are left unprovided for are those who do not bother themselves much about the matter, one way or another (Bierce 1912, p. 35).

John Wesley Powell, the son of a Methodist minister who became a famous explorer and geologist, dismissed the Christianity in which he had been reared as "ghostlore" (Carter 1971, p. 5).

Other survivors of the war were attracted to spiritualist movements on the fringes of Christianity. These groups offered answers to questions raised by the war about life after death. Although American spiritualism had its beginnings in the 1840s, with the Fox sisters of Hydesville, New York, and their mysterious abilities of "channeling" the spirits of the departed, the movement grew rapidly in the years after 1865, as thousands of bereaved families asked for "messages" from loved ones killed in battle. First Lady Mary Todd Lincoln gave the movement additional publicity by consulting spiritualists in the White House after the death of her son Willie in 1863 and even more frequently after her husband's assassination in 1865 (Ahlstrom 1973, p. 489).

Robert Dale Owen (1801–1877), the founder of a utopian community in New Harmony, Indiana, was converted to spiritualism in 1856 while serving the Pierce administration as a diplomat in Italy. After publishing a book about his experiences of the occult in 1860, Owen received an official invitation to the White House in 1862 to give a lecture on his new beliefs. Owen's presentation prompted a classic comment from President Lincoln: "Well, for those who like that sort of thing, I should think it is just about the sort of thing they would like" (Fornell 1964, p. 118). Although the national organization of spiritualists formed in 1863 counted only 50,000 members by 1893, spiritualism proved to be a long-lasting reservoir from which later investigators of the occult—from people fascinated by astrology and paranormal phenomena to the New Age enthusiasts of the late twentieth century—would freely draw.

BIBLIOGRAPHY

Ahlstrom, Sydney E. *A Religious History of the American People*. New Haven, CT: Yale University Press, 1973.

Bainton, Roland H. *Yale and the Ministry*. New York and San Francisco: Harper & Row, 1985.

Beecher, Lyman. "A Plea for the West." Cincinnati, OH: Truman & Smith, 1835.

Bierce, Ambrose. *A Cynic Looks at Life*. Girard, KS: Haldeman-Julius Company, 1912.

Bonhoeffer, Dietrich. *No Rusty Swords: Letters, Lectures, and Notes, 1928–1936*, ed. Edwin H. Robinson. New York: Harper & Row, 1965.

"Burning of the Charlestown Convent." *Boston Evening Transcript*, August 12, 1834, n.p.

Carter, Paul A. *The Spiritual Crisis of the Gilded Age*. DeKalb: Northern Illinois University Press, 1971.

Fornell, Earl Wesley. *Unhappy Medium: Spiritualism and the Life of Margaret Fox*. Austin: University of Texas Press, 1964.

Latourette, Kenneth Scott. *A History of the Expansion of Christianity*. Grand Rapids, MI: Zondervan Publishing House, 1970.

Lyon, Mary. *A Missionary Offering, or, Christian Sympathy, Personal Responsibility, and the Present Crisis in Foreign Missions*. Boston: Crocker & Brewster, 1843.

Marsden, George M. *Understanding Fundamentalism and Evangelicalism*. Grand Rapids, MI: Wm. B. Eerdmans Publishing Co., 1991.

Maxfield, Charles A. "The Legacy of Jeremiah Evarts." *International Bulletin of Missionary Research* 22 (1998): 172–175.

Nelson, E. Clifford, ed. *The Lutherans in North America*. Philadelphia: Fortress Press, 1980.

Rich, Lawson Carter. "The Deaconesses of the Church in Modern Times." *The Churchman*, May 4, 1907.

Stark, Rodney, and William S. Bainbridge. "Of Churches, Sects, and Cults: Preliminary Concepts for a Theory of Religious Movements." *Journal for the Scientific Study of Religion* 18 (1979): 117–131.

Weiser, Frederick S. *Love's Response: A Story of Lutheran Deaconesses in America.* Philadelphia: Board of Publication, United Lutheran Church in America, 1962.

Rebecca J. Frey

■ Revivals

From 1720 to the end of the Civil War, the United States was roiled by religious revivals or, as they were called, "awakenings." Historians generally ascribe the first such revival, the Great Awakening, to the period 1720 to 1790, although some modern scholars have attempted to narrow it to 1739 to 1745, during the itinerant preaching of George Whitefield (1714–1770) in British North America. Whitefield's preaching contained four elements that resurfaced in subsequent American revivals. First, his preaching did not offer an explication of biblical text; instead, it was an emotional call for a new birth for Christians. Second, his evangelical fervor was directed against the sins of avarice and consumption, which he saw as triumphant in America; people seemed more interested in the fruits of this world than in those of the next (though Whitefield himself was not above using secular methods such as printed circulars and advance men to increase attendance at his meetings). Third, although he apparently visited every part of the British American colonies,

he was particularly successful in the cities, including Philadelphia, New York, and Boston. Fourth, and perhaps most importantly for subsequent revivals, Whitefield's call to Christ and salvation occurred outside the confines of established churches and doctrine and without the permission of the local ministries. His revivals featured open-air preaching that reached thousands; he was said to have addressed 23,000 people on Boston Common. Open-air meetings, to which all were invited, regardless of denomination, meant that individuals could make their own decisions about spiritual matters, and this represented an indirect assault on the spiritual authority of the established religions in the colonies.

The Second Great Awakening

The Second Great Awakening occurred from 1800 to 1835 (though it persisted in many forms until the eve of the Civil War). Its most famous camp meeting—so called because participants would camp outdoors at the selected site, opening the event to vast numbers of seekers and creating a community, however ephemeral, organized on Christian principles—was in August 1801 in Cane Ridge, Kentucky. A crowd estimated at 10,000 came to hear local ministers, at least twenty-two, in nearly nonstop preaching over several days. The crowd was so overcome with religious fervor that men and women threw themselves on the ground in fits of religious ecstasy, and were beset by convulsions where they stood and barked like dogs. An eyewitness

Revival meeting. Many Americans attended religious revival meetings, listening to traveling ministers in outdoor settings who spread evangelical Christianity. *© North Wind Picture Archives*

reported on this improbable outpouring of the Holy Spirit:

> Men and women rolled over and over like a wheel or stretched in a prostrate manner … Still more demeaning and mortifying were the jerks … it appeared that the transfixed were being goaded by "a red hot iron." … The last possible grade of mortification seemed to be couched in the barks … both men and women would be forced to personate that animal. (M'Nemar 2007, p. 80)

The meeting at Cane Ridge differed in degree from subsequent meetings of the period. "While revivals were almost always emotional affairs with crying, shouting and sometimes falling, excesses such as barking or tree-ing the devil … were limited. With the possible exceptions of the early meetings, they never became regular features of the Second Great Awakening" (Hankins 2004, p. 11).

The Second Great Awakening spread north and east and had soon encompassed most of the Northern states, reaching its greatest intensity in western New York and Ohio. Indeed, an area of western New York became known as the "burned-over district" because it was repeatedly racked by successive waves of revivalism and the camp meetings (and the camp fires that went with them) that were essential to spreading the Gospel.

One of the Protestant evangelists who had preached in the burned-over district was Charles G. Finney (1792–1875). Finney had been a teacher and a law student until he had an epiphany in 1821, then became a minister ordained in the Presbyterian Church in 1824. Immensely popular, Finney is recognized as the leader of the Second Great Awakening. His sermons and organization were quite radical; he permitted women to pray in mixed groups with men, and prayed for people by name—unconventional ideas for his time. He employed the "anxious bench," where a sinner struggling with acceptance of faith might come and sit in the front of the assembly to be prayed for by everyone present, a practice that prefigures modern evangelism's invitation to the newly saved to come to the front of the church to acknowledge their new birth.

Finney accepted a faculty post at Oberlin Collegiate Institute in 1835 and eventually became the school's president. He molded Oberlin into a training ground for young evangelists and "left men and women eager to demonstrate their virtue through social action" (Walters 1976, p. 38). Although he was staunchly antislavery, Finney, like many other otherwise outspoken evangelists, was hesitant to take a firm public stand for abolition, and he avoided advocating political action. He feared that to do so would divide the church and distract its ministers from their ordained mission, which was the saving of souls. Evangelicals believed that America was God's chosen land selected to evangelize the world, an idea that had persisted since the days of the Massachusetts Bay Colony; political disunion would threaten America's divine mission. They were also tormented by a fundamental conundrum—could the proponents of Christian love advocate force of arms to destroy the evil that was slavery?

The Second Great Awakening prefigured modern evangelistic moments in some significant ways. It continued the expansion of lay influence in organized religion, as many revivals took place outside established churches. Finney himself, although ordained in the Presbyterian Church, admitted that he had no knowledge of the Westminster Confession, the faith's central tenet. For Finney and his many followers, the emotionalism of revivalism demonstrated convincingly that the Holy Spirit could touch anyone. Finney eschewed the sensationalism that had marked the Cane Ridge Revival, but his camp meetings were open to all, regardless of formal religious affiliation. This reinforced the idea of interdenominational brotherhood present in earlier awakenings, an idea that spread quickly throughout Protestant America.

In the Second Great Awakening, moral choices and ethical questions replaced dogma as the central concern of a committed Christian, and suggested individual action as a means to triumph over sin:

> The revivals' doctrinal innovations related to free will and the agency of man in conversion. The Calvinist doctrine of predestination held that man, by nature sinful, could do nothing to assure his own salvation. But revivals could only work if man was not inherently depraved; and revivalists preached that man could, by an act of will, achieve harmony with God and thus salvation. Moreover, and perhaps more important, the use of revivals to promote conversions implied that men had the power to save others. These tenets had two important implications for the development of the antislavery movement: they declared slavery to be an unacceptable social institution, and they acknowledged that men had the capacity to eliminate evil in the world. (Hammond 1974, p. 183).

In theological terms, the concepts of Arminian doctrine began to replace those of Calvinism. Arminian doctrine stressed "free will, free grace, and unlimited hope for the conversion of all men" (Smith 1980, pp. 88–89). It held that humanity, by God's grace, could either accept or reject salvation and strive for a life of perfection. God's will, to the evangelical revivalists, is to save all who will partake of salvation, that is, by coming to Christ. To the evangelicals, human will is eternally corrupt, but by God's will, humanity is given the freedom to choose to turn to God for salvation. Humanity, however, must live in God's way. Christ's sacrifice, therefore, atones for all, as opposed to Calvinism's somewhat strained belief in Christ's limited atonement only for the elect or those predestined to receive grace. As a consequence of such beliefs converging in the revivals, the once culturally and dogmatically dominant

Congregationalists, Presbyterians, and Anglicans (whose sway held through the Revolutionary period) were displaced by Methodists and Baptists, which grew to become the two largest denominations in the United States (Smith 1980, p. 20).

There were two undercurrents to American revivalism that manifested themselves in different ways—perfectionism and millennialism. Perfectionism, which grew out of the teachings of John Wesley (1703–1791), held that humankind could achieve perfect love of God; to be sanctified was to love God and one's neighbor perfectly. Once sanctified, a Christian would no longer feel any inward inclination toward sin. Evangelists put great emphasis on human effort in sanctification—although it was a gift from God, a committed Christian could use that grace to grow in holiness and achieve perfection through adherence to moral law. Public testimony became important because it was a sign of the Holy Spirit acting through an individual's emotions that gave witness to sanctification. Many evangelists believed that sanctification could be squandered, and it was a Christian's duty to continue to strive for perfection even after sanctification occurred. The main denominational expression of the perfectionist or holiness movement during this era was the Free Methodist Church, founded in the burned-over district of western New York in 1860. It was staunchly and vocally opposed to slavery, and many of its members were active in the Underground Railroad, smuggling escaped slaves to freedom in Canada.

Both Charles Finney and Phoebe Palmer (1807–1874), the best known female evangelist of the period, integrated the need for Christian perfection into their preaching. Most importantly, the idea of Christian perfection meant that a striving mankind could advance the advent of the kingdom of heaven through right living—perfectionism could lead to the "early inauguration of the Kingdom of God on earth" (Smith 1980, p. 105). This idea intertwined with the concept of millennialism—the belief in a golden age, Christ's thousand-year reign on earth. Many antebellum revivalists believed that the Second Great Awakening and the burgeoning social reform movements were signs that the millennium was fast approaching. One evangelist, William Miller (1815–1874), even calculated the exact date for Christ's return as October 22, 1844. Although Miller and his followers were disappointed and ridiculed when Christ did not appear on the appointed day, the idea of the millennium was not completely discredited in evangelical thought; in fact, it "seemed increasingly expected to be ushered in by political movements . . ." (Smith 1980, p. 15). Thus revivalism came to be linked to perfection and humanitarian reform through ethical principles that applied to the entire sphere of human activity—daily life, commerce, and the eradication of social evil.

The Awakening of 1858

The last of the antebellum awakenings occurred in 1857 to 1858 and is known variously as the Awakening of 1858, the Revival of 1857 to 1858, or, most colorfully, the Businessmen's Revival. Although it shared many of the characteristics of the two earlier awakenings, it was fundamentally different.

In September 1857 the New York City missionary Jeremiah Lanphier organized a noontime prayer meeting at the Old Dutch Church on Fulton Street in lower Manhattan. His first meeting was sparsely attended, but by the following spring, 10,000 people—predominantly young professionals—were attending the prayer meetings. The awakening spread rapidly to cities in the North, West, and as far south as Baltimore. The *Cleveland Herald*, reporting on events in New York, noted that "A very general religious interest now prevails in many churches," and that the churches were so crowded that they had to open at nine in the morning to accommodate the masses of mostly young people who sought spiritual release (*Cleveland Herald*, December 12, 1857). In January the same newspaper reported that as the awakening continued to grow, "Meetings are held nightly, penitents throng the altar, and a general awakening has taken place" (*Cleveland Herald*, January 16, 1858).

The revival was characterized by fluidly organized meetings without a prepared plan or liturgy. Anyone present might pray, testify, or sing as long as they stayed within the agreed-upon five-minute time limit and avoided controversial topics such as water baptism and slavery. The *New York Herald* reproduced a notice from a noontime revival meeting in its February 21, 1858, edition that read: "Prayers and Exhortations Not to exceed five minutes In order to give all an opportunity Not more than two consecutive prayers or exhortations. No controverted points discussed" (*New York Herald* 1858).

Like earlier revivals, the Businessmen's Revival was interdenominational and placed ethical concerns and a united front against Satan above the doctrine of any one denomination. Unlike earlier revivals, these were essentially prayer meetings without a presiding minister and were urban in character. Earlier revivals had spread from west to east; the Businessmen's Revival first engulfed the cities of the North and then spread west and into the rural North. Meetings focused almost exclusively on individual salvation and avoided any discussion of controversial social issues; news of the revival and the revival fires themselves were fanned by repeated articles in large metropolitan dailies in New York City, perhaps with an eye to increasing circulation (Long 1998).

The antecedents of the Revival of 1857 to 1858 are unclear. The Old Dutch Church was near Wall Street, and a stock-market collapse in October 1857 (the Panic of 1857) may have been seen by the servants of mammon as an omen and warning that they should attend more assiduously to their souls than to their pocketbooks. The Panic of 1857 may also have meant that un- or underemployed stockbrokers, clerks, and other office workers now had time to spare during the day. Historian Sandra Sizer discounts such economic causes for the revival by observing that the United States had suffered panics before without engendering corresponding revivals. She believes that a concatenation of events precipitated the awakening—the long, increasingly bitter struggle around the slavery issue was more in the public consciousness following the Dred Scott Supreme Court decision in 1857 and the publication of *Uncle Tom's Cabin*, first serialized in 1851, which by 1857 had sold two million copies. In addition, the earlier Second Great Awakening had led more Americans to agree that slavery was a national sin. Indeed, some might have seen the Panic of 1857 as God's punishment for the sins of both slavery and avarice. The sin of slavery touched whites in the North and South alike—white Northerners for their complicity and white Southerners for the damage slavery inflicted on social and political institutions. Sizer writes, "Portraits of the slave system in the South increasingly emphasized not only its political tyranny but also its perversion of the family, and therefore of the minds and hearts of whites as well as blacks" (Sizer 1979, p. 88). The revival may have been seen by some as a way to purify themselves and, by extension, the country, by acts of public contrition and conversion.

This view was not necessarily shared by newspapers of the time:

> It may not be impertinent to request these expounders of the word to leave the black man to the politicians, and to shower their hardest apostolic knocks against the devil and all his works, as developed in the daily life of the white man in Wall street and elsewhere.... no class needs saving grace more the Wall Street editors and the Wall street financiers.... (*New York Herald*, February 19, 1858)

Sizer notes, in discussing the antebellum revivals:

> Despite the intention of the Northerners, who had thought that slavery could be contained, the wrong people—people of an aristocratic and parasitical temperament—had seized the reins of government and intended to spread their pernicious system throughout the land. The situation could only be rectified, from an evangelical perspective, by an inward purification which would lead to a reformation of morals and appropriate political action. (Sizer 1979, p. 91)

There seems little doubt that the antebellum revivals had an impact on the antislavery movement; what is not as clear is the character and extent of that impact. The historian Ronald Walters points out the "long gap between religious awakenings and reform" (Walters 1976, p. 39), but he also observes that "Antislavery

could not, in fact, have been what it was after 1830 if there had not been an evangelical Protestant tradition behind it and if there had not been evangelical Protestants in it from beginning to end" (p. 37).

As historian Vernon Burton and other scholars have observed, "religion played a large role in pro- and anti-slavery movements" (2007, p. 42). Some proslavery theologians advanced justifications of slavery based upon both the Old Testament, where slavery is mentioned, and the New, where it is not, interpreting this silence as assent. This equivocation widened the split between the militant abolitionists and religion.

It may be that it was the very failure of revivalism to define the state as a moral agent for transformation or to advocate vigorous political action to end slavery that led men and women to join antislavery organizations that advocated political means to achieve their ends. Religious beliefs informed political attitudes, then as they do now, and may have prepared the larger population to support those means at the polls. As Burton observes:

> Most Americans remained content to imagine that fervent prayer and steady labor would be sufficient until God brought forth his government on earth. For those few who were not content to wait for the Lord, their moral choices made all the difference in driving the nation toward Civil War.... It was not the slavery of sin that looked to destroy the nation and confound the millennium, but the sin of slavery. (2007, p. 49)

BIBLIOGRAPHY

Burton, Orville V. *The Age of Lincoln*. New York: Hill and Wang, 2007.

Cleveland Herald, December 12, 1857.

Cleveland Herald, January 16, 1858.

Hankins, Barry. *The Second Great Awakening and the Transcendentalists*. Westport, CT: Greenwood Press, 2004.

Hammond, John L. "Revival Religion and Antislavery Politics." *American Sociological Review* 39, no. 2 (1974): 175–186.

Long, Kathryn T. *The Revival of 1857–58: Interpreting an American Religious Awakening*. New York: Oxford University Press, 1998.

M'Nemar, Richard. "The Kentucky Revival." In *Encyclopedia of Religious Revivals in America*, ed. Michael McClymond. Westport, CT: Greenwood, 2007.

New York Herald, February 19, 1858.

New York Herald, February 21, 1858.

Sizer, Sandra. "Politics and Apolitical Religion: The Great Urban Revivals of the Late Nineteenth Century." *Church History* 48, no. 1 (March 1979): 81–98.

Smith, Timothy L. *Revivalism and Social Reform: American Protestantism on the Eve of the Civil War*. Baltimore: Johns Hopkins University Press, 1980.

Walters, Ronald. *The Antislavery Appeal: American Abolitionism after 1830.* Baltimore: Johns Hopkins University Press, 1976.

James Onderdonk

■ The Sunday School Movement

The tradition of Sunday schools, while familiar in the early twenty-first century as places where the children of church-going families are taught the tenets of their faith, was not part of the popular lexicon prior to the late 1700s. Once organized, however, Sunday schools quickly grew in popularity and influence, spreading literacy and moral values while also providing evangelical Christianity with young converts. The strength of the Sunday school movement inspired some of the greatest minds of the age—among them the economist Adam Smith (1723–1790), the philosopher Thomas Malthus (1766–1836), and the Methodist theologian John Wesley (1703–1791)—to note its virtues in promoting popular education generally. As Smith noted, "No plan has promised to effect a change of manners, with equal ease and simplicity" as did the morals-based literacy training provided in the eighteenth-century Sunday school (Trumbull 1888, p. 118).

Although the first actual Sunday school was established by Hannah Ball in Buckinghamshire, England, in 1769, the systematization of faith-based education for children is credited to one of one of Ball's countrymen. As publisher and editor of the *Gloucester Journal*, Robert Raikes (1736–1811) viewed with concern the many poor children living in England's slums who found their way into crime. "The world marches forth on the feet of small children," the editor was known to proclaim in the pages of his newspaper. As the parents of these children were forced by necessity into factory jobs, Raikes realized that the task of instilling positive moral values in these children must be taken up by others.

Working with a local pastor, Raikes established a Sunday school for the poor and orphaned in July 1780. Promoted in his newspaper, Raikes's school soon had hundreds of students. At first only boys attended, but within a year, girls were also invited. As word of his work spread, Sunday schools soon appeared in other communities throughout England. By 1800, 200,000 children were enrolled in English Sunday schools, and the number had risen to 1,250,000 by 1830. By 1850, approximately two million British children attended weekly religious classes (Laqueur 1976, p. 44).

Because facilities were not available in most English parish churches, the first Sunday school classes were held either in the homes of paid teachers or in rented rooms. Some were free while others charged a modest tuition, although promising but needy students often gained a financial sponsor from the upper classes. The instruction included reading, rudimentary mathematics, and catechesis; it usually lasted four or five hours each week. For many children, Sunday school was the only education they would ever receive.

Francis Asbury (1745–1816). Primarily a late eighteenth-century development, the first Sunday schools sought to promote moral and religious education in children from the poorer classes, as well as some basic instruction in reading, math, and writing. Methodist bishop Francis Asbury extended these religious classes to reach slave children throughout the South, decades prior to the Civil War. *The Library of Congress.*

The Movement Comes to America

Like other aspects of British culture, the Sunday school movement quickly jumped the Atlantic. While the Sunday instruction of children was probably ongoing in the New England colonies by 1670, the first school modeled on Raikes's system was begun by William Elliott in Accomac County, Virginia, in the mid-1780s. The philanthropic Elliott hosted the children of poor white families in his home for Bible study, and also established a second school for slaves. The instruction of slaves became a unique outgrowth of the Sunday school movement in the United States as Elliott's efforts inspired others in the antebellum South, such as the Methodist bishop Francis Asbury (1745–1816), to establish schools for black slaves. White adults also benefited from the Sunday school system by either learning basic skills from their children or attending the schools themselves.

Many supporters of Sunday schools came from the reform-minded upper classes. Many hoped to instill discipline, a work ethic, and literacy in the working-class families that now crowded into the cities as a result of industrialization. Teachers, both men and women, also dedicated themselves to this task. James M. Garnett, a Sunday-school teacher in Virginia, reportedly encouraged his young students to "become more dutiful and affectionate children; more kind and loving brothers and sisters; more friendly and benevolent to your companions…and more devoted to the constant discharge of all your duties in relation to both this word and the next" (*Maryland Gazette and Political Intelligencer*, July 12, 1821). As Raikes had also reported, the crime rate among young people who attended a Sunday school dropped significantly, improving the safety of the community at large. Remarking on the effects of the first session of a Sunday school established in Northampton, Massachusetts, in 1817, one correspondent reported in the *Daily National Intelligencer* that "this experiment," in which "the improvement of the scholars was generally great, and in some instances astonishing," demonstrates "conclusively that these schools may be rendered as useful in our small towns, as in our large cities" (November 26, 1817).

Part of the success of the Sunday school movement was its voluntary nature. Young participants, some of whom worked long hours in factories and lived in squalor, cherished their half-day of focused study. The Rev. J. Fisk may have been only slightly overdramatizing the situation in his speech before the Vermont Sunday School Union in the winter of 1827 when he recalled one boy, "whose parents were too poor to provide him with shoes, who was found by his teacher on one snowy Sabbath in autumn, sewing old rags upon his feet, 'because,' said he, with tears in his eyes, 'I cannot stay away from the Sabbath School'" (*Vermont Watchman and State Gazette*, December 4, 1827). Referring to the pervasive state of "unbelief and error" that the Rev. Lyman Beecher (1775–1863), a leader of the Second Great Awakening, had famously confronted over a half-century before in his "Waste Places of New England" sermon, Henry Clay Trumbull contended in 1888 that "America has been practically saved to Christianity and the religion of the Bible by the Sunday-school" (Trumbull 1888, p. 122).

Educating the Urban Poor

Fuelled by the country's growing nationalistic fervor, the Sunday school movement of the early 1800s established its deepest roots in America's most established towns and cities. In Boston; Baltimore; Hartford, Connecticut; Charleston, South Carolina; and New York City independent schools were soon replaced by schools organized and monitored by societies and unions. One of the first, the First Day School Society, was established in Philadelphia in 1791 for the purpose of providing for the education of impoverished girls. In 1824 the American Sunday School Union (ASSU) was formed. The first National Sunday School Convention convened in Philadelphia in 1832, with 15 states represented among its 220 delegates (Brown 1901, p. 71). The efforts of organizing bodies such as the ASSU were reinforced by the many books and periodicals that soon appeared to guide both students and teachers: *The Baptist Teacher*, *Sunday School Journal*, *Sunday School World*, *Sunday School Helper*, *Earnest Worker*, and the Philadelphia-based and nationally circulating *Sunday School Times*. Bible societies, which sprang up during the late 1800s to facilitate international Christian outreach, often set as their first task obtaining copies of the Holy Bible for every Sunday school student who desired one and showed dedication to its study. To create a uniform common curriculum for American Sunday schools, the National Sunday School Convention adopted the *International Uniform Lesson* in 1872. This curriculum did not find favor with all schools, however, and soon there were other similar lesson systems available, such as the *International Graded Series* (also known as the *Closely Graded Lessons*), and the *Group Graded Lessons* (also known as the *Departmental Graded Lessons*), which provided teachers with age-appropriate curricula.

Although the Sunday school movement rode the positive spirit of social reform characteristic of the Industrial Revolution, the movement also had its detractors. Raikes was hailed for his achievement, but those in class-conscious England who were concerned by the nation's upwardly mobile middle class also expressed concern as to whether a literate and intellectually stimulated lower class would be satisfied with their so-called proper station in life. Some U.S. churches also regarded the secular origins of Sunday schools with the same suspicion as Bible societies, tract societies, temperance societies, the Masonic order, and other similar groups. For Christian reformers such as Alexander Campbell (1788–1866), this secularism posed a different kind of threat: it opposed his effort to encourage all Christians, whatever their denomination, to unite under one single creed based in the New Testament. In January of 1827 Campbell warned in the pages of his periodical *The Christian Baptist:* "If children are taught to read in a Sunday school, their pockets must be filled with religious tracts, the object of which is either directly or indirectly to bring them under the domination of some creed or sect."

Sunday Schools and the Civil War

In the United States, the Sunday school movement travelled along with the tides of migration to points west and south, and within four years of its founding the ASSU had shepherded the spread of Sunday schools across twenty-eight states. In addition to producing Christian literature attractive to younger children, the organization also sent missionaries into the Mississippi Valley, one of which, Stephen Paxson, traveled by horseback throughout the region, organizing more than 1,300 Sunday schools. The distribution of Sunday schools between the North and the South, however, was uneven in the years leading up to the Civil War. As the Massachusetts statesman, Charles Sumner (1811–1874), reported while arguing for the admission of Kansas to the Union as a free state in June of 1860: "In the Free States the Sunday-school libraries are 1,713, and contain 474,241 volumes; in the Slave States they are 275, and contain 68,080 volumes" (Sumner 1872, p. 42).

After America became fractured by the Civil War, the effects of the Sunday school movement reached the battle lines. Among the many male Sunday school teachers to enlist in the service of their country was an Ohio Baptist, Thomas Shaw, who fought for the Union Army. Called "one of the most pious and devoted [of] Christians" by the memoirist Rev. James B. Rogers, Shaw, "as a poor young man, an orphan," … "was greatly loved for his simple, fervent piety. He was a devoted and faithful Sunday School teacher" and "his influence in the regiment was most blessed. He had more spiritual power over the men than almost any chaplain; held prayer-meetings and exhorted his fellow soldiers to come to Jesus and follow him." Noting Shaw's death on the battlefield, Rogers added that "among both officers and men there is the savor of the true Christian salt. The fact may encourage those who…have mourned over the ungodliness that too much prevails in the patriot army" (Rogers 1863, p. 242). In his *Army Life in a Black Regiment*, Thomas Wentworth Higginson also attested to the dedication on the part of many soldiers to provide education among the Negro troops, noting in one entry: "This afternoon our good quartermaster establishes a Sunday-school for our little colony of [black] 'contrabands,' now numbering seventy" (Higginson 1870, p. 119).

Although the Sunday school movement had reached its zenith by the 1840s, its after-effects reverberated throughout the remainder of the nineteenth century and into the twentieth. Noting the power of organized morals-based education to instill "the democratic sentiment" of compassion in even the youngest future citizens, the Pennsylvania congressman William D. Kelley (1814–1890), a Quaker, stated in a speech before the House of Representatives in 1863, "Once in seven days comes the Sabbath; and from hillside and valley, from the lanes and alleys, as well as from the broad streets of the city, the children gather in the church and Sunday School: there they learn that Christianity enforces while it refines … ; thus the religious sentiment adds its great power to the political" (Kelley 1863, p. 24).

BIBLIOGRAPHY

Brown, Arlo Ayres, *A History of Religious Education in Recent Times.* New York, NY: Abingdon Press, 1901.

Campbell, Alexander. *Christian Baptist*, January 1827.

Daily National Intelligencer (Washington, DC), November 26, 1817.

Garnett, James M. "Address to a Sunday School in Essex County, Virginia, on Distributing Bibles to the Scholars." *Maryland Gazette and Political Intelligencer*, Issue 28, July 12, 1821.

Higginson, Thomas Wentworth. *Army Life in a Black Regiment.* Boston, MA: Fields, Osgood & Co., 1870.

Kelley, William Darrah. *The Conscription. Also Speeches of the Hon. W. D. Kelley of Pennsylvania, in the House of Representatives.* Philadelphia, PA: privately printed, 1863.

Laqueur, Thomas Walter. *Religion and Respectability: Sunday Schools and Working Class Culture.* New Haven, CT: Yale University Press, 1976.

Rice, Edwin Wilbur. *The Sunday School Movement 1780–1917, and the American Sunday-School Union.* New York, NY: Arno Press, 1971.

Rogers, Rev. James B. *War Pictures: Experiences and Observations of a Chaplain in the U.S. Army, in the War of the Southern Rebellion.* Chicago: Church & Goodman, 1863.

Sumner, Charles. *Works of Charles Sumner*, vol. 5. Boston, MA: Lee & Shepard, 1872.

Trumbull, Henry Clay. *The Sunday-School: Its Origins, Mission, Methods, and Auxiliaries.* Philadelphia, John D. Wattles, 1888.

Vermont Watchman and State Gazette (Montpelier, VT), issue 1102, December 4, 1827.

Pamela L. Kester

■ Religion and Reform

During the Civil War, the nation's religious community was not immune from involvement in the political conflict between North and South. Clergymen associated their side's cause with divine providence and guidance. Proslavery and antislavery ministers alike infused their sermons with political sentiment. According to *The Liberator,*

> [t]he religion of a country should be its most active and vigorous helper in the renunciation of evil-doing and the commencement of practical reform. As far as the vice of slaveholding is concerned, our readers are aware that the churches of our popular religion have been its main bulwark;

not only doing nothing to overthrow it, but holding active complicity with it, and placing active obstruction in the way of those who *would* overthrow it. ("Present Relation of the Presbyterian Church to Slavery," November 1, 1861, p. 174)

Reverend Samuel Johnson of Lynn, Massachusetts, acknowledged such complacency on the church's part during an 1863 sermon:

[The] Christ of American civilization is the slave. Only through his emancipation can she [the country] be restored. The Church has proved apostate, shrinking from the duty of the hour. . . . Hatred of the negro in the North is more cruel than slavery in the South. It alone stands between us and the suppression of the rebellion to-day. We must be bruised more and more severely by the mill-stone of God's retributive justice, until this vice is eradicated. ("A Sermon for the Present Hour," *The Liberator*, May 1, 1863, p. 70)

Sermons that advocated slavery and secession provided support for the assertion that the church has been slavery's "main bulwark": "How eloquent and earnest men become—and the ministers of religion too—when pleading for 'slavery' in the name of 'liberty,' and braving all the miseries of war for its sake" (Stanton 1864, p. 158). For example, during a sermon the Reverend James H. Thornwell "urged the whole doctrine of secession on the ground of constitutional right, the alleged encroachment upon slavery being given as the justifying cause" (Stanton 1864, p. 156). Reverend Thornwell believed that the South had received the greatest of endorsements, but that for the sake of "the institution," it might have to "meet the horrors of war and carnage": "Even though our cause be just, and our course approved of Heaven," he declared, "our path to victory may be through a baptism of blood. Liberty has its martyrs and confessors, as well as religion" (Stanton 1864, p. 157).

Rather than advocating the abolition of slavery, Southern religious organizations urged followers to lobby for the transformation of the institution to make it more humane and "Christian." For example, a "Pastoral Letter from the Bishops of the Protestant Episcopal Church, to the Clergy and Laity of the Church of the Confederate States of America" expressed the belief that the Church had a duty to lobby lawmakers of the Confederacy to change the "system of labor" so as to preserve familial relationships. The Pastoral Letter stated in part:

It is likewise the duty of the Church to press upon the masters of the country their obligation, as Christian men, so to arrange this institution (slavery) as not to necessitate the violation of those sacred relations which God has created, and which man cannot, consistently with Christian duty, annul. The systems of labor which prevail in Europe, and which are, in many respects, more severe than ours, are so arranged as to prevent all necessity for the separation of parents and children, and of husbands and wives; and a very little care upon our part would rid the system, upon which we are about to plant our national life, of these unchristian features. (Stanton 1864, p. 181)

In the North, there were some churches that supported the more drastic measure of abolition. For instance, the Synod at Allegheny, Pennsylvania, selected a committee of six to travel to Washington "for the purpose of pressing upon the attention of the President and his Cabinet, as well as upon other officers of the Government, the duty and necessity of taking immediate steps to put away our national sins, that we may be restored to the favor of God" ("Present Relation of the Presbyterian Church to Slavery," *The Liberator*, November 1, 1861, p. 174).

After the Civil War began, Southern religious organizations were restructured to reflect geographical and political alliances. For example,

The leading ministers, and other influential men in the respective Churches of all denominations, at the earliest moment, brought all the religious bodies of the South to break their connection with those of the North—that is, with those religious organizations which hitherto were co-extensive with the Union—[and] changed their formularies of Church Polity, their Prayer-Books, and Directories for worship, so as to give in their adhesion to the Government set up by the rebels, and thus recognize it as a lawfully established Civil Power (Stanton 1864, p. 177)

In addition, "the words 'United States of America' were blotted out, and the words 'Confederate States of America' took their places, in the Liturgies, Prayers, and Standards of Faith, of every Church in the rebel dominions" (Stanton 1864, p. 177).

Southern churches also issued addresses and resolutions directed at members of their own organizations and the Christian world at large. These addresses outlined organizational changes and expressed the organizations' allegiance to the Confederate cause. For example, in one address, the Presbyterian Church in the Confederate States of America "renounced the jurisdiction of [the General Assembly of the Presbyterian Church in the Unites States of America,] and dissolved the ties which bound them ecclesiastically with their brethren of the North" (Stanton 1864, p. 179).

A pastoral letter from the Protestant Episcopal Church of the Confederate States of America stated that it had been "[f]orced by the Providence of God to separate . . . from the Protestant Episcopal Church in the United States . . . at a moment when civil strife had dipped its foot in blood, and cruel war was desolating our homes and firesides" (Stanton 1864, p. 180). The Church believed "with a wonderful unanimity, that the providence of God had guided our footsteps, and for His own inscrutable purposes had forced us into a separate organization" (Stanton 1864, p. 181). It also expressed solidarity with its secular neighbors: "In our case, we go forward with the leading minds of our new Republic cheering us on by their communion with us, and with no prejudications to overcome, save those which arise from a lack of acquaintance with our doctrine and worship" (p. 181). The pastoral letter also informed followers that the prayer book was unaltered, except "where a change of our Civil Government and the formation of a new nation have made alteration essentially requisite" (p. 181).

Religious organizations also involved themselves more formally in social and political movements, such as the temperance movement.

The Temperance Movement

Temperance advocates encouraged their fellow Americans to reduce the amount of alcohol they consumed. Many favored the absolute prohibition of the sale and consumption of alcohol, because they believed that alcohol caused people to behave in immoral ways. Social reformer Margaret Chappellsmith stated an understanding of temperance that was embraced by most within the movement:

> What is duty? It is a natural obligation to so rule our lives and actions, that we may contribute to the production of the greatest amount of happiness of the greatest number of human beings. This requires us to have a regard for what is good for ourselves, as well as for others; it includes regard for truth, justice, kindness, love, and that temperance in all our habits that experience proves to be necessary to mental and bodily health. ("Can Atheism Abrogate Duty?" *Boston Investigator*, May 15, 1861)

Churches and religious organizations were quite active in the temperance movement. In fact, according to the *Vermont Chronicle*:

> The church as a body has done more to promote [the temperance movement] than all other organizations. While men out of the church have done nobly, the members of the church so far as we have known, and we have been careful observers for forty years, have been the main pillars of the movement. All our Congregational churches, (and we presume that the same is true of Methodist and Baptist churches,) are temperance organizations. … Neither temperance nor any other moral movement ever has or ever can succeed in this world without the aid of the church and its ministers. ("Forcing the Law," February 6, 1864, p. 4)

However, not all clergymen felt that churches should engage in social reform. In an article focusing on the Reverend Dr. Blagden, the *Boston Daily Advertiser* declared that

in endeavoring to reform men, we must adopt the doctrine of total depravity, and so begin at the origin of all evil, the human heart, instead of being satisfied with mere outward reform. The contrary course had been the great mistake of many churches, and one against which he [Blagden] had frequently warned his people. He spoke of the temperance and anti-slavery reforms as examples, saying that those who take it upon themselves to make any act a sin, which is not of necessity a crime, were wise beyond what is written. This practice tends to make men too censorious, and to do more harm than good. ("Sermon of Dr. Blagden," September 30, 1861)

Many churches established temperance societies, which hosted lectures on temperance and engaged in other activities to encourage temperance in society. For example, the Father Mathew Temperance Society was established in Massachusetts, while the Sons of Temperance Society was quite active in New York. The American Temperance Union met at churches, including ones in New York. Religious organizations, such as the United States Christian Commission (USCC), also distributed temperance pamphlets. By January of 1863, the USCC had distributed 300,000 temperance documents (*North American and United States Gazette*, January 30, 1863).

The proponents of temperance did more than meet among themselves and talk about the evils of alcohol. Their battle extended from churches and lecture halls to the halls of justice and lawmaking. In 1861 a meeting was scheduled in San Francisco's Mission Baptist Church regarding establishing a temperance party. Notice was published in the San Francisco *Daily Evening Bulletin*, and an invitation was extended to "[a]ll persons, irrespective of sect in religion or party in politics, who are in favor of promoting to public office moral men, and such men as totally abstain from the manufacture, sale and use of all intoxicating liquors as a beverage" ("Movement toward a Temperance Party," May 6, 1861).

Members of the temperance movement were often successful in their missions, resulting in temperance laws throughout the country. Both Massachusetts and Vermont, for example, had temperance laws. "Where the liquor law has been thoroughly successful," declared Judge Marston, district attorney for Vermont's Cape District, "it has resulted in increase in order, in strengthening the law in the estimation of its friends and the friends of quiet, and making delinquents feel there was really a power in it" ("Massachusetts Temperance Law," *Vermont Chronicle*, February 25, 1865, p. 4).

The *Vermont Chronicle* likewise extolled the virtues of Vermont's temperance law:

> [W]hile our excellent Temperance Law may not entirely prevent the sale of intoxicating drinks as a beverage, by wicked men, for the love of gain, yet we believe such sales are greatly circumscribed by

its salutary terror over evil doers; and we have the fullest confidence in this legal agent, in the hands of a virtuous people, as fully equal when properly enforced, to the great work of reform. ("Local and State Matters: Addison County Temperance Society," March 18, 1865, p. 8).

BIBLIOGRAPHY

"Can Atheism Abrogate Duty?" *Boston Investigator*, May 15, 1861.

"Forcing the Law." *Vermont Chronicle*, February 6, 1864, p. 4.

"Local and State Matters: Addison County Temperance Society." *Vermont Chronicle*, March 18, 1865, p. 8.

"Massachusetts Temperance Law." *Vermont Chronicle*, February 25, 1865, p. 4.

"Movement toward a Temperance Party." *San Francisco Daily Evening Bulletin*, May 6, 1861.

North American and United States Gazette, Friday, January 30, 1863.

"Present Relation of the Presbyterian Church to Slavery." *The Liberator*, November 1, 1861, p. 174.

"A Sermon for the Present Hour." *The Liberator*, May 1, 1863, p. 70.

"Sermon of Dr. Blagden." *Boston Daily Advertiser*, September 30, 1861.

Stanton, Robert Livingston. *The Church and the Rebellion: A Consideration of the Rebellion against the Government of the United States; and the Agency of the Church, North and South, in Relation Thereto.* New York: Derby & Miller, 1864.

Jodi M. Savage

■ Religion and Slavery

From the beginning of the Atlantic slave trade, Western nations used religious doctrine to justify the enslavement of Africans. Although the bodies of the slaves were suffering, their souls were saved through conversion to Christianity. At the time of the Civil War, religion was still used to rationalize slavery, but it was also used by abolitionists to oppose the institution, and by the slaves themselves to resist bondage.

Christianizing Slaves

Converting slaves to Christianity involved educating slaves to some degree, but the abolitionist movement made Southern slaveholders question the wisdom of instructing slaves. On the one hand, the fear that abolitionist literature would incite slave rebellions had a chilling effect on any effort to educate slaves: The distribution of abolitionist literature in the South aroused a distrust of all missionaries coming into the region to promote religion. On the other hand, abolitionist arguments against slavery challenged proslavery apologists to push slave evangelization: If slavery was to be defended as a positive good, the slaves had to be converted to Christianity and master-slave relations had to be conducted along biblical lines. Schisms over the question of slavery resulted in the formation of the Methodist Episcopal Church, South in 1844 and the Southern Baptist Convention in 1845. The divisions, which relieved some of the anxiety among slaveholders that churches were sympathetic to abolitionism, also created greater urgency among Southern churches to convert the slaves.

The division also fostered the development of a proslavery analysis of the Bible, particularly in the Old Southwest. Preachers in Mississippi and Alabama began in the 1850s to perfect a proslavery religious argument. Samuel Baldwin of Mississippi argued that Adam's fall negated all human rights. God occasionally chose to return a few of these rights, but He withheld some as a curse on certain men and their descendants. Baldwin insisted that God cursed Ham and his offspring to eternal servitude, and that slavery was, as a consequence, an important feature of God's plan (Bailey 1985, pp. 79–80). Other slavery apologists cited the numerous biblical passages, particularly in the Old Testament, that discuss slavery and give little support to the belief that God was an abolitionist. Whereas abolitionists contended that the New Testament contains Christ's repudiation of slavery, supporters of slavery argued that the relationship of master and slave was sanctioned by God. Emancipation, therefore, was contrary to God's will.

Proslavery religious activists also argued that Christianity benefited slaves as well as masters. They contended that Christianity would regularize and pacify relations between slaves and masters. To achieve this end, plantation missionaries attempted to convince masters that they had duties toward their slaves. Masters and, particularly, mistresses, were urged to take an active part in catechizing slaves by reading sermons to them, including them in family prayers, and teaching them in Sabbath schools. Religion had to influence the owner's physical as well as spiritual treatment of his slaves. This ideal picture of a Christianized master-slave relationship contributed to the Southern myth of the benevolent planter-patriarch presiding benignly over his happy flock of slaves.

But slaves provided numerous accounts that depict devoutly religious masters as being the most difficult of owners. In testimony in 1863 before the American Freedman's Inquiry Commission, the former slave Mrs. Joseph Smith explained why she thought Christian slaveholders made the worst masters:

> Well, it is something like this—the Christians will oppress you more. For instance, the biggest dinner must be got on Sunday. Now, everybody that has got common sense knows that Sunday is a day of rest. And if you do the least thing in the world that they don't like, they will mark it down against you, and Monday you have got to take a

whipping. Now the card-player and horse-racer won't be there to trouble you. They will eat their breakfast in the morning and feed their dogs, and then be off, and you won't see them again till night. I would rather be with a card-player or sportsman, by half, than a Christian. (Raboteau 2004, p. 166)

Isaac Throgmorton, testifying before the same commission, recalled,

I believe the people that were not religious treated their slaves better than those who were religious. A religious man will believe whatever the overseer says, and he has control of the hands in the field.... If he says, "John has acted impudent," the master will come round and say, "Chastise him for it," and the overseer will give him two or three hundred lashes.... Then, in the next place, they don't feed nor clothe their slaves as well as irreligious man. (Raboteau 2004, p. 166)

Slaveholders who practiced the Christian principles of thrift and careful management spent less money on slaves and disciplined them more quickly. A Northern white journalist, Charles Nordhoff, made the same discovery when he reported his conversations with South Carolina slaves in 1863. Nordhoff wrote,

I find the testimony universal, that the masters were "mean." Now there was one Fripps, a planter on one of the islands, of whom the blacks habitually speak as "good Mr. Fripps." "Come now, Sam," said the questioner, "there was good Mr. Fripps, he could not have been mean." "Yes, sah, he bad to his people same as any of 'em." "Why do you call him 'good Mr. Fripps,' then?" "Oh!" said Sam, "dat no tell he good to we; call him good 'cause he good Metodis' man—he sing and pray loud on Sundays." (Raboteau 2004, pp. 167–168)

It is not clear how many African Americans were Christian during the time of the Civil War. Undoubtedly, many slaves learned the tenets of Christianity, accepted them, and attended church, without actually appearing on the official rolls of any church. By 1860 the black membership of the Baptist Church is estimated to have been 600,000, but church membership figures are not known for their accuracy. By the start of the war, Christianity pervaded the slave community. The vast majority of slaves were American-born, and the cultural and linguistic barriers that had impeded the evangelization of earlier generations of slaves was no longer a problem. The doctrines, symbols, and vision of life preached by Christianity were familiar to most blacks.

Slave Worship

Slave preachers were common in the South, despite periodic attempts by whites to suppress them. Although many slaves were encouraged to attend white churches, they often felt inhibited by the presence of whites. Sarah Fitzpatrick, once a slave in Alabama, recalled,

Niggers commence ta wanna go to church by de'selves, even ef dey had to meet in de white church. So white folks have deir service in de mornin' an' Niggers have deirs in de evenin', a'ter dey clean up, wash de dishes, an' look a'ter ever'-thing.... Ya' see Niggers lack ta shout a whole lot an' wid de white folks al' round em, dey couldn't shout jes' lack dey want to. (Raboteau 2004, p. 226)

Another former slave, Robert Anderson, recalled, "We would gather out in the open on summer nights, gather around a big bonfire, to keep the mosquitoes away, and listen to our preachers preach sometimes half the night" (Raboteau 2004, p. 221).

Religious interpretations by slaves, which sometimes were limited by the prohibition on slave literacy, focused not merely on the attainment of spiritual freedom but also on the attainment of physical freedom. Traditional African religions had a distinctly nonmessianic cast, emphasized community and fidelity to tradition as a means of fulfillment, and promoted the long view on immediate issues of social justice. To Africans, time was cyclical. Accordingly, slave clergy preached an eventual reversal of fortune, conveying the message that in time, the bottom rail would be on top. Imbued with African sensibility, slave preachers constructed a universe that was morally self-correcting, one in which justice would be restored and imbalances of power reversed over the vast stretch of time.

Traditional attempts to catechize slaves had been unsuccessful, for the most part because whites tried to persuade blacks to accept alien ritual, worship, and theology. When evangelical whites invited blacks to participate in worship through singing, praying, and preaching in ways similar to African traditions, more blacks were prompted to become Christians. Slave preachers also promoted an African style of worship. Robert Anderson remembered of his slave community, "There would be singing and testifying and shouting" (Raboteau 2004, p. 221). Mose Hursey, a freed man, remembered,

On Sundays they had meetin', sometimes at our house, sometime at 'nother house.... They'd preach and pray and sing—shout too. I heard them git up with a powerful force of the spirit, clappin' they hands and walkin' round the place. They'd shout, "I got the glory. I got that old time 'ligion in my heart." I seen some powerful 'figurations of the spirit in them days. (Raboteau 2004, p. 221)

Whites often observed slave religious meetings. Mary Boykin Chesnut reported on one gathering in her diary in the 1860s: "The Negroes sobbed and shouted and swayed backward and forward, some with aprons to their eyes, most of them clapping their hands and responding in shrill tones, 'Yes, God!' 'Jesus!'

'Savior!' 'Bless de Lord, amen,' etc. It was a little too exciting for me. I would very much have liked to shout too" (Raboteau 2004, p. 221). Some whites found the black style of worship to be humorous, but just as many apparently found them as affecting as Chesnut did.

Spirituals were an integral part of slave worship. Drawing from the Bible, Protestant hymns, sermons, and African styles of singing, slaves fashioned a religious music of their own. Spirituals were communal songs that were performed with hand-clapping, foot-stamping, head-shaking excitement. They were sung as prayer meetings for full effect. Harris Barrett, writing after slavery had ended, recalled,

> Those who have never heard these songs in their native setting can have no conception of the influence they exert upon the people. I have sat in a gathering where everything was as quiet and placid as a lake on a summer day, where the preacher strove in vain to awaken an interest; I have heard a brother or sister start one of these spirituals, slowly and monotonously; I have seen the congregation irresistible drawn to take up the refrain; I have seen the entire body gradually worked up from one degree of emotion to another until, like a turbulent, angry sea, men and women, to the accompaniment of the singing, and with shouting, moaning, and clapping of hands, surged and swayed to and fro. I have seen men and women at these times look and express themselves as if they were conversing with their Lord and Master, with their hands in His.... (Raboteau 2004, p. 244)

Not all slaves cared about religion. Some complained that they were too tired from a week of work to participate in services. The former slave Margaret Nickerson recalled, "On Sunday after working' hard all de week dey would lay down to sleep and be so tired; soon ez yo' sleep, de overseer would come an' wake you up 'an make you go to church" (Raboteau 2004, p. 225). Other African Americans spent Sundays in the same activities as nonreligious whites: hunting, fishing, marble shooting, storytelling, and resting. Sunday also served as market day for those slaves who were allotted individual plots to produce vegetables or poultry for their own use.

The clash between religion and slavery continued after the conclusion of the Civil War. Freedmen's aid societies were private charitable associations active during the Civil War and the immediate postwar years that provided both short-term welfare and educational opportunities for ex-slaves. By 1867 the societies were under attack for welfare paternalism that promoted negative views of the freedmen. When the American Missionary Association tried to induce the American Freedmen's and Union Commission to combine evangelicalism with teaching duties, the freedmen's commission collapsed in 1869, a casualty of religious controversy.

BIBLIOGRAPHY

Bailey, David T. *Shadow on the Church: Southwestern Evangelical Religion and the Issue of Slavery, 1783–1860*. Ithaca, NY: Cornell University Press, 1985.

Davis, David Brion. *In the Image of God: Religion, Moral Values, and Our Heritage of Slavery*. New Haven, CT: Yale University Press, 2001.

Genovese, Eugene D. *Roll, Jordan, Roll: The World the Slaves Made*. New York: Vintage, 1976.

Mathews, Donald G. "Religion and Slavery—The Case of the American South." In *Anti-Slavery, Religion, and Reform: Essays in Memory of Roger Anstey*, ed. Christine Bolt and Seymour Drescher. Hamden, CT: Archon, 1980.

Owens, Leslie Howard. *This Species of Property: Slave Life and Culture in the Old South*. New York: Oxford University Press, 1976.

Raboteau, Albert J. *Slave Religion: The "Invisible Institution" in the Antebellum South*. New York: Oxford University Press, 2004.

Caryn E. Neumann

■ Abolitionism

The objectives of the abolition movement of the nineteenth century in the United States were the ending of enslavement on the basis of race and the securing of social justice. Before the American colonies declared their independence from Great Britain in 1776, however, there had been a small but potent antislavery crusade to end the Atlantic slave trade as well as to eliminate the institution of slavery itself. This campaign was part of a larger struggle in the Atlantic world. As a result of these efforts, the system of human bondage that had existed throughout the British, Dutch, French, Portuguese, and Spanish empires in the Western Hemisphere since the 1740s had slowly disappeared by the late 1780s. Most of these efforts, however, remained relatively isolated and muted until well into the early 1790s. It was not until the early antebellum years that the call for the immediate end to slavery gained broader support and overshadowed many of the various other social reform movements in the United States. The prominence of the antislavery campaign led at least in part to the coming of the Civil War.

Early Abolitionism

As soon as slavery had been imported into the American colonies, Africans and African Americans tried to free themselves from bondage through such activities as court actions, self-purchases, and running away. For instance, Venture Smith (1729–1805), an enslaved African from Anamaboe, Guinea, successfully purchased his

THE ANTISLAVERY MOVEMENT

The outset abolitionism in America during the Civil War, whether led by either African Americans or white Americans, consisted of two movements distinguished by geography and chronology. The first movement began in the South. It was led mostly by enslaved persons of color but involved some free black Americans and a few sympathetic Caucasians. Active in the eighteenth century, before the American Revolution, these antislavery advocates and their organizations merely sought to free persons in bondage but did not seek to destroy the entire system. In essence, however, this first phase of the antislavery movement and the activities that followed contributed to the elimination of slavery in the North during and soon after the American Revolution.

The second wave of the antislavery movement of the American Civil War, which occurred during the antebellum period, was based primarily in the North. In these states, Caucasian involvement and control was enormous because Caucasians led most of the larger antislavery organizations above the Mason-Dixon Line; however, many black Americans used their personal narratives and life experiences to influence the entire movement. For example, Frederick Douglass (1818–1895) escaped from enslavement in Maryland and became a powerful orator, abolitionist, and political activist throughout the rest of his adult life. His third autobiography, *The Life and Times of Frederick Douglass*, written in 1881 and revised in 1892, spoke volumes when it described the harshness, brutality, and horror acts associated with the inhumanity of slavery.

ERIC R. JACKSON

BIBLIOGRAPHY

Douglass, Frederick. *The Life and Times of Frederick Douglass*. New York: Collier Books, 1962 [1892].

Harrold, Stanley. *American Abolitionists*. New York: Longman, 2001.

freedom from his Connecticut owner in 1765. More rarely—an action that had a greater psychological, emotional, and physical impact—some enslaved persons began to resort to overt rebellion to gain their freedom. One of the first recorded cases occurred in 1676, when some eighty Africans joined the white rebel Nathaniel Bacon's failed campaign to overthrow the ruling class of gentry in colonial Virginia (Aptheker 1993, p. 37). Several decades later, in 1712, another incident occurred when thirty enslaved Africans, along with several Native Americans and a group of white indentured servants, participated in a sporadic rebellion in New York City that led to the burning of several buildings and the death of at least nine innocent people (Aptheker 1963, p. 173). Finally, in 1739, approximately one hundred fugitives in rural South Carolina armed themselves with

guns, knives, and sticks, and started a revolt to obtain their freedom. These African rebels began to march south toward the Spanish settlement of St. Augustine, Florida, but were quickly headed off before they could attract a larger following (Wood 2000, p. 96). Despite the lack of success of most slave insurrections, some white Americans began to argue that slavery should be done away with immediately.

One of the first groups of antislavery whites that emerged was the Society of Friends, commonly known as the Quakers. Labeled as religious dissenters and thus persecuted during their early years in Great Britain, a small group of Quakers first arrived in New Jersey during the 1670s. In 1681 William Penn (1644–1718), himself a member of the Society, established the colony of Pennsylvania for them. Many Quakers settled in other American colonies and became slaveholders; however, others believed that the Christian faith required them to teach that God loves all human beings, that people should not go to war with one another, and that slaves who had received Christian baptism should be free according to civil law (Nash 1988, p. 17). A few Quakers even believed that God would punish all people who held slaves in any capacity. Such a stance led to members of the Society of Friends in Germantown, Pennsylvania, adopting a resolution in early 1688 that declared slavery evil, and immoral, and contrary to their Christian faith. Several years later, in 1693, a Philadelphia Quaker named George Keith (1638–1716) echoed similar sentiments in a´ publication titled "An Exhortation and Caution to Friends Concerning Buying and Keeping of Negroes" (Aptheker 1993, p. 74).

During the 1730s, Benjamin Lay, who had lived in Barbados for several years and owned a number of enslaved Africans, moved to Pennsylvania and quickly joined the local antislavery movement. Here he was befriended by Anthony Bénézet (1713–1784), a French immigrant who had become a Quaker in 1727, and Benjamin Franklin (1706–1790), already well known as a journalist and inventor. It was Bénézet, along with John Woolman (1720–1772), an itinerant preacher, who dominated the Quaker antislavery movement from the 1740s through the 1760s. Woolman traveled primarily throughout New Jersey, Maryland, Virginia, and into the New England colonies in order to spread his antislavery message, while Bénézet became a proliferate antislavery writer who fiercely denounced slavery in many of his publications, such as *A Short Account of that Part of Africa Inhabited by the Negroes* (1762) and *A Caution and Warning to Great Britain and her Colonies* (1767). Most importantly, most of Bénézet's essays and articles rested on the notion that African Americans were not an inferior race (Aptheker 1993, p. 79). A schoolmaster for many years, Bénézet held night classes for black slaves in the Philadelphia area from 1750 onward and started a school for black children in 1770.

Abolitionism during the Revolutionary Era

It took a major religious, economic, and ideological upheaval during the late eighteenth century to transform the assault on human bondage from an African American- and Quaker-led struggle to a widely held assumption that all people deserve to be free. Among the various important developments that led to this change was the spread of such powerful social and intellectual movements as evangelicalism, revivalism, rationalism, and political revolution.

In contrast to the more traditional forms of religious doctrine that had dominated earlier decades throughout the American colonies, the widespread religious movement known as the Great Awakening, which took place during the early and mid-eighteenth century, began to weaken some forms of church organization, de-emphasize some traditional religious rituals, and stress the belief that all who had faith in God, despite differences of race, class, and gender, could gain salvation and everlasting life through a personal and intimate relationship with the Creator. This religious trend enabled George Whitefield (1714–1770), Samuel Davis, Gilbert Tennent (1703–1764), Isaac Backus (1724–1806), and other evangelical leaders to establish a movement that was "nothing short of guerilla warfare"

(Hatch 1989, p. 34). In other words, these "new" religious leaders were using a more earthy language, everyday reasoning, and a commonsense approach to appeal to regular people in ways in which the previously established church-leaders could not counter.

Simultaneously, rationalist tendencies in philosophy, which emerged from the European intellectual movement known as the Enlightenment, began to dominate political thought in the American colonies. Influenced by such individuals as the physicist Isaac Newton (1643–1727) and the political philosophers Francis Bacon (1561–1626), David Hume (1711–1766), and John Locke (1632–1704), some American colonists began to argue that there must be natural laws to assist human beings in ordering a society. It was the American Revolution, however, that fused these various intellectual movements into a broader socioeconomic and political campaign that transformed abolitionism from a struggle led primarily by Quakers and African Americans to a more broadly based movement. The American Revolution helped to spread the notion that natural rights, equality, and liberty apply to all people (Frey 1991, p. 45).

Rise of Immediate Abolitionism

The aggressive proslavery arguments that began to circulate in the South during the late 1790s helped in part to create an atmosphere in which a more integrated, vocal, comprehensive, and militant Northern assault on slavery could take shape during the late 1820s and early 1830s. Another important factor was the activities and ultimate objectives of the American Colonization Society (ACS). Formed in 1816 by a group of prominent white Virginians, most members of the ACS wanted to resettle free blacks in what is now Liberia without challenging the idea of individual property rights or disturbing the Southern way of life. The ACS believed that slavery was unsustainable over the long term but did not consider the integration of free blacks into American society a viable option.

As the previous generation of isolated and passive antislavery individuals and organizations faded away, however, a new cadre of African American and white abolitionists appeared and began to argue for the immediate emancipation of all enslaved persons of color from a Christian, nationwide, and self-reflective standpoint. Gradually such abolitionist figures as James G. Birney (1792–1857), Frederick Douglass (1818–1895), Lewis Hayden (1811–1889), George Julian (1817–1898), Elijah Lovejoy (1802–1837), Charles Sumner (1811–1874), and Thaddeus Stevens (1792–1868) spread their militant antislavery message to all of who would listen. By the mid-1830s, internal divisions began to appear in the movement, however, as disagreements developed over tactics, political action, the role of the church, race, and especially the participation of women.

Thaddeus Stevens (1792–1868), early antebellum abolitionist. A leading member of the early antebellum abolitionist movement, Thaddeus Stevens advocated eliminating slavery in the United States on the grounds that human bondage was against Christian teachings. *The Library of Congress.*

Abolitionism and Gender

The role of gender in the abolition movement was both powerful and complex. More specifically, immediate abolitionism during the 1830s led to the origins of the early women's rights movement that began with the Seneca Falls, New York, meeting in 1848. Once the two movements were linked, women participated in almost every aspect of the abolition crusade from political action to the formation of local organizations to working with fugitive slaves. Women were not only welcomed as participants by male abolitionists, but they were also encouraged to challenge wider societal norms regarding the role of women. For example, while Elizabeth Chandler (1807–1834), a white woman from Delaware, wrote a monthly column for Benjamin Lundy's antislavery newspaper, the *Genius of Universal Emancipation*, and helped to organize women's antislavery groups in Pennsylvania and Michigan, Maria W. Stewart (1803–1879), an African American widow from Boston, traveled to several East Coast cities to encourage all women who would listen to her to strive for both gender and racial equality. Despite the various activities and powerful speeches of many women such as Chandler and Stewart, most female abolitionists occupied separate and subordinate positions in the antislavery movement compared to their male counterparts.

Race and Abolitionism

When the American Anti-Slavery Society (AASS) was established in 1833, its leaders announced five main goals: 1) an immediate end to slavery; 2) to constitute the AASS as an interracial organization; 3) to strive for racial equality for all African Americans; 4) to reject any plan to end slavery based on colonization; and 5) to reject violence as a tactic to be used to end slavery. What black and white abolitionists, both men and women, meant when they agreed to these objectives were not necessarily the same, however. For instance, a precursor to the rise of the immediate abolition movement was the effort of some individuals to send black Americans as colonists to West Africa, Haiti, and other locations outside the United States mainland. During the early 1800s, when white supremacy and racial intolerance became were intense throughout the United States, some African American abolitionists, such as Bishop Henry McNeal Turner (1834–1915) and Martin Delany (1812–1885), found the prospect of migrating to another country very appealing. They maintained that African Americans should consider emigrating to Latin America or the Caribbean Islands (Painter 1988, p. 155). As a result of these discussions, most black abolitionists had to make an individual decision on the merits of any colonization plan or idea.

In the area of interracial cooperation, despite their great efforts, most white abolitionists never overcame their racial and cultural biases. White abolitionists could easily oppose the system of human bondage, but to embrace the entire African American community as an equal partner was a different matter. Many white abolitionists tended to associate only with those black American abolitionists whom they deemed respectable and intelligent, such as Samuel Cornish (1790–1859), Frederick Douglass, James Forten (1766–1842), Henry Highland Garnet (1815–1882), and Robert Purvis (1810–1898). Even white women abolitionists maintained this same elitist perspective when it came to their African American counterparts Thus, many black female abolitionists eventually had to establish separate antislavery facilities and organizations.

Violence and Abolitionism

As abolitionists became more aggressive and vocal during the middle of the antebellum period, the reference to violence in many antislavery speeches as well as in the some of the deeds that were carried out by various individuals gradually surfaced. More specifically, many abolitionists who had pledged nonviolence had not only begun to take part in some violent activities but also started to openly express admiration for those who used force to oppose slavery, such as Denmark Vesey (1767–1822), David Walker (1785–1830), Nat Turner (1800–1831), Augustus W. Hanson, and Henry Highland Garnet. Influenced by the Underground Railroad and other forms of resistance to the fugitive slave laws, many of the activities and the rhetoric around these actions brought many African American and white abolitionists closer together. Such an alliance reached its high point with the failed attempt by John Brown (1800–1859) to end slavery with an assault on a federal armory in Harpers Ferry, Virginia, in 1859. Yet, despite this internal dilemma and many heated debates, for the most part abolitionists remained on the side of peaceful persuasion (Harrold 2001, p. 73).

BIBLIOGRAPHY

Aptheker, Herbert. *American Negro Slave Revolts.* New York: International Publishers, 1963.

Aptheker, Herbert. *Abolitionism: A Revolutionary Movement.* Boston: Twayne Publishers, 1989.

Aptheker, Herbert. *Anti-Racism in U.S. History: The First Two Hundred Years.* Westport, CT: Praeger Publishers, 1993.

Collins, Patricia Hill. *Black Feminist Thought: Knowledge, Consciousness, and the Politics of Empowerment.* New York: Routledge, 1990.

Davis, Angela Y. *Women, Race and Class.* New York: Vintage Books, 1983.

DuBois, Ellen Carol, and Lynn Dumenil. *Through Women's Eyes: An American History with Documents.* Boston: Bedford and St. Martin's, 2005.

Frey, Sylvia R. *Water from the Rock: Black Resistance in a Revolutionary Age.* Princeton, NJ: Princeton University Press, 1991.

Harrold, Stanley. *American Abolitionists.* New York: Longman, 2001.

Hatch, Nathan O. *The Democratization of American Christianity.* New Haven, CT: Yale University Press, 1989.

Nash, Gary B. *Forging Freedom: The Formation of Philadelphia's Black Community, 1720–1840.* Cambridge, MA: Harvard University Press, 1988.

Nash, Gary B. *Race and Revolution.* Madison, WI: Madison House, 1990.

Painter, Nell Irvin. "Martin R. Delany: Elitism and Black Nationalism." In *Black Leaders of the Nineteenth Century*, ed. Leon Litwack and August Meier. Urbana: University of Illinois Press, 1988.

Ripley, C. Peter, et al., eds. *Witness for Freedom: African American Voices on Race, Slavery, and Emancipation.* Chapel Hill: University of North Carolina Press, 1993.

Wood, Peter H. *Black Majority: Negroes in Colonial South Carolina — From 1670 through the Stono Rebellion.* New York: Alfred A. Knopf, 1974.

Wood, Peter H. "Africans in Eighteenth-Century North America." In *Upon These Shores: Themes in the African American Experience—1600 to the Present*, ed. William R. Scott and William G. Shade. New York: Routledge, 2000.

Eric R. Jackson

■ The Slavery Apologists

The role of the church in the Civil War and the events leading up to it was primarily one of moral guidance. In the North, the abolitionist cause was the driving force behind the message from religious institutions and theologians. In the South, however, clergy were confronted with trying to defend slavery. While many members of the Southern clergy (some of whom were men of national distinction) privately had questions about slavery, many others did not—and in fact saw slavery as sanctioned by the Bible. For the most part, Southern ministers embraced (and often championed) the Southern cause.

Splits in the Church

The split between Northern and Southern religious leaders began well before the start of the Civil War. Slavery had been an important economic institution in the South from early colonial days, less so in the more industrialized North. Still, by the beginning of the nineteenth century a large number of Southerners in fact opposed slavery (Hudson 1987, p. 190). Faced with growing criticism by a largely Northern-based abolition movement, however, people in the Southern states felt compelled to defend themselves and to show solid justifications for keeping slaves. Economists and business leaders did this by pointing out that the agricultural South needed the labor provided by slaves. The economic argument, however, failed to address the exploitative nature of slavery. What justification, after all, did white landowners have to enslave Africans except that slavery was a source of cheap labor? The moral component of the argument fell into the hands of the clergy—and a surprisingly large number of Southern ministers offered a rational moral justification for slavery.

The Presbyterian Church divided itself into two factions—the "Old School" (which did not condemn slavery) in the South and the "New School" (staunchly antislavery) in the North. By 1838, the split between the two factions had grown so strong that there were in effect two Presbyterian churches in the United States. The Methodist Church, which had been founded in part on antislavery principles, followed suit in 1844 with the formation of the Methodist Episcopal Church, South (Boles 1994, pp. 78–79). Such other denominations as the Lutherans, Episcopalians, and Roman Catholics were affected by the slavery issue, although they did not have any formal separations until after the secession began (Hudson 1987, p. 193). This outcome was in part the result of different forms of church government; all three of these churches were organized into dioceses (or synods, in the case of the Lutherans) that were largely defined by territory; thus extreme abolitionist and proslavery views did not meet at the national level in these bodies. In the case of the Episcopalians, several Southern dioceses seceded to form the Episcopal Church, C.S.A. in 1861.

Preserving a Way of Life

The Southern clergy who accommodated slavery did so for two main reasons. The first was their loyalty to the South and to the Southern way of life. Frustrated with decades of what they saw as attacks on their morality by the abolitionist movement, many Southerners dug in their heels and became increasingly suspicious of the North. By the beginning of the Civil War, many Southerners saw themselves as morally superior to Northerners; after all, they had never tried to force their way of life onto the North. One anonymous contributor to the Richmond-based *Southern Literary Messenger*, a magazine devoted to literature and the fine arts, wrote a piece for the June 1860 issue in which the claim was made that Northerners were themselves of an inferior stock, "wild, savage, bold, fond of freedom" (p. 404) and who, despite being deeply religious, "yet nearly approach infidelity [unbelief]." Southerners, in contrast, were quiet, gentle, thoughtful, and given on occasion to "flights of genius" (p. 406).

God bless you massa! you feed and clothe us. When we are sick you nurse us, and when too old to work, you provide for us!

These poor creatures are a sacred legacy from my ancestors and while a dollar is left me, nothing shall be spared to increase their comfort and happiness.

"God bless you, massa!" Many Southern slaveholders rationalized their perceived right to own slaves by claiming that African Americans were unable to care for themselves independently. As shown in this illustration, some anti-abolitionists believed slaves actually appreciated their master's efforts and showed contentment with their bondage. *The Library of Congress*

Members of the Southern clergy, who had their own feelings of devotion toward their home states, approved the notion that a well-intentioned South was being morally condemned by a self-righteous and arrogant North. In the years leading up to the Civil War and through the war years, Southern ministers brought this concept into their pulpits, often using extreme language, such as referring to Northerners as "atheists" and "infidels" (Farmer 1999, p. 11). One of the most prominent Southern Presbyterian preachers of the time, James Henley Thornwell (1812–1862), pointedly referred to the conflict at hand as being "not merely [between] abolitionists and slaveholders—they are atheists, socialists, communists, red republicans, jacobins [the radical party in the French Revolution, responsible for the Reign of Terror of 1793–1794] on the one side, and the friends of order and regulated freedom on the other" (Farmer 1999, p. 11).

Southerners believed that their way of life was the natural, moral order, while the Northern way of life—faster-paced, more industrialized, more cosmopolitan—was an unnatural and in fact immoral way to exist (Farmer 1999, pp. 10–11).

Many Southerners compared their cause to that of the American Revolution of nearly a century earlier, and religious leaders eagerly helped popularize that notion. Moses Drury Hoge (1918–1899), once the personal minister to Jefferson Davis, noted that those who praised the colonial soldiers of the American Revolution and those who praised the Confederate soldiers did "homage to virtue."(Wilson 1980, p. 40). In his famous thanksgiving sermon in New Orleans in November 1860, the Presbyterian minister Benjamin Morgan Palmer (1818–1902) stated bluntly, "I throw off the yoke of this union as readily as did our ancestors the yoke of King George III, and for causes immeasurably stronger than those pleaded in their celebrated declaration" (Palmer 1860, p. 14).

A Duty to Protect Slaves

A second and, to the clergy who espoused it, more compelling argument in favor of slavery is that they believed slaves benefited from the system that controlled their lives. This belief arose primarily from the widespread conviction that slaves could not take care of themselves if left to their own devices. Some felt that slaves would be too frightened and confused to be able to make a living for themselves. Others felt that slaves were too irresponsible to try to live on their own. Maintaining slavery, many Southerners believed, was doing the slaves a favor.

Interestingly, many white preachers made it a point of preaching to slave congregations; some turned their ministries exclusively to slaves. Curiously, despite their status as personal property rather than as individuals, slaves were welcomed and even encouraged to attend church services. In fact, the churches in many communities were biracial; although the slaves and their white masters did not mix with each other socially within the church, both worshipped there together (Boles 1994, p. 46).

Moreover, many prominent Southern ministers made special efforts to provide religious instruction to slaves, whether in church or on their own plantations. Such preachers as Charles Colcock Jones (1804–1863) of Liberty County, Georgia, traveled from plantation house to plantation house to preach to the slave populations there. He would travel from early morning to late evening, and he was well received by the slaves.

John Adger (1810–1899), who preached in a Presbyterian church in Charleston, South Carolina, served as a missionary in what are now Turkey and Armenia for a dozen years; he returned to the United States in 1846 and wished to return to his missionary work. His wife, however, had inherited several slaves. The American Board of Foreign Missions (specifically its Northern members) refused to send him on a new mission unless he gave up the slaves. Adger chose instead to forego his missionary work overseas and to focus closer to home,

where he could be of benefit to the slaves and their owners (White 1911, pp. 299–300).

John Lafayette Girardeau (1825–1898), the Presbyterian preacher at a small church off the coast of South Carolina, held services for both white and black parishioners and then separate services for slaves. He had been John Adger's successor in the Second Presbyterian Church of Charleston for several years. The slaves in particular enjoyed Girardeau's sermons, and he noted their enthusiasm:

> [They] pour in and throng the seats vacated by their masters—yes, crowding the building up to the pulpit. I have seen them rock to and fro under the influence of their feelings, like a wood in a storm. What singing! What hearty handshakings after the service. I have had my finger joints stripped of the skin in consequence of them (White 1911, p. 301).

Girardeau served as a Confederate chaplain during the war; after the war ended, his former slave congregants, now free men and women, implored him to "come back to preach to them as of old" (White 1911, p. 304). The enthusiasm with which slaves embraced Christianity was in part a result of their desire to find a faith that they could embrace in a new land—and that would embrace them. Because they were welcomed into the churches, they felt a sense of belonging that they felt in almost no other sphere of their existence. Moreover, in addition to their sincerity of faith, the slaves valued religion because it gave them an opportunity to communicate with their fellow slaves in a more relaxed and natural way. Those who attended churches where the slaves of several families were active had a chance as well to meet others in their unique predicament; they could have relatively normal conversations without feeling constrained by the yoke they usually wore (Boles 1994, p. 55).

When the Second Presbyterian Church of Charleston opened in 1850 to serve the slave and free black community, James Henley Thornwell delivered the dedication sermon to a crowd of both white and black congregants—a sermon that underscores how the average Southern preacher saw how slavery and religious values could coexist:

> The slave has rights, all the rights which belong essentially to humanity, and without which his nature could not be human or his conduct susceptible of praise or blame. In the enjoyment of these rights, religion demands he should be protected. The right which the master has is a right not to the *man*, but to his *labor* (White 1911, p. 298).

Extolling "our faith that the negro is one blood with us," Thornwell goes on to admit that slavery itself may not be a perfect system: "Slavery is a part of the curse which sin has introduced into the world and stands in the same general relation to Christianity as poverty, sickness, disease and death. That it is inconsistent with a perfect state—that it is not absolutely a good, a blessing—the most strenuous defender of slavery ought not to permit himself to deny" (White 1911, p. 298). In other words, Thornwell explains, slavery is simply part of the human condition that highlights human imperfections and that should make individuals work harder to tackle those imperfections.

Palmer's Thanksgiving Sermon: A Call to Unity

To many Southern ministers, slavery conferred upon slaveholders a sense of responsibility for the souls of their slaves. The master-slave relationship was frequently compared to a parent-child relationship. One of the clearest documents highlighting this and other important aspects of the complex relationship between slavery and religion is the sermon delivered by Benjamin Morgan Palmer. The sermon, entitled "The South: Her Peril, and Her Duty" was delivered as part of a thanksgiving service on November 29, 1860 at the First Presbyterian Church of New Orleans, Louisiana, where Palmer was a minister. So popular was the sermon that afterwards two separate groups from his congregation wrote to him imploring him to publish it for widespread distribution. This he did, convinced that the response he got was "sufficient proof that I have spoken to the heart of this community" (Palmer 1860, p. 2).

The sermon, which reads in part almost like the Declaration of Independence, notes that a nation "often has a character as well defined and intense as that of the individual" (Palmer 1860, p. 6). "The particular trust assigned to such a people becomes the pledge of the divine protection, and their fidelity to it determines the fate by which it is finally overtaken." he continues. Palmer then poses the question, "If the South is such a people, what, at this juncture, is their providential trust?" His answer: "[I]t is *to conserve and perpetuate the institution of slavery as now existing*" (Palmer 1860, p. 6).

Palmer continues with the practical dimension of his argument:

> Need I pause to show how this system of servitude underlies and supports our material interests? Need I pause to show how this system of servitude underlies and supports our material interests; that our wealth consists in our lands and in the serfs who till them; that from the nature of our products they can only be cultivated by labor which must be controlled in order to be certain; that any other than a tropical race must faint and wither beneath a tropical sun? (Palmer 1860, p. 8).

Then he moves on with an appeal to emotional and spiritual elements:

> Need I pause to show how this system is interwoven with our entire social fabric; that these slaves form parts of our households, even as our children; and that, too, through a relationship recognized and sanctioned in the Scriptures of

God even as the other? Must I pause to show how it has fashioned our modes of life, and determined all our habits of thought and feeling, and moulded the very type of our civilization? How then can the hand of violence be laid upon it without involving our existence? (Palmer 1860, p. 8).

Palmer also argues that the slaves are better off with slavery, in part because of their own nature: "We know better than others that every attribute of their character fits them for dependence and servitude. By nature the most affectionate and loyal of all races beneath the sun, they are also the most helpless: and no calamity can befal [*sic*] them greater than the loss of that protection they enjoy under this patriarchal system" (Palmer 1860, pp. 8–9).

Palmer then swings back to a more practical argument: that the North—and the world beyond—needs to maintain the status quo in the South just as much as the South needs it: "[The] world has grown more and more dependent on [slavery] for sustenance and wealth ... the enriching commerce ... has been largely established upon the products of our soil: and the blooms upon southern fields gathered by black hands, have fed the spindles and looms of Manchester and Birmingham not less than of Lawrence and Lowell" (Palmer 1860, pp. 9–10).

The rest of Palmer's sermon is an exhortation to stand firm against the reformers and the North—even if that means secession. The sermon, in fact, has been widely credited with giving the moral and popular push to Louisiana's decision to secede from the Union.

Message to Slaves and Slave Owners

Through the days leading up to the secession and during the war itself, Palmer and other preachers delivered the same message. Curiously, while most of them do note that the Bible sanctions slavery, they fail to give definitive proof in the way of specific passages. Rather, they note that the master-slave relationship has existed since the beginning of humanity—and, that as long as masters understand their obligation to slaves (including the provision of spiritual sustenance), the system is overall an acceptable one.

More important, from the point of view of the congregants, both black and white, is the message sent from Southern pulpits that protection was the watchword. Slaveholders were told that they must protect the system of slavery, and doing so would protect their financial interests. Slaves were told that their masters would protect them, giving them a safe home and access to their own church communities. This message was accepted gladly both by whites and a significant number of slaves. Although the support of the clergy did nothing to alter the outcome of the war, it did provide Southerners with a sense of having done the right thing. For decades afterward, veterans and civilian survivors of the war, even those who agreed that slavery was an indefensible system, commemorated the Confederacy's spirited fight for self-determination.

BIBLIOGRAPHY

Boles, John B. *The Irony of Southern Religion*. New York: Peter Lang Publishing, 1994.

"The Difference in Race between Northern and Southern People." *Southern Literary Messenger* 30, no. 6 (June 1860): 401–409.

Farmer, James O., Jr. *The Metaphysical Confederacy: James Henley Thornwell and the Synthesis of Southern Values*. Macon, GA: Mercer University Press, 1999.

Gallagher, Gary W., and Alan T. Nolan, eds. *The Myth of the Lost Cause and Civil War History*. Bloomington: Indiana University Press, 2000.

Hudson, Winthrop S. *Religion in America*. New York: Macmillan, 1987.

Johnson, Thomas Cary. *The Life and Letters of Benjamin Morgan Palmer*. Richmond, VA: Presbyterian Committee of Publication, 1911.

Palmer, Benjamin Morgan. "The South: Her Peril and Her Duty." Sermon delivered in the First Presbyterian Church, New Orleans, Louisiana, November 29, 1860. New Orleans, LA: n.p., 1860.

Stout, Harry S. *Upon the Altar of the Nation: A Moral History of the Civil War*. New York: Viking, 2006.

Stringfellow, Thornton. *Scriptural and Statistical Views in Favor of Slavery*. Richmond, VA: J. W. Randolph, 1856.

White, Henry Alexander. *Southern Presbyterian Leaders*. New York: Neale Publishing Company, 1911.

Wilson, Charles Reagan. *Baptized in Blood: The Religion of the Lost Cause, 1865–1920*. Athens: University of Georgia Press, 1980.

George A. Milite

■ Hymns

Hymns, in their purest form, are communications from believers to God. They can express praise, supplication, adoration, and a host of other positive emotions and attitudes. In human terms, they can serve as teaching tools, encourage flagging spirits, and bring comfort to the dying. As a musical form, they were an integral part of nineteenth-century culture, found not only in the churches, but also on the front pages of the nation's newspapers. Given that prominence, it is little wonder that hymns figured prominently in Civil War daily life.

During the early days of the conflict, both sides sought especially to emphasize that God was on their side. Theologians and preachers attempted to lay biblical foundations for their respective causes, and the songwriters and musicians did their part. Even poets joined the mad rush for validation. In July 1861 a Boston

"Battle Hymn of the Republic." Written in 1862, Julia Ward Howe's "Battle Hymn of the Republic" became a unifying song for the North, suggesting parallels between the suffering of Jesus Christ and the sacrifice of Union soldiers. *Written by Julia Ward Howe, variations by Louis Weber.*

newspaper published Oliver Wendell Holmes Sr.'s "Army Hymn" (sung to the tune of "Old Hundred"), which concludes with the fierce passage: "God of all Nations! Sovereign Lord / In thy dread name we draw the sword, / We lift the starry flag on high / That fills with light our stormy sky" (*New Hampshire Statesman*, July 6, 1861).

On both sides of the Mason-Dixon line, politicians, newspapermen, and other interested parties sought a national hymn that would claim God's favor, enunciate their goals, and like Holmes's work, properly threaten the enemy. With the offer of a $1,000 prize, many entries were submitted, but none took the prize. The "Star Spangled Banner" was dismissed as being too difficult to sing (*Frank Leslie's Illustrated Newspaper*, June 3, 1865). Yet, on the Union side, one hymn above all captured the spirit of the age: Julia Ward Howe's "Battle Hymn of the Republic." In it, she transformed a soldiers' simple marching tune, "John Brown's Body," into Christological justification of the Union cause by proclaiming the Union army to be an instrument of God and comparing the soldiers' sacrifices to

"HOLD THE FORT, FOR I AM COMING"

"Hold the Fort" is a hymn written shortly after the Civil War (1870) by Philip Paul Bliss (1838–1876), based on the events of a battle that took place near Atlanta, Georgia, on October 5, 1864. Bliss wrote the lyrics as well as the tunes for this and many other hymns, sometimes using the pen name "Pro Phundo Basso." Bliss's Gospel songs were very popular with Dwight L. Moody (1837–1899) and his lay missionaries in Chicago. The composer sometimes performed as a vocal soloist at Moody's revivals, with his wife as his accompanist. Husband and wife were killed in a train wreck in Ohio in 1876; Bliss was only 38.

The battle that inspired "Hold the Fort" took place on October 5, 1864, at at Allatoona Pass, a key Union supply depot at a railroad cut on the Western & Atlantic Railroad about forty miles northwest of Atlanta, Georgia. Confederate general John Bell Hood (1831–1879) saw an opportunity to cut Union General William T. Sherman's supply line by seizing the pass. A small group of Union defenders at Altoona were forced backward to a fort at the top of a hill overlooking the pass. They refused a Confederate order to surrender, even though prolonging the battle seemed hopeless. One of the Union officers then saw a signal flag from Sherman's headquarters on Kennesaw Mountain fifteen miles (24 kilometers) away. The flag conveyed the message: "Hold the fort; I am coming. W. T. Sherman." Bliss may have been thinking of the reference to Jesus as the "captain of our salvation" in Hebrews 2:10 when he compared Sherman's signal to Jesus's message of encouragement.

> Ho, my comrades, see the signal,
> Waving in the sky!
> Reinforcements now appearing,
> Victory is nigh.

Refrain
> 'Hold the fort, for I am coming,'
> Jesus signals still;
> Wave the answer back to heaven,
> 'By thy grace we will.'

> See the mighty host advancing,
> Satan leading on,
> Mighty men around us falling,
> Courage almost gone!

> (Refrain repeated)
> See the glorious banner waving,
> Hear the trumpet blow!
> In our Leader's name we'll triumph,
> Over every foe.

> (Refrain repeated)

> Fierce and long the battle rages,
> But our help is near,
> Onward comes our great Commander,
> Cheer, my comrades, cheer.

> 'Hold the fort, for I am coming,'
> Jesus signals still;
> Wave the answer back to heaven,
> 'By thy grace we will.'

REBECCA J. FREY

SOURCE: *"Hold the Fort." Public Domain Music. Available from* http://www.pdmusic.org/bliss/ppb70htf.mid.

Christ's with the line "as He died to make men holy, let us die to make men free." If it was not the national anthem, it certainly became the anthem for abolitionism. Within weeks of the song's publication, William Lloyd Garrison's *Liberator* declared, "The negro boys around Annapolis have caught the 'Army Hymn' and Old John Brown's 'Glory, Hallelujah,' from the New England soldiers. As for the latter, an Annapolis resident says, 'the negroes are clear carried away with it'" (*The Liberator*, January 10, 1862).

Though the Confederates tried, they never found a hymn to match the power of Howe's. At about the same time that the "Battle Hymn" took hold in the North, a Savannah newspaper published the lyrics to a rather tepid hymn sung to the tune of Britain's "God Save the King," which it described as being "Suitable for the Times" in the Confederacy. It went: "God of the brave and free, / Father of all, to Thee / Our voice we raise. / For all Thy blessings shown, / For deeds of mercy done, / Thy guardian care we own; / Accept our praise" (*Daily Morning News*, February 22, 1862). It was reverent, praiseful, and theologically correct; but it did not capture the imagination of many Confederates. Later in 1862 that same newspaper proclaimed "The Oath of Freedom" as the Confederate national hymn, not at all recognizing the irony. Perhaps its opening line, "Liberty is always won where there exists the unconquerable will to be free" made some Southerners uncomfortable (*Daily Morning News*, October 21, 1862).

Aside from broad characterizations of their respective causes, hymn writers wrote about anything that struck them as noteworthy, and not always successfully. One hymnist, perhaps envious of Howe's success, penned "The Battle Hymn of the West," a truly ponderous hymn, triple the length of the original "Battle Hymn" but with none of its grace (*The Dakotian*, June 3, 1862). Then there was the "Battle Hymn for Midsummer 1862," which was as unimaginative as its name (*Frank Leslie's Illustrated Newspaper*, August 23, 1862).

Civil War–era hymns also spoke to civilian life, the mundane, and the tragic. In Vermont in 1863, a newspaper published "A Hymn on the Death of a Child," and in San Francisco, "The Hymn of the Harvesters" and "Hymn to the Flowers" invoked God's blessing in a pastoral setting (*Vermont Chronicle*, March 3, 1863; *Daily Evening Bulletin*, October 15, 1862; *Daily Evening Bulletin*, November 20, 1863). Some hymns were written for the National Day of Fasting, others commemorated the national feast of Thanksgiving, and at least one letter to an editor complained that there were not enough hymns on temperance and intemperance (*Daily Cleveland Herald*, April 29, 1863, November 26, 1862; *The Congregationalist*, April 21, 1865).

The conclusion of the war inspired a flurry of new hymns. According to one newspaper, Robert E. Lee's surrender of the Army of Northern Virginia in April 1865 put the nation in a grateful mood, claiming "the people in many places gave vent to the joy and gratitude by the singing of psalms, hymns, chants, & c" (*Union and Dakotaian*, September 16, 1865). But the joy did not last long, for John Wilkes Booth (1838–1865) took Lincoln's life less than a week later, prompting an outpouring of grief that often manifested itself in hymns. One hymn called Lincoln "The people's friend—the friend of God"; another, returning to Julia Ward Howe's sacrificial theme, lamented, "His voice in clarion notes rang out / The bondsmen's Jubilee; / His name is on Freedom's tongue, / Watchword of liberty. / Thy might, O God, was in his heart; / Thy wisdom made him wise; / He lived a man—he rule a prince— / He died a sacrifice" (*The Congregationalist*, April 28, 1865).

Ultimately, hymns of the Civil War era represented people's belief in and desire to influence God, whom they believed was active in everyday affairs. When good things happened, such as a victory on the battlefield, the harvest of a bountiful crop, or even the blooming of a pretty flower, people felt it worthy of mentioning to God in song. Conversely, when things went terribly wrong, as in the death of a child, a defeat of arms, or the loss of a beloved president, people sought comfort in solemn song. Hymns, in everyday life during the Civil War, thus were like their conception of God—omnipresent.

BIBLIOGRAPHY

The Congregationalist, Boston, April 21, 1865.

The Congregationalist, Boston, April 28, 1865.

The Daily Cleveland Herald, Cleveland, OH, November 26, 1862.

The Daily Cleveland Herald, Cleveland, OH, April 29, 1863.

Daily Evening Bulletin, San Francisco, October 15, 1862.

Daily Evening Bulletin, San Francisco, November 20, 1863.

Daily Morning News, Savannah, GA, February 22, 1862.

The Dakotian, Yankton, SD, June 3, 1862.

Frank Leslie's Illustrated Newspaper, New York, August 23, 1862.

Frank Leslie's Illustrated Newspaper, New York, June 3, 1865.

The Liberator, Boston, January 10, 1862.

New Hampshire Statesman, Concord, NH, July 6, 1861.

Union and Dakotaian, Yankton, SD, September 16, 1865.

Vermont Chronicle, Bellows Falls, VT, March 3, 1863.

David H. Slay

■ Religious Tracts

During the Civil War, major religious revivals were taking place across the country as well as within both the Union and Confederate Armies (Olsen 1998). In addition, many churches believed that building good Christian character among the soldiers would make them better soldiers. In contrast to "unbelieving and careless comrades," a Christian soldier would be "disciplined, brave, persevering, and in all ways manly, for religious courage elevated men above the fear of mere physical death" (Shattuck 1987, p. 46). To meet the spiritual need of soldiers, win new converts, and keep Christian young men from being led astray by the drinking and gambling prevalent in the army camps, churches and Bible societies sent the armies Bibles, tracts, and preachers (Woodworth 2001, p. 161). Many evangelical denominations also sent prayer books and hymnals, and the religious military press began publishing numerous newspapers designed particularly with the needs of soldiers in mind. Missionaries whose chief role was to distribute religious literature were called colporteurs. Colporteurs were often well received by the soldiers because the soldiers had a lot of free time on their hands between war campaigns and they were often desperate for any kind of reading material that would relieve the boredom of camp life (Woodworth 2001, p. 163).

The American Tract Society, one of the earliest providers of evangelical literature, was organized in 1825 in New York City by members of several Protestant denominations. Its goal was "to diffuse the knowledge of our Lord Jesus Christ as the Redeemer of sinners" through the distribution of inexpensive religious tracts and the use of colporteurs (Gaustad 1982, p. 332). Tracts were a cost-effective means of distributing the Gospel. A ten-page tract could be printed in 1825 for one cent, and this same tract could be passed on and read by many families. Tracts could be read a little at a time at one's leisure, and they contained "instruction important and weighty enough for the sage, and yet simple enough to be accommodated to the taste and intelligence of a child," thus making it easy for readers to remember the content (Gaustad 1982, p. 333).

The Rev. Dr. A. E. Dickinson, superintendent for several years of the Virginia Baptist colportage board, wrote that "in a few hours a colporteur may place a tract in the hands of hundreds of our most promising young men, may urge upon them the claims of the Gospel, and in many ways do them good. How many leisure hours may be rescued from scenes of vice and turned to good account by having a colporteur in every regiment?" (Jones 1888, p. 24)

Northern Efforts

In the North, most of the need for tracts was supplied by the U.S. Christian Commission, an interdenominational evangelical organization formed by the Young Men's Christian Association in November 1861 in cooperation with the American Bible Society and the American Tract Society, with the goal of meeting the spiritual needs of soldiers. One effort of the Christian Commission was to provide quality reading materials for the troops. The organization raised more than $500 million and distributed thirty million religious tracts (Olsen 1998) and nearly one million Bibles among the troops to try to curb the swearing, gambling, drinking, and other immoral behavior among the soldiers (Volo and Volo 1998, p. 169).

The Christian Commission received donations from the British and Foreign Bible Society in London, who in March 1863 sent to the Christian Commission 14,000 volumes valued at $1,677.79, and offered more if requested (Moss 1868, p. 696). In addition, according to the *Annals of the U.S. Christian Commission*, many other societies also cooperated with the Christian Commission to provide reading materials. These included the American Sunday-School Union, the Tract Society of the Methodist Episcopal Church, the Presbyterian Board of Publication, the Presbyterian Publication Committee, the American Baptist Publication Society, the Protestant Episcopal Book Society, the American Reform Tract and Book Society, and many others (Moss 1868, p. 700). Many of the denominational organizations forwarded cash donations collected by their constituent churches, sometimes as much as $1,000 or more, "with the request that its value in publications be sent to the Christian Commission" (Moss 1868, p. 700). Many of these organizations also sent their own contributions to the troops in addition to their contributions to the Christian Commission, as did the American Tract Society, which according to its website, distributed over 39 million pages of tracts to the soldiers in the war camps.

Southern Efforts

In the South much of the soldiers' religious literature was supplied by the Evangelical Tract Society of the Confederacy, which was supported by various Southern denominations. During the war, the tract society issued more than a hundred different tracts with a total print run estimated at some 50 million pages (Woodworth 2001, p. 165).

Southern churches not only sent chaplains to minister to soldiers, but also sent religious tracts and newspapers, Bibles, hymnals, and prayer books to the troops. The tracts were seen as the most effective way to save the army from the "demoralizing influences of camp life" (Shattuck 1987, p. 48). The Southern Baptists' Sunday School and Colportage Board had been distributing tracts before the war, so they were ready to send representatives of their denomination to the troops with plenty of reading materials. The demand for tracts and other devotional materials increased so greatly during the war that new agencies were created during this time to produce religious literature for the troops (Shattuck 1987, p. 49). The largest and most prolific of these was the interdenominational Evangelical Tract Society of Petersburg, Virginia. In addition, five religious newspapers designed for circulation among the Confederate troops were founded in 1863 alone.

Robert Franklin Bunting, a chaplain of Terry's Texas Rangers, the Eighth Texas Cavalry, wrote regular letters to several newspapers to keep them informed of how the troops were doing both physically and spiritually. In a letter to the *Houston Tri-Weekly Telegraph*, published May 1, 1863, Bunting wrote that the constant migration of the troops had left the troops "almost entirely deficient in religious reading" (Cutrer 2006, p. 151).

Fulfilling the demand for tracts and other religious reading materials was a more difficult task in the South, however, than it was in the North. At the beginning of the war, most of the religious publishing houses were located in the North. The Rev. J. William Jones, a chaplain in the Army of Northern Virginia under the command of General Robert E. Lee, wrote that

> ... our people generally did their Bible and tract work in connection with societies whose headquarters were in Northern cities, and our facilities for publishing were very scant. The great societies at the North generally declared Bibles and Testaments 'contrabands of war,' and we had at once to face the problem of securing supplies through the blockade, or manufacturing them with our poor facilities. (Jones 1888, p. 148)

To solve the problem of the blockade, the Rev. Dr. M. D. Hoge of Virginia visited England during the war to obtain religious reading matter for the Confederate soldiers. The British and Foreign Bible Society gave to the Confederate Bible Society 10,000 Bibles, 50,000 New Testaments, and 250,000 portions of the Scriptures. In addition, the American Bible Society donated 20,000 Testaments to the Baptist Sunday-school Board (Jones 1888, p. 150). Hoge was able to elicit from Christians in Great Britain donations of "many very valuable books and tracts," some of which were republished for use in the Confederate armies (Jones 1888,

p. 150). Some of the Bibles and other supplies secured by Dr. Hoge did not make it through the Union block-ade of the ports, however (Jones 1888, p. 151).

Content of the Tracts

Many of the tracts dealt with the subject of salvation and sought to win soldiers to active commitment to Christianity. Such titles as "Prepare to Meet Thy God" and "Where Are You Going?" are examples of the many tracts aimed at assuring soldiers of salvation in case they died in the conflict. "For the Soldiers: Are You Ready?" reminds soldiers that death is certain although they can-not know when it will happen. The tract urges soldiers to be certain of the state of their soul, telling them that

> … this is a most momentous event. It will sunder all your relations to the present world: it will break every tie of mortality—strip off every disguise—expose every error and deception—bring out to light your whole character, even to every secret thing—present you before a just and holy Judge, and introduce you to an unchangeable condition of joy or sorrow. This event is DEATH; and the question is, 'Are you ready to die?' ("Are You Ready?", 1861–1865).

Such other tracts as "A Word of Comfort for the Sick Soldiers" and "The Wounded Soldier" aimed at comforting wounded soldiers as they lay in the hospital recovering. "In the Hospital," written by the Rev. G. B. Taylor of Staunton, Virginia, tells its readers,

> … your cheerful suffering, your heroic endurance are seen to be no less valuable qualities than the courage that would charge a battery. … Do not, then, I beseech you, yield to a feeling of discon-tent, because you are laid aside from active duty. Yours is now the more difficult, and the no less useful part. Every right thinking person regards the sick or wounded soldier, who patiently and cheerfully suffers his appointed time, as no less heroic than when marching or fighting; and doubtless, the historian of this war will refer to our hospitals as being not less glorious to our people than our bloody and victorious battle fields.

Other tracts dealt with moral issues, particularly the drinking and gambling that were prevalent among the troops. "Liquor and Lincoln" urged soldiers to abstain from drinking whiskey. Written by a physician, it stated "That the Total Abstinence regiments, can endure more labor, more cold, more heat, more expo-sure, and more privations than those who have their regular grog rations" ("Liquor and Lincoln," 1861–1865). Other titles dealing with moral issues included "Advice to Soldiers" (Royal 1861–1865) and "The Evils of Gaming: A Letter to a Friend in the Army" (Jeter 1861–1865).

Soldiers' Reception of Religious Reading Materials

Much evidence suggests that soldiers were more than eager to receive such reading materials. One colporteur, the Rev. W. J.W. Crowder, reported that within the space of several weeks he had distributed 200,000 pages of tracts and had over 2,800 conversations about reli-gion with soldiers in the camps and hospitals (Wood-worth 2001, p. 164). Another colporteur working in an army hospital in Atlanta reported distributing 20,000 pages of tracts in a single day and speaking to more than 3,000 sick men during his entire time there (p. 165).

The Confederate army chaplain, Rev. J. William Jones, wrote,

> I had a pair of large 'saddle-bags' which I used to pack with tracts and religious newspapers, and with Bibles and Testaments when I had them, and besides this I would strap packages behind my saddle and on the pommel. Thus equipped I would sally forth, and as I drew near the camp some one would raise the cry, 'Yonder comes the Bible and tract man,' and such crowds would rush out to meet me, that frequently I would sit on my horse and distribute my supply before I could even get into the camp. (Jones 1888, p. 155)

He describes how the men formed "reading clubs," gathering around a "good reader" who would read aloud portions of Scriptures for several hours. He observed, "I have never seen more diligent Bible-readers than we had in the Army of Northern Virginia" (Jones 1888, p. 155).

A letter published in a Southern Baptist paper on March 17, 1864, further illustrates the eagerness of the soldiers to receive the tracts. The article reports that

> … a chaplain arrived in Staunton, [Virginia,] with several large packages of Testaments and tracts, which he was anxious to get to Winchester, but had despaired of doing so as he had to walk, when a party of several soldiers volunteered to lug them the whole distance—ninety-two miles—so anxious were they that their comrades should have the precious messengers of salvation. (Jones 1888, p. 153)

Dr. W. W. Bennett, the Superintendent of the Sol-diers' Tract Association, reported that "the number of religious tracts and books distributed by the colporters, chaplains, and missionaries in the army, we can never know. But as all the churches were engaged in the work of printing and circulating, it is not an overestimate to say that hundreds of millions of pages were sent out by the different societies" (Jones 1888, p. 156).

BIBLIOGRAPHY

"Are You Ready? [Tract No. 26, For the Soldiers]."
    Raleigh, NC: n.p., 1861–1865. University of North

Carolina at Chapel Hill, *Documenting the American South*. Available online at http://docsouth. unc.edu/.

Berends, Kurt. O. "'Wholesome Reading Purifies and Elevates the Man'": The Religious Military Press in the Confederacy." In *Religion and the American Civil War*, ed. Randall M. Miller, Harry S. Stout, and Charles Reagan Wilson. New York: Oxford University Press, 1998.

Cutrer, Thomas W., ed. *Our Trust is in the God of Battles: The Civil War Letters of Robert Franklin Bunting, Chaplain, Terry's Texas Rangers, C.S.A.* Knoxville: University of Tennessee Press, 2006.

Gaustad, Edwin, ed. *A Documentary History of Religion in America to the Civil War*. Grand Rapids, MI: William B. Eerdmans Publishing Co., 1982.

Jeter, Rev. Jeremiah Bell. "The Evils of Gaming. A Letter to a Friend in the Army." Raleigh, NC: n.p., 1861–1865. University of North Carolina at Chapel Hill, *Documenting the American South*. Available online at http://docsouth.unc.edu/.

Jones, Rev. J. William. *Christ in the Camp or Religion in Lee's Army*. Richmond, VA: B.F. Johnson & Co., 1888.

"Liquor and Lincoln." Petersburg, VA [?], n.p.: 1861–1865. University of North Carolina at Chapel Hill, *Documenting the American South*. Available online at http://docsouth.unc.edu/.

Moss, Rev. Lemuel. *Annals of the United States Christian Commission*. Philadelphia: J.B. Lippincott & Co., 1868.

Olsen, Ted. "Memorializing the Civil War." *Christianity Today*, Christian History and Biography, May 22, 1998. Available online at http://www.christianitytoday. com/.

Royal, William. "Advice to Soldiers" [Tract No. 44]. Raleigh, NC: n.p., 1861–1865. University of North Carolina at Chapel Hill, *Documenting the American South*. Available online at http://docsouth.unc.edu/.

Shattuck, Gardiner H., Jr. *A Shield and Hiding Place: The Religious Life of the Civil War Armies*. Macon, GA: Mercer University Press, 1987.

Taylor, George Boardman. "In the Hospital." N.p, 1861–1865. University of North Carolina at Chapel Hill, *Documenting the American South*. Available online at http://docsouth.unc.edu/.

Volo, Dorothy Denneen, and James M. Volo. *Daily Life in Civil War America*. Westport, CT: Greenwood Press, 1998.

Woodworth, Steven E. *While God Is Marching On: The Religious World of Civil War Soldiers*. Lawrence: University Press of Kansas, 2001.

Sandra Johnston

■ Young Men's Christian Association

The Young Men's Christian Association, known today as the YMCA, is familiar to most for its family fitness centers and recreational programs for youth. In the Civil War era, however, the organization was active throughout the nation, tending to the spiritual and social needs of the communities they served.

Origins of the YMCA

In 1844 unhealthy social conditions in England at the end of the Industrial Revolution led George Williams (1821–1905) to begin a Bible study and prayer group for the men who roamed the streets searching for jobs. The idea caught on, and other groups formed throughout Great Britain and other parts of the world. In 1851 the first YMCA in North America was established in Montreal, Canada, on November 25, followed by the first YMCA in the United States in Boston, Massachusetts, on December 29. Anthony Bowen (c. 1805–1872), a freed slave, founded the first YMCA for African Americans two years later in Washington, DC. By 1854 total membership worldwide had grown to 30,369 members, with 397 YMCAs in seven nations.

During the Civil War membership in the United States dwindled as men went off to war, until at the end of the war there were only fifty-nine chapters. However, the popularity of the YMCA and the organization's war efforts among the troops helped to revive membership when the war was over, and four years later there were more than 600 chapters. Women were not admitted as members until the beginning of the 1850s, but they served the YMCS before then by teaching classes, raising funds, and functioning like a church's Ladies Auxiliary.

Although begun by evangelical Christians, the concept of the YMCA was unusual and appealing because it fostered an openness that crossed the boundaries between different churches and social classes, and it focused on social need in the communities it served. The focus of the YMCA in the early years "was on saving souls, with saloon and street corner preaching," but by 1866 the New York YMCA adopted the fourfold purpose of improving the "spiritual, mental, social, and physical condition of men" ("History of the YMCA Movement").

Areas of Service

One area of focus for the YMCA was recreation for youth. In the 1860s the YMCA got involved with camping when the Vermont Y's boy's missionary took a group of boys to Lake Champlain for a summer encampment. In 1860 the Brooklyn YMCA planned a building that would cost $50,000 and would be large enough for meeting rooms, a library, reading room, baths, a bowling alley, and a gymnasium (*Boston Investigator*, February 29, 1860).

Another recreational activity sponsored by the YMCA was reading clubs. Male clubs were attended by businessmen and professionals who founded many social projects. Middle- and upper-class women enjoyed their own versions of these clubs, which provided intellectual stimulation beyond domestic and church activities. The clubs typically met twice per month to discuss literature, history, and art (Volo and Volo 1998, p. 219).

In addition to literary societies and reading clubs, YMCAs also offered lectures to the public. By charging admission, usually 50 cents per person, the chapter could raise money to benefit the poor in their communities. A notice in the *Weekly Raleigh Register* on January 11, 1860, indicated that the proceeds from a lecture sponsored by the Raleigh YMCA would "be given to the poor, and want, and suffering to some extent be relieved by the tickets sold, while a rich moral and intellectual treat will be enjoyed." The lecture by Duncan K. McRae, Esquire, was a repeat performance, and McRae had agreed to repeat his lecture only if half the proceeds went to the poor. The YMCA responded by raising the ticket price to 50 cents and giving the entire proceeds to the poor.

These lectures were generally well received by the public. An editorial in the *Daily Evening Bulletin* of San Francisco, California, on January 13, 1860, extolled the virtues of public lectures and praised the YMCA as "calling upon 'superior men and men of high consideration to address the public in their name.'" The topics presented varied greatly, but were all educational in nature. The Philadelphia YMCA sponsored Dr. Henry M. Scudder to deliver a course of five lectures on India at the Musical Fund Hall, according to an advertisement in the *North American and United States Gazette* (January 21, 1860). The *New York Herald* reported on January 29, 1860, that a local chapter of the YMCA would sponsor Mrs. Ellen Key Blunt to give sacred poetry readings. A similar meeting in Raleigh, North Carolina, featured the Reverend Dr. Deems, who lectured on "The Poetry and Ethics of Trade" (*Weekly Raleigh Register*, February 8, 1860). In addition to educational topics, the YMCAs also addressed social problems. The *Boston Investigator* reported on February 8, 1860, that a Reverend Dr. Miller gave a talk on "Bigotry in the Town Hall, Birmingham."

Charitable service was another focus of the YMCA. An advertisement in the *Daily National Intelligencer* on January 4, 1860, revealed that the Washington, DC, chapter was holding a Grand Concert to benefit the Western Mission Sunday School of the YMCA, and children of the school would participate in the concert. In late March 1863 the YMCA distributed bread, meat, rice, and other foodstuffs to the needy in response to a food shortage that developed in urban areas of the South (Volo and Volo 1998, p. 58).

The YMCA also held public prayer meetings. In 1857, in response to a "severe economic reversal" in the nation, the New York YMCA sponsored noonday prayer meetings at the Fulton Street Dutch Reformed Church, which "began drawing overflow crowds" (Moorhead 1978, p. 20). The *Scioto Gazette* (March 20, 1860), of Chillicothe, Ohio, advertised daily prayer meetings from 8:30 to 9:00 A.M. every day at the local YMCA, and the *New York Herald* (December 16, 1860) advertised meetings of prayer for the Union being held in Boston. The *Daily Cleveland Herald* reported on December 10, 1860, that members of the Cleveland YMCA went to the county jail to provide "religious exercise in company with the prisoners." They took a vote to determine if they should do it again, and "the prisoners were unanimous in favor of it."

Shortly before the Civil War broke out, the YMCA of Alexandria, Virginia, sent letters to various Northern chapters "imploring them to set apart the last Friday in January (1860) as a day of special prayer to Almighty God for the preservation of the Union of the States, and for the restoration of kindness and good feeling among the citizens thereof" (*New York Herald*, February 5, 1860). Though the Connecticut members refused to participate, the *Detroit Free Press* reported that the meeting held in that city "under the auspices of the Young Men's Christian Association, was quite numerously attended by citizens of all classes, a large number of clergymen, and many ladies" (quoted in the *New York Herald*, February 5, 1860). The one-hour meetings included reading of Scriptures, singing, and "brief, voluntary prayers by those who felt prompted to lead in these devotions." The editor of the *New York Herald* noted that in spite of the negative response of the Connecticut chapter, similar meetings were being held all over the country, and that "the influence of such meetings cannot but be good upon the whole country at the present time" (February 5, 1860).

Founding of the U.S. Christian Commission

When the Civil War broke out, many charitable organizations formed to provide assistance in response to the needs of the war. The United States Christian Commission was founded by delegates from YMCAs in the Northern states in 1861 to form "a single national agency to minister to the spiritual needs of the Union soldiers" and to win "the soldiers' souls to Christ" (Shattuck 1987, pp. 26, 24). George H. Stuart (1816–1890), a Presbyterian lay leader, was elected its first president in November 1861. The organization grew tremendously; by the war's end it had become a "vast interdenominational fellowship" of nearly 5,000 unpaid workers who visited the armies and led revival meetings, distributed tracts, and gave spiritual counsel.

Volunteers also wrote letters, helped to tend the sick and wounded, operated lending libraries to provide quality reading materials, and ran soup kitchens to provide additional nourishment beyond what the soldiers received from the government. According to James Moorhead, more than $6 million in cash, goods, and services were received and disbursed among the soldiers (1978, p. 66). Rufus Kinsley, a soldier in the Union Army, wrote about a visit from "two old ladies from Michigan" who were sent by the Michigan Christian Commission. The women visited the hospitals and camps, distributing "thousands of garments, and thousands of dollars worth of table fixings to the sick and suffering" (Rankin 2004, p. 149). Although some felt that the Christian Commission should leave "temporal matters" such as nursing the wounded to the Sanitary Commission, Stuart replied that "there is a good deal of religion in a warm shirt and a good beefsteak" (Shattuck 1987, p. 29).

Other Northern War Efforts

In addition to the work of the U.S. Christian Commission, the YMCA assisted the war effort in other ways. In May 1861 the New York Association formed the Army Committee. New York and Chicago YMCA chapters helped to recruit troops for the army, and were so successful that membership of local chapters dwindled as men went to join the troops. Some military units, especially in the South, started their own YMCA chapters, as did the federal prisoner-of-war camp at Johnson's Island in Sandusky, Ohio, for the purpose of looking after the prison hospital and holding weekly lectures. Beyond caring for wounded soldiers, their goal was to give the men hope. The Reverend R. W. Cridlin wrote about a Confederate captive who had arrived at Johnson's Island following the Gettysburg campaign and found "rampant profanity, gambling, slacking and other unchristian habits." The new prisoner initiated prayer meetings and Bible classes which soon grew in frequency and number (Lutz 2001). Though there were tensions between the Northern and Southern chapters of the YMCA, the Northern YMCA–U.S. Christian Commission workers at Johnson's Island were commended by forty-eight Confederate officers at the prison, who stated in a October 31, 1863, letter to the Confederate government in Richmond that the YMCA–U.S. Christian Commission workers "make no difference or discrimination between Confederate or Federal.... We trust, that the authorities at Richmond and elsewhere will treat any said delegates ... with kindness justly due them and grant them speedy return to their Christian work" (Lutz 2001).

Southern Efforts

When nearly 3,000 soldiers were wounded in the Battle of Manassas in July 1861, the Charleston YMCA chapter asked the Richmond chapter to oversee the collection and distribution of supplies for the sick and wounded.

The Richmond chapter responded by turning its building into a "supply depot" (Lutz 2001). In mid-August of the same year, three Richmond homes were converted into hospitals that were attended by physicians who were YMCA members. In addition, Southern chapters founded a lodge to provide food, shelter, and other supplies to transient soldiers. By the end of the year nearly 4,700 soldiers had passed through the facility. The Charlottesville, Virginia, YMCA also made wooden legs to distribute free to disabled soldiers (Lutz 2001). In winter 1863 to 1864, one Mississippi Brigade YMCA fasted once a week in order to send the saved rations to the poor in Richmond.

In addition to the relief efforts of Southern chapters, some army units formed their own chapters of the YMCA. James Street, a minister serving in the Ninth Texas Regiment, reported in a letter to his wife that "a Young Men's Christian Association, composed of fifty men of all denominations had been formed in his brigade" (Shattuck 1987, p. 101). He wrote that he had heard that the chaplains were attempting to form a YMCA in every brigade of the Army of Tennessee. He felt that this might lead to revival among the Southern troops, which in turn might "assure the triumph of the South" because "only God could give victory to one side or the other" (Shattuck 1987, p. 101).

BIBLIOGRAPHY

"History of the YMCA Movement." YMCA Web site. Available from http://www.ymca.net/.

Lutz, Stephen D. "Coffee, Bibles, and Wooden Legs: The YMCA Goes to War." *Civil War Times Illustrated* 40, no. 1 (2001): 32–37.

Moorhead, James H. *American Apocalypse: Yankee Protestants and the Civil War.* New Haven, CT: Yale University Press, 1978.

Rankin, David C. *Diary of a Christian Soldier: Rufus Kinsley and the Civil War.* New York: Cambridge University Press, 2004.

Shattuck, Gardiner H., Jr. *A Shield and a Hiding Place: The Religious Life of the Civil War Armies.* Macon, GA: Mercer University Press, 1987.

Volo, Dorothy Denneen, and James M. Volo. *Daily Life in Civil War America.* Westport, CT: Greenwood Press, 1998.

Sandra Johnston

■ U.S. Christian Commission

Before the outbreak of the American Civil War, civilians had paid little attention to the spiritual needs of soldiers. By the end of 1861, however, with the mobilization of large volunteer forces, the opportunity for an organization devoted to soldiers' spiritual needs arose. The United

States Christian Commission (USCC) was organized at a Young Men's Christian Association (YMCA) meeting held in New York from November 14 to November 15, 1861, with the passage of a resolution by thirty-six delegates. This document recognized one of the YMCA's duties as promoting "the spiritual and temporal welfare of soldiers and sailors, and created a Christian Commission of twelve members, who were to serve gratuitously appoint necessary agents, and report their accomplishments to the Young Men's Christian Association and to the public" (Cannon 1951, pp. 63–64).

The new USCC was hierarchically structured. George Hay Stuart (1816–1890), a Philadelphia merchant and Presbyterian lay leader, was named the chairman of the organization. In August 1862, John A. Cole was appointed general field agent—the man in charge of all the paid field agents in each army corps. These individuals supervised volunteer delegates—those ministers who performed the grassroots work of the organization, serving in both hospitals and in battlefield regiments. According to the historian M. Hamlin Cannon, those delegates sent to the battlefield served a two-week tour of duty while those stationed in camps or at hospitals served for six weeks (1951, pp. 64, 66). At the height of the USCC's influence, about 5,000 volunteer delegates worked for the organization (Woodworth 2001, p. 167).

Goals and Activities

The main goal of the USCC was "to bring men to Christ," an objective achieved through two main activities (Cannon 1951, p. 70). First, USCC delegates strove to help regimental chaplains in all aspects of their jobs: providing pastoral care for their men, distributing tracts, and assisting with worship services. The USCC proved especially helpful in constructing chapels for men in camp. William R. Eastman, a chaplain for the Seventy-second New York Regiment, recalled that during the winter of 1863–1864, "the Christian Commission lent a large canvas to cover any log chapel that might be built and there were several brigade chapels that winter near Brandy Station, each seating more than a hundred men" (Eastman 2003, pp. 120–121). The USCC also maintained their own prayer spaces, such as the chapel at City Point, Virginia, the main supply depot for the Union armies operating in Virginia from 1864 to 1865. Described by Thomas Scott Johnson, a USCC delegate stationed at City Point, two services were held there daily, "the one a prayer meeting held at two o'clock and the other a regular evening service with preaching at 7 o'clock" (Kaliebe 1966, p. 45).

Second, the USCC delegates provided for the physical needs of the soldiers themselves. This undertaking included providing soldiers with stationery and stamped envelopes. Moses Smith, Chaplain of the Eighth Connecticut Volunteers, Army of the James, explained in *The Congregationalist* that "the Commission Tent allowed

me to draw daily a quire of paper and package of envelopes for our men" (January 20, 1865). In addition, the USCC delegates tended the wounded, serving as nurses. At Gettysburg, Surgeon General William Alexander Hammond (1828–1900) praised the assistance of the USCC in a letter sent to George Hay Stuart dated July 20, 1863, and reprinted in the *Bangor* (ME) *Daily Whig & Courier*. Hammond noted that without the aid of USCC delegates at the battle "the suffering would have been much greater" (July 31, 1863).

Commended by such prominent civilians as Surgeon General Hammond for their dedication and hard work, USCC delegates were beloved by many of those soldiers who had been in their care. An article printed in the *Vermont Chronicle* in 1864 related the message quite clearly, explaining that "The delegate who passes through the hospitals with his shining badge upon his breast continually hears the testimony of these men, saying, 'You saved my life!' 'Many of us would have been in our graves but for you'—and similar things" (August 6, 1864).

The Union military establishment also helped the USCC in any possible manner. Its assistance most was explicitly seen in Grant's order pertaining to USCC delegates, dated December 12, 1863, and reprinted in the San Francisco *Daily Evening Bulletin* the following year. Promulgated in Chattanooga, Tennessee, this order gave delegates permission "to pass to all parts within the lines, without hindrance or molestation" and charged the Commissary Department to sell goods to USCC delegates. It also allowed delegates to use military telegraph lines. Perhaps most useful to the USCC, however, was that Grant charged the Quartermaster's Department with providing delegates with "free transportation upon all government steamers and military railroads to and from such points within the military divisions as their duties may require them to visit" (May 5, 1864).

The Home Front's Support

The work of the USCC among the soldiers in the field and in hospitals would not have been successful or even attempted without money raised by the organization on the home front. Collections for the organization were taken throughout the Northern states. At the anniversary meeting of the USCC held in Philadelphia in 1863, the *Bangor* (ME) *Daily Whig & Courier* stated, "a very large collection was taken up at the close, and rings, brooches, and other jewelry were found in it" (February 13, 1863). The city of Boston was another major contributor. George H. Stuart noted in the *North American and United States Gazette* that the citizens of Boston had given twenty-six thousand dollars and had not yet completed their fundraising activities (July 13, 1863).

Later in the conflict, Stuart made a specific appeal for more donations to the cause. In one notable example, Stuart published a "Thanksgiving Appeal for the Nation's Defenders" in the *Milwaukee Daily Sentinel*.

DWIGHT L. MOODY

Dwight Lyman Moody (1837–1899) was a member of the U.S. Christian Commission who became a well-known nineteenth-century evangelist and the founder of a Bible training school now known worldwide as Moody Bible Institute in Chicago. Moody's institute, which opened in 1886, was intended to train laypeople to do evangelism; it was not a seminary for clergy.

Born in Northfield, Massachusetts, Moody went to Boston to work for an uncle in the shoe business while he was still a teenager. He had always been a devout church member, but after a conversion experience in 1854 he became interested in the Sunday School movement. Moody continued to be a Sunday School worker after he moved to Chicago in 1856. He was doing so well in the shoe business that his new employer sent him out as a commercial traveler, but after the Civil War began, Moody decided to give up secular employment for full-time evangelistic work.

As a member of the wartime U.S. Christian Commission Moody visited prisoner of war camps for Confederate soldiers in the Chicago area, handing out pocket-sized Bibles and holding revival meetings. After the war he traveled to England to study British methods of evangelism and to hear Charles Spurgeon (1834–1892), a famous English preacher. Moody himself began to preach in Scotland and Ireland as well as in England, drawing crowds as large as twenty thousand. He drew similarly large crowds after returning to the United States; President Ulysses S. Grant (1822–1885) attended one of Moody's worship services in 1876. Moody was also invited to preach at the Chicago World's Fair in 1893. He died in 1899 after a series of heart attacks.

Moody's preaching was noteworthy for the period because there was nothing sensationalist or flamboyant about his sermons. He was not attracted to controversy with other clergy, and he strove to be "homey" and sincere rather than entertaining or provocative. An example of Moody's warm and positive approach to faith is a sermon that he preached in 1873 called "The Qualifications for Soul-Winning." Here is an excerpt from that sermon:

> I have observed that God never uses a man that is always looking on the dark side of things: what we do for Him let us do cheerfully, not because it is our duty—not that we should sweep away the word but because it is our

privilege. What would my wife or children say if I spoke of loving them because it was my *duty* to do so? . . .

A London minister, a friend of mine, lately pointed out a family of seven, all of whom he was just receiving into the Church. Their story was this: going to church, he had to pass by a window, looking up at which one day, he saw a baby looking out; he smiled—the baby smiled again. Next time he passes he looks up again, smiles, and the baby smiles back. A third time going by, he looks up, and seeing the baby, throws it a kiss—which the baby returns to him. Time after time he has to pass the window, and now cannot refrain from looking up each time: and each time there are more faces to receive his smiling greeting; till by-and-by he sees the whole family grouped at the window—father, mother, and all. The father conjectures the happy, smiling stranger must be a minister, and so, next Sunday morning, after they have received at the window the usual greeting, two of the children, ready dressed, are sent out to follow him: they enter his church, hear him preach, and carry back to their parents the report that they never heard such preaching; and what preaching could equal that of one who had so smiled on them? Soon the rest come to the church too, and are brought in—all by a smile. Let us not go about, hanging our heads like a bulrush; if Christ gives joy, let us live it! The whole world is in all matters for the very best thing—you always want to get the best possible thing for your money; let us show, then, that our religion is the very best thing: men with long, gloomy faces are never wise in the winning of souls.

REBECCA J. FREY

BIBLIOGRAPHY

Marsden, George M. *Understanding Fundamentalism and Evangelicalism,* pp. 20–22. Grand Rapids, MI: Wm. B. Eerdmans Publishing Co., 1991.

Moody, Dwight L. *"The Qualifications for Soul-Winning,"* December 7, 1873. Available from http://www.biblebelievers.com/moody_sermons/m1.html.

Here, he made a plea to the newspaper's readers for aid "in behalf of our country's defenders, for Thanksgiving day collections." He further elaborated: "Contributions of clothing, and comforts, as well as money, are needed" (November 9, 1863). In another request for money printed in the *North American and United States Gazette,* Stuart attempted to appeal to the Union population's religious base. He stated on behalf of the USCC delegates, "It remains for the Christian philanthropic people of the land to keep [the delegates] supplied with the means of carrying on and increasing their labors of love" (May 26, 1864).

Relations between the USCC and the USSC

During the course of the war, tensions arose between the USCC and another philanthropic organization, the United States Sanitary Commission (USSC). According to historian Gardiner Shattuck, this tension occurred due to the inherent differences between "two rival theological wings of American Protestantism—evangelical [the USCC] and liberal [the USSC]." Moreover, "the practical work that they both performed was similar" (Shattuck 1987, p. 29). Some chaplains in the field, such as Hallock Armstrong of the Fiftieth Regiment, Pennsylvania Veteran Volunteers of the Ninth Corps of the

Men of U.S. Christian Commision at field headquarters. Recognizing a need to minister to the Union troops, the Young Men's Christian Association created the United States Christian Commission whose primary aim was to provide spiritual support for the soldiers. Funded primarily by Northerners, the organization also assisted in hospitals and gathered extra supplies to distribute in the army camps. *Alexander Gardner/George Eastman House/Getty Images.*

Army of the Potomac, appeared to think that the USCC @was more beneficial than the USSC. Armstrong related an incident in a letter to his wife Mary, in which he saw the delegates at the USCC headquarters in Virginia "distributing a large number of beautiful medals, on which was inscribed the pledge 'Rum and tobacco I'll not use, Nor take God's name in vain,' yet when approaching the USSC headquarters, he "found them issuing large quantities of tobacco free to the boys" (March 23, 1865; quoted in Raup 1961, p. 13). Yet other chaplains felt both organizations were performing valuable work. The Reverend Andrew Jackson Hartsock, chaplain of the One Hundred and Tenth and the One Hundred and Thirty-third Pennsylvania Regiments, noted in a diary entry dated February 3, 1863, that "the agents of these organizations [the USCC and the USSC] are gentleman and Christians, and are doing a noble work" (Duram 1979, p. 59).

The United States Christian Commission provided for the spiritual and physical well-being of Union soldiers throughout the American Civil War. The USCC delegates, although serving only for a limited period of time and without pay, augmented the strength of the official paid military chaplains assigned to both

regiments in the field and hospitals. Supported by donations from the home front, USCC delegates successfully spread evangelical Christianity while at the same time providing for the physical needs of soldiers. Soldiers, chaplains, and even General Grant acknowledged the USCC's important role, yet over the course of the conflict tensions sometimes flared between the USCC and the other large philanthropic body that aided the troops, the United States Sanitary Commission (USSC).

BIBLIOGRAPHY

Cannon, M. Hamlin. "The United States Christian Commission." *Mississippi Valley Historical Review* 38, no. 1 (June 1951): 61–80.

Duram, James C., and Eleanor A. Duram, eds. *Soldier of the Cross: The Civil War Diary and Correspondence of Rev. Andrew Jackson Hartsock.* Manhattan, KS: Military Affairs/Aerospace Historian Publishing for the American Military Institute, 1979.

Eastman, William R. "A Yankee Chaplain Remembers." In *Faith in the Fight: Civil War Chaplains*, John W. Brinsfield, William C. Davis, Benedict Maryniak, and James I. Robertson Jr., eds. Mechanicsburg, PA: Stackpole Books, 2003.

Fredrickson, George M. *The Inner Civil War: Northern Intellectuals and the Crisis of the Union.* Urbana: University of Illinois Press, 1993 [1965].

Kaliebe, Jon Edward. "The Letters of Thomas Scott Johnson: His Work among the Negro as Christian Commission Delegate and Chaplain, 1864–1866." Master's thesis, University of Wisconsin, 1966.

Moorhead, James H. *American Apocalypse: Yankee Protestants and the Civil War, 1860–1869.* New Haven: Yale University Press, 1978.

Raup, Hallock F., ed. *Letters from a Pennsylvania Chaplain at the Siege of Petersburg, 1865.* London: The Eden Press, 1961.

Shattuck, Jr., Gardiner H. *A Shield and Hiding Place: The Religious Life of the Civil War Armies.* Macon, GA: Mercer University Press, 1987.

Smith, Moses. "The U.S. Christian Commission." *The Congregationalist,* January 20, 1865.

"Special Notices U.S. Christian Commission." *North American and United States Gazette,* July 13, 1863.

Stuart, George H. Letter to the editor, *North American and United States Gazette,* May 26, 1864.

"U.S. Christian Commission." *Bangor* (ME) *Daily Whig & Courier,* February 13, 1863.

"U.S. Christian Commission." *Bangor* (ME) *Daily Whig & Courier,* July 31, 1863.

"The U.S. Christian Commission." *Daily Evening Bulletin,* San Francisco, May 5, 1864.

"U.S. Christian Commission Thanksgiving Appeal for the Nation's Defenders." *Milwaukee Daily Sentinel,* November 9, 1863.

"U.S. Christian Commission: The Present Campaign in Virginia,—Marches and Battles," *Vermont Chronicle* (Bellows Falls), August 6, 1864.

Woodworth, Steven E. *While God Is Marching On: The Religious World of Civil War Soldiers.* Lawrence: University Press of Kansas, 2001.

Benjamin L. Miller

■ Catholic Christianity

Anti-Catholic sentiment was pronounced in the mid-nineteenth-century United States. Powerful nativist impulses found political voice in the Know Nothing (American) Party, which had reached its zenith during the 1850s, but prejudices against Catholics remained on the eve of the Civil War in 1861. The fact that American Catholics increased their numbers from approximately 1 percent of the total population during the Revolutionary period to become one of the largest Christian denominations in the United States by 1860 (Wagner, Gallagher, and Finkelman 2002, p. 82) seems to have exacerbated the hostility that white Anglo-Saxon Protestants felt towards immigrant Catholics. These complex religious and ethnic conflicts produced particularly inflammatory tensions in the cities in the Northeast and Midwest, where most of the poor German and Irish Catholic immigrants lived.

Many Americans were particularly suspicious of these immigrant Catholics because of their purported loyalty to the Pope. Fearing the inroads of papal influence on domestic politics, nativist Protestants sought to deny immigrant Catholics the vote. During the 1860 election, Catholics generally voted in favor of the Democratic Party because they disagreed with the Republican Party's support of temperance and emancipation (McPherson 2003, p. 176). Although the Catholic Church opposed the institution of slavery on moral grounds, working-class American Catholics feared that if the Republican Party freed the slaves, then the competition for low-paying industrial jobs would increase, potentially leaving them unemployed.

After the Civil War began on April 12, 1861, the Catholic Church took no official position on the war so as not to cause a schism among its followers. Some Catholics were initially leery about the conflict and, later, about emancipation, but many, both civilian and clergy, rallied to their respective causes in the North and South. They were motivated by a mixture of patriotism, a desire to silence nativist attitudes, and, like many Protestant volunteers, a need to obtain a steady income through military enlistment.

Catholicism in Camp, on the March, and under Fire

Catholic soldiers and clergy who served in the Northern and Southern armies continued to practice their religion despite the fact that they constituted a minority of both Union and Confederate forces. Catholic soldiers turned to God and Catholic theology to sustain them in combat, to prepare them for death, and to see them through the trials of their daily lives in camp and on the march.

Because of the predominant anti-Catholic sentiment, the number of Catholic chaplains on both the Union and Confederate sides was small in proportion to their population when compared to the number of Protestant chaplains. Catholic priests were assigned only to regiments whose ranks were composed entirely of Catholics because Protestant officers commonly refused priests' services for their Catholic soldiers (Shattuck 1987, p. 55). Army regiments fortunate enough to have a Catholic chaplain, such as the Irish Brigade of the Union Army of the Potomac and the Fourteenth Louisiana Infantry of the Confederate Army of Northern Virginia, had their spiritual needs fulfilled on a regular basis.

Chaplains believed in the causes for which they fought, emphasized the exemplary nature of the Catholic soldier, and honored the opportunity to save soldiers' souls through conversion, absolution, or the administration of last rites. Reverend Sheeran of the Fourteenth Louisiana summarized his devotion to God, the

Sunday morning mass. Time permitting, Catholic priests conducted worship services for soldiers, giving the troops a sense of normalcy during the war and admonishing them to avoid temptations while away from their families. *The Library of Congress.*

Confederate cause, and his men by saying, "The interest I feel in the Cause for which our brave men are sacrificing the comforts of society and periling their lives as well as the salvation of their souls prompted me to do all in my power to keep them in the friendship of their God" (Sheeran 1960, p. 5). These priests believed that a man's commitment to God and the Catholic faith translated into heroic service on the battlefield. Father Corby of the Irish Brigade likened the commitment that men make to soldiering to the promise made in marriage, because both covenants bound men until death. Because of this commitment, the Irish priest held that "there is no braver soldier in this world ... than a consistent Catholic" because these men realize that their power "comes from the 'God of battles,' not from man" (Corby 1992 [1893], pp. 6, 296).

In order to ensure that their men were ready to meet God at any moment, Catholic chaplains labored tirelessly in camp, on the battlefield, and as members of burial details. Catholic priests heard many confessions and administered absolution to soldiers individually or en masse, as was the case of Father Corby and the Irish Brigade before battle at Gettysburg on July 2, 1863. Observers noted that absolution brought peace of mind to both Catholic and, at Gettysburg, non-Catholic soldiers because it enabled them, in the words Major St. Clair Mulholland, to "receive every benefit of divine grace that could be imparted through the instrumentality of the Church ministry" before God called them home (Corby 1992 [1893], p. 184).

Religious practices also brought comfort, order, and some of the familiarity of home to the unfamiliar world of the army. If the armies were not actively campaigning on Sundays, both Union and Confederate soldiers constructed rustic altars in their camps where a congregation could gather to celebrate Mass. In their sermons, chaplains exhorted men against the temptations of liquor, gambling, immorality, and blasphemy, all readily accessible in the army. Chaplains also helped soldiers manage their money by forwarding soldiers' pay to their families in order to keep it from being squandered (Blied 1945, p. 115).

The religious life of the army also provided men with leisure activities during the holidays. Saint Patrick's Day in the Irish Brigade never passed without mass and festivities such as a steeplechase. Catholic regiments also observed the Easter and Christmas holidays. Reverend Sheeran recalled that in 1862, at his request, the men of the Fourteenth Louisiana donated the money they had raised to purchase him a Christmas present—a sum of $1,206—to Saint Joseph's Asylum in Richmond. On Easter Sunday the following year, Sheeran was moved by the sight of "a large number of the Catholics" gathered in the morning "knee-deep in the snow, cheerfully awaiting the offering of the Holy Sacrifice of the Mass" (Sheeran 1960, p. 39).

Priests and Nuns Tending to the Wounded

The presence of Catholic priests and nuns in military hospitals or on burial details bridged the sectional divide between Union and Confederate soldiers. Following the fighting at Fair Oaks (Seven Pines), Virginia on June 1, 1862, Captain David Power Conyngham of the Irish Brigade praised the work of chaplains as they tended to fallen soldiers, and noted that the clergy "know no distinction between rebel or Federal" because their mission was "to console the mind and heal the body, and in this they know no distinction" (Conyngham 1994 [1866], p. 161). Following the battle of Malvern Hill in early July 1862, Conyngham noted that Catholic chaplains remained on the field until all the wounded, dead, and dying were treated and "cheerfully allowed themselves to fall into the enemy's hands sooner than neglect the spiritual or temporal welfare of our brave sufferers" (p. 226).

Reverend Sheeran reported that on September 15, 1862, he encountered Union soldiers burying their comrades who had fallen in the recent siege of Harpers Ferry. The Yankee soldiers, who turned out to be Catholic, "rejoiced" to learn that Sheeran was a priest and forgot "for the moment that they were in the hands of the enemy." Following the fighting at Chancellorsville, Virginia on May 4, 1863, Sheeran visited a Union field hospital. After administering the sacraments to a number of wounded Catholic soldiers, the men informed Sheeran that Federal surgeons "had paid no attention to them." Upon hearing this, Sheeran found the Union doctors and "requested them as a matter of humanity not to neglect the men" (Sheeran 1960, p. 44). A year later, following an engagement at Spotsylvania Court House, Virginia, Sheeran took it upon himself to care for the Union wounded, Catholics who happened to belong to the Union Irish Brigade (p. 88).

Catholic nuns played a significant role in caring for wounded Civil War soldiers. By the mid-nineteenth century there were approximately 1,500 nuns in the United States whose mission was to carry out the works of Christian charity by teaching, caring for orphans, nursing the sick, and providing spiritual assistance to the dying (Maher 1989, pp. 2, 14). The nuns' antebellum mission was rare, and they were the only source of trained nurses at the outset of the Civil War (p. 27). Many orders of nuns worked in military hospitals, or turned their convents into medical wards. The specific orders that ministered to the wounded and dying included the Sisters of Charity, the Sisters of Mercy, the Sisters of Saint Joseph, and the Sisters of the Holy Cross. Many soldiers and civilians, however, made no distinction among the orders, and commonly referred to all nuns as "Sisters of Charity" (Barton 1897, p. 3).

Doctors specifically requested Catholic sisters to assist the wounded and dying because of their medical expertise (Maher 1989, p. 69). The Sisters of Charity of Emmittsburg, Maryland, had great demands placed on their service: These nuns traveled to Richmond in June 1861 to serve at the city's Confederate Military Hospital. On May 24, 1863, five Sisters of Charity fulfilled a request to minister to wounded soldiers in Atlanta, Georgia (Barton 1897, pp. 86, 90). Although sometimes they were negatively received, the sisters worked in the hospitals tirelessly and without pay, bringing food to the hungry, writing letters home on the behalf of dying soldiers, and bringing spiritual and physical comfort to those in pain. After benefiting from treatment at the Atlanta hospital, one wounded soldier confessed to the Catholic nurse that when he learned that the nurses were nuns his "heart was filled with hatred," but that he later recognized "the unintentional blackness" of his heart and saw the sisters "in their true light" (p. 91).

Although the Catholic sisters devoted a large amount of their time to nursing wounded soldiers, they did not forsake their commitment to aiding orphans during the Civil War. On November 9, 1864, the Washington, DC, *Daily National Intelligencer* ran an ad for a fair benefiting orphan girls, soliciting donations to "relieve the necessities of the numerous orphan girls of St. Vincent's Orphan Asylum…where they will partake of the maternal and judicious care of the Sisters of Charity of St. Joseph." The paper praised the nuns' noble devotion to caring for the suffering regardless of creed, and commended their "devoted attention and zealous labors in nursing the sick, wounded, and dying soldiers in our military hospitals during the present war."

Catholicism as Sustaining Motivation

Catholicism not only sustained Civil War soldiers on a day-to-day basis, it also gave them and civilians at home a reason to continue supporting the war. As both the Union and the Confederacy suffered heavy losses during the latter part of 1862 and early 1863, patriotic rhetoric

The Propagation Society.   As immigration propelled Catholicism to become one of the largest Christian denominations in the United States at the start of the Civil War, many native-born Protestants feared the United States would become unduly influenced by the Pope and actively sought to curb the rising political power of Catholic immigrants.   *The Library of Congress.*

became steeped with religious metaphors, particularly that of the martyr and Christian warrior (Fellman, Gordon, and Sutherland 2003, p. 179). The requiem mass for the repose of the souls of the Irish Brigade held on January 16, 1863, at Saint Patrick's Cathedral in New York, and the sermon titled "Patriotism, a Christian Virtue" preached by the Reverend Joseph Fransioli at the same location on July 26, 1863, reveal the role that religion played in consoling the bereaved and sustaining civilians' and soldiers' motivation. Many Union soldiers attached religious significance to the preservation of the United States (Woodworth 2001, p. 111). The requiem mass, accordingly, honored the country's fallen and praised "Men who had pledged to this land their troth, and died to defend her, ere break there oath" (Conyngham 1994 [1866], p. 358).

The Reverend Fransioli's sermon echoed the requiem mass's reverence for the dead, and exhorted men and women to support the Union cause by contending that patriotism "is not only a social virtue, commanding respect, but a Christian virtue to be rewarded by the blessings of God here and hereafter." The priest concluded by advising the congregation to love God

above all, then country and family, and stated that "the Christian patriot brings before the altar of his country, his property and his life cheerfully ready for the sacrifice when it is demanded." Ultimately, soldiers' and civilians' Catholic faith inspired them to see the Civil War through to its end and helped them to cope with human loss. Catholic soldiers' participation in the conflict, however, did little to quell anti-Catholic sentiment, which continued in the postwar years.

BIBLIOGRAPHY

"A Friend to the Orphan: The Fair for the Benefit of the Orphan Girls." *Daily National Intelligencer*, Washington, DC, November 9, 1864.

Barton, George. *Angels of the Battlefield: A History of the Labors of the Catholic Sisterhoods in the Late Civil War.* Philadelphia: Catholic Art Publishing Company, 1897.

Blied, Benjamin J. *Catholics and the Civil War.* Milwaukee, WI: Author, 1945.

Conyngham, David Power. *The Irish Brigade and Its Campaigns* [1866], ed. Lawrence Frederick Kohl. New York: Fordham University Press, 1994.

Corby, William. *Memoirs of Chaplain Life: Three Years with the Irish Brigade in the Army of the Potomac* [1893], ed. Lawrence Frederick Kohl New York: Fordham University Press, 1992.

Fellman, Michael, Lesley J. Gordon, and Daniel E. Sutherland. *This Terrible War: The Civil War and Its Aftermath.* New York: Longman, 2003.

Fransioli, Joseph. "Patriotism, A Christian Virtue." New York: Loyal Publication Society, 1863.

Gould, Virginia. "'Oh I Pass Everywhere': Catholic Nuns in the Gulf South." In *Battle Scars: Gender and Sexuality in the American Civil War*, ed. Catherine Clinton and Nina Silber. New York: Oxford University Press, 2006.

Maher, Mary Denis. *To Bind Up the Wounds: Catholic Sister Nurses in the U.S. Civil War.* New York: Greenwood Press, 1989.

McPherson, James M. *The Illustrated Battle Cry of Freedom: The Civil War Era.* New York: Oxford University Press, 2003.

Ochs, Stephen J. *A Black Patriot and a White Priest: André Cailloux and Claude Paschal Maistre in Civil War New Orleans.* Baton Rouge: Louisiana State University Press, 2000.

Shattuck, Gardiner H., Jr, *A Shield and Hiding Place: The Religious Life of the Civil War Armies.* Macon, GA: Mercer University Press, 1987.

Sheeran, James B. *Confederate Chaplain: A War Journal of Rev. James B. Sheeran, c.ss.r. 14th Louisiana, C.S.A.*, ed. Joseph T. Durkin, S. J., preface, Bruce Catton. Milwaukee, WI: Bruce Publishing Company, 1960.

Wagner, Margaret E., Gary W. Gallagher, and Paul Finkelman, eds. *The Library of Congress Civil War Desk Reference.* New York: Simon and Schuster, 2002.

Woodworth, Steven E. *While God Is Marching On: The Religious World of Civil War Soldiers.* Lawrence: University Press of Kansas, 2001.

Angela M. Zombek

■ Unitarianism

Unitarians in antebellum America led battles to reform society. In particular, Unitarians fought against slavery; indeed, Unitarian ministers were at the forefront of much of the most radical abolitionist activity. One leader in particular, Theodore Parker, influenced abolitionist leaders of other denominations, including the famous William Lloyd Garrison.

Unitarians believe in the unity of God and reject the Christian belief in a Trinity and the divinity of Jesus. Believers stress the importance of rational thinking and of a person's direct relationship with God. Throughout American history, Unitarians have had great influence.

Famous Unitarians include John and Abigail Adams, Benjamin Rush, John Quincy Adams, Lydia Child, Bronson and Abigail Alcott, Louisa May Alcott, Julia Ward Howe, Horace Mann, Harriet Martineau, and Mary White Ovington. Unitarians have been prominently involved in a variety of reform movements, including those seeking educational reform, prison reform, the overhaul of orphanages, temperance, poor relief, abolition, and peace.

The institutional organization of Unitarianism began as three separate movements, in Poland, Transylvania, and England. In America, Unitarianism took root in the 1740s as a reaction to the emotional revivalism of the Great Awakening. Some liberal Puritans embraced the rationalist approach to Christianity that Unitarianism offered. Whereas more evangelical Christianity appealed to all classes of Congregationalists, the calmer, more benevolent God of liberal Unitarianism appealed particularly to New England elites, with Boston being the hub. Unitarians tended to be wealthier than members of other denominations, and to have higher social status and more education. This gave them significant social influence.

Dorothea Dix (1802–1887). Known for her work helping the mentally ill, Unitarian activist Dorothea Dix served as superintendent of United States Army Nurses during the Civil War and emphasized the need to care for all wounded soldiers during the conflict, no matter the color of the uniform. © *Corbis.*

Around 1815, a young minister, William Ellery Channing, began sending articles and letters to liberal religious publications. In 1819, Channing delivered a sermon, "Unitarian Christianity," that soon became the Unitarian manifesto. In it, Channing declared:

Our leading principle in interpreting Scripture is this, that the Bible is a book written for men, in the language of men, and that its meaning is to be sought in the same manner as that of other books.... With these views of the Bible, we feel it our bounden duty to exercise our reason upon it perpetually, to compare, to infer, to look beyond the letter to the spirit, to seek in the nature of the subject, and the aim of the writer, his true meaning; and, in general to make use of what is known, for explaining what is difficult, and for discovering new truths. (Channing 1875, pp. 367–368)

Channing's sermon gave liberal Christians a coherent theology, centered around belief in the unity of Christ, humankind's inferiority to God, and humanity's moral responsibility. Unitarians believed that conversion should be calm and deliberative, and they stressed the importance of character improvement, a rational and gradual process through which individuals came to understand accepted moral truths. Unitarians believed that a moral society was as important as eternal salvation. Interest in Unitarianism spread from Boston to other urban areas of New England, and as a result, many Congregationalist churches became Unitarian.

In 1825, the American Unitarian Association (AUA) was established, not as a group of churches, but as a group of individuals. Many Unitarians were wary of this organization, however, fearing it might threaten religious liberty by exerting control over their churches. The AUA received minimal financial support from Unitarians and its primary activity proved to be the publication of religious tracts.

As New England society grew more industrialized, the mostly middle- and upper-class Unitarians realized they needed to minister to the poor and address the societal problems that poverty created. In 1834, nine churches formed the Benevolent Fraternity of Christian Churches. These Unitarian ministers commonly offered pastoral care to the poor, with the goal of adding them to their congregations. The ministers led campaigns for free public education, temperance, and penal reform, and created efficient social reform organizations. Unitarians coordinated with other denominations, as well as secular organizations. Male Unitarians gathered information on various social problems, allowing charities to determine the most effective method of distributing funds and dispensing charity. Women raised funds by collecting subscriptions, sewing clothing, and visiting families. Though Unitarians worked to improve the economic lot of the poor and to alleviate various social problems, their primary goal was to bring about moral improvement through a demonstration of Christian benevolence. In their view, the act of charity not only helped recipients, it also helped givers through cultivating acts of conscience.

In 1830, Harvard Divinity School appointed Unitarian Henry Ware Jr. to a newly created professorship of "pulpit eloquence and pastoral care" (Rose 1981, pp. 31–32). He was to revitalize the classical curriculum of Greek and Latin, biblical criticism, and didactic theology with exercises in extemporaneous preaching. Ware introduced informal discussions of current topics to promote philanthropy and social responsibility among the young men. Students collected information on the reformation of criminals, the success of missions, the conditions of sailors, and, importantly, slavery. Ministers were thus trained not only to promote religion but also to engage in disciplined social reform. Ware belonged to a number of reform societies and served as a model and an inspiration for a generation of young ministerial students.

Theodore Parker, the Unitarian minister with the greatest influence on the abolition movement, was born in 1810 in Lexington, Massachusetts. An impressive scholar, he mastered twenty languages while studying at Harvard Divinity School, from which he graduated in 1836. Parker left the Congregationalist Church to become a Unitarian in the early 1840s. By the 1850s Parker was an immensely popular minister, preaching to two thousand in the Boston Music Hall and thousands more on his lecture tours. Other influential reformers attended and were influenced by Parker's fiery sermons and radical ideas. His followers were sometimes called *Parkites* or *Parkerites* and included William Lloyd Garrison, Elizabeth Cady Stanton, Julia Ward Howe, Samuel Gridley Howe, and Louisa May Alcott.

Parker's radical abolitionist views led to resistance from more mainstream Unitarians; other Unitarian ministers criticized him and refused to exchange pulpits with him. Undeterred, Parker continued to argue for the ending of slavery, and to champion temperance and educational reform. His sermons included statistics and analysis of social classes, along with Biblical commentary. He advocated the integration of Boston schools and churches and served as a minister to fugitive slaves.

After the passage of the Fugitive Slave Act in 1850, Parker strenuously criticized Massachusetts Senator Daniel Webster for voting for it. Parker hid one of the fugitives in his congregation, Ellen Craft, in his house until he could arrange for her to get to Canada. In 1854, a fugitive slave from Virginia, Anthony Burns, was captured in Boston. Parker led protests to prevent Burns from being forcibly returned to slavery. After one of these protests turned violent and resulted in the death of a jailer, a grand jury indicted Parker for obstructing a federal marshal. The charges, however, were subsequently dismissed.

WILLIAM LLOYD GARRISON

Abolitionist William Lloyd Garrison was born in 1805 in New-buryport, Massachusetts. When he was a young boy, his father abandoned the family, forcing him to work small jobs to help his mother support the family. This left him with a lifelong sympathy for the poor and a passionate urge to fight social injustice. Garrison was apprenticed as a printer, then worked for a newspaper as both a writer and an editor. He became strongly opposed to slavery by his mid-twenties, and briefly joined the American Colonization Society, which was engaged in transporting freed blacks to a newly established "homeland" in Liberia. In 1828 Garrison met the Quaker abolitionist Benjamin Lundy, who asked him to edit his Baltimore newspaper, *The Genius of Universal Emancipation*. Under Lundy's influence, he became convinced that the issue of slavery could only be resolved through the immediate emancipation of all slaves.

In 1830, after spending forty-nine days in jail for libeling a slave trader, Garrison moved to Boston and started his own publication, *The Liberator*. It was in this newspaper that he issued his famous declaration: "I am in earnest—I will not equivocate—I will not excuse—I will not retrench a single inch—and I will be heard" (Garrison 1831, p. 1). For thirty-four years *The Liberator* served as the principal organ of radical abolitionism. Garrison believed that slavery was a sin, slaveholders were sinners, and Northerners shared in the guilt by not ending slavery. Through what they often called "moral suasion," he sought to convince both Southerners and Northerners of the righteousness of the abolitionist cause.

After the Thirteenth Amendment passed in 1865, ending slavery, Garrison ceased publication of *The Liberator*. He spent the remainder of his life campaigning for other causes, including women's suffrage and temperance.

MINOA UFFELMAN

BIBLIOGRAPHY

Garrison, William Lloyd. The Liberator. *January 1, 1831, p. 1.*

Mayer, Henry. All on Fire: William Lloyd Garrison and the Abolition of Slavery. *New York: St. Martin's Press, 1998.*

Stewart, James Brewer. William Lloyd Garrison and the Challenge of Emancipation. *Arlington Heights, IL: Harlan Davidson, 1992.*

Thomas, John L. The Liberator: William Lloyd Garrison: A Biography. *Boston: Little, Brown, 1963.*

Parker also raised money for John Brown's raid on Harpers Ferry, hoping that the slave insurrection would inspire others throughout the South. Parker's participation became known when Virginian authorities seized correspondence following Brown's arrest. The aborted insurrection convinced many Southerners that Northerners, even ministers, were willing to use any means to end slavery, regardless of how much blood was spilt. This further confirmed to them that only by withdrawing from the Union could they preserve a way of life based on slavery.

BIBLIOGRAPHY

Channing, William Ellery. *The Works of William E. Channing.* New and rearranged ed. Boston: American Unitarian Association, 1875.

Rose, Anne C. *Transcendentalism as a Social Movement, 1830–1850.* New Haven: Yale University Press, 1981.

Stange, Douglas C. *Patterns of Antislavery among American Unitarians, 1831–1860.* Cranbury, NJ: Associated University Presses, 1977.

Wilbur, Earl Morse. *A History of Unitarianism: In Transylvania, England, and America.* Boston: Beacon Press, 1952.

Minoa Uffelman

■ Judaism

Jews migrated to America from various parts of Europe in large numbers during the 1850s and 1860s, fleeing religious persecution, denial of the right to travel, and many other restrictions in their native lands. With them they brought their culture and their religion, Judaism. The America they arrived in was then divided over the issue of states' rights and the morality of slavery. Although many Jews in the antebellum South participated in the development of the institution of slavery—some owned slaves and others were slave traders as well—Jews as a whole were as divided on the issue as were other Americans.

Judaism, largely speaking, played no role in the molding of public sentiment regarding slavery. This is not to say, however, that Jewish leaders were silent. One of the most highly publicized rabbinical pronouncements on slavery was an argument for its merits made at the very peak of the secession crisis by Dr. Morris J. Raphall of New York City, one of the most celebrated orators in the American rabbinate of his time:

> I would therefore ask the Reverend gentlemen from Brooklyn and his compeers, how dare you. . . Denounce slaveholding as a sin? When you Remember that Abraham, Isaac, Jacob, Job, The men with whom the Almighty conversed, With whose names he emphatically connects His own only name . . . they all these men were Slaveholders, does it not strike you that you Are guilty of something very little short of Blasphemy? And if you answer me, "oh, in Their time slaveholding was lawful, but now it Has become a sin," I in turn ask you, "when And by which authority you draw the line? Tell us the precise time when slaveholding Ceased to be permitted, and became sinful?" (Korn 1951, p. 17)

What Raphall did was to place Judaism squarely in opposition to the philosophy of abolitionism. He denied that any statement or law in the Bible could be

Rabbi David Einhorn (1809–1879), abolitionist. While noting the existence of slavery in the Old Testament, Rabbi David Einhorn nonetheless pronounced slavery a moral wrong, forcing him to flee his Maryland congregation in fear of his personal safety. *Dover Publications, Inc.*

opened his art collection to the public and swelled the coffers of the Sanitary Commission with the proceeds from admission fees. Three Jewish firms in San Francisco contributed one thousand dollars each to the Commission's California campaign. Nathan Grossmeyer of Washington, DC, contributed ideas as well as money for relief purposes; he was the first to suggest the establishment of a national veterans' hospital and home. In a letter to President Abraham Lincoln on November 16, 1864, Grossmeyer called the president's attention to the provisions for disabled veterans made by various European governments and urged that the United States do no less. President Lincoln was assassinated before he could carry out the suggestion; however, Grossmeyer then wrote Andrew Johnson about the idea and suggested that the home be designated a memorial to Lincoln. Congress adopted the proposal in 1866 (Korn 1951, p. 99).

BIBLIOGRAPHY

Diner, Hasia R. "Jewish People in America." *A Time for Gathering: The Second Migration 1820–1880*, vol. 5, *Striving for the Sacred*, ed. Hasia R. Diner. Baltimore and London: Johns Hopkins University Press, 1992.

Korn, Bertram Wallace. *American Jewry and the Civil War*. Philadelphia: Jewish Publication Society of America, 1951.

St. John, Robert. *Jews, Justice, and Judaism: A Narrative of the Role Played by the Bible People in Shaping American History*. Garden City, NY: Doubleday, 1969.

Deliah K. Brown

interpreted to prohibit slavery, and insisted that, to the contrary, biblical tradition and law guaranteed the right to own slaves. Raphall accused Henry Ward Beecher and other abolitionists of attempting to pervert the meaning of biblical texts and challenged them to produce factual evidence to back up their contention that biblical law mandated the abolishment of slavery (Korn 1951, p. 17).

Never had an American rabbi created such a stir. His sermon was reprinted in newspapers, pamphlets, and books. It was both praised and denounced. Rabbi David Einhorn of Har Sinai Temple, Baltimore, suggested that Jews should be concerned with the spirit and not the literal wording of the Bible, which in his interpretation, acknowledged the existence of slavery in pre-biblical times, but made it clear that it was an evil to be abolished (St. John 1969, p. 153).

During the war, Jews fought valiantly for both the Confederacy and the Union despite the fact that many Americans were as anti-Semitic as they were racist. In addition, many Jews participated in a range of relief efforts as private citizens. For example, August Belmont

■ Chaplains

The Continental Congress officially laid the foundations for the future U.S. Chaplaincy Corps on July 29, 1775, when it authorized Washington to procure a chaplain for each regiment serving in the Continental army. Between the Revolution and Civil War, just like the regular army, the chaplaincy generally languished in peacetime and was rapidly expanded in wartime, when each U.S. brigade was authorized to secure the service of at least one chaplain. In 1838, the U.S. Army set up a new system that provided funding for chaplain positions at West Point and the army's various Western forts and bases. On the eve of the Civil War this system had expanded to thirty post chaplain positions for the nineteen regiments, or 16,000 troops, of the U.S. regular army. But Lincoln's July 22, 1861, call for 500,000 additional volunteers meant that the army's prewar chaplaincy could not possibly address the enormous spiritual needs of the rapidly expanding Union Army (Hourihan 2004).

In May 1861, the federal government dramatically expanded the size of the U.S. Chaplaincy Corps. President Abraham Lincoln ordered the colonels of all regular and volunteer regiments to appoint regimental chaplains to help maintain "the social happiness and moral improvement of the troops" and issue regular reports on the "moral and religious condition" of their units. President Lincoln took a personal interest in the project, convinced that an expanded chaplaincy would not only address Union soldiers' religious needs, but also raise Northern morale by helping volunteers adjust to army life and become better integrated into their units (Shattuck 1987, pp. 52–63).

Not Clearly Defined

Theoretically, the selection process for chaplains mirrored that for other regimental officers, with field officers and company commanders voting to confirm or reject the colonel's nominee, but numerous "unofficial" chaplains served without commissions. The regulations also specified that chaplains were to be "regularly ordained ministers of some Christian denomination," a provision that was later amended by Congress in July 1862 to include spiritual representatives from other prominent religious denominations, such as Jewish rabbis (Wagner 2002, p. 440). During the conflict, more than 3,000 official and unofficial chaplains eventually served in the Union armies, but there were never more than 1,000 chaplains in active service in the army's regiments, hospitals and military posts (Hourihan 2004).

The official rank, uniform, and daily duties of the chaplain were not clearly defined in Lincoln's initial orders. Although they received a cavalry captain's salary and horse from the government, and thus frequently dressed as officers, the government did not officially define them as captains or provide them with uniforms, officers' rations, or forage for their animals (Woodworth 2001, pp. 145–146). Some chaplains' practice of riding behind Union battle lines bearing the weapons and insignia of a cavalry captain provoked enough resentment in the ranks for Congress to issue additional regulations clarifying the chaplains' dress and rank. The government specified that they were to wear a plain black frock coat and cap without any insignia, and that they held the "rank of chaplain, without command" (Hourihan 2004).

Although most Union Army chaplains were dedicated ministers of the Gospel who worked tirelessly to meet their troops' spiritual and physical needs, and bravely accompanied them into battle, too many of the early nominees turned out to be personally or professionally unqualified for their wartime ministries. This was mainly due to the unprecedented demand for chaplains in all the new Northern regiments; the demand had rapidly exhausted the pool of qualified applicants. Few accomplished Northern ministers felt "called" to abandon their successful, well-established ministries in the North for the spartan and highly dangerous life of an underpaid chaplain. Veteran pastors probably also knew from experience how difficult it would be to carve out new ministries among hardened men living outside the normal constraints of society. The other major problem was the high attrition rate in the chaplaincy during the war. Men of the cloth proved highly susceptible to disease, and many returned home after becoming seriously ill or realizing their physical constitution was not up to the task of heavy marching and sleeping outdoors in inclement weather.

Practically Unfit for Their Work

In any event, the successful confirmation of numerous unqualified candidates tarnished the reputation of the entire chaplaincy. According to some soldiers, during the first eighteen months of the war more than half of the chaplains were neither spiritually nor professionally qualified for their posts. After listening to a sermon by a chaplain from the Thirty-third Massachusetts on Sunday, August 16, 1863, John T. McMahon wrote, "I have come to the conclusion that our Chaplains are a class of men who could not get employment at home and by underhanded work have got to be Chaplains. At any rate I never heard a good sermon from a Chaplain yet" (McMahon 1863, p. 60). A lieutenant colonel in the Fifth Massachusetts believed that "at least seventy-five per cent of the chaplains commissioned during the first year of the war were practically unfit for their work"; Milton Bailey of the Forty-third Indiana noted that "over half the preachers that our Government employs at such high prices turn out to be the most deprave siners in the world our firs Chaplain maid no scruples to take things out of houses wher people had left them and was always in the company with abandoned women" (Woodworth 2001, pp. 149–150).

In the first year of the war the charismatic, hard-working chaplain was apparently more the exception than the general rule in the Union Army. In 1863, Sergeant George Chapin told his brother—who coincidentally also happened to be a preacher—that the Twenty-seventh Indiana Infantry Regiment's "chaplain has gone home on furlough tho' we do not miss him for he has been very little account to our regiment.... Thomas A Witted has not preached over a dozen times to the 27th regiment & never held social religious meetings & what is far worse than this he has not walked circumspectly before his men. His example is exceedingly inconsistent resembling more that of a renegade than a Teacher of Christ" (Chapin, February 17, 1863).

Some religious soldiers were extremely disappointed when they discovered that their spiritual shepherds were more interested in pursuing the pleasures of this world than ensuring the safe arrival of their flock in the next. In the fall of 1863, First Lieutenant John Blackwell informed his wife of the "sad state" of religious affairs in his brigade: "I wrote you that one of our chaplains has been sent home for drunkenness & now I have had the painful duty of reporting another, the 116th chaplain, for lending his pants to a lewd woman about camp to conceal her sex" (Blackwell, October 24, 1863).

Notwithstanding this behavior, the reputation of the Civil War chaplaincy was largely redeemed by the dedicated chaplains who did perform their duties extraordinarily well, and by the much larger crop of inspired and competent official and unofficial chaplains who began filling the existing regimental vacancies in late 1862. By then the worst of their kind had mostly returned home for health reasons or easier jobs, or because their wartime ministries had foundered due to their professional or spiritual shortcomings. Meanwhile, most of the chaplains still serving in the ranks had gradually earned the respect of their units and commanders through their steadfast dedication, courage under fire, and sacrificial service for their commands, thus ensuring the future success of their wartime ministries. Having come to recognize the

Henry McNeal Turner (1834–1915), first black chaplain in the Civil War. Chaplains in the Union army not only tended to the spiritual health of their wartime congregation, but also assisted doctors in battlefield hospitals, taught illiterate soldiers to read, and helped notify the kin of deceased soldiers. Across enemy lines, however, the Confederate army did not actively seek chaplains, and the few who did serve generally fought alongside the soldiers in battle. *© North Wind Picture Archive.*

valuable services rendered by a good chaplain, colonels and company officers also were exercising greater caution and care when replacing previously unsuitable candidates.

"I Don't Know How I Could Live Here Without Him"

Another major reason for the improved performance of the Union chaplains was that the physical requirements, dress, and duties of the chaplaincy were now more clearly defined—in books such as Reverend W. Y. Brown's *The Army Chaplain: His Office, Duties, and Responsibilities and Means of Aiding Him* (1863), a first-rate guidebook written by a highly successful Northern hospital chaplain. Brown emphasized that successful chaplains needed to do more than just preach weekly sermons, conduct prayer meetings, and administer last rites. In addition to performing their regular spiritual duties, chaplains also cared for the wounded, both on and off the battlefield; distributed stationary and helped soldiers write letters home to their families; wrote to the families of dead soldiers to inform them of their loved one's heroic sacrifice; secured and maintained regimental libraries containing books on both spiritual and secular topics; served as regimental postmasters and messengers; and in their free time, taught illiterate soldiers and contrabands how to read and write. Their service in the regiment reflected Christ's principle of servant leadership. On long marches they offered to haul the soldiers' heavier equipment on their horses or offered their mounts to sick soldiers, and when the regiment had to perform a hard manual-labor or foraging assignment, they energetically pitched in with the rest of the men.

From late 1862 on, the soldiers' correspondence generally documented a growing appreciation for their chaplains' ministries. In October 1863, Elisha Hunt Rhodes kept urging his fellow officers to nominate a new chaplain after their first spiritual shepherd proved to be a miserable failure: "Some of the officers were opposed and were afraid that we might get another man like Jameson," but were later persuaded, and "after much talk, I nominated Mr. Beugless .... He has already made himself very popular, and I trust God will bless his labors.... Many of the soldiers are good Christian men, but need some one to guide them. I feel greatly rejoiced over the prospect for the future" (Rhodes 1985, pp. 125–126). Private David King also rejoiced at the arrival of his new chaplain: "Our Pastor has come at last and he is a fine man and a good preacher" (King, April 16, 1864). In late December 1863, Andrew J. McGarrah of the Sixty-third Indiana expressed his appreciation for the religious books and tracts his unit's "fine little" chaplain was distributing: "he furnishes us with good Books tracts and papers and is going to establish a Bible class" (McGarrah, December 16, 1863). Vermont soldier Charles A. Manson also boasted that his unit "had

JEWISH CHAPLAINS IN THE CIVIL WAR

The Civil War was the first American conflict in which the military chaplaincy was opened to Jewish rabbis as well as to Christian clergy. There were about 6,500 Jews in the Union Army in 1861, as well as 2,000 in the Confederate Army, but there was no provision for their religious needs at the beginning of the war. Although Congress recognized the need for regimental chaplains to serve the rapidly expanding Union Army, the act that was passed in August 1861 stipulated that they must be "regularly ordained ministers of some Christian denomination and were to be selected and appointed as the President may direct" (Bates 1864, p. 280). Arnold Fischel, a Philadelphia rabbi, lobbied various congressmen for the next eleven months to have the wording of the law changed. In addition to Fischel, the Board of Delegates of American Israelites petitioned President Abraham Lincoln (1809–1865) to open the military chaplaincy to Jewish rabbis as well as to Christian clergy.

Lincoln then made a recommendation to Congress in favor of the change. On July 17, 1862, the wording of the act providing for regimental chaplains was altered to read as follows:

> That no person shall be appointed a chaplain in the United States Army who is not a regularly ordained minister of some religious denomination, and who does not present testimonials of his good standing as such minister, with a recommendation of his appointment as an Army chaplain from some authorized ecclesiastical body, or not less than five accredited ministers belonging to said religious denomination (U.S. War Department 1862, p. 521).

After the law was changed Rabbi Fischel served as a civilian chaplain during the Civil War, ministering to Jewish personnel in the Army of the Potomac.

The first rabbi to be officially commissioned as a chaplain in the Union Army was Rabbi Jacob Frankel of Congregation Rodeph Shalom in Philadelphia, Pennsylvania. Frankel came from a musical family and was known as "the sweet singer of Israel" for his beautiful voice. He was commissioned by President Lincoln on September 18, 1862, and served until July 1, 1865. Rabbi Frankel ministered to wounded soldiers in military hospitals in the Philadelphia area, singing and praying with them. He valued his years as a chaplain so highly that he had his commission framed and displayed in his home.

The first Jewish chaplain who saw combat in the Civil War was Rabbi Ferdinand Leopold Samer, who emigrated to the United States from Germany. Rabbi Samer was elected by the largely German-speaking soldiers of the 54th New York Volunteer Regiment, the so-called *Schwarze Jäger*, to be their chaplain. He was commissioned on April 10, 1863. Following a severe wound received at the Battle of Gettysburg (1863), Rabbi Samer was discharged for medical disabilities in October 1864.

REBECCA J. FREY

BIBLIOGRAPHY

Bates, Edward. "Opinion of Attorney General Bates on Paying a Colored Chaplain." *The Political History of the United States of America during The Great Rebellion,* ed. Edward McPherson. Washington, DC: Philp and Solomons, 1864.

Patrick, Bethanne Kelly. "Jacob Frankel." *Military.com.* Available from http://www.military.com/.

Slomovitz, Albert Isaac. *The Fighting Rabbis: Jewish Military Chaplains and American History. New York:* New York University Press, 1999.

U.S. War Department. Revised Regulations for the Army of the United States, 1861. *Philadelphia: George W. Childs, 1862.*

one of the best chaplains," because recently, "he had had given every soldier in the regiment a Soldiers prayer Book" (Manson, October 18, 1862).

Most soldiers apparently believed that the unofficial chaplains serving short-term missions in the army with the U.S. Christian Commission came the closest to exemplifying Brown's ideal of a military chaplain, but by late 1862, the energetic preaching and teaching of conscientious, hardworking official chaplains was also finally beginning to bear fruit. In a late September 1862 diary entry, Berea M. Willsey recorded that "Nothing has been talked of this forenoon but the sermon we had yesterday. I hope good results will follow" (Willsey 1995, p. 49). First Lieutenant Dwight Fraser told his sisters, "Our Chaplain is a very fine man and is the highest sense a Christian gentleman..... It is quite a treat for us to get together once in a while and have preaching and singing and prayer. It seems a good deal like a Camp Meeting to me, and I think these exercises are calculated to do much good among the men" (Fraser, June 25–26, 1864). W. S. Bower told his sister that his chaplain's prayer meetings were very "profitable to us.... There was 18 present last time [and] our number is increasing. Some are beginning to enquire the way our chaplain is loved by all. I don't know how I could live here without him" (Bower, April 17, 1863). Many Union chaplains' exemplary service after 1862 apparently helped atone for the earlier sins and failures of their peers. Three Union chaplains even received the Congressional Medal of Honor for their heroic wartime service—either fighting at the front or caring for wounded soldiers while under fire.

The Sword over the Gown

On the Confederate side, Jefferson Davis initially opposed the creation of a Southern military chaplaincy because he thought the South needed soldiers, not ministers, and because, like most Southerners reared with the Spirituality of the Church doctrine espoused by the Presbyterian minister James Henley Thornwell (1812–1862), he believed such religious concerns were best left to individual churches, not the state. Although the Richmond government later reluctantly organized a chaplaincy to placate the spiritual concerns of prominent Southern Christians and churches, Southern chaplains were paid significantly less than their Northern counterparts, were issued even fewer instructions regarding their duties, and received virtually no support from their government. As a result, there was always a severe shortage of Confederate chaplains serving in the army, and less than half of the Confederate units ever received one. Lacking detailed orders concerning their military status, many of those who did serve became "fighting chaplains," and were thus far more likely to be wounded or killed in combat than their Northern counterparts (Shattuck 1987, pp. 47, 63–68).

In the first years of the war most Southern churchmen seemed more interested in embracing the role of an Old Testament warrior—such as Joshua or King David—than in ministering to the spiritual needs of Southern soldiers. When Jefferson Davis asked his former West Point roommate, the Episcopal bishop Leonidas Polk (1806–1864), to accept a commission as major general in the Confederate States Army, Polk immediately suspended his religious duties so he could buckle his "sword over the gown" and serve the South as a warrior-priest. Over the next year, many other Southern clergymen apparently felt inspired to follow his lead. In Richmond, Sallie Putnam noted that Virginia clergymen such as William N. Pendleton (1809–1883) and Dabney Harrison were shedding their clerical vestments and girding on "the armor of the soldier ... not with a wish to lead in a rebellion ... but from a stern sense of divine direction and the whisperings of patriotism to which conscience and an innate feeling of duty prompted and would not be stilled" (Putnam [1867] 1961, p. 49).

Ministers from other denominations across the South seemed to share Polk's sentiment that fighting the war should take precedence over their local ministries or any spiritual outreach to the troops. Catherine Hopley, an English subject living in Virginia during the war, was shocked when the local Baptist minister she invited to dinner suddenly exclaimed: "I cannot rest here, I believe I must enlist too. I feel that my country calls me, and that I might be as useful on the battlefield as in my church. Has not Bishop Polk set me an example? And there is S. who has volunteered, and M. intends to do the same" (Hopley [1861] 1971, pp. 329–330). Perhaps Hopley's dinner guest and colleagues were among the dozens of Baptist ministers across Georgia, North Carolina, and Virginia who organized local companies and marched off to war, leaving their congregations to fend for themselves. The Methodist camp was

also decimated by fever for war. Bishop George Foster Pierce noted that so many Methodist ministers had enlisted in the Confederate army that the work of the December 1861 Atlanta Conference was impaired (Smith 1888, p. 447). Increasingly concerned with the excessive "war spirit among our preachers," Bishop Pierce announced that in the future, Methodist preachers should only go to war as chaplains, not soldiers (Owen 1998, pp. 103–105). The Virginian Presbyterian, Robert Lewis Dabney, also believed that ministers like himself should not compromise their moral power "to act as peace-makers and mediators," and urged Virginia's Christians to "arise and conquer in this war by the power of prayer." After taking a leave of absence from his seminary to serve as a chaplain in Beauregard's army, however, Dabney's earlier convictions and noncombatant status did not prevent him from serving as a battlefield courier in the First Battle of Manassas (July 1861), or from later serving as "Stonewall" Jackson's chief of staff (Johnson 1903, pp. 221–272).

The Eternal Message of Grace and Love to Perishing Sinners

Shortly before his death in 1863, General Stonewall Jackson urgently requested that the Southern churches send additional clergymen to his army to care for the spiritual needs of his men. In response to Jackson's request, despite a critical shortage of local clergy, the 1863 Annual Council of the Episcopal Diocese of Virginia temporarily stripped some hard-pressed clergymen of their parishes so they could serve short-term mission trips with the Rebel army. In what appeared to be the beginning of a gradual shift in policy, the Episcopal Council also asked that its ministers stop preaching sermons "on the times and the war and the objects of our country's hopes" and instead focus on "the glad tidings of salvation, [or] just the eternal message of grace and love to perishing sinners" (Episcopal Church, Diocese of Virginia 1863, p. 39). In other words, the churches should shift the emphasis of their preaching away from a Yankee-appropriated Confederate jeremiad and back to the more urgent and traditional spiritual business of individual salvation.

This return to the gospel of individual salvation later reaped handsome rewards, as major revivals began to blaze through the Army of Northern Virginia. Having failed to redeem the home front, the Southern churches continued to dispatch spiritual emissaries or eleventh-hour "chaplains" to help feed the burgeoning revivals at the front. At home, popular interest in the army revivals soared as many hoped the spiritual enthusiasm in the army would somehow spill over to their communities and help spiritually renew the home front as well.

Military events in 1864 and the spring of 1865, however, soon dispelled such illusions. Instead of unlocking the spiritual door to victory, the Southern revivals had apparently just sanctified soldiers for their imminent deaths at places such as Spotsylvania Courthouse and Petersburg. The final defeat of the Confederacy provoked a profound spiritual crisis as the Southern churches and their emissaries to the troops tried to ascertain what had gone wrong with the Confederate experiment. Still convinced of the righteousness of their lost cause, they could only conclude that like the examples of Job and Christ, the life and death of the Confederacy was intended to accomplish some higher, presently unknown, purpose. Southern Christians took comfort in a literal, common-sense exegesis of the scriptures that assured them that God had never intended His Church's final victory to come in this world. When the Confederate chaplains returned from the war, they helped their churches pursue revival at home with the same spirit it had been pursued in the army.

BIBLIOGRAPHY

Bennet, William W. *A Narrative of the Great Revival Which Prevailed in the Southern Armies during the Late Civil War.* [1876]. Harrisonburg, VA: Sprinkle Publications, 1989.

Blackwell, John A. Civil War Letters. Indiana State Historical Society, Indianapolis.

Bower, W. S. In Robert Steele Papers. State Historical Society of Wisconsin. Madison, Wisconsin.

Brown, William Young. *The Army Chaplain: His Office, Duties, and Responsibilities, and the Means of Aiding Him.* Philadelphia: Martien, 1863.

Chapin, George T. Civil War Papers. Indiana State Historical Society, Indianapolis.

Fraser, Dwight. Civil War Letters. Indiana State Historical Society, Indianapolis.

Episcopal Church, Diocese of Virginia. "Journal of the Sixty-eighth Annual Council of the Protestant Episcopal Church in Virginia. Held in St. Paul's Church, Richmond on the 20th, 21st and 22nd May, 1863." Richmond, VA: B. R. Wren, 1863. Available from http://docsouth.unc.edu/.

Hopley, Catherine C. *Life in the South; From the Commencement of the War by a Blockaded British Subject Being a Social History of Those Who Took Part in the Battles, From a Personal Acquaintance with Them in Their Homes from the Spring of 1860 to August 1862*, vol. 1. [1861]. New York: A. M. Kelley, 1971.

Hourihan, William J. "A Brief History of the United States Chaplain Corps: Pro Deo Et Patria." 2004. Available from http://www.usachcs.army.mil/.

Johnson, Thomas C. *The Life and Letters of Robert Lewis Dabney.* Richmond, VA: Presbyterian Committee of Publication, 1903.

King, David, Jr. King Family Papers. Illinois State Historical Library. Springfield, Illinois.

Manson, Charles A. Papers. Robert W. Woodruff Library. Emory University. Atlanta, Georgia.

McGarrah, Andrew J. Civil War Letters. Indiana State Historical Society. Indianapolis.

McMahon, John T. *John T. McMahon's Diary of the 136th New York 1861-1864.* Edited by John Michael Priest. Shippenberg, PA: White Mane, 1993.

Norton, Herman A. *Struggling for Recognition: The United States Army Chaplaincy, 1791–1865.* Washington, DC: Office of the Chief of Chaplains, Department of the Army, 1977.

Owen, Christopher H. *The Sacred Flame of Love: Methodism and Society in Nineteenth-Century Georgia.* Athens: University of Georgia Press, 1998.

Putman, Sallie A. *In Richmond during the Confederacy: By a Lady of Richmond.* [1867], ed. Sally Brock. New York: G.V. Carlton, 1961.

Rhodes, Elisha Hunt. *All for the Union: The Civil War Diary and Letters of Elisha Hunt Rhodes.* Edited by Robert Hunt Rhodes. New York: Orion Books, 1985.

Rolfs, David W. "No Peace For the Wicked: How Northern Christians Justified Their Participation in the American Civil War." Ph.D. diss. Florida State University, 2002.

Shattuck, Gardiner H., Jr. *A Shield and a Hiding Place: The Religious Life of the Civil War Armies.* Macon, GA: Mercer University Press, 1987.

Smith, George G. *The Life and Times of George Foster Pierce, D.D., LL.D. Bishop of the Methodist Church, South with His Sketch of Lovick Pierce, D.D., His Father.* Sparta, GA: Hancock Publishing Company, 1888.

Wagner, Margaret E., Gary W. Gallagher, and Paul Finkelman., eds. *The Library of Congress Civil War Desk Reference.* New York: Simon and Schuster, 2002.

Willsey, Berea M. *The Civil War Diary of Berea M. Willsey*, ed. Jessica H. Demay. Bowie, MD: Heritage Books, 1995.

Woodworth, Steven E. *While God Is Marching On: The Religious World of Civil War Soldiers.* Lawrence: University Press of Kansas, 2001.

David W. Rolfs

■ Army Missionaries

Army missionaries ministered to both the Confederate and Union Armies. These persons were defined by the historian Steven Woodworth as "ministers who had no official role in the military establishment and did not necessarily intend to remain permanently with the army" (2001, p. 160). As opposed to chaplains, these individuals were not attached to a specific regiment or brigade and thus could move from place to place as needed. Father Paul E. Gillen's missionary work in the Army of the Potomac as a Roman Catholic priest serves as a perfect example. He moved "from regiment to regiment, and wherever he found a few dozen Catholics, there he 'pitched his tent,' staid a day or two, heard all their confessions, celebrated holy Mass, and communicated those ready to receive" (Corby 1992, p. 309).

Missionaries' Roles

As Gillen's experience illustrates quite clearly, missionaries functioned much like chaplains, providing care in hospitals and distributing Bibles and other religious literature as well as preaching to troops in camp. Their temporary positions allowed churches on the home front to continue to hold services. The missionaries' role also prevented the waste of their talents during times of the year when preaching services were usually not held.

In both the North and South, the main role of the missionaries was the distribution of tracts, Bibles, and other forms of religious literature. The specific missionaries who participated in this work were known as colporteurs. A prominent Methodist missionary, William W. Bennett, served on the Confederate side. Bennett noted in his 1876 *A Narrative of the Great Revival Which Prevailed in the Southern Armies During the Late Civil War Between the States of the Federal Union,* that the missionaries as a group sought "to turn the thoughts of the soldiers not to a sect, but to Christ, to bring them into the great spiritual temple, and to show them the wonders of salvation" (p. 71). These individuals were quite inclusive and represented several denominations that had large memberships in the Southern states—the Baptists, the Presbyterians, the Episcopalians, and the Methodists—each of which sent their own contingent of colporteurs.

As Bennett further explained in his text, in the South the Baptists were the first to organize, setting themselves up under the General Association of the Baptist churches in Virginia in May 1861. Subsequently, the Presbyterians organized as the Presbyterian Board of Publication, directed by the Reverend Dr. Leyburn. Next, the Virginia Episcopal Mission Committee formed under the direction of the Reverend Messrs. Gatewood and Kepler of the Protestant Episcopal Church. The Virginia Episcopal Mission was formed after the Episcopal dioceses in the South formed the Episcopal Church in the C.S.A. Finally, the Methodist Episcopal Church formed their colporteur group in March of 1862 (Bennett 1876, pp. 72, 74–76).

In addition to these missions provided to members of specific Christian denominations within the Confederacy, the Evangelical Tract Society, organized in July 1861, included within its ranks an interdenominational group of Christians. According to Bennett, this body issued over a hundred different tracts (pp. 72, 74–76). Noting the importance of this devotional literature to the soldiers at war, the historian Beth Schweiger asserts that the tracts and Bibles themselves served as "the great evangelists of the war" (2000, p. 101).

The United States Christian Commission

Many missionaries served within the Union armies, under the auspices of the United States Christian Commission (USCC), a national group formed in November 1861 upon the urging of the New York Young Men's Christian Association (YMCA). No comparable institution existed within the Confederacy. According to Woodworth, the USCC at the height of its power contained about five thousand delegates from various denominations across the North, "with field superintendents in each army corps" (2001, p. 167).

Historian Gardiner Shattuck relates that the USCC had two main goals during the war, one spiritual and the other more physical. First and foremost, the missionaries were to help regimental chaplains in all aspects of their jobs: in providing pastoral care for their men, distributing tracts, and also helping with worship services. Second,

Rep. John Hyatt Smith (1824–1886) of New York. Smith served with the U.S. Christian Commission in Virginia in 1862. Many individuals contributed to the war effort in the North and South by working as independent missionaries among the troops, conducting religious services, offering spiritual advice, and distributing reading material. *The Library of Congress*

they were to provide for the physical needs of the soldiers themselves (1987, p. 27).

An example of meeting the latter goal took place at Petersburg in 1864. The USCC gave Chaplain Henry Clay Trumbull of the Army of the Potomac a basket of fresh peaches, which he distributed "among the men on duty in the advanced trenches, one peach to each man" (Trumbull 1898, p. 116). In another example, at Fortress Monroe in Virginia in August 1864, a Christian Commission delegate, Thomas Scott Johnson, explained in one of his letters that the USCC provided supplies for both the hospitals in the area as well as "the hospital transports that load at this point." He subsequently concluded, "We are thus reaching as far as may be all the cases of suffering among our brave boys" (Kaliebe 1966, p. 28).

Not all Union missionaries, however, were affiliated with the United States Christian Commission. Some worked for independent tract societies or missionary associations. In a letter written to his brother Ned, Chaplain Joseph Hopkins Twichell of the Seventy-First New York Infantry Regiment noted the impressive work of the missionary John Vassar of the New York Tract Society during a period of revival within the Army of the Potomac. Twichell described Vassar as "the most wonderful Christian I ever saw ... He, by fervent prayers and exhortations, stirred us mightily" (Messant and Courtney 2006, p. 274). According to a Massachusetts newspaper, the *Lowell Daily Citizen and News* (October 7, 1861), another missionary, the Reverend L. C. Lockwood, affiliated with the American Missionary Association, was commissioned and sent to Fortress Monroe to teach the contraband laborers.

Missionaries admirably ministered in both the Union and Confederate armies during the Civil War, augmenting and aiding the work of chaplains in fostering religious devotion within the armies. Their most important duty, however, was as colporteurs distributing religious tracts and Bibles to those troops enduring the profaneness of army life. This literature aided greatly in promoting revivals within both the Union and Confederate armies, yielding men reborn into the Christian faith by the trials and tribulations of war.

BIBLIOGRAPHY

Bennett, William W. *A Narrative of the Great Revival Which Prevailed in the Southern Armies During the Late Civil War between the States of the Federal Union.* Philadelphia: Claxton, Remsen and Haffelfinger, 1876.

Corby, William. *Memoirs of Chaplain Life: Three Years with the Irish Brigade in the Army of the Potomac,* ed. Lawrence Frederick Kohl. New York: Fordham University Press, 1992.

Kaliebe, Jon Edward. "The Letters of Thomas Scott Johnson: His Work among the Negro as Christian Commission Delegate and Chaplain, 1864–1866." Master's thesis, University of Wisconsin, 1966.

Messent, Peter, and Steve Courtney, eds. *The Civil War Letters of Joseph Hopkins Twichell: A Chaplain's Story.* Athens: University of Georgia Press, 2006.

"Missionaries among the 'Contraband,'" *Lowell* (MA) *Daily Citizen and News,* October 7, 1861.

Schweiger, Beth Barton. *The Gospel Working Up: Progress and the Pulpit in Nineteenth-Century Virginia.* New York: Oxford University Press, 2000.

Shattuck, Jr., Gardiner H. *A Shield and Hiding Place: The Religious Life of the Civil War Armies.* Macon, GA: Mercer University Press, 1987.

Trumbull, Henry Clay. *War Memories of an Army Chaplain.* New York: Charles Scribner's Sons, 1898.

Woodworth, Steven E. *While God Is Marching On: The Religious World of Civil War Soldiers.* Lawrence: University Press of Kansas, 2001.

Benjamin L. Miller

Popular Culture

■ Popular Culture Overview

The forms of popular culture Americans experienced and participated in during the Civil War era varied according to the part of the country in which they lived and their personal preferences. Residents of the rural interior had different opportunities for diversion than did denizens of the relatively cosmopolitan cities, and Americans' ideas about desirable use of leisure time differed as widely in the mid-nineteenth century as they do in the twenty-first, even if many of the specific activities and attractions are much different.

One of the forms of entertainment available in many cities and towns was the theater. British theater was also popular in America. The British actress Laura Keene (1826–1873) came to America in 1852 and became an immediate favorite. In New York in 1855 she opened Laura Keene's Theater, which she managed until 1863. Thereafter she continued to star in her own traveling theater troupe, performing a variety of plays including the British playwright Tom Taylor's popular 1858 farcical comedy "Our American Cousin," which Keene and her company presented at Ford's Theater in Washington, DC, for an audience that included President and Mrs. Abraham Lincoln on April 14, 1865. That performance was disastrously cut short midway through Scene 2 of Act III when Lincoln was assassinated by John Wilkes Booth (1838–1865).

Traveling thespians were not unusual during this era, and performances even by the most renowned actors of the day were not entirely limited to East coast cities, even if they were more frequent and abundant there. America's most famous acting family, the Booths, appeared in many cities, towns, and smaller venues during the decades preceding the Civil War. Junius Brutus Booth Sr. (1796–1852) and his son Edwin Booth (1833–1893) famously toured gold rush California, performing Shakespeare for the Forty-niners. In 1864 the Booths performed *Julius Caesar* in New York City, the only performance in which Junius Brutus Sr. and Edwin appeared on stage with the youngest member of the family, John Wilkes Booth, who was by then famous in his own right. Reputed to be the most handsome man in America, the youngest Booth son was already known for his energetic performances and onstage acrobatics. Less well known was his bitter racism and deep sympathy for the Confederate cause.

More readily accessible to most Americans than the theater was popular literature. The romantic novel was the favorite light reading material of many. The British novelist Sir Walter Scott (1771–1832) was a favorite of Americans of both the North and South before the war, and his books continued to be popular long after Appomattox. Scott had his American imitators, most notably William Gilmore Simms (1806–1870), a South Carolinian who tried to cultivate a distinctly Southern literature. At the opposite extreme of sectional literature was Harriet Beecher Stowe's enormously popular 1852 novel *Uncle Tom's Cabin*. Based on interviews with escaped slaves, Stowe's book was aimed at illustrating the evils of the system of slavery. Naturally, it was anathema south of the Mason-Dixon line. Louisa May Alcott (1832–1888) was not yet well known at the time of the Civil War, though her first book, *Flower Fables*, had appeared in 1854, and her 1864 novel, *Moods*, was received well by critics. She gained far more recognition for her 1863 nonfiction work, *Hospital Sketches*, which drew on her experience as a volunteer nurse in Union hospitals. Much greater fame awaited her 1868 book, *Little Women*. The Civil War was also the era of Transcendentalist authors such as Herman Melville (1819–1891) and the poet Walt Whitman (1819–1892), though their works had somewhat less appeal to popular audiences.

A significant segment of the American population looked somewhat askance at the reading of novels, and at most or all of the theater. For some devout Christians, novel reading and theater going represented worldly distractions that might draw them away from God. Other Americans, whether strongly religious or not, saw such pursuits as unprofitable and intellectually stultifying distractions for idle minds. For them, serious books and educational lectures were preferable.

Appropriately, therefore, a popular and educational feature of American culture during the antebellum period was the lyceum. The teacher and traveling lecturer Josiah Holbrook (1778–1854) founded the first American lyceum in 1826 in Millbury, Massachusetts. Holbrook believed learning should be a life-long passion, and he hoped to spread the concept of the lyceum as a regular venue for educational lectures in each locality. By the 1850s his dream had largely become a reality, with lyceums established throughout the country, sponsoring lectures on topics ranging from literature to science to current events and issues. Large eastern lyceums paid impressive fees to major figures of the day such as Ralph Waldo Emerson (1803–1882) and Henry David Thoreau (1817–1862), and top orators such as Edward Everett Hale (1822–1909) regularly worked the lyceum circuit. More remote lyceums might have had to turn to local talent, as when the Springfield Young Men's Lyceum in January 1838 heard up-and-coming twenty-eight-year-old Springfield lawyer and politician Abraham Lincoln speak on "The Preservation of Our Political Institutions." After the Civil War, lyceums gradually came to present more drama and entertainment and less lecture.

More active, if less intellectual, entertainment was to be found in physical activities. Children might play active games such as crack the whip or leapfrog, but adults usually did not. Some might play card games, though others eschewed such pastimes as sinful because of their close association with gambling. The closest means in which adults usually came to active physical play was by making some communal work activity into something like a game. This might be a corn-husking, a barn-raising, or a chopping bee. Those who did not have religious scruples against it might also engage in dancing. Also, the Civil War brought an exception to the usual rule that adults did not play physical games. The soldiers, many of whom were very young men barely out of their teens, often referred to themselves as "the boys." It made sense then that when boredom weighed heavily on them in camp, they took up some of the games they recently had played in the schoolyard. A favorite was known as "drive ball" or "town ball," and involved a player with a stick trying to hit some sort of ball thrown by one of the other players. It may be that the war, by bringing together thousands of young men with much unavoidable and generally tedious leisure time in the army camps, helped them to develop, regularize, and spread this game, which later came to be called "baseball." However, contrary to legend, it was not invented by the Civil War general Abner Doubleday (1819–1893).

Reading, playing, dancing, attending lyceum, theater, or religious worship, Americans of the Civil War era had many options for amusing themselves and occupying their free time, but of course work was the activity that took up the majority of the time of most adults, and to a far greater extent than is true in the twenty-first century.

Steven E. Woodworth

■ Performing Arts

PERFORMING ARTS: AN OVERVIEW
   Kerry L. Pimblott

MINSTREL SHOWS
   Eric R. Jackson

THEATER
   John L. Reilly

PERFORMING ARTS: AN OVERVIEW

The social upheaval of the Civil War disrupted and transformed the world of performing arts and the nature of the theatergoing public. As the nation mobilized for war, theaters throughout the country were forced to close their doors under the dual strains of mass enlistment and reallocation of vital resources. Those that continued to operate sought to attract new audiences by altering their schedules in accordance with a broader transformation of cultural tastes. Accordingly, the age group, gender, and class distinctions that had characterized the theater during the early nineteenth century were challenged, allowing women—as both performers and spectators—to redefine the boundaries of the public sphere and transform the theatergoing experience for all Americans. The minstrel show, however, remained the nation's most popular theatrical pursuit, bringing into relief the limits of wartime inclusion and the ongoing significance of white supremacy in the era of emancipation.

Initial Effects of the War

During the initial stages of the war, theaters across the country struggled to maintain regular operations. In New York, the *Herald* lamented the decline in theater attendance, complaining that there were frequently "more people upon the stage than in the audience" (August 5, 1861, p. 3). By the following year little had changed, with the *Herald* reporting that most of the leading theaters were still closed, "not only in New York, but in all the other large cities," and that "great uncertainty prevails as to the arrangements of many of them for the coming season" (August 18, 1862, p. 2). In an effort to rationalize matters, New Orleans's *Daily Picayune* contended that it could "hardly be expected that the theatres should be very liberally patronized" during wartime when the "theatre of war, with its stirring incidents of terrible reality, absorbs more of the popular interest than the theatre of mimic and amusing representations" (September 14, 1862, p. 1).

Dwindling audiences and the widespread closure of local theaters left many actors seeking employment. Some of the more prestigious actors looked outside the United States for a renewed supply of challenging and innovative roles. For example, after performing before small audiences at New York's Winter Garden, the celebrated actor Edwin Booth (1833–1893), the older brother of John Wilkes Booth, accepted an offer from the Haymarket Theatre in London to play Shylock in Shakespeare's *The Merchant of Venice* during the summer of 1861. The vast majority of dramatic artists, however, looked for work domestically in segments of the performing arts formerly beneath their notice. As Horace Greeley's *Daily Tribune* reported, the general shutdown of theaters resulted in actors from across the country relocating to New York to gain employment in the city's minstrel shows (August 19, 1861). Opera singers such as David Miranda, Brookhouse Bowler, and Aynsley Cook donned blackface and appeared with local minstrel troupes. Similarly, the celebrated singers Agnes Sutherland, George Crozier, and Johanna Ficher all took jobs in the city's concert saloon scene.

Cultivating New Audiences

Theaters that survived the challenges of wartime sought to attract new audiences by altering their schedules in accordance with the broader transformation of cultural tastes then taking place. One of the most popular strategies among theater managers was to cultivate new markets by appealing to women and children. During the early nineteenth century, theaters were widely considered unseemly and unsafe for females to attend without a male escort. The economic depression of the mid-1850s and declining profits during the Civil War, however, encouraged theater managers to challenge Victorian mores that limited female appearances in the public sphere.

During the war it became much more acceptable for women to attend theaters unescorted, a fact that theater managers capitalized on by establishing matinee (afternoon) performances geared specifically to women. For example, P. T. Barnum announced in December 1862 that his theater would feature a matinee performance for the first time. According to coverage in the *Boston Herald*, Barnum had taken "every precaution" to ensure "that ladies or children can visit the establishment unattended without fear of annoyance" (December 17, 1862, p. 4). As the war continued unabated, the trend toward matinees increased. In the spring of 1865, the *New York Clipper* reported that matinees "are on the increase" and that "ladies are the chief patrons of these day entertainments" (April 8, 1865, p. 414).

The increased attendance of women also affected theater managers' decisions about the types of productions they would feature on their stages as well as the scheduling of afternoon performances. As the historian Richard Butsch has demonstrated, sensational melodramas were particularly popular with female theatergoers during the

1860s. Moreover, these plays often replaced the traditional manly hero with an assertive female protagonist. For example, Dio Boucicault's *The Colleen Bawn* featured two strong female leads.

According to Butsch, however, the feminization of the theater had adverse affects on the male theatergoing population, many of whom found sentimental melodrama tedious and went in search of other forms of entertainment (Butsch 1994, p. 391). This dynamic was enhanced during the war by an emphasis on masculine virility and heroism associated with the soldier. In the theater, a variety of efforts were made to appeal to male audiences. Increasing numbers of middle-class males attended working-class concert saloons to watch women perform in burlesque shows. The elite counterpart of the burlesque show came in the form of the musical extravaganza, which emerged as a genre during wartime. These performances included a combination of comical acts and ballet dancers in revealing costumes. An early and popular example was the Laura Keene Theatre's *Seven Sisters*, which ran for 253 performances in 1860–1861 and saved the theater from closure. The actress Adah Isaacs Menken (1835–1868) also capitalized on the relaxation of sexual norms during wartime in *Mazeppa*, causing a sensation by riding a horse on stage in flesh-colored tights that gave the illusion of nudity. *Mazeppa* ran for eight months on Broadway and then went on tour in 1863, earning Menken more than $100,000.

Rise of Popular Entertainment

The efforts of elite theaters to maintain wartime attendance and profits were significant, but were ultimately eclipsed by the tremendous success of more popular forms of entertainment. Magical acts, burlesques, concert saloons, beer gardens, and, most notably, minstrel shows prospered by catering to a predominantly urban working-class male audience. While other theaters were quickly going out of business, New York's Bryant Minstrels were performing to large audiences at Mechanics' Hall throughout the war. Among the many other groups active in New York were Hooley and Campbell's Minstrels, Lloyd's Minstrels, and Sharpley's Minstrels. This pattern was not confined to New York City. The *Boston Herald* reported in 1861 that the city's Opera House had reopened with the Morris Brothers, Pell and Trowbridge Minstrels performing before "a crammed audience" (August 6, 1861, p. 2).

The replacement of more traditional forms of theater with minstrel shows and these new shows' predominantly working-class audiences raised concern amongst segments of the elite. Despite giving Hooley and Campbell's Minstrels a positive review for their performances at the Walnut Street Theatre in Philadelphia, the *North American and United States Gazette* lamented that such success could not be shared more broadly across the city's theater scene:

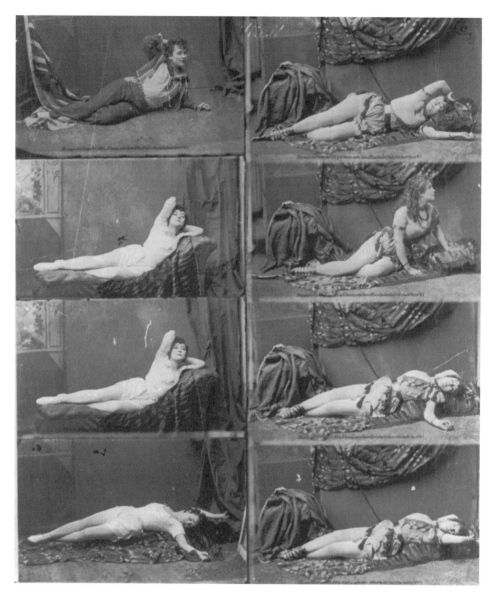

Actress Adah Isaacs Menken (1835–1868). As attendance dwindled at theaters during the Civil War, promoters looked for new avenues of entertainment. Adah Isaacs Menken, pictured here, filled theaters with her suggestive performance in *Mazeppa*, where she donned a flesh-colored body suit and rode bareback on a horse across the stage. *The Library of Congress*

We greatly regret that all our theatres are not open at this time, and that our citizens will not recognize the need of making the city attractive at a time when so many people usually travel for recreation or health. New York has always found it to her interest to do so. If we are answered that the state of the times does not admit of much traveling, we must urge that many thousands of fugitives from the south are constantly seeking protection at the north, and will be likely to remain here at least through the summer. As the war progresses southward, the number of these fugitives will of course increase extensively, and it would not be strange if southern

people of fortune generally were to seek refuge with us. (July 8, 1861, p. 802)

The *Gazette* reporter subtly invoked both a commercial and a moral interest in balancing minstrel shows with more elite leisure activities that "people of fortune" could enjoy, and that in turn would render Philadelphia a more "attractive" city.

Minstrel Shows

In spite of elite disapproval, minstrel shows—with their combination of comic skits, dance routines, and musical acts performed by white people in blackface—remained extraordinarily popular. Central to the narrative structure of minstrelsy was the mockery of African Americans through a series of disparaging stereotypes. Minstrel skits depicted a world in which slaves were happy, docile beings who loved their masters and dreaded leaving their plantation homes. Left to their own devices, these skits implied, African Americans lacked the motivation and intelligence to participate in society as coequals with whites. Therefore, the minstrel shows suggested, African Americans were better kept in slavery with white slaveholders functioning as their benevolent caretakers. Taken collectively, the stereotypes propagated by the minstrel show functioned as a powerful political defense of slavery.

During the Civil War, proslavery arguments remained a staple of the minstrel show both north and south of the Mason-Dixon Line. According to the historian Richard C. Toll, many Northern minstrel performers were fierce nationalists whose main objective was to restore the Union despite the important sectional differences that existed over slavery. Therefore, Northern minstrel troupes mobilized the myth of the docile slave to demonstrate that the abolition of slavery was unnecessary to the preservation of the Union. White minstrels in blackface depicted slaves as confused by the war and resentful of the disruption it brought to their idyllic plantation home.

The real villains of the minstrel shows were the abolitionists and profiteers who exacerbated the conflict for their own political and material benefit. According to the minstrel shows, abolitionists manipulated slaves to gain political power and prestige. In addition, the minstrel shows attacked Northern corporate elites who, they believed, were benefiting financially from the prolonged war. In a skit poignantly titled "I Wish I had a Fat Contract," one performer charged that the war would not end until the "Army contractors' pockets are full." Similarly, in "Shoddy Contracts" a parallel was drawn between cynical war profiteers and the gallant soldiers who died for the Union as a result of inadequate supplies:

> Shoddy contracts all de go, and money fur de
> same;
> And if you're a politician, you're sure to git de
> game.
> No matter what the job is either shoddy or a ram
> For all you've got to do is, charge the bill to Uncle
> Sam
> (Converse 1863, pp. 15–16, 45–46).

Designated as enemies of the Union, abolitionists and profiteers fell victim to some of the minstrel shows' harshest criticisms, bringing into relief the racialized working-class politics of both performers and audience.

Racist characterizations of blacks continued unabated in minstrel shows even after African American troops began fighting for the Union. The most popular minstrel skit involving African American troops was called "Black Brigade" (or "Greeley's Brigade") and characterized black soldiers as cowardly and incompetent. Likewise, in "Raw Recruits," the minstrels lampooned black soldiers as children incapable of performing the most basic duties of military life. This characterization of African Americans as ignorant and childlike extended into all areas of life. As early as 1863, the skit "High, Low, Jack" warned, "Let him vote and he's what you call a mighty sassy chile." Sentiments like these demonstrated the widespread belief that African Americans were racially inferior and incapable of participating as coequals with whites either in the military or in a postwar interracial democracy.

BIBLIOGRAPHY

"Affairs about Home." *Boston Herald*, December 17, 1862, p. 4.

"Affairs about Home: Opening of the Morris Brothers, Pell and Trowbridge Opera House." *Boston Herald*, August 6, 1861, p. 2.

Butsch, Richard. "Bowery B'hoys and Matinee Ladies: The Re-Gendering of Nineteenth-Century American Theater Audiences." *American Quarterly* 46, no. 3 (1994): 374–405.

"City Summary." *New York Clipper*, April 8, 1865, p. 414.

Converse, Frank. *Frank Converse's Old Cremona Songster*. New York: Dick and Fitzgerald, 1863.

Cornelius, Steven H. *Music of the Civil War Era*. Westport, CT: Greenwood Press, 2004.

"Hooley & Campbell's Minstrels Remain at the Walnut Street Theatre One Week Longer." *North American and United States Gazette*, July 8, 1861, p. 802.

Lawrence, Vera Brodsky. *Strong on Music: The New York Music Scene in the Days of George Templeton Strong.* Vol. 3, *Repercussions, 1857–1862.* Chicago: University of Chicago Press, 1999.

"Musical and Dramatic Chat." *New Orleans Daily Picayune*, September 14, 1862, p. 1.

"Musical and Theatrical Matters." *New York Herald*, August 5, 1861, p. 3.

"Musical and Theatrical Matters." *New York Herald*, August 18, 1862, p. 2.

Saxton, Alexander. "Blackface Minstrelsy and Jacksonian Ideology." *American Quarterly* 27, no.1 (1975): 3–28.

" 'Suspense,' at the Winter Garden." *New York Herald*, July 2, 1861, p. 4.

Toll, Robert C. *Blacking Up: The Minstrel Show in Nineteenth-Century America*. New York: Oxford University Press, 1974.

Wilmeth, Don B., and C. W. E. Bigsby, eds. *The Cambridge History of American Theatre*. Vol. 1: *Beginnings to 1870*. Cambridge, U.K.: Cambridge University Press, 1998.

Kerry L. Pimblott

MINSTREL SHOWS

One of the most popular forms of musical entertainment in the United States during the second half of the nineteenth century, minstrel shows reflected the era's prevailing racism and an ethos of white supremacy that permeated much of American society. The history of blackface itself can be traced to the 1820s, when the white entertainer Thomas "T. D." Rice rubbed burnt cork on his face and performed a song titled "Jump Jim Crow" at a local theater. Rice's act became a nationwide success almost immediately and thus led numerous theaters, both in the North and South, to create similar stage performances with white casts for various audiences to enjoy. However, at the same time, many African Americans formed their own minstrelsy groups that at least to some degree enabled a small cadre of black American entertainers to perfect their craft—such as William Henry Lane and Bert A. Williams, who developed a new musical genre and dance routine. According to scholar John Strausbaugh

Sheet music cover depicting Jim Crow, the happy slave. Highly popular throughout the United States, minstrel shows reinforced attitudes of white supremacy, as African Americans were portrayed by white actors in blackface as slothful, ignorant, and loose in their sexual mores. *The Library of Congress*

(2006), minstrelsy, for all its humiliations, enabled many African Americans to acquire positions as performers and composers that they never had during the earlier decades of the antebellum period.

Before and during the Civil War, however, minstrel shows were mostly performed by whites. Mostly of Irish descent, these performers blackened their faces with burnt cork, cooled ashes, or dirt and presented a grotesque and highly stereotypical portrayal of African American slave culture and life in the American South. Popular stock characters included an ignorant, stumbling, but happy-go-lucky African American buffoon named "Sambo," as well as Rice's invention, Jim Crow, who expressed enormous fondness for the system of slavery (and whose name was later appropriated to refer to the South's system of racial segregation). One typical minstrel show presented a group of about fifteen or sixteen men seated in a semicircle, facing the audience, telling jokes about each other, accompanied by music, while another person danced and played the banjo in front of them.

While these types of shows were most popular in the South, many white Northerners who had very little familiarity with African American life also enjoyed minstrel shows. Northern-based minstrelsy in part was popular because it reinforced notions of white supremacy, and ridiculed African American and white abolitionists who promoted racial equality during the early to mid-antebellum period. During the Civil War era, minstrel shows continued to be popular and frequently portrayed African American soldiers as incompetent, lazy, and cowardly.

After the war, white minstrel shows, partly in response to increasing competition from African American–led minstrel groups, expanded their repertoire to include what became known as "freak" shows, which were popularized by P. T. Barnum and various entertainment companies. The nature of many minstrel shows also changed as a result of the inclusion of overtly sexual material, as well as the addition of white female performers. At the same time, minstrel shows began to gain much popularity in Britain and throughout Europe. Indeed, large minstrel groups now were seen in both small towns and big cities abroad, as well as throughout the United States.

The popularity of the music used in minstrel shows also started to take off during these years, with various show tune hits selling 100,000 copies in less than a year. For example, songs such as "Camptown Races," "My Old Kentucky," and "O Susanna" were all popularized in minstrel shows and became hit songs during the decades that followed the end of the Civil War, when they were appropriated by such respectable musicians as Al Jolson and Irving Berlin. Indeed, songs that originated in minstrel shows perpetuated stereotypes about blacks and supported an ideology of white superiority well into the twentieth century.

BIBLIOGRAPHY

Blair, John G. "Blackface Minstrels in Cross-Cultural Perspective." *American Studies International* 28, no. 2 (1990): 52–65.

Carlyon, David. *Dan Rice: The Most Famous Man You've Never Heard Of.* New York: Public Affairs, 2001.

Chude-Sokei, Louis. *The Last "Darky": Bert Williams, Black-on-Black Minstrelsy, and the African Diaspora.* Durham, NC: Duke University Press, 2005.

Cockrell, Dale. *Demons of Disorder: Early Blackface Minstrels and Their World.* New York: Cambridge University Press, 1997.

Fee, Frank E., Jr. "Blackface in Black and White: Race, Ethnicity, and the Gender in Frederick Douglass' Hometown Newspapers, 1847." *American Journalism* 20 (Summer 2003): 73–92.

Gilmore, Paul. "William Wells Brown, Blackface Minstrelsy, and Abolitionism." *American Literature* 69, no. 4 (1997): 743–780.

Goldman, Herbert G. *Jolson: The Legend Comes to Life.* New York: Oxford University Press, 1988.

Lott, Eric. *Love and Theft: Blackface Minstrelsy and the American Working Class.* New York: Oxford University Press, 1993.

Meer, Sarah. *Uncle Tom Mania: Slavery, Minstrelsy, and Transatlantic Culture in the 1850s.* Athens: University of Georgia, 2005.

Strausbaugh, John. *Black Like You: Blackface, Whiteface, Insult, and Imitation in American Popular Culture.* New York: Penguin Books, 2006.

Toll, Robert C. *Blacking Up: The Minstrel Show in Nineteenth Century America.* New York: Oxford University Press, 1974.

Eric R. Jackson

THEATER

The state of American theater in the decades prior to the Civil War was, according to David S. Reynolds's 1995 biography *Walt Whitman's America*, a democratic and participatory experience for playgoers. Outbursts from the audience were commonplace. The leading tragedian, Junius Brutus Booth (1796–1852), the father of Lincoln's assassin John Wilkes Booth (1838–1865), welcomed those outbursts and was, as one Washington paper wrote, "a distinguished favorite in America" (*Daily National Intelligencer*, July 26, 1821).

The exuberance of Booth's performance was described by a Boston newspaper thus: "He lost himself in the part he was performing, to such a degree that it became for the time being a sort of insanity, which was sometimes dangerous to his antagonists in the play" (*Boston Daily Atlas*, December 3, 1852). According to Reynolds, "[Booth]

Junius Brutus Booth (1796–1852). A daguerreotype of Junius Brutus Booth, the patriarch of an acting family popular in the years prior to the Civil War. His son John Wilkes Booth earned a different type of notoriety after he assassinated President Abraham Lincoln on April 14, 1865. *The Library of Congress*

could become so carried away as Othello trying to suffocate Desdemona with a pillow that he had to be pulled away by other actors for fear he would actually kill her. As the sword-wielding Richard he sometimes inflicted real wounds" (1995, p. 160). Although born in England, Booth represented an American style of acting that "had to compete with ranting revivalists, ebullient blackface shows, and the popular frontier screamer" (Reynolds 1995, p. 159).

In November 1847 the Astor Place Opera House in New York opened, primarily for upper-class theater patrons. A popular British actor who often performed there, William Charles Macready (1793–1873), had made his first stage appearance in June 1810 in Birmingham, England, and after finding success there as a Shakespearean tragedian, moved to the United States in 1843 (*New York Herald*, July 22, 1863). His rival, the American actor Edwin Forrest (1806–1872), was known for his "muscular, turbulent style" and his appreciation for the local roughnecks that were partial to his flamboyant acting.

The *New York Herald* recounted the rivalry between Macready and Forrest, saying, "On account of some misunderstanding with another play actor [Macready] aroused the anti-English feeling of a portion of the people of this city" ("Additional Particulars," May 12, 1849). After Forr-

est hissed at Macready's performance of Hamlet in March 1846, Macready publicly stated, "I feel I cannot stomach the United States as a nation" (Reynolds 1995, p. 164). In May 1849 Macready was "ignominiously driven from the Astor Place Theatre . . . by a mob after vainly endeavoring to perform the part of Macbeth" (*North American and United States Gazette*, May 12, 1849). Days later, when Macready attempted to continue his performance, a mob of "no less than 25,000 persons" tried to force their way into the opera house.

Earlier that day, according to the *New York Herald*, "rumors were abundant that a riotous organization" had purchased firearms. In addition to rumors of firearms, it was reported that throughout the city, flyers were posted proclaiming, "Americans! Arouse! The great crisis has come!! Decide now whether English aristocrats!!! And foreign rule! Shall triumph in this, America's metropolis" ("Additional Particulars," May 12, 1849). The local militia was called out and eventually was ordered to fire upon the crowd, killing twenty-two and wounding more than fifty (Reynolds 1995, p. 165).

Beyond common melodrama and the works of Shakespeare, theater during and around the Civil War also consisted of dramatic performances of popular literature. In 1852 Harriet Beecher Stowe's *Uncle Tom's Cabin* was adapted and performed on stages in both Boston and New York. *Frederick Douglass' Paper* reported that "the practice of dramatizing a popular novel, as soon as it takes a run, has become very common. In many instances, and particularly with regard to the highly dramatic graphic novels of Dickens, these new plays have been very successful, giving pleasure and satisfaction to the public, and putting money into the pockets of the chuckling manager" (October 8, 1852). Although the play "sold by thousands," it was seen as an artistic failure, with one critic calling it a "crude and aggravated affair."

BIBLIOGRAPHY

"Additional Particulars of the Terrible Riot at the Astor Place Opera House." *New York Herald*, New York, May 12, 1849.

Boston Daily Atlas, Boston, December 3, 1852.

Daily National Intelligencer, Washington, DC, July 26, 1821.

Frederick Douglass' Paper, Rochester, NY, October 8, 1852.

"Obituary for Macready." *New York Herald*, New York, July 22, 1863.

North American and United States Gazette, Philadel phia, May 12, 1849.

Reynolds, David S. *Walt Whitman's America: A Cultural Biography*. New York: Vintage Books, 1995.

John L. Reilly

■ Music

MUSIC: AN OVERVIEW

The social upheaval of the Civil War disrupted musical traditions and gave rise to forms that were more readily applicable to wartime realities. In the military Confederate and Union armies employed field and band musicians entrusted with the task of promoting soldier morale, regimenting camp life, and delivering commands on the battlefield. On the home front popular music and civic bands served many of the same functions, with patriotic tunes serving to solidify support for the war and aiding in the recruitment of troops. African American music traditions were also transformed as the power of the southern planter elite eroded. Spirituals, as well as folk and abolitionist songs served as expressions of racial pride and newly acquired freedoms. Moreover, contacts between Northern white soldiers and former slaves facilitated the dissemination of African American music traditions to a broader audience in the postwar era.

In 1864 Robert E. Lee (1807–1870) emphasized the centrality of music to successful military operations, stating: "I don't believe we can have an army without music." Indeed, musicians were involved in all aspects of soldierly life from the camp to the battlefield and performed a variety of musical and non-musical duties.

Military music fell into two main categories: field music and band music. Field musicians included fifers, drummers, and buglers who were responsible for memorizing and transmitting orders essential to the day-to-day functioning of the regiment. Often only twelve or thirteen years old, many field musicians were too young to enlist as troops and were thus classified as noncombatants. Fourteen-year-old Charles W. Bardeen, for example, joined the 1st Massachusetts Infantry drum corps after learning he was too young to enlist as an army regular. Bardeen, like many other field musicians, lacked formal musical training and was relatively unprepared for the realities of war. Celebrated in popular songs like Will S. Hays's 1863 "The Drummer Boy of Shiloh," young field musicians were forced to grow up quickly if they were to survive the perils of conflict and camp life.

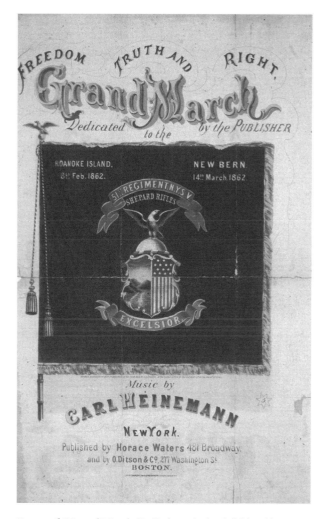

Cover of "Grand March." Both on the battlefield and in army camps, music was used as a communications device, relaying a variety of instructions to soldiers. The sound of fife, drum, and bugle related tactical commands to soldiers, such as marching speed and orders to charge or retreat. *MPI/Hulton Archive/Getty Images*

The primary responsibility of field musicians was to deliver the regulatory calls that served to structure daily life in the army. From "Drummers Call" in the morning to "Taps" at the end of the day, field musicians provided army camps with a rigid and familiar routine. Describing a typical morning with 17th Maine Regiment, Edwin B. Houghton recalled in Francis A. Lord's and Arthur Wise's 1966 edited work *Bands and Drummer Boys of the Civil War* "the clear notes of the bugle" piercing his ears as "the first beams of the rising sun [began] to tinge the eastern skies." The sound of the bugle was quickly followed by the "noisy rataplan" of the drum corps thundering about the camp. "At the last tap of the drum," Houghton wrote, "every man is supposed to be "up and dressed" the companies formed, the roll called by the first sergeants, and woe to the absentees!" (pp. 82–84). Throughout the day, field musicians performed a variety of familiar ensembles to alert soldiers to events and important camp duties, and their tunes established the rhythm of military life.

On the battlefield, field musicians were charged with the essential duty of relaying important tactical signals, such as instructions to march slower or faster, load and fire, rally to the flag, charge, halt, or retreat. These calls were memorized and performed primarily by the drum corps and buglers, who could relay them from a significant distance. In addition to their musical responsibilities, field musicians also performed a miscellany of non-musical duties. George T. Ulmer of the 8th Maine Infantry described his experiences in Lord's and Wise's *Bands and Drummer Boys of the Civil War* working as an anesthetist in a camp hospital at the age of sixteen as an "ordeal I never wish to go through again" (1966 p. iii). Working as stretcher-bearers and hospital assistants was a common duty of field musicians throughout the Civil War.

In addition to an extensive array of field musicians, many regiments also featured a military band. During the initial stages of the war civilian bands from across the country offered their services to individual regiments by enlisting as a group. The renowned American Brass Band from Providence, for example, enlisted with the 1st Regiment Rhode Island Militia in April 1861, whereupon it performed for dress parades and served with the medical corps. Maintaining a military band, however, was costly and as the war continued unabated, the federal government opted to cut music expenditure significantly. On July 29, 1862, the war department passed General Order 91 restricting bands to the brigade level and limiting their size to no more than sixteen musicians. In contrast, the Confederate army continued to permit sixteen-member ensembles to operate within regiments as well as brigades. Despite these cutbacks, it is estimated that more than 400 bands were represented in the ranks of the Union army and 125 in the Confederate army during the course of the war.

Military bands were largely brass-and-percussion ensembles. Although considerable variation existed, bands usually consisted of two E-flat cornets, two B-flat cornets two alto horns, two tenor horns, one baritone horn, one bass horn, and a percussion section of one snare drum, a bass drum, and cymbals. Woodwind instruments were relatively rare, though some piccolos and clarinets were represented.

Band repertoires were equally diverse, consisting of marches, patriotic melodies, popular songs, traditional dances, and hymns. Though considerable crossover existed in the repertoires of Confederate and Union forces, both sides developed their own patriotic songs with which to rally the troops and overawe the enemy. Northern favorites included "Yankee Doodle" and "Battle Hymn of the Republic" while Southerners preferred "Dixie" and "La Marseillaise." In some cases, opposing military bands dueled as a prelude to battle. Colonel George A. Bruce of the 20th Massachusetts Volunteers recalled in Lord's and Wise's *Bands and Drummer Boys of the Civil War* his band playing the "Star-Spangled Banner" only to be countered by a Confederate band playing "Bonnie Blue Flag" and "My Maryland." The musical duel climaxed when Confederate forces fired on Northern troops after hearing the introductory bars of "Old John Brown" (p. 396).

On the battlefield military bands were used to inspire and motivate soldiers. According to Francis H. Buffum of the 14th Regiment of the New Hampshire Volunteers, in *Bands and Drummer Boys of the Civil War*, the presence of a band during military operations "tends to promote morale, strengthening the discipline and elevating the sentiment" of the soldiers (pp. 130–132). The use of patriotic songs was an obvious strategy for raising troop's morale, but certainly not the only one. In her study of sixty popular Civil War songs, historian Lenora Cuccia contends in the 2004 edited work *Bugle Resounding: Music and Musicians of the Civil War Era* that lyrical representations of women as wives and mothers also served as powerful inspiration for soldiers going into battle. Popular songs such as "The Yellow Rose of Texas" invoked a sense of patriotism infused with dominant understandings of manliness.

Back at camp, military bands entertained soldiers and provided music for special occasions. It was at these special camp performances that accomplished bands often experimented with newer and more challenging operatic or classical pieces. In April 1862, a solider with the 24th Massachusetts Regiment wrote a letter home in which he testified to the importance of these special camp performances to soldiers morale. "I don't know what we should have done without our band," he wrote, as Bell I. Wiley recounted in *The Life of Billy Yank: The Common Soldier of the Union*. "Every night about sun down [Patrick] Gilmore gives us a splendid concert, playing selections from the operas and some very pretty marches, quicksteps, waltzes and the like, most of which are composed by himself or by Zohler, a member of his band" (p. 158). In this way military bands brought excitement to the often dull and monotonous days of camp life and offered soldiers an important reprieve from the horrors of war.

Military bands were also tremendously popular on the home front. In cities and towns across the country the performances of military or civic bands served many of the same functions as they did for soldiers: fostering patriotism and offering vital relief from the tragedies of war. Bands in cities across the nation led parades and performed concerts. In New York's Central Park, celebrated bandmaster Henry Dodsworth held military band concerts that regularly attracted audiences of more than 20,000 people. In Washington, DC, military bands serenaded the president with patriotic favorites from the lawn of the executive mansion. Moreover, contemporary composers set about immortalizing significant battles and war heroes in the popular sheet music of the era. Songs such as P. Rivinac's "General Bragg's Grand March" (1861) emphasized the heroism of military leaders while others, such as Walter Kittredge's "Tenting on the Old Camp Ground" (1864) focused on the daily lives of soldiers.

Cover of "Beauregard's March."   Inspired by feelings of patriotism, musicians penned military marches for both Union and Confederate troops.   *MPI/Hulton Archive/Getty Images*

As European Americans on both sides of the Mason-Dixon Line utilized music to express nationalist fervor and provide solace for wartime horrors, African Americans in the southern states continued to engage in their own distinctive music traditions. In the context of enslavement, music had functioned as an important vehicle for African American community building and the preservation of folk culture. Musical festivities provided people of African descent with a rare opportunity to join together and participate in an activity devoid of white supervision. Through the singing of spirituals and work songs, African Americans asserted their humanity and collective desire for freedom.

In the social upheaval of the Civil War Northern whites came into direct contact with African American music traditions, often for the first time. While African American music and dance styles had long been the subject of parody by minstrel show performers, it was not until the Civil War and the concomitant movement of Northern soldiers and teachers into Southern states that a large percentage of Northern whites experienced music produced and performed by people of African descent. Through the per-

formance of spirituals, abolitionist songs, and folk songs, African Americans challenged the authenticity of the minstrel show and the dehumanizing racial stereotypes it perpetuated.

Wartime accounts of African American music and dance revealed the ongoing influence of West African cultural traditions. In her diary, Charlotte Forten, an African American schoolteacher from Salem, Massachusetts working in the Sea Islands, described how local children would "form a ring, and move around in a kind of shuffling dance, singing all the time" According to Forten's account, reproduced as "Life on the Sea Islands" in the 1997 compilation *Work of Teachers in America: A Social History through Stories,* several of the children would "stand apart, and sing very energetically, clapping their hands, stamping their feet, and rocking their bodies to and fro" while others shouted in time (p. 129). Thomas Wentworth Higginson, a white colonel of an African American regiment in South Carolina, also provided accounts of a ring dance being performed. In *Army Life in a Black Regiment* [1962], Higginson described how "a circle forms, winding monotonously round some one in the center; some 'heel and toe' tumultuously, others merely tremble and stagger on, others stoop and rise, others whirl, others caper sideways, all keep steadily circling like dervishes" while the "spectators applaud special strokes of skill" (pp. 17–18). Historian Sterling Stuckey has contended that this practice, widely recognized as "the ring shout", has roots in West Africa and that its continuation represents the ongoing importance of West African retentions in African American culture.

As the power of the southern planter class eroded African Americans also composed and performed songs that addressed the material realities of a seemingly new world. Spirituals and abolitionist songs were particularly popular genres with which former slaves expressed their newly acquired freedoms. While traveling with troops in 1864, Boston journalist and historian Charles Carlton Coffin observed that African Americans who had fled local plantations celebrated their emancipation with songs of praise. A middle-aged woman asked Coffin: "Will it disturb you if we have a little singing? You see we feel so happy to-day that we would like to praise the Lord" (pp. 110–112). On Helena Island, South Carolina, Charlotte Forten recalled how former slaves sang the abolitionist song "John Brown" passionately as they "drove through the pines and palmettos." "Oh, it was good to sing that song in the very heart of Rebeldom!" Forten declared (p. 128). Singing spirituals and abolitionist songs was a dangerous, yet empowering act for African Americans in the southern states during the war.

While abolitionist songs were liberating for many former slaves, Northern white military leaders used the same genre as a tool for policing African American regiments. Historian Keith P. Wilson contends that white officers used music to impress their own social values on their men. Many of the abolitionist songs played for African American regiments were written by white composers and contained lyrics that emphasized the moral and economic responsibilities of emancipation. In this sense abolitionist songs were often reflective of the deeper concerns of Northern whites about a postwar interracial democracy. Despite these efforts African American soldiers also brought their own musical and expressive traditions to bear on army life. Spirituals played a particularly important role in providing solace and inspiration for African American soldiers. In contrast to the patriotic songs of their white counterparts, spirituals drew on the history of enslavement and the prophetic call for freedom that was central to African American life and culture.

BIBLIOGRAPHY

Bardeen, Charles William. *A Little Fifer's War Diary.* Syracuse, NY: C.W. Bardeen, 1910.

Buffum, Francis Henry. *A Memorial of the Great Rebellion: Being a History of the Fourteenth Regiment New-Hampshire Volunteers.* Boston: Franklin Press: Rand, Avery, and Company, 1882.

Bruce, George Anson. *The Twentieth Regiment of Massachusetts Volunteer Infantry, 1861–1865* Boston: Houghton Mifflin, 1906.

Catton, Bruce. *A Stillness at Appomattox.* Garden City, NY: Doubleday, 1953.

Corneluis, Steven H. *Music of the Civil War Era.* Westport, CT: Greenwood Press, 2004.

Cuccia, Lenora. "They Weren't All Like Lorena: Musical Portraits of Women in the Civil War Era." In *Bugle Resounding: Music and Musicians of the Civil War Era*, ed. Bruce C. Kelley and Mark A. Snell. Columbia: University of Missouri Press, 2004.

Epstein, Dena J. *Sinful Tunes and Spirituals: Black Folk Music to the Civil War.* Urbana: University of Illinois Press, 1977.

Forton, Charlotte L. "Life on the Sea Islands." In *Work of Teachers in America: A Social History through Stories*, ed. Rosetta Marantz Cohen and Samuel Scheer. Mahwah, NJ: Lawrence Erlbaum Associates, 1997.

Hays, Will S. "The Drummer Boy of Shiloh," 1863. *Musica International.* Available from http://musicanet.org/.

Higginson, Thomas Wentworth. *Army Life in a Black Regiment* [1900]. Boston: Beacon Press, 1962.

Lord, Francis A., and Arthur Wise. *Bands and Drummer Boys of the Civil War.* New York: Thomas Yoseloff, 1966.

Olson, Kenneth E., *Music and Musket: Bands and Bandsmen of the American Civil War.* Westport, CT: Greenwood Press, 1981.

Wiley, Bell I. *The Life of Billy Yank: The Common Soldier of the Union* [c. 1952]. New York: Doubleday, 1971.

Wilson, Keith P., *Campfires of Freedom: The Camp Life of Black Soldiers during the Civil War.* Kent, OH: Kent State University, 2002.

Kerry L. Pimblott

WAR MUSIC

During the American Civil War, soldiers and civilians alike wrote and sang songs that captured the experience of war. The lyrics of these songs ranged from accounts of famous battles to sentimental thoughts of family and home. The Union and Confederacy each had specific songs that celebrated their cause and praised their troops. Particularly in the North, some songs were political in nature, either supporting or criticizing President Abraham Lincoln. Many of the same melodies were popular in both the North and the South, resulting in numerous variants with different lyrics. These words and melodies helped to build morale, fight the doldrums of military life, and unite people. In the end, this music formed a lasting record of what people considered the most pressing aspects of life during the war.

Soldiers and the Army

Music was a common form of entertainment during the Civil War era, and musicians were in abundance in both civilian and military life. A corporal in the 44th Massachusetts Volunteer Militia commented that "each company has its excellent choir of singers, but Company F affords instrumental as well as vocal music." He added that "the Cobb brothers, who are excellent violinists, delight a numerous auditory nightly assembled about their bunks" (Haines 1863, p. 11). Eventually the men of the 44th organized a regimental choir and obtained some instruments so that they could start a band. Besides offering comforting diversion, military bands could have tactical importance as well. For example, Confederate bands played during the evacuation of Richmond, Virginia, at the end of the war, in order to mask the sounds of troops and equipment being moved out of the Confederate capital.

Wartime songs could inspire soldiers, and help them deal with the perils and hardships of military life. In his 1866 regimental history of the 3rd Louisiana Infantry, W. H. Tunnard recalled how during a rainstorm, "the Louisianians marched cheerfully forward, shouting forth with stentorian voices the chorus of the 'Bonny Blue Flag' and other patriotic songs" (p. 124). A wartime rallying song gave one Union soldier a similar, yet more crucial, burst of stamina. The soldier lost an arm to a Rebel cannon ball, yet he sang the chorus of "Battle Cry of Freedom" as the surgeon tended to his ghastly wound. Soon, other patients joined in the chorus: "We will rally round the flag, boys, rally once again, shouting the battle cry of freedom" (Denison 1864, p. 319).

Published Music

Public demand for music was so high during the war that publishers in the North printed lyrics and music in many different forms, including songbooks (also called *songsters*) written specifically for the war effort. George F. Root, an author of numerous Union songs, published a songbook titled *The Bugle Call* in 1863. Root explained that his book was "designed for loyal people, whether around the campfire or the hearth-stone," in order to "arouse every true heart to a greater love of the Union, and a sterner determination to protect it to the last" (p. 1). Another book, *Songs and Ballads of Freedom*, was available from a New York publisher in 1863 for fifteen cents and included both sentimental tunes and patriotic songs. Several of the songs conjured up visions of the home front and loved ones, including "Who Will Care for Mother Now," "When Johnny Comes Marching Home," and "When This Cruel War is Over." Soldiers enjoyed writing their own lyrics to existing songs, such as Stephen Foster's "Hard Times Come Again No More," which some Federals reworked as "Hard Crackers Come Again No More" in honor of the almost inedible rations the Union Army issued its troops.

Southerners appreciated songs that praised secession and the Confederacy, but music had the added challenge of creating a feeling of Confederate nationalism. It is no small irony that the best-known Southern anthem, "Dixie," was written before the war by a Northerner, Daniel Decatur Emmett. Before the war, most of the South's sheet music came from Northern publishers, but there was an increase in Southern-produced sheet music and songbooks until paper shortages at the end of the war limited publishing. Confederate songsters were generally marketed to soldiers, but there is evidence that publishers intended to sell these books and sheet music to the public as well. One example of a Southern songbook is *The Jack Morgan Songster* (1864), which a captain in the Confederate army compiled. The book's title and first song paid homage to General John Hunt Morgan, a Confederate cavalry raider from Kentucky. Not all of the selections were so militant; the songster also included a Confederate version of "When This Cruel War is Over" that was similar to the Northern favorite, but mentioned "Southern boys" and the "Southern banner" in the final verse.

Northern Political Music

In the North, popular songs addressed the political nature of the conflict, particularly the debates concerning Lincoln's leadership, the war, and emancipation. The Republican Party produced such songbooks as *The President Lincoln Campaign Songster* and *The Republican Songster* for the 1864 election. Besides songs extolling Lincoln's presidency, these songsters included lyrics that criticized "Copperheads," as Northern Democrats who opposed emancipation and demanded an immediate end to the war were called. Lincoln's detractors had their own tunes, including the ones published in *Copperhead Minstrel*, an 1863 songbook compiled by Andrew Dickson White, the future co-founder of Cornell University. These antiwar Democrats blamed Lincoln for the war's hardships and loss of life. A Copperhead version of "We are Coming, Father Abraham," addressed to Lincoln,

---

SONGSTERS

To keep the public and the troops entertained and inspired, publishers in both the Union and the Confederacy brought out what they called songsters—that is, booklets of song lyrics. Musical notation was rarely included, however, as the songs were sung to familiar tunes. Examples of songsters include *War Songs of the South* (1862), *The Beauregard Songster* (1864), and *Songs & Ballads of Freedom: A Choice Collection, Inspired by the Incidents and Scenes of the Present War* (1864) (Schultz 2004, p. 136).

Soldiers of both camps also wrote their own lyrics to existing songs, and if they were lucky could make some money for their talent. The *Boston Daily Advertiser* ran this advertisement in 1864: "George F. Root of Chicago offers $10 each for five Union campaign songs to these tunes, 'Old Shady,' 'Uncle Ned,' 'Out of the Wilderness,' 'John Brown,' and 'America,' or 'God Save the Queen'" (September 14, 1864, col. C). Writing about war songs of the South in the *Charleston Courier, Tri-Weekly*, an unnamed critic called the songs "the spontaneous outburst of popular feeling. They show the sentiments of the people, and give the lie to the assertion of our enemy, that this revolution is the work of politicians and party leaders alone" (May 31, 1862).

JEANNE M. LESINSKI

BIBLIOGRAPHY
Schultz, Kirsten M. "The Production and Consumption of Confederate Songsters." In Bugle Resounding: Music and Musicians of the Civil War Era, ed. Bruce C. Kelley and Mark A. Snell. Columbia: University of Missouri Press, 2004.

"War Songs of the South." Charleston Courier, Tri-Weekly, May 31, 1862, col. C.

---

declared, "Your dark and wicked doings a god of mercy sees, and the wail of homeless children is heard on every breeze" (White 1863, p. 14). A songbook bearing the nickname ("Little Mac") of the 1864 Democratic candidate, former General George McClellan, used music to criticize Lincoln's leadership and policies, including the president's emancipation policy (*The Little Mac Campaign Songster*, 1864).

Songs of Freedom

Some songs supported emancipation, such as the compositions of songwriter Henry C. Work, whose songs "Kingdom Coming" and "Babylon Is Falling" championed freeing and enlisting Southern slaves as a suitable retaliation for Southern disloyalty. African Americans wrote and sang songs to express their feelings about the war and emancipation. Versions of "John Brown's Body" were very popular, including the song of the 1st Arkansas Colored Regiment, which stated, "We are fightin' for de Union, We are fightin' for de law" (Cornelius 2004, p. 29). Further, hymns and spirituals used religious imagery to celebrate and promote the cause of emancipation. Even the Union rallying song, "Battle Cry of Freedom," included a reference to emancipation in the line "although he may be poor, not a man shall be a slave" (Cornelius 2004, p. 47).

Regardless of what their sentiments were, soldiers and civilians alike relied on music to help them shoulder the burdens of war.

BIBLIOGRAPHY

Abel, E. Lawrence. *Singing the New Nation: How Music Shaped the Confederacy, 1861–1865.* Mechanicsburg, PA: Stackpole Books, 1999.

Cornelius, Steven H. *Music of the Civil War Era.* Westport, CT: Greenwood Press, 2004.

Denison, Charles Wheeler. *The Tanner-Boy and How He Became Lieutenant-General.* Boston: Roberts Brothers, 1864.

Haines, Zenas T. *Letters from the Forty-Fourth Regiment M.V.M.: A Record of the Experience of a Nine Months' Regiment in the Department of North Carolina in 1862–3.* Boston: Herald Job Office, 1863.

The Little Mac Campaign Songster. New York: T.R. Dawley, 1864.

Olson, Kenneth E. *Music and Musket: Bands and Bandsmen of the American Civil War.* Westport, CT: Greenwood Press, 1981.

Root, George F., ed. *The Bugle Call.* Chicago: Root & Cady, 1863.

Schultz, Kirsten M. "The Production and Consumption of Confederate Songsters." In *Bugle Resounding: Music and Musician of the Civil War Era*, ed. Bruce C. Kelley and Mark A. Snell. Columbia: University of Missouri Press, 2004.

Tunnard, W. H. *A Southern Record: The History of the Third Regiment Louisiana Infantry.* Baton Rouge, LA: Author, 1866.

White, Andrew Dickson. *Copperhead Minstrel: A Choice Collection of Democratic Poems and Songs, for the Use of Political Clubs and the Social Circle.* New York: Feeks & Bancker, 1863.

Stephen Rockenbach

SLAVE, ABOLITIONIST, AND CIVIL RIGHTS SONGS

In an era when literacy was not universal—indeed, slaves were forbidden to learn to read—song took on many roles: entertainment, worship, and propaganda. Many colonists, including the enslaved Africans, came to America from cultures in which music played an important role; thus the creation of new forms of music was a natural development.

Slave Songs

In the African homeland of American slaves, music was thoroughly integrated into the activities of everyday life. Thus it is understandable—even if surprising to nineteenth-

century white Americans—that the slaves expressed their emotions through music and entertained themselves with songs while doing such repetitive tasks as spinning, weaving, hoeing, picking crops, plowing, or washing clothes. In fact, the repetitive rhythms of the task often entered into the music, while conversely, the music helped maintain the momentum of the task. On the eve of the outbreak of the Civil War, Daniel Robinson Hundley noted in his *Social Relations in Our Southern States* (1860) that:

> No matter where they may be or what they may be doing, indeed, whether alone or in crowds, at work or at play, ploughing through the steaming maize in the sultry heat of June, or bared to the waist and with deft hand mowing down the yellow grain, or trudging homeward in the dusky twilight after the day's work is done—always and everywhere they [the Negroes] are singing (Hundley 1860, pp. 344–345).

In addition to the activities Hundley enumerates, such events as corn shucking, threshing parties, slave "frolics," and religious services also lent themselves to singing. The slaves sang a variety of songs, ranging from hymns to folksongs and improvised pieces. Though songs could be created individually, most often they were created through communal improvisation. Slave singing used African rhythms, tonalities, and vocal embellishments. Rhythms were often syncopated and set against each other in complicated patterns. The scale on which the music was based might be pentatonic (that is, it used only five notes) or employ microtones (intervals between the standard Western pitches). The vocal embellishments might include yodeling, pitch-bending, and melismata (singing several notes to one syllable of text). In addition, grunts, yells, cries, and moans were common. Writing in the June 13, 1874, edition of *Inter Ocean*, an anonymous commentator remarked, "[f]or forty years or more plantation songs have been extraordinarily popular in all quarters.... They are valuable as an expression of the character and life of the race which has played such a conspicuous part in the history of our nation" (p. 6).

Abolitionist Songs

In the early 1840s abolitionist songs joined temperance tunes as staples of American repertoires. The November 16, 1843, issue of the *Emancipator and Free American*, for example, advertised a *Liberty and Anti-Slavery Song Book*, and contained an anonymous letter to the editor telling of an abolitionist meeting in New Bedford, Massachusetts, that ended "after singing an antislavery song" (p. 67). The most popular songwriter of the antebellum period, Stephen Foster, portrayed African Americans in a positive light in his works. This treatment contrasted with the racist caricatures of slaves found in minstrel shows, which were popular entertainments performed by whites who darkened their faces with burnt cork. For example, although the lyrics to Foster's "Oh! Susanna" seem nonsensical at first, they in fact subtly criticize slavery:

Stephen Foster (1826–1864). Considered by many the most beloved songwriter prior to the Civil War, Stephen Foster offered a humanizing look at the life of a slave in his popular works, including "Oh! Susanna" and "Old Kentucky Home." *The Library of Congress.*

> I come from Alabama with my banjo on my knee
> I'se gwine to Lou'siana My true lub for to see
> It rain'd all night de day I left, De wedder it was dry;
> The sun so hot I froze to def—Susanna don't you cry.
> Oh! Susanna, do not cry for me;
> I come from Alabama, Wid my Banjo on my knee.

The banjo and dialect indicate that the singer is an African American—but slaves would not have been allowed to travel freely and certainly not simply to see a loved one. Foster thus encouraged listeners to think differently about slaves—to consider them human beings—and thus elicited sympathy for the abolitionist cause (Kelley and Snell 2004, pp. 42, 44).

Commenting on several Foster tunes, the former slave and abolitionist leader Frederick Douglass wrote, "'Old Kentucky Home' and 'Uncle Ned' can make the heart sad as well as merry, and can call forth a tear as well as a smile. They awaken the sympathies for the slave, in which antislavery principles take root and flourish" (Douglass 1950 [1855], pp. 356–357).

The campaign song for the first antislavery party, the Liberty Party, was written in 1844 by a white vocal group, the Hutchinson Family Singers. Their combination of harmonized folk music and personal convictions was potent. They performed often and widely throughout the Northern states, though sometimes they were forced to cancel performances because of the likelihood of violence. Recalling a time when "the twin offenses of singing antislavery songs and admitting colored people to hear them" had caused the Hutchinsons to be driven from a hall, an article in the April 22, 1877, *St. Louis Globe-Democrat* described the family's career: "[They] had drawn enormous houses wherever they appeared, but being of pronounced antislavery sentiment, and having always introduced this sentiment into their songs, they had frequently met, even in the very heart of New England, with disapprobation" (p. 11). In 1864 the Hutchinson Family Singers put their talents to work for Lincoln, publishing "Lincoln and Liberty" in *Hutchinson's Republican Songster.* After the Civil War, however, the group largely lost its following and fell apart due to personal conflicts.

Political Songs

Songs became an important part of the political landscape beginning with the 1840 presidential race between the challenger, William Henry Harrison, and the incumbent, President Martin Van Buren. In addition to individual songs, writers composed entire songsters—booklets of songs written to popular tunes (some by Stephen Foster). During the 1864 presidential election, songsters were published for both President Lincoln and his challenger, George B. McClellan: Lincoln's was the *Republican Songster for the Campaign of 1864*; McClellan's *The Little Mac Campaign Songster.* The former included such titles as "Abe Lincoln Knows the Ropes," "Forward for Lincoln and the Union," "Lincoln, Freedom, Victory," and "Rally Boys for Uncle Abe." On the other hand, McClellan's songster contained more anti-Lincoln songs than it did pro-McClellan ones. The anti-Lincoln songs included such titles as "Do I Love Abe or Not?" "Abraham Lover of My—Smell," "Lincoln Written Down an Ass," and "Abe's Brother of Negro Descent." Pro-McClellan songs, which drew on the challenger's storied career as a Civil War general, included the wrapped-in-the-flag number "Hurrah for McClellan":

> Come, brothers, and unite with us,
> Come, join us one and all.
> United we must conquer,
> But divided we shall fall;
> Our Union flag we're raising
> For McClellan—tried and true,
> Who'll uphold it—and revere it—
> 'Tis the Red, White and Blue.
>
> Then hurrah, for McClellan
> Hurrah for McClellan,
> Hurrah for McClellan,
> And the Red, White, and Blue.

(*The Little Mac Campaign Songster*, 1864, p. 9)

In contrast, "Uncle Abe," from the Lincoln songster, is more down to earth in its patriotism:

> Uncle Abe, Uncle Abe! Here we are again!
> We've got a platform now, we think that will not bend or strain.
> Beat the drum, unfurl the flag, Freedom is for all.
> And so we fling it to the breeze as in the ranks we fall.
> Ho Uncle Abe! Listen, Uncle Abe, and see!
> We sing for you, work for you, Hurrah for Liberty!
> (*Republican Songster*, 1864, p. 41)

Whatever their style or political leaning, campaign songs were here to stay.

Slave, abolitionist, and political songs were, of course, only a part of the body of music that enriched American culture during the Civil War era. Operas and orchestral works by classical European composers as well as American music composed for brass bands or piano, and the ethnic tunes and songs of immigrants, all blended to create a rich musical landscape.

BIBLIOGRAPHY

Douglass, Frederick. "The Anti-Slavery Movement: Lecture Delivered before the Rochester [New York] Ladies' Anti-Slavery Society, January 1855." In *The Life and Writings of Frederick Douglass*, ed. Philip S. Foner. New York: International Publishers, 1950.

Emancipator and Free American, November 16, 1843, p. 116.

Epstein, Dena J. *Sinful Tunes and Spirituals: Black Folk Music to the Civil War*. Music in American Life Series. Champaign: University of Illinois Press, 1977.

Foster, Stephen. *Susanna*. Louisville, KY: W. C. Peters, 1848.

Gac, Scott. *Singing for Freedom: The Hutchinson Family Singers and the Nineteenth-Century Culture of Reform*. New Haven, CT: Yale University Press, 2007.

Hundley, Daniel Robinson. *Social Relations in Our Southern States*. New York: Henry B. Price, 1860.

Keck, George Russell, and Sherrill V. Martin. *Feel the Spirit: Studies in Nineteenth-Century Afro-American Music*. Contributions in Afro-American and African Studies 119. Westport, CT: Greenwood Press, 1988.

Kelley, Bruce C., and Mark A. Snell, eds. *Bugle Resounding: Music and Musicians of the Civil War Era*. Columbia: University of Missouri Press, 2004.

The Little Mac Campaign Songster. New York: T. R. Dawley, 1864.

McNeil, Keith, and Rusty McNeil, eds. *Civil War Songbook: With Historical Commentary*. Riverside, CA: WEM Records, 1999.

"Plantation Melodies." *Inter Ocean* (Chicago), June 13, 1874, p. 6.

Republican Songster for the Campaign of 1864. Cincinnati, OH: T. R. Hawley, 1864.

St. Louis (MO) *Globe-Democrat*, April 22, 1877, p. 11.

Silverman, Jerry. *Songs and Stories of the Civil War*. Brookfield, CT: Twenty-First Century Books, 2002.

"Songs of the Blacks." *The Boston Liberator*, September 9, 1859, n.p.

Southern, Eileen. *The Music of Black Americans: A History*, 2nd ed. New York: Norton, 1983.

White, Shane, and Graham White. *The Sounds of Slavery: Discovering African American History through Songs, Sermons, and Speech*. Boston: Beacon Press, 2005.

Jeanne M. Lesinski

ARMY BANDS

From the regimental field bands (fife and drum corps) of colonial America to the U.S. army bands of the early twenty-first century, music has always been a vital part of American military tradition (Cornelius 2004, p. xiii). The Civil War, often called the "singing war," epitomized the centrality of music to military life. In *America's Musical Life: A History* (2001), the music historian Richard Crawford stated that "music was used for "morale building (or esprit de corps), camp duties (which included signaling), public ceremonies, and recreation" (pp. 83–84). It was the duty of military musicians to facilitate these tasks.

Functions of Army Musicians

There were two types of army musicians: field musicians and bandsmen. Field musicians were often young boys who served as drummers, fifers, and buglers. They sounded camp calls and, in battle, relayed commands through musical signals, allowing officers to communicate quickly with their soldiers over great distances. After 1863 the U.S. Army permitted boys twelve years and older to enlist as field musicians, even though most could not read music. The recollections of Augustus Meyer, who joined the army in 1854 when he was twelve, describe the life of a young field musician in training at the School of Practice for U.S.A. Field Musicians at Governor's Island, New York. Meyer, who enlisted as a fifer, described the living quarters of field musicians, or "music boys," as sparse, and the meals as "meager" (Meyer 1914, pp. 1–4). He also recounted learning the various signals that controlled the lives of every soldier. For example, he wrote, "I was awakened . . . at daylight by a drummer beating the first call for 'Reveille,'" followed by a corporal shouting to "Get up! You lazy fellows." Soon after dressing, a drummer sounded the beat for "Assembly," calling for the soldiers to gather outside for roll call. Drums also signaled soldiers to report for sick call, guard duty, and at night, "Taps" signaled when soldiers should go to sleep (Meyer 1914, pp. 4–5).

The duties of military musicians detailed to bands were different from those of the "music boys." Army bands played at parades, funerals, and executions, and also gave concerts for high-ranking civilian and military officials. Often during the war, both the U.S. president Abraham Lincoln and the Confederate president Jefferson Davis were serenaded by army brass bands. The bands' most important function was performing for the troops, and in diaries and letters to their families and friends, Union and Confederate soldiers expressed gratitude and pride in the army service bands. On one occasion, a Union soldier from the Twenty-fourth Massachusetts Regiment remarked in 1862 that "I don't know what we should have done without our band. It is acknowledged by everyone to be the best in the division" (U.S. Army, "The Civil War").

It was customary at the time for army commanders to recruit accomplished musicians and bandleaders to serve in volunteer civilian bands or the regular army. The renowned bandleader Patrick Gilmore (1829–1892), who is credited with writing the popular Civil War–era song "When Johnny Comes Marching Home," enlisted with his band of formally trained musicians (Patrick Gilmore's Band); they were attached to the Twenty-fourth Massachusetts Infantry in September 1861. The trooper from the Twenty-fourth Massachusetts related: "Every night about sundown Gilmore gives us a splendid concert, playing selections from the operas and some very pretty marches, quicksteps, waltzes and the like" (U.S. Army, "The Civil War"). Many other musicians joined the war effort as well, and by the end of 1861 the U.S. Army had more than 28,000 musicians and 618 bands (U.S. Army, "The Civil War"). The Army of the Confederate States of America also had bands, but the scarcity of brass instruments and musicians in the South kept their numbers small.

Bands in Battle

Military bands accompanied troops to battle. The First Regiment of Artillery Band (also known as Chandler's Band of Portland, Maine) was present at the first engagement of the Civil War in April 1861 to witness Major Robert Anderson (1805–1871) surrendering the Fort Sumter garrison to Brigadier General P.G.T Beauregard (1818–1893), commander of the provisional Confederate forces at Charleston, South Carolina.

Army bands sometimes played at forward positions in the midst of battles. Union and Confederate officers knew the power of music to inspire troops encamped in the field and in combat. To encourage his men to fight on, Union general Philip H. Sheridan (1831–1888) ordered the band to play during the Battle of Dinwiddie Court House, part of the Appomattox Campaign that led to the surrender of Confederate general Robert E. Lee's Army of Northern Virginia to Union general Ulysses S. Grant in 1865. Gen-

eral Sheridan commanded the bandsmen to "play the gayest tunes in their books . . . play them loud and keep on playing them, and never mind if a bullet goes through a trombone, or even a trombonist, now and then" (U.S. Army, "The Civil War"). In another story, Confederate soldiers stationed near Union forces in Fredericksburg, Virginia, during the winter of 1862 to 1863 could hear the Union band playing. A Confederate soldier called from across the Rappahannock River, "Now give us some of ours," and the Union band broke into a lively rendition of "Dixie," which was written in 1859 by a Northerner, Daniel Decatur Emmett from Ohio, but was adopted widely as "a rallying cry for the patriots of the Confederacy" and "a battle song for her soldiers" (Harwell 1950, p. 41).

Army bandsmen and field musicians also experienced the terror of battle. John A. Cockerill, a sixteen-year-old regimental musician, wrote: "I passed . . . the corpse of a beautiful boy in gray who lay with his blond curls scattered about his face and his hand folded peacefully across his breast. . . . His neat little hat lying beside him bore the number of a Georgia regiment. . . . At the sight of the poor boy's corpse, I burst into a regular boo-hoo" (Mintz). The dead Confederate soldier probably had been a drummer or bugler; many of the young boys who enlisted in the Union and Confederate armies were.

Death was a constant in the war, and casualties among army field musicians and bandsmen were high. Only ten bandsmen of the original thirty-six members of the One Hundred Twenty-fifth Ohio Regimental Band (known as the Tiger Band) survived the war (U.S. Army, "The Civil War"). Nevertheless, bravery was high among the field musicians and bandsmen. Thirty-two army musicians have received the Medal of Honor, which is awarded by the U.S. Congress for distinguished action in battle; twenty of them served in the Civil War. According to the award citation for William J. Carson, a Civil War recipient:

> At a critical stage in the battle [at Chickamauga, Georgia on September 19, 1863] when the 14th Corps lines were wavering and in disorder he on his own initiative bugled "to the colors" amid the 18th U.S. Infantry who formed by him, and held the enemy. Within a few minutes he repeated his action amid the wavering 2d Ohio Infantry. This bugling deceived the enemy who believed reinforcements had arrived. Thus, they delayed their attack. (U.S. Army Center of Military History)

When not engaged in musical functions on the field, army field musicians and bandsmen performed noncombatant duties such as assisting the medical staff. They served as stretcher bearers for the wounded, collected wood for splints, helped set up field hospitals, and assisted surgeons with amputations. Whether performing music in noncombatant areas or in the midst of combat, or assisting injured soldiers at the rear of the battle lines, army musicians served the Union and the Confederacy with distinction. Unfortunately, the expense of maintaining army bands after the Civil War seemed unwarranted as Congress faced the

Elmira Cornet Band.   In addition to using field musicians to relay commands on the battlefield by drum, fife, and bugle, most regiments in the Union army also had a military band to provide entertainment to the troops as well as play at parades, funerals, and other ceremonious events.   *The Library of Congress.*

enormous cost of reconstructing the South. The Army Act of 1869 abolished regimental bands. By the early 1900s, however, military officials lobbied successfully to reestablish bands in the regular army, citing the positive impact on the troops (U.S. Army, "The Civil War").

BIBLIOGRAPHY

Cornelius, Steven H. *Music of the Civil War Era.* Westport, CT: Greenwood Press, 2004.

Crawford, Richard. *America's Musical Life: A History.* New York: W.W. Norton, 2001.

Harwell, Richard Barksdale. *Confederate Music.* Chapel Hill: University of North Carolina Press, 1950.

Library of Congress, Music Division. Presents Music, Theater and Dance. "When Johnny Comes Marching Home Again." Patriotic Melodies. Available from http://lcweb2.loc.gov/.

Meyer, Augustus. *Ten Years in the Ranks: U.S. Army.* New York: Stirling Press, 1914.

Mintz, Steven. "Children and the American Civil War." Digital History Web site. Available from http://www.digitalhistory.uh.edu/.

U.S. Army. "Bands from 1830–1860: Rise of the Brass Band." U.S. Army Bands Web site. Available from http://bands.army.mil/.

U.S. Army. "The Civil War." U.S. Army Bands Web site. Available from http://bands.army.mil/.

U.S. Army Center of Military History. "Medal of Honor." Available from http://www.army.mil/.

Carol J. Gibson

■ Dancing

Dance is an expression of feeling, a social communication, and a means of identifying with a group. It releases tension and serves as a means of sexual display. The types of dance that could be most commonly found in Civil War America reflected the ethnic backgrounds of the dancers. Slaves and freed people performed dances with African roots, whereas white Americans adopted forms of European dance. Americans' social attitudes toward dancing were those common to the European middle classes. The main

SOLDIERS' BALL AT HUNTSVILLE, ALABAMA—DANCING THE "VIRGINIA REEL."—[See Page 235.]

Dancing the "Virginia Reel."   Dancing was an important social activity around the time of the Civil War, and learning to dance was considered an important part of a young person's education. New dances, such as the "Virginia Reel" pictured here, became popular among young Americans looking for entertainment.   *© Corbis*

attraction of dance lay in the steps and the pleasure of movement.

Some religious groups, such as the Baptists and Methodists, frowned upon dance as lewd. Most Americans viewed dancing as a perfectly acceptable form of relaxation and exercise. In upper-class schools, social dancing formed part of the instruction. *Godey's Lady's Book*, the most popular women's magazine in the mid-nineteenth century, included instructional articles on the correct way to dance.

However, some dances provoked the wrath of secular observers, particularly bystanders from an older generation. Alfred L. Carroll, writing in *Harper's New Monthly Magazine* in 1865, sharply criticized the new craze for round dances as immoral. Round dances echoed the ring dances of medieval times in that a group of people moved in a circle. Carroll complained that once upon a time,

> No pure woman would suffer a man to retain her hand in his, much less to encircle her with his arm, in the ordinary relations of social life; and yet, at the bidding of fashion, and because the additional stimulus of music is superadded, she will not only permit these liberties, but will remain willingly strained to his breast for a quarter of an hour at a time, publicly exhibiting herself in a position which in itself she virtuously condemns. (Thompson 1998, p. 178)

Carroll preferred the waltz, a dance first greeted with alarm but accepted by the 1830s and common throughout the rest of the nineteenth century. The waltz originated with the peasantry of Germany and gradually spread across Europe before coming to America. Dancers performing a waltz engage in whirls, arms-embracing gyrations, and more intimate contact as they move face-to-face in a three-four rhythm. The contact and the energy between dance partners was initially viewed as improper, especially if the partners were not husband and wife. But by the 1860s, Confederate and Union officers were dancing the waltz as well as the polka. The polka also came from Europe. Originally a folk dance from Bohemia, it became a craze in Paris and London in the 1840s before spreading to America. An energetic social dance, the one and two, one and two rhythm captured fans from every social class.

Some Americans objected to dances chiefly because they had trouble performing them. Mark Twain (Samuel Clemens) lamented his tendency to step on the dresses of young ladies and tear their hems. Twain wrote in January 1863 about a ball sponsored by the United States Sanitary Commission to raise funds for sick and wounded Union soldiers, at which the partygoers performed a new dance, the Virginia Reel. As he humorously described it, "The dancers are formed in two long ranks, facing each other, and the battle opens with some light skirmishing between the pickets, which is gradually resolved into a general engagement along the whole line; after that, you have nothing to do but stand by and grab every lady that drifts within reach of you, and swing her" (Thompson 1998, p. 191).

Unlike whites, African Americans did not always have a choice about whether or where to dance. Depending on the whim of the master, slaves would hold dances on their own plantations, or they would obtain a pass to visit another plantation. Some masters encouraged their slaves to dance, and frequently asked (or forced) them to entertain whites at the "Big House." A former slave, Dan Barton, recollected that, "They'd dance the buck and wing and another step [probably the chica] that nobody does any more. It went two steps to the right, two steps to the left. The womens shake their skirts and the mens dance 'round them" (Emery 1972, p. 89). Slaves often danced at festivals; the Cake-Walk was a common festival dance. This dance—a straight walk along a path with the dancers balancing a pail of water—was named after the prize given to the couple that spilled the least amount of water: a cake. When left to themselves, without white interference, slaves performed a variety of dances including the ring dance, buzzard lope, water dance, and juba. All of these dances have roots in Africa. The ring dance, possibly originating in the Congo, involved dancing in a ring to celebrate the harvest. The buzzard lope mimicked the act of a bird eating carrion, whereas the water dance involved dancing while balancing a bucket of water on the head. The juba, apparently known in Africa as the *Djouba*, was characterized by stamping, clapping, and slapping of arms, chest, and thighs, with dancers sometimes balancing pails of water on their heads. Africans habitually carried almost everything on their heads, a custom that persisted in the water dances of the New World.

BIBLIOGRAPHY

Clarke, Mary, and Clement Crisp. *The History of Dance.* London: Orbis, 1981.

Emery, Lynne Fauley. *Black Dance in the United States from 1619 to 1970.* Palo Alto, CA: National Press Books, 1972.

Thompson, Alison, ed. *Dancing through Time: Western Social Dance in Literature, 1400–1918: Selections.* Jefferson, NC: McFarland, 1998.

Caryn E. Neumann

■ Lyceum Lectures

Established in the late 1820s the American lyceum was a diffuse circuit of public lectures, debates, and dramatic performances utilized to promote civic education and moral uplift. During its early years the lyceum movement was comprised of local mutual-education societies situated predominantly in the villages and towns of the Northeast.

Affluent Anglo-American Protestant men met together to read scholarly works, hold debates, and present and hear lectures on topics of importance from the realms of science, art, and industry. By the start of the Civil War the lyceum movement had expanded into the Old Northwest and parts of the South with the public lecture emerging as its most prominent and profitable activity. Renowned orators prepared lectures and followed a well-traveled circuit across the country. The outbreak of sectional conflict, however, transformed the lyceum and its lecture circuit irrevocably as wartime realities resulted in altered cultural tastes. The antebellum lyceum's emphasis on scientific and literary pursuits was quickly supplanted by lectures addressing contemporary political affairs and light entertainment that offered solace from the tragedies of warfare.

The outbreak of the Civil War marked the demise of local lyceums across the country. Laboring under the dual pressures of mass enlistment and lack of resources, many local lyceums were forced to limit operations or close their doors entirely.. With increasing numbers of young men enlisted in the military, the ranks of Ohio's lyceum movement were depleted, leaving responsibility for the organization's upkeep in the charge of older residents who lacked the energy and enthusiasm to maintain its formerly robust program. Newspaper editorials across the country lamented the dissolution of local lyceums and expressed considerable concern about the broader implications for American culture and society. An article published in the *Dayton Journal* on November 18, 1862, expressed concern that in the absence of the local lyceum residents might turn to the kind of "bar-room clubs, surprise parties, and political plotting and mutual criminations, which culminate in the murderous spirit of the mob, by which peace, morality and public reputation are destroyed" (Mead 1951, p. 201). Long understood to be a space for civic and moral instruction, the demise of the lyceum was received with considerable apprehension at the local level.

Lyceums that continued to operate during the war years altered their programs in accordance with the broader transformation of cultural tastes initiated by the war. In a significant departure from prewar traditions, many surviving lyceums offered comedy routines, musical acts, and other popular performances in the place of scientific or literary pursuits. Comedic lecturer Charles Farrar Browne (1834–1867) entertained lyceum audiences across the country with performances like "Children in the Wood," which consisted of a series of satirical and humorous anecdotes. In a review of Browne's performance in Cleveland in February 1862, a correspondent for *Plain Dealer* contended: "[That] the affected seriousness, the pauses here and there to be followed by something immensely ridiculous and comical all combined to make it irresistible" (Mead 1951, p. 214). Performances like those delivered by Browne served as an important, albeit temporary, distraction from the painful traumas of war.

Free black abolitionist Frances Ellen Watkins Harper (1825–1911). Educated white Protestant men often gathered together to discuss science, attend debates, and listen to lectures in lyceums across the country. The Civil War expanded the variety of participants in lyceums, with abolitionists such as Frances Ellen Watkins Harper, a free black woman, delivering speeches denouncing slavery. *Harper, Frances E. W., photograph.*

Despite the widespread appreciation of comedy acts, it was the public lecture circuit that remained the lyceums' most popular activity. Before the war, lectures addressing explicitly political topics were widely believed to be inappropriate and improper. As broader cultural tastes were transformed by wartime realities, however, public lectures took on an increasingly political tenor. As early as 1854 the Ohio Mechanics Institute presented a course of lectures entitled "American Slavery," with speakers including the prominent abolitionists Frederick Douglass (1817–1895), William Lloyd Garrison (1805–1979), Theodore Parker (1810–1860), and Wendell Phillips (1811–1884). Similarly, the Young Men's Lyceum in Milwaukee, Wisconsin, held a lecture in March 1861, on the unjust and immoral character of slavery. As the war began lyceums across the nation attempted to satisfy the heightened demand for political lectures by requesting the participation of reform-minded and patriotic orators. In Salem, Massachusetts, lectures such as Charles Sumner's (1811–1874) "The Rebellion," Charles C. Coffin's "Battle Scenes,"

and George William Curtis's (1824–1892) "Political Infidelity," provided important information about the war and helped consolidate support for the Union.

Not all contemporary observers understood the new political and reformist focus of the lecture circuit to be a positive one. Rather, political lectures were widely characterized as moneymaking ventures that tainted the original function of the lyceum as a site for the production of serious scholarship and moral improvement. Opponents argued that political lectures were in poor taste and rendered the lyceum little more than a lucrative public spectacle. An area of particular contestation was the behavior of figures like the staunch Tennessee unionist William G. Brownlow, whose provocative onstage performances challenged contemporary conventions of public speaking.

On January 1, 1863, Brownlow spoke before a full house in Cleveland, Ohio. According to historian David Mead, Brownlow referred to his lecture as a "stump speech" and launched into a bitter attack on the Confederacy during which he asserted that there were better men in the depths of hell than there were amongst the ranks of Southern leaders. Mead relays that, in a review of Brownlow's lecture, a correspondent for *Plain Dealer* declared in the January 2, 1863 edition that Brownlow's audience, while "intensely interested," was "disgusted and shocked at some of his low and vulgar expressions." According to the writer, it appeared doubtful that there was "another man in America who could make use of such vulgarities during a public address without being hissed down at once." (1951, p. 205) In this manner, the controversial style of political lecturers like Brownlow challenged the conventions of public speaking and raised concern in certain quarters.

While the *Plain Dealer* reporter took pains to distinguish between Brownlow and his more refined audience, however, press coverage of other political lectures complicates this characterization of audience responses. Addressing a lecture held in New Orleans on February 3, 1863, a journalist for the *Vermont Chronicle* reported that pro-Union speeches by military leaders were "loudly applauded" and that "the horrible tales they told of the intolerance and barbarism of the rebels toward them, roused the audience to a high pitch of enthusiasm and intense excitement." In similar lectures around the country, lyceum audiences responded to political and reformist lectures with an enthusiasm and revelry unmatched in the antebellum era.

Thus many of the tensions that emerged around the Civil War lyceum movement were tied both to the changing nature of the public lecture and the audiences that attended them. Indeed, while some historians have depicted the Civil War as having a destructive effect on the lyceum as a more holistic educational institution, others have pointed to the lecture circuit as an example of the lyceums' ongoing vitality and increasing inclusion. Political and social upheaval wrought by the Civil War opened up the lyceum movement not only to political and reformist discourse, but also to a wider variety of lecturers. During the Civil War, African American orators such as Frederick Douglass and Frances Ellen Watkins Harper, and white suffragists including Mary Ashton Livermore (1820–1905) and Susan B. Anthony (1820–1906) were able to take the stage alongside the affluent white men who had traditionally dominated the lyceum movement. Through the lyceum lecture circuit, speakers such as Douglass, Watkins Harper, Livermore, and Anthony issued powerful critiques of the status quo that were disseminated to a national audience.

BIBLIOGRAPHY

Bode, Carl. *The American Lyceum: Town Meeting of the Mind.* New York: Oxford University Press, 1956.

Cameron, Kenneth Walter, comp. *The Massachusetts Lyceum during the American Renaissance; Materials for the Study of the Oral Tradition in American Letters: Emerson, Thoreau, Hawthorne, and Other New-England Lecturers.* Hartford, CT: Transcendental Books, 1969.

Mead, David C. *Yankee Eloquence in the Middle West: The Ohio Lyceum 1850–1870.* East Lansing: Michigan State College Press, 1951.

Ray, Angela G. *The Lyceum and Public Culture in the Nineteenth-century United States.* East Lansing: Michigan State University Press, 2005.

"Union Demonstrations." *Vermont Chronicle* 5, (February 3, 1863): 19, col. B.

"The Young Men's Lyceum." *Milwaukee Daily Sentinel* 65, (March 16, 1861): col. F.

"Young Men's Lyceum." *Tri-weekly Miner's Register* 59, (December 10, 1862): col. B.

Kerry L. Pimblott

■ Fraternal Organizations

Fraternal organizations have a storied and prominent place in the history and development of the United States; however, during the American Civil War fraternal institutions were largely dormant outside the military because the nation was preoccupied with the war. Prior to the Civil War, fraternal organizations had experienced an increase in popularity, while organizations that opposed them experienced a decline. For example, the 1832 presidential candidate of the Anti-Masonic Party was William Wirt (1772–1834), a former Attorney General of the United States and, coincidentally, a member of the Freemasons. College fraternities were slowly gaining popularity until the Civil War, when many colleges shut down or distanced themselves from their fraternal organizations. These trends, however, would prove to be temporary.

Military Lodges

Even though the three largest fraternal organizations at the time of the Civil War—the Freemasons, the Odd Fellows, and the Knights of Pythias—were for the most part institutionally inactive outside the military, the fraternities' conceptions of manhood and the importance of individual character famously endured the war. Several Masonic lodges were founded as military lodges, and the practice of Masonry was continued by soldiers as a bonding experience, a connection to home life, and a kind of quasi-religious activity.

Many stories and legends were told of opposing soldiers coming to aid wounded brethren in battle, which surely appealed to those considering joining a military lodge. One story particularly treasured by contemporary Masons concerns Horatio Rogers of Rhode Island, a general in the Union Army and a Mason, discovering Masonic documents in the pocket of a fallen Confederate soldier. Rogers ensured that the soldier's body received a proper Masonic burial "by fraternal hands" (Dumenil 1984, pp. 101–102). Such stories are told among Masons in the early twenty-first century to teach that Masonic brotherhood transcends political or religious quarrels (Lowe 2001).

Toward the end of the Civil War and immediately following, a controversy erupted among several Masonic lodges regarding the accommodation of handicapped members in their facilities. Following the Masonic ideal of physical ability and bodily perfection, brothers who had lost limbs were often permitted to continue lodge membership, but handicapped new members were barred from joining the lodge as a means of emphasizing cultural norms of manhood of the time. Some Masons feared that if handicapped persons could join the lodge, women—who were considered physically inferior to men—would be next (Carnes 1989, pp. 142–143).

Other Fraternal Organizations

Following the Civil War, however, fraternal organizations flourished and multiplied. Such temperance societies as the Sons of Temperance, the Sons of Honor, and the Independent Order of Grand Templars, all founded before the war, grew in numbers and influence. The Order of the Star-Spangled Banner, an anti-immigrant fraternity founded in 1844 that would later become the nucleus for the Know-Nothing and American Republican parties, spawned the Knights of the Golden Circle in 1861. A group of Knights organized themselves in "Castles." These "Castles" were largely safe spaces for Copperheads—Union men who sympathized with the Confederacy—to gather. The Ku Klux Klan was organized in Pulaski, Tennessee, in 1866, though its influence directly after the war was not of much consequence (Carnes 1989, pp. 7–9).

Oliver Hudson Kelley (1826–1913), a clerk for the U.S. Department of Agriculture, tried to capitalize on

BIRTHPLACE OF THE G. A. R.

BIRTH·PLACE₅ G·A·R

The above shows the front of the building on the south side of Central Park, Decatur, Ill., where Post 1, Grand Army of the Republic, was organized on the night of April 6, 1866, by the founder of the order, Dr. B. F. Stephenson.

Etching of the birthplace of the Grand Army of the Republic, 1866. Despite experiencing a lull in membership during the Civil War years, fraternal organizations found new life at war's end as former soldiers sought to join groups such as the Grand Army of the Republic (for Northern soldiers) and the United Confederate Veterans (for Southern soldiers). *Al Fenn/Time Life Pictures/Getty Images*

the popularity of postwar fraternal organizations by establishing the Order of the Patrons of Husbandry in 1867. Later known as the Grange, the Order promoted farming and animal husbandry. In 1880 several Grangers formed the National Farmers' Alliance. It had similar rituals and enjoyed significant political influence. New veterans' associations were created and emphasized ritual more than the veterans' organizations that predated the Civil War, such as the Military Order of the Loyal Legion (1865), the Grand Army of the Republic (1866), the Union Veteran Legion (1884), and the United Confederate Veterans (1888) (Carnes 1989, p. 8).

Postwar Fraternal and Anti-Masonic Groups

Many new fraternal organizations emerged following the war as insurance societies. The first of these was the Ancient Order of United Workmen in 1868, which blended Masonic and Odd Fellows rituals. Another, the Noble and Holy Order of the Knights of Labor was formed primarily for workers in the skilled trades, although it also admitted employers, women, and (after 1878) blacks. The order became so prominent—it claimed 730,000 members by 1886—that its rituals and activities became part of the day-to-day life of many tradespeople (Carnes 1989, pp. 8–9). These groups and others later became the foundation of the modern trade union movement.

The anti-Masonic movement also revived and gained new influence following the war. Mormons, whose religion and history are closely tied to both the Freemasons and the Anti-Masonic Party, were forbidden to join Masonic groups and largely suppressed the history of their denomination's Masonic origins. An "Anti-Secrecy Crusade" began among evangelical Christians. The movement aimed to restore transparency to all aspects of American life, but particularly focused its attention upon Freemasonry. The Anti-Secrecy movement was largely initiated by Jonathan Blanchard, founder of the National Christian Association; and spread by the revivalist Charles Finney, whose book *The Character, Claims, and Practical Workings of Freemasonry*, launched a mainstream religious attack on Masons and other secret societies that continues into the early twenty-first century. Despite the influence of anti-Masonic groups, by the turn of the twentieth century 5 million American men belonged to at least one fraternal organization; 854,000 of these were Masons (Vaughn 1990, pp. 9–13).

The Civil War provided the context for much of the mystery, excitement, and ritual surrounding fraternal organizations in the twentieth century. One example of this influence is the lore and revisionist history exhibited in D. W. Griffith's 1915 film, *Birth of a Nation*, which portrayed the Ku Klux Klan as saviors of the South, complete with a cameo appearance of Jesus Christ himself. The popularity of the film was partially responsible for the resurgence of the Klan, leading to its expansion to nearly 4 million members in the United States and Canada by the early 1920s. Another well-documented example of the ongoing fascination with the Civil War is the Zeta Chapter of the Alpha Pi fraternity in Dover, Ohio, whose rituals, perhaps as early as 1905, involved

the skull of William Quantrill (1837–1865), a guerrilla leader who had grown up in Dover and is best known for his role in the Lawrence Massacre of 1863 (Leslie 1995, pp. 53–54, 58–60).

BIBLIOGRAPHY

Carnes, Mark. *Secret Ritual and Manhood in Victorian America.* New Haven, CT: Yale University Press, 1989.

Dumenil, Lynn. *Freemasonry and American Culture, 1880–1930.* Princeton, NJ: Princeton University Press, 1984.

Finney, Charles G. *The Character, Claims, and Practical Workings of Freemasonry.* Cincinnati, OH: Western Tract and Book Society, 1869.

Leslie, Edward. "Quantrill's Bones." *American Heritage* 46, no. 4 (1995): 53–60.

Lowe, Justin "Freemasonry and the Civil War: A House Undivided." *California Mason Online,* (2001). Available at http://www.freemason.org/.

Roberts, Allen. *House Undivided: The Story of Freemasonry and the Civil War.* Fulton, MO: Ovid Bell, 1961.

Vaughn, William. "The Reverend Charles G. Finney and the Post-Civil War Antimasonic Crusade." *Social Science Journal* 27, no. 2 (1990): 209–222.

Christopher D. Rodkey

◼ Sports

Sports—that is, athletic activities requiring skill or physical prowess and often competitive in nature, have existed since ancient times, when the Greeks and Romans held contests that evolved into the modern Olympic Games. In the nineteenth century, Americans enjoyed such sports as baseball, fishing, hunting, horse racing, rowing, skating, cockfighting, running, bowling, and boxing. Although newspapers did not report much about sports until Reconstruction, the articles that do exist from earlier years give glimpses into the history of American sports.

Game Hunting

Hunting and fishing can be considered sports only when they become optional instead of necessary to the subsistence of the hunter or fisherman. The methods employed to hunt game in the period of the Civil War were much different from the managed game hunts of later centuries. Newspaper articles dating from the first decades of the nineteenth century describe organized hunts involving dozens of shooters that took place over large tracts of land in New York and Connecticut. During the hunt the hunters would move systemically so that the game was shepherded into crossfire. Wholesale slaughter ensued. For example, during a two-day outing

Skating pond in Central Park, 1863.   Ice skating, sledding, and curling were all seen as pleasant winter pastimes that proved beneficial to one's health.   *Hulton Archive/Getty Images*

in North Carolina in 1820, sixty-one men killed 4,028 squirrels (July 14, 1820, n.p.)

The same technique was used with fishing, if this excerpt from the "Cape Cod" section of the *Lowell (MA) Daily Citizen and News* is any indication: "Four boats . . . succeeded in driving ashore at Brewster a large school of blackfish, which, with the aid of the people on shore, they slaughtered with spears, lances, scythes, and whatever came to hand" (August 23, 1859, n.p.) With this approach to hunting, it is easy to see why the passenger pigeon became extinct, and why the American bison was reduced to a few hundred animals by the mid-1880s.

Fighting Sports

Fighting sports consisted of cockfighting, dogfighting, and bare-knuckle boxing. In 1859 a *Vermont Chronicle* contributor noted an increase in cockfighting, in which two trained roosters fight until one kills the other. The writer remarked, "The effect of such exhibitions upon the populace is demoralizing in the extreme" (November 22, 1859, n.p.). Boxing, a sport that dates from antiquity, was not thought to be more uplifting, especially when it became the subject of gambling. In fact, in 1849 the State of Massachusetts banned prizefighting; yet bare-knuckle

boxing (without gloves) continued on a limited basis along the East Coast. On October 20, 1858, a match held in Long Point, Ontario, between John Morrissey (1831–1878), "Old Smoke," and John Carmel Heenan (1833–1873), "the Benicia Boy," sparked the public's imagination and revived the sport, which eventually evolved into gloved boxing (Mee 2001, pp. 137–139).

Water Sports

Water sports of the time included swimming, rowing, and boating. The Eastern colleges such as Yale, Brown, the University of Pennsylvania, and Harvard fielded rowing teams in annual regattas. In the winter, inland bodies of water became the sites of skating parties. On natural lakes and ponds, and at artificial ponds in places such as the forty-acre rink in Central Park in New York City and Jamaica Pond in Boston, men, women, and children could take part in this "most delightful, agreeable and health-giving of winter recreations," to quote a *New York Herald* writer (December 11, 1859, p. 4).

Sleighing (or sledding) might take place wherever there was a snowy incline. The Scots brought curling (a game resembling bowling, played with granite stones that slid across a sheet of ice) with them when they immigrated.

Racing

People had long liked to gamble on a race, whether human or animal. Any harvest festival or other gathering—such as a Fourth of July picnic—might become the site of a horse race, though horses were usually reserved for more important work during the war years. Human track and field events took somewhat longer to become popular than the equine versions, yet by the late 1850s a Philadelphia Pedestrian Association had been formed to help its members become better athletes. Foot races were also one of the activities with which Union soldiers filled their idle hours (Cumming 1981, p. 49).

The civilian version of foot racing, which went dormant during the war years, resumed quickly after the cessation of hostilities. Distance races and challenges from across the nation appeared in the newspaper *New York Clipper* and were soon followed with competitions of jumping, sprinting, and throwing. Cumming describes the usual events of a typical athletic meeting in the mid-1860s as walking, running, leaping, taking a standing leap over a height, taking a standing leap over a width, a running leap over a height, a running leap over a width, the hop-step-and-jump, and the pole vault. It was not uncommon for such unusual types of races as sack races, or sprints run while carrying weights, to find their way into the competition as well (Cumming 1981, pp. 64–65).

Bowling

Bowling or similar games have existed for centuries. During the Middle Ages in Germany, bowling was an integral part of such gatherings as village dances and festivals. The French, English, and Spanish also played games that were forerunners of modern bowling. They were played outdoors or indoors; the number, shape, and configuration of pins varied. Although the British settlers first brought the game to the colonies, the German immigrants, who arrived in several waves in the mid-1800s, had the greatest impact on the popularity of the game in the United States (Weiskopf 1978, pp. 25–26). In 1854, according to one witness, "the only bowlers were Germans and the only alleys were the very crude ones at the picnic groves and other German resorts" (Hemmer & Kenna 1904, p. 30).

Yet the popularity of bowling was not dimmed by its early crude surroundings. Conversely, it continued to grow. The largest German population was located in New York City, where the first indoor bowling alley was opened in Manhattan in 1840. Like racing and boxing, bowling later suffered from the gambling and cheating that disreputable people brought to it and was banned in some areas. After the Civil War, however, bowling again grew in popularity.

America's National Pastime

Baseball beat out other stick-and-ball games (rounders, cricket, stickball) to become the premier organized American team sport. Although some variation of baseball had existed since the early 1800s, it was not until 1842 that the first club was founded—the Knickerbocker Base Ball Club—and until 1845 that the rules of the game were first recorded.

Prior to the Civil War, most organized teams were located in cities, with the largest number located in the New York City area, the Hudson River valley, central and upstate New York, Philadelphia, and Boston. Yet such Midwestern and Western cities as Chicago, Cleveland, Detroit, Milwaukee, St. Paul, San Francisco, and Sacramento also hosted organized teams (Kirsch 2003, p. 20). "[Baseball] has become almost universal, every State in the Union having its clubs, and the rules of the game are laid down by a regular convention," wrote a *New York Herald* reporter in September of 1859. "The growth and popularity which this fine game has attained within a few years is amazing. Young men of all classes and ages indulge in it, and the matches are witnessed by immense crowds of spectators" (Kirsch 2003, p. 4).

Shortly before the outbreak of the war, newspapers began covering baseball and cricket games, as is evident in this headline from the *New York Times*, "The New and Philadelphia Cricket Match" (July 6, 1860). "Next to swimming, which is the finest exercise in the world," wrote a *New York Herald* writer, "we think base ball is the best exercise" (July 27, 1859, p. 4). Though the press coverage helped popularize the game further, it still developed more slowly in the antebellum South, where New Orleans, Louisville, St. Louis, and Houston had teams (Kirsch 2003, p. 25).

Yet one of the most significant events affecting the popularization of baseball was the gathering together of large groups of men who were idle a portion of each day. Whether in the military or in prison camps, Civil War soldiers played baseball (Kirsch 2003, p. 135). Although the growth in popularity of baseball slowed during the war, the conflict contributed to the eventual diffusion of the sport. After the war, newspapers began regular coverage of sports, creating the first sports columns (p. xiv).

BIBLIOGRAPHY

"The College Regatta Yesterday—Progress of Athletic Sports." *New York Herald*, July 27, 1859, p. 4, col. E.

Cumming, John. *Runners & Walkers: A Nineteenth Century Sports Chronicle*. Chicago: Regnery Gateway, 1981.

"Demoralizing Sports." *Vermont Chronicle* (Bellows Falls), November 22, 1859, issue 47; column E, n.p.

"Gymnastic Sports—Base Ball and Cricket." *New York Herald*, September 10, 1859, p. 4, col. F.

Hemmer, John G., and W. J. Kenna, eds. *Bowling Encyclopedia*. Chicago: Western Bowlers' Journal, 1904.

Kirsch, George B. *Baseball in Blue and Gray: The National Pastime during the Civil War*. Princeton, NJ: Princeton University Press, 2003.

Mee, Bob. *Bare Fists: The History of Bare-Knuckle Prize-Fighting*. New York: Overlook Press, 2001.

"Sports of the Forest." *Raleigh Register and North-Carolina Gazette* (Raleigh, NC) July 14, 1820, issue 1086, col. B.

Weiskopf, Herman. *The Perfect Game: The World of Bowling*. Englewood Cliffs, NJ: Prentice-Hall, 1978.

"Winter in Central Park." *New York Herald*, December 11, 1859, p. 4, col. D.

Jeanne M. Lesinski

■ Games

Throughout the Civil War years, card and board games, gambling, and multiple sports were among the favorite activities for ordinary Americans as well as for Union and Confederate soldiers. These activities offered physical and mental breaks from the intense realities of war for both civilians and soldiers (Varhola 1999, p. 96). Examining Americans' interests in games during the 1860s allows glimpses into the recreation and social details of daily life during the Civil War.

Games Move from Cities to Camps

In American homes, apartments, boardinghouses, and tenements, people welcomed both familiar and new forms of recreation during the difficult years of the war. Games were widespread and played in cities, on rural farms or shipboards, or at soldiers' campsites. For Northerners and Southerners, card and board games were popular forms of entertainment. Euchre, seven-up, twenty-one, poker, checkers, cribbage, dice, and backgammon, were among the favorites. Soldiers, for instance, could pass the time at camps carrying on conversations about life back home or share insights about the enemy while also engaged in contests of skill (Sutherland 1989, p. 13). Multiple efforts were made to enliven the hours, even a little, during the long days and nights at camp.

The Civil War created the need for portable entertainment. Shortly after the war started in 1861, Milton Bradley (1836–1911), a printer who worked out of Springfield, Massachusetts, developed a small kit called *Games for Soldiers*. This set included several popular games, such as checkers and backgammon, and it was designed to fit in a soldier's knapsack for easy transport between camps (Adams and Edmonds 1977, p. 373). Many organizations in the Northeast purchased the kits to donate to the Union soldiers, helping Milton Bradley to turn his enterprise into

an established company, both financially and in terms of popularity. The methods of mass printing available in the 1860s allowed a wide circulation of such products as games advertised with war themes. These themes were extended to multiple markets, including children's games. Some games were explanatory and educational, while others appealed more to the public's natural interest in and preoccupation with the war (Marten 1998, p. 16).

Manufactured card decks with military images and patriotic symbols were common; playing cards used by soldiers and ordinary Americans often had military or political figures and flags. The Union Playing Card Company manufactured such cards used by soldiers in the North, while a card company in the South had images of Confederate generals on the face cards. Regardless of the deck type, soldiers frequently participated in "throwing the papers" (a vernacular phrase for playing cards), including poker and gambling. Although gambling was widespread, particularly among soldiers, many people considered it sinful, and soldiers often eliminated evidence of their participation before leaving to fight (Varhola 1999, p. 98). There are reports of card games played for high stakes as well; in some cases, cheaters as well as unpopular officers were marked for assassination (Sutherland 1989, p. 13).

Aside from the manufactured games, soldiers created their own game pieces, including dice, out of available materials. Such handmade designs took on creative shapes and construction. Dice could be imperfectly carved out of wood and used to play craps or to play out simple bets. One game called for placing bets on the numbers that would appear when dice were thrown from a cup (Sutherland 1989, p. 13). Although the risks of betting were high and game materials less than perfect, soldiers sought frequent entertainment through games. Another form of competition that involved making do with what was available in a military camp involved racing lice or cockroaches across strips of canvas and betting on the outcome ("Life in a Civil War Army Camp," 2002).

Family Activities and Socializing

For families, evenings and weekends were times for social activities with friends or members of the extended family. Similar to board and card game popularity among soldiers, life at home frequently included activities for relief from such typical daily events as chores or the general stresses of war. Croquet offered one such outlet. During the 1860s, croquet became extremely popular for families, and the game's equipment was a common sight on lawns when weather allowed. Friends and family, both males and females, could gather to socialize on the croquet lawn, which also marked their middle-class social status. Men and women even courted each other during such gatherings. The wide variety of participants, including children and members of both sexes, allowed the game's social nature to flourish rather than just its competitive aspect. Within croquet's social context, however, the competitive

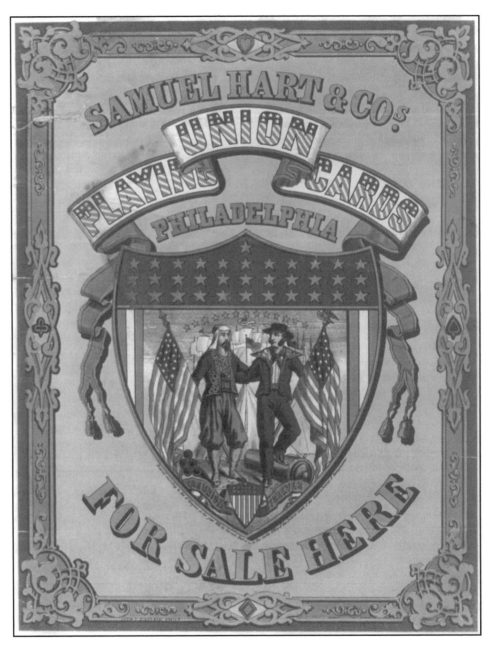

A box of Union playing cards. Though families back home would disapprove, many soldiers gambled with cards for entertainment. During times of battle, soldiers would remove their playing cards from their belongings so if killed, family members would not learn of their wartime habits. *The Library of Congress*

spirit existed, even thrived. According to historian Jon Sterngass in "Cheating, Gender Roles, and the Nineteenth-Century Croquet Craze," women were particularly clever and competitive croquet players who often defeated male players—and enjoyed doing so (Sterngass 1998, p. 309).

Popular Sports

Such other types of games as baseball were also increasing in national popularity during the early 1860s. Large venues for baseball parks were less common in the South than the North due to the North's greater urbanization and diversified population. Immediately before the Civil War began in 1861, baseball's popularity had been increasingly evident in such Northeastern cities as Boston, Philadelphia, and New York City. From schoolboys to townsmen, groups across the Northeast gathered to play. With the onset of war, however, the nation's focus shifted. As soldiers arrived in the Northeastern cities, they became interested in the game, which offered social and physical outlets. Soldiers and officers gathered for recreation and formed baseball teams based on their athletic talents rather than their military ranks (Smithsonian Associates, 2004).

Southerners played such other team sports as cricket and football, in addition to baseball. As with board games, materials used in sports could be homemade or creative, especially for soldiers with limited resources. Commonly, a stick or fence rail became a bat, and rags or string could entwine available objects to serve as balls. Thus, men from different social classes played together and developed interests in games they could take home to various parts of the country after the war.

BIBLIOGRAPHY

Adams, David W., and Victor Edmonds. "Making Your Move: The Educational Significance of the American Board Game, 1832 to 1904." *History of Education Quarterly* 17, no. 4 (1977): 359–383.

"Life in a Civil War Army Camp." *Civil War Armies,* 2002. Available online at http://www.civilwarhome.com/camplife.htm.

Marten, James. *The Children's Civil War.* Chapel Hill: University of North Carolina Press, 1998.

Smithsonian Associates. "The 1860's—When Men Were Men and They Played Baseball in Washington." 2004. *Smithsonian Associates Civil War E-Mail Newsletter.* Available online at http://civilwarstudies.org/.

Sterngass, Jon. "Cheating, Gender Roles, and the Nineteenth-Century Croquet Craze." *Journal of Sports History* 25, no. 3 (1998): 398–418.

Sutherland, Daniel D. *The Expansion of Everyday Life, 1860–1876.* New York: Harper & Row, Publishers, 1989.

Varhola, Michael J. *Everyday Life during the Civil War.* Cincinnati, OH: Writer's Digest Books, 1999.

Jenny Lagergren

■ Holidays

Despite a few early military victories by the Confederacy, the harsh reality of wartime subsistence began to surface in the south shortly after the war began. With their local economies stunted due to the faltering of imports and exports, and with inflation and unemployment rising, the civilian population inflicted further hardships on themselves by their sacrificial giving of food and clothing stores to their troops. Perhaps more than at any other time of the year, Christmas correspondence offered an insight into everyday condition of life during the war.

Sensing the impending hardship that a Union naval blockade and occupation of the port of New Orleans would incur, J. F. H Claiborne wrote in a letter to the editor of the local newspaper in Jackson, Mississippi on December 25, 1861, "Our people live by the transportation of cord wood, charcoal, [and several more items are mentioned] to New Orleans, bringing . . . in return, corn and flour and other articles of prime necessity that our soil refuses to produce . . . There are not breadstuffs in the seashore counties to subsist the population one month" (*The Weekly Mississippian*, December, 25, 1861).

Many young men were off from home, perhaps for the first time. Their recollections of past holidays were evidenced in the letters they sent home. Isaac Howard, Private, C.S.A., wrote to his father on December 25, 1862, "There isn't much preparation for Christmas in camp, the boys are in excellent spirits however, not much doing in the egg-nog line . . . I wish I could send some apples, nice rosy cheeked fellows to Nellie and Susie, bless their little hearts." Seven months later, Howard was killed in Pennsylvania at the battle of Gettysburg (Howard Papers).

For all of the tragedies and hardships the war brought to those on both sides of the conflict, there were lighter moments too. The editor of the *Vicksburg Sun* relives his 1861 Christmas time eggnog experience with some of his friends and their quest to concoct the perfect nog. This story was published in the *Fayetteville* (NC) *Observer*, in January 1862:

> Egg-nog is a very difficult thing to compound to suit one's palate. We tried the experiment yesterday and after drinking one glass . . . there was too much egg. We diluted the mixture with old Otard (cognac) . . . after two glasses . . . we discovered it was not sufficiently sweet . . . we diluted the mixture . . . but this time it involved opening a second bottle of brandy, which proved to be rather fiery after sipping three or four glasses, so we qualified the mixture with rum. We then smoked a cigar and imbibed three or four (more) glasses . . . we waited for our friends to come, but as they didn't, we drank to their health . . . on looking up we saw two doors, and as we knew our room had but one, we thought we would we would wait til our friends . . . should return and show us the way out.

Some prominent Southern families fared better during the conflict in its third year. Mary Boykin Chesnut, wife of Confederate General James Chestnut and a diarist of the Confederacy, wrote of the Christmas of 1863 in Columbia, South Carolina, of a rather festive dinner despite the shortages that abounded for most families: "Yesterday dined at the Preston's with one of my handsomest Paris dresses . . . we had for dinner oyster soup, soup a la reine . . . boiled mutton, ham, boned turkey, wild ducks, partridges, plum pudding . . . and Madeira wine" (*The Roanoke Times*, December 3, 2007).

The holidays offered little respite for anyone in uniform, North or South; not even the Generals were immune. A newspaper article published on December 16, 1864 in Columbia, South Carolina, wrote of an apparent false alarm that the Confederate forces were in retreat: "The holiday season is fast approaching and it is not improbable the (Union) General Grant, who was hurried away from New York by the absurd rumor of the evacuation of Petersburg

[Virginia] may revisit his family to spend Christmas with them" (*The Daily South Carolinian*, December 16, 1864).

By 1864, with many thousands having been killed and many thousands more wounded, hardly a family was left untouched by the ravages of the war. Christmas would never be the same for this generation or for many generations to come. An editorial in the *Daily Picayune*, [New Orleans], published on December 18, 1864, evinces the somber mood of the times: "Jolly old elf! He comes but once a year. On this his annual visit, he will pass over many broken shrines and desolate fields—over many new graves…under which rest unknown soldiers who have fought their last battle…"

As far away as California, reports of the war back East made their way into the local newspapers. Not all of the accounts related directly to the battles of the day. A story of cultural competition reported in the *Richmond* (VA) *Whig* in December 1864 was also reported in a San Francisco paper:

> The *Richmond Whig* notices the proposition of the Yankees…to furnish a dinner to their soldiers in the field, and proposes to our farmers to imitate their example, one of the few…that can be imitated with propriety. The *Whig* says to the farmers: Send every turkey, chicken or pig they can possibly spare…Don't wait for your neighbor to commence the good work, but right away…conscribe certain fat gobblers of your flock and give them a furlough until the 20th of December. (*Daily Evening Bulletin*, December 24, 1864)

For the ordinary soldier, thoughts of home and hearth were always present. Christmas was not only time for the festivities of family, food, and friends, but also a time of religious reflection. To his niece Martha, Jasper Cockerham wrote from near the Petersburg-Richmond, Virginia, front line on December 26, 1864, " The soldiers all look sad and lonely. We have nothing spiritual or refreshing in camp. Have not seen one case of intoxification during our Christmas Holiday" (*Surry County Genealogical Association Journal*, July 3, 1985).

Federal occupation of the port of New Orleans in 1862 and the capture of the port of Vicksburg in 1863 effectively denied the Confederacy's use of inland waterways. The final crushing tactics of Union General William T. Sherman's march from Chattanooga, Tennessee, through Atlanta, Georgia and onward to the sea effectively cut the South in two. General Sherman sent a telegram to President Lincoln on December 22, 1864: "I beg to present you, as a Christmas gift, the city of Savannah, with 150 heavy guns and plenty of ammunition, and also about 25,000 bales of cotton" (U.S. War Department, p. 783).

The war had cost hundreds of thousands lives through combat and disease. The number of families affected is incalculable and the letters to and from home by both soldiers and civilians reflected the extreme hardships of wartime life. On occasion, humor recorded as well. The conflict ended in April but it would not be until Christmas of 1865 that the country would once again celebrate the holidays with some sense of normalcy.

BIBLIOGRAPHY

Daily Evening Bulletin, San Francisco, December 24, 1864.

The Daily Picayune, New Orleans, December 18, 1864.

The Daily South Carolinian, Columbia, December 16, 1864.

Fayetteville Observer, Fayetteville, North Carolina, January 6, 1862.

Howard Papers, Southern Historical Collection, University of North Carolina at Chapel Hill.

"Letter from Jasper Cockerham to his Niece Martha Cockerham, during the Civil War." *Surry County Genealogical Association Journal*. vol. 5, no. July 3, 1985.

The Roanoke Times, Virginia, December 3, 2007.

U. S. War Department. *The War of Rebellion: A Compilation of the Official Records of the Union and Confederate Armies*. (Washington, DC, 1880–1901), series 1. vol. 44. serial No. 92, p. 783.

The Weekly Mississippian, Jackson, December 25, 1861.

Thomas J. Fehn

■ Agricultural Fairs

Agricultural fairs and livestock shows were familiar events for Americans in the first half of the nineteenth century. The public face of local and state agricultural societies, they ostensibly operated without political or social ideologies. In fact, they supported a class-based view of farming, privileging rural elites and promoting modernization that undermined the community relations, which supported small-scale farming. Although the agricultural societies and the fairs they sponsored were limited in scope and duration—few societies lasted more than a decade—the sporadic appearance of agricultural societies and fairs should not obscure their influence in their own time and their legacy in postbellum fairs and farm organizations.

Farm organizations and agricultural fairs operated to encourage scientific planting practices, improve stock-breeding, and promote crop diversification. In both the North and the South, agricultural societies and fairs flourished in areas where emigration to the West had left a more stable population to deal with land at risk from erosion, overuse, and poor farming practices. For these farmers and planters, the only alternative to migration or poverty was better farming. The more substantial farmers formed agricultural societies to address the problem and sponsored lectures on land management and stock breeding, published farm journals, and conducted experiments to determine the best planting practices. To promote acceptance of their ideas, farmers of the "better class" offered premiums for improved crops and livestock at local and regional fairs, believing this would encourage poorer farmers to incorporate scientific practices into their farm routines.

From the beginning, class differences were apparent in fair activities and in the reactions of farmers. With time and capital to invest in unproven ideas, wealthier planters took the prizes and premiums, and celebrated with dinners that excluded their poorer neighbors. Unable to win prizes or attend the after-fair festivities, working farmers complained bitterly and sometimes ignored the fairs altogether. That was the case for the Brighton Cattle Show, founded in 1816 by the Massachusetts Agricultural Society. By 1837 class differences had become so pronounced that most farmers no longer attended the show. In the South Carolina Low Country, the planter-dominated agricultural society promoted reform by offering premiums to progressive overseers. But again, the larger planters used their influence to obtain awards that reflected well on their own plantations. In contrast, yeomen farmers were more likely to attend local county fairs. Rural elites looked at county fairs—with their horseracing, circuses, and sideshows—with scarcely concealed disdain. But to hardworking farm families, the county fair offered a long-anticipated respite from the year's labor and the less rigorous criteria for premiums gave them a chance to demonstrate their agricultural skills.

Agricultural fairs were conflicted ground in other respects as well, incorporating tensions between rural communities and emerging manufacturing interests and sectional disputes that increasingly characterized American political life. Thus, when Tennessee's Mark Cockrill won the premium for the finest example of wool fleece in the world at the London Exposition of 1851, Southern farmers interpreted his award as a sectional victory. News of state agricultural fairs regularly appeared in Southern farm journals, always with claims that they were superior to Northern fairs in presentation and attendance. Because of these claims of cultural superiority over Northern industrialism, Southern agriculturalists wavered between the need to demonstrate new farming techniques and the fear that any admission of the need for reform would reflect badly on them.

Observers, North and South, were more reluctant to comment on the tension between farming and manufacturing interests that also characterized displays and demonstrations at agricultural and county fairs. The wealthiest planters and farmers often invested in mills and factories that processed agricultural commodities. The transition in the countryside from frontier subsistence-farming to commercial agriculture and small-scale manufacturing transformed labor and community relations as capital undermined or replaced the bonds of kinship and friendship that sustained small-scale agriculture, substituting paid labor and capital investment for communal work and shared interests. Increasingly, promoters of manufacturing used local fairs as a means to introduce rural people to the potential benefits of incorporating farm machines into planting and harvesting routines, hiring short-term labor, and maximizing the use of female labor in home manufacturing and local mills. Smaller producers understood that commercialization of agriculture and the increasing reliance on capital investment placed their farms at risk in periods of economic decline. Although they lined up to view the newest machines, they recognized that a way of life was passing.

Agricultural fairs provided an opportunity for women to demonstrate their skills as well. Kitchen garden displays, cooking demonstrations, preservation presentations, and sewing and horticultural exhibits were included in areas set aside for women. Larger fairs erected tents and pavilions for women's exhibits. In the post–Civil War era, no fair was complete without a Women's Pavilion, and women increasingly took responsibility for the design of the space devoted to their work.

The influence of prewar agricultural fairs is apparent in rural reform efforts after the Civil War. Southern agriculturalists, such as Tennessee's Joseph B. Killebrew, organized farmer clubs, published agricultural newspapers, and revived local and regional fairs. Promoters of New South industrialization organized state and regional fairs and expositions to publicize the reconstruction of the Southern economy and to entice Northern capital investment in agriculture and manufacturing.

Despite their influence on the postwar South, the prewar fairs largely failed to meet their founders' goals. Regardless of their intent to promote better farming practices, antebellum reformers were limited in their efforts. Their experiments were conducted within limited parameters and, despite their efforts to generalize from their own experiences, the claims of men such as John Taylor or Edmund Ruffin did not apply to most farms. After the Civil War, however, a more comprehensive approach to the development of better agricultural practices was instituted through federal and state programs—the land-grant college system of education, agricultural experiment stations, the agricultural extension service, and state departments of agriculture. Thus, while their immediate effect was limited, antebellum agricultural fairs and shows—and the agricultural societies that produced them—influenced rural change and established a legacy that helped shape American life in the twentieth century.

BIBLIOGRAPHY

Kelly, Catherine E. " 'The Consummation of Rural Prosperity and Happiness': New England Agricultural Fairs and the Construction of Class and Gender, 1810–1860." *American Quarterly* 49, no. 3 (1997): 574–602.

Nelson, Lynn A. *Pharsalia: An Environmental Biography of a Southern Plantation, 1780–1880.* Athens: University of Georgia Press, 2007.

Steffen, Charles G. "In Search of the Good Overseer: The Failure of the Agricultural Reform Movement in Lowcountry South Carolina, 1821–1834." *Journal of Southern History* 63, no. 4 (1997): 753–802.

Summerhill, Thomas. *Harvest of Dissent: Agrarianism in Nineteenth-Century New York.* Champaign: University of Illinois Press, 2005.

Winters, Donald L. *Tennessee Farming, Tennessee Farmers: Antebellum Agriculture in the Upper South.* Knoxville: University of Tennessee Press, 1994.

Connie L. Lester

■ Newspapers and Magazines

As critic Brayton Harris characterized it in his 1999 book *Blue & Gray in Black & White: Newspapers in the Civil War*, the early nineteenth century newspaper was less a place to report news than a "journal of opinion," and a "vehicle for cultured discourse" (1999, p. 3). During the Civil War, however, the telegraph transformed how readers received their news from the front. "For the first time," writes historian Phillip Knightly, "it was possible for the public to read what had happened yesterday, rather than someone's opinion on what had happened last week" (2002, p. 20). In turn, this possibility of "rapid transmission" fed an insatiable consumer appetite for battlefield news and images on the homefront. Knightley notes that the pressures of immediacy and of consumer demand created inaccuracy and bias, as one Northern daily correspondent was directed by his editor to "Telegraph fully all the news you can get, and when there's no news send rumors" (p. 23). Regardless of their publication cycle (most southern newspapers operated as weekly publications) reporters on both sides of the conflict—perhaps in the tradition of the earlier opinion journals—felt it their responsibility to maintain their readers' morale, which often led to the exaggeration or outright fabrication of reported events.

Newspapers in camp. Technological developments such as the telegraph allowed newspapers to publish up-to-date accounts of wartime events. Newspapers provided an important distraction for soldiers and gave them a temporary reprieve from the hardships of the battlefield. *The Library of Congress.*

Another conflict arose during the Civil War that has yet to be fully resolved: How to reconcile the military need to maintain the security of its operations with the journalist's job to report the news, especially if the information could divulge strategic information, aid an adversary, and influence the events of the war. Thus Civil War correspondents encountered varying degrees of cooperation.

In a July 1861 diary entry, London *Times* correspondent William Howard Russell (1820–1907) recalls in his 1863 book *My Diary North and South* an encounter with Irvin McDowell in which the general assured the journalist, "I shall be happy, indeed, to take you with me. I have made arrangements for the correspondents... to take the field under certain regulations, and I have suggested to them they should wear a white uniform, to indicate the purity of their character" (p. 424). Though Russell suggests no apparent irony in the conversation, other commanders proved less accommodating.

Two months earlier, in April 1861, Gen. Benjamin F. Butler (1818–1893) arrested Edward Grandval, who had been discovered communicating with the editor of the *Baltimore Sun*. The *Sun*, according to Butler, was "a known enemy of the Union" whom Grandval knew when he contracted with the newspaper's editor "to place himself at or as near as possible to Annapolis," where he would "gather what information he could of the movements and numbers of the troops," and forward it to the editor (1917, p. 59). Butler's claims, if considered carefully, are exactly the job of the correspondent—to gather information and report the news. Butler, however, appreciated the sensitivity and potential threat of what he regarded as military intelligence being gathered and conveyed to readers, which doubtless included Confederate military and government officials. In a letter to General Winfield Scott (1786–1866), Butler charged that the prisoner had been "lurking" around a colonel's quarters, where he had examined confidential papers and stolen a revolver; that he had queried the soldiers about troop strength; and that he had attempted to "tamper with the men" by trying convert federal soldiers into secessionists (p. 59). Though he wrote for orders from his superior, Butler had already formed his own convictions about Grandval. "From the evidence, I have no doubt that he was sent as a Spy upon our movements... My own opinion is that the utmost severity is needed towards such a person" (p. 60). In closing, he railed, "Under the guise of bearers of dispatches and reporters of newspapers we are overrun by the meanest and most despicable kind of Spies, who add impudence and brazen effrontery to traitorous and lying reports with which to injure us" (p. 60).

General William T. Sherman (1820–1891) apparently shared Butler's appraisal of the press. In his postwar memoir, Fenwick Y. Hedley, a former subordinate of Sherman's recalled of the general, "Newspaper correspondents were a special abomination in his eyes, provoking him to great wrath and spasmodic profanity of a highly original pattern" (Hedley 1890, p. 67). While occupying Savannah as a military post, Sherman issued Special Field Order 143, establishing guidelines for the city's occupants while under military jurisdiction. Among other regulations, the order restricted the city to a maximum of two newspapers and warned that the publication's editors and proprietors would be "held to the strictest accountability, and... punished severely in person and property, for any libelous publication, mischievous matter, premature news, exaggerated statements, or any comments whatever upon the acts of the constituted authorities..." (Tenney 1865, p. 623). The same accountability applied even when the publishers copied such articles from other newspapers, as was common practice at the time.

Despite the antagonism between the media and the military the value of newspapers and magazines in the daily lives of soldiers was apparently observed both by officers and relief organizations. Ulysses S. Grant (1822–1885) found that issuing the daily eighteen ounce ration in the form of bread rather than flour stretched his budget to "furnish many extra comforts to the men " (Grant 1865, p. 180). In his postwar memoir, *Personal Memoirs of U.S. Grant*, published in 1885, Grant recalled having rented a bakery, hired bakers, and purchased fuel, all to convert the rations. After two months he had "made more money... than my pay amounted to during the entire war." He used the proceeds to "furnish many extra comforts to the men," including regimental libraries and magazine subscriptions (p. 180).

Similarly, Jonathan Hammond's 1863 book *Army Chaplain's Manual, Designed as a help to Chaplains in the Discharge of their Various Duties* includes instructions for establishing a hospital library and reading room. According to the manual, "Many of our newspaper and magazine publishers will cheerfully send their publications to such hospitals as may be established in their respective States, or in which they may feel some special interest" (p. 83). The job of stocking the library lay with the chaplain, whose duty was to "make personal application" to the publishers and to solicit cast off periodicals from friends (p. 83). Though such donations were old to the contributors, the manual assured, "they will be new to the soldiers" (p. 83). At other times daily news vendors sold copies of their papers in camp, where the publications sparked political debates that eased the psychological hardships. As army surgeon J. A. Mowris recorded in the history of his regiment in his 1865 book *A History of the One Hundred and Seventeenth Regiment, N.Y. Volunteers*: "There were times when soldier life seemed intolerably heavy and dull. No wonder the boys sometimes felt despondent as they soliloquized: 'Our work is digging, we could have done that at home.' 'We came to fight and end the war by extinguishing the rebellion.' 'We are now nearly a half year in the service and yet at the Capital instead of at the front.' 'Burnside, with our great army, has just been repulsed with heavy loss.'" But according to

Mowris, the "hopeful tone" of "pro-administration journals" provided an anecdote to the soldiers' dejection. "The good effect of these papers" was felt among the troops as "an efficient moral tonic." (pp. 55–56).

Anthony M. Keiley describes a different use during his time as a prisoner of war. "If newspapers, especially the illustrated ones," could be procured after the construction of a shelter, "the walls are papered inside, increasing the comfort as well as bettering the appearance of the room" (Keiley 1865, p. 72).

A few soldiers also published their own camp newspapers. Some may have used the same printing presses retained to print military administration forms. Others used whatever resources were available, including wrapping paper and wallpaper. Most regimental newspapers published infrequently or only for a short time, especially if the troops were often on the move. For the enlisted men who comprised the vast majority of the publishers, the newspapers provided sources of occupation and media for expression. With the caveat that camp newspapers could not publish sensitive strategic information, they were largely uncensored. According to historian Chandra Miller Manning in her 2002 dissertation "What this Cruel War is Over," the columns of these regimental newspapers "offered soldiers outlets for complaining about everything from the weather to politics to their officers." In so doing, they served "important functions" for the soldiers by "allowing them not only to release pent up frustrations, or explore their own emotions but also to deliberate the meaning of the war" (p. 11). In his journal of life in the Confederate army published after the war, the 1876 book *Fourteen Hundred and 91 Days in the Confederate Army,* W. W. Heartsill recalls the process by which his colleagues issued their camp newspaper. According to Heartsill:

> [A]t Lancaster and Hudson there was published, or rather written, a Newspaper, which for patience and perseverance will be hard to beat, they get up one copy in regular Newspaper style, then copy off as many as they wish, then let those who wish a copy to write it off; thus [of] each issue there is several copies, which are sent back home.... These Papers are of course on the burlesque order; but are as eagerly looked for as any Paper, and long years from now, copies can be found safely stowed away as mementos of frontier life by the "W.P. Lane Rangers." (p. 56)

A copy of the weekly paper, which Heartsill reproduces in his published journal, includes the obituary of a regimental surgeon, a letter from a correspondent at Ft. Lancaster, and subscription rates as follows: one-year subscription, $5.00; six-month subscription, $3.00; and three-month subscription, $2.00. No subscriptions, the publishers declared, would be accepted for less than three months. The regimental newspaper that published that long, however, was a rare exception.

BIBLIOGRAPHY

Butler, Benjamin Franklin. "Letter from Benjamin Franklin Butler to Winfield Scott, April 30, 1861." In *Private and Official Correspondence of Gen. Benjamin F. Butler, during the Period of the Civil War.* Vol. 1. [Norwood, MA: Plimpton Press], 1917.

Frank, Joseph Allan, and Barbara Duteau. "Measuring the Political Articulateness of United States Civil War Soldiers: The Wisconsin Militia." *Journal of Civil War History* 64, no. 1. (January 2000): 53–77.

Grant, Ulysses S. *Personal Memoir of U.S. Grant.* Vol. 1, 1885–1886. Old Saybrook, CT: William S. Konecky, [1999.]

Hammond, Jonathan Pinkney. *The Army Chaplain's Manual, Designed as a help to Chaplains in the Discharge of their Various Duties.* Philadelphia, PA: J. B. Lippincot, 1863. Sources in U.S. History Online: Civil War. Gale. Available from http://galenet.galegroup.com/.

Harris, Brayton. *Blue & Gray in Black & White: Newspapers in the Civil War.* Washington, DC: Brassey's, 1999.

Heartsill, William Williston. *Fourteen Hundred and 91 Days in the Confederate Army: A Journal Kept by W. W. Heartsill, for Four Years, One Month, and One Day, or, Camp Life: Day-by-Day of the W. P. Lane Rangers, from April 19th 1861, to May 20th 1865.* [Marshall, TX: W. W. Heartsill, 1876]. Sources in U.S. History Online. Gale . Available from http://galenet.galegroup.com/.

Hedley, Fenwick Y. *Marching through Georgia : Pen-Pictures of Every-Day Life in General Sherman's Army, from the Beginning of the Atlanta Campaign until the Close of the War* Chicago: Donohue, Henneberry, and Co., 1890. Sources in U.S. History Online. Gale. Available from http://galenet.galegroup.com/.

Keiley, Anthony M. *In Vinculis: Or, the Prisoner of War Being the Experience of a Rebel in Two Federal Pens, Interspersed with Reminiscences of the Late War.* New York: Blelock & Co., 1866.

Knightley, Phillip. *The First Casualty: The War Correspondent as Hero and Myth-Maker from the Crimea to Kosovo.* Baltimore, MD: Johns Hopkins University Press, 2002.

Manning, Chandra Miller. "When this Cruel War is Over: Why Union and Confederate Soldiers Thought They Were Fighting the Civil War." Ph.D. diss. Harvard University, Cambridge, MA, 2002.

Mowris, James. A. *A History of the One Hundred and Seventeenth Regiment, N.Y. Volunteers, (Fourth Oneida), from the Date of Its Organization, August 1862, till that of Its Muster Out, June 1865.* Hartford, CT: Case, Lockwood, Printers, 1866.

Sources in U.S. History Online. Gale. Available from http://galenet.galegroup.com/.

Richards, Eliza. "U.S. Civil War Print Culture and Popular Imagination." *American Literary History* 17, no. 2 (2005).

Russell, William Howard. "Diary of William Howard Russell, July, 1861." In *My Diary North and South*. Boston: T.O.H.P. Burnham, 1863.

Tenney, William Jewett. *The Military and Naval History of the Rebellion in the United States*. New York: D. Appleton & Company, 1865.

United States Army. Military Division of the Mississippi. *General and Field Orders: Campaign of the Armies of the Tennessee, Ohio and Cumberland, Maj. Gen. W. T. Sherman, Commanding, 1864–5*. St. Louis, MO: R. P. Studley and Co., Printers, 1865.

Christina Adkins

■ Literature

American Literature in the nineteenth century was seen in Europe as a poor emulation of European literature. In the 1850s, a number of authors made national calls for a wholly unique American literature to emerge to distinguish itself from what was being viewed as imitation, particularly of a British style. Essaying and critic E. P. Whipple wrote in an 1850 edition of the newspaper *Greenville Mountaineer*, "No matter how meritorious a composition may be, as long as any foreign nation can say that it has done the same thing better, so long shall we be spoken of with contempt, or in a spirit of impertinent patronage." Ralph Waldo Emerson (1803–1882), whose transcendentalist philosophy placed a premium on individuality, similarly wrote in an 1858 edition of *The Kansas Herald of Freedom*, "Insist on yourself; never imitate. Your own gift you can present every moment the emulative force of a whole life's cultivation, but of the adopted talent of another, you have only an extemporaneous half-possession."

If the previously criticized literature was being produced as the last throes of the United States's cultural connection with England, then the authors who answered Whipple and Emerson's calls produced their literature out of the social and political strife of the Civil War era.

Harriet Beecher Stowe (1811–1896)

When President Abraham Lincoln (1809–1865) finally met Harriet Beecher Stowe, he was said to remark, as noted in the introduction to Beecher's 1852 book *Uncle Tom's Cabin*, "So this is the little lady who made the big war" (p. xvi). The book Lincoln referred to was *Uncle Tom's Cabin*, or *Life among the Lowly*, and perhaps no other work of literature caused so great a stir in the national character as Stowe's serialized novel of the life

Cover of *Little Women* by Louisa May Alcott (1832–1888) Before her success as the author of the classic children's story *Little Women*, Louisa May Alcott volunteered as a nurse in a Union hospital. Though typhoid fever cut her service short, Alcott recorded her wartime experiences in a series of letters to her family, which were published in *Commonwealth* magazine and a collection of essays. *Baldwin Library, University of Florida Library.*

of a slave. *Uncle Tom's Cabin* was published in 1852 and met with unprecedented success, selling more than ten thousand copies in the first week and more than three hundred thousand copies in the first year. The success of the novel was due in part, according to editor Darryl Pinckney, to "innovations in printing, such as the development of the cylinder press, which made possible the mass production and distribution of inexpensive editions" (p. ix). The novel chronicles the life of the slave Uncle Tom, who is sold between different masters of varying compassion only to wind up in the hands of Simon Legree, a cruel plantation owner who eventually orders Tom beaten to death for refusing to tell the whereabouts of other escaped slaves. As Tom is beaten, he forgives Legree's cruelties and thereby reaffirms the value of Christian forgiveness that Stowe discusses throughout the novel, saying:

Mas'r, if you was sick, or in trouble, or dying, and I could save ye, I'd *give* ye my heart's blood; and, if taking every drop of blood in this poor old body would save your precious soul, I'd give 'em freely, as the Lord gave his for me. Oh, Mas'r! don't bring this great sin on your soul! It will hurt you more than 't will me! Do the worst you can, my troubles'll be over soon; but, if ye don't repent, yours will *never* end. (p. 446)

Stowe affirmed her reason for writing the novel, saying, "The Carthagenian women in the last peril of their state cut off their hair for bow strings to give to the defenders of their country; and such peril and shame as now hangs over this country is worse than Roman slavery, and I hope every woman who can write will not be silent" (p. ix).

Throughout the novel, Stowe addresses the reader directly. After Simon Legree decides to beat Tom for what will be the last time, the narrative breaks with the following passage: "Ye say that the *interest* of the master is a sufficient safeguard for the slave. In the fury of man's mad will, he will wittingly, and with open eye, sell his own soul to the devil to gain his ends; and will he be more careful of his neighbor's body?" (p. 443).

The book was met with harsh criticism in the South, where its descriptions of cruelty were seen as an exaggeration. The *Fayetteville Observer* in 1855 reported that "the picture of [slavery's] cruelties and atrocities given by Mrs. Stowe in her celebrated novel are either gross exaggerations, or so exceptionable as not at all to be taken into the account when forming a judgment of the institution itself." In order to refute the critics as to the validity of the narrative, in 1853 Stowe published *A Key to Uncle Tom's Cabin*, in which specific accounts of slave cruelty are chronicled. In the *Key*, according to Pinckney, Stowe is "eager to give examples of abiding Christian faith among blacks" in order to provide evidence of her "depiction of the system of slavery, because many whites were distressed that she had made a black man sensitive and intelligent" (p. xvii). A Florida newspaper, the *Pensacola Gazette*, refuted *Key* in 1853, saying:

The Uncle Tom was so profitable a speculation, that the "*Key*" followed as a matter of course. Should the Key turn a good penny for the author, it will probably be succeeded by a "*Peg*" to hang it on; and this, in the event of further success, by a "*Hammer*," to drive the peg home . . . One must be desperately in love with the garbage of Abolition newspapers to read a dozen consecutive pages of this book; and the man whose patience can hold out to the end of it, can get through anything.

As a testament to the power of *Uncle Tom's Cabin*, Pinckney asserts that "in the three years following [the book], at least fourteen pro-slavery novels were issued, some of which branded Stowe a mad woman or a plain liar" (p. xx). Whether it was loved or hated, her novel "was

so popular that it helped to break the prejudice of church people like herself against novel reading—and theater going—as unworthy pursuits (p. xxii).

Rebecca Harding Davis (1831–1910)

Uncle Tom's Cabin was to slavery what Rebecca Harding Davis's 1861 novella *Life in the Iron Mills* was to American capitalism. The story contains detailed descriptions of the working and living conditions of mill workers contrasted with their profiteering overseer, who mistreats them. Hugh, an artistic mill worker, steals a lump of pig iron and sculpts it into an abstract statue of a struggling worker. Hugh is later arrested and subsequently dies in prison, but Davis ends on a hopeful and religious note: "While the room is yet steeped in heavy shadow, a cool, gray light suddenly touches its head like a blessing hand, and its groping arm points through the broken cloud to the far East, where, in the flickering, nebulous crimson, God has set the promise of the Dawn" (p. 65). Davis's descriptions were one of the first in American history that cataloged the harsh conditions of the working class while simultaneously presenting a scathing criticism of the factory owner Kirby, who at one point says, "I wash my hands of all social problems, — slavery, caste, white or black. My duty to my operatives has a narrow limit, —the pay-hour on Saturday night. Outside of that, if they cut korl, or cut each other's throats, (the more popular amusement of the two,) I am not responsible" (p. 35).

Walt Whitman (1819–1892)

Walt Whitman's literary masterpiece, *Leaves of Grass*, was first self-published in 1855 with less than glowing reviews, some calling it, as the 2003 edition of the *Norton Anthology of American Literature* notes "indecent, bold, curious, lawless, [and] obscene" (p. 36). According to the *Norton Anthology* Whitman, unsatisfied with the lack of positive book reviews, "wrote a few himself to be published anonymously" (p. 18). When Whitman released his second edition in 1860, the reviews still did not meet his hopes. One Washington newspaper, the *Daily National Intelligencer*, in assuming the reaction of another literary critic, Jeffery, wrote in 1860:

We do not know that Jeffery would have pronounced "The Leaves of Grass" to be the *worst* poem ever honored with exquisite typography, imprinted on paper of irreproachable quality, but we are pretty certain he would have conceded to it the merit of being the strangest-born among all the intellectual freaks of nature he had ever been called to inspect and analyze.

That same review goes on to say that "It were no great wonder, after the success of Walt Whitman, if many persons who have never talked anything but the most unmitigated nonsense should congratulate themselves on the discovery that they have all the while been Miltons in

AMBROSE BIERCE

Ambrose Bierce (1842–1914?) was a journalist, short-story writer, and literary critic known as "Bitter Bierce" by his friends as well as his many readers. Bierce joined the Ninth Indiana Volunteer Infantry in 1861 and remained in the Union Army until his discharge in 1865. He fought at Shiloh, Chickamauga, Kennesaw Mountain (where he received a serious head wound), Franklin, and Nashville; his injuries weakened his health for the rest of his life.

Bierce's war experiences were the source of a number of his short stories, which are considered some of the finest ever written by an American author and continue to be included in anthologies. "An Occurrence at Owl Creek Bridge" (1890) describes the hanging of a Confederate sympathizer by a group of Union soldiers and is well known for its surprise ending, which was often imitated by later writers.

After the end of the Civil War Bierce joined an expedition to inspect army outposts in the West, which eventually brought him to San Francisco. There he worked as a journalist and newspaper editor, becoming highly controversial for his biting satire and social commentary. He began to publish occasional sarcastic word definitions as part of a weekly column in the *San Francisco Examiner* titled "Prattle." These definitions were eventually brought together in *The Devil's Dictionary* (1911), first published as *The Cynic's Word Book* in 1906. The entries in the *Dictionary* reflect Bierce's bleak view of life as well as his wit:

CONTROVERSY. , n. A battle in which spittle or ink replaces the injurious cannon-ball and the inconsiderate bayonet.

DICTIONARY. , n. A malevolent literary device for cramping the growth of a language and making it hard and inelastic. This dictionary, however, is a most useful work.

GRAVE. , n. A place in which the dead are laid to await the coming of the medical student.

HISTORY. , n. An account mostly false, of events mostly unimportant, which are brought about by rulers mostly knaves, and soldiers mostly fools.

JUSTICE. , n. A commodity which is a more or less adulterated condition the State sells to the citizen as a reward for his allegiance, taxes and personal service.

MAN. , n. An animal so lost in rapturous contemplation of what he thinks he is as to overlook what he indubitably ought to be. His chief occupation is extermination of other animals and his own species, which, however, multiplies with such insistent rapidity as to infest the whole habitable earth and Canada.

NEIGHBOR. , n. One whom we are commanded to love as ourselves, and who does all he knows how to make us disobedient.

YANKEE. , n. In Europe, an American. In the Northern States of our Union, a New Englander. In the Southern States the word is unknown. (See **DAMN YANK**.)

At the end of his life Bierce became one of the most famous missing persons in American history. He went to Texas in October 1913 to tour Civil War battlefields and crossed into Mexico, then undergoing an internal revolution. He sent a last letter to a friend in December 1913 and disappeared. Some think he was shot by Mexican revolutionaries, died of disease, committed suicide, or was killed by robbers preying on tourists. His disappearance, however, remains an unsolved mystery almost a century later.

REBECCA J. FREY

BIBLIOGRAPHY

Bierce, Ambrose. *The Devil's Dictionary.* Cleveland, OH: World Publishing Co., 1911.

Carter, Paul A. *The Spiritual Crisis of the Gilded Age.* DeKalb: Northern Illinois University Press, 1971.

Churchill, Allan. *They Never Came Back.* Garden City, NY: Doubleday and Co., 1960.

---

disguise." Whitman was criticized for his lack of poetic meter, for emulating a biblical tone, for openly discussing sexual content, and for using long catalogues and lists of American places and people. It was not until Whitman released other editions of *Leaves of Grass* that these criticisms became the very arguments used in modern times to celebrate his genius.

Future editions of *Leaves of Grass* include expanded selections of poems and revisions of previous poems, most notably "Song of Myself." The 1855 edition begins:

> I celebrate myself,
> And what I assume you shall assume,
> For every atom belonging to me as good belongs
>   to you.

> I loafe and invite my soul,
> I lean and loafe at my ease . . . observing a spear of
>   summer grass.
> Houses and rooms are full of perfumes . . . the
>   shelves are crowded with perfumes,
> I breathe the fragrance myself, and know it and
>   like it,
> The distillation would intoxicate me also, but I
>   shall not let it.

The final 1881 edition of the same poem begins the same, but then changes dramatically from the original:

> I celebrate myself, and sing myself,
> And what I assume you shall assume,
> For every atom belonging to me as good belongs
>   to you.

I loafe and invite my soul,
I lean and loafe at my ease observing a spear of
    summer grass.
My tongue, every atom of my blood, form'd from
    this soil, this air,
Born here of parents born here from parents the
    same, and their parents the same,
I, now thirty-seven years old in perfect health begin,
Hoping to cease not till death.

Before the Civil War began, Whitman made visits to hospitals to cheer patients, and when war broke out, he soon found himself working as a wound dresser for the North. These war experiences became the subject of *Drum Taps*, a series of poems set during the war. *The Civil War: A Treasury of Art and Literature*, edited by Stephen W. Sears in 1992, quotes Whitman as once saying, "Future years will never know the seething hell and the black and infernal background of countless minor scenes and interiors (not the official surface courteousness of the generals, not the few great battles) of the Secession War, and it is best they should not. The real war will never get in the books" (p. 13). Despite these words Whitman was able to give readers of his day a taste of the brutalization of war with poems such as "Beat! Beat! Drums," "Vigil Strange I Kept on the Field One Night," and "The Wound-Dresser."

Whitman's response to President Lincoln's assassination was cataloged in the poems "O Captain! My Captain!" and "When Lilacs Last in the Dooryard Bloom'd." For twelve years after the war had ended, Whitman gave a lecture on the anniversary of Lincoln's death to memorialize the president and to show the political importance of the event. One newspaper, in reporting Whitman's words about Lincoln, wrote:

> Abraham Lincoln will take first place in the history of the future. He will be like the heroes of the Homeric wars . . . The final use of a heroic eminent life—especially of a heroic eminent death, is its indirect filterings into the nation and the race, and to give also at many removes, age after age, color and fibre to the personalism of the youth and the maturity of that age and mankind . . . Why, if the old Greeks had this man, what trilogies of plays, what epics would have been made out of him . . . When, centuries hence, . . . the leading historians and dramatists seek for some personage, some special event incisive enough to mark with deepest cut this turbulent nineteenth century of ours, . . . the absolute extirpation of slavery from the States, these historians, these dramatists, will seek in vain for any point to serve more thoroughly their purpose than Abraham Lincoln.

BIBLIOGRAPHY

Anthology of Modern American Poetry, ed. Cary Nelson. New York: Oxford University Press, 2000.

Boston Daily Advertiser (Boston) December 24, 1868; col. B.

The Civil War: A Treasury of Art and Literature, ed. Stephen W. Sears. New York: Macmillan, 1992.

Daily Evening Bulletin (San Francisco) January 12, 1861; col. B.

Daily National Intelligencer (Washington, DC) July 14, 1860; col. C.

Davis, Rebecca Harding. *Life in the Iron Mills and Other Stories*. Ed. Tillie Olsen. Old Westbury, NY: Feminist Press, 1972.

Fayetteville Observer (Fayetteville, NC) October 18, 1855; col. D.

Frank Leslie's Illustrated Newspaper (New York) July 11, 1868; p. 259; col. D.

Frederick Douglass' Paper (Rochester, NY) June 17, 1853; col. B.

Freedom's Champion (Atchison, KS) April 28, 1864; col. F.

Greenville Mountaineer (Greenville, SC) March 1, 1850; col. C.

The Kansas Herald of Freedom (Wakarusa, KS) August 14, 1858; col. H.

Milwaukee Daily Sentinel (Milwaukee, WI) May 10, 1865; col. B.

The North American (Philadelphia) June 23, 1892; pg. 5; col. E.

The Norton Anthology of American Literature, ed. Nia Baym. 6th ed., vol. C. New York: W. W. Norton, 2003.

Pensacola Gazette (Pensacola, FL) May 7, 1853; col F.

Poetry and Eloquence from the Blue and the Gray: The Photographic History of the Civil War, ed. Francis Trevelyan Miller. New York: Castle Books, 1957.

Rocky Mountain News (Denver, CO) March 22, 1896; p. 8; col. A.

St. Louis Globe-Democrat (St. Louis, MO) April 19, 1882; p. 6; col. F.

Stowe, Harriet Beecher. *Uncle Tom's Cabin*, [1852] ed. Darryl Pinckney. New York: Penguin Books, [1998.]

John L. Reilly

■ Children's Literature

Although literature for children and young adults is a well-developed genre in the twenty-first century, in the 1800s it was in its beginning stages in both the United States and England. Children learned to read from hornbooks (sheets of parchment or paper mounted on a piece of wood and covered with a transparent layer of horn), and then primers (first readers). The material they read was meant to instruct them on good moral values. At this time, children were treated as small adults rather than as having unique needs. Yet, as views on childrearing evolved toward a greater awareness of children's developmental needs, the material written for children began to change as well. At the same time, public education was expanding, adding to the pool of readers. Most juvenile books were geared toward ten-year-olds, though a few were designed for younger children.

Technical advances made during the industrial revolution also had an impact on reading: They made printed material (magazines, pamphlets, and books) affordable for a wider range of readers. Magazines were often sold for 2 to 3 cents, "dime novels"—the equivalent of a cheap paperback in the twenty-first century—for 10 cents, and hardbound books for 50 cents to $1.50. However, during the war years, in regions where Americans suffered economically, even such modestly priced reading material became a luxury.

Boys' Adventure Stories

By the mid-1860s adventure stories geared toward boys had become very popular. Full of action and suspense, they usually appeared serially in juvenile or general readership magazines before being sold in book form. Numerous magazines for children were founded over the course of the nineteenth century. They were often published by such civic-minded organizations as churches, which meant that the emphasis was more on moral development than entertainment. During the war years, a reader could choose from some dozen magazines, such as *All the Year Round*, *The Student and Schoolmate*, *Child's World*, and *The Boy's Own Magazine*. This last title enjoyed a healthy existence from 1855 to 1874 because its publishers, the husband-and-wife team of John and Mary Bennett, knew their audience and offered the magazine at a reasonable price (2 cents, gradually increasing to 6 cents). It contained adventure stories illustrated with woodcuts, stories of school life, articles on cricket, and articles on scientific topics. There were also puzzles and contests in which winners would receive such prizes as watches and pencil cases. *The Boy's Own Magazine* was quite a success, for in 1863 subscriptions numbered 40,000 (Meigs et al 1969, p. 249).

The Irvin P. Beadle Company of New York specialized in dime novels—pocket-sized booklets printed on white rag paper and sporting a colored cover. Beadle titles included detective stories, mysteries, and frontier adventures that were often printed in series. Edward Sylvester Ellis wrote approximately two hundred such novels, eighteen of them during the Civil War period. His most popular title, selling more than 600,000 copies, was the 1860 tale *Seth Jones; or the Captives of the Frontier* (Bingham 1980, pp. 191–192). Another prominent author of this period was the Unitarian minister Horatio Alger, whose *Frank's Campaign* (1864) was the first of many rags-to-riches stories published by Loring, a Boston firm (Bingham 1980, p. 197). An anonymous reviewer for *Frank Leslie's Illustrated Newspaper* called Alger's debut novel a "well written story, full of unpretentious interest, and inspired by genial feeling and good moral motive" (December 17,

The poet Christina Georgina Rossetti (1830–1894). Christina Georgina Rossetti was one of the few reputable poets that wrote for children in newspapers. Her famous piece, *Goblin Market* (1862), includes evil fairies that are changed with love. *Rossetti, Christina, portrait by James Collinson.*

1864, p. 203). While the attraction of Alger's books for juvenile readers was their entertainment value, parents could be assured that good moral values were being imparted, even if the writing was often lackluster. Another type of adventure tale was the travel adventure, such as the Woodville Series (1861–1871), popularized by former schoolteacher William Taylor Adams, who wrote under the pseudonym Oliver Optic.

Realistic Domestic Stories

Whereas publishers gave boys tales of adventure, they offered girls realistic stories of American life. Jane Andrews introduced readers to *The Seven Little Sisters Who Live on the Round Ball That Floats in the Air* (1861), a story about girls who live in different countries, and Adeline Dutton Train Whitney, who published as Mrs. A. D. T. Whitney, released the popular tale *Faith Gartney's Childhood* (1863) (Meigs et al 1969, p. 204). Aiming for the attention of somewhat younger readers was Sophie May, writing as Rebecca Clarke. In 1863 she introduced a series of books based on the character Little Prudy (*Little Prudy* [1863], *Little Prudy's Sister Susy* [1864], *Little Prudy's Captain Horace* [1864], etc.), which ran until 1865 (Meigs et al 1969, p. 204). While A. R. Baker of the *Lowell Daily*

"THE MAN WITHOUT A COUNTRY"

One of the most popular stories of the Civil War era, "The Man without a Country" (1863), was first published in the *Atlantic Monthly* in December of 1863. This tale, written by the Reverend Edward E. Hale under the pseudonym Frederick Ingham, U.S.N., recounts the life of Philip Nolan, a man found guilty of participating in Aaron Burr's failed efforts to create a republic in the Southwest. During his trial Nolan angrily declares that his wish is to never hear of the United States again. The court takes him at his word and sentences him to stay aboard various ships, and for more than fifty years he is not allowed to set foot on or even see the United States.

While the story is fictional, its verisimilitude struck many contemporary readers. An anonymous reviewer for the *Daily Cleveland Herald* described the tale as "extraordinary," adding, "Whatever may be the truth of the story—and it seems impossible to be believed—it is one of those extraordinary narratives that impress the reader with its truthfulness, even when known to be pure fiction" (November 24, 1863, col. C). As well as impressing readers with its realism, the tale had another effect: It engendered feelings of loyalty in the North and thus encouraged enlistment (Meigs et al. 1969, p. 207).

JEANNE M. LESINSKI

BIBLIOGRAPHY

"The Atlantic Monthly for December." Daily Cleveland Herald (Cleveland, OH), November 24, 1863, col. C.

Meigs, Cornelia, et al. A Critical History of Children's Literature: A Survey of Children's Books in English, *rev. ed. London: Macmillan, 1969, p. 207.*

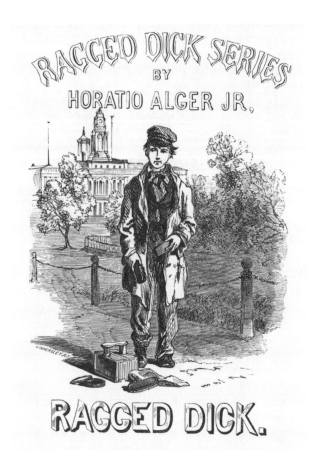

Cover of *Ragged Dick*, a book by Horatio Alger Jr. Horatio Alger Jr. was a Unitarian minister and prominent author of the Civil War era, writing many adventures for boys. This title, along with *Frank's Campaign*, are two examples of his tales of rags-to-riches. *The Library of Congress.*

Citizen and News described *Little Prudy* as "excellent and pleasant for the little folks" (Baker 1864, n.p.), the following year a critic complained about *Cousin Grace*, from the same series: "It contains many things which are quite too good for their surroundings, and much that is really excellent; but altogether it confirms the opinion which is frequently forced upon us, that the work of preparing juvenile books in series is carried out too fast" (*Boston Daily Advertiser*, October 26, 1864, n.p.).

Other Genres

Such other genres as the fairy tale, fantasy, poetry, and novelty had also formed part of juvenile offerings since the 1850s. The fairy tales of the Danish writer Hans Christian Andersen (such as "The Ugly Duckling") and of the German folklorists Jacob and Wilhelm Grimm (such as "Hansel and Gretel") were widely popular. Another enduring tale of the time is the 1865 fantasy *Alice's Adventures in Wonderland* by Lewis Carroll (Charles Dodgson). Although many of the poems for children that appeared in the newspapers were trite, there were such notable exceptions as Christina Georgina Rossetti's *Goblin Market* (1862), in which the evil fairies are changed through the power of love. Coventry Patmore attempted to gather the best children's verse of the time in his 1863 compilation *The Children's Garland from the Best Poets*. Novelty books, among them puzzle books, books containing silhouettes to be cut out, and illusion books held great appeal. J. H. Brown's *Spectropia; or Surprising Spectral Illusions* (1864) was printed in black and white, and hand-painted in bright colors. If the reader stared at the pictures for a time and then turned their attention to the ceiling or wall, a "ghost" in complementary colors could be seen. In *Shadow and Substance* (1860), the illustrator Charles Henry Bennett produced drawings of human figures casting unusual shadows (Quayle 1971, pp. 133–135).

Some of what were to become among the best-loved children's classics were written during the last third of the century, after the Civil War: Louisa May Alcott's *Little Women* (1868–1869), Mark Twain's *The Adventures of Tom Sawyer* (1876), Robert Louis Stevenson's *Treasure Island* (1883), and Rudyard Kipling's *The Jungle Books*

(1894–1895). A new generation of literate children were ready to make these works their own.

BIBLIOGRAPHY

Baker, A. R. *Lowell Daily Citizen and News* (Lowell, MA), January 1, 1864.

Bingham, Jane, and Grayce Scholt. *Fifteen Centuries of Children's Literature: An Annotated Chronology of British and American Works in Historical Context.* Westport, CT: Greenwood Press, 1980.

Boston Daily Advertiser (Boston), October 26, 1864, col. H.

Frank Leslie's Illustrated Newspaper (New York), December 17, 1864.

Meigs, Cornelia, et al. *A Critical History of Children's Literature: A Survey of Children's Books in English,* rev. ed. London: Macmillan, 1969.

Quayle, Eric. *The Collector's Book of Children's Books.* London: Clarkson N. Potter, 1971.

Jeanne M. Lesinski

■ Photography

PHOTOGRAPHY: AN OVERVIEW
Richard C. Keenan

WAR PHOTOGRAPHY
Christina Adkins

CIVILIAN PHOTOGRAPHY
Christina Adkins

PHOTOGRAPHY: AN OVERVIEW

The American Civil War was the first war to be extensively documented by photography. The photographic process was still in its infancy in the first quarter of the nineteenth century; by modern standards it was a cumbersome and primitive process. With the advent of the war, photography, which had been largely limited to portraiture and the visual recording of landmarks, both natural and humanly constructed, took a new direction and discovered a new purpose. It recorded history with a graphic reality unrealized in any written description; it largely dispelled the romantic imagery of equestrian prowess, flashing sabers, and desperate but heroic stands by larger-than-life figures—images derived from paintings and illustrations that had been the more commonly depicted views of war before the photograph. Photography presented to the public the devastation of war and its destructive aftermath in all their grim reality. Although the Civil War was not definitively documented on film, there were approximately one million photographs taken between 1860 and 1865, and there were more than 3,000 photographers actively practicing their profession in the United States (Schwarz 2000, p. 1515).

Among these photographers was a relatively small group who worked as the first photographers of the devastations of war. The most notable members of the group were Alexander Gardner (1821–1882), Timothy H. O'Sullivan (c. 1840–1882), and James F. Gibson (b. 1828), all of whom began their careers working for Mathew Brady (1823–1896), an enterprising producer of daguerreotypes whose name became all but synonymous with Civil War photography.

Popular American photography began in the 1840s with the daguerreotype, a process for reproducing images on a light-sensitive, silver-coated metal sheet. The process, patented in 1839, had been developed by Louis Daguerre (1787–1851), a French artist and chemist. There was one image produced with each sitting, and the subject was required to hold completely still for a period of time that could last up to a full sixty seconds in order to effect the proper exposure. These proto-photographs were generally kept in decorative boxes designed to protect the product. Daguerreotype studios flourished in New York City in the 1840s, and one of the more successful of these studios was owned by the enterprising Mathew Brady.

Brady's Early Work

Brady, the son of Irish immigrants, began as an art student who also made watch and instrument cases, including cases for daguerreotypes, which awakened his interest in this new technology. He took lessons in the daguerreotype method from Samuel F. B. Morse (1791–1872), an art instructor and portrait painter who learned the process from its inventor, Louis Daguerre (Morse is better known to posterity as the inventor of the single-wire telegraph and the Morse code).

Brady enjoyed great success with daguerreotypes, and in 1842 opened his own studio and portrait gallery in New York. In 1849 he opened a second gallery in Washington, DC In 1854 he opened an additional gallery in New York. He became world-renowned, winning prizes for his work at the 1851 World Exposition in London and the 1853 World's Fair in New York. Brady photographed every president of the United States from John Quincy Adams to William McKinley, with the exception of William Henry Harrison, who died in 1841 after a little more than a month in office. Brady's best-known presidential photographs are those of Abraham Lincoln, most notably the one that for many years appeared on the American five-dollar bill.

In the 1850s Brady began to turn his attention from the daguerreotype to a new method of photography known as the wet plate process, developed by an Englishman named Frederick Scott Archer. This process used a mixture of nitrocellulose dissolved in acetone called collodion. The collodion was mixed with additional chemicals, applied to a carefully cleaned glass plate, and allowed to stand until it formed a glutinous, jelly-like consistency. The plate was then immersed in liquid silver nitrate in a darkroom,

War dead at Gettysburg. Images captured by Civil War photographers delivered the brutality of the conflict to the American public in a way never before seen. *Photograph by Alexander Gardner. The Library of Congress.*

creating sensitivity to light in the gelatinous collodion that would last only as long as the plate remained wet. The wet plate was then placed in an opaque holder and subsequently transferred to the focused and positioned camera, with the subject already in place for the exposure. After exposure, the collodion plate was removed from the camera, again in its opaque holder, and returned to the darkroom, where it was placed in a bath of chemical developer followed by a bath of fixer, usually potassium cyanide. The plate was then washed in water, dried, and given a protective coat of light varnish. The wet plate process was less expensive and gave a sharper image with a greater contrast on the gray scale, unlike the darker quality of the daguerreotype. Moreover, the wet plate process produced a negative from which the photographer could make additional positive photographs in the darkroom.

With the addition of the wet plate process, Brady's studios went on to even greater success. Brady placed particular emphasis on large portraits, some as large as 17 by 21 inches, which were called "Brady Imperials." An Imperial could be carefully retouched with paint or ink to create an impressive lifelike portrait that would sell for fifty to a hundred dollars on average. Brady favored

the Imperials, both for the money they brought to the studio and, in particular, for their artistic prestige.

Cartes de visite and the Civil War

Brady's assistant, later the manager of his Washington, DC, studio, Alexander Gardner, wanted to place greater emphasis on the *carte de visite*, a smaller photograph (2 ½ x 4 inches) printed on thin cardboard. This process had first been developed by a Frenchman, André Disdéri, who patented his concept in 1854. His process allowed eight negatives to be taken on an 8 x 10 glass plate. The *carte de visite*, a descendant of the Victorian calling card, from which it derives its name, was extremely popular with the public. The paper print photograph could also be mounted on a slightly larger and heavier piece of card stock with a sentiment (usually a poem or quotation) printed below. The photograph might be a famous landmark or person, or a family member. During the Civil War, thousands of proud young soldiers in new uniforms, on duty and far from home, would stand in line at the photographer's wagon found at almost every encampment to have a *carte de visite* taken. It would then be mailed home, where it would be placed in the family album for posterity.

The *carte de visite* also went the other way, and many a soldier carried with him a small likeness of his wife, children, mother or sweetheart. Brady was initially resistant to making these mementos and wanted to concentrate more of the studio's time on the Imperial portrait, with its greater immediate profit and prestige. Gardner, an astute businessman as well as a talented photographer, saw greater profit in the volume that *cartes de visite*, which sold individually for between ten and twenty cents, would bring. Using existent equipment, Gardner improvised a four-lens camera that could make four images on one glass plate, quadrupling the studio's volume of production of the small photographs. At Gardner's urging, Brady entered into an agreement with the Anthony Brothers, who operated the largest photographic supply company in the country, to produce and distribute the small photographs. The Brady studios would supply the negatives and in return would receive a substantial royalty from the sales (Sullivan 2004, pp. 26–27).

Perhaps the most poignant story concerning the *carte de visite* is that of an unknown soldier, a sergeant who served with the 154th New York Volunteer Regiment. On July 1, the first day of the battle of Gettysburg, the sergeant was mortally wounded and died before he was able to reach the safety of the Union lines on Cemetery Ridge. After the battle, his body was found, but without identification. In his hand was an ambrotype photograph of three small children. The young woman who found the body gave the photograph to her father, the owner of a local tavern. The tavern keeper displayed the photograph, and it became a curiosity and conversation piece.

Some months later, in November 1863, Dr. John Francis Bourns, a Philadelphia physician who had come to the battlefield hospital to lend assistance to the sick and wounded, saw the photograph and became intrigued with the case of this unknown soldier. After first locating and marking the grave where the sergeant was buried, he set out to identify and locate the children. Bourns had the photograph of the children duplicated as a *carte de visite*. Because the format was not expensive, he made multiple copies and circulated them widely. On October 19, 1863, the *Philadelphia Inquirer* carried the story, and other newspapers throughout the Northeast gave it widespread distribution. Finally, in Portville, New York, Mrs. Philinda Humiston responded to the story. She was the wife of Sgt. Amos Humiston and the mother of eight-year old Franklin, six-year-old Alice, and four-year-old Frederick. She had sent the photograph to her husband months before but had not heard from him since the conclusion of the Gettysburg battle. Sgt. Humiston was thus conclusively identified. The public was greatly moved by the story, and Dr. Bourns sold hundreds of copies of the *carte de visite* with the poignant image of the orphan children. He donated the proceeds of the sales to Mrs. Humiston and her family (Dunkleman 1999, pp. 12–17).

Stereographs

Another photographic innovation that became extremely popular in the 1850s was the stereograph. The stereograph was a set of photographs (paper prints from glass negatives) printed side by side, with one print having a slightly different, all but indiscernible depth of field, taken by a double-lens specially designed camera. These dual photographs, placed side by side on cardboard, were viewed through a handheld binocular frame with a slight magnification. The view for the spectator was a single three-dimensional image. The stereograph remained a popular entertainment device in American homes into the early twentieth century. It brought to quiet domestic parlors not only the visual pleasures of faraway places with strange-sounding names never before seen, but also the destruction and devastation of the American Civil War.

The continuing demand for *cartes de visite* and stereographs greatly increased Brady's profits and reputation. In 1864 he opened a new and highly luxurious studio at Broadway and Tenth Street in New York City. *Frank Leslie's Illustrated Newspaper*, one of the most popular periodicals of the time, waxed eloquent about the studio's "costly carpet...elegant and luxurious couches...and artistic gas fixtures." There was also a private entrance for ladies arriving in evening dress "to obviate the unpleasant necessity of passing, so attired, through the public gallery." The greatest experience of Brady's career came with the visit of the Prince of Wales, Albert Edward, son of Queen Victoria, and heir to the British throne. The prince, later King Edward VII (1841–1910), was on a diplomatic visit to Canada and North America, the first member of the British royal family to visit the United States. Brady invited the prince and his entourage to visit the studio, and the prince readily accepted. He and others sat for individual and group portraits, and spent several hours touring the studio and viewing Brady's prized collection of photographs of prominent Americans. *The New York Times* reported that the royals "complimented Brady highly upon his proficiency and art" (Sullivan 2004, 28–29).

Brady at the peak of his career enjoyed his artistic recognition and high social standing, but he was not a man with a sound fiscal sense. He lived a life of luxury, traveled often, made some bad investments, and spared little or no expense for the equipment and interior decoration of his studios. In later years he lost everything, including a large collection of negatives held by the Anthony Brothers as security for the purchase of photographic supplies.

Battlefield Photography

The relatively new technology of photography and the American Civil War came together on July 21, 1861. Brady, among a handful of Washington photographers, followed the Federal Army to Manassas, Virginia, just south of the capital, where Union troops engaged the new Confederate Army near Bull Run Creek in the first land battle of the war.

B-5077

Mathew Brady (1822–1896) and company, Petersburg, Virginia. Developments in photography allowed the Civil War to be the first conflict to be captured on still media. Mathew Brady, already a well-known professional photographer before the war, and his staff became famous for images capturing different aspects of Civil War battles. *The Library of Congress.*

Initially Brady was motivated by the opportunity for business profit, but gradually he developed the idea of photographing the war as an important contribution to the new visual dimension of history presented by photography. This first experience, however, produced no known photographs whatever. The newly formed Confederate Army overwhelmed the Federal troops, and the engagement turned into a rout. Brady and other photographers had to hastily pack up their equipment (delicate and easily damaged in the great urgency) and toss it into darkroom wagons as they joined the hasty retreat of soldiers and civilian spectators back to Washington.

Brady's studios continued to be in the forefront of efforts to document the war in photographs, although Brady, afflicted with deteriorating eyesight, gradually took a less active part in on-site photography. Others, particularly Gardner and O'Sullivan, along with James Gibson, took many of the photographs that came to the public's attention as the work of "Mathew Brady Studios." This identification became a point of contention, particularly

with Gardner, who resented not receiving credit for his work. Sometime in 1862 or 1863, he left Brady and opened his own studio in Washington with his brother James. Timothy O'Sullivan and others also left Brady and went to work for Gardner. Both Gardner and O'Sullivan went on to distinguish themselves in the annals of photography, receiving due recognition for their compositions. Gardner photographed the meeting between McClellan and President Lincoln, formally posed with military staff outside McClellan's tent, which is perhaps his best-known photograph, as well as much of the destruction of the city of Richmond. At the end of the war Gardner photographed the conspirators convicted in Lincoln's assassination and their subsequent execution. Another associate of Gardner's, George Barnard, followed General Sherman's Army on its march through Georgia and made memorable photographs of the stark devastation of the countryside and the destruction of Atlanta.

Gardner's and Gibson's photographs of the aftermath of the Antietam battlefield were the first graphic images of battlefield dead to reach the American public. The photographs could not be directly reproduced in newspapers because the half-tone process that enables such reproduction of photographs was not invented until the 1880s. Engravings, however, were made from the photographs, depicting such scenes as the Confederate dead who fell near the Burnside Bridge and along the fenced area known as Bloody Lane. The engravings were initially reproduced in *Harper's Weekly*, and the original photographs, displayed at Brady's New York studio, both horrified and fascinated the public, who came to see them in great numbers (Schwarz 2000, p. 1516).

A reporter for the *New York Times* visited the studio during the Antietam exhibit, and recognized a deeper significance and value that transcended the more lurid and sensational aspects of the exhibit. In the October 20, 1862 edition of the newspaper, the unidentified reporter wrote the following: "Mr. Brady has done something to bring home to us the terrible reality and earnestness of war. If he has not brought bodies and laid them in our door-yards and along streets, he has done something very like it" (Frassanito 1978, p. 16). O'Sullivan's photographs of the Gettysburg battlefield, appearing in a later exhibit, produced a similar reaction—particularly the photograph of the bloated bodies of Federal dead lying in a field near the McPherson woods, titled "A Harvest of Death" (Schwarz 2000, p. 1446).

In addition to corpses on the battlefield, skeletonized buildings, and devastated countryside, photographers of the Civil War period recorded in both quantity and detail soldiers posing on captured breastworks and gun emplacements, regiments on parade or drilling in the fields, army encampments, and the formidable and growing ironclad navy. The only missing element is the actual combat. There are no photographs of armies moving into active combat or the explosions, caught at the moment of impact, that are such a distinctive part of war photography in later generations.

This omission had nothing to do with the courage or initiative of the photographers; it was the primary limitation of photography at the time. The exposure time for the wet plate process took approximately ten to thirty seconds, depending on the intensity of the light. Officers and enlisted men could hold such poses without difficulty, but horses, mules, and flying flags could be a problem. Any movement before the exposure was complete would produce a blur in the final image. The photographing of actual battle or combat action was not possible in the 1860s. To compensate for this limitation, photographers would often recreate a particular battlefield scene to enhance its dramatic effect, moving corpses, equipment and weapons into a variety of poses. A good example of this technique is the often-reproduced photograph taken by Alexander Gardner of a dead Confederate sharpshooter in the Devil's Den area of the battle of Gettysburg. William Frassanito, after a painstaking analysis of the photograph and of others taken in the same area, demonstrated conclusively that the body of the sharpshooter had been moved and rearranged, and a number of exposures had been taken of the various positions (Frassanito 1975, pp. 191–192).

Most of the Civil War photographs that have survived were taken by Northerners. Southern photographers were active in the beginning of the war, and were in fact the first Civil War photographers on record. The photographs of the Confederate general staff that appear most often in books about the war, along with other high-ranking officers in Southern uniforms, were taken by photographers in the South. Noted Southern photographers include Andrew Lytle of Baton Rouge and George S. Cook of Charleston, among others. As the Union blockade gradually but effectively reduced all commerce with the world outside the Confederacy only contraband goods were readily obtainable. Photographic supplies and necessary chemicals, including cameras and replacement parts, became increasingly scarce and were simply unavailable in the South by 1863.

By the end of the four-year conflict, several hundred thousand photographs had been taken; a large percentage of those were portraits. Mathew Brady's photographic collection consisted of some 6,000 negatives and photographs taken by his studio and those of other photographers, which he purchased during his lifetime. These photographs were acquired by the War Department in 1874 and are now stored in the National Archives. In addition, there are major collections in the Library of Congress and the Connecticut State Library in Hartford. Other substantial collections can be found in the Boston Public Library, Princeton University's Firestone Library, and the George Eastman House in Rochester, New York.

BIBLIOGRAPHY

Dunkelman, Mark H. *Gettysburg's Unknown Soldier: The Life, Death, and Celebrity of Amos Humiston.* Westport, CT: Praeger, 1999.

Frassanito, William A. *Antietam: The Photographic Legacy of America's Bloodiest Day.* New York: Charles Scribner's Sons, 1978.

Frassanito, William A. *Early Photography at Gettysburg.* Gettysburg, PA: Thomas Publications, 1995.

Frassanito, William A. *Gettysburg: A Journey in Time.* Gettysburg, PA: Thomas Publications, 1975.

Schwarz, Angela. "Photography." In *Encyclopedia of the American Civil War: A Political, Social, and Military History,* ed. David S. and Jeanne T. Heidler. New York: W. W. Norton & Co., 2000.

Sullivan, George. *In the Wake of Battle: The Civil War Images of Mathew Brady.* Munich and New York: Prestel Verlag, 2004.

Richard C. Keenan

WAR PHOTOGRAPHY

The Civil War was the first conflict to be extensively documented by photographers. Between 1860 and 1865, about one million photographs depicted some aspect of a nation at war (Sullivan 2004, p. 6). During this time, military photography radically altered the vision of battle held in America's popular imagination. In illustrated weeklies, popular histories, and children's textbooks, antebellum print culture produced scenes that celebrated and romanticized war with little acknowledgment of its attendant loss (Frassanito 1978, pp. 27–28). Though images of battlefield casualties constituted only a small portion of the photographs taken during the war, the pictures of the dead captured by such Civil War photographers as Mathew Brady (1823–1896) and his associates confronted the public with drastically different and haunting tableaus.

Though a few photographic images of war had been produced during the Crimean War (1853–1856) in Europe and the Mexican-American War (1846–1848) in the Southwest, they were not widely circulated in the United States. Rather, the most abundant visual representations of combat were artist illustrations, particularly woodcut engravings. The technology did not yet exist to replicate photographs in newspapers or magazines, so during the Civil War these publications employed graphic artists to redraw photographic images for their readers. But before that, artists worked without photographic referents, and the illustrations they produced, according to historian William Frassanito, depicted war as "a glorious adventure." Most depicted action scenes of troops in the midst of battle or of individual soldiers in heroic postures. The dead and wounded were pictured, but their presence was subordinated to the unity of the heroic battle scene. The casualties were almost never shown as mutilated, dismembered, or rotting (Frassanito 1978, p. 28).

The 1862 Antietam Exhibit

That type of representation changed when a series of battlefield photographs, titled "The Dead at Antietam" went on display in Mathew Brady's New York studio. The photographs had been made by Alexander Gardner (1821–1882), one of Brady's associates. Portable photo laboratories in horse-drawn wagons gave photographers the mobility to perform field work and follow the military engagements (Bleiler 1959 [1866]). But as the photo process required extended exposure, the technology did not lend itself to recording action shots of engagements, nor did the obvious hazards of setting up equipment in the middle of combat zones (Cobb 1962, pp. 128–129). The process was also complicated by possession of the battlefield after the fighting had ended. Thus, the most dramatic battlefield images taken by photographers were necessarily taken afterward. If burial details had finished clearing the battlefield and interring the dead before the photographers arrived, they documented the aftermath by focusing on the scarred landscape. Alexander Gardner and his assistant made their well-known death studies at Antietam soon after the battle ended. Many of the dead remained where they had fallen on the battlefield in abject postures and in various stages of decomposition (Frassanito 1978, pp. 51–52). Gardner's images presented a terrible spectacle to the viewers who studied the images in Brady's gallery.

A reporter who covered the story for *The New York Times* acknowledged that though most civilians "recognize the battle-field as a reality…it stands as a remote one." The photos in the exhibit had begun to change that conception. According to the *Times*, the photographer had "done something to bring home to us the terrible reality and earnestness of war. If he has not brought bodies and laid them in our dooryards and along the streets, he has done something very like it" (October 20, 1862, p. 5).

Some of the battlefield scenes were so graphic that when they were redrawn as magazine illustrations, artists and editors had to select the subjects carefully so as not to offend the sensibilities of their readers. According to the historian Donald Keyes, however, "There was no escaping the truth of the photograph when the camera dispassionately surveyed the carnage and wreckage of humanity and buildings" (Keyes 1976–1977, p.121). As the *Times* reporter noted, the photos bore a "terrible distinctiveness" so that with the use of a magnifying glass, "the very features of the slain may be distinguished" (October 20, 1862, p. 5). The reporter also speculated that "Of all objects of horror one would think the battle-field should stand preeminent." But rather than the repulsiveness one would anticipate, the photographs elicited "a terrible fascination…that draws one near these pictures, and makes him loth [*sic*] to leave them." The article continued, "You will see hushed, reverend groups standing around these weird copies of carnage, bending down to look in the pale faces of the dead, chained by the strange spell that dwells in dead men's eyes" (October 20, 1862, p. 5).

In a study of photography that was published in the July 1863 *Atlantic Monthly*, Oliver Wendell Holmes Sr. (1809–1894), an eminent Boston physician, discussed the Antietam exhibit as evidence that "the field of photography is extending itself to embrace subjects of strange and sometimes fearful interest." Holmes had traveled to the site in search of his son soon after the battle ended, and the photographs in "The Dead at Antietam" captured the consequences that Holmes had witnessed firsthand. He testified to the realism of the photographs by declaring, "Let him who wishes to know what war is look at this series of illustrations" (Holmes 1863, p. 11). Holmes also described his own experience of viewing these "terrible mementos" and their capacity to "thrill or revolt those whose soul sickens at such sights" (pp. 11–12). Looking over the prints, Holmes remarked, was "so nearly like visiting the battlefield" that "all the emotions excited by the actual sight of the stained and sordid scene … came back to us, and we hurried them in the recesses of our cabinet as we would have buried the mutilated remains of the dead they too vividly represented" (Holmes 1863, p. 12).

Stereographs and Portraits

What no doubt increased the vividness of the photographs and amplified the viewer's response was that many of the photographs were produced as three-dimensional, or stereoscopic, images. A camera containing two side-by-side lenses would capture almost identical images. When viewed simultaneously under a stereograph viewer—the forerunner of children's 3D View-Master toys—the two distinct images were combined by the viewer's brain to create the optical illusion of a single image with depth (Zeller 1997, pp. 13, 16). Oliver Wendell Holmes Sr. was an avid collector of stereographs and had invented the first practical handheld viewer in 1859 (Zeller 1997, p. 14). The images from "The Dead at Antietam" were reproduced and sold widely—stereographs for fifty cents each, two-dimensional *cartes de visite* and album cards for a quarter. The scenes were also redrawn by artists and printed in the illustrated magazine *Harper's Weekly* (Zeller 1997, p. 38).

While the battlefield photos generated the most reaction from viewers, they actually constituted only a small portion of the photographs taken to document the war. More than three thousand photographers were working in the United States at the time (Sullivan 2004, p. 6); at least three hundred of those photographed some aspect of the war (Moyes 2001, p. 17). Most worked as portrait artists, taking pictures of individual soldiers (Zeller 2005, p. 88). In his study of the Union soldier, *The Life of Billy Yank,* the historian Bell Irvin Wiley cites an official from the U.S. Sanitary Commission who commented on the "immense number" of soldiers who had their likenesses taken by photographers (Wiley 1971, p. 367). According to Wiley, "during their first weeks in uniform countless soldiers visited the 'daguerrean artists' who set up shop in camp or in near-by towns" (Wiley 1971, p. 25). In a letter dated February 1862, Warren Hapgood Freeman wrote to his father, "There is a photograph artist about the camp, but he has such a crowd about his saloon all the time that I have not been able to get a picture yet" (Freeman 1871).

A few photographers, such as Alexander Gardner, who left Brady and established his own gallery in 1863, reproduced maps, took images of large landscape views, and documented various aspects and activities of army life. Of the extensive collections of Civil War photographs that survive in the National Archives, "Soldiers at Rest after a Drill" depicts troops seated on the ground reading letters and playing cards. Other prints include regimental group portraits, an army blacksmith's forge, cavalry columns, refugees fleeing a combat zone, religious services, railroad bridges, the construction of telegraph lines, councils of senior generals with President Lincoln, people and places related to Lincoln's assassination, and fugitives who fled slavery as they arrived at Union lines.

MATHEW BRADY

Mathew Brady was perhaps the preeminent figure of Civil War photography, but his role in photographing the war has often been misunderstood. Brady was the first person to dispatch a corps of photographers to document the war (Trachtenberg 1985, p. 3). While the images that resulted were copyrighted in the names of individual photographers, the press largely credited Brady for the work of his employees. Many have speculated that this fact ultimately led to Alexander Gardner's decision to leave Brady's employ in 1863 (Zeller 2005, p. 103). Brady's reputation remains largely unchallenged throughout the postwar nineteenth century—for example, an 1891 *New York World* article referred to Brady as "the grand old man of American photography" and as "a man who has photographed more prominent men than any other artist in the country" (Townsend 1891, p. 26).

Later, however, as scholars began to differentiate the work of several photographers, some questioned whether Brady's name was merely the equivalent of a corporate brand (Panzer 1997, p. 3). In fact, Brady did personally continue to produce images consistent with his earlier portraits of famous subjects. But he also devoted much of his effort to compiling as comprehensive a collection as he could, through directing the work of his employees and buying negatives of pictures taken by other photographers (Library of Congress, n.p.). He spent $100,000 to finance his war enterprise, but sold his collection to the U.S. government for approximately $25,000 to pay his debts (Townsend 1891, p. 26; Panzer 1997, p. 19). "No one will ever know what I went through to secure those negatives," Brady later lamented. "The world can never appreciate it. It changed the whole course of my life" (Library of Congress, n.p.).

CHRISTINA ADKINS

BIBLIOGRAPHY

Library of Congress. "Mathew B. Brady: Biographical Note." In American Memory: Selected Civil War Photographs. Available from http://memory. loc.gov/ammem/cwphtml/cwbrady.html.

Panzer, Mary. Mathew Brady and the Image of History. Washington, DC: Smithsonian Books, 1997.

Townsend, George Alfred. "Still Taking Pictures." New York World, April 12, 1891, p. 26. Reprinted in Mary Panzer's Mathew Brady and the Image of History. Washington, DC: Smithsonian Books, 1997.

Trachtenberg, Alan. "Albums of War: On Reading Civil War Photographs." Representations 9 (Winter 1985): 1–32.

Zeller, Bob. The Blue and Gray in Black and White: A History of Civil War Photography. Westport, CT: Praeger Publishers, 2005.

Between November 1861 and March 1862, Timothy O'Sullivan (c. 1840–1882) visited the war zone in Beaufort, South Carolina, where defeated planters had abandoned their lands but former slaves were not yet recognized as free by U.S. government policy (Wilson 1999, p. 108). During his time in Beaufort, O'Sullivan photographed the African Americans of the "Old Fort Plantation," which became the largest group photo of enslaved men and women ever

Union artillery unit posed with cannons and horses.   More than one million photos are thought to have been taken during the Civil War, capturing numerous facets of army life.   *Photograph by Mathew Brady. The Library of Congress.*

recorded (Wilson 1999, p. 108). Photo collector and author Jackie Napolean Wilson notes the symbolism in the photograph as the subjects "stand in a wake of light emerging from the darkness of shadows." As Wilson explains, the men and women in the photograph are bewildered survivors of an American tragedy (Wilson 1999, p. 108).

A Military Photographer

Most of the photographers who documented the war, either for their own enterprise or as military contractors, did so as civilians (Zeller 2005, p. 88). A notable exception was a Union officer, Captain Andrew J. Russell (1830–1902), who was uniquely positioned to capture much more with his camera. Officially, Russell's assignment as the photographer of military railroads required him to photograph aspects of railroad infrastructure. The photos were then reproduced and distributed to various military and government authorities (Zeller 2005, pp. 89–90).

But Russell also photographed war scenes because he was often traveling with the troops. Most notably, he took rare shots of the second battle of Fredericksburg. Russell photographed soldiers huddled together ready to move on a moment's notice. He also set up his camera on the periphery of the battle and documented the engagement as it progressed. His photos include pictures of what may be smoke from an artillery battery and images of casualties

taken twenty minutes after the battle (Zeller 2005, pp. 91–99). Russell is credited with raising the bar of Civil War photographic achievement in that he was able to follow an army in action (Zeller 2005, p. 91).

Other Applications of Civil War Photography

But the documentary value of photography was employed for other purposes as well. The U.S. Congress commissioned photographs to record the condition of prisoners at Andersonville, Georgia, the site of a notorious Confederate prison camp (Orvell 2003, p. 65). The images, which revealed prisoners near starvation, were used as evidence in the trial of the jailer in charge of the camp, Henry Wirz, who was ultimately convicted and executed for war crimes. The *Daily National Intelligencer* reported the testimony of a U.S. Army surgeon, V. A. Vanderkief, who supervised the treatment of reclaimed prisoners at Annapolis, Maryland. The *Intelligencer* reported that "a photograph of a man . . . reduced to a mere skeleton was exhibited," to which the witness testified that "a large number of prisoners who came from Andersonville were of the appearance of that exhibited by the photograph" (August 30, 1865, col. A).

In addition, a report issued by the Surgeon General's Office gauging the material available for a medical history of the war recounted the early uses of medical photography.

Ravages of war. Although photographic technology did not yet allow for images of actual fighting, some camera operators would take images of the battlefield after the hostilities ended, before dead soldiers were removed. Newspaper editors often sanitized the etchings based on those pictures, fearing their readership would be too unsettled by the graphic nature of war captured by the photos. *The Library of Congress*

In 1862, the Surgeon General's Office directed army medical officers to forward monthly reports with details of their surgical cases and pathological specimens. The plan was to establish the Army Medical Museum for the advancement of medical study. Eventually a photograph gallery was also established at the museum. According to George Otis, the author of the Surgeon General's report, "Typical specimens were reproduced, and the photographs, accompanied by brief printed histories, were distributed to medical directors, to be shown to the medical officers serving with them. [. . .] Numerous patients in hospitals were photographed, and the Museum now possesses four quarto volumes, with

over a thousand photographic representations of wounded or mutilated men" (Otis 1865, p. 7). This early medical photography allowed army surgeons to document and disseminate knowledge of injuries and treatments that were developed during the war.

After the Civil War, the commercial market for military photographs rapidly disappeared. In 1865 and 1866, Alexander Gardner published two volumes of *Gardner's Photographic Sketch Book of the War*. Rather than reproducing the original photographs with artist sketches, the book was produced with actual photographic positives pasted into the pages. The collection was expensive to produce and sold few copies (Bleiler 1959 [1866]). By then, many Americans eschewed reminders of the devastating conflict, especially images that so vividly preserved its violence.

BIBLIOGRAPHY

Bleiler, E.F. Introduction to *Gardner's Photographic Sketch Book of the Civil War,* by Alexander Gardner. New York: Dover Publications, Inc., 1959 [1866].

"Brady's Photographs: Pictures of the Dead at Antietam." *New York Times,* October 20, 1862. p. 5.

Cobb, Josephine. "Photographers of the Civil War." *Military Affairs* 26, no 3 (1962): 127–135.

Frassanito, William A. *Antietam: The Photographic Legacy of America's Bloodiest Day.* New York: Charles Scribner's Sons, 1978.

Freeman, Warren Hapgood. "Letter from Warren Hapgood Freeman to J. D. Freeman." In *Letters from Two Brothers Serving in the War for the Union to Their Family at Home in West Cambridge, Mass.* Cambridge, MA: H.O. Houghton and Co., 1871.

Holmes, Oliver Wendell, Sr. "Doings of the Sunbeam." *Atlantic Monthly,* July 1863, 1–15.

Keyes, Donald. "The Daguerreotype's Popularity in America." *Art Journal* 36, no. 2 (1976–1977): 116–122.

Moyes, Norman B. *American Combat Photography from the Civil War to the Gulf War.* New York: MetroBooks, 2001.

Otis, George Alexander. *Reports on the Extent and Nature of the Materials Available for the Preparation of a Medical and Surgical History of the Rebellion.* Philadelphia: J. B. Lippincott & Co., 1865.

Sullivan, George. *In the Wake of Battle: The Civil War Images of Mathew Brady.* New York: Prestel Publishing, 2004.

"Trial of Henry Wirz: The Proceedings of Yesterday." *Daily National Intelligencer.* August 30, 1865, col. A.

Wiley, Bell Irvin. *The Life of Billy Yank: The Common Soldier of the Union.* Garden City, NY: Doubleday & Company, Inc., 1971 [1952].

Wilson, Jackie Napolean. *Hidden Witness: African American Images from the Dawn of Photography to the Civil War.* New York: St. Martin's Press, 1999.

Zeller, Bob. *The Civil War in Depth: History in 3-D.* San Francisco, CA: Chronicle Books, 1997.

Zeller, Bob. *The Blue and Gray in Black and White: A History of Civil War Photography.* Westport, CT: Praeger Publishers, 2005.

Christina Adkins

CIVILIAN PHOTOGRAPHY

During the Civil War, photography became an important medium through which Americans documented the conflict in their own private collections, communicated sentiment to loved ones, and mourned the losses they endured.

At the beginning of the Civil War, new army recruits and civilians on the home front rushed to take portraits for exchange with distant loved ones. By one account, nearly twenty thousand letters and "two or three bushels" of photographs were mailed daily from a single post office at Nashville (Fitch 1863, p. 313).

Portrait photography was so prevalent that newspaper articles offered advice on "How to Photograph Pleasing Countenances" and "How to Dress for a Photograph." The *Washington* (DC) *Daily National Intelligencer* advised that when dressing for a photograph, "violent contrasts of color should be especially guarded against." It also advocated the use of the powder "puff box," as freckles appeared "most painfully distinct" when photographed (February 3, 1865). The *San Francisco Daily Evening Bulletin* reported that a photographer in Cleveland, Ohio, had attempted to alleviate the "stereotyped solemnity" of the portrait-sitter by placing a mirror next to the camera. Subjects could then see their own expressions as they were captured by the camera. Reportedly, the result was that the "stern scowl is suddenly changed to a pleasant smile" (April 25, 1863).

As a corollary to the small card-mounted portraits known as *cartes de visite*, photo albums became popular, as they allowed people to arrange their own personal photo archives and place them on display in their homes (Trachtenberg 1985, pp. 6–7).

Newspaper classifieds regularly contained advertisements for new types of photo albums. Eastman's Book and Stationary Store in Lowell, Massachusetts, for example, claimed to offer the best albums on the market, purportedly manifesting "decided improvements over any heretofore made"—though what these innovations might have been they did not specify (*Lowell Daily Citizen,* February 19, 1862). An 1865 article in the *Daily Cleveland Herald* announced the introduction of a new type of album, the Photograph Family Record, which was intended to preserve the "likeness, descriptions, and records" of each family member. Each record included spaces for two photographs taken at different times in a person's life, a blank marriage certificate, and places to record birth dates, genealogy, education, politics, and various other personal information up to the date of death and place of burial. The article concluded that the new album "affords opportunity for a complete family history, which cannot but become a highly-prized memorial" (August 3, 1865).

Indeed, these personal photo collections were among the valuables saved in times of crisis. For example, one witness to the Confederate raid on Chambersburg, Pennsylvania, recalled seeing "ladies escaping from their houses with nothing but a few photographs or an album" (Schneck 1864, p. 64). Another resident who lived near the soon-to-be-burned courthouse recalled salvaging a few books, the family Bible, and a photograph album by stowing them in a neighbor's house (Schneck 1864, p. 47). While the fact that so few things were salvaged was due to the desperation of the situation, the choice of what to save reveals much about the importance of photographs.

For hospital supervisor Elvira Powers, the photo album she received from her patients was a token of mutual esteem. The album had her name engraved on it and was "of a size to hold one hundred pictures." No gift, she declared, was "more acceptable than the album, especially . . . [if it contained] the faces of the donors" (Powers 1866, pp. 201–202).

By the 1860s, though, photo collecting was not exclusively a personal matter; photo-reproduction processes had created new commercial possibilities. Whereas the earlier daguerreotype portrait had allowed for only a single copy of a photograph, the *carte de visite* process, developed in 1850, allowed for multiple prints from a single negative. Meanwhile, the reproduction and sale of celebrity portraits meant that in addition to pictures of their nearest and dearest, people could purchase small portrait prints of famous figures. Whereas enthusiasts previously had to attend galleries to view images of the most prominent public figures of the time, they could now collect prints of such images in their own album archive.

This became the pastime of Southern diarist Mary Chesnut, who in 1861 recorded a peculiar morning encounter with South Carolina Governor John Manning. When Manning arrived for breakfast in full formal attire as if dressed to attend a ball, Chesnut "looked at him in amazement." But Manning assured her, "I am not mad. . . . I am only going to the photographer." Manning's wife wanted a portrait taken in his dress attire. Chesnut accompanied Manning to the studio, along with her husband James Chesnut Jr. and the former governor, John Means. Afterward, the diarist received a gift of a photo album in which she was to "pillory all celebrities" (Chesnut 1981, p. 37). Though Chesnut's social circle comprised a veritable who's who of famous Confederates, she may have acquired photographs for her album not only from personal acquaintances but also from the portrait copies that were widely available for sale. Chesnut later wrote that her photograph book contained "one of all the Yankee generals" (Chesnut 1981, p. 731). To amuse the young son of a Confederate colonel, Chesnut handed him a photo album; on flipping through it, the child exclaimed "You have Lincoln in your book! I am astonished at you" (Chesnut 1981, p. 412).

Chesnut also recorded an instance in which a suitor submitted his portrait to his intended, a common ritual in nineteenth-century courtships. Sally "Buck" Preston was the object of a Confederate major's attentions—though only after her own older sister had rejected him. The officer, Chesnut noted, sent Sally his photograph, and in

due time "cannonaded" her with marriage proposals (Chesnut 1981, p. 445).

Photography was so integral a part of the cultural experience of the war that it became the subject of literary compositions. For example, an anonymous poem titled "The Carte de Visite" appeared in the September 1862 issue of *Harper's New Monthly Magazine*. It tells the story of a soldier who stops to rest on a stranger's front porch. During this respite, he describes a terrible battle to a mother and daughter. An unidentified youth killed in action becomes the subject of particular concern, as the daughter begins to worry that the soldier is referring to her beloved. When the soldier reveals a photograph of the young ensign, the image confirms the daughter's worst fears. The poem concludes, "when we buried our dead that night / I took from his breast this picture—see! / It is as like him as like can be / . . . One glance, and a look, half sad, half wild, / passed over her face, which grew more pale, / Then a passionate, hopeless, heart-broken wail" (pp. 479–480).

While this poem is fictional, during the war it indeed became common practice to identify casualties from family photographs and other items they carried on their person. "Ordinarily," wrote Edward Parmelee Smith, who ministered among the casualties, "in the inside breast pocket of the blouse, there would be a letter from friends, a photograph, a Christian Commission Testament or Hymn Book, with the name and regiment and home address" (Smith 1869, p. 236).

At Gettysburg, a soldier was found slain on the battlefield with no identification but the ambrotype of his three children. In *Incidents of the United States Christian Commission* (1869), Smith reflected that perhaps no other story of the war "became so widely known or excited such deep sympathy." According to Smith, the soldier was found clutching the photograph so that it "must have met his dying gaze" (pp. 175–176). The case came to the attention of civilian doctor J. Francis Bourns. To discover the identity of the soldier and notify his family, Bourns had the photograph reproduced, then furnished the image and details to the press. The incident and the search became a national story, and copies of the children's image were reproduced and sold for the benefit of the family. Eventually, the soldier was identified as Sergeant Amos Humiston. When the Humiston family was finally located, Bourns arranged to meet them. According to the *Washington Daily National Intelligencer*, Bourns "found them living in the same humble house in which the father had left them when he went forth to the service of his country; and when the children gathered together and grouped as they are in the ambrotype, it was seen that there could be no mistake in the family" (February 24, 1864). Bourns returned the original portrait to Humiston's widow, along with the money collected from the sale of the photo reprints and various contributions. Copies of the children's photograph, the article added, were still available for sale at a Seventh Street bookstore and in the Patent Office at the National Fair. On January 23, 1866, the *Scioto Gazette* (Chillicothe, OH)

Last thought of a dying father. Soldiers on both sides of the Civil War often kept pictures of their loved ones close to their person. After the Battle of Gettysburg, an unknown fallen soldier clutching a portrait of his children became famous after a doctor reproduced the image in newspapers, hoping to identify the man. *The Library of Congress.*

reported continued fundraising efforts for the support of Frank, Frederick, and Alice, the children of the patriot martyr of Gettysburg" (*The Scioto Gazette*, January 23, 1866). A musical composition entitled "The Children of the Battle-field" was published and sold with a brief narrative of the family history and a reproduction of the children's likenesses. The music sold for fifty cents per copy, and card-sized photographs for a quarter. According to the *Gazette*, the music would be a welcome addition "in every circle where music is a part of home enjoyment, and where are those who with gratitude remember our country's brave defenders." According to Smith, the Humiston family relocated to the National Orphan Homestead, founded at Gettysburg, where Mrs. Humiston worked as an under-matron and where seventy war orphans then resided. Offering an appropriate conclusion to the sentimental story, Smith reported that the "morning after the children came to the institution, it was found that they had gone out quietly and decked their father's grave with beautiful flowers" (Smith 1869, p. 176).

While the case of the Humiston family was exceptional for the amount of media attention it received, William Howell Reed recounted a similar scene of pathos in his memoir *Hospital Life in the Army of the Potomac* (1866). Reed recalled conducting a roadside funeral and interment for a man who had died on an ambulance bivouac. The man had no identification, and Reed found in the man's packet "only a photograph of a little infant, which showed that there was one tie at least to bind him to this world." After placing the photo "upon his breast, and covering it with his blouse," Reed began the burial and the man "was laid down to rest" (pp. 16–17).

Such stories, however fact-based, were influenced by a cultural association between mourning and photography. Since the development of the daguerreotype in the 1830s, it had become common to commission memorial photographs of recently deceased loved ones. As the genre developed, subjects were commonly posed in lifelike postures. Children, whose memorial photos were sometimes their only recorded likenesses, were pictured as if sleeping.

According to historian Miles Orvell (2003), such images were consistent with the Victorian view of death as a bodily sleep from which the deceased would awaken in heaven, and thus offered comfort to the bereaved (pp. 24–25).

"Spirit photography," the discovery of which coincided with the Civil War, also became a popular form of memorial image in the nineteenth century. In March 1861, William Mumler photographed himself alone in his studio, but when he developed the plate he found an additional figure in the frame. Several people claimed that this "spirit extra" was the ghost of Mumler's dead cousin, to whom the image bore a strong resemblance (Kaplan 2003, p. 18). Soon, other photographers began to discover their own "spirit extras." Though spirit images were the result of double exposures superimposed by these photographers, some photographers may have actually believed in the authenticity of their apparition ("Gone but Not Forgotten," p. 6).

Oliver Wendell Holmes Sr., a photo collector and doctor by profession, dismissed spirit photographs as the result of overwrought mourners and unscrupulous photographers. "The actinic influence of a ghost on a sensitive plate is not so strong as might be desired," Holmes wrote sarcastically, "but considering that spirits are so nearly immaterial...the effect is perhaps as good as ought to be expected." Holmes elaborated on what he perceived to be the usual scenario: "Mrs. Brown, for instance, has lost her infant, and wishes to have its spirit-portrait taken with her own. A special sitting is granted, and a special fee is paid. In due time the photograph is ready, and, sure enough, there is the misty image of an infant in the background. Or, it may be, across the mothers lap." It may be impossible to identify the child. But, wrote Holmes, "it is enough for the poor mother, whose eyes are blinded with tears, that she sees a print of drapery like an infant's dress, and a rounded something, like a foggy dumpling, which will stand for a face: she accepts the spirit-portrait as a revelation from the world of shadows" (Holmes 1862, p. 14). But even after belief in the authenticity of spirit photography had subsided, the genre maintained its popularity ("Gone but Not Forgotten," p. 6). According to art historian Louis Kaplan (2003), spirit photography during the Civil War helped mourners to feel connected with dead loved ones and to withstand the daily tragedies and losses that surrounded them.

BIBLIOGRAPHY

Chesnut, Mary. *Mary Chesnut's Civil War*, ed. C. Vann Woodward. New Haven: Yale University Press, 1981.

Fitch, John. *Annals of the Army of the Cumberland: Comprising Biographies, Descriptions of Departments, Accounts of Expeditions, Skirmishes, and Battles*, 5th ed. Philadelphia: J. B. Lippincott, 1864.

"Gone but Not Forgotten." Special online feature prepared in conjunction with the *P.O.V.*
documentary *A Family Undertaking*. PBS.org, 2004. Available from http://www.pbs.org/.

Holmes, Oliver Wendell, Sr. "Doings of the Sunbeam." *Atlantic Monthly*, July 1863, pp. 1–15.

"How to Dress for a Photograph." *Washington* (DC) *Daily National Intelligencer*, February 3, 1865.

"How to Photograph Pleasing Countenances." *San Francisco Daily Evening Bulletin*, April 25, 1863.

Kaplan, Louis. "Where the Paranoid Meets the Paranormal: Speculations on Spirit Photography." *Art Journal* 62, no. 3 (2003): 18–29.

Orvell, Miles. *American Photography*. New York: Oxford University Press, 2003.

"Photograph Albums: Just Received a Large and Well Selected Stock Direct from the Manufacturers." Advertisement. *Lowell* (MA) *Daily Citizen and News*, February 19, 1862.

"Photograph Family Record." *Daily Cleveland* (OH) *Herald*, August 3, 1865.

Powers, Elvira J. *Hospital Pencillings: Being a Diary While in Jefferson General Hospital, Jeffersonville, Ind., and Others at Nashville, Tennessee, as Matron and Visitor*. Boston: Edward L. Mitchel, 1866.

Reed, William Howell. *Hospital Life in the Army of the Potomac*. Boston: W. V. Spencer, 1866.

Schneck, B. S. *The Burning of Chambersburg, Pennsylvania*, 2nd rev. ed. Philadelphia: Lindsay & Blakiston, 1864.

The Scioto Gazette, Tuesday, January 23, 1866, issue 49, col C.

"Sergeant Humiston." *Washington* (DC) *Daily National Intelligencer*, February 24, 1864.

Smith, Edward Parmelee. *Incidents of the United States Christian Commission*. Philadelphia: J. B. Lippincott, 1869.

Trachtenberg, Alan. "Albums of War: On Reading Civil War Photographs." *Representations* 9 (Winter 1985): 1–32.

Christina Adkins

■ Reading and Reading Groups

Civil War soldiers avidly read newspapers to learn about news from home. Newspapers obtained by soldiers were sometimes traded with the enemy in picket exchanges. All types of paper were used for these newspapers, from wallpaper to wrapping paper. The exchange of letters, newspapers, and fiction among soldiers and their families helped them to maintain their emotional connections even while at a physical distance. Soldiers gained access to books from shipments from home, picket exchanges, religious and charitable sources, and traveling loan libraries. Men also read while convalescing after battle injuries.

A field nurse, Jane Stuart Woolsey, wrote in her 1870 book *Hospital Days* that "Soldiers were omnivorous readers, but many wanted a better order of books than novels and magazines. One of the forwsiest of the 'inv'lids' was a devourer of everything Mr. Sumner wrote. Files of the 'Scientific American' were in demand. The personage of Cicero and the store-room of Shakespeare went about the wards. Dickens was very popular. I think David Copperfield was the favorite story" (p. 59).

Novels by well-known British and American authors were among the favorites read aloud in camp, both North and South. In their letters and journals some soldiers mentioned reading Walter Scott (1771–1832), Charles Dickens (1812–1870), James Fenimore Cooper (1789–1851), William Makepeace Thackeray (1811–1863), and Edward Bulwer-Lytton (1831–1891). The chaplain of the 8th Connecticut Volunteers in wrote home: "Dickens has a great run. The tales of Miss Edgeworth and T. S. Arthur are very popular. The Army and Navy Melodies are hailed with delight" (Koch 1918, p. 4). George Williams, a Union soldier, recalled reading groups in camp in his 1884 article "Lights and Shadows of Army Life": "Especially when the army was in winter quarters and books were in short supply, a good reader with a copy of Bulwer-Lytton, Scott or Dickens could be assured that his hut would be filled with listeners. The standard rule about extinguishing lights at taps was seldom enforced under such conditions" (p. 808).

For soldiers of both armies a camp fire served as a makeshift memory of the family hearth. George Freeman Noyes recalled in his 1863 book *The Bivouac and the Battlefield, Campaign in Virginia and Maryland*, "Around each pyramid of flame sat the men, engaged in various avocations; some, of course, cooking, for no camp fire was ever without a soldier making coffee, no matter what the hour; some reading or playing cards." Noyes said that he regretted the boredom of do-nothingism in camp during the war:

> If you wish to demoralize a man, to dilute his manliness, corrode his patriotism, steal away his cheerfulness, destroy his enthusiasm, and impair his health, pen him up in an isolated camp with little to do, no books to read, no resources against idleness; if you wish to demoralize an army, march it off from a severely contested battle-field into the woods, and condemn it to a month or two of listless do-nothinginsm. At such a time the men need, as never so much before, books of a cheerful and moderately exciting character, strong, bracing stories like those of Charles Kingsley, quiet pictures of homelife like that fascinating sketch of "John Halifax, Gentleman," military tales like those of Lever, the wonderful character pieces of Charles Dickens, and choice productions of our American authors. (p. 224)

Cheap fiction was popular in camp. Soldiers often read nickel and dime novels. These 4 inch by 6 inch, 100-page volumes could fit into a soldier's pocket and their low price appealed to many. Private Dwight Henry Cory, a Union soldier who had a good voice and liked to sing, was one of these readers of popular fiction. In his journal on Friday, March 3, 1865, reproduced in the "Dwight Henry Cory Letters," he wrote: "Read storys or novels as they are commonly called and answer letters. In fact these two vocations are the chief employment of the soldier in camp."

When Civil War soldiers mentioned their reading in their letters home, they often spoke of reading from the Bible or prayer books. Robert Cruikshank, for example, wrote to his wife Mary on September 21, 1862, from Arlington Heights, Virginia, that "They read their Bibles every day." He asked his wife on November 15, "Send me papers with the war news." Henry Cory told his wife: "Dear, you sent a big letter but not much reading .... They call me their chaplain. I have a testament in my pocket. I read a chapter every day."

One source of soldiers' reading material was the regimental library. Alonzo Hall Quint, a Union soldier who kept the volumes within one of these, preserved his writings in the 1863 published work *The Potomac and the Rapidan and Army Notes, 1861–63*. He wrote,

> Among devices for this vacation period we have a small regimental library .... I owe public thanks for this especially to Mr. MH Sargent, who interested himself most generously and heartily in obtaining and forwarding the books ... the nest egg of which was a kind donation from Mr. Tolman's church at Wilmington ... If the donors could see the eagerness with which the books are read, they would feel still happier in doing good (p. 94).

Among the most read of these books, Quint noted, were those of Dickens. "Among the most read (I take from the book where I charge volumes, to show the taste) are Deacon Safford, Winthrop's John Brent, Dickens's Christmas Stories, Abbot's Practical Christianity, Dexter's Street Thoughts, the Lives of Washington, Jackson, Fremont, Franklin, and Boone" (p. 94).

While marching through the south, Louis J. Dupré, in Knoxville, Tennessee, saw books in southern homes. He wrote in his 1881 book *Fagots from the Campfire*, "In every house there was Weems 'Life of Washington,' Jefferson's 'Notes on Virginia.' and Brownlow's 'Whig' and the National Intelligencer" (p. 137). Likewise, August Joseph Hickey Duganne wrote in his 1865 book *Camps and Prisons, Twenty Months in the Department of the Gulf* of seeing books while he was part of a Northern occupying force:

> Meanwhile, here we sit, hostile strangers from the North, amidst the dusty lumber of a southern home. The family portraits rest against the wall, backs turned upon us. I handle many a duplicate of favorite authors in my home library. Here stand, in line, battalia of books, which show the classic taste of their collector. The British Poets muster, rank on rank, some ninety strong; the British Essayists beneath, and here are Dickens, Irving, Cooper, Bulwer, Thackeray; with hundreds, rank and file, of literary yeomen, and brave historians. (p. 56)

Reading was also practiced by prisoners of war. Confederate captain Robert E. Park of the 12th Alabama Regiment wrote on February 8, 1865 from a Baltimore prison, "Some read novels and histories, others study ancient and modern languages and mathematics, and these divert for the time, their minds from the painful, desperate, hopeless surroundings" (Park 1877, p. 46).

Reading fiction aloud was a popular pastime in many homes. Families and friends often gathered in the front room parlor of a home or by the fireplace to read aloud to each other. In the North free blacks were among those who met in reading circles. In one southern home Bill Arp read *The Arabian Nights* aloud to his family, as he noted in his 1903 book *From the Uncivil War to Date*: "We love to read the Arabian Nights, and we rejoice with Ali Baba who outwitted the forty thieves and with Alladin who found the wonderful lamp. Just so we rejoice in Cinderella for marrying the prince, and we take comfort in it, although we know it never happened" (p. 188).

Books were also vocalized in Joseph Waddell's household in Augusta, Virginia. He notes in his diary that on Thursday evening September 25, 1857, "Kate was reading The Life of Charlotte Bronte and would persist in reading passages aloud, not withstanding my restlessness." Waddell was then reading *Count Robert of Paris* and *The Pira*. He had just finished reading *The Ocean* by Gipe. The night that Kate read aloud from Elizabeth Gaskell's biography of Charlotte Bronte, he had been reading the newspaper.

Belle Kearney of Vernon, Mississippi, recalls in her 1900 book *A Slaveholder's Daughter* that she made a bargain with her younger brothers, enticing them to house work in return for reading aloud to them from Dickens or Scott.

"Well," I answered, "suppose we make a bargain? If you will cook every time mother gets sick, I will tell you one of Dickens's stories or one of Walter Scott's novels as regularly as the nights roll around." "All right! I'll do it!" was the ready assent; — and the compact was sealed. It was never broken.

As the days went by and mother's health failed to improve, and my work failed correspondingly to grow lighter, the younger boys were pressed into service by similar agreements … Every night after our lessons were learned for the next day, we gathered around the hearth in mother's room and I told the boys the promised stories; going into the smallest details; dwelling on peculiarities of characters, painting minutely their environment, waxing humorous or pathetic according to the situation; all the while watching closely the faces of my auditors. There they would sit for hours, my little brothers, listening intently to every word that was uttered; at time clapping their chubby hands with intense enjoyment, or doubling up their bodies with convulsive laughter, or holding their lips together with fore-finger and thumb to prevent too boisterous an

explosion of hilarity, at other times allowing the great tears to roll down their cheeks, or with bowed heads sobbing aloud. My precious little comrades! They constituted my first audience and it was the most sympathetic and inspiring that has ever greeted me in all the after years (p. 25).

Stories were available in Northern homes as well as southern ones. In some cases the younger children just looked at the pictures. While Charles Dickens's *Our Mutual Friend* was being serialized in *Harper's* in 1864, one reader wrote about the fondness of her children for the visual content of the magazine:

The appearance of Harpers Magazine at our house is an event of great importance with my children. The illustrations in it are the chief cause of this. [On one page there is an] illustration of winged children as "Angels of the Household." All the children are mischievous. One of them raids a cookie jar as her sister looks on and reaches up for it; three children slide down a banister; one pulls at a cat's tail; another breaks a mirror. Meanwhile, a little girl with wings holds up torn pages in her hand and stomps over shattered shards on the floor as her parents look on (pp. 820–821).

BIBLIOGRAPHY

Arp, Bill. *From the Uncivil War to Date*, ed. Marian Arp Smith. Atlanta, GA: Hudgins, 1903.

Cory, Dwight Henry. *Dwight Henry Cory Letters*. Ehistory.com. Available from http://ehistory.osu.edu/.

Cruishank, Robert. "Robert Cruishank Collection: Letter to his wife Mary of September 21, 1862." Ehistory.com. Available from http://ehistory.osu.edu/.

Dupré, Louis J. *Fagots from the Campfire*. Washington, DC: Emily Thornton Charles and Co., 1881.

Duganne, August Joseph Hickey. *Camps and Prisons, Twenty Months in the Department of the Gulf*. New York: J. P. Robens, 1865.

Harper's New Monthly Magazine (August 1864): 820–821.

Kaser, David. *Camp and Battle: The Civil War Experience*. Westport, CT: Greenwood Press, 1984.

Kearney, Belle. *A Slaveholder's Daughter*. New York: Abbey Press, 1900. Documenting the American South. Available from http://docsouth.unc.edu/.

Koch, Theodore Wesley. *War Libraries and Allied Studies*. New York: G. E. Stechert and Co., 1918.

McHenry, Elizabeth. *Forgotten Readers: Recovering the History of African-American Literary Societies*. Durham, NC: Duke University Press, 2002.

Noyes, George Freeman. *The Bivouac and the Battle Field, or Common Sketches in Virginia and Maryland.* New York: Harpers, 1863

Park, Robert E. "Diary of Captain Robert E. Park." *Southern Historical Society Papers, Richmond* 3, no.1, January 1877, p. 46.

Quint, Alonzo Hall. *The Potomac and the Rapidan: Army Notes from the Failure at Winchester to the Re-enforcements of Rosencrans, 1861–3.* Boston: Crosby and Nichols, 1864.

Waddell, Joseph. *The Diary of Joseph Waddell (1855–1865).* Valley of the Shadow. Available from http://etext.virginia.edu/.

Williams, George F. "Lights and Shadows of Army Life." *Century Magazine* (October 1884): 808.

Woolsey, Jane Stuart. *Hospital Days.* New York: D. Van Nostrand, 1870.

Robert P. McParland

■ Vices on the Home Front

VICES ON THE HOME FRONT: AN OVERVIEW
  Adrienne M. Petty

GAMBLING
  Aileen E. McTiernan

ALCOHOL
  Anurag Biswas

SMOKING AND TOBACCO
  Adrienne M. Petty

VICES ON THE HOME FRONT: AN OVERVIEW

In December 2006 the Pennsylvania Gaming Control Board voted against a plan to open a casino near the historic Gettysburg battlefield, one of the most sacred sites of the Civil War. The plan failed, in large measure, because of public opposition: Modern-day residents of Gettysburg feared that the casino would tarnish the battlefield's legacy and harm its appeal as a family tourist attraction (Foster 2006). This controversy is in many ways similar to how people living during the Civil War responded to activities that were considered bad habits at the time. Although some people freely indulged in gambling, smoking, and drinking alcohol for fun and to escape the uncertainty of war, others decried these vices as outside the boundaries of respectability.

Gambling

During the colonial era and early nineteenth century, public lotteries were an accepted and common means of raising money for cities, states, and even Protestant churches. Revenue generated in lotteries helped these institutions complete essential but costly building projects such as schools, bridges, roads, and jails. Denmark Vesey, the former slave in South Carolina who planned a slave insurrection in 1822, had purchased his freedom with $1,500 he won in a lottery intended to support work on East Bay Street in Charleston (Fabian 1990, p. 126).

People also gambled in more informal ways. As eighteenth-century aristocrats had done, Southern slaveholders organized and bet on horse races, cockfights, and card games. Among the Northern working class, betting on dogs, cocks, cards, and dice was a common pastime in urban taverns. At public gatherings such as markets and fairs, professional gamblers even made their livings by swindling unsuspecting people out of their money (Fabian 1990, pp. 1–2).

By the late 1830s, however, reformers had begun to argue that the social and moral cost of lotteries far outweighed the benefits. They also argued that gambling threatened the very foundations of the American republic. In addition to undermining people's personal well-being, they argued that gambling was dangerous to public welfare and the Protestant work ethic because it falsely deluded people into thinking that they could make a quick buck. In the 1840s and 1850s Northern newspapers focused particularly on gambling by African American men and women who engaged in "policy play." Policy dealers let poor people wager pennies or nickels on the numbers drawn in official and unofficial lotteries (Fabian 1990, p. 136). Opposition to policy play and other forms of gambling waned during the Civil War era, but picked up momentum during the last quarter of the nineteenth century.

On the American frontier, gambling thrived because of the unsettled nature of life there. Many in gold rush California made their fortunes not from frugality and hard work, but from taking on enormous risk that generated lucky windfalls. Even those who did some of the most demanding jobs found amusement in gambling. In their leisure time, cowboys and sailors gambled in cattle towns and port cities (Fabian 1990, pp. 5–6).

The Civil War was a watershed moment in the history of gambling in the United States. With the consolidation of capitalism during the Civil War, people turned to new forms of gambling. Angry farmers began to decry the greed of those who profited from speculations in agricultural commodities. According to Ann Fabian in *Card Sharps, Dream Books, and Bucket Shops: Gambling in Nineteenth-Century America*, farmers alleged that these traders were the direct descendants of evil gamblers who "lived as parasites on the productive economy" (1990, p. 9). Despite the efforts of reformers, gambling flourished before, during, and after the war. Gambling continued in private even though laws against it had become widespread by the 1890s. In the early twenty-first century, of course, gambling is legal and prevalent.

"Our patriots." Despite efforts by Northerners to curtail tobacco consumption, sales of cigars increased in the 1860s. *MPI/Hulton Archive/Getty Images*

Smoking

Just as gambling became a target for reformers during the 1830s, tobacco use also rankled reformers, particularly in the North. It was offensive because it was considered unhealthy, rude, and a waste of money. At the same time, many Americans, particularly Southerners, did not attach any social stigma to tobacco. During the nineteenth century chewing tobacco and cigar smoking were the dominant forms of tobacco consumption among men of all classes in all regions of the country. In 1850 Americans bought ten cigars per capita; by 1860 they were buying twenty-six cigars per capita (Burnham 1993, p. 88). Women in the South had a penchant for pipe smoking and dipping snuff. Many Union soldiers expressed amazement in their letters and diaries over the extent to which women in the South used tobacco.

Cigarette use started in the nineteenth century as a practice among people who were considered deviant. People characterized cigarettes as effeminate, and argued that no "real man" would be caught smoking them. Robert Sobel in *They Satisfy: The Cigarette in American Life* quotes

a writer in 1854 New York who criticized women on the fringe of society who "are aping the silly ways of some pseudo-accomplished foreigners in smoking tobacco through a weaker and more feminine article, the cigarette" (Sobel 1978, pp. 9–10).

But after the Crimean War (1853–1856) and Civil War, soldiers who had turned to the quick smoke of cigarettes on the battlefield continued to use them when they returned home, helping to spread the habit. During the 1880s, dramatic changes in manufacturing and marketing secured the place of cigarettes as the most popular form of tobacco consumption (Burnham 1993, p. 89). Reformers warned about the temptation that cigarettes posed to young people, but they never succeeded in outlawing them. In contrast to gambling, which became socially unacceptable and illegal by the early twentieth century (only to regain legitimacy by the end of the twentieth century), tobacco use continued to be regarded as a minor vice until the late twentieth century, when health concerns made cigarettes less socially acceptable.

Alcohol

In their cautionary tales against the evils of gambling, ex-gamblers of the nineteenth century often connected gaming with alcohol and cigars. It is not surprising, then, that reformers viewed these minor vices as part of the same problem. Although alcoholic beverages were socially acceptable and even preferred during the early 1800s because they posed less of a threat to people's health than polluted water, reformers began to define them as morally unacceptable by the mid-nineteenth century. The years before the war witnessed the spread of temperance societies devoted to either decreasing or totally eliminating alcohol manufacturing and use.

During the war, the temperance movement lost some of its momentum because reformers were preoccupied with the more pressing work of either fighting as soldiers or aiding the war effort. At the same time, the use of alcohol among civilians paralleled soldiers' use of spirits. In addition to seeking an escape from the cruelty of war, Union and Confederate soldiers drank to prove their manhood. The ritual of drinking also became important among working-class immigrants in the North. The Civil War reinforced opposition to alcohol consumption by unleashing an increase in its popularity as a means of escape (Burnham 1993, p. 59). Use of alcohol among soldiers and civilians during the Civil War was one of several factors that contributed to passage of the Eighteenth Amendment to the U.S. Constitution and the Prohibition movement during the Progressive Era.

Despite reformers' efforts to curb this constellation of vices—gambling, tobacco use and smoking, and alcohol use—Americans indulged in them before, during, and after the Civil War. Even with the successful defeat of efforts to build a casino near the hallowed Gettysburg battleground, Americans now, as then, continue to gamble and engage in other pastimes as an escape from the sometimes brutal realities of life.

BIBLIOGRAPHY

Burnham, John C. *Bad Habits: Drinking, Smoking, Taking Drugs, Gambling, Sexual Misbehavior, and Swearing in American History.* New York and London: New York University Press, 1993.

Fabian, Ann. *Card Sharps, Dream Books, and Bucket Shops: Gambling in Nineteenth-Century America.* Ithaca, NY, and London: Cornell University Press, 1990.

Foster, Margaret. "Gettysburg Casino Denied." *Preservation Online*, December 21, 2006. Available from http://www.nationaltrust.org/.

Sobel, Robert. *They Satisfy: The Cigarette in American Life.* Garden City, NY: Doubleday, 1978.

Adrienne M. Petty

GAMBLING

Throughout the Civil War, gambling was perceived by the majority of the populace as an immoral and pernicious practice. Still, roulette parlors, gambling saloons, and secret card rooms operated across the country from New York to San Francisco. Opponents criticized gambling as "the most dangerous of all vices" (*Daily Cleveland Herald*, January 10, 1862), arguing it posed nothing but a nuisance to the nation. In accordance with public perspective, the legislature elevated the vice to criminal status. In fact, in March 1864, the *Daily Miners' Register* reported gambling was an indictable crime "in every loyal State and Territory of the Union, except Colorado, New Mexico and Idaho."

Public Opposition

Public condemnation of gambling stemmed from the belief that it served no purpose besides contaminating society by promoting a lifestyle of crime and obtaining money by illegitimate means. An editorial from the San Francisco *Daily Evening Bulletin* addressed the evils of gambling; the author attributed a laundry list of moral damages that society has suffered to the existence of gambling establishments:

> . . . the sudden and unaccountable failures among business men, resulting on account of their suddenness in injury to creditors and the impairing of the general credit; the coming, unforeseen, of utter desolation upon the happy homes of love and plenty; the degradation and disgrace of honorable men; the hopeless ruin of many a promising youth; the following of suicide upon suicide in rapid succession; and worst of all, because fraught with all the ills society is heir to—the alarming

increase among us of gamblers and other thieves and robbers. (1862)

The same newspaper reflected (February 3, 1863) on the prevalence and the perils of gambling since the settlement of the Lower Mississippi Valley. The appeal of games of chance was pervasive: gambling sites ranged from public hotels to private homes, sparing no segment of society from the resultant catalogue of crimes. Such common-law crimes as murder, robbery, larceny, and arson threatened to corrupt society, sparking a "crusade against the evil" of gambling (*Daily Evening Bulletin*, December 18, 1862). The apparent menace of wagering was continuously pointed out, but warnings did little to eradicate the practice.

Mysterious gambling rooms hidden from the public allowed obscure card and roulette games to be conducted very quietly behind secret walls within legitimate establishments. Conducting business under such underground pretexts sparked speculation about what occurred behind closed doors—causing the public imagination to assume only the worst. In San Francisco, the ground floor of an old gambling hall was rumored to conceal a deadfall, a trap in which men were entombed after being robbed and murdered. When the hall was demolished in 1864, however, the *Daily Evening Bulletin* disappointed its readers' expectations by reporting that no bones or human remains were found (May 25, 1864).

The police proved rather ineffective at suppressing gambling establishments, and were often compensated for turning a blind eye to any activities they did observe (*Fayetteville Observer*, October 19, 1863). While some men were arrested and indicted for illegal gambling, Judge Blake observed that gambling prosecutions were not sufficiently representative of its prevalence in San Francisco. In his charge to a grand jury in 1862, he further lamented: "I do not suppose that gambling can be entirely prevented, but it may be reduced to a small proportion and compelled to hide itself in that obscurity which becomes its ruinous and demoralizing tendencies" (*Daily Evening Bulletin*, November 10, 1862).

Gamblers and Gambling Establishments

Gambling dens were frequented by prominent middle- and upper-class businessmen as well as by men engaged in professional gambling. Some entertained gambling as a sport—or even a fashionable social activity. Noting the appeal of the element of risk over the financial aspect of the game, the *New Haven* (CT) *Daily Palladium* reported that it had become "fashionable" to form exclusive clubs of wealthy men to play cards for small stakes, using the money merely "to give piquancy to the game" (July 27, 1864).

In South Carolina, the *Camden Confederate*, described the bifurcation in gambling practices in the city of Richmond. The so-called House of Lords was strict about admitting only invited guests, and only those in possession of considerable wealth, including quartermasters and commissaries. The House of Commons, less luxurious yet more accessible, was maintained for those of less extravagant means; it welcomed congressmen as well as army and naval officers (October 23, 1863). Though congressmen were not considered to be heavy gamblers themselves, according to the *Daily Evening Bulletin*, the gamers in the Western states executed considerable control over their cohorts in the lobby: they were the ultimate manipulators of the legislature (March 8, 1864).

Yet wherever gambling had been sanctioned by law, inevitably misguided laborers could be found squandering their savings. Destroying the honest independence of men, and embodying the very essence of sin, gambling halls threatened to corrupt society. Gamblers cheated and robbed each other on a regular basis. In fact, a stranger entering into a certain gambling den in Cleveland "was as sure to be plundered as if he were found on the highway and robbed with a pistol at his throat" (*Lowell Daily Citizen and News*, January 21, 1863).

Every gambling hall had its professionals—regulars permanently residing there. The *Daily Evening Bulletin* relayed the chronicle (originally reported in the *Territorial Enterprise* of Virginia City, Nevada) of a gambler appearing as a witness at trial. Inquiring as to the witness's profession, the judge was rather astonished to hear his response:

> "Rough gambling!" repeated the Judge—"I would ask you, sir, what you mean by 'rough gambling!'"
>
> "I means, yer Honor, that my style is, where the run o' the cards doesn't fetch me a feller's money, I knocks him down and takes it anyhow." (February 27, 1864)

Some of these professionals utilized gambling as their sole source of income, though many lost everything they had and more. Thinking they could win back their life savings if they had just another hundred dollars—then another hundred, then another—many men found themselves homeless and penniless upon departure. The tale of one inveterate gambler was recounted in the *Milwaukee Daily Sentinel*: after losing every penny he had, followed by his land, his house, and his furniture, he lost his young and beautiful wife in a game of cards (July 28, 1863).

Gambling and the Churches

While social gambling was publicly denounced across the country, fairs and raffles organized for the benefit of religious institutions created much contention. In 1862 the *Boston Investigator* denounced church festivals—only decades prior these gatherings had been "patronized only by the worst characters" (December 24, 1862). Such religiously sponsored lotteries or gambling involved such prizes as doll-babies, plum cakes, or paintings to raise money for "heathens," orphanages, or other virtuous causes. In 1861, an editorial in the *Boston Investigator* epitomized the irony of the practice, noting: "[t]he *principle* is certainly the same, whatever the *form* of the *game* or the object of the *stake*" (May 22, 1861; emphasis in original).

Objections to gaming under the guise of the religious institutions included the preservation of the innocence of youth. Impressionable children attending such religious fairs would be misguided by the fascination and the pleasure of games of chance and their associated transgressions. Church-sanctioned gambling was condemned as worse than "the lowest gambling hell," due to its nature as "sugar-coated, heaven-liveried, and hence all the more fascinating and dangerous," reported the *Boston Investigator* (December 24, 1862).

By 1863, the Church was treated no differently than public or private establishments that promoted lotteries; church festivals or bazaars employing such games were required to take out a license for the practice. The license for practicing lottery games required a fee of one thousand dollars, but the penalty for failing to obtain the license cost three thousand dollars (*Vermont Chronicle*, April 14, 1863).

Even with lotteries, raffles and games of chance sanctioned by clergymen and regulated by the government, the practice, though frequented by the majority, was not universally sanctioned. By 1864, with the Civil War well underway, some Christians sought to raise money to aid the suffering soldiers through games of chance. Such pretenses were endorsed by the *New York Times*, but the *Vermont Chronicle* objected, emphasizing, "We are not under obligations to do it in any particular way [especially such means as are] subversive of the great principles of morality and religion" (February 6, 1864).

BIBLIOGRAPHY

"Early Lessons in Gambling." *Boston Investigator*, December 24, 1862.

"Gambling." *Camden* (SC) *Confederate*, October 23, 1863.

"Gambling." *Fayetteville* (NC) *Observer*, October 19, 1863.

"Gambling at Fairs." *Vermont Chronicle* (Bellows Falls, Windsor, and Montpelier, VT), February 6, 1864.

"Gambling for a Wife." *Milwaukee Daily Sentinel*, July 28, 1863.

"Gambling in Cleveland." *Daily Cleveland Herald*, January 10, 1862.

"Gambling in San Francisco." *Daily Evening Bulletin* (San Francisco), February 3, 1863.

"Gambling in San Francisco, and Its Remedy—No. 1." *Daily Evening Bulletin* (San Francisco), December 18, 1862.

"Judge Blake's Charge as to Gambling." *Daily Evening Bulletin* (San Francisco), November 10, 1862.

"One of the Gambling Dens in Cleveland." *Lowell* (MA) *Daily Citizen and News*, July 21, 1863.

"Police Intelligence: Descent on an Alleged Gambling House." *New York Herald*, January 9, 1861.

"Progress of Gambling." *New York Herald*, December 14, 1861.

"Religious Gambling, &c." *Boston Investigator*, May 22, 1861.

"Rough Gambling." *Daily Evening Bulletin* (San Francisco), February 27, 1864.

"Saratoga: The Ladies' Fashions–Gambling." *New Haven* (CT) *Daily Palladium*, July 27, 1864.

"Transforming an Old Gambling Hall." *Daily Evening Bulletin* (San Francisco), May 25, 1864.

"Uncle Sam on Religious Gambling." *Vermont Chronicle* (Bellows Falls, Windsor, and Montpelier, VT), April 14, 1863.

[Untitled.] *Daily Miners' Register* (Central City, CO), March 1, 1864.

Aileen E. McTiernan

ALCOHOL

In the early 1800s alcoholic beverages were consumed at levels far above present-day per capita consumption. Milk was often a premium commodity and fruit juices were rare. Water was oftentimes unclean, whereas alcohol was distilled and germ-free. As a result, whisky quickly became a staple. It was made in the mills and while price of production varied according to time and place, especially in the Confederacy, many found the beverage affordable. Most people also believed in the medicinal value of alcohol, as many tonics and elixirs of the time contained a high percentage of alcohol. As industrialization progressed and American cities prospered, saloons became a social hub for the working class. In an effort to draw more patrons, saloons created the "free lunch"—free only after the patron had laid down his money for drinks. As the Civil War dragged on, most American distilleries were closed, as they were considered "nonessential industries" in the war effort (Jahns 2003, p. 11). This led to an increase in the production of illegal alcohol, and moonshining, bootlegging, and the smuggling of alcohol from Canada and the tropics flourished.

Temperance Societies

During the initial decades of the nineteenth century, wine and beer were not looked down upon, but as the mid-century approached, the notion developed that all spirits were sinful and wrong. T. S. Arthur (1809–1885) expressed the sentiments of an increasing number of concerned citizens when he declared in *Grappling with the Monster* (1877), "[t]he CURSE is upon us, and there is but one CURE: Total Abstinence, by the help of God, for the Individual, and Prohibition for the State" (Furnas 1965, p. 15).

Such beliefs led to the growth of the temperance movement, which held that drinking was a serious threat to family life and that the use of alcohol should be limited, if not banned outright. The U.S. temperance movement originated around 1826, with the formation of the American Society for the Promotion of Temperance. The efforts of this group led to a decrease in per capita consumption of pure alcohol, from a high of more than seven gallons per year in 1830 to just over three per year in 1840, the largest ten-year drop in U.S. history ("Alcohol," 1998 p. 149). Over the next few years, more temperance organizations of a general and national character were formed than during any other period in U.S. history. By 1832 all but three states had societies. The Washingtonian movement, organized in Baltimore in 1840, was followed by the Martha Washington movement in 1841. The Sons of Temperance formed in 1842, as did the Order of Rechabites, and the Congressional Temperance Society of 1833 was revived on the basis of total abstinence (Cherrington 1920, p. 94).

The first state to adopt a law prohibiting the sale and manufacture of alcohol was Maine, in 1851. The famous Presbyterian clergyman Lyman Beecher exclaimed from the pulpit "This thing is of God, that glorious Maine law was a square and grand blow right between the horns of the Devil" (Eddy 1887, p. 425). Soon Delaware, following Maine's example, passed its first prohibition law, only to have it declared unconstitutional the following year. Over the following years, similar laws were enacted in New York, Pennsylvania, Connecticut, Rhode Island, Massachusetts, Ohio, Illinois, and Minnesota. They met with varying fates, including veto by governors, repeal by legislatures, and invalidation by state supreme courts.

Not all members of the public were opposed to drinking. In the 1850s, citizens of Chicago fought against the enforcement of Sunday closing laws, which prohibited saloons from serving alcohol on the Sabbath. According to Virgil W. Peterson (1949), an armed mob of protesters burst into the city's business district, only to be met by police. Fortunately, the mob was dispersed before the mayor found it necessary to use the cannon he had hurriedly planted around City Hall (p. 120). Conversely, in 1865, women in the town of Greenfield, Ohio, frustrated with their drunk and disorderly men, took it upon themselves to break into the local saloon and wreck the establishment; they then proceeded to Linn's drug store, where they smashed more casks of alcohol (July 28, 1865).

The Civil War years were anomalous ones for the temperance movement. Those involved in the crusade against the immoralities of alcohol were either off fighting in the war or too busy aiding the war effort. Upon the war's end, temperance societies once again took up the fight. In 1874, the Woman's Christian Temperance Union (WCTU) was founded. The only temperance organization still in operation, the WCTU has worked continuously since its inception to educate the public and to influence policies that discourage the use of alcohol and other drugs ("Alcohol," 1998, p. 149).

Politics and Alcohol

When asked his opinion of whiskey, one Southern senator remarked:

> Well, if by whiskey you mean that degradation of the noble barley, that burning fluid which sears

Tree of Temperance. One of a pair of prints issued by A. D. Fillmore in 1855 extolling the social and moral benefits of temperance and condemning the evils of alcohol. *The Library of Congress*

the throats of the innocent, that vile liquid that sets men to fighting in low saloons, from whence they go forth to beat their wives and children, that liquor the Devil spawns which reddens the eye, coarsens the features, and ages the body beyond its years, then I am against it with all my soul. But, sir, if by whiskey you mean that diadem of the distiller's art, that nimble golden ambrosia which loosens the tongue of the shy, gladdens the heart of the lonely, comforts the afflicted, rescues the snake-bitten, warms the frozen and brings the joys of conviviality to men during their hard-earned moments of relaxation, then I am four-square in favor of whiskey. From these opinions I shall not waver. (Lowry 1994, p. 6)

These words summarize the contradictory positions many politicians held. The temperance movement shaped political rhetoric, and parties with names such as the "Rum Democrats" and the "Temperance Men" sprang up. When Father Theobald Matthew of Ireland toured the United States from 1849 to 1851, administering the pledge of total abstinence to some 600,000 persons in twenty-five states, he was awarded with a White House dinner and a Senate reception (Couling 1862, p. 326). Ironically, the same government that had praised Father Matthew for his anti-drinking campaign concluded a treaty with King Kamehameha III of Hawaii in 1850 permitting the sale of liquor in the king's formerly sovereign nation.

If some fought against alcohol, other fought to protect its availability. In response to the repeal of the Maine's 1851 law prohibiting alcohol, John Pendleton Kennedy remarked: "Many quack politicians have been wasting their energies for years, upon the abortive attempt to legislate peaceable families into the disuse of spirituous liquors, by bringing alcohol into platforms and making parties upon it: —but alcohol has gained the day and the Maine Liquor Law has become a dead letter" (Kennedy 1861, p. 37). Temperance advocates such as Senator Henry Wilson of Massachusetts (1812–1875) and Senator Samuel C. Pomeroy (1816–1891) of Kansas criticized the idea of federal revenues coming from the liquor industry.

With the onset of the Civil War, the federal government reinstituted excise taxes on whiskey and tobacco in an effort to fund the Union army, and in 1862 it imposed a liquor and beer tax. Rates increased several times between 1863 and 1868, and the initial tax of 20 cents per gallon eventually rose to $2 per gallon (McGrew 1972). In response, alcohol producers engaged in mass tax-evasion schemes and organized the first industry lobby—the United States Brewers Association. The Association rapidly launched a legislative campaign and succeeded in 1863 in reducing the tax rate on beer from $1 to 60 cents (Cherrington 1969 [1920], p. 157).

Following the war, alcohol taxes were kept in place as a means to help finance the rebuilding of the nation. Faced with enormous debt, both state and federal governments continued to collect and enforce the whisky taxes. Yet, the federal government noted an interesting phenomenon: As the rates increased, the revenues did not. In fact, the number of gallons reported actually declined. Various attempts were made to enforce the tax laws; for example, in 1868 the sum of $25,000 was appropriated for the detection of violators. Still, fraud continued almost unabated. Liquor was stockpiled to hedge against future tax increases, as taxes were not applicable to liquor on hand. Congress eventually reduced the tax from a high of $2 per gallon to 50 cents in 1869. The happy result was a rise in collections from $13.5 million in 1868, to $45 million in 1869, and $55 million the following year. Taking further precautions, the government stipulated that new stamps be developed for alcohol containers to preclude counterfeiting and tampering (Cherrington 1969 [1920], pp.156–162).

While the Civil War marked a hiatus in nineteenth-century struggles over alcohol consumption, following the war temperance societies resumed and expanded their activities. These activities eventually led to the Eighteenth Amendment to the U.S. Constitution, which banned the manufacture, sale, and transportation of alcohol from its passage in 1919 until its repeal in 1933.

BIBLIOGRAPHY

"Alcohol." *West's Encyclopedia of American Law.* St. Paul, MN: West Group, 1998.

Cherrington, Ernest H. *The Evolution of Prohibition in the United States of America.* Westerville, Ohio: American Issue Press, 1920. Reprint, Montclair, NJ: Patterson Smith, 1969.

Couling, Samuel. *History of the Temperance Movement in Great Britain and Ireland.* London: William Tweedie, 1862.

Eddy, Richard. *Alcohol in History: An Account of Intemperance in All Ages.* New York: The National Temperance Society and Publication House, 1887.

"Female Riot in Greenfield, Ohio—Putting Down Rum." *Washington* (DC) *Daily National Intelligencer,* Friday, July 28, 1865.

Furnas, J. C. *The Life and Times of the Late Demon Rum.* New York: Putnam, 1965.

Jahns, Art. "The Windsor/Walkerville Connection." *Walkerville Times,* March 2003.

Kennedy, John Pendleton. *The Border States: Their Power and Duty in the Present Disordered Condition of the Country.* Philadelphia: J. B. Lippincott, 1861.

Lowry, Thomas P. *The Story the Soldiers Wouldn't Tell: Sex in the Civil War.* Mechanicsburg, PA: Stackpole Books, 1994.

McGrew, Jane Lang. "History of Alcohol Prohibition." National Commission on Marihuana and Drug Abuse, 1972.

Peterson, Virgil W. "Vitalizing Liquor Control." *Journal of Criminal Law and Criminology* 40, no. 2. (1949): 119–134.

Anurag Biswas

SMOKING AND TOBACCO

Though they were bitter enemies, at least one thing united many men in the Union with both women and men in the Confederacy: their fondness for tobacco. The plant was the stimulant of choice for soldiers, as well as for southern women on the home front. Over the course of the war, smoking hand-rolled cigarettes became popular among Union and Confederate soldiers. The use of cigarettes on the battlefield laid the groundwork for the mass production and consumption of cigarettes that began during the 1880s and became popular among both women and men by the 1920s.

A chewing tobacco emblem. Prior to the Civil War, Americans either chewed, dipped, or smoked tobacco in pipes. Lacking the time and equipment needed for these consumption methods, many soldiers took to smoking cigarettes, a habit they continued in civilian life. *The Library of Congress*

Tobacco Use before the Civil War

Tobacco, whether chewed or smoked, was an early and popular product of the New World. After learning its use from Native Americans during the colonial period, Europeans who had spent time in North, Central, and South America took the practice back to Europe. Indigenous people in the Chesapeake region of North America often smoked tobacco in pipes. By 1612 English settlers in Virginia were cultivating the plant and it soon became the main export crop of the North American colonies.

The cigarette, in particular, had its origins in South and Central America, where the Maya smoked tobacco wrapped in banana skin, bark, and maize leaves. The Spanish gave these leaf-wrapped tobacco sticks the name "papalettes," and replaced the maize-wrappers with fine paper. By the mid-nineteenth century papalettes crossed into France, where the tobacco monopoly there named them cigarettes.

In the United States people indulged in tobacco even though they suspected it was unhealthy and found it socially unpleasant. One encyclopedia published during the nineteenth century described tobacco as "bitter, acrid, and poisonous." John Quincy Adams (1767–1848) was quoted in the February 25, 1861, edition of the *Fayetteville Observer* as contending that "abandonment of the use of tobacco would add five years to the average human life." Nevertheless, pipe smoking emerged as the most popular form of tobacco consumption during the colonial period, and it continued into the antebellum era among men in both sections and women in the South. Even president's wives smoked pipes, including Rachel Donelson Jackson (1767–1828), the Tennessee-reared wife of Andrew Jackson (1767–1845), the seventh president of the United States, and Margaret Mackall Taylor (1788–1852), the Maryland-born wife of Zachary Taylor (1784–1850), the twelfth U.S. president. Members of the elite

TOBACCO ADVERTISING AND THE CIVIL WAR

From the stereotypical Indian chief to the contemporary image of the Marlboro Man, tobacco manufacturers have exploited American iconography to promote their products. It is not surprising, then, that the Civil War, a decisive moment in United States history, emerged as a popular theme in tobacco packaging and advertising. During the war itself, companies targeted tobacco users on both sides of the conflict with advertisements that reflected their divergent political beliefs. In the years following the war, however, manufacturers used advertising images to bring about reconciliation between the North and the South.

As sectional tensions heated up, tobacco companies marketed snuff, chewing tobacco, and cigars to Southerners with package labels that depicted images of slavery and Southern political leaders. An 1859 label perpetuated the myth of the happy slave by featuring a smiling slave family enjoying the father's banjo playing. On another label, a manufacturer of Cuban cigars featured John C. Calhoun, the South Carolina politician who first advocated states' rights and later became the seventh Vice President of the United States (Quigley 2006, p. 55).

During the war, tobacco package labels continued to reflect the allegiances of both sides. A Petersburg, Virginia, manufacturer portrayed cannons on its product labels. One 1862 label featured Union soldiers under the banner, "Our Country's Pride." "The Twin Sisters," an 1863 label by C. S. Allen & Company, depicted profile images of embracing sisters who represented Liberty and Union. Labels intended to appeal to Unionists also used eagles, shields, and the Stars and Stripes as symbols of liberty (Quigley 2006, pp. 55–56).

After the Reconstruction era, manufacturers once again used Civil War images to generate a mass market for the burgeoning cigarette industry. One historian has written that tobacco companies in the North and South used themes of Civil War reconciliation to appeal to consumers. The *News and Observer* in Raleigh, North Carolina, published an advertisement containing sketches of Northern and Southern senators accompanied by testimonies about Blackwell's Bull Durham Tobacco (August 2, 1884, col. D).

Likewise, the Duke Tobacco Company of Durham, North Carolina, published a twenty-nine-page souvenir album in 1889 titled "The Heroes of the Civil War." It featured multicolored images of Confederate General Robert E. Lee, Union General Ulysses S. Grant, and other war heroes interspersed between advertisements for the company's various brands of cigarettes. The company's purpose in producing the album was to promote "kindly feeling" between the sections (Blight 2001, p. 201). According to Blight, "those famous generals, dead and alive, depicted in colorful sketches by the Duke Company ... had become commodities; their images were salable memories in the name of good will and good business" (Blight, p. 201).

ADRIENNE M. PETTY

BIBLIOGRAPHY

Blight, David W. *Race and Reunion: The Civil War in American Memory.* Cambridge, MA: Harvard University Press, 2001.

"Images of Native Americans in Advertisements." Available online at http://www.cwrl.utexas.edu/.

News and Observer (Raleigh, NC), August 2, 1884; issue 66; col. D.

Quigley, Paul D. H. "Tobacco's Civil War: Images of the Sectional Conflict on Tobacco Package Labels." Southern Cultures 12 (2006): 53–57.

---

also dabbled in the use of snuff during the revolutionary era, in imitation of European aristocrats, and took up cigar smoking after soldiers adopted the practice during the Mexican War (1846–1848).

By far the most common form of consuming tobacco before the Civil War, however, was chewing tobacco. Chewing tobacco was distinctly American and could be found in the mouths of yeoman farmers in the South as well as settlers on the expanding frontier. The practice was especially prevalent in the rural South. "The South Carolina Gentleman," a song included in *Songs of the War...*, published in 1863, mocked a tobacco-chewing slave owner:

> This South Carolina gentleman, one of the present time.
> He chews tobacco by the pound, and spits upon the floor,
> If there is not a box of sand behind the nearest door;
> And when he takes a weekly spree he clears a mighty track

Of everything that bears the shape of whiskey-skin, gin and sugar—brandy sour, peach and honey,
Irrepressible cocktail, rum and gum and luscious Apple-jack (p. 28)

Although they were teetotalers for the most part, some slaves also had a healthy appetite for pipe smoking and chewing tobacco, whether they were working, enjoying leisure time or celebrating a rare holiday. In his classic 1974 book *Roll, Jordan, Roll: The World the Slaves Made,* Eugene Genovese explains that slaves traded and bartered goods for tobacco and, if possible, grew their own. They soaked tobacco in sugar and honey in order to chew it.

Another way of consuming tobacco prevalent in the South was snuff, a form of powdered tobacco, usually flavored, that people typically packed between their cheek and gum in a practice known as dipping. The manufacture of chewing tobacco and snuff was based in Richmond, Virginia. The city boasted a sizable slave labor force and convenient access for shipping the finished product to major markets. In his 1996 book *Ashes to Ashes: America's Hundred-Year Cigarette War, the Public Health, and the Unabashed Triumph of Philip Morris,* Richard Kluger writes that, on the eve of the Civil War, more than fifty tobacco factories were operating in Richmond, Virginia.

Tobacco Use during the Civil War

The outbreak of the Civil War not only disrupted tobacco production in Richmond's factories but also hampered the growing of tobacco in the southern countryside. In March 1862 the Confederate Congress passed a joint resolution recommending that states plant food crops instead of tobacco. After the First Battle of Manassas, several tobacco warehouses in Richmond were converted into prisons for Union soldiers. These limits on tobacco planting and manufacturing, however, did not curb southerners' robust appetite for it. In account after account Union soldiers unaccustomed to seeing women use tobacco were shocked when they observed women engaged in the practice. Zenas T. Haines, a member of the Massachusetts Forty-fourth Regiment, wrote a letter from Washington, North Carolina, on March 20, 1863, where he and other troops occupied the home of an enslaved woman in order to seek shelter from a drenching downpour. He sat watching "Aunt Fanny" in amazement as she dipped snuff:

> Our presence must have caused a large consumption of this consoling article. She transferred the snuff from a tin box to her mouth with a sweet gum wood stick, which she used like a toothbrush, and then left the handle sticking out of her mouth. Aunt Fanny afforded me the first opportunity I ever had of witnessing the operation of "dipping," [. . .] which is said to prevail among the white women as well as the black ones at the South. (p. 87)

Bell Irvin Wiley, author of *The Life of Billy Yank: The Common Soldier of the Union,* quotes soldier John Tallman, who wrote, "thare are some nice looking girls, but they will chew tobacco, Sweet little things. Don't you think 'I' for instance would . . . make a nice showing riding [*sic*] along in a carriage with a young lady, me spitting tobacco juice out of one side of the carriage and she out the other . . . wall aint that nice, oh, cow!" (1971, p. 101).

Even some Confederate soldiers found tobacco chewing and snuff dipping among women to be unladylike and distasteful, as Wiley notes in *The Life of Billy Yank.* Philip Daingerfield Stephenson of the 13th Arkansas Infantry and Washington Artillery expressed amazement about the snuff habit of a woman who visited him while he was sick: "I found, oh I found that my pretty Josephine 'dipped!' Dipped snuff! Alas, alas! How rude the awakening. The sweet ideal shattered irreparably. For no conceivable future enchantment could reconstruct that ideal—with a snuff stick in her mouth" (p. 368).

Civilians in the border states indulged in tobacco use too. In a January 7, 1863, article in *The Daily Cleveland,* it was reported that in Missouri, "tobacco is used among natives in the rural districts indiscriminately by both sexes, children as well as adults, both for chewing and smoking."

So popular was tobacco among women and men in the Confederacy that ordinary citizens expressed their appreciation to the troops with gifts of tobacco. Washington Lafayette Gammage, in his history of the Fourth Arkansas regiment, reported that hundreds of "weary soldiers" in his regiment received "shoes and hats and coats and tobacco from the grateful people" as they marched through Lexington, Kentucky, in September 1863.

Northern women also sent tobacco to their loved ones serving in the Union army, but they eschewed the use of tobacco themselves. During the 1830s, in fact, many Northern women reformers became involved in the temperance movement. In addition to condemning alcohol consumption and gambling, these women targeted tobacco use for health reasons and on moral grounds. An 1841 issue of *The Emancipator,* warned readers, "if your children ever hanker after the vile weed, so as to form any of these slavish disgusting habits, it will, in nine cases out of ten, be your own fault. If you cling even stealingly to the loathsome wormleaf yourself, they will find it out, and you cannot expect to deter them" (Humphrey 1841, p. 172).

Cigarette Smoking after the War

The temperance movement ebbed during the Civil War, but it regained momentum later, when cigarette manufacturing and smoking became more widespread. During the war more and more soldiers turned to cigarettes as a way to achieve a quick escape from the harshness of the battlefield. Many Union soldiers who had become hooked on tobacco during the war exposed civilians to the practice once they returned home. As various manufacturers found ways to market cigarettes after the war, many civilians and veterans alike became prime consumers of the new product. In response, some women's groups in the North stepped up their campaign against tobacco. The Women's Christian Temperance Movement targeted the evils of cigarettes, in particular, and expressed alarm over their growing use not only among men but also among boys. In Connecticut, according to the article "To Be Taught Good Habits" in an 1886 issue of the *Boston Daily Advertiser,* a temperance advocate named Miss Greenwood secured passage of a bill that authorized teaching public school children the evil effects of using tobacco and liquor. Jerome E. Brooks reprints in his 1954 book *The Mighty Leaf: Tobacco through the Centuries* a message the temperance movement distributed in a pamphlet:

> "I'll never use tobacco, no;
> It is a filthy weed;
> I'll never put it in my mouth."
> Said Little Robert Reed.
> "It hurts the health; it makes bad breath;
> 'Tis very bad indeed.
> I'll never, never use it, no!"
> Said Little Robert Reed (pp. 242–243)

Although some middle class women in the South increasingly became active in the temperance movement, most rural women continued to crave tobacco. According to an 1896 article in the *News and Observer*, "In Court for Failing to Provide His Wife with Snuff and Tobacco," a woman in Mooresville, North Carolina, even went so far as to take her husband to court for failing to provide for her needs because he went off and "stayed some two or three days, and not a chew of tobacco or a dip of snuff in the house."

BIBLIOGRAPHY

Brooks, Jerome E. *The Mighty Leaf: Tobacco through the Centuries*. Boston: Little, Brown, 1952.

Fayetteville Observer, (Fayetteville, NC) Monday, February 25, 1861; issue 999; col. F.

Gammage, Washington Lafayette. *The Camp, the Bivouac, and the Battlefield, Being the History of the Fourth Arkansas Regiment, from Its First Organization Down to the Present Date*. Little Rock: Arkansas Southern Press, 1958.

Genovese, Eugene. *Roll, Jordan, Roll: The World the Slaves Made*. New York: Pantheon Books, 1974.

Gottsegen, Jack J. *Tobacco: A Study of Its Consumption in the United States*. New York: Pitman Publishing Corp., 1940.

Haines, Zenas T. *Letters from the Forty-fourth Regiment M.V.M.: A Record of the Experience of a Nine Months' Regiment in the Department of North Carolina in 1862–3*. Boston: Printed at the Herald Job Office, 1863. *Sources in U.S. History Online: Civil War*. Gale. Available from http://galenet.galegroup.com/.

Humphrey. "Keep Your Children from Using Tobacco." *The Emancipator*, February 18, 1841; issue 43, p. 172, col C.

"In Court for Failing to Provide His Wife with Snuff and Tobacco." *The News and Observer*, (Raleigh, NC) July 21, 1896; issue 122, pg. 3, col D.

Kluger, Richard. *Ashes to Ashes: America's Hundred-Year Cigarette War, the Public Health, and the Unabashed Triumph of Philip Morris*. New York: Vintage Books, 1997.

Palmer, George Putnam. *Soldiers' and Sailors' Patriotic Songs: New York, May, 1864*. New York: Loyal Publication Society, 1864.

Songs of the War . . ., Albany: J. Munsell, 1863. *Sources in U.S. History Online: Civil War*. Gale. Available from http://galenet.galegroup.com/.

"To Be Taught Good Habits: A Bill to Instruct School Children of the Evil Effects of Alcohol and Tobacco Passes the Connecticut House." *Boston Daily Advertiser*, February 25, 1886; issue 48, col F.

Wiley, Bell Irvin. *The Life of Billy Yank: The Common Soldier of the Union*. Garden City, NY: Doubleday, [1971].

"Women and Children Chewing Tobacco." *The Daily Cleveland*, January 7, 1863; issue 5; col C.

Adrienne M. Petty

Annotated Bibliography

The following resources, which provide overviews of the American Civil War, are recommended for their broad scope and availability.

GENERAL READING

Ash, Stephen. *When the Yankees Came: Conflict and Chaos in the Occupied South.* Chapel Hill, NC: University of North Carolina Press, 1999. A comprehensive and thoughtful account of life in areas of the South that experienced Union military occupation.

Davis, William C. *A Taste for War: The Culinary History of the Blue and Gray.* Mechanicsburg, PA: Stackpole Books, 2003.

Gallman, J. Matthew. *The North Fights the Civil War: The Home Front.* Chicago: I. R. Dee, 1994. A useful overview of the Northern home front during the Civil War.

Gallman, J. Matthew, ed. *The Civil War Chronicle: The Only Day-by-Day Portrait of America's Tragic Conflict as Told by Soldiers, Journalists, Politicians, Farmers, Nurses, Slaves, and Other Eyewitnesses.* New York: Crown Publishers, 2000.

Marten, James. *Civil War America: Voices from the Home Front.* Santa Barbara, CA: ABC-CLIO, 2003.

Paludan, Phillip Shaw. *A People's Contest: The Union and Civil War, 1861–1865.* New York: Harper & Row, 1988. An examination of the impact of the Civil War on Northern society, especially in connection with the growth of industrialization.

Rubin, Anne Sarah. *A Shattered Nation: The Rise and Fall of the Confederacy, 1861–1868.* Chapel Hill: University of North Carolina Press, 2005.

Selby, John G. *Virginians at War: The Civil War Experiences of Seven Young Confederates.* Wilmington, DE: Scholarly Resources, 2002. A study of four Virginia soldiers and three women on the home front (who nevertheless sometimes experienced the passing of armies), this fascinating work seeks the reasons that a generation of Virginians supported the Confederacy and the war.

Sutherland, Daniel E. *The Expansion of Everyday Life, 1860–1876.* New York: Harper & Row, 1989. A popularly written overview of daily life in America during the era of the Civil War and Reconstruction, built on the testimony of those who lived through the period and emphasizing the quest for middle-class status.

Volo, Dorothy Denneen, and James M. Volo. *Daily Life in Civil War America.* Westport, CT: Greenwood Press, 1998.

Williams, David. *Rich Man's War: Class, Cast, and Confederate Defeat in the Lower Chattahoochee Valley.* Athens: University of Georgia Press, 1998. An examination of the impact of the Civil War in southwestern Georgia and southeastern Alabama, with particular emphasis on class divisions.

Woodworth, Steven E., ed. *Cultures in Conflict: The American Civil War.* Westport, CT: Greenwood Press, 2000. A collection of first-person accounts of Civil War life in both the North and the South.

A SOLDIER'S LIFE

Barton, Michael. *Goodmen: The Character of Civil War Soldiers.* University Park: Pennsylvania State

University Press, 1981. A quantitative analysis of the collective personality of Civil War soldiers on the basis of their writings.

Barton, Michael, and Larry M. Logue. eds. *The Civil War Soldier: A Historical Reader*. New York: New York University Press, 2002. Excerpts from some of the memoirs of the Civil War soldiers.

Billings, John D. *Hardtack and Coffee; or, The Unwritten Story of Army Life*. Boston: G. M. Smith, 1887. Reprint, Alexandria, VA: Time-Life Books, 1982. A description of the soldier's life written by a soldier.

Davis, William C. *Rebels and Yankees: The Fighting Men of the Civil War*. New York: Smithmark Publishers, 1991.

Glatthaar, Joseph T. *The March to the Sea and Beyond: Sherman's Troops in the Savannah and Carolinas Campaigns*. New York: New York University Press, 1985.

Grimsley, Mark. *The Hard Hand of War: Union Military Policy toward Southern Civilians, 1860–1865*. New York: Cambridge University Press, 1997. An excellent account and analysis of the behavior of Union troops toward Confederate civilians.

Kennett, Lee B. *Marching through Georgia: The Story of Soldiers and Civilians during Sherman's Campaign*. New York: HarperCollins, 1995.

Marvel, William. *Andersonville: The Last Depot*. Chapel Hill: University of North Carolina Press, 1994. A good account of the worst prison camp of the Civil War.

McPherson, James M. *What They Fought For, 1861–1865*. New York: Anchor Books, 1995. A preliminary to McPherson's *For Cause and Comrades*, this book is nevertheless eminently readable and useful.

McPherson, James M. *For Cause and Comrades: Why Men Fought in the Civil War*. New York: Oxford University Press, 1997. The definitive examination of the motivations of Civil War soldiers.

Mitchell, Reid. *Civil War Soldiers: Their Expectations and Their Experiences*. New York: Viking, 1988. A study of the thought and motivations of the Civil War soldiers.

Mitchell, Reid. *The Vacant Chair: The Northern Soldier Leaves Home*. New York: Oxford University Press, 1993. A discussion of the emotional and psychological effects of the separation entailed by the war, both for Civil War soldiers and their families. Informed by modern scholarly ideas of gender.

Moore, Albert Burton. *Conscription and Conflict in the Confederacy*. New York: Macmillan, 1924. Reprint, New York: Hillary House, 1963.

Murdock, Eugene C. *One Million Men: The Civil War Draft in the North*. Madison: State Historical Society of Wisconsin, 1971. An investigation of how the Civil War draft worked—or failed to work—and why.

Power, J. Tracy. *Lee's Miserables: Life in the Army of Northern Virginia from the Wilderness to Appomattox*. Chapel Hill: University of North Carolina Press, 1998. An outstanding analysis of the devolution of morale within the Army of Northern Virginia during its last year of existence.

Robertson, James I., Jr. *Soldiers Blue and Gray*. New York: Warner Books, 1991.

Silber, Nina, and Mary Beth Sievens, eds. *Yankee Correspondence: Civil War Letters between New England Soldiers and the Home Front*. Charlottesville: University Press of Virginia, 1996. A selection of interesting letters between New England soldiers and their families back home.

Wert, Jeffry D. *A Brotherhood of Valor: The Common Soldiers of the Stonewall Brigade, C.S.A., and the Iron Brigade, U.S.A*. New York: Simon & Schuster, 1999.

Wiley, Bell Irvin. *The Life of Johnny Reb: The Common Soldier of the Confederacy*. Indianapolis, IN: Bobbs-Merrill, 1943. By making extensive use of soldiers' diaries and letters, this book pioneered the modern literature of the Civil War's common soldier.

Wiley, Bell Irvin. *The Life of Billy Yank: The Common Soldier of the Union*. Indianapolis, IN: Bobbs-Merrill, 1952. A highly successful sequel to Wiley's groundbreaking *The Life of Johnny Reb*.

Wiley, Bell Irvin. *The Common Soldier in the Civil War*. New York: Grosset & Dunlap, 1958.

Williams, David. *Johnny Reb's War: Battlefield and Homefront*. Abilene, TX: McWhiney Foundation Press, 2000. A brief but helpful overview of the common Confederate soldier.

Woodworth, Steven E., ed. *The Loyal, True, and Brave: America's Civil War Soldiers*. Wilmington, DE: SR Books, 2002. A collection of writings by and about soldiers.

FAMILY AND COMMUNITY

Attie, Jeanie. *Patriotic Toil: Northern Women and the Civil War*. Ithaca, NY: Cornell University Press, 1998. A study that shows how localism and individualism continued to be characteristic of relief work for the soldiers, despite the efforts of the leadership of the United States Sanitary Commission to impose order and central control.

Campbell, Edward D. C., Jr., and Kym S. Rice, eds. *A Woman's War: Southern Women, Civil War, and the*

Confederate Legacy. Charlottesville: University Press of Virginia, 1996. A collection of six essays examining the wartime experiences of Southern black women as well as white women of various social classes.

Cashin, Joan E., ed. *The War Was You and Me: Civilians in the American Civil War*. Princeton, NJ: Princeton University Press, 2002. A collection of essays dealing with the interconnections between the war and the home front in the North, the South, and on the western frontier.

Clinton, Catherine, ed. *Southern Families at War: Loyalty and Conflict in the Civil War South*. New York: Oxford University Press, 2000. A collection of twelve essays dealing with Southern families and family ties during the Civil War.

Clinton, Catherine, and Nina Silber, eds. *Divided Houses: Gender and the Civil War*. New York: Oxford University Press, 1992. A collection of eighteen essays by different authors examining various aspects of the Civil War from the perspective of modern scholarly ideas of gender.

DeCredico, Mary A. *Mary Boykin Chesnut: A Confederate Woman's Life*. Madison, WI: Madison House, 1996. A biography of the highly perceptive diarist whose husband was a Southern planter, U.S. senator, and Confederate staff officer.

Edwards, Laura F. *Scarlet Doesn't Live Here Anymore: Southern Women in the Civil War Era*. Urbana: University of Illinois Press, 2000.

Faust, Drew Gilpin. *Mothers of Invention: Women of the Slaveholding South in the American Civil War*. Chapel Hill: University of North Carolina Press, 1996. A highly acclaimed account of how upper-class Southern women tried to hold their world together in the midst of the upheavals and dislocations brought on by war and emancipation.

Gallman, J. Matthew. *Mastering Wartime: A Social History of Philadelphia during the Civil War*. New York: Cambridge University Press, 1990. A study of how the war affected Philadelphia socially, economically, and psychologically.

Inscoe, John C., and Gordon B. McKinney. *The Heart of Confederate Appalachia: Western North Carolina in the Civil War*. Chapel Hill: University of North Carolina Press, 2000.

Karamanski, Theodore J. *Rally 'Round the Flag: Chicago and the Civil War*. Rowman & Littlefield Publishers, 2006. A wide-ranging narrative examining the impact Chicagoans had on the war and how the war affected Chicago.

Leonard, Elizabeth D. *Yankee Women: Gender Battles in the Civil War*. New York: W. W. Norton, 1994. A study focusing on three Northern women and their roles within the Union war effort. Leonard argues that the war was a major watershed that changed ideas about women's role in society.

Marten, James. *The Children's Civil War*. Chapel Hill: University of North Carolina Press, 1998.

Marten, James. *Lessons of War: The Civil War in Children's Magazines*. Wilmington, DE: SR Books, 1999.

Marten, James. *Children for the Union: The War Spirit on the Northern Home Front*. Chicago: Ivan R. Dee, 2004. An account of how the war was presented to children in literature and popular culture and of how children reacted and remembered the war.

McCaslin, Richard B. *Tainted Breeze: The Great Hanging at Gainesville, Texas, 1862*. Baton Rouge: Louisiana State University Press, 1994. An excellent account of the hanging of a number of Texas Unionists in one North Texas town.

Moore, Frank. *Women of the War: Their Heroism and Self-Sacrifice*. Chicago: R. C. Treat, 1866. Reprint, Alexander, NC: Blue Gray Books, 1997. One of the first books to be written about the role of women in the Civil War. Moore stresses women's roles in caring for suffering soldiers.

Noe, Kenneth W., and Shannon H. Wilson, eds. *The Civil War in Appalachia: Collected Essays*. Knoxville: University of Tennessee Press, 1997.

Rable, George C. *Civil Wars: Women and the Crisis of Southern Nationalism*. Urbana: University of Illinois Press, 1989. A comprehensive account of the impact of the Civil War on Southern women, showing how traditional roles quickly reestablished themselves after the upheaval of war.

Rose, Anne C. *Victorian America and the Civil War*. New York: Cambridge University Press, 1992. Looking at seventy-five upper-middle-class Victorians in America, this study examines their attitudes on an array of subjects and argues that the war changed them little but did enhance their self-confidence.

Rosen, Robert H. *Confederate Charleston: An Illustrated History of the City and People during the Civil War*. Columbia: University of South Carolina Press, 1994. A brief but profusely illustrated account of wartime life in the city where the Civil War began.

Silber, Nina. *Daughters of the Union: Northern Women Fight the Civil War*. Cambridge, MA: Harvard University Press, 2005.

Spann, Edward K. *Gotham at War: New York City, 1860–1865*. Wilmington, DE: SR Books, 2002. This excellent examination of many facets of wartime New York provides a case study in the impact of wartime pressures on civilian society.

Sutherland, Daniel E. *Seasons of War: The Ordeal of a Confederate Community, 1861–1865.* New York: Free Press, 1995. A highly readable account of the impact of the Civil War in Culpeper County, Virginia, told from the viewpoint of and based on the accounts of the many soldiers and civilians who either lived in the county or passed through it during the war.

Taylor, Amy Murrell. *The Divided Family in Civil War America.* Chapel Hill: University of North Carolina Press, 2005.

Werner, Emmy E. *Reluctant Witnesses: Children's Voices from the Civil War.* Boulder, CO: Westview Press, 1998.

RELIGION

Bailey, David T. *Shadow on the Church: Southwestern Evangelical Religion and the Issue of Slavery, 1783–1860.* Ithaca, NY: Cornell University Press, 1985.

Bennett, William W. *A Narrative of the Great Revival Which Prevailed in the Southern Armies during the Late Civil War between the States of the Federal Union.* Philadelphia: Claxton, Remsen & Haffelfinger, 1877. A Southern minister draws on the reports of his fellow ministers to describe the upsurge in piety that occurred in the Confederate armies. Along with Jones's *Christ in the Camp* (below), this is a favorite of Lost Cause apologists seeking to present the Confederacy as morally superior to the Union.

Blied, Benjamin J. *Catholics and the Civil War.* Milwaukee, WI: Author, 1945.

Boles, John B. *The Irony of Southern Religion.* New York: Peter Lang Publishing, 1994. A brief but fascinating exploration of the multiple ironies involved in the way in which Christianity was adapted to the purposes of antebellum Southern society and, along with this, used to defend slavery.

Brinsfield, John W., William C. Davis, Benedict Maryniak, and James I. Robertson Jr., eds. *Faith in the Fight: Civil War Chaplains.* Mechanicsburg, PA: Stackpole Books, 2003.

Brown, William Young. *The Army Chaplain: His Office, Duties, and Responsibilities, and the Means of Aiding Him.* Philadelphia: Martien, 1863.

Farmer, James O., Jr. *The Metaphysical Confederacy: James Henley Thornwell and the Synthesis of Southern Values.* Macon, GA: Mercer University Press, 1999. A discussion of the shift in religious philosophy behind secession and the Confederacy.

Jones, Rev. J. William. *Christ in the Camp or Religion in Lee's Army.* Richmond, VA: B. F. Johnson, 1888. An account of religious revivals in the Army of Northern Virginia. Along with Bennett's *Great Revival* (above), this is a favorite of Lost Cause apologists seeking to present the Confederacy as morally superior to the Union.

Miller, Randall M., Harry S. Stout, and Charles Reagan Wilson, eds. *Religion and the American Civil War.* New York: Oxford University Press, 1998. A collection of essays exploring various aspects of American religion during the Civil War.

Moorhead, James H. *American Apocalypse: Yankee Protestants and the Civil War.* New Haven, CT: Yale University Press, 1978. Moorhead uses pamphlet sermons and nineteenth-century religious periodicals to argue that Northern Protestant denominations too readily identified the Union war effort with the Christian apocalypse and the ushering in of the millennium—leading to a religious crisis after the war.

Moss, Rev. Lemuel. *Annals of the United States Christian Commission.* Philadelphia: J. B. Lippincott, 1868. An early history of this organization, which was founded as an offshoot of the YMCA for the purpose of bringing both Christian witness and material comfort to the Union soldiers in the field.

Owen, Christopher H. *The Sacred Flame of Love: Methodism and Society in Nineteenth-Century Georgia.* Athens: University of Georgia Press, 1998. An interesting account of the growth of Methodism in Georgia and of the efforts of Georgia Methodists to reconcile their religion with slavery.

Rhodes, Elisha Hunt. *All for the Union: The Civil War Diary and Letters of Elisha Hunt Rhodes.* Ed. Robert Hunt Rhodes. New York: Orion Books, 1985. Made famous by the 1990 Ken Burns PBS Civil War series, Rhodes was a devout Christian who had much to say on the subject of religion in the Civil War armies.

Shattuck, Gardiner H., Jr. *A Shield and Hiding Place: The Religious Life of the Civil War Armies.* Macon, GA: Mercer University Press, 1987. A brief comparative study of religion in the Union and Confederate armies, which suggests that the individualistic nature of Southern religion made it less able to sustain the South in war.

Smith, Edward Parmelee. *Incidents of the United States Christian Commission.* Philadelphia: J. B. Lippincott, 1869.

Smith, Timothy L. *Revivalism and Social Reform: American Protestantism on the Eve of the Civil War.* Baltimore, MD: Johns Hopkins University Press, 1980. An account of the revival of 1857, with a focus on its contribution to reform movements.

Trumbull, Henry Clay. *The Sunday-School: Its Origins, Mission, Methods, and Auxiliaries.* Philadelphia: John D. Wattles, 1888. An account by the chaplain of the 10th Connecticut, discussing the birth and growth of a popular nineteenth-century religious institution.

Trumbull, Henry Clay. *War Memories of an Army Chaplain.* New York: Charles Scribner's Sons, 1898.

Wilson, Charles Reagan. *Baptized in Blood: The Religion of the Lost Cause, 1865–1920.* Athens: University of Georgia Press, 1980. A broad examination of civil religion in the post–Civil War South.

Woodworth, Steven E. *While God Is Marching On: The Religious World of Civil War Soldiers.* Lawrence: University Press of Kansas, 2001. An account of religion within the Civil War armies, focusing on what soldiers thought, said, and did.

POPULAR CULTURE

Abel, E. Lawrence. *Singing the New Nation: How Music Shaped the Confederacy, 1861–1865.* Mechanicsburg, PA: Stackpole Books, 1999. A popularly written account of music as it was performed, published, and composed in the Confederacy, along with an examination of the experiences of bandsmen in the Confederate army.

Bernard, Kenneth A. *Lincoln and the Music of the Civil War.* Caldwell, ID: Caxton Printers, 1966. An account of the music of wartime Washington, DC, focusing on songs related to Lincoln—songs Lincoln heard, songs about Lincoln, songs he liked—including his favorites, "Dixie" and "La Marseillaise."

Bode, Carl. *The American Lyceum: Town Meeting of the Mind.* New York: Oxford University Press, 1956.

Burnham, John C. *Bad Habits: Drinking, Smoking, Taking Drugs, Gambling, Sexual Misbehavior, and Swearing in American History.* New York and London: New York University Press, 1993. This excellent and thought-provoking study of "minor vices" in American history places such activities in the Civil War era within a broader context.

Cornelius, Steven H. *Music of the Civil War Era.* Westport, CT: Greenwood Press, 2004.

Epstein, Dena J. *Sinful Tunes and Spirituals: Black Folk Music to the Civil War.* Urbana: University of Illinois Press, 1977. Documents period accounts of African American music and its development before and during the Civil War.

Gac, Scott. *Singing for Freedom: The Hutchinson Family Singers and the Nineteenth-Century Culture of Reform.* New Haven, CT: Yale University Press, 2007. Tells the story of the Hutchinson Family, America's most popular singing group of the era leading up to the Civil War. Rooted in revival meetings, the Hutchinsons specialized in songs promoting temperance and abolition.

Kirsch, George B. *Baseball in Blue and Gray: The National Pastime during the Civil War.* Princeton, NJ: Princeton University Press, 2003. A brief, popular account of how baseball, already the national pastime, survived and developed during the Civil War.

Lott, Eric. *Love and Theft: Blackface Minstrelsy and the American Working Class.* New York: Oxford University Press, 1993. A history of blackface minstrelsy from its beginnings around 1830 through the Civil War.

Mead, David C. *Yankee Eloquence in the Middle West: The Ohio Lyceum, 1850–1870.* East Lansing: Michigan State College Press, 1951. A detailed study of the lyceum movement in Ohio, focusing on the fifteen most popular lecturers in the state.

Meer, Sarah. *Uncle Tom Mania: Slavery, Minstrelsy, and Transatlantic Culture in the 1850s.* Athens: University of Georgia, 2005. An analysis of the intersections among minstrelsy, abolitionism, American literature, and British-American relations in the nineteenth century.

Morgan, Jo-Ann. *Uncle Tom's Cabin As Visual Culture.* Columbia: University of Missouri Press, 2007. A study of how the various illustrations associated with Harriet Beecher Stowe's famous abolitionist novel influenced popular conceptions.

Ray, Angela G. *The Lyceum and Public Culture in the Nineteenth-Century United States.* East Lansing: Michigan State University Press, 2005.

Reynolds, David S. *Walt Whitman's America: A Cultural Biography.* New York: Vintage Books, 1995.

Silverman, Jerry. *Songs and Stories of the Civil War.* Brookfield, CT: Twenty-First Century Books, 2002.

Sullivan, George. *In the Wake of Battle: The Civil War Images of Mathew Brady.* Munich and New York: Prestel Verlag, 2004. A collection of Brady's photographs, along with helpful explanations.

Toll, Robert C. *Blacking Up: The Minstrel Show in Nineteenth-Century America.* New York: Oxford University Press, 1974. Relates minstrelsy, the most popular entertainment form of the mid-nineteenth century, to American society.

Zeller, Bob. *The Blue and Gray in Black and White: A History of Civil War Photography.* Westport, CT: Praeger Publishers, 2005.

HEALTH AND MEDICINE

Adams, George Worthington. *Doctors in Blue: The Medical History of the Union Army in the Civil*

War. New York: Henry Schuman, 1952. Reprint, Dayton, OH: Press of Morningside, 1985. One of the early pioneering studies of Civil War surgeons, Adams's book is still a classic.

Alcott, Louisa May. *Hospital Sketches.* Boston: J. Redpath, 1863. Published in a local newspaper during the war, these accounts, which originated as letters home, describe the future author of *Little Women*'s service as a volunteer nurse in the District of Columbia's Union Hotel Hospital.

Apperson, John Samuel. *Repairing the "March of Mars": The Civil War Diaries of John Samuel Apperson, Hospital Steward in the Stonewall Brigade, 1861–1865.* Ed. John Herbert Roper. Macon, GA: Mercer University Press, 2001.

Bollet, Alfred Jay. *Civil War Medicine: Challenges and Triumphs.* Tucson, AZ: Galen Press, 2002. A lengthy (475-page), highly documented study encompassing all aspects of Civil War medical practice.

Brinton, John H. *Personal Memoirs of John H. Brinton, Major and Surgeon U.S.V., 1861–1865.* New York: Neale Publishing Company, 1914.

Cumming, Kate. "A Nurse's Diary." In *A Journal of Hospital Life in the Confederate Army of Tennessee, from the Battle of Shiloh to the End of the War: With Sketches of Life and Character, and Brief Notices of Current Events during That Period.* Louisville, KY: John P. Morgan, 1866.

Cunningham, H. H. *Doctors in Gray: The Confederate Medical Service.* Baton Rouge: Louisiana State University Press, 1958. Along with Adams's *Doctors in Blue*, this was one of the early pioneering studies of Civil War surgeons.

Denney, R. E. *Civil War Medicine: Care and Comfort of the Wounded.* New York: Sterling Publishing, 1994. A compilation of first-person observations of Civil War medical care, arranged in an almost day-by-day chronological order.

Dyer, J. Franklin. *The Journal of a Civil War Surgeon.* Ed. Michael B. Chesson. Lincoln: University of Nebraska Press, 2003. Dyer, who served from 1861 to 1864, started the war as surgeon of the 19th Massachusetts and rose to be chief medical officer of the Second Division, Second Corps.

Ellis, Thomas T. *Leaves from the Diary of an Army Surgeon; or, Incidents of Field, Camp, and Hospital Life.* New York: J. Bradburn, 1863.

Flannery, Michael A. *Civil War Pharmacy: A History of Drugs, Drug Supply and Provision, and Therapeutics for the Union and Confederacy.* New York: Pharmaceutical Products Press, 2004. A comprehensive history of pharmaceuticals and the practice of pharmacy in both the Union and Confederate armies.

Freemon, Frank R. *Gangrene and Glory: Medical Care during the American Civil War.* Madison, NJ: Fairleigh Dickinson University Press, 2001. This lavishly illustrated book is organized into twenty-four brief chapters, each dealing with a particular aspect of Civil War medical care.

Giesberg, Judith Ann. *Civil War Sisterhood: The United States Sanitary Commission and Women's Politics in Transition.* Lebanon, NH: University Press of New England, 2006. Giesberg argues that women took an active role in directing the activities of the U.S.S.C. and thus advanced the cause of women fulfilling previously male roles during the years that followed.

Hart, Albert G. *The Surgeon and the Hospital in the Civil War.* Palmyra, VA: Old Soldier Books, 1987.

Parsons, Emily Elizabeth. *Civil War Nursing: Memoir of Emily Elizabeth Parsons.* Boston: Little, Brown, 1880. Reprint, New York: Garland, 1984.

Powers, Elvira J. *Hospital Pencillings: Being a Diary While in Jefferson General Hospital, Jeffersonville, Ind., and Others at Nashville, Tennessee, as Matron and Visitor.* Boston: Edward L. Mitchel, 1866.

Reed, William Howell. *Hospital Life in the Army of the Potomac.* Boston: W. V. Spencer, 1866.

Rutkow, I. M. *Bleeding Blue and Gray: Civil War Surgery and the Evolution of American Medicine.* New York: Random House, 2005. A comprehensive history of Civil War medical care, focusing on the progress made during the course of the war.

Schroeder-Lein, Glenna R. *The Encyclopedia of Civil War Medicine.* Armonk, NY: M. E. Sharpe, 2008. A comprehensive reference guide to all aspects of Civil War medicine.

Smith, Adelaide W. *Reminiscences of an Army Nurse during the Civil War.* New York: Greaves Publishing Company, 1911.

Straubing, Harold Elk, ed. *In Hospital and Camp: The Civil War through the Eyes of Its Doctors and Nurses.* Mechanicsburg, PA: Stackpole Books, 1993. A compilation of eyewitness accounts of medical care during the Civil War.

Woolsey, Jane Stuart. *Hospital Days: Reminiscences of a Civil War Nurse.* New York: D. Van Nostrand, 1870.

WORK AND ECONOMY

Ball, Douglas B. *Financial Failure and Confederate Defeat.* Urbana: University of Illinois Press, 1991. Ball suggests that the Confederacy suffered from an unwillingness to face financial reality, in particular an unwillingness to raise taxes to a level sufficient to finance the war.

Dew, Charles B. *Ironmaker to the Confederacy: Joseph R. Anderson and the Tredegar Iron Works.* New Haven, CT, and London: Yale University Press, 1966. An examination of the business career of the director of the Confederacy's largest and most important industrial concern, showing how Anderson favored the Confederacy but favored his own profits even more.

Dew, Charles B. *Bond of Iron: Master and Slave at Buffalo Forge.* New York: W. W. Norton, 1994. A study of a small iron-making establishment near Lexington, Virginia, demonstrating that although slaves could be used successfully in such industrial work, the system of slavery inhibited technological innovation and placed limits on productivity.

Dublin, Thomas. *Women at Work: The Transformation of Work and Community in Lowell, Massachusetts, 1826–1860.* New York: Columbia University Press, 1979. A study of the social origins and motivations of the young women who made up the work force of one of America's first textile mills during the decades leading up to the Civil War.

Fite, Emerson David. *Social and Industrial Conditions in the North during the Civil War.* New York: Macmillan, 1910.

Gates, Paul W. *Agriculture and the Civil War.* New York: Alfred A. Knopf, 1965. While the war stimulated rapid growth in agricultural mechanization in the North, in the South government policies led to a decline in agricultural production, handicapping the Confederate war effort.

Hareven, Tamara K., and Randolph Langenbach. *Amoskeag: Life and Work in an American Factory-City.* New York: Pantheon Books, 1978. A history of the workers in the Manchester, New Hampshire, textile mills.

Johnson, Russell L. *Warriors into Workers: The Civil War and the Formation of Urban-Industrial Society in a Northern City.* New York: Fordham University Press, 2003. A study of the culture and society of Dubuque, Iowa, during the Civil War.

Massey, Mary Elizabeth. *Ersatz in the Confederacy: Shortages and Substitutes on the Southern Homefront.* Columbia: University of South Carolina Press, 1952. Massey discusses not only the shortages, which were severe and endemic within the Confederacy, but also analyzes their causes, of which Confederate government policies such as impressment and the tax-in-kind were chief.

Otto, John Solomon. *Southern Agriculture during the Civil War Era, 1860–1880.* Westport, CT:

Greenwood Publishing Group, 1994. A brief overview of Southern agricultural developments during the Civil War era.

Palladino, Grace. *Another Civil War: Labor, Capital, and the State in the Anthracite Regions of Pennsylvania, 1840–1868.* Urbana: University of Illinois Press, 1990.

Thornton, Mark, and Robert B. Ekelund Jr. *Tariffs, Blockades, and Inflation: The Economics of the Civil War.* Wilmington, DE: SR Books, 2004. An examination of government fiscal policy during the Civil War, showing that the Confederate government pursued policies that ultimate hurt its cause.

Wilson, Mark R. *The Business of Civil War: Military Mobilization and the State, 1861–1865.* Baltimore, MD: Johns Hopkins University Press, 2006.

POLITICS

Abrahamson, James L. *The Men of Secession and Civil War, 1859–1861.* Wilmington, DE: SR Books, 2000. A brief narrative and analysis of the secession crisis, emphasizing that it was not a spontaneous popular outburst but rather a carefully engineered revolution for which secessionist leaders had worked long and hard.

Bernstein, Iver. *The New York Draft Riots: Their Significance for American Society and Politics in the Age of the Civil War.* New York: Oxford University Press, 1990.

Boritt, Gabor. *The Gettysburg Gospel: The Lincoln Speech That Nobody Knows.* New York: Simon & Schuster, 2006.

Cooper, William J. Jr. *Jefferson Davis, American.* New York: Alfred A. Knopf, 2000.

Davis, William C. *Jefferson Davis: The Man and His Hour.* New York: HarperCollins, 1991.

Davis, William C. *A Government of Our Own: The Making of the Confederacy.* New York: Free Press, 1994.

Dew, Charles B. *Apostles of Disunion: Southern Secession Commissioners and the Causes of the Civil War.* Charlottesville: University of Virginia Press, 2001. This study of the rhetoric of commissioners sent by seceding states to other wavering slave states reveals that the overriding motive for secession was the preservation of slavery.

Guelzo, Allen C. *Abraham Lincoln: Redeemer President.* Grand Rapids, MI: W. B. Eerdmans, 1999. This award-winning book looks at Lincoln's thought and sees him as an heir to the classical liberalism of John Locke.

Guelzo, Allen C. *Lincoln and Douglas: The Debates That Defined America*. New York: Simon & Schuster, 2008.

Harris, Brayton. *Blue and Gray in Black and White: Newspapers in the Civil War*. Washington, DC: Brassey's, 1999. An overview of how Civil War newspapers reported and often attempted to influence the course of events.

Holzer, Harold. *Lincoln at Cooper Union: The Speech That Made Abraham Lincoln President*. New York: Simon & Schuster, 2004. A fascinating account of one of Lincoln's greatest speeches. Holzer describes the circumstances leading up to the speech, its delivery, and its reception, and also provides a profound discussion of its meaning, showing Lincoln's eagerness to "think as the Founders thought, and act as the Founders acted."

Jaffa, Harry V. *Crisis of the House Divided: An Interpretation of the Issues in the Lincoln-Douglas Debates*. Garden City, NY: Doubleday, 1959.

Jaffa, Harry V. *A New Birth of Freedom: Abraham Lincoln and the Coming of the Civil War*. Lanham, MD: Rowman & Littlefield Publishers, 2000. A challenging and profoundly thought-provoking meditation on Lincoln's commitment to the truth that "all men are created equal."

Neely, Mark E., Jr. *The Fate of Liberty: Abraham Lincoln and Civil Liberties*. New York; Oxford University Press, 1991. Dispels the myth that the Lincoln administration was unduly harsh or unmindful of the importance of civil liberties.

Neely, Mark E., Jr. *Confederate Bastille: Jefferson Davis and Civil Liberties*. Milwaukee, WI: Marquette University Press, 1993. Dispels the myth that the Confederate government strictly respected civil liberties.

Neely, Mark E., Jr. *The Divided Union: Party Conflict in the Civil War North*. Cambridge, MA: Harvard University Press, 2002.

Rable, George C. *The Confederate Republic: A Revolution against Politics*. Chapel Hill: University of North Carolina Press, 1994. An exploration of Confederate politics. It points up the irony that while many Southerners expressed a desire to get away from politics as they had known it in the old Union, they nonetheless recreated it in a more corrosive form in their new republic.

Walther, Eric H. *The Fire-Eaters*. Baton Rouge: Louisiana State University Press, 1992.

Walther, Eric H. *The Shattering of the Union: America in the 1850s*. Wilmington, DE: Scholarly Resources, 2004. An account of the political struggles of the 1850s that lead the country to the brink of secession and Civil War.

Walther, Eric H. *William Lowndes Yancey and the Coming of the Civil War*. Chapel Hill: University of North Carolina Press, 2006.

Waugh, John C. *Reelecting Lincoln: The Battle for the 1864 Presidency*. New York: Crown Publishers, 1997.

Waugh, John C. *On the Brink of Civil War: The Compromise of 1850 and How It Changed the Course of American History*. Wilmington, DE: Scholarly Resources, 2003. A fascinating and thoughtful narrative of the struggle for passage of the Compromise of 1850, which may have delayed the Civil War by a decade.

Weber, Jennifer L. *Copperheads: The Rise and Fall of Lincoln's Opponents in the North*. New York and Oxford: Oxford University Press, 2006. An account of Northerners who opposed the Union war effort.

White, Ronald C., Jr. *The Eloquent President: A Portrait of Lincoln through His Words*. New York: Random House, 2005. A discussion of Lincoln as one of history's most skillful practitioners of the art of using the English language to communicate with and motivate the American people.

Yearns, Wilfred Buck. *The Confederate Congress*. Athens: University of Georgia Press, 1960.

EFFECTS OF THE WAR ON SLAVES AND FREEDPEOPLE

Bentley, George R. *A History of the Freedmen's Bureau*. Philadelphia: University of Pennsylvania Press, 1955.

Berlin, Ira, Joseph P. Reidy, and Leslie S. Rowland, eds. *Freedom's Soldiers: The Black Military Experience in the Civil War*. New York: Cambridge University Press, 1998. A collection of documents relating to the service of black troops in the Union army. Includes a collection of photographs and a lengthy introductory essay.

Berlin, Ira, and Leslie S. Rowland, eds. *Families and Freedom: A Documentary History of African-American Kinship in the Civil War Era*. New York: New Press, 1997.

Cornish, Dudley Taylor. *The Sable Arm: Negro Troops in the Union Army, 1861–1865*. New York: Longmans, Green, 1956. Reprint, New York: W. W. Norton, 1966. The classic account of black troops in the Union army. Cornish discusses the policy debates leading to black enlistment, the raising and equipping of black units, and their impressive operational performance, including in combat.

Durden, Robert F. *The Gray and the Black: The Confederate Debate on Emancipation*. Baton

Rouge: Louisiana State University Press, 1972. An account of one of the most curious incidents of the war, the tentative (and ultimately stillborn) decision by the Davis administration to attempt to induce slaves to fight for the Confederacy.

Foner, Eric. *Nothing but Freedom: Emancipation and Its Legacy*. Baton Rouge: Louisiana State University Press, 1984. A discussion of emancipation and its effects.

Forbes, Ella. *African American Women during the Civil War*. New York: Garland, 1998.

Frankel, Noralee. *Freedom's Women: Black Women and Families in Civil War Era Mississippi*. Bloomington: Indiana University Press, 1999.

Franklin, John Hope. *The Emancipation Proclamation*. Garden City, NY: Anchor Books, 1965. A discussion of the purposes and impact of the Emancipation Proclamation.

Glatthaar, Joseph T. *Forged in Battle: The Civil War Alliance of Black Soldiers and White Officers*. New York: Free Press, 1990.

Guelzo, Allen C. *Lincoln's Emancipation Proclamation: The End of Slavery in America*. New York: Simon & Schuster, 2004. A study of Lincoln's cautious progress toward emancipation, which balanced his desire to free the slaves with his respect for constitutional limitations.

Hansen, Joyce. *Between Two Fires: Black Soldiers in the Civil War*. New York: Franklin Watts, 1993.

Hargrove, Hondon B. *Black Union Soldiers in the Civil War*. Jefferson, NC: McFarland, 1988.

Levine, Bruce. *Confederate Emancipation: Southern Plans to Free and Arm Slaves during the Civil War*. New York: Oxford University Press, 2006.

McPherson, James M. *The Negro's Civil War: How American Negroes Felt and Acted during the War for the Union*. New York: Pantheon Books, 1965. An early but classic work on the subject by one of the most respected Civil War historians.

Robinson, Armstead L. *Bitter Fruits of Bondage: The Demise of Slavery and the Collapse of the Confederacy, 1861–1865*. Charlottesville: University of Virginia Press, 2005. This long-awaited book, published posthumously from the notes and manuscripts of the late University of Virginia professor, argues that "class conflict based on defense of slavery eroded the Southern will to national independence" (p. 10).

Smith, John David, ed. *Black Soldiers in Blue: African American Troops in the Civil War Era*. Chapel Hill: University of North Carolina Press, 2002. A collection of fourteen essays exploring various aspects of the African American military experience during the Civil War.

Taylor, Susie King. *A Black Woman's Civil War Memoirs*. Ed. by Patricia W. Romero and Willie Lee Rose. Princeton, NJ: Markus Wiener, 1988.

Wiley, Bell Irvin. *Southern Negroes, 1861–1865*. New Haven: Yale University Press, 1938.

Wilson, Keith P. *Campfires of Freedom: The Camp Life of Black Soldiers during the Civil War*. Kent, OH: Kent State University Press, 2002. Wilson not only relates the experiences of black soldiers in military camps, but also places those experiences within the broader setting of the political and social transformation that took place during the Civil War years.

RECONCILIATION AND REMEMBRANCE

Adams, Jessica. *Wounds of Returning: Race, Memory, and Property on the Postslavery Plantation*. Chapel Hill: University of North Carolina Press, 2007.

Blight, David W. *Race and Reunion: The Civil War in American Memory*. Cambridge, MA: Belknap Press of Harvard University Press, 2001.

Blight, David W. *Beyond the Battlefield: Race, Memory, and the American Civil War*. Amherst: University of Massachusetts Press, 2002. Both this book and the one above discuss shifting memories of the war along with ways in which the late-nineteenth-century movement toward reunion had an impact on issues of race.

Brown, Thomas J. *The Public Art of Civil War Commemoration: A Brief History with Documents*. New York: Bedford/St. Martin's, 2004.

Fahs, Alice, and Joan Waugh, eds. *The Memory of the Civil War in American Culture*. Chapel Hill: University of North Carolina Press, 2004.

Foster, Gaines M. *Ghosts of the Confederacy: Defeat, the Lost Cause, and the Emergence of the New South, 1865 to 1913*. New York: Oxford University Press, 1987. A thought-provoking study of Confederate veterans groups and memorial associations.

McConnell, Stuart. *Glorious Contentment: The Grand Army of the Republic, 1865–1900*. Chapel Hill: University of North Carolina Press, 1992. A social history of the great Union veterans' organization.

Neff, John R. *Honoring the Civil War Dead: Commemoration and the Problem of Reconciliation*. Lawrence: University Press of Kansas, 2005. A thoughtful discussion of the commemoration of war dead and how it reflected the difficulties of reconciliation.

Reardon, Carol. *Pickett's Charge in History and Memory*. Chapel Hill: University of North Carolina Press,

1997. An examination of how one of the most famous incidents of the Civil War has evolved in popular memory.

Shaffer, Donald R. *After the Glory: The Struggles of Black Civil War Veterans.* Lawrence: University Press of Kansas, 2004.

Smith, Timothy B. *This Great Battlefield of Shiloh: History, Memory, and the Establishment of a Civil War National Military Park.* Knoxville: University of Tennessee Press, 2004. A history of the Shiloh battlefield, showing its significance to public memory of the war.

Smith, Timothy B. *The Golden Age of Battlefield Preservation: The Decade of the 1890s and the Establishment of America's First Five Military Parks.* Knoxville: University of Tennessee Press, 2008. A fascinating account of the process that led to the creation of the first and most important National Military Parks at battlefields, including Chickamauga, Shiloh, Vicksburg, and Antietam.

Index

This index is sorted word-by-word. Bold page locators indicate main essays. Italic page locators indicate images. Page locators with a *t* indicate tabular material.

Anti-Masonic Party, 1:256, 258

Antietam Exhibit, 1862, 1:278–279, 280–281

Antietam National Battlefield, 2:249, 267–269
See also Battle of Antietam, 1862

Antietam National Cemetery, 2:271

Antietam Plan, 2:249, 250, 267, 269

Antietam Wavelet, 2:267

Antislavery movement. *See* Abolitionism

Apostles of Disunion (Dew), 2:160

Appeal to the Coloured Citizens of the World (Walker), 2:218–219

Appomattox Campaign, 1865, 1:48, 112, 251, 2:239

Arkansas
Arkansas Post National Memorial (national park), 2:250
black churches, 1:120
contraband and, 2:92
military units, 1:247, 299
pro-Unionists, 2:169
secession, 2:160

Arlington National Cemetery, 2:246, 252, 270

Armies. *See* Confederate States of America Army; United States Army; *specific military units*

Arminian doctrine, 1:191

Armory Square Hospital, Washington, DC, 2:20

Arms manufacturing, 2:75–78, 77
Colt revolvers, 2:67, 68, 100
Northern states, 2:65–66, 67, 68
war profiteers, 2:100
See also Military weapons

Armstrong, Hallock, 1:218–219

Army Act, 1869, 1:252

Army bands, 1:35–36, 243–244, 250–252, 252

The Army Chaplain (Brown), 1:229

Army Chaplain's Manual (Hammond), 1:267

Army Corps of Engineers, 1:126, 129

"Army Hymn" (Holmes), 1:209

Army life. *See* Soldiers' lives

Army Life in a Black Regiment (Wentworth), 1:196, 245

Army missionaries, 1:**232–234**

Army of the Cumberland, 2:247, 254–255, 256

Army of the Ohio, 2:258

Army of the Potomac
army bands and, 1:35
health of soldiers and, 2:26
Hooker, Joe and, 1:62
McClellan, George B. and, 1:77, 2:14

Mead, G. G. and, 2:263
medical reforms and, 2:9, 11, 14, 31, 59
military chaplains and, 1:218–219, 233, 234
remembrances and memorials, 2:243, 254
Reynolds, J. F. and, 2:263
Seven Days Battles, 1862 and, 2:156
Sheridan, William T. and, 1:85

The Army of the Potomac (Castleman), 2:26

Army officers
abolitionists, 1:71
black units, 1:45, 52, 69–70, 71, 72, 73
desertion, 1:28, 31
draft, 1:10
drill and training, 1:13
election of, 1:7
foraging and looting, 1:83, 84, 87
furloughs, 1:44
headquarters, 1:19
military prisons, 1:45, 46, 47
prisoner exchanges, 1:45
soldiers' relationships with, 1:33, 41–42
vices, 1:37, 66
West Point, 1:126–129
wives of, 1:62–63

Arnold, Isaac Newton, 1:153–154

Arp, Bill, 1:289, 2:190

"The Arsenal at Springfield" (Longfellow), 2:76

Arthur, T. S., 1:97, 288, 294

Artillery, 1:58, 251, 282, 2:3–5

An Artilleryman's Diary (Jones), 2:27

Asbury, Francis, 1:194, 194–195

Ashcraft, James A., 2:258

Ashes to Ashes (Kluger), 1:299

Asian Exclusion Act, 1875, 1:173

ASSU (American Sunday School Union), 1:195, 196

Atlanta Constitution, 2:190

Atlantic Coast. *See* Blockades and blockade running

Atlantic Monthly, 1:119, 280

Atlantic States, 2:70, 86
See also specific states

Atwood, J., "Advice to Young Women," 1:98

AUA (American Unitarian Association), 1:225

Augusta Factory, 2:105

Augusta Powder Works, 2:63, 64

Augusta Purveying Association, 2:105

Autenrieth wagon, 2:9

Awakening of 1858, 1:192–193

B

Backus, Isaac, 1:203

Bacon, Georgeanna Muirson Woolsey, 2:34, 35

Bacon, Leonard, 2:28

Bacot, Ada W., 1:138

Baker, Lafayette, 2:171

Ball, Charles, 1:129, 2:213

Ball, Hannah, 1:194

Ballads, 1:165–166, 247

Ballou's Dollar Magazine, 1:97

Baltimore Riot, 1861, 2:170, 170

Baltimore Sun, 1:267, 2:145

Bandits and bummers looting, 1:87

Bands. *See* Army bands

Bands and Drummer Boys of the Civil War (Wise and Lord), 1:243, 244

Bangor Daily Whig & Courier, 1:217, 2:143

Banking industry, 2:101, 102–103, 109

Baptist Teacher, 1:195

Baptists
dance and, 1:253
history of, 1:192
slavery and, 1:184, 2:163

Barnard, George, 1:278

Barnard, John Gross, 2:94

Barnes, David M., 1:157

Barnes, Samuel Denham, 2:278

Barnum, P. T., 1:237, 241

Barrett, Harris, 1:201

Barrett, James, 2:75

Barton, Clara, 1:59, 137, 2:37–38, 38, 132

Barton, William E., 2:138–139

Bartow, Francis Stebbins, 2:260

Baseball, 1:2, 236, 260, 262–263

Bate, William B., 2:260–261

Battery Wagner, 1:73

Battle casualties. *See* War casualties

"Battle Hymn of the Republic" (Howe), 1:209, 209–210

Battle of Antietam, 1862, 1:278–279, 280–281, 2:268
ambulance corps and, 2:31
commemoration, 2:247
effects of, 2:205
first aid stations and, 2:14
Northern Virginia Confederate States of America Army, 2:96
victor of, 1:7
women and, 1:58
See also Antietam National Battlefield

Battle of Cedar Mountain, 1862, 1:59

on execution of deserters, 1:30

on GAR, 2:241

on health, 1:27

history of, 2:188

illustration of Battle at Antietam, 1:279

literature for soldiers, 1:32

political humor and cartoons, 2:188, 189, 190

propaganda and, 2:184

on surgeons, 2:17

on telegraph system, 2:114

on uniforms, 1:20, 2:100

Harris, Brayton, *Blue & Gray in Black & White,* 1:266

Harris, J. Andrews, 1:155

Harris, William C., 1:51, 275

Harrison, Benjamin, 2:255

Harrison, Dabney, 1:231

Hart, Albert G., *The Surgeon and the Hospital in the Civil War,* 2:3

Harvard Divinity School, 1:225

Harvard University, 1:185, 186

Haskell, John, 2:13–14

Hauptman, Laurence M., *Between Two Fires,* 1:77

Hayes, Rutherford B., 2:177

Hayes-Tilden Compromise, 1877, 1:122

Hays, Will S., 1:243

Hazen, William B., 2:260

Health and medicine

overview, 2:1–2

advances in medicine, 2:31, 42, 44–45, 45, 46, 58–60

amputations, 2:1, 16–17, 29

anesthesia and, 2:1, 2, 17, 42–44

artificial limbs and, 2:16, 52

civilian health care, 2:56–58

dentistry, 2:59

epidemics and, 1:108, 163, 2:1, 23, 25–26, 42

excisions and, 2:17

food and nutrition, 1:18, 27, 50, 66, 2:25

home remedies, 1:110, 2:44

homeopathy and, 2:57

infections, 1:26–27, 2:1, 8–9, 10, 17, 25, 44, 46

manuals, 1:109, 2:43

medicines and, 2:1–2, 42–44, 58

military prisons, 1:47, 50, 50–52, 2:25

PTSD and, 2:43, 60

recovery of health, 2:42–46

slaves, 2:56

surgeons, 2:8, 17, 21, 27–32

USSC, 2:48–52

venereal disease and, 1:39, 66, 2:22, 26

war photography and, 1:282–283

See also Battlefield wounds; Disease; Field hospitals; Food and nutrition; Nursing; Public health and sanitation

Heartsill, William Williston, 1:268

Hébert, Paul O., 2:129

Hedley, Fenwick Yellowley, 1:267

Helper, Hinton Rowan, *The Impending Crisis of the South,* 2:197

Henderson, David, 2:258

Heroes of America, 1:167, 2:176

Heth, Henry, 2:267, 268

Hickman, Lucretia S., 1:155

Higginson, Thomas Wentworth, 1:73–74, 245

"High with Courage and Hope" (Hunt), 1:146

Hill, Daniel H., 1:44, 55

Hill, Sarah, 1:170–171

Hinton, Thomas H. C., 2:277

History of the Army of the Cumberland (Horne), 2:281

History of the Civil War (Abbott), 2:231

History of Kershaw's Brigade (Dickert), 2:280

A History of the One Hundred and Seventeenth Regiment, N.Y. Volunteers (Mowris), 1:267–268

Histories of the Several Regiments and Battalions from North Carolina (Clark), 2:281

History of the Thirty-Sixth Regiment Illinois Volunteers (Bennett and Haigh), 2:280

Hitchcock, Henry, 1:86

H.L. Hunley (ship), 2:79

Hodges, Jenny. *See* Cashier, Albert D. J.

Hoffman, William, 1:51

Hoge, Jane, 2:50, 51, 52

Hoge, Moses Drury, 1:207, 212–213

Holbrook, Josiah, 1:236

Holcombe, William Henry, 2:162–163, 166

"Hold the Fort" (Bliss), 1:210

Holden, William Woods, 2:177

Holidays, 1:**263–264**

See also Memorial and Decoration Days

Holmes, Frank, 1:142

Holmes, Oliver Wendell, Sr., 1:209, 280–281, 287, 2:57, 243

Holstein, Anna Morris Ellis, 2:141

Home front, 1:**152–153**

army bands and, 1:244

attitudes of civilians, 1:88–89, 91, 102, 103

attitudes of Northerners, 1:88–89

attitudes of Southerners, 1:88–89, 103

battles on, 1:59

Catholicism and, 1:222–223

effects of recruitment on black wives and children, 1:136

free blacks on, 1:153

games, 1:139, 144, 145, 180, 236

holidays, 1:263–264

letters from, 1:43, 140, 145, 148–149, 151, 168–171, 169, 170

men on, 1:152–153

newspapers and magazines, 1:266

support from, 1:217–218, 2:62

writing letters and embroidering, 1:169

See also Civilians; Family and community life; Games; Sports; Vices on home front

Homeopathy, 2:57

Homespun cloth, 2:82, 83, 84

Homestead Act, 1862, 1:121–122, 2:88

Hood, John Bell, 1:210

Hoodoo practices, 2:217

Hooker, Joseph, 1:66

Hooper, Samuel, 1:122

Hopkins, John Henry, 1:149–151

Horne, Thomas Van, *History of the Army of the Cumberland,* 2:281

Horrocks, William, 2:81

Hospital Days (Woolsey), 1:287–288, 2:22

Hospital Life in the Army of the Potomac (Reed), 1:286, 2:51

Hospital Sketches (Alcott), 1:159, 171, 235, 2:41

Hospital volunteers, 1:69, 159, 171, 222, 272

See also Nursing

Hospitals

overview, 1:222, 230, 2:18–23, 19

Boston and, 2:32

design and building, 2:2, 20–21

disease and, 2:18, 22

hospital ships, 2:11, 51

military chaplains and, 1:222, 230

military hospitals, 2:60

Northern states, 2:2, 19–21, 30, 32, 59, 132

Philadelphia and, 1:165, 2:19, 20, 22, 32, 39, 60

Southern states, 2:19, 19, 20, 21, 59

Washington, DC, and, 2:21

women's role in, 2:21–22, 33–37, 34, 40, 40, 60

See also Field hospitals

on resignation speech of Jefferson
Davis, 2:143
revivals, 1:192
salaries and, 2:123
on sports, 1:259, 260
textile trade, 2:83, 84
on theater, 1:236, 242, 260
U.S. Army and, 2:124, 125
on war profiteers, 2:100
YMCA lectures, 1:215
New York Illustrated News, 2:190
New York Monthly Magazine, 1:151
New York (NY)
Central Park, 1:*259,* 2:55
Department of Police, 1:10,
2:181, 182
Draft Riots of 1863, 1:*154,*
157–158, 177, 2:170, 180–182,
181, 224
hospitals and, 2:20, 32
immigrants and, 1:172, 2:63, 68
manufacturing, 2:73
public health and sanitation,
2:47–48
sanitary fairs and, 2:52, *53,* 54
shipbuilding and, 2:79
sports and, 1:262
New York Observer, 2:89
New York Observer and Chronicle,
2:90
New York Reader, 1:114
New York Times
Antietam Exhibit, 1862, 1:279,
280
on blue-gray reunions, 2:275
eyewitness account of Gettysburg
Address, 2:141–142
on food riots, 2:89, 90
gambling, 1:293
on hospitals, 2:19, 21
on Memorial Day celebration,
2:245
obituaries, 2:281–282
on photography, 1:277
on press censorship, 2:124
on Robert E. Lee monument,
2:238
on sanitary fairs, 2:54
sports, 1:260
status of veterans, 2:243
on USSC, 2:52
on visiting husbands and relatives
on battlefield, 1:62–64
on women's volunteer efforts,
2:49, 50, 51
New York Tribune, 2:124, 181,
191, 231
New York World, 1:281, 2:125,
140, 192
Newark Advocate, 2:148
Newell, Robert, 2:279
News and Observer, 1:300

Newspapers and magazines,
1:**266–269,** 273
biased reporting, 2:183–185,
191–193
neutrality and, 2:191
obituaries and local memorials to
dead, 2:281–283
press censorship, 1:267,
2:123–125, 170
propaganda and, 2:183–185, 195
reactions to Gettysburg Address,
2:139–140
soldiers' lives, 1:*266,* 267–268,
287
U.S. Army and, 2:124, 125
*See also specific newspapers and
magazines*
Nichols, Charles H., 2:43
Nightingale, Florence, 2:32–33, 35,
36, 38
9th Texas Regiment, 1:216
9th Vermont Infantry Regiment,
2:267
9th Wisconsin Infantry Regiment,
1:76
95th Illinois Infantry Regiment, 1:60
Nolan, Philip, 1:274
Nondenominational religious organizations, 1:32
Nordhoff, Charles, 1:200
Norris, William, 1:80
*North American and United States
Gazette,* 1:215, 217, 218, 237–238
North Atlantic Blockading Squadron,
1:154, 2:94
North Carolina
education system, 1:115
military units, 1:35, 2:177
pro-Unionists, 2:169
secession, 2:160
North Carolina Standard, 2:176
The North Reports the Civil War
(Andrews), 2:191
North Star, 2:118
Northeastern United States. *See* New
England; *specific states*
Northern states
abolitionism and, 1:202, 204,
2:118, 166–167
agriculture, 1:99–100, 2:86
arms manufacturing, 2:65–66, 68
attitudes about blacks in, 2:197
attitudes about slavery, 2:197–198
attitudes of Southerners about,
1:205–206, 2:163
attitudes on home front,
1:88–89, *91*
biased newspapers and,
2:191–192
black market, 2:92–93

bounties for volunteers, 1:8, 9,
70, 152, 178
child labor and, 2:107
class tensions, 1:175, 177–178
common school movement,
1:123–126
concept of Union and, 2:165
currency, 2:100–101, 102–103
declaration of war, 2:134
domestic life, 1:95, *96,* 99–100
draft riots and resistance, 1:10,
154, 157–158, 177, 2:170,
180–182, *181,* 224
effects of War, 2:229
emancipation of slaves and,
2:169–270
expansion of slavery to western
territories and, 2:159, 165–166
freedpeople and, 1:119–120,
2:167
Grand Review of the Armies,
1:135
histories of War and, 2:231–232
hospitals, 2:2, 19–21, 30, 32, 59,
132
housing, 1:179, *179*
immigrants and, 2:72
labor, 2:105–106
lost cause myth, 2:231–232
manufacturing and, 2:62–63,
64–65, 67–69, 70t, 112
motherhood, 1:139
pacifism and, 2:178–179,
178–180
party politics, 2:115
patriotism, 1:*291*
political humor and cartoons,
2:188–190
press censorship in, 2:123–125
pro-Union refugees in, 2:177,
198
propaganda and, 2:183–185
reactions to first inaugural address
of Abraham Lincoln, 2:144–146
reactions to inaugural address of
Jefferson Davis, 2:144
reactions to inaugural addresses of
Abraham Lincoln, 2:134, 138
religion and, 1:184
religious tracts and, 1:212
shipbuilding, 2:79–80
smoking and tobacco use, 1:291,
291, 299
songs, 1:132–133, 247
support for the War, 2:154,
155–157, 165–168
textile manufacturing, 2:83–84
volunteer work, 1:158–159, *160,*
162
women laborers, 1:99–100, 139,
2:110–111, *111*
YMCA, 1:214–216
See also New England; *specific
states*